The Definitive Guide to DAX: Business intelligence with Microsoft Power BI, SQL Server Analysis Services, and Excel

Second Edition

Marco Russo and Alberto Ferrari

Published with the authorization of Microsoft Corporation by:

Pearson Education, Inc.

Copyright © 2020 by Alberto Ferrari and Marco Russo

ISBN-13: 978-1-5093-0697-8

ISBN-10: 1-5093-0697-8

Library of Congress Control Number: 2019930884

1 2019

Trademarks

Microsoft and the trademarks listed at http://www.microsoft.com on the "Trademarks" webpage are trademarks of the Microsoft group of companies. All other marks are property of their respective owners.

Warning and Disclaimer

Every effort has been made to make this book as complete and as accurate as possible, but no warranty or fitness is implied. The information provided is on an "as is" basis. The authors, the publisher, and Microsoft Corporation shall have neither liability nor responsibility to any person or entity with respect to any loss or damages arising from the information contained in this book.

Special Sales

For information about buying this title in bulk quantities, or for special sales opportunities (which may include electronic versions; custom cover designs; and content particular to your business, training goals, marketing focus, or branding interests), please contact our corporate sales department at corpsales@pearsoned.com or (800) 382-3419.

For government sales inquiries, please contact governmentsales@pearsoned.com.

For questions about sales outside the U.S., please contact intlcs@pearson.com.

EDITOR-IN-CHIEF
Brett Bartow

EXECUTIVE EDITOR
Loretta Yates

DEVELOPMENT EDITOR
Mark Renfrow

MANAGING EDITOR
Sandra Schroeder

SENIOR PROJECT EDITOR
Tonya Simpson

COPY EDITOR
Chuck Hutchinson

INDEXER
Ken Johnson

PROOFREADER
Abigail Manheim

TECHNICAL EDITOR
Daniil Maslyuk

EDITORIAL ASSISTANT
Cindy Teeters

COVER DESIGNER
Twist Creative, Seattle

COMPOSITOR
codeMantra

Contents at a Glance

Contents

Chapter 6   Variables   175

Chapter 7   Working with iterators and with *CALCULATE*   187

Chapter 8   Time intelligence calculations   217

Foreword

You may not know our names. We spend our days writing the code for the software you use in your daily job: We are part of the development team of Power BI, SQL Server Analysis Services, and...yes, we are among the authors of the DAX language and the VertiPaq engine.

The language you are going to learn using this book is our creation. We spent years working on this language, optimizing the engine, finding ways to improve the optimizer, and trying to build DAX into a simple, clean, and sound language to make your life as a data analyst easier and more productive.

But hey, this is intended to be the foreword of a book, so no more about us! Why are we writing a foreword for a book published by Marco and Alberto, the SQLBI guys? Well, because when you start learning DAX, it is a matter of a few clicks and searches on the web before you find articles written by them. You start reading their papers, learning the language, and hopefully appreciating our hard work. Having met them many years ago, we have great admiration for their deep knowledge of SQL Server Analysis Services. When the DAX adventure started, they were among the first to learn and adopt this new engine and language.

The articles, papers, and blog posts they publish and share on the web have become the source of learning for thousands of people. We write the code, but we do not spend much time teaching developers how to use it; Marco and Alberto are the ones who spread the knowledge about DAX.

Alberto and Marco's books are among a few bestsellers on this topic, and now with this new guide to DAX, they have truly created a milestone publication about the language we author and love. We write the code, they write the books, and you learn DAX, providing unprecedented analytical power to your business. This is what we love: working all together as a team—we, they, and you—to extract better insights from data.

Marius Dumitru, Architect, Power BI CTO's Office

Cristian Petculescu, Chief Architect of Power BI

Jeffrey Wang, Principal Software Engineer Manager

Christian Wade, Senior Program Manager

Acknowledgments

Writing this second edition required an entire year's worth of work, three months more than the first edition. It has been a long and amazing journey, connecting people all around the world in any latitude and time zone to be able to produce the result you are going to read. We have so many people to thank for this book that we know it is impossible to write a complete list. So, thanks so much to all of you who contributed to this book—even if you had no idea that you were doing so. Blog comments, forum posts, email discussions, chats with attendees and speakers at technical conferences, analysis of customer scenarios, and so much more have been useful to us, and many people have contributed significant ideas to this book. Moreover, big thanks to all the students of our courses: By teaching you, we got better!

That said, there are people we must mention personally, because of their particular contributions.

We want to start with Edward Melomed: He has inspired us, and we probably would not have started our journey with the DAX language without a passionate discussion we had with him several years ago and that ended with the table of contents of our first book about Power Pivot written on a napkin.

We want to thank Microsoft Press and the people who contributed to the project: They all greatly helped us along the process of book writing.

The only job longer than writing a book is the studying you must do in preparation for writing it. A group of people that we (in all friendliness) call "ssas-insiders" helped us get ready to write this book. A few people from Microsoft deserve a special mention as well, because they spent a lot of their precious time teaching us important concepts about Power BI and DAX: They are Marius Dumitru, Jeffrey Wang, Akshai Mirchandani, Krystian Sakowski, and Cristian Petculescu. Your help has been priceless, guys!

We also want to thank Amir Netz, Christian Wade, Ashvini Sharma, Kasper De Jonge, and T. K. Anand for their contributions to the many discussions we had about the product. We feel they helped us tremendously in strategic choices we made in this book and in our career.

We wanted to reserve a special mention to a woman who did an incredible job improving and cleaning up our English. Claire Costa proofread the entire manuscript and made it so much easier to read. Claire, your help is invaluable—Thanks!

The last special mention goes to our technical reviewer: Daniil Maslyuk carefully tested every single line of code, text, example, and reference we had written. He found any and all kinds of mistakes we would have missed. He rarely made comments that did not require a change in the book. The result is amazing for us. If the book contains fewer errors than our original manuscript, it is only because of Daniil's efforts. If it still contains errors, it is our fault, of course.

Thank you so much, folks!

Errata, updates, and book support

We've made every effort to ensure the accuracy of this book and its companion content. You can access updates to this book—in the form of a list of submitted errata and their related corrections—at https://MicrosoftPressStore.com/DefinitiveGuideDAX/errata

For additional book support and information, please visit https://MicrosoftPressStore.com/Support.

Please note that product support for Microsoft software and hardware is not offered through the previous addresses. For help with Microsoft software or hardware, go to *http://support.microsoft.com*.

Stay in touch

Let's keep the conversation going! We are on Twitter: *http://twitter.com/MicrosoftPress*.

Introduction to the second edition

When we decided it was time to update this book, we thought it would be an easy job: After all, not many things have changed in the DAX language, and the theoretical core of the book was still very good. We believed the focus would mainly be on updating the screenshots from Excel to Power BI, adding a few touch-ups here and there, and we would be done. How wrong we were!

As soon as we started updating the first chapter, we quickly discovered that we wanted to rewrite nearly everything. We felt so not only in the first chapter, but at every page of the book. Therefore, this is not really a second edition; it is a brand new book.

The reason is not that the language or the tools have changed so drastically. The reason is that over these last few years we—as authors and teachers—have evolved a lot, hopefully for the better. We have taught DAX to thousands of users and developers all around the world; we worked hard with our students, always striving for the best way to explain complex topics. Eventually, we found different ways of describing the language we love.

We increased the number of examples for this edition, showing practical uses of the functionalities after teaching the theoretical foundation of DAX. We tried to use a simpler style, without compromising on precision. We fought with the editor to increase the page count, as this was needed to cover all the topics we wanted to share. Nevertheless, we did not change the leitmotif of the book: we assume no previous knowledge of DAX, even though this is not a book for the casual DAX developer. This is a book for people who really want to learn the language and gain a deep understanding of the power and complexity of DAX.

Yes, if you want to leverage the real power of DAX, you need to be prepared for a long journey with us, reading the book from cover to cover, and then reading it again, searching for the many details that—at first sight—are not obvious.

Introduction to the first edition

We have created considerable amounts of content on DAX: books about Power Pivot and SSAS Tabular, blog posts, articles, white papers, and finally a book dedicated to DAX patterns. So why should we write (and, hopefully, you read) yet another book about DAX? Is there really so much to learn about this language? Of course, we think the answer is a definite yes.

When you write a book, the first thing that the editor wants to know is the number of pages. There are very good reasons why this is important: price, management, allocation of resources, and so on. In the end, nearly everything in a book goes back to the number of pages. As authors, this is somewhat frustrating. In fact, whenever we write a book, we have to carefully allocate space to the description of the product (either Power Pivot for Microsoft Excel or SSAS Tabular) and of to the DAX language. This has always left us with the bitter feeling of not having enough pages to describe all we wanted to teach about DAX. After all, you cannot write 1,000 pages about Power Pivot; a book of such size would be intimidating for anybody.

Thus, for years we wrote about SSAS Tabular and Power Pivot, and we kept the project of a book completely dedicated to DAX in a drawer. Then we opened the drawer and decided to avoid choosing what to include in the next book: We wanted to explain everything about DAX, with no compromises. The result of that decision is this book.

Here you will not find a description of how to create a calculated column, or which dialog box to use to set a property. This is not a step-by-step book that teaches you how to use Microsoft Visual Studio, Power BI, or Power Pivot for Excel. Instead, this is a deep dive into the DAX language, starting from the beginning and then reaching very technical details about how to optimize your code and model.

We loved each page of this book while we were writing it. We reviewed the content so many times that we had it memorized. We continued adding content whenever we thought there was something important to include, thus increasing the page count and never cutting something because there were no pages left. Doing that, we learned more about DAX and we enjoyed every moment spent doing so.

But there is one more thing. Why should you read a book about DAX?

Come on, you thought this after the first demo of Power Pivot or Power BI. You are not alone; we thought the same the first time we tried it. DAX is so easy! It looks so similar to Excel! Moreover, if you have already learned other programming and/or query languages, you are probably used to learning a new language by looking at examples of the syntax, matching patterns you find to those you already know. We made this mistake, and we would like you to avoid doing the same.

DAX is a mighty language, used in a growing number of analytical tools. It is very powerful, but it includes a few concepts that are hard to understand by inductive reasoning. The evaluation context, for instance, is a topic that requires a deductive approach: You start with a theory, and then you see a few examples that demonstrate how the theory works. Deductive reasoning is the approach of this book. We know that a number of people do not like learning this way, because they prefer a more practical approach—learning how to solve specific problems, and then with experience and practice, they understand the underlying theory with an inductive reasoning. If you are looking for that approach, this book is not for you. We wrote a book about DAX patterns, full of examples and without any explanation of why a formula works, or why a certain way of coding is better. That book is a good source for copying and pasting DAX formulas. The goal of this book here is different: to enable you to master DAX. All the examples demonstrate a DAX behavior; they do not solve a specific problem. If you find formulas that you can reuse in your models, good for you. However, always remember that this is just a side effect, not the goal of the example. Finally, always read any note to make sure there are no possible pitfalls in the code used in the examples. For educational purposes we have often used code that was not the best practice.

We really hope you will enjoy spending time with us in this beautiful trip to learn DAX, at least in the same way we enjoyed writing it.

Who this book is for

If you are a casual user of DAX, then this book is probably not the best choice for you. Many books provide a simple introduction to the tools that implement DAX and to the DAX language itself, starting from the ground up and reaching a basic level of DAX programming. We know this very well, because we wrote some of those books, too!

If, on the other hand, you are serious about DAX and you really want to understand every detail of this beautiful language, then this is your book. This might be your first book about DAX; in that case you should not expect to benefit from the most advanced topics too early. We suggest you read the book from cover to cover and then read the most complex parts again, once you have gained some experience; it is very likely that some concepts will become clearer at that point.

DAX is useful to different people, for different purposes: Power BI users might need to author DAX formulas in their models, Excel users can leverage DAX to author Power Pivot data models, business intelligence (BI) professionals might need to implement DAX code in BI solutions of any size. In this book, we tried to provide information to all these different kinds of people. Some of the content (specifically the optimization part) is probably more targeted to BI professionals, because the knowledge needed to optimize a DAX measure is very technical; but we believe that Power BI and Excel users too should understand the range of possible performance of DAX expressions to achieve the best results for their models.

Finally, we wanted to write a book to study, not only a book to read. At the beginning, we try to keep it easy and follow a logical path from zero to DAX. However, when the concepts to learn start to become more complex, we stop trying to be simple, and we remain realistic. DAX is simple, but it is not easy. It took years for us to master it and to understand every detail of the engine. Do not expect to be able to learn all this content in a few days, by reading casually. This book requires your attention at a very high level. In exchange for that, we offer an unprecedented depth of coverage of all aspects of DAX, giving you the option to become a real DAX expert.

Assumptions about you

We expect our reader to have basic knowledge of Power BI and some experience in the analysis of numbers. If you have already had prior exposure to the DAX language, then this is good for you—you will read the first part faster—but of course knowing DAX is not necessary.

There are references throughout the book to MDX and SQL code; however, you do not really need to know these languages because they just reflect comparisons between different ways of writing expressions. If you do not understand those lines of code, it is fine; it means that that specific topic is not for you.

In the most advanced parts of the book, we discuss parallelism, memory access, CPU usage, and other exquisitely geeky topics that not everybody might be familiar with. Any developer will feel at home there, whereas Power BI and Excel users might be a bit intimidated. Nevertheless, this information is required in order to discuss DAX optimization. Indeed, the most advanced part of the book is aimed more towards BI developers than towards Power BI and Excel users. However, we think that everybody will benefit from reading it.

Organization of this book

The book is designed to flow from introductory chapters to complex ones, in a logical way. Each chapter is written with the assumption that the previous content is fully understood; there is nearly no repetition of concepts explained earlier. For this reason, we strongly suggest that you read it from cover to cover and avoid jumping to more advanced chapters too early.

Once you have read it for the first time, it becomes useful as a reference: For example, if you are in doubt about the behavior of *ALLSELECTED*, then you can jump straight to that section and clarify your mind on that. Nevertheless, reading that section without having digested the previous content might result in some frustration or, worse, in an incomplete understanding of the concepts.

With that said, here is the content at a glance:

- Chapter 1 is a brief introduction to DAX, with a few sections dedicated to users who already have some knowledge of other languages, namely SQL, Excel, or MDX. We do not introduce any new concept here; we just give several hints about the differences between DAX and other languages that might be known to the reader.

- Chapter 2 introduces the DAX language itself. We cover basic concepts such as calculated columns, measures, and error-handling functions; we also list most of the basic functions of the language.

- Chapter 3 is dedicated to basic table functions. Many functions in DAX work on tables and return tables as a result. In this chapter we cover the most basic table functions, whereas we cover advanced table functions in Chapter 12 and 13.

- Chapter 4 describes evaluation contexts. Evaluation contexts are the foundation of the DAX language, so this chapter, along with the next one, is probably the most important in the entire book.

- Chapter 5 only covers two functions: *CALCULATE* and *CALCULATETABLE*. These are the most important functions in DAX, and they strongly rely on a good understanding of evaluation contexts.

- Chapter 6 describes variables. We use variables in all the examples of the book, but Chapter 6 is where we introduce their syntax and explain how to use variables. This chapter will be useful as a reference when you see countless examples using variables in the following chapters.

- Chapter 7 covers iterators and CALCULATE: a marriage made in heaven. Learning how to use iterators, along with the power of context transition, leverages much of the power of DAX. In this chapter, we show several examples that are useful to understand how to take advantage of these tools.

- Chapter 8 describes time intelligence calculations at a very in-depth level. Year-to-date, month-to-date, values of the previous year, week-based periods, and custom calendars are some of the calculations covered in this chapter.

- Chapter 9 is dedicated to the latest feature introduced in DAX: calculation groups. Calculation groups are very powerful as a modeling tool. This chapter describes how to create and use calculation groups, introducing the basic concepts and showing a few examples.

- Chapter 10 covers more advanced uses of the filter context, data lineage, inspection of the filter context, and other useful tools to compute advanced formulas.

- Chapter 11 shows you how to perform calculations over hierarchies and how to handle parent/child structures using DAX.

- Chapters 12 and 13 cover advanced table functions that are useful both to author queries and/or to compute advanced calculations.

- Chapter 14 advances your knowledge of evaluation context one step further and discusses complex functions such as *ALLSELECTED* and *KEEPFILTERS*, with the aid of the theory of expanded tables. This is an advanced chapter that uncovers most of the secrets of complex DAX expressions.

- Chapter 15 is about managing relationships in DAX. Indeed, thanks to DAX any type of relationship can be set within a data model. This chapter includes the description of many types of relationships that are common in an analytical data model.

- Chapter 16 contains several examples of complex calculations solved in DAX. This is the final chapter about the language, useful to discover solutions and new ideas.

- Chapter 17 includes a detailed description of the VertiPaq engine, which is the most common storage engine used by models running DAX. Understanding it is essential to learning how to get the best performance in DAX.

- Chapter 18 uses the knowledge from Chapter 17 to show possible optimizations that you can apply at the data model level. You learn how to reduce the cardinality of columns, how to choose columns to import, and how to improve performance by choosing the proper relationship types and by reducing memory usage in DAX.

- Chapter 19 teaches you how to read a query plan and how to measure the performance of a DAX query with the aid of tools such as DAX Studio and SQL Server Profiler.

- Chapter 20 shows several optimization techniques, based on the content of the previous chapters about optimization. We show many DAX expressions, measure their performance, and then display and explain optimized formulas.

Conventions

The following conventions are used in this book:

- **Boldface** type is used to indicate text that you type.

- *Italic* type is used to indicate new terms, measures, calculated columns, tables, and database names.

- The first letters of the names of dialog boxes, dialog box elements, and commands are capitalized. For example, the Save As dialog box.

- The names of ribbon tabs are given in ALL CAPS.

- Keyboard shortcuts are indicated by a plus sign (+) separating the key names. For example, Ctrl+Alt+Delete means that you press Ctrl, Alt, and Delete keys at the same time.

About the companion content

We have included companion content to enrich your learning experience. The companion content for this book can be downloaded from the following page:

MicrosoftPressStore.com/DefinitiveGuideDAX/downloads

The companion content includes the following:

- A SQL Server backup of the Contoso Retail DW database that you can use to build the examples yourself. This is a standard demo database provided by Microsoft, which we have enriched with several views, to make it easier to create a data model on top of it.

- A separate Power BI Desktop model for each figure of the book. Every figure has its own file. The data model is almost always the same, but you can use these files to closely follow the steps outlined in the book.

CHAPTER 1

What is DAX?

DAX, which stands for Data Analysis eXpressions, is the programming language of Microsoft Power BI, Microsoft Analysis Services, and Microsoft Power Pivot for Excel. It was created in 2010, with the first release of PowerPivot for Microsoft Excel 2010. In 2010, PowerPivot was spelled without the space. The space was introduced in the Power Pivot name in 2013. Since then, DAX has gained popularity, both within the Excel community, which uses DAX to create Power Pivot data models in Excel, and within the Business Intelligence (BI) community, which uses DAX to build models with Power BI and Analysis Services. DAX is present in many different tools, all sharing the same internal engine named *Tabular*. For this reason, we often refer to *Tabular models*, including all these different tools in a single word.

DAX is a simple language. That said, DAX is different from most programming languages, so becoming acquainted with some of its new concepts might take some time. In our experience, having taught DAX to thousands of people, learning the basics of DAX is straightforward: you will be able to start using it in a matter of hours. When it comes to understanding advanced concepts such as evaluation contexts, iterations, and context transitions, everything will likely seem complex. Do not give up! Be patient. When your brain starts to digest these concepts, you will discover that DAX is, indeed, an easy language. It just takes some getting used to.

This first chapter begins with a recap of what a data model is in terms of tables and relationships. We recommend readers of all experience levels read this section to gain familiarity with the terms used throughout the book when referring to tables, models, and different kinds of relationships.

In the following sections, we offer advice to readers who have experience with programming languages such as Microsoft Excel, SQL, and MDX. Each section is focused on a certain language, for readers curious to briefly compare DAX to it. Focus on languages you know if a comparison is helpful to you; then read the final section, "DAX for Power BI users," and move on to the next chapter where our journey into the DAX language truly begins.

Understanding the data model

DAX is specifically designed to compute business formulas over a data model. The readers might already know what a data model is. If not, we start with a description of data models and relationships to create a foundation on which to build their DAX knowledge.

A data model is a set of tables, linked by relationships.

We all know what a table is: a set of rows containing data, with each row divided into columns. Each column has a data type and contains a single piece of information. We usually refer to a row in a table as a record. Tables are a convenient way to organize data. A table is a data model in itself although in its simplest form. Thus, when we write names and numbers in an Excel workbook, we are creating a data model.

If a data model contains many tables, it is likely that they are linked through relationships. A relationship is a link between two tables. When two tables are tied with a relationship, we say that they are related. Graphically, a relationship is represented by a line connecting the two tables. Figure 1-1 shows an example of a data model.

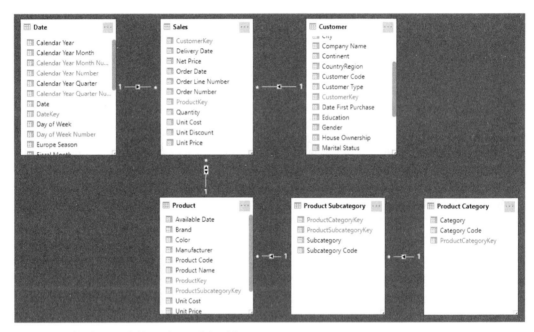

FIGURE 1-1 This data model is made up of six tables.

Following are a few important aspects of relationships:

- Two tables in a relationship do not have the same role. They are called the *one-side* and the *many-side* of the relationship, represented respectively with a 1 and with a *. In Figure 1-1, focus on the relationship between Product and Product Subcategory. A single subcategory contains many products, whereas a single product has only one subcategory. Therefore, Product Subcategory is the one-side of the relationship, having one subcategory, while Product is the many-side having many products.

- Special kinds of relationships are 1:1 and weak relationships. In 1:1 relationships, both tables are the one-side, whereas in weak relationships, both tables can be the many-side. These special kinds of relationships are uncommon; we discuss them in detail in Chapter 15, "Advanced relationships."

- The columns used to create the relationship, which usually have the same name in both tables, are called the keys of the relationship. On the one-side of the relationship, the column needs to have a unique value for each row, and it cannot contain blanks. On the many-side, the same value can be repeated in many different rows, and it often is. When a column has a unique value for each row, it is called a key for the table.

- Relationships can form a chain. Each product has a subcategory, and each subcategory has a category. Thus, each product has a category. To retrieve the category of a product, one must traverse a chain of two relationships. Figure 1-1 includes an example of a chain made up of three relationships, starting with Sales and continuing on to Product Category.

- In each relationship, one or two small arrows can determine the *cross filter direction*. Figure 1-1 shows two arrows in the relationship between Sales and Product, whereas all other relationships have a single arrow. The arrow indicates the direction of the automatic filtering of the relationship (*cross filter*). Because determining the correct direction of filters is one of the most important skills to learn, we discuss this topic in more detail in later chapters. We usually discourage the use of bidirectional filters, as described in Chapter 15. They are present in this model for educational purposes only.

Understanding the direction of a relationship

Each relationship can have a unidirectional or bidirectional cross filter. Filtering always happens from the one-side of the relationship to the many-side. If the cross filter is bidirectional—that is, if it has two arrows on it—the filtering also happens from the many-side to the one-side.

An example might help in understanding this behavior. If a report is based on the data model shown in Figure 1-1, with the years on the rows and *Quantity* and *Count of Product Name* in the values area, it produces the result shown in Figure 1-2.

Calendar Year	Quantity	Count of Product Name
CY 2007	44,310	1258
CY 2008	40,226	1478
CY 2009	55,644	1513
Total	**140,180**	**2517**

FIGURE 1-2 This report shows the effect of filtering across multiple tables.

Calendar Year is a column that belongs to the *Date* table. Because *Date* is on the one-side of the relationship with *Sales,* the engine filters *Sales* based on the year. This is why the quantity shown is filtered by year.

With *Products,* the scenario is slightly different. The filtering happens because the relationship between the *Sales* and *Product* tables is bidirectional. When we put the count of product names in the report, we obtain the number of products sold in each year because the filter on the year propagates to *Product* through *Sales.* If the relationship between *Sales* and *Product* were unidirectional, the result would be different, as we explain in the following sections.

If we modify the report by putting *Color* on the rows and adding *Count of Date* in the values area, the result is different, as shown in Figure 1-3.

Color	Quantity	Count of Product Name	Count of Date
Azure	546	14	2556
Black	33,618	602	2556
Blue	8,859	200	2556
Brown	2,570	77	2556
Gold	1,393	50	2556
Green	3,020	74	2556
Grey	11,900	283	2556
Orange	2,203	55	2556
Pink	4,921	84	2556
Purple	102	6	2556
Red	8,079	99	2556
Silver	27,551	417	2556
Silver Grey	959	14	2556
Transparent	1,251	1	2556
White	30,543	505	2556
Yellow	2,665	36	2556
Total	**140,180**	**2517**	**2556**

FIGURE 1-3 This report shows that if bidirectional filtering is not active, tables are not filtered.

The filter on the rows is the *Color* column in the *Product* table. Because *Product* is on the one-side of the relationship with *Sales*, *Quantity* is filtered correctly. *Count of Product Name* is filtered because it is computing values from the table that is on the rows, that is *Product*. The unexpected number is *Count of Date*. Indeed, it always shows the same value for all the rows—that is, the total number of rows in the *Date* table.

The filter coming from the *Color* column does not propagate to *Date* because the relationship between *Date* and *Sales* is unidirectional. Thus, although *Sales* has an active filter on it, the filter cannot propagate to *Date* because the type of relationship prevents it.

If we change the relationship between *Date* and *Sales* to enable bidirectional cross-filtering, the result is as shown in Figure 1-4.

The numbers now reflect the number of days when at least one product of the given color was sold. At first sight, it might look as if all the relationships should be defined as bidirectional, so as to let the filter propagate in any direction and always return results that make sense. As you will learn later in this book, designing a data model this way is almost never appropriate. In fact, depending on the scenario you are working with, you will choose the correct propagation of relationships. If you follow our suggestions, you will avoid bidirectional filtering as much as you can.

Color	Quantity	Count of Product Name	Count of Date
Azure	546	14	41
Black	33,618	602	811
Blue	8,859	200	408
Brown	2,570	77	169
Gold	1,393	50	106
Green	3,020	74	188
Grey	11,900	283	499
Orange	2,203	55	142
Pink	4,921	84	226
Purple	102	6	11
Red	8,079	99	286
Silver	27,551	417	722
Silver Grey	959	14	63
Transparent	1,251	1	14
White	30,543	505	750
Yellow	2,665	36	110
Total	**140,180**	**2517**	**2556**

FIGURE 1-4 If we enable bidirectional filtering, the *Date* table is filtered using the *Color* column.

DAX for Excel users

Chances are you already know the Excel formula language that DAX somewhat resembles. After all, the roots of DAX are in Power Pivot for Excel, and the development team tried to keep the two languages similar. This similarity makes the transition to this new language easier. However, there are some important differences.

Cells versus tables

Excel performs calculations over cells. A cell is referenced using its coordinates. Thus, we can write formulas as follows:

```
= (A1 * 1.25) - B2
```

In DAX, the concept of a cell and its coordinates does not exist. DAX works on tables and columns, not cells. As a consequence, DAX expressions refer to tables and columns, and this means writing code differently. The concepts of tables and columns are not new in Excel. In fact, if we define an Excel range as a table by using the *Format as Table* function, we can write formulas in Excel that reference tables and columns. In Figure 1-5, the *SalesAmount* column evaluates an expression that references columns in the same table instead of cells in the workbook.

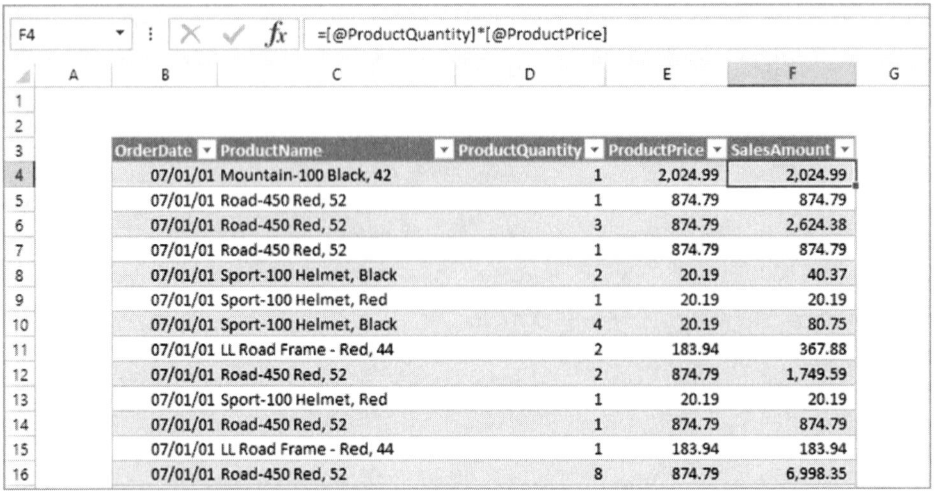

FIGURE 1-5 Excel can reference column names in tables.

Using Excel, we refer to columns in a table using the *[@ColumnName]* format. *ColumnName* is the name of the column to use, and the @ symbol means "take the value for the current row." Although the syntax is not intuitive, normally we do not write these expressions. They appear when we click a cell, and Excel takes care of inserting the right code for us.

You might think of Excel as having two different ways of performing calculations. We can use standard cell references, in which case the formula for F4 would be E4*D4, or we can use column references inside a table. Using column references offers the advantage that we can use the same expression in all the cells of a column and Excel will compute the formula with a different value for each row.

Unlike Excel, DAX works only on tables. All the formulas must reference columns inside tables. For example, in DAX we write the previous multiplication this way:

```
Sales[SalesAmount] = Sales[ProductPrice] * Sales[ProductQuantity]
```

As you can see, each column is prefixed with the name of its table. In Excel, we do not provide the table name because Excel formulas work inside a single table. However, DAX works on a data model containing many tables. As a consequence, we must specify the table name because two columns in different tables might have the same name.

Many functions in DAX work the same way as the equivalent Excel function. For example, the *IF* function reads the same way in DAX and in Excel:

```
Excel IF ( [@SalesAmount] > 10, 1, 0)
DAX   IF ( Sales[SalesAmount] > 10, 1, 0)
```

One important aspect where the syntax of Excel and DAX is different is in the way to reference the entire column. In fact, in *[@ProductQuantity]*, the @ means "the value in the current row." In DAX, there is no need to specify that a value must be from the current row, because this is the default behavior of the language. In Excel, we can reference the entire column—that is, all the rows in that column—by removing the @ symbol. You can see this in Figure 1-6.

	A	B	C	D	E	F	G
	G4		f_x	=SUM([SalesAmount])			
3		OrderDate	ProductName	ProductQuantity	ProductPrice	SalesAmount	AllSales
4		07/01/01	Mountain-100 Black, 42	1	2,024.99	2,024.99	47,993.66
5		07/01/01	Road-450 Red, 52	1	874.79	874.79	47,993.66
6		07/01/01	Road-450 Red, 52	3	874.79	2,624.38	47,993.66
7		07/01/01	Road-450 Red, 52	1	874.79	874.79	47,993.66
8		07/01/01	Sport-100 Helmet, Black	2	20.19	40.37	47,993.66
9		07/01/01	Sport-100 Helmet, Red	1	20.19	20.19	47,993.66
10		07/01/01	Sport-100 Helmet, Black	4	20.19	80.75	47,993.66
11		07/01/01	LL Road Frame - Red, 44	2	183.94	367.88	47,993.66
12		07/01/01	Road-450 Red, 52	2	874.79	1,749.59	47,993.66
13		07/01/01	Sport-100 Helmet, Red	1	20.19	20.19	47,993.66
14		07/01/01	Road-450 Red, 52	1	874.79	874.79	47,993.66
15		07/01/01	LL Road Frame - Red, 44	1	183.94	183.94	47,993.66
16		07/01/01	Road-450 Red, 52	8	874.79	6,998.35	47,993.66
17		07/01/01	Sport-100 Helmet, Black	3	20.19	60.56	47,993.66
18		07/01/01	Sport-100 Helmet, Red	4	20.19	80.75	47,993.66
19		07/01/01	LL Road Frame - Red, 48	2	183.94	367.88	47,993.66

FIGURE 1-6 In Excel, you can reference an entire column by omitting the @ symbol before the column name.

The value of the *AllSales* column is the same in all the rows because it is the grand total of the *SalesAmount* column. In other words, there is a syntactical difference between the value of a column in the current row and the value of the column as a whole.

DAX is different. In DAX, this is how you write the *AllSales* expression of Figure 1-6:

```
AllSales := SUM ( Sales[SalesAmount] )
```

There is no syntactical difference between retrieving the value of a column for a specific row and using the column as a whole. DAX understands that we want to sum all the values of the column because we use the column name inside an aggregator (in this case the *SUM* function), which requires a column name to be passed as a parameter. Thus, although Excel requires an explicit syntax to differentiate between the two types of data to retrieve, DAX does the disambiguation automatically. This distinction might be confusing—at least in the beginning.

Excel and DAX: Two functional languages

One aspect where the two languages are similar is that both Excel and DAX are functional languages. A functional language is made up of expressions that are basically function calls. In Excel and DAX, the concepts of statements, loops, and jumps do not exist although they are common to many programming languages. In DAX, everything is an expression. This aspect of the language is often a challenge for programmers coming from different languages, but it should be no surprise at all for Excel users.

Iterators in DAX

A concept that might be new to you is the concept of iterators. When working in Excel, you perform calculations one step at a time. The previous example showed that to compute the total of sales, we create one column containing the price multiplied by the quantity. Then as a second step, we sum it to compute the total sales. This number is then useful as a denominator to compute the percentage of sales of each product, for example.

Using DAX, you can perform the same operation in a single step by using iterators. An iterator does exactly what its name suggests: it iterates over a table and performs a calculation on each row of the table, aggregating the result to produce the single value requested.

Using the previous example, we can now compute the sum of all sales using the *SUMX* iterator:

```
AllSales :=
SUMX (
    Sales,
    Sales[ProductQuantity] * Sales[ProductPrice]
)
```

This approach brings to light both an advantage and a disadvantage. The advantage is that we can perform many complex calculations in a single step without worrying about adding columns that would end up being useful only for specific formulas. The disadvantage is that programming with DAX is less visual than programming with Excel. Indeed, you do not see the column computing the price multiplied by the quantity; it exists only for the lifetime of the calculation.

As we will explain later, we can create a calculated column that computes the multiplication of price by quantity. Nevertheless, doing so is seldom a good practice because it uses memory and might slow down the calculations, unless you use DirectQuery and Aggregations, as we explain in Chapter 18, "Optimizing VertiPaq."

DAX requires theory

Let us be clear: The fact that DAX requires one to study theory first is not a difference between programming languages. This is a difference in mindset. You are probably used to searching the web for complex formulas and solution patterns for the scenarios you are trying to solve. When you are using Excel, chances are you will find a formula that almost does what you need. You can copy the formula, customize it to fit your needs, and then use it without worrying too much about how it works.

This approach, which works in Excel, does not work with DAX, however. You need to study DAX theory and thoroughly understand how evaluation contexts work before you can write good DAX code. If you do not have a proper theoretical foundation, you will find that DAX either computes values like magic or it computes strange numbers that make no sense. The problem is not DAX but the fact that you do not yet understood exactly how DAX works.

Luckily, the theory behind DAX is limited to a couple of important concepts, which we explain in Chapter 4, "Understanding evaluation contexts." When you reach that chapter, be prepared for some intense learning. After you master that content, DAX will have no secrets for you, and learning DAX will mainly be a matter of gaining experience. Remember: knowing is half the battle. So do not try to go further until you are somewhat proficient with evaluation contexts.

DAX for SQL developers

If you are accustomed to the SQL language, you have already worked with many tables and created joins between columns to set relationships. From this point of view, you will likely feel at home in the DAX world. Indeed, computing in DAX is a matter of querying a set of tables joined by relationships and aggregating values.

Relationship handling

The first difference between SQL and DAX is in the way relationships work in the model. In SQL, we can set foreign keys between tables to declare relationships, but the engine never uses these foreign keys in queries unless we are explicit about them. For example, if we have a *Customers* table and a *Sales* table, where *CustomerKey* is a primary key in *Customers* and a foreign key in *Sales,* we can write the following query:

```
SELECT
    Customers.CustomerName,
    SUM ( Sales.SalesAmount ) AS SumOfSales
FROM
    Sales
    INNER JOIN Customers
    ON Sales.CustomerKey = Customers.CustomerKey
GROUP BY
    Customers.CustomerName
```

Though we declare the relationship in the model using foreign keys, we still need to be explicit and state the join condition in the query. Although this approach makes queries more verbose, it is useful because you can use different join conditions in different queries, giving you a lot of freedom in the way you express queries.

In DAX, relationships are part of the model, and they are all *LEFT OUTER JOINs*. When they are defined in the model, you no longer need to specify the join type in the query: DAX uses an automatic *LEFT OUTER JOIN* in the query whenever you use columns related to the primary table. Thus, in DAX you would write the previous SQL query as follows:

```
EVALUATE
SUMMARIZECOLUMNS (
    Customers[CustomerName],
    "SumOfSales", SUM ( Sales[SalesAmount] )
)
```

Because DAX knows the existing relationship between *Sales* and *Customers,* it does the join automatically following the model. Finally, the *SUMMARIZECOLUMNS* function needs to perform a group by *Customers[CustomerName],* but we do not have a keyword for that: *SUMMARIZECOLUMNS* automatically groups data by selected columns.

DAX is a functional language

SQL is a declarative language. You define what you need by declaring the set of data you want to retrieve using *SELECT* statements, without worrying about how the engine actually retrieves the information.

DAX, on the other hand, is a functional language. In DAX, every expression is a function call. Function parameters can, in turn, be other function calls. The evaluation of parameters might lead to complex query plans that DAX executes to compute the result.

For example, if we want to retrieve only customers who live in Europe, we can write this query in SQL:

```
SELECT
    Customers.CustomerName,
    SUM ( Sales.SalesAmount ) AS SumOfSales
FROM
    Sales
    INNER JOIN Customers
    ON Sales.CustomerKey = Customers.CustomerKey
WHERE
    Customers.Continent = 'Europe'
GROUP BY
    Customers.CustomerName
```

Using DAX, we do not declare the *WHERE* condition in the query. Instead, we use a specific function (*FILTER*) to filter the result:

```
EVALUATE
SUMMARIZECOLUMNS (
    Customers[CustomerName],
    FILTER (
        Customers,
        Customers[Continent] = "Europe"
    ),
    "SumOfSales", SUM ( Sales[SalesAmount] )
)
```

You can see that *FILTER* is a function: it returns only the customers living in Europe, producing the expected result. The order in which we nest the functions and the kinds of functions we use have a strong impact on both the result and the performance of the engine. This happens in SQL too, although in SQL we trust the query optimizer to find the optimal query plan. In DAX, although the query optimizer does a great job, you, as programmer, bear more responsibility in writing good code.

DAX as a programming and querying language

In SQL, a clear distinction exists between the query language and the programming language—that is, the set of instructions used to create stored procedures, views, and other pieces of code in the database. Each SQL dialect has its own statements to let programmers enrich the data model with code. However, DAX virtually makes no distinction between querying and programming. A rich set of functions manipulates tables and can, in turn, return tables. The *FILTER* function in the previous query is a good example of this.

In that respect, it appears that DAX is simpler than SQL. When you learn it as a programming language—its original use—you will know everything needed to also use it as a query language.

Subqueries and conditions in DAX and SQL

One of the most powerful features of SQL as a query language is the option of using subqueries. DAX features similar concepts. In the case of DAX subqueries, however, they stem from the functional nature of the language.

For example, to retrieve customers and total sales specifically for the customers who bought more than US$100 worth, we can write this query in SQL:

```
SELECT
    CustomerName,
    SumOfSales
FROM (
    SELECT
    Customers.CustomerName,
    SUM ( Sales.SalesAmount ) AS SumOfSales
    FROM
    Sales
    INNER JOIN Customers
      ON Sales.CustomerKey = Customers.CustomerKey
    GROUP BY
    Customers.CustomerName
    ) AS SubQuery
WHERE
    SubQuery.SumOfSales > 100
```

We can obtain the same result in DAX by nesting function calls:

```
EVALUATE
FILTER (
    SUMMARIZECOLUMNS (
        Customers[CustomerName],
        "SumOfSales", SUM ( Sales[SalesAmount] )
    ),
    [SumOfSales] > 100
)
```

In this code, the subquery that retrieves *CustomerName* and *SumOfSales* is later fed into a *FILTER* function that retains only the rows where *SumOfSales* is greater than 100. Right now, this code might seem unreadable to you. However, as soon as you start learning DAX, you will discover that using subqueries is much easier than in SQL, and it flows naturally because DAX is a functional language.

DAX for MDX developers

Many Business Intelligence professionals start learning DAX because it is the new language of Tabular. In the past, they used the MDX language to build and query Analysis Services Multidimensional models. If you are among them, be prepared to learn a completely new language: DAX and MDX do not share much in common. Worse, some concepts in DAX will remind you of similar existing concepts in MDX though they are different.

In our experience, we have found that learning DAX after learning MDX is the most challenging option. To learn DAX, you need to free your mind from MDX. Try to forget everything you know about multidimensional spaces and be prepared to learn this new language with a clear mind.

Multidimensional versus Tabular

MDX works in the multidimensional space defined by a model. The shape of the multidimensional space is based on the architecture of dimensions and hierarchies defined in the model, and this, in turn, defines the set of coordinates of the multidimensional space. Intersections of sets of members in different dimensions define points in the multidimensional space. You may have taken some time to realize that the *[All]* member of any attribute hierarchy is indeed a point in the multidimensional space.

DAX works in a much simpler way. There are no dimensions, no members, and no points in the multidimensional space. In other words, there is no multidimensional space at all. There are hierarchies, which we can define in the model, but they are different from hierarchies in MDX. The DAX space is built on top of tables, columns, and relationships. Each table in a Tabular model is neither a measure group nor a dimension: it is just a table, and to compute values, you scan it, filter it, or sum values inside it. Everything is based on the two simple concepts of tables and relationships.

You will soon discover that from the modeling point of view, Tabular offers fewer options than Multidimensional does. In this case, having fewer options does not mean being less powerful because you can use DAX as a programming language to enrich the model. The real modeling power of Tabular is the tremendous speed of DAX. In fact, you probably try to avoid overusing MDX in your model because optimizing MDX speed is often a challenge. DAX, on the other hand, is amazingly fast. Thus, most of the complexity of the calculations is not in the model but in the DAX formulas instead.

DAX as a programming and querying language

DAX and MDX are both programming languages and query languages. In MDX, the difference is made clear by the presence of the MDX script. You use MDX in the MDX script, along with several special statements that can be used in the script only, such as *SCOPE* statements. You use MDX in queries when you write *SELECT* statements that retrieve data. In DAX, this is somewhat different. You use DAX as a programming language to define calculated columns, calculated tables, and measures. The concept of calculated columns and calculated tables is new to DAX and does not exist in MDX; measures are similar to calculated members in MDX. You can also use DAX as a query language—for example, to retrieve data from a Tabular model using Reporting Services. Nevertheless, DAX functions do not have a specific role and can be used in both queries and calculation expressions. Moreover, you can also query a Tabular model using MDX. Thus, the querying part of MDX works with Tabular models, whereas DAX is the only option when it comes to programming a Tabular model.

Hierarchies

Using MDX, you rely on hierarchies to perform most of the calculations. If you wanted to compute the sales in the previous year, you would have to retrieve the *PrevMember* of the *CurrentMember* on the *Year* hierarchy and use it to override the MDX filter. For example, you can write the formula this way to define a previous year calculation in MDX:

```
CREATE MEMBER CURRENTCUBE.[Measures].[SamePeriodPreviousYearSales] AS
(
    [Measures].[Sales Amount],
    ParallelPeriod (
        [Date].[Calendar].[Calendar Year],
        1,
        [Date].[Calendar].CurrentMember
    )
);
```

The measure uses the *ParallelPeriod* function, which returns the cousin of the *CurrentMember* on the *Calendar* hierarchy. Thus, it is based on the hierarchies defined in the model. We would write the same calculation in DAX using filter contexts and standard time-intelligence functions:

```
SamePeriodPreviousYearSales :=
CALCULATE (
    SUM ( Sales[Sales Amount] ),
    SAMEPERIODLASTYEAR ( 'Date'[Date] )
)
```

We can write the same calculation in many other ways using *FILTER* and other DAX functions, but the idea remains the same: instead of using hierarchies, we filter tables. This difference is huge, and you will probably miss hierarchy calculations until you get used to DAX.

Another important difference is that in MDX you refer to *[Measures].[Sales Amount]*, and the aggregation function that you need to use is already defined in the model. In DAX, there is no predefined aggregation. In fact, as you might have noticed, the expression to compute is *SUM(Sales[Sales Amount])*. The predefined aggregation is no longer in the model. We need to define it whenever we want to use it. We can always create a measure that computes the sum of sales, but this would be beyond the scope of this section and is explained later in the book.

One more important difference between DAX and MDX is that MDX makes heavy use of the *SCOPE* statement to implement business logic (again, using hierarchies), whereas DAX needs a completely different approach. Indeed, hierarchy handling is missing in the language altogether.

For example, if we want to clear a measure at the *Year* level, in MDX we would write this statement:

```
SCOPE ( [Measures].[SamePeriodPreviousYearSales], [Date].[Month].[All] )
    THIS = NULL;
END SCOPE;
```

DAX does not have something like a *SCOPE* statement. To obtain the same result, we need to check for the presence of filters in the filter context, and the scenario is much more complex:

```
SamePeriodPreviousYearSales :=
IF (
    ISINSCOPE ( 'Date'[Month] ),
    CALCULATE (
        SUM ( Sales[Sales Amount] ),
        SAMEPERIODLASTYEAR ( 'Date'[Date] )
    ),
    BLANK ()
)
```

Intuitively, this formula returns a value only if the user is browsing the calendar hierarchy at the month level or below. Otherwise, it returns a *BLANK*. You will later learn what this formula computes in detail. It is much more error-prone than the equivalent MDX code. To be honest, hierarchy handling is one of the features that is really missing in DAX.

Leaf-level calculations

Finally, when using MDX, you probably got used to avoiding leaf-level calculations. Performing leaf-level computation in MDX turns out to be so slow that you should always prefer to precompute values and leverage aggregations to return results. In DAX, leaf-level calculations work incredibly fast and aggregations serve a different purpose, being useful only for large datasets. This requires a shift in your mind when it is time to build the data models. In most cases, a data model that fits perfectly in SSAS Multidimensional is not the right fit for Tabular and vice versa.

DAX for Power BI users

If you skipped the previous sections and directly came here, welcome! DAX is the native language of Power BI, and if you do not have experience in Excel, SQL, or MDX, Power BI will be the first place where you learn DAX. If you do not have previous experience in building models with other tools, you will learn that Power BI is a powerful analytical and modeling tool, with DAX as the perfect companion.

You might have started using Power BI a while ago and now you want to get to the next level. If this is the case, be prepared for a wonderful journey with DAX.

Here is our advice to you: do not expect to be able to write complex DAX code in a matter of a few days. DAX requires your time and dedication, and mastering it requires some practice. Based on our experience, you will be excited at first when you are rewarded with a few simple calculations.

The excitement fades away as soon as you start learning about evaluation contexts and *CALCULATE*, the most complex topics of the language. At that point, everything looks complex. Do not give up; most DAX developers had to move past that level. When you are there, you are so close to reaching a full understanding that it would be a real pity to stop. Read and practice again and again because a lightbulb will go off much sooner that you would expect. You will be able to finish the book quickly, reaching DAX guru status.

Evaluation contexts are at the core of the language. Mastering them takes time. We do not know anyone who was able to learn all about DAX in a couple of days. Besides, as with any complex topic, you will learn to appreciate a lot of the details over time. When you think you have learned everything, give the book a second read. You will discover many details that looked less important at first sight but, with a more trained mindset, really make a difference.

Enjoy the rest of this book!

CHAPTER 2

Introducing DAX

In this chapter, we start talking about the DAX language. Here you learn the syntax of the language, the difference between a calculated column and a measure (also called calculated field, in certain old Excel versions), and the most commonly used functions in DAX.

Because this is an introductory chapter, it does not cover many functions in depth. In later chapters, we explain them in more detail. For now, introducing the functions and starting to look at the DAX language in general are enough. When we reference features of the data model in Power BI, Power Pivot, or Analysis Services, we use the term *Tabular* even when the feature is not present in all the products. For example, "DirectQuery in Tabular" refers to the DirectQuery mode feature available in Power BI and Analysis Services but not in Excel.

Understanding DAX calculations

Before working on more complex formulas, you need to learn the basics of DAX. This includes DAX syntax, the different data types that DAX can handle, the basic operators, and how to refer to columns and tables. These concepts are discussed in the next few sections.

We use DAX to compute values over columns in tables. We can aggregate, calculate, and search for numbers, but in the end, all the calculations involve tables and columns. Thus, the first syntax to learn is how to reference a column in a table.

The general format is to write the table name enclosed in single quotation marks, followed by the column name enclosed in square brackets, as follows:

```
'Sales'[Quantity]
```

We can omit the single quotation marks if the table name does not start with a number, does not contain spaces, and is not a reserved word (like *Date* or *Sum*).

The table name is also optional in case we are referencing a column or a measure within the table where we define the formula. Thus, *[Quantity]* is a valid column reference, if written in a calculated column or in a measure defined in the *Sales* table. Although this option is available, we strongly discourage you from omitting the table name. At this point, we do not explain why this is so important, but the reason will become clear when you read Chapter 5, "Understanding CALCULATE and CALCULATETABLE." Nevertheless, it is of paramount importance to be able to distinguish between measures (discussed later) and columns when you read DAX code. The de facto standard is to always use the table name in column references and always avoid it in measure references. The earlier you start adopting this standard, the easier your life with DAX will be. Therefore, you should get used to this way of referencing columns and measures:

```
Sales[Quantity] * 2          -- This is a column reference
[Sales Amount] * 2           -- This is a measure reference
```

You will learn the rationale behind this standard after learning about context transition, which comes in Chapter 5. For now, just trust us and adhere to this standard.

Comments in DAX

The preceding code example shows comments in DAX for the first time. DAX supports single-line comments and multiline comments. Single-line comments start with either -- or //, and the remaining part of the line is considered a comment.

```
= Sales[Quantity] * Sales[Net Price]    -- Single-line comment
= Sales[Quantity] * Sales[Unit Cost]    // Another example of single-line comment
```

A multiline comment starts with /* and ends with */. The DAX parser ignores everything included between these markers and considers them a comment.

```
= IF (
    Sales[Quantity] > 1,
    /* First example of a multiline comment
       Anything can be written here and is ignored by DAX
    */
    "Multi",
    /* A common use case of multiline comments is to comment-out a part of
       the existing code
       The next IF statement is ignored because it falls within a multiline comment
       IF (
           Sales[Quantity] = 1,
           "Single",
           "Special note"
       )
    */
    "Single"
)
```

It is better to avoid comments at the end of a DAX expression in a measure, calculated column, or calculated table definition. These comments might be not visible at first, and they might not be supported by tools such as DAX Formatter, which is discussed later in this chapter.

DAX data types

DAX can perform computations with different numeric types, of which there are seven. Over time, Microsoft introduced different names for the same data types, creating some sort of confusion. Table 2-1 provides the different names under which you might find each DAX data type.

TABLE 2-1 Data Types

DAX Data Type	Power BI Data Type	Power Pivot and Analysis Services Data Type	Correspondent Conventional Data Type (e.g., SQL Server)	Tabular Object Model (TOM) Data Type
Integer	Whole Number	Whole Number	Integer / INT	int64
Decimal	Decimal Number	Decimal Number	Floating point / DOUBLE	double
Currency	Fixed Decimal Number	Currency	Currency / MONEY	decimal
DateTime	DateTime, Date, Time	Date	Date / DATETIME	dateTime
Boolean	True/False	True/False	Boolean / BIT	boolean
String	Text	Text	String / NVARCHAR(MAX)	string
Variant	-	-	-	variant
Binary	Binary	Binary	Blob / VARBINARY(MAX)	binary

In this book, we use the names in the first column of Table 2-1 adhering to the de facto standards in the database and Business Intelligence community. For example, in Power BI, a column containing either *TRUE* or *FALSE* would be called *TRUE/FALSE*, whereas in SQL Server, it would be called a *BIT*. Nevertheless, the historical and most common name for this type of value is Boolean.

DAX comes with a powerful type-handling system so that we do not have to worry about data types. In a DAX expression, the resulting type is based on the type of the term used in the expression. You need to be aware of this in case the type returned from a DAX expression is not the expected type; you would then have to investigate the data type of the terms used in the expression itself.

For example, if one of the terms of a sum is a date, the result also is a date; likewise, if the same operator is used with integers, the result is an integer. This behavior is known as *operator overloading*, and an example is shown in Figure 2-1, where the *OrderDatePlusOneWeek* column is calculated by adding 7 to the value of the *Order Date* column.

```
Sales[OrderDatePlusOneWeek] = Sales[Order Date] + 7
```

The result is a date.

Order Date	OrderDatePlusOneWeek
10/08/2008	10/15/2008
10/10/2008	10/17/2008
10/12/2008	10/19/2008
09/05/2008	09/12/2008
09/07/2008	09/14/2008
09/23/2008	09/30/2008
11/05/2008	11/12/2008
11/07/2008	11/14/2008
11/09/2008	11/16/2008
11/17/2008	11/24/2008

FIGURE 2-1 Adding an integer to a date results in a date increased by the corresponding number of days.

In addition to operator overloading, DAX automatically converts strings into numbers and numbers into strings whenever required by the operator. For example, if we use the & operator, which concatenates strings, DAX converts its arguments into strings. The following formula returns "54" as a string:

```
= 5 & 4
```

On the other hand, this formula returns an integer result with the value of 9:

```
= "5" + "4"
```

The resulting value depends on the operator and not on the source columns, which are converted following the requirements of the operator. Although this behavior looks convenient, later in this chapter you see what kinds of errors might happen during these automatic conversions. Moreover, not all the operators follow this behavior. For example, comparison operators cannot compare strings with numbers. Consequently, you can add one number with a string, but you cannot compare a number with a string. You can find a complete reference here: https://docs.microsoft.com/en-us/power-bi/desktop-data-types. Because the rules are so complex, we suggest you avoid automatic conversions altogether. If a conversion needs to happen, we recommend that you control it and make the conversion explicit. To be more explicit, the previous example should be written like this:

```
= VALUE ( "5" ) + VALUE ( "4" )
```

People accustomed to working with Excel or other languages might be familiar with DAX data types. Some details about data types depend on the engine, and they might be different for Power BI, Power

Pivot, or Analysis Services. You can find more detailed information about Analysis Services DAX data types at http://msdn.microsoft.com/en-us/library/gg492146.aspx, and Power BI information is available at https://docs.microsoft.com/en-us/power-bi/desktop-data-types. However, it is useful to share a few considerations about each of these data types.

Integer

DAX has only one *Integer* data type that can store a 64-bit value. All the internal calculations between integer values in DAX also use a 64-bit value.

Decimal

A *Decimal* number is always stored as a double-precision floating-point value. Do not confuse this DAX data type with the *decimal* and *numeric* data type of *Transact-SQL*. The corresponding data type of a DAX decimal number in SQL is *Float*.

Currency

The *Currency* data type, also known as *Fixed Decimal Number* in Power BI, stores a fixed decimal number. It can represent four decimal points and is internally stored as a 64-bit integer value divided by 10,000. Summing or subtracting *Currency* data types always ignores decimals beyond the fourth decimal point, whereas multiplication and division produce a floating-point value, thus increasing the precision of the result. In general, if we need more accuracy than the four digits provided, we must use a *Decimal* data type.

The default format of the *Currency* data type includes the currency symbol. We can also apply the currency formatting to *Integer* and decimal numbers, and we can use a format without the currency symbol for a *Currency* data type.

DateTime

DAX stores dates as a *DateTime* data type. This format uses a floating-point number internally, wherein the integer corresponds to the number of days since December 30, 1899, and the decimal part identifies the fraction of the day. Hours, minutes, and seconds are converted to decimal fractions of a day. Thus, the following expression returns the current date plus one day (exactly 24 hours):

```
= TODAY () + 1
```

The result is tomorrow's date at the time of the evaluation. If you need to take only the date part of a *DateTime,* always remember to use *TRUNC* to get rid of the decimal part.

Power BI offers two additional data types: *Date* and *Time*. Internally, they are a simple variation of *DateTime*. Indeed, *Date* and *Time* store only the integer or the decimal part of the *DateTime*, respectively.

Boolean

The *Boolean* data type is used to express logical conditions. For example, a calculated column defined by the following expression is of *Boolean* type:

```
= Sales[Unit Price] > Sales[Unit Cost]
```

You will also see *Boolean* data types as numbers where *TRUE* equals 1 and *FALSE* equals 0. This notation sometimes proves useful for sorting purposes because *TRUE* > *FALSE*.

String

Every string in DAX is stored as a *Unicode* string, where each character is stored in 16 bits. By default, the comparison between strings is not case sensitive, so the two strings "Power BI" and "POWER BI" are considered equal.

Variant

The *Variant* data type is used for expressions that might return different data types, depending on the conditions. For example, the following statement can return either an integer or a string, so it returns a variant type:

```
IF ( [measure] > 0, 1, "N/A" )
```

The *Variant* data type cannot be used as a data type for a column in a regular table. A DAX measure, and in general, a DAX expression can be *Variant*.

Binary

The *Binary* data type is used in the data model to store images or other nonstructured types of information. It is not available in DAX. It was mainly used by Power View, but it might not be available in other tools such as Power BI.

DAX operators

Now that you have seen the importance of operators in determining the type of an expression, see Table 2-2, which provides a list of the operators available in DAX.

TABLE 2-2 Operators

Operator Type	Symbol	Use	Example
Parenthesis	( )	Precedence order and grouping of arguments	(5 + 2) * 3
Arithmetic	+ – * /	Addition Subtraction/negation Multiplication Division	4 + 2 5 – 3 4 * 2 4 / 2
Comparison	= <> > >= < <=	Equal to Not equal to Greater than Greater than or equal to Less than Less than or equal to	[CountryRegion] = "USA" [CountryRegion] <> "USA" [Quantity] > 0 [Quantity] >= 100 [Quantity] < 0 [Quantity] <= 100
Text concatenation	&	Concatenation of strings	"Value is" & [Amount]
Logical	&& || IN NOT	AND condition between two Boolean expressions OR condition between two Boolean expressions Inclusion of an element in a list Boolean negation	[CountryRegion] = "USA" && [Quantity]>0 [CountryRegion] = "USA" || [Quantity] > 0 [CountryRegion] IN {"USA", "Canada"} NOT [Quantity] > 0

Moreover, the logical operators are also available as DAX functions, with a syntax similar to Excel's. For example, we can write expressions like these:

```
AND ( [CountryRegion] = "USA", [Quantity] > 0 )
OR ( [CountryRegion] = "USA", [Quantity] > 0 )
```

These examples are equivalent, respectively, to the following:

```
[CountryRegion] = "USA" && [Quantity] > 0
[CountryRegion] = "USA" || [Quantity] > 0
```

Using functions instead of operators for Boolean logic becomes helpful when writing complex conditions. In fact, when it comes to formatting large sections of code, functions are much easier to format and to read than operators are. However, a major drawback of functions is that we can pass in only two parameters at a time. Therefore, we must nest functions if we have more than two conditions to evaluate.

Table constructors

In DAX we can define anonymous tables directly in the code. If the table has a single column, the syntax requires only a list of values—one for each row—delimited by curly braces. We can delimit multiple rows by parentheses, which are optional if the table is made of a single column. The two following definitions, for example, are equivalent:

```
{ "Red", "Blue", "White" }
{ ( "Red" ), ( "Blue" ), ( "White" ) }
```

If the table has multiple columns, parentheses are mandatory. Every column should have the same data type throughout all its rows; otherwise, DAX will automatically convert the column to a data type that can accommodate all the data types provided in different rows for the same column.

```
{
    ( "A", 10, 1.5, DATE ( 2017, 1, 1 ), CURRENCY ( 199.99 ), TRUE ),
    ( "B", 20, 2.5, DATE ( 2017, 1, 2 ), CURRENCY ( 249.99 ), FALSE ),
    ( "C", 30, 3.5, DATE ( 2017, 1, 3 ), CURRENCY ( 299.99 ), FALSE )
}
```

The table constructor is commonly used with the *IN* operator. For example, the following are possible, valid syntaxes in a DAX predicate:

```
'Product'[Color] IN { "Red", "Blue", "White" }

( 'Date'[Year], 'Date'[MonthNumber] ) IN { ( 2017, 12 ), ( 2018, 1 ) }
```

This second example shows the syntax required to compare a set of columns (tuple) using the *IN* operator. Such syntax cannot be used with a comparison operator. In other words, the following syntax is not valid:

```
( 'Date'[Year], 'Date'[MonthNumber] ) = ( 2007, 12 )
```

However, we can rewrite it using the *IN* operator with a table constructor that has a single row, as in the following example:

```
( 'Date'[Year], 'Date'[MonthNumber] ) IN { ( 2007, 12 ) }
```

Conditional statements

In DAX we can write a conditional expression using the *IF* function. For example, we can write an expression returning MULTI or SINGLE depending on the quantity value being greater than one or not, respectively.

```
IF (
    Sales[Quantity] > 1,
    "MULTI",
    "SINGLE"
)
```

The *IF* function has three parameters, but only the first two are mandatory. The third is optional, and it defaults to *BLANK*. Consider the following code:

```
IF (
    Sales[Quantity] > 1,
    Sales[Quantity]
)
```

It corresponds to the following explicit version:

```
IF (
    Sales[Quantity] > 1,
    Sales[Quantity],
    BLANK ()
)
```

Understanding calculated columns and measures

Now that you know the basics of DAX syntax, you need to learn one of the most important concepts in DAX: the difference between calculated columns and measures. Even though calculated columns and measures might appear similar at first sight because you can make certain calculations using either, they are, in reality, different. Understanding the difference is key to unlocking the power of DAX.

Calculated columns

Depending on the tool you are using, you can create a calculated column in different ways. Indeed, the concept remains the same: a calculated column is a new column added to your model, but instead of being loaded from a data source, it is created by resorting to a DAX formula.

A calculated column is just like any other column in a table, and we can use it in rows, columns, filters, or values of a matrix or any other report. We can also use a calculated column to define a relationship, if needed. The DAX expression defined for a calculated column operates in the context of the current row of the table that the calculated column belongs to. Any reference to a column returns the value of that column for the current row. We cannot directly access the values of other rows.

If you are using the default *Import Mode* of Tabular and are not using DirectQuery, one important concept to remember about calculated columns is that these columns are computed during database processing and then stored in the model. This concept might seem strange if you are accustomed to SQL-computed columns (not persisted), which are evaluated at query time and do not use memory. In Tabular, however, all calculated columns occupy space in memory and are computed during table processing.

This behavior is helpful whenever we create complex calculated columns. The time required to compute complex calculated columns is always process time and not query time, resulting in a better user experience. Nevertheless, be mindful that a calculated column uses precious RAM. For example, if we have a complex formula for a calculated column, we might be tempted to separate the steps of computation into different intermediate columns. Although this technique is useful during project development, it is a bad habit in production because each intermediate calculation is stored in RAM and wastes valuable space.

If a model is based on DirectQuery instead, the behavior is hugely different. In DirectQuery mode, calculated columns are computed on the fly when the Tabular engine queries the data source. This might result in heavy queries executed by the data source, therefore producing slow models.

Computing the duration of an order

Imagine we have a *Sales* table containing both the order and the delivery dates. Using these two columns, we can compute the number of days involved in delivering the order. Because dates are stored as number of days after 12/30/1899, a simple subtraction computes the difference in days between two dates:

```
Sales[DaysToDeliver] = Sales[Delivery Date] - Sales[Order Date]
```

Nevertheless, because the two columns used for subtraction are dates, the result also is a date. To produce a numeric result, convert the result to an integer this way:

```
Sales[DaysToDeliver] = INT ( Sales[Delivery Date] - Sales[Order Date] )
```

The result is shown in Figure 2-2.

Order Date	Delivery Date	DaysToDeliver
01/02/2007	01/08/2007	6
01/02/2007	01/09/2007	7
01/02/2007	01/10/2007	8
01/02/2007	01/11/2007	9
01/02/2007	01/12/2007	10
01/02/2007	01/13/2007	11
01/02/2007	01/14/2007	12

FIGURE 2-2 By subtracting two dates and converting the result to an integer, DAX computes the number of days between the two dates.

Measures

Calculated columns are useful, but you can define calculations in a DAX model in another way. Whenever you do not want to compute values for each row but rather want to aggregate values from many rows in a table, you will find these calculations useful; they are called *measures*.

For example, you can define a few calculated columns in the *Sales* table to compute the gross margin amount:

```
Sales[SalesAmount] = Sales[Quantity] * Sales[Net Price]
Sales[TotalCost] = Sales[Quantity] * Sales[Unit Cost]
Sales[GrossMargin] = Sales[SalesAmount] - Sales[TotalCost]
```

What happens if you want to show the gross margin as a percentage of the sales amount? You could create a calculated column with the following formula:

```
Sales[GrossMarginPct] = Sales[GrossMargin] / Sales[SalesAmount]
```

This formula computes the correct value at the row level—as you can see in Figure 2-3—but at the grand total level the result is clearly wrong.

SalesKey ▲	SalesAmount	TotalCost	GrossMargin	GrossMarginPct
20070104611301-0002	$72.19	$38.74	$33.45	46.34%
20070104611301-0003	$23.75	$11.50	$12.25	51.58%
20070104611320-0006	$216.57	$116.22	$100.35	46.34%
20070104611320-0007	$23.75	$11.50	$12.25	51.58%
20070104611506-0002	$72.19	$38.74	$33.45	46.34%
20070104611506-0003	$23.75	$11.50	$12.25	51.58%
20070104611914-0002	$64.59	$38.74	$25.85	40.02%
20070104611914-0003	$21.25	$11.50	$9.75	45.88%
20070104611952-0004	$64.59	$38.74	$25.85	40.02%
20070104611952-0005	$21.25	$11.50	$9.75	45.88%
20070104611998-0002	$64.59	$38.74	$25.85	40.02%
20070104611998-0003	$63.75	$34.50	$29.25	45.88%
Total	**$732.23**	**$401.92**	**$330.31**	**551.46%**

FIGURE 2-3 The *GrossMarginPct* column shows a correct value on each row, but the grand total is incorrect.

The value shown at the grand total level is the sum of the individual percentages computed row by row within the calculated column. When we compute the aggregate value of a percentage, we cannot rely on calculated columns. Instead, we need to compute the percentage based on the sum of individual columns. We must compute the aggregated value as the sum of gross margin divided by the sum of sales amount. In this case, we need to compute the ratio on the aggregates; you cannot use an aggregation of calculated columns. In other words, we compute the ratio of the sums, not the sum of the ratios.

It would be equally wrong to simply change the aggregation of the *GrossMarginPct* column to an average and rely on the result because doing so would provide an incorrect evaluation of the percentage, not considering the differences between amounts. The result of this averaged value is visible in Figure 2-4, and you can easily check that (330.31 / 732.23) is not equal to the value displayed, 45.96%; it should be 45.11% instead.

SalesKey	SalesAmount	TotalCost	GrossMargin	Average of GrossMarginPct
20070104611301-0002	$72.19	$38.74	$33.45	46.34%
20070104611301-0003	$23.75	$11.50	$12.25	51.58%
20070104611320-0006	$216.57	$116.22	$100.35	46.34%
20070104611320-0007	$23.75	$11.50	$12.25	51.58%
20070104611506-0002	$72.19	$38.74	$33.45	46.34%
20070104611506-0003	$23.75	$11.50	$12.25	51.58%
20070104611914-0002	$64.59	$38.74	$25.85	40.02%
20070104611914-0003	$21.25	$11.50	$9.75	45.88%
20070104611952-0004	$64.59	$38.74	$25.85	40.02%
20070104611952-0005	$21.25	$11.50	$9.75	45.88%
20070104611998-0002	$64.59	$38.74	$25.85	40.02%
20070104611998-0003	$63.75	$34.50	$29.25	45.88%
Total	**$732.23**	**$401.92**	**$330.31**	**45.96%**

FIGURE 2-4 Changing the aggregation method to *AVERAGE* does not provide the correct result.

The correct implementation for *GrossMarginPct* is with a measure:

```
GrossMarginPct := SUM ( Sales[GrossMargin] ) / SUM (Sales[SalesAmount] )
```

As we have already stated, the correct result cannot be achieved with a calculated column. If you need to operate on aggregated values instead of operating on a row-by-row basis, you must create measures. You might have noticed that we used := to define a measure instead of the equal sign (=). This is a standard we used throughout the book to make it easier to differentiate between measures and calculated columns in code.

After you define *GrossMarginPct* as a measure, the result is correct, as you can see in Figure 2-5.

SalesKey	SalesAmount	TotalCost	GrossMargin	GrossMarginPct
20070104611301-0002	$72.19	$38.74	$33.45	46.34%
20070104611301-0003	$23.75	$11.50	$12.25	51.58%
20070104611320-0006	$216.57	$116.22	$100.35	46.34%
20070104611320-0007	$23.75	$11.50	$12.25	51.58%
20070104611506-0002	$72.19	$38.74	$33.45	46.34%
20070104611506-0003	$23.75	$11.50	$12.25	51.58%
20070104611914-0002	$64.59	$38.74	$25.85	40.02%
20070104611914-0003	$21.25	$11.50	$9.75	45.88%
20070104611952-0004	$64.59	$38.74	$25.85	40.02%
20070104611952-0005	$21.25	$11.50	$9.75	45.88%
20070104611998-0002	$64.59	$38.74	$25.85	40.02%
20070104611998-0003	$63.75	$34.50	$29.25	45.88%
Total	**$732.23**	**$401.92**	**$330.31**	**45.11%**

FIGURE 2-5 *GrossMarginPct* defined as a measure shows the correct grand total.

Measures and calculated columns both use DAX expressions; the difference is the context of evaluation. A measure is evaluated in the context of a visual element or in the context of a DAX query. However, a calculated column is computed at the row level of the table it belongs to. The context of the visual element (later in the book, you will learn that this is a filter context) depends on user selections in the report or on the format of the DAX query. Therefore, when using *SUM(Sales[SalesAmount])* in a measure, we mean the sum of all the rows that are aggregated under a visualization. However, when we use *Sales[SalesAmount]* in a calculated column, we mean the value of the *SalesAmount* column in the current row.

A measure needs to be defined in a table. This is one of the requirements of the DAX language. However, the measure does not really belong to the table. Indeed, we can move a measure from one table to another table without losing its functionality.

Differences between calculated columns and measures

Although they look similar, there is a big difference between calculated columns and measures. The value of a calculated column is computed during data refresh, and it uses the current row as a context. The result does not depend on user activity on the report. A measure operates on aggregations of data defined by the current context. In a matrix or in a pivot table, for example, source tables are filtered according to the coordinates of cells, and data is aggregated and calculated using these filters. In other words, a measure always operates on aggregations of data under the evaluation context. The evaluation context is explained further in Chapter 4, "Understanding evaluation contexts."

Choosing between calculated columns and measures

Now that you have seen the difference between calculated columns and measures, it is useful to discuss when to use one over the other. Sometimes either is an option, but in most situations, the computation requirements determine the choice.

As a developer, you must define a calculated column whenever you want to do the following:

- Place the calculated results in a slicer or see results in rows or columns in a matrix or in a pivot table (as opposed to the Values area), or use the calculated column as a filter condition in a DAX query.

- Define an expression that is strictly bound to the current row. For example, *Price * Quantity* cannot work on an average or on a sum of those two columns.

- Categorize text or numbers. For example, a range of values for a measure, a range of ages of customers, such as 0–18, 18–25, and so on. These categories are often used as filters or to slice and dice values.

However, it is mandatory to define a measure whenever one wants to display calculation values that reflect user selections, and the values need to be presented as aggregates in a report, for example:

- To calculate the profit percentage of a report selection
- To calculate ratios of a product compared to all products but keep the filter both by year and by region

We can express many calculations both with calculated columns and with measures, although we need to use different DAX expressions for each. For example, one can define the *GrossMargin* as a calculated column:

```
Sales[GrossMargin] = Sales[SalesAmount] - Sales[TotalProductCost]
```

However, it can also be defined as a measure:

```
GrossMargin := SUM ( Sales[SalesAmount] ) - SUM ( Sales[TotalProductCost] )
```

We suggest you use a measure in this case because, being evaluated at query time, it does not consume memory and disk space. As a rule, whenever you can express a calculation both ways, measures are the preferred way to go. You should limit the use of calculated columns to the few cases where they are strictly needed. Users with Excel experience typically prefer calculated columns over measures because calculated columns closely resemble the way of performing calculations in Excel. Nevertheless, the best way to compute a value in DAX is through a measure.

Using measures in calculated columns

It is obvious that a measure can refer to one or more calculated columns. Although less intuitive, the opposite is also true. A calculated column can refer to a measure. This way, the calculated column forces the calculation of a measure for the context defined by the current row. This operation transforms and consolidates the result of a measure into a column, which will not be influenced by user actions. Obviously, only certain operations can produce meaningful results because a measure usually makes computations that strongly depend on the selection made by the user in the visualization. Moreover, whenever you, as the developer, use measures in a calculated column, you rely on a feature called *context transition*, which is an advanced calculation technique in DAX. Before you use a measure in a calculated column, we strongly suggest you read and understand Chapter 4, which explains in detail evaluation contexts and context transitions.

Introducing variables

When writing a DAX expression, one can avoid repeating the same expression and greatly enhance the code readability by using variables. For example, look at the following expression:

```
VAR TotalSales = SUM ( Sales[SalesAmount] )
VAR TotalCosts = SUM ( Sales[TotalProductCost] )
```

```
VAR GrossMargin = TotalSales - TotalCosts
RETURN
    GrossMargin / TotalSales
```

Variables are defined with the *VAR* keyword. After you define a variable, you need to provide a *RETURN* section that defines the result value of the expression. One can define many variables, and the variables are local to the expression in which they are defined.

A variable defined in an expression cannot be used outside the expression itself. There is no such thing as a global variable definition. This means that you cannot define variables used through the whole DAX code of the model.

Variables are computed using lazy evaluation. This means that if one defines a variable that, for any reason, is not used in the code, the variable itself will never be evaluated. If it needs to be computed, this happens only once. Later uses of the variable will read the value computed previously. Thus, variables are also useful as an optimization technique when used in a complex expression multiple times.

Variables are an important tool in DAX. As you will learn in Chapter 4, variables are extremely useful because they use the definition evaluation context instead of the context where the variable is used. In Chapter 6, "Variables," we will fully cover variables and how to use them. We will also use variables extensively throughout the book.

Handling errors in DAX expressions

Now that you have seen some of the basics of the syntax, it is time to learn how to handle invalid calculations gracefully. A DAX expression might contain invalid calculations because the data it references is not valid for the formula. For example, the formula might contain a division by zero or reference a column value that is not a number while being used in an arithmetic operation such as multiplication. It is good to learn how these errors are handled by default and how to intercept these conditions for special handling.

Before discussing how to handle errors, though, we describe the different kinds of errors that might appear during a DAX formula evaluation. They are

- Conversion errors

- Arithmetic operations errors

- Empty or missing values

Conversion errors

The first kind of error is the conversion error. As we showed previously in this chapter, DAX automatically converts values between strings and numbers whenever the operator requires it. All these examples are valid DAX expressions:

```
"10" + 32 = 42
"10" & 32 = "1032"
```

```
10 & 32 = "1032"
DATE (2010,3,25) = 3/25/2010
DATE (2010,3,25) + 14 = 4/8/2010
DATE (2010,3,25) & 14 = "3/25/201014"
```

These formulas are always correct because they operate with constant values. However, what about the following formula if *VatCode* is a string?

```
Sales[VatCode] + 100
```

Because the first operand of this sum is a column that is of *Text* data type, you as a developer must be confident that DAX can convert all the values in that column into numbers. If DAX fails in converting some of the content to suit the operator needs, a conversion error will occur. Here are some typical situations:

```
"1 + 1" + 0 = Cannot convert value '1 + 1' of type Text to type Number
DATEVALUE ("25/14/2010") = Type mismatch
```

If you want to avoid these errors, it is important to add error detection logic in DAX expressions to intercept error conditions and return a result that makes sense. One can obtain the same result by intercepting the error after it has happened or by checking the operands for the error situation before-hand. Nevertheless, checking for the error situation proactively is better than letting the error happen and then catching it.

Arithmetic operations errors

The second category of errors is arithmetic operations, such as the division by zero or the square root of a negative number. These are not conversion-related errors: DAX raises them whenever we try to call a function or use an operator with invalid values.

The division by zero requires special handling because its behavior is not intuitive (except, maybe, for mathematicians). When one divides a number by zero, DAX returns the special value *Infinity*. In the special cases of 0 divided by 0 or *Infinity* divided by *Infinity*, DAX returns the special *NaN* (not a number) value.

Because this is unusual behavior, it is summarized in Table 2-3.

TABLE 2-3 Special Result Values for Division by Zero

Expression	Result
10 / 0	Infinity
7 / 0	Infinity
0 / 0	NaN
(10 / 0) / (7 / 0)	NaN

It is important to note that *Infinity* and *NaN* are not errors but special values in DAX. In fact, if one divides a number by *Infinity*, the expression does not generate an error. Instead, it returns 0:

```
9954 / ( 7 / 0 ) = 0
```

Apart from this special situation, DAX can return arithmetic errors when calling a function with an incorrect parameter, such as the square root of a negative number:

```
SQRT ( -1 ) = An argument of function 'SQRT' has the wrong data type or the result is too
large or too small
```

If DAX detects errors like this, it blocks any further computation of the expression and raises an error. One can use the *ISERROR* function to check if an expression leads to an error. We show this scenario later in this chapter.

Keep in mind that special values like *NaN* are displayed in the user interface of several tools such as Power BI as regular values. They can, however, be treated as errors when shown by other client tools such as an Excel pivot table. Finally, these special values are detected as errors by the error detection functions.

Empty or missing values

The third category that we examine is not a specific error condition but rather the presence of empty values. Empty values might result in unexpected results or calculation errors when combined with other elements in a calculation.

DAX handles missing values, blank values, or empty cells in the same way, using the value *BLANK*. *BLANK* is not a real value but instead is a special way to identify these conditions. We can obtain the value *BLANK* in a DAX expression by calling the *BLANK* function, which is different from an empty string. For example, the following expression always returns a blank value, which can be displayed as either an empty string or as "(blank)" in different client tools:

```
= BLANK ()
```

On its own, this expression is useless, but the *BLANK* function itself becomes useful every time there is the need to return an empty value. For example, one might want to display an empty result instead of 0. The following expression calculates the total discount for a sale transaction, leaving the blank value if the discount is 0:

```
=IF (
    Sales[DiscountPerc] = 0,              -- Check if there is a discount
    BLANK (),                            -- Return a blank if no discount is present
    Sales[DiscountPerc] * Sales[Amount]  -- Compute the discount otherwise
)
```

BLANK, by itself, is not an error; it is just an empty value. Therefore, an expression containing a *BLANK* might return a value or a blank, depending on the calculation required. For example, the following expression returns *BLANK* whenever *Sales[Amount]* is *BLANK*:

```
= 10 * Sales[Amount]
```

In other words, the result of an arithmetic product is *BLANK* whenever one or both terms are *BLANK*. This creates a challenge when it is necessary to check for a blank value. Because of the implicit conversions, it is impossible to distinguish whether an expression is 0 (or empty string) or *BLANK* using an equal operator. Indeed, the following logical conditions are always true:

```
BLANK () = 0      -- Always returns TRUE
BLANK () = ""     -- Always returns TRUE
```

Therefore, if the columns *Sales[DiscountPerc]* or *Sales[Clerk]* are blank, the following conditions return *TRUE* even if the test is against 0 and empty string, respectively:

```
Sales[DiscountPerc] = 0  -- Returns TRUE if DiscountPerc is either BLANK or 0
Sales[Clerk] = ""        -- Returns TRUE if Clerk is either BLANK or ""
```

In such cases, one can use the *ISBLANK* function to check whether a value is *BLANK* or not:

```
ISBLANK ( Sales[DiscountPerc] )  -- Returns TRUE only if DiscountPerc is BLANK
ISBLANK ( Sales[Clerk] )         -- Returns TRUE only if Clerk is BLANK
```

The propagation of *BLANK* in a DAX expression happens in several other arithmetic and logical operations, as shown in the following examples:

```
BLANK () + BLANK () = BLANK ()
10 * BLANK () = BLANK ()
BLANK () / 3 = BLANK ()
BLANK () / BLANK () = BLANK ()
```

However, the propagation of *BLANK* in the result of an expression does not happen for all formulas. Some calculations do not propagate *BLANK*. Instead, they return a value depending on the other terms of the formula. Examples of these are addition, subtraction, division by *BLANK*, and a logical operation including a *BLANK*. The following expressions show some of these conditions along with their results:

```
BLANK () - 10 = -10
18 + BLANK () = 18
4 / BLANK () = Infinity
0 / BLANK () = NaN
BLANK () || BLANK () = FALSE
BLANK () && BLANK () = FALSE
( BLANK () = BLANK () ) = TRUE
( BLANK () = TRUE ) = FALSE
( BLANK () = FALSE ) = TRUE
( BLANK () = 0 ) = TRUE
( BLANK () = "" ) = TRUE
ISBLANK ( BLANK() ) = TRUE
FALSE || BLANK () = FALSE
FALSE && BLANK () = FALSE
TRUE || BLANK () = TRUE
TRUE && BLANK () = FALSE
```

Empty values in Excel and SQL

Excel has a different way of handling empty values. In Excel, all empty values are considered 0 whenever they are used in a sum or in a multiplication, but they might return an error if they are part of a division or of a logical expression.

In SQL, null values are propagated in an expression differently from what happens with *BLANK* in DAX. As you can see in the previous examples, the presence of a *BLANK* in a DAX expression does not always result in a *BLANK* result, whereas the presence of *NULL* in SQL often evaluates to *NULL* for the entire expression. This difference is relevant whenever you use DirectQuery on top of a relational database because some calculations are executed in SQL and others are executed in DAX. The different semantics of *BLANK* in the two engines might result in unexpected behaviors.

Understanding the behavior of empty or missing values in a DAX expression and using *BLANK* to return an empty cell in a calculation are important skills to control the results of a DAX expression. One can often use *BLANK* as a result when detecting incorrect values or other errors, as we demonstrate in the next section.

Intercepting errors

Now that we have detailed the various kinds of errors that can occur, we still need to show you the techniques to intercept errors and correct them or, at least, produce an error message containing meaningful information. The presence of errors in a DAX expression frequently depends on the value of columns used in the expression itself. Therefore, one might want to control the presence of these error conditions and return an error message. The standard technique is to check whether an expression returns an error and, if so, replace the error with a specific message or a default value. There are a few DAX functions for this task.

The first of them is the *IFERROR* function, which is similar to the *IF* function, but instead of evaluating a Boolean condition, it checks whether an expression returns an error. Two typical uses of the *IFERROR* function are as follows:

```
= IFERROR ( Sales[Quantity] * Sales[Price], BLANK () )
= IFERROR ( SQRT ( Test[Omega] ), BLANK () )
```

In the first expression, if either *Sales[Quantity]* or *Sales[Price]* is a string that cannot be converted into a number, the returned expression is an empty value. Otherwise, the product of *Quantity* and *Price* is returned.

In the second expression, the result is an empty cell every time the *Test[Omega]* column contains a negative number.

Using *IFERROR* this way corresponds to a more general pattern that requires using *ISERROR* and *IF*:

```
= IF (
    ISERROR ( Sales[Quantity] * Sales[Price] ),
    BLANK (),
    Sales[Quantity] * Sales[Price]
)

= IF (
    ISERROR ( SQRT ( Test[Omega] ) ),
    BLANK (),
    SQRT ( Test[Omega] )
)
```

In these cases, *IFERROR* is a better option. One can use *IFERROR* whenever the result is the same expression tested for an error; there is no need to duplicate the expression in two places, and the code is safer and more readable. However, a developer should use *IF* when they want to return the result of a different expression.

Besides, one can avoid raising the error altogether by testing parameters before using them. For example, one can detect whether the argument for *SQRT* is positive, returning *BLANK* for negative values:

```
= IF (
    Test[Omega] >= 0,
    SQRT ( Test[Omega] ),
    BLANK ()
)
```

Considering that the third argument of an *IF* statement defaults to *BLANK*, one can also write the same expression more concisely:

```
= IF (
    Test[Omega] >= 0,
    SQRT ( Test[Omega] )
)
```

A frequent scenario is to test against empty values. *ISBLANK* detects empty values, returning *TRUE* if its argument is *BLANK*. This capability is important especially when a value being unavailable does not imply that it is 0. The following example calculates the cost of shipping for a sale transaction, using a default shipping cost for the product if the transaction itself does not specify a weight:

```
= IF (
    ISBLANK ( Sales[Weight] ),          -- If the weight is missing
    Sales[DefaultShippingCost],         -- then return the default cost
    Sales[Weight] * Sales[ShippingPrice] -- otherwise multiply weight by shipping price
)
```

If we simply multiply product weight by shipping price, we get an empty cost for all the sales transactions without weight data because of the propagation of *BLANK* in multiplications.

When using variables, errors must be checked at the time of variable definition rather than where we use them. In fact, the first formula in the following code returns zero, the second formula always throws an error, and the last one produces different results depending on the version of the product using DAX (the latest version throws an error also):

```
IFERROR ( SQRT ( -1 ), 0 )               -- This returns 0

VAR WrongValue = SQRT ( -1 )             -- Error happens here, so the result is
RETURN                                   -- always an error
    IFERROR ( WrongValue, 0 )            -- This line is never executed

IFERROR (                                -- Different results depending on versions
    VAR WrongValue = SQRT ( -1 )         -- IFERROR throws an error in 2017 versions
    RETURN                               -- IFERROR returns 0 in versions until 2016
        WrongValue,
    0
)
```

The error happens when *WrongValue* is evaluated. Thus, the engine will never execute the *IFERROR* function in the second example, whereas the outcome of the third example depends on product versions. If you need to check for errors, take some extra precautions when using variables.

Avoid using error-handling functions

Although we will cover optimizations later in the book, you need to be aware that error-handling functions might create severe performance issues in your code. It is not that they are slow in and of themselves. The problem is that the DAX engine cannot use optimized paths in its code when errors happen. In most cases, checking operands for possible errors is more efficient than using the error-handling engine. For example, instead of writing this:

```
IFERROR (
    SQRT ( Test[Omega] ),
    BLANK ()
)
```

It is much better to write this:

```
IF (
    Test[Omega] >= 0,
    SQRT ( Test[Omega] ),
    BLANK ()
)
```

This second expression does not need to detect the error and is faster than the previous expression. This, of course, is a general rule. For a detailed explanation, see Chapter 19, "Optimizing DAX."

Another reason to avoid *IFERROR* is that it cannot intercept errors happening at a deeper level of execution. For example, the following code intercepts any error happening in the conversion of the *Table[Amount]* column considering a blank value in case *Amount* does not contain a number. As discussed previously, this execution is expensive because it is evaluated for every row in *Table*.

```
SUMX (
    Table,
    IFERROR ( VALUE ( Table[Amount] ), BLANK () )
)
```

Be mindful that, due to optimizations in the DAX engine, the following code does not intercept the same errors intercepted by the preceding example. If *Table[Amount]* contains a string that is not a number in just one row, the entire expression generates an error that is not intercepted by *IFERROR*.

```
IFERROR (
    SUMX (
        Table,
        VALUE ( Table[Amount] )
    ),
    BLANK ()
)
```

ISERROR has the same behavior as *IFERROR*. Be sure to use them carefully and only to intercept errors raised directly by the expression evaluated within *IFERROR/ISERROR* and not in nested calculations.

Generating errors

Sometimes, an error is just an error, and the formula should not return a default value in case of an error. Indeed, returning a default value would end up producing an actual result that would be incorrect. For example, a configuration table that contains inconsistent data should produce an invalid report rather than numbers that are unreliable, and yet it might be considered correct.

Moreover, instead of a generic error, one might want to produce an error message that is more meaningful to the users. Such a message would help users find where the problem is.

Consider a scenario that requires the computation of the square root of the absolute temperature measured in Kelvin, to approximately adjust the speed of sound in a complex scientific calculation. Obviously, we do not expect that temperature to be a negative number. If that happens due to a problem in the measurement, we need to raise an error and stop the calculation.

In that case, this code is dangerous because it hides the problem:

```
= IFERROR (
    SQRT ( Test[Temperature] ),
    0
)
```

Instead, to protect the calculations, one should write the formula like this:

```
= IF (
    Test[Temperature] >= 0,
    SQRT ( Test[Temperature] ),
    ERROR ( "The temperature cannot be a negative number. Calculation aborted." )
)
```

Formatting DAX code

Before we continue explaining the DAX language, we would like to cover an important aspect of DAX—that is, formatting the code. DAX is a functional language, meaning that no matter how complex it is, a DAX expression is like a single function call. The complexity of the code translates into the complexity of the expressions that one uses as parameters for the outermost function.

For this reason, it is normal to see expressions that span over 10 lines or more. Seeing a 20-line DAX expression is common, so you will become acquainted with it. Nevertheless, as formulas start to grow in length and complexity, it is extremely important to format the code to make it human-readable.

There is no "official" standard to format DAX code, yet we believe it is important to describe the standard that we use in our code. It is likely not the perfect standard, and you might prefer something different. We have no problem with that: find your optimal standard and use it. The only thing you need to remember is: *format your code and never write everything on a single line; otherwise, you will be in trouble sooner than you expect.*

To understand why formatting is important, look at a formula that computes a time intelligence calculation. This somewhat complex formula is still not the most complex you will write. Here is how the expression looks if you do not format it in some way:

```
IF(CALCULATE(NOT ISEMPTY(Balances), ALLEXCEPT (Balances, BalanceDate)),SUMX (ALL(Balances
[Account]), CALCULATE(SUM (Balances[Balance]),LASTNONBLANK(DATESBETWEEN(BalanceDate[Date],
BLANK(),MAX(BalanceDate[Date])),CALCULATE(COUNTROWS(Balances)))))),BLANK())
```

Trying to understand what this formula computes in its present form is nearly impossible. There is no clue which is the outermost function and how DAX evaluates the different parameters to create the complete flow of execution. We have seen too many examples of formulas written this way by students who, at some point, ask for help in understanding why the formula returns incorrect results. Guess what? The first thing we do is format the expression; only later do we start working on it.

The same expression, properly formatted, looks like this:

```
IF (
    CALCULATE (
        NOT ISEMPTY ( Balances ),
        ALLEXCEPT (
            Balances,
            BalanceDate
        )
    ),
    SUMX (
        ALL ( Balances[Account] ),
        CALCULATE (
            SUM ( Balances[Balance] ),
            LASTNONBLANK (
                DATESBETWEEN (
                    BalanceDate[Date],
                    BLANK (),
                    MAX ( BalanceDate[Date] )
                ),
                CALCULATE (
                    COUNTROWS ( Balances )
                )
            )
        )
    ),
    BLANK ()
)
```

The code is the same, but this time it is much easier to see the three parameters of *IF*. Most important, it is easier to follow the blocks that arise naturally from indenting lines and how they compose the complete flow of execution. The code is still hard to read, but now the problem is DAX, not poor formatting. A more verbose syntax using variables can help you read the code, but even in this case, the formatting is important in providing a correct understanding of the scope of each variable:

```
IF (
    CALCULATE (
        NOT ISEMPTY ( Balances ),
        ALLEXCEPT (
            Balances,
            BalanceDate
        )
    ),
    SUMX (
        ALL ( Balances[Account] ),
        VAR PreviousDates =
            DATESBETWEEN (
                BalanceDate[Date],
                BLANK (),
                MAX ( BalanceDate[Date] )
            )
```

```
        VAR LastDateWithBalance =
            LASTNONBLANK (
                PreviousDates,
                CALCULATE (
                    COUNTROWS ( Balances )
                )
            )
        RETURN
            CALCULATE (
                SUM ( Balances[Balance] ),
                LastDateWithBalance
            )
    ),
    BLANK ()
)
```

DAXFormatter.com

We created a website dedicated to formatting DAX code. We created this site for ourselves because formatting code is a time-consuming operation and we did not want to spend our time doing it for every formula we write. After the tool was working, we decided to donate it to the public domain so that users can format their own DAX code (by the way, we have been able to promote our formatting rules this way).

You can find the website at www.daxformatter.com. The user interface is simple: just copy your DAX code, click FORMAT, and the page refreshes showing a nicely formatted version of your code, which you can then copy and paste in the original window.

This is the set of rules that we use to format DAX:

- Always separate function names such as *IF*, *SUMX*, and *CALCULATE* from any other term using a space and always write them in uppercase.

- Write all column references in the form *TableName[ColumnName]*, with no space between the table name and the opening square bracket. Always include the table name.

- Write all measure references in the form *[MeasureName]*, without any table name.

- Always use a space following commas and never precede them with a space.

- If the formula fits one single line, do not apply any other rule.

- If the formula does not fit a single line, then

  - Place the function name on a line by itself, with the opening parenthesis.

  - Keep all parameters on separate lines, indented with four spaces and with the comma at the end of the expression except for the last parameter.

  - Align the closing parenthesis with the function call so that the closing parenthesis stands on its own line.

These are the basic rules we use. A more detailed list of these rules is available at http://sql.bi/daxrules.

If you find a way to express formulas that best fits your reading method, use it. The goal of formatting is to make the formula easier to read, so use the technique that works best for you. The most important point to remember when defining your personal set of formatting rules is that you always need to be able to see errors as soon as possible. If, in the unformatted code shown previously, DAX complained about a missing closing parenthesis, it would be hard to spot where the error is. In the formatted formula, it is much easier to see how each closing parenthesis matches the opening function call.

Help on formatting DAX

Formatting DAX is not an easy task because often we write it using a small font in a text box. Depending on the version, Power BI, Excel, and Visual Studio provide different text editors for DAX. Nevertheless, a few hints might help in writing DAX code:

- To increase the font size, hold down Ctrl while rotating the wheel button on the mouse, making it easier to look at the code.
- To add a new line to the formula, press Shift+Enter.
- If editing in the text box is not for you, copy the code into another editor, such as Notepad or DAX Studio, and then copy and paste the formula back into the text box.

When you look at a DAX expression, at first glance it may be hard to understand whether it is a calculated column or a measure. Thus, in our books and articles we use an equal sign (=) whenever we define a calculated column and the assignment operator (:=) to define measures:

```
CalcCol = SUM ( Sales[SalesAmount] )          -- is a calculated column
Store[CalcCol] = SUM ( Sales[SalesAmount] )   -- is a calculated column in Store table
CalcMsr := SUM ( Sales[SalesAmount]  )        -- is a measure
```

Finally, when using columns and measures in code, we recommend to always put a table name before a column and never before a measure, as we do in every example.

Introducing aggregators and iterators

Almost every data model needs to operate on aggregated data. DAX offers a set of functions that aggregate the values of a column in a table and return a single value. We call this group of functions *aggregation functions*. For example, the following measure calculates the sum of all the numbers in the *SalesAmount* column of the *Sales* table:

```
Sales := SUM ( Sales[SalesAmount] )
```

SUM aggregates all the rows of the table if it is used in a calculated column. Whenever it is used in a measure, it considers only the rows that are being filtered by slicers, rows, columns, and filter conditions in the report.

There are many aggregation functions (*SUM*, *AVERAGE*, *MIN*, *MAX*, and *STDEV*), and their behavior changes only in the way they aggregate values: *SUM* adds values, whereas *MIN* returns the minimum value. Nearly all these functions operate only on numeric values or on dates. Only *MIN* and *MAX* can operate on text values also. Moreover, DAX never considers empty cells when it performs the aggregation, and this behavior is different from their counterpart in Excel (more on this later in this chapter).

> **Note** *MIN* and *MAX* offer another behavior: if used with two parameters, they return the minimum or maximum of the two parameters. Thus, *MIN* (1, 2) returns 1 and *MAX* (1, 2) returns 2. This functionality is useful when one needs to compute the minimum or maximum of complex expressions because it saves having to write the same expression multiple times in *IF* statements.

All the aggregation functions we have described so far work on columns. Therefore, they aggregate values from a single column only. Some aggregation functions can aggregate an expression instead of a single column. Because of the way they work, they are known as *iterators*. This set of functions is useful, especially when you need to make calculations using columns of different related tables, or when you need to reduce the number of calculated columns.

Iterators always accept at least two parameters: the first is a table that they scan; the second is typically an expression that is evaluated for each row of the table. After they have completed scanning the table and evaluating the expression row by row, iterators aggregate the partial results according to their semantics.

For example, if we compute the number of days needed to deliver an order in a calculated column called *DaysToDeliver* and build a report on top of that, we obtain the report shown in Figure 2-6. Note that the grand total shows the sum of all the days, which is not useful for this metric:

```
Sales[DaysToDeliver] = INT ( Sales[Delivery Date] - Sales[Order Date] )
```

SalesKey	Order Date	Delivery Date	DaysToDeliver
200701022CS425-0013	01/02/2007	01/08/2007	6
200701022CS425-0014	01/02/2007	01/09/2007	7
200701022CS425-0015	01/02/2007	01/10/2007	8
200701022CS425-0016	01/02/2007	01/11/2007	9
200701022CS425-0017	01/02/2007	01/12/2007	10
200701022CS425-0018	01/02/2007	01/13/2007	11
200701023CS425-0202	01/02/2007	01/08/2007	6
200701023CS425-0203	01/02/2007	01/09/2007	7
200701023CS425-0204	01/02/2007	01/10/2007	8
200701023CS425-0205	01/02/2007	01/11/2007	9
Total			**848075**

FIGURE 2-6 The grand total is shown as a sum, when you might want an average instead.

A grand total that we can actually use requires a measure called *AvgDelivery* showing the delivery time for each order and the average of all the durations at the grand total level:

```
AvgDelivery := AVERAGE ( Sales[DaysToDeliver] )
```

The result of this new measure is visible in the report shown in Figure 2-7.

SalesKey	Order Date	Delivery Date	DaysToDeliver	AvgDelivery
200701022CS425-0013	01/02/2007	01/08/2007	6	6.00
200701022CS425-0014	01/02/2007	01/09/2007	7	7.00
200701022CS425-0015	01/02/2007	01/10/2007	8	8.00
200701022CS425-0016	01/02/2007	01/11/2007	9	9.00
200701022CS425-0017	01/02/2007	01/12/2007	10	10.00
200701022CS425-0018	01/02/2007	01/13/2007	11	11.00
200701023CS425-0202	01/02/2007	01/08/2007	6	6.00
200701023CS425-0203	01/02/2007	01/09/2007	7	7.00
200701023CS425-0204	01/02/2007	01/10/2007	8	8.00
200701023CS425-0205	01/02/2007	01/11/2007	9	9.00
Total			**848075**	**8.46**

FIGURE 2-7 The measure aggregating by average shows the average delivery days at the grand total level.

The measure computes the average value by averaging a calculated column. One could remove the calculated column, thus saving space in the model, by leveraging an iterator. Indeed, although it is true that *AVERAGE* cannot average an expression, its counterpart *AVERAGEX* can iterate the *Sales* table and compute the delivery days row by row, averaging the results at the end. This code accomplishes the same result as the previous definition:

```
AvgDelivery :=
AVERAGEX (
    Sales,
    INT ( Sales[Delivery Date] - Sales[Order Date] )
)
```

The biggest advantage of this last expression is that it does not rely on the presence of a calculated column. Thus, we can build the entire report without creating expensive calculated columns.

Most iterators have the same name as their noniterative counterpart. For example, *SUM* has a corresponding *SUMX*, and *MIN* has a corresponding *MINX*. Nevertheless, keep in mind that some iterators do not correspond to any aggregator. Later in this book, you will learn about *FILTER*, *ADDCOLUMNS*, *GENERATE*, and other functions that are iterators even if they do not aggregate their results.

When you first learn DAX, you might think that iterators are inherently slow. The concept of performing calculations row by row looks like a CPU-intensive operation. Actually, iterators are fast, and no performance penalty is caused by using iterators instead of standard aggregators. Aggregators are just a syntax-sugared version of iterators.

Indeed, the basic aggregation functions are a shortened version of the corresponding X-suffixed function. For example, consider the following expression:

```
SUM ( Sales[Quantity] )
```

It is internally translated into this corresponding version of the same code:

```
SUMX ( Sales, Sales[Quantity] )
```

The only advantage in using *SUM* is a shorter syntax. However, there are no differences in performance between *SUM* and *SUMX* aggregating a single column. They are in all respects the same function.

We will cover more details about this behavior in Chapter 4. There we introduce the concept of evaluation contexts to describe properly how iterators work.

Using common DAX functions

Now that you have seen the fundamentals of DAX and how to handle error conditions, what follows is a brief tour through the most commonly used functions and expressions of DAX.

Aggregation functions

In the previous sections, we described the basic aggregators like *SUM*, *AVERAGE*, *MIN*, and *MAX*. You learned that *SUM* and *AVERAGE*, for example, work only on numeric columns.

DAX also offers an alternative syntax for aggregation functions inherited from Excel, which adds the suffix A to the name of the function, just to get the same name and behavior as Excel. However, these functions are useful only for columns containing *Boolean* values because *TRUE* is evaluated as 1 and *FALSE* as 0. Text columns are always considered 0. Therefore, no matter what is in the content of a column, if one uses *MAXA* on a text column, the result will always be a 0. Moreover, DAX never considers empty cells when it performs the aggregation. Although these functions can be used on nonnumeric columns without retuning an error, their results are not useful because there is no automatic conversion to numbers for text columns. These functions are named *AVERAGEA*, *COUNTA*, *MINA*, and *MAXA*. We suggest that you do not use these functions, whose behavior will be kept unchanged in the future because of compatibility with existing code that might rely on current behavior.

> **Note** Despite the names being identical to statistical functions, they are used differently in DAX and Excel because in DAX a column has a data type, and its data type determines the behavior of aggregation functions. Excel handles a different data type for each cell, whereas DAX handles a single data type for the entire column. DAX deals with data in tabular form with well-defined types for each column, whereas Excel formulas work on heterogeneous cell values without well-defined types. If a column in Power BI has a numeric data type, all the values can be only numbers or empty cells. If a column is of a text type, it is always 0 for these functions (except for *COUNTA*), even if the text can be converted into a number, whereas in Excel the value is considered a number on a cell-by-cell basis. For these reasons, these functions are not very useful for Text columns. Only *MIN* and *MAX* also support text values in DAX.

The functions you learned earlier are useful to perform the aggregation of values. Sometimes, you might not be interested in aggregating values but only in counting them. DAX offers a set of functions that are useful to count rows or values:

- *COUNT* operates on any data type, apart from *Boolean*.

- *COUNTA* operates on any type of column.

- *COUNTBLANK* returns the number of empty cells (blanks or empty strings) in a column.

- *COUNTROWS* returns the number of rows in a table.

- *DISTINCTCOUNT* returns the number of distinct values of a column, blank value included if present.

- *DISTINCTCOUNTNOBLANK* returns the number of distinct values of a column, no blank value included.

COUNT and *COUNTA* are nearly identical functions in DAX. They return the number of values of the column that are not empty, regardless of their data type. They are inherited from Excel, where *COUNTA* accepts any data type including strings, whereas *COUNT* accepts only numeric columns. If we want to count all the values in a column that contain an empty value, you can use the *COUNTBLANK* function. Both blanks and empty values are considered empty values by *COUNTBLANK*. Finally, if we want to count the number of rows of a table, you can use the *COUNTROWS* function. Beware that *COUNT-ROWS* requires a table as a parameter, not a column.

The last two functions, *DISTINCTCOUNT* and *DISTINCTCOUNTNOBLANK*, are useful because they do exactly what their names suggest: count the distinct values of a column, which it takes as its only parameter. *DISTINCTCOUNT* counts the *BLANK* value as one of the possible values, whereas *DISTINCT-COUNTNOBLANK* ignores the *BLANK* value.

Note   *DISTINCTCOUNT* is a function introduced in the 2012 version of DAX. The earlier versions of DAX did not include *DISTINCTCOUNT*; to compute the number of distinct values of a column, we had to use *COUNTROWS (DISTINCT (table[column]))*. The two patterns return the same result although *DISTINCTCOUNT* is easier to read, requiring only a single function call. *DISTINCTCOUNTNOBLANK* is a function introduced in 2019 and it provides the same semantic of a *COUNT DISTINCT* operation in SQL without having to write a longer expression in DAX.

Logical functions

Sometimes we want to build a logical condition in an expression—for example, to implement different calculations depending on the value of a column or to intercept an error condition. In these cases, we can use one of the logical functions in DAX. The earlier section titled "Handling errors in DAX expressions" described the two most important functions of this group: *IF* and *IFERROR*. We described the *IF* function in the "Conditional statements" section, earlier in this chapter.

Logical functions are very simple and do what their names suggest. They are *AND*, *FALSE*, *IF*, *IFERROR*, *NOT*, *TRUE*, and *OR*. For example, if we want to compute the amount as quantity multiplied by price only when the *Price* column contains a numeric value, we can use the following pattern:

```
Sales[Amount] = IFERROR ( Sales[Quantity] * Sales[Price], BLANK ( ) )
```

If we did not use *IFERROR* and if the *Price* column contained an invalid number, the result for the calculated column would be an error because if a single row generates a calculation error, the error propagates to the whole column. The use of *IFERROR*, however, intercepts the error and replaces it with a blank value.

Another interesting function in this category is *SWITCH*, which is useful when we have a column containing a low number of distinct values, and we want to get different behaviors depending on its value. For example, the column *Size* in the *Product* table contains S, M, L, XL, and we might want to decode this value in a more explicit column. We can obtain the result by using nested *IF* calls:

```
'Product'[SizeDesc] =
IF (
    'Product'[Size] = "S",
    "Small",
    IF (
        'Product'[Size] = "M",
        "Medium",
        IF (
            'Product'[Size] = "L",
            "Large",
            IF (
                'Product'[Size] = "XL",
                "Extra Large",
                "Other"
            )
        )
    )
)
```

A more convenient way to express the same formula, using *SWITCH*, is like this:

```
'Product'[SizeDesc] =
SWITCH (
    'Product'[Size],
    "S", "Small",
    "M", "Medium",
    "L", "Large",
    "XL", "Extra Large",
    "Other"
)
```

The code in this latter expression is more readable, though not faster, because internally DAX translates *SWITCH* statements into a set of nested *IF* functions.

> **Note** *SWITCH* is often used to check the value of a parameter and define the result of a measure. For example, one might create a parameter table containing *YTD*, *MTD*, *QTD* as three rows and let the user choose from the three available which aggregation to use in a measure. This was a common scenario before 2019. Now it is no longer needed thanks to the introduction of calculation groups, covered in Chapter 9, "Calculation groups." Calculation groups are the preferred way of computing values that the user can parameterize.

> **Tip** Here is an interesting way to use the *SWITCH* function to check for multiple conditions in the same expression. Because *SWITCH* is converted into a set of nested *IF* functions, where the first one that matches wins, you can test multiple conditions using this pattern:
>
> ```
> SWITCH (
>     TRUE (),
>     Product[Size] = "XL" && Product[Color] = "Red", "Red and XL",
>     Product[Size] = "XL" && Product[Color] = "Blue", "Blue and XL",
>     Product[Size] = "L" && Product[Color] = "Green", "Green and L"
> )
> ```
>
> Using *TRUE* as the first parameter means, "Return the first result where the condition evaluates to *TRUE*."

Information functions

Whenever there is the need to analyze the type of an expression, you can use one of the information functions. All these functions return a *Boolean* value and can be used in any logical expression. They are *ISBLANK*, *ISERROR*, *ISLOGICAL*, *ISNONTEXT*, *ISNUMBER*, and *ISTEXT*.

It is important to note that when a column is passed as a parameter instead of an expression, the functions *ISNUMBER*, *ISTEXT*, and *ISNONTEXT* always return *TRUE* or *FALSE* depending on the data type of the column and on the empty condition of each cell. This makes these functions nearly useless in DAX; they have been inherited from Excel in the first DAX version.

You might be wondering whether you can use *ISNUMBER* with a text column just to check whether a conversion to a number is possible. Unfortunately, this approach is not possible. If you want to test whether a text value is convertible to a number, you must try the conversion and handle the error if it fails. For example, to test whether the column *Price* (which is of type *string*) contains a valid number, one must write

```
Sales[IsPriceCorrect] = NOT ISERROR ( VALUE ( Sales[Price] ) )
```

DAX tries to convert from a string value to a number. If it succeeds, it returns *TRUE* (because *ISERROR* returns *FALSE*); otherwise, it returns *FALSE* (because *ISERROR* returns *TRUE*). For example, the conversion fails if some of the rows have an "N/A" string value for price.

However, if we try to use *ISNUMBER*, as in the following expression, we always receive *FALSE* as a result:

```
Sales[IsPriceCorrect] = ISNUMBER ( Sales[Price] )
```

In this case, *ISNUMBER* always returns *FALSE* because, based on the definition in the model, the *Price* column is not a number but a string, regardless of the content of each row.

Mathematical functions

The set of mathematical functions available in DAX is similar to the set available in Excel, with the same syntax and behavior. The mathematical functions of common use are *ABS*, *EXP*, *FACT*, *LN*, *LOG*, *LOG10*, *MOD*, *PI*, *POWER*, *QUOTIENT*, *SIGN*, and *SQRT*. Random functions are *RAND* and *RANDBETWEEN*. By using *EVEN* and *ODD*, you can test numbers. *GCD* and *LCM* are useful to compute the greatest common denominator and least common multiple of two numbers. *QUOTIENT* returns the integer division of two numbers.

Finally, several rounding functions deserve an example; in fact, we might use several approaches to get the same result. Consider these calculated columns, along with their results in Figure 2-8:

```
FLOOR = FLOOR ( Tests[Value], 0.01 )
TRUNC = TRUNC ( Tests[Value], 2 )
ROUNDDOWN = ROUNDDOWN ( Tests[Value], 2 )
MROUND = MROUND ( Tests[Value], 0.01 )
ROUND = ROUND ( Tests[Value], 2 )
CEILING = CEILING ( Tests[Value], 0.01 )
ISO.CEILING = ISO.CEILING ( Tests[Value], 0.01 )
ROUNDUP = ROUNDUP ( Tests[Value], 2 )
INT = INT ( Tests[Value] )
FIXED = FIXED ( Tests[Value], 2, TRUE )
```

Test	Value	FLOOR	TRUNC	ROUNDDOWN	MROUND	ROUND	CEILING	ISO.CEILING	ROUNDUP	INT	FIXED
A	1.123450	1.12	1.12	1.12	1.12	1.12	1.13	1.13	1.13	1	1.12
B	1.265000	1.26	1.26	1.26	1.26	1.27	1.27	1.27	1.27	1	1.27
C	1.265001	1.26	1.26	1.26	1.27	1.27	1.27	1.27	1.27	1	1.27
D	1.499999	1.49	1.49	1.49	1.50	1.50	1.50	1.50	1.50	1	1.50
E	1.511110	1.51	1.51	1.51	1.51	1.51	1.52	1.52	1.52	1	1.51
F	1.000001	1.00	1.00	1.00	1.00	1.00	1.01	1.01	1.01	1	1.00
G	1.999999	1.99	1.99	1.99	2.00	2.00	2.00	2.00	2.00	1	2.00

FIGURE 2-8 This summary shows the results of using different rounding functions.

FLOOR, *TRUNC*, and *ROUNDDOWN* are similar except in the way we can specify the number of digits to round. In the opposite direction, *CEILING* and *ROUNDUP* are similar in their results. You can see a few differences in the way the rounding is done between *MROUND* and *ROUND* function.

Trigonometric functions

DAX offers a rich set of trigonometric functions that are useful for certain calculations: *COS, COSH, COT, COTH, SIN, SINH, TAN,* and *TANH.* Prefixing them with A computes the arc version (arcsine, arccosine, and so on). We do not go into the details of these functions because their use is straightforward.

DEGREES and *RADIANS* perform conversion to degrees and radians, respectively, and *SQRTPI* computes the square root of its parameter after multiplying it by pi.

Text functions

Most of the text functions available in DAX are similar to those available in Excel, with only a few exceptions. The text functions are *CONCATENATE, CONCATENATEX, EXACT, FIND, FIXED, FORMAT, LEFT, LEN, LOWER, MID, REPLACE, REPT, RIGHT, SEARCH, SUBSTITUTE, TRIM, UPPER,* and *VALUE.* These functions are useful for manipulating text and extracting data from strings that contain multiple values. For example, Figure 2-9 shows an example of the extraction of first and last names from a string that contains these values separated by commas, with the title in the middle that we want to remove.

Name	Comma1	Comma2	FirstLastName	SimpleConversion
Ferrari, Alberto	8		Alberto Ferrari	Ferrari, Alberto Ferrari
Ferrari, Mr., Alberto	8	13	Alberto Ferrari	Alberto Ferrari
Russo, Mr., Marco	6	11	Marco Russo	Marco Russo

FIGURE 2-9 This example shows first and last names extracted using text functions.

To achieve this result, you start calculating the position of the two commas. Then we use these numbers to extract the right part of the text. The *SimpleConversion* column implements a formula that might return inaccurate values if there are fewer than two commas in the string, and it raises an error if there are no commas at all. The *FirstLastName* column implements a more complex expression that does not fail in case of missing commas:

```
People[Comma1] = IFERROR ( FIND ( ",", People[Name] ), BLANK ( ) )
People[Comma2] = IFERROR ( FIND ( " ,", People[Name], People[Comma1] + 1 ), BLANK ( ) )
People[SimpleConversion] =
MID ( People[Name], People[Comma2] + 1, LEN ( People[Name] ) )
    & " "
    & LEFT ( People[Name], People[Comma1] - 1 )
People[FirstLastName] =
TRIM (
    MID (
        People[Name],
        IF ( ISNUMBER ( People[Comma2] ), People[Comma2], People[Comma1] ) + 1,
        LEN ( People[Name] )
    )
)
    & IF (
```

```
        ISNUMBER ( People[Comma1] ),
        " " & LEFT ( People[Name], People[Comma1] - 1 ),
        ""
    )
```

As you can see, the *FirstLastName* column is defined by a long DAX expression, but you must use it to avoid possible errors that would propagate to the whole column if even a single value generates an error.

Conversion functions

You learned previously that DAX performs automatic conversions of data types to adjust them to operator needs. Although the conversion happens automatically, a set of functions can still perform explicit data type conversions.

CURRENCY can transform an expression into a Currency type, whereas *INT* transforms an expression into an Integer. *DATE* and *TIME* take the date and time parts as parameters and return a correct *DateTime*. *VALUE* transforms a string into a numeric format, whereas *FORMAT* gets a numeric value as its first parameter and a string format as its second parameter, and it can transform numeric values into strings. *FORMAT* is commonly used with *DateTime*. For example, the following expression returns "2019 Jan 12":

```
= FORMAT ( DATE ( 2019, 01, 12 ), "yyyy mmm dd" )
```

The opposite operation, that is, converting strings into *DateTime* values, is performed using the *DATEVALUE* function.

DATEVALUE with dates in different format

DATEVALUE displays a special behavior regarding dates in different formats. In the European standard, dates are written with the format "dd/mm/yy", whereas Americans prefer to use "mm/dd/yy". For example, the 28th of February has different string representations in the two cultures. If you provide to *DATEVALUE* a date that cannot be converted using the default regional setting, instead of immediately raising an error, it tries a second conversion switching months and days. *DATEVALUE* also supports the unambiguous format "yyyy-mm-dd". As an example, the following three expressions evaluate to February 28, no matter which regional settings you have:

```
DATEVALUE ( "28/02/2018" )    -- This is February 28 in European format
DATEVALUE ( "02/28/2018" )    -- This is February 28 in American format
DATEVALUE ( "2018-02-28" )    -- This is February 28 (format is not ambiguous)
```

Sometimes, *DATEVALUE* does not raise errors when you would expect them. However, this is the behavior of the function by design.

Date and time functions

In almost every type of data analysis, handling time and dates is an important part of the job. Many DAX functions operate on date and time. Some of them correspond to similar functions in Excel and make simple transformations to and from a *DateTime* data type. The date and time functions are *DATE*, *DATEVALUE*, *DAY*, *EDATE*, *EOMONTH*, *HOUR*, *MINUTE*, *MONTH*, *NOW*, *SECOND*, *TIME*, *TIMEVALUE*, *TODAY*, *WEEKDAY*, *WEEKNUM*, *YEAR*, and *YEARFRAC*.

These functions are useful to compute values on top of dates, but they are not used to perform typical time intelligence calculations such as comparing aggregated values year over year or calculating the year-to-date value of a measure. To perform time intelligence calculations, you use another set of functions called time intelligence functions, which we describe in Chapter 8, "Time intelligence calculations."

As we mentioned earlier in this chapter, a *DateTime* data type internally uses a floating-point number wherein the integer part corresponds to the number of days after December 30, 1899, and the decimal part indicates the fraction of the day in time. Hours, minutes, and seconds are converted into decimal fractions of the day. Thus, adding an integer number to a *DateTime* value increments the value by a corresponding number of days. However, you will probably find it more convenient to use the conversion functions to extract the day, month, and year from a date. The following expressions used in Figure 2-10 show how to extract this information from a table containing a list of dates:

```
'Date'[Day] = DAY ( Calendar[Date] )
'Date'[Month] = FORMAT ( Calendar[Date], "mmmm" )
'Date'[MonthNumber] = MONTH ( Calendar[Date] )
'Date'[Year] = YEAR ( Calendar[Date] )
```

Date	Day	Month	Year
1/1/2010	1	January	2010
1/2/2010	2	January	2010
1/3/2010	3	January	2010
1/4/2010	4	January	2010
1/5/2010	5	January	2010
1/6/2010	6	January	2010
1/7/2010	7	January	2010
1/8/2010	8	January	2010
1/9/2010	9	January	2010

FIGURE 2-10 This example shows how to extract date information using date and time functions.

Relational functions

Two useful functions that you can use to navigate through relationships inside a DAX formula are *RELATED* and *RELATEDTABLE*.

You already know that a calculated column can reference column values of the table in which it is defined. Thus, a calculated column defined in *Sales* can reference any column of *Sales*. However, what if one must refer to a column in another table? In general, one cannot use columns in other tables unless a relationship is defined in the model between the two tables. If the two tables share a relationship, you can use the *RELATED* function to access columns in the related table.

For example, one might want to compute a calculated column in the *Sales* table that checks whether the product that has been sold is in the "Cell phones" category and, in that case, apply a reduction factor to the standard cost. To compute such a column, one must use a condition that checks the value of the product category, which is not in the *Sales* table. Nevertheless, a chain of relationships starts from *Sales*, reaching *Product Category* through *Product* and *Product Subcategory*, as shown in Figure 2-11.

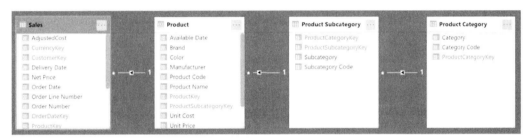

FIGURE 2-11 Sales has a chained relationship with *Product Category*.

Regardless of how many steps are necessary to travel from the original table to the related table, DAX follows the complete chain of relationships, and it returns the related column value. Thus, the formula for the *AdjustedCost* column can look like this:

```
Sales[AdjustedCost] =
IF (
    RELATED ( 'Product Category'[Category] ) = "Cell Phone",
    Sales[Unit Cost] * 0.95,
    Sales[Unit Cost]
)
```

In a one-to-many relationship, *RELATED* can access the one-side from the many-side because in that case, only one row in the related table exists, if any. If no such row exists, *RELATED* returns *BLANK*.

If an expression is on the one-side of the relationship and needs to access the many-side, *RELATED* is not helpful because many rows from the other side might be available for a single row. In that case, we can use *RELATEDTABLE*. *RELATEDTABLE* returns a table containing all the rows related to the current row. For example, if we want to know how many products are in each category, we can create a column in *Product Category* with this formula:

```
'Product Category'[NumOfProducts] = COUNTROWS ( RELATEDTABLE ( Product ) )
```

For each product category, this calculated column shows the number of products related, as shown in Figure 2-12.

Category	NumOfProducts
Audio	115
Cameras and camcorders	372
Cell phones	285
Computers	606
Games and Toys	166
Home Appliances	661
Music, Movies and Audio Books	90
TV and Video	222

FIGURE 2-12 You can count the number of products by using *RELATEDTABLE*.

As is the case for *RELATED*, *RELATEDTABLE* can follow a chain of relationships always starting from the one-side and going toward the many-side. *RELATEDTABLE* is often used in conjunction with iterators. For example, if we want to compute the sum of quantity multiplied by net price for each category, we can write a new calculated column as follows:

```
'Product Category'[CategorySales] =
SUMX (
    RELATEDTABLE ( Sales ),
    Sales[Quantity] * Sales[Net Price]
)
```

The result of this calculated column is shown in Figure 2-13.

Category	CategorySales
Audio	$384,518.16
Cameras and camcorders	$7,192,581.95
Cell phones	$1,604,610.26
Computers	$6,741,548.73
Games and Toys	$360,652.81
Home Appliances	$9,600,457.04
Music, Movies and Audio Books	$314,206.74
TV and Video	$4,392,768.29

FIGURE 2-13 Using *RELATEDTABLE* and iterators, we can compute the amount of sales per category.

Because the column is calculated, this result is consolidated in the table, and it does not change according to the user selection in the report, as it would if it were written in a measure.

Conclusions

In this chapter, you learned many new functions and started looking at some DAX code. You may not remember all the functions right away, but the more you use them, the more familiar they will become.

The more crucial topics you learned in this chapter are

- Calculated columns are columns in a table that are computed with a DAX expression. Calculated columns are computed at data refresh time and do not change their value depending on user selection.

- Measures are calculations expressed in DAX. Instead of being computed at refresh time like calculated columns are, measures are computed at query time. Consequently, the value of a measure depends on the user selection in the report.

- Errors might happen at any time in a DAX expression; it is preferable to detect the error condition beforehand rather than letting the error happen and intercepting it after the fact.

- Aggregators like SUM are useful to aggregate columns, whereas to aggregate expressions, you need to use iterators. Iterators work by scanning a table and evaluating an expression row by row. At the end of the iteration, iterators aggregate a result according to their semantics.

In the next chapter, you will continue on your learning path by studying the most important table functions available in DAX.

CHAPTER 3

Using basic table functions

In this chapter, you learn the basic table functions available in DAX. Table functions are regular DAX functions that—instead of returning a single value—return a table. Table functions are useful when writing both DAX queries and many advanced calculations that require iterating over tables. The chapter includes several examples of such calculations.

The goal of this chapter is to introduce the notion of table functions, but not to provide a detailed explanation of all the table functions in DAX. A larger number of table functions is included in Chapter 12, "Working with tables," and in Chapter 13, "Authoring queries." Here, we explain the role of most common and important table functions in DAX, and how to use them in common scenarios, including in scalar DAX expressions.

Introducing table functions

Until now, you have seen that a DAX expression usually returns a single value, such as a string or a number. An expression that results in a single value is called a *scalar expression*. When defining a measure or a calculated column, you always write scalar expressions, as in the following examples:

```
= 4 + 3
= "DAX is a beautiful language"
= SUM ( Sales[Quantity] )
```

Indeed, the primary goal of a measure is to produce results that are rendered in a report, in a pivot table, or in a chart. At the end of the day, the source of all these reports is a number—in other words, a scalar expression. Nevertheless, as part of the calculation of a scalar value, you are likely to use tables. For example, a simple iteration like the following uses a table as part of the calculation of the sales amount:

```
Sales Amount := SUMX ( Sales, Sales[Quantity] * Sales[Net Price] )
```

In this example, *SUMX* iterates over the *Sales* table. Thus, though the result of the full calculation is a scalar value, during the computation the formula scans the *Sales* table. The same code could iterate the result of a table function, like the following code. This code computes the sales amount only for rows greater than one:

```
Sales Amount Multiple Items :=
SUMX (
    FILTER (
        Sales,
        Sales[Quantity] > 1
    ),
    Sales[Quantity] * Sales[Net Price]
)
```

In the example, we use a *FILTER* function in place of the reference to *Sales*. Intuitively, *FILTER* is a function that filters the content of a table based on a condition. We will describe *FILTER* in full later. For now, it is important to note that whenever you reference the content of a table, you can replace the reference with the result of a table function.

 Important In the previous code you see a filter applied to a sum aggregation. This is not a best practice. In the next chapters, you will learn how to use *CALCULATE* to implement more flexible and efficient filters. The purpose of the examples in this chapter is not to provide best practices for DAX measures, but rather to explain how table functions work using simple expressions. We will apply these concepts later in more complex scenarios.

Moreover, in Chapter 2, "Introducing DAX," you learned that you can define variables as part of a DAX expression. There, we used variables to store scalar values. However, variables can store tables too. For example, the previous code could be written this way by using a variable:

```
Sales Amount Multiple Items :=
VAR
    MultipleItemSales = FILTER ( Sales, Sales[Quantity] > 1 )
RETURN
    SUMX (
        MultipleItemSales,
        Sales[Quantity] * Sales[Unit Price]
    )
```

MultipleItemSales is a variable that stores a whole table because its expression is a table function. We strongly encourage using variables whenever possible because they make the code easier to read. By simply assigning a name to an expression, you already are documenting your code extremely well.

In a calculated column or inside an iteration, one can also use the *RELATEDTABLE* function to retrieve all the rows of a related table. For example, the following calculated column in the *Product* table computes the sales amount of the corresponding product:

```
'Product'[Product Sales Amount] =
SUMX (
    RELATEDTABLE ( Sales ),
    Sales[Quantity] * Sales[Unit Price]
)
```

Table functions can be nested too. For example, the following calculated column in the *Product* table computes the product sales amount considering only sales with a quantity greater than one:

```
'Product'[Product Sales Amount Multiple Items] =
SUMX (
    FILTER (
        RELATEDTABLE ( Sales ),
        Sales[Quantity] > 1
    ),
    Sales[Quantity] * Sales[Unit Price]
)
```

In the sample code, *RELATEDTABLE* is nested inside *FILTER*. As a rule, when there are nested calls, DAX evaluates the innermost function first and then evaluates the others up to the outermost function.

Note As you will see later, the execution order of nested calls can be a source of confusion because *CALCULATE* and *CALCULATETABLE* have a different order of evaluation from *FILTER*. In the next section, you learn the behavior of *FILTER*. You will find the description for *CALCULATE* and *CALCULATETABLE* in Chapter 5, "Understanding *CALCULATE* and *CALCULATETABLE*."

In general, we cannot use the result of a table function as the value of a measure or of a calculated column. Both measures and calculated columns require the expression to be a scalar value. Instead, we can assign the result of a table expression to a *calculated table*. A calculated table is a table whose value is determined by a DAX expression rather than loaded from a data source.

For example, we can create a calculated table containing all the products with a unit price greater than 3,000 by using a table expression like the following:

```
ExpensiveProducts =
FILTER (
    'Product',
    'Product'[Unit Price] > 3000
)
```

Calculated tables are available in Power BI and Analysis Services, but not in Power Pivot for Excel (as of 2019). The more you use table functions, the more you will use them to create more complex data models by using calculated tables and/or complex table expressions inside your measures.

Introducing *EVALUATE* syntax

Query tools such as DAX Studio are useful to author complex table expressions. In that case, a common statement used to inspect the result of a table expression is *EVALUATE*:

```
EVALUATE
FILTER (
    'Product',
    'Product'[Unit Price] > 3000
)
```

One can execute the preceding DAX query in any tool that executes DAX queries (DAX Studio, Microsoft Excel, SQL Server Management Studio, Reporting Services, and so on). A DAX query is a DAX expression that returns a table, used with the *EVALUATE* statement. *EVALUATE* has a complex syntax, which we fully cover in Chapter 13. Here we only introduce the more commonly used *EVALUATE* syntax, which is as follows:

```
[DEFINE { MEASURE <tableName>[<name>] = <expression> }]
EVALUATE <table>
[ORDER BY {<expression> [{ASC | DESC}]} [, …]]
```

The initial *DEFINE MEASURE* part can be useful to define measures that are local to the query. It becomes useful when we are debugging formulas because we can define a local measure, test it, and then deploy the code in the model once it behaves as expected. Most of the syntax is optional. Indeed, the simplest query one can author retrieves all the rows and columns from an existing table, as shown in Figure 3-1:

```
EVALUATE 'Product'
```

ProductKey	Product Code	Product Name	Manufacturer	Brand	Color	
1707	0702001	MGS Dal of Honor Airbor...	Tailspin Toys	Tailspin Toys	Silver	
1708	0702002	MGS Collector's M160	Tailspin Toys	Tailspin Toys	Black	
1709	0702003	MGS Gears of War M170	Tailspin Toys	Tailspin Toys	Blue	
1710	0702004	MGS Age of Empires III: T...	Tailspin Toys	Tailspin Toys	Silver	
1711	0702005	MGS Age of Empires III: T...	Tailspin Toys	Tailspin Toys	Black	
1712	0702006	MGS Flight Simulator X A...	Tailspin Toys	Tailspin Toys	Silver	

FIGURE 3-1 The result of the query execution in DAX Studio.

The *ORDER BY* clause controls the sort order:

```
EVALUATE
FILTER (
    'Product',
    'Product'[Unit Price] > 3000
)
ORDER BY
    'Product'[Color],
    'Product'[Brand] ASC,
    'Product'[Class] DESC
```

> **Note** Please note that the Sort By Column property defined in a model does not affect the sort order in a DAX query. The sort order specified by *EVALUATE* can only use columns included in the result. Thus, a client that generates a dynamic DAX query should read the Sort By Column property in a model's metadata, include the column for the sort order in the query, and then generate a corresponding *ORDER BY* condition.

EVALUATE is not a powerful statement by itself. The power of querying with DAX comes from the power of using the many DAX table functions that are available in the language. In the next sections, you learn how to create advanced calculations by using and combining different table functions.

Understanding *FILTER*

Now that we have introduced what table functions are, it is time to describe in full the basic table functions. Indeed, by combining and nesting the basic functions, you can already compute many powerful expressions. The first function you learn is *FILTER*. The syntax of *FILTER* is the following:

```
FILTER ( <table>, <condition> )
```

FILTER receives a table and a logical condition as parameters. As a result, *FILTER* returns all the rows satisfying the condition. *FILTER* is both a table function and an iterator at the same time. In order to return a result, it scans the table evaluating the condition on a row-by-row basis. In other words, it iterates the table.

For example, the following calculated table returns the Fabrikam products (Fabrikam being a brand).

```
FabrikamProducts =
FILTER (
    'Product',
    'Product'[Brand] = "Fabrikam"
)
```

FILTER is often used to reduce the number of rows in iterations. For example, if a developer wants to compute the sales of red products, they can author a measure like the following one:

```
RedSales :=
SUMX (
    FILTER (
        Sales,
        RELATED ( 'Product'[Color] ) = "Red"
    ),
    Sales[Quantity] * Sales[Net Price]
)
```

You can see the result in Figure 3-2, along with the total sales.

Category	Sales Amount	RedSales
Audio	384,518.16	33,123.82
Cameras and camcorders	7,192,581.95	1,514.39
Cell phones	1,604,610.26	38,227.47
Computers	6,741,548.73	240,222.29
Games and Toys	360,652.81	19,938.31
Home Appliances	9,600,457.04	770,373.33
Music, Movies and Audio Books	314,206.74	6,702.49
TV and Video	4,392,768.29	
Total	**30,591,343.98**	**1,110,102.10**

FIGURE 3-2 *RedSales* shows the amount of sales of only red products.

The *RedSales* measure iterated over a subset of the *Sales* table—namely the set of sales that are related to a red product. *FILTER* adds a condition to the existing conditions. For example, *RedSales* in the Audio row shows the sales of products that are both of Audio category and of Red color.

It is possible to nest *FILTER* in another *FILTER* function. In general, nesting two filters produces the same result as combining the conditions of the two *FILTER* functions with an *AND* function. In other words, the following two queries produce the same result:

```
FabrikamHighMarginProducts =
FILTER (
    FILTER (
        'Product',
        'Product'[Brand] = "Fabrikam"
    ),
    'Product'[Unit Price] > 'Product'[Unit Cost] * 3
)

FabrikamHighMarginProducts =
FILTER (
    'Product',
    AND (
        'Product'[Brand] = "Fabrikam",
        'Product'[Unit Price] > 'Product'[Unit Cost] * 3
    )
)
```

However, performance might be different on large tables depending on the selectivity of the conditions. If one condition is more selective than the other, applying the most selective condition first by using a nested *FILTER* function is considered best practice.

For example, if there are many products with the Fabrikam brand, but few products priced at three times their cost, then the following query applies the filter over *Unit Price* and *Unit Cost* in the innermost *FILTER*. By doing so, the formula applies the most restrictive filter first, in order to reduce the number of iterations needed to check for the brand:

```
FabrikamHighMarginProducts =
FILTER (
    FILTER (
        'Product',
        'Product'[Unit Price] > 'Product'[Unit Cost] * 3
    ),
    'Product'[Brand] = "Fabrikam"
)
```

Using *FILTER*, a developer can often produce code that is easier to read and to maintain over time. For example, imagine you need to compute the number of red products. Without using table functions, one possible implementation might be the following:

```
NumOfRedProducts :=
SUMX (
    'Product',
    IF ( 'Product'[Color] = "Red", 1, 0 )
)
```

The inner *IF* returns either 1 or 0 depending on the color of the product, and summing this expression returns the number of red products. Although it works, this code is somewhat tricky. A better implementation of the same measure is the following:

```
NumOfRedProducts :=
COUNTROWS (
    FILTER ( 'Product', 'Product'[Color] = "Red" )
)
```

This latter expression better shows what the developer wanted to obtain. Moreover, not only is the code easier to read for a human being, but the DAX optimizer is also better able to understand the developer's intention. Therefore, the optimizer produces a better query plan, leading in turn to better performance.

Introducing *ALL* and *ALLEXCEPT*

In the previous section you learned *FILTER*, which is a useful function whenever we want to restrict the number of rows in a table. Sometimes we want to do the opposite; that is, we want to extend the number of rows to consider for a certain calculation. In that case, DAX offers a set of functions designed for that purpose: *ALL, ALLEXCEPT, ALLCROSSFILTERED, ALLNOBLANKROW,* and *ALLSELECTED*. In this section, you learn *ALL* and *ALLEXCEPT*, whereas the latter two are described later in this chapter and *ALLCROSSFILTERD* is introduced in Chapter 14, "Advanced DAX concepts."

ALL returns all the rows of a table or all the values of one or more columns, depending on the parameters used. For example, the following DAX expression returns a *ProductCopy* calculated table with a copy of all the rows in the Product table:

```
ProductCopy = ALL ( 'Product' )
```

> **Note** *ALL* is not necessary in a calculated table because there are no report filters influencing it. However, *ALL* is useful in measures, as shown in the next examples.

ALL is extremely useful whenever we need to compute percentages or ratios because it ignores the filters automatically introduced by a report. Imagine we need a report like the one in Figure 3-3, which shows on the same row both the sales amount and the percentage of the given amount against the grand total.

Category	Sales Amount	Sales Pct
Audio	384,518.16	1.26%
Cameras and camcorders	7,192,581.95	23.51%
Cell phones	1,604,610.26	5.25%
Computers	6,741,548.73	22.04%
Games and Toys	360,652.81	1.18%
Home Appliances	9,600,457.04	31.38%
Music, Movies and Audio Books	314,206.74	1.03%
TV and Video	4,392,768.29	14.36%
Total	**30,591,343.98**	**100.00%**

FIGURE 3-3 The report shows the sales amounts and each percentage against the grand total.

The *Sales Amount* measure computes a value by iterating over the *Sales* table and performing the multiplication of *Sales[Quantity]* by *Sales[Net Price]*:

```
Sales Amount :=
SUMX (
    Sales,
    Sales[Quantity] * Sales[Net Price]
)
```

To compute the percentage, we divide the sales amount by the grand total. Thus, the formula must compute the grand total of sales even when the report is deliberately filtering one given category. This can be obtained by using the *ALL* function. Indeed, the following measure produces the total of all sales, no matter what filter is being applied to the report:

```
All Sales Amount :=
SUMX (
    ALL ( Sales ),
    Sales[Quantity] * Sales[Net Price]
)
```

In the formula we replaced the reference to *Sales* with *ALL (Sales)*, making good use of the *ALL* function. At this point, we can compute the percentage by performing a simple division:

```
Sales Pct := DIVIDE ( [Sales Amount], [All Sales Amount] )
```

Figure 3-4 shows the result of the three measures together.

The parameter of *ALL* cannot be a table expression. It needs to be either a table name or a list of column names. You have already learned what *ALL* does with a table. What is its result if we use a column instead? In that case, *ALL* returns all the distinct values of the column in the entire table. The *Categories* calculated table is obtained from the *Category* column of the *Product* table:

```
Categories = ALL ( 'Product'[Category] )
```

Figure 3-5 shows the result of the *Categories* calculated table.

Category	Sales Amount	All Sales Amount	Sales Pct
Audio	384,518.16	30,591,343.98	1.26%
Cameras and camcorders	7,192,581.95	30,591,343.98	23.51%
Cell phones	1,604,610.26	30,591,343.98	5.25%
Computers	6,741,548.73	30,591,343.98	22.04%
Games and Toys	360,652.81	30,591,343.98	1.18%
Home Appliances	9,600,457.04	30,591,343.98	31.38%
Music, Movies and Audio Books	314,206.74	30,591,343.98	1.03%
TV and Video	4,392,768.29	30,591,343.98	14.36%
Total	**30,591,343.98**	**30,591,343.98**	**100.00%**

FIGURE 3-4 The *All Sales Amount* measure always produces the grand total as a result.

Category
Audio
Cameras and camcorders
Cell phones
Computers
Games and Toys
Home Appliances
Music, Movies and Audio Books
TV and Video

FIGURE 3-5 Using *ALL* with a column produces the list of distinct values of that column.

We can specify multiple columns from the same table in the parameters of the *ALL* function. In that case, *ALL* returns all the existing combinations of values in those columns. For example, we can obtain the list of all categories and subcategories by adding the *Product[Subcategory]* column to the list of values, obtaining the result shown in Figure 3-6:

```
Categories =
ALL (
    'Product'[Category],
    'Product'[Subcategory]
)
```

Throughout all its variations, *ALL* ignores any existing filter in order to produce a result. We can use *ALL* as an argument of an iteration function, such as *SUMX* and *FILTER*, or as a filter argument in a *CALCULATE* function. You learn the *CALCULATE* function in Chapter 5.

If we want to include most, but not all the columns of a table in an *ALL* function call, we can use *ALLEXCEPT* instead. The syntax of *ALLEXCEPT* requires a table followed by the columns we want to exclude. As a result, *ALL-EXCEPT* returns a table with a unique list of existing combinations of values in the other columns of the table.

Category	Subcategory
Audio	Bluetooth Headphones
Audio	MP4&MP3
Audio	Recording Pen
Cameras and camcorders	Camcorders
Cameras and camcorders	Cameras & Camcorders Accessories
Cameras and camcorders	Digital Cameras
Cameras and camcorders	Digital SLR Cameras
Cell phones	Cell phones Accessories
Cell phones	Home & Office Phones
Cell phones	Smart phones & PDAs
Cell phones	Touch Screen Phones

FIGURE 3-6 The list contains the distinct, existing values of category and subcategory.

ALLEXCEPT is a way to write a DAX expression that will automatically include in the result any additional columns that could appear in the table in the future. For example, if we have a *Product* table with five columns (*ProductKey, Product Name, Brand, Class, Color*), the following two expressions produce the same result:

```
ALL ( 'Product'[Product Name], 'Product'[Brand], 'Product'[Class] )
ALLEXCEPT ( 'Product', 'Product'[ProductKey], 'Product'[Color] )
```

However, if we later add the two columns *Product[Unit Cost]* and *Product[Unit Price]*, then the result of *ALL* will ignore them, whereas *ALLEXCEPT* will return the equivalent of:

```
ALL (
    'Product'[Product Name],
    'Product'[Brand],
    'Product'[Class],
    'Product'[Unit Cost],
    'Product'[Unit Price]
)
```

In other words, with *ALL* we declare the columns we want, whereas with *ALLEXCEPT* we declare the columns that we want to remove from the result. *ALLEXCEPT* is mainly useful as a parameter of *CALCULATE* in advanced calculations, and it is seldomly adopted with simpler formulas. Thus, even if we included its description here for completeness, it will become useful only later in the learning path.

Top categories and subcategories

As an example of using *ALL* as a table function, imagine we want to produce a dashboard that shows the category and subcategory of products that sold more than twice the average sales amount. To produce this report, we need to first compute the average sales per subcategory and then, once the value has been determined, retrieve from the list of subcategories the ones that have a sales amount larger than twice that average.

The following code produces that table, and it is worth examining deeper to get a feeling of the power of table functions and variables:

```
BestCategories =
VAR Subcategories =
    ALL ( 'Product'[Category], 'Product'[Subcategory] )
VAR AverageSales =
    AVERAGEX (
        Subcategories,
        SUMX ( RELATEDTABLE ( Sales ), Sales[Quantity] * Sales[Net Price] )
    )
VAR TopCategories =
    FILTER (
        Subcategories,
        VAR SalesOfCategory =
            SUMX ( RELATEDTABLE ( Sales ), Sales[Quantity] * Sales[Net Price] )
        RETURN
            SalesOfCategory >= AverageSales * 2
    )
RETURN
    TopCategories
```

The first variable (*Subcategories*) stores the list of all categories and subcategories. Then, *AverageSales* computes the average of the sales amount for each subcategory. Finally, *Top-Categories* removes from *Subcategories* the subcategories that do not have a sales amount larger than twice the value of *AverageSales*.

The result of this table is visible in Figure 3-7.

Category	Subcategory
Cameras and camcorders	Camcorders
Cameras and camcorders	Digital SLR Cameras
Computers	Laptops
Computers	Projectors & Screens
Home Appliances	Washers & Dryers

FIGURE 3-7 These are the top subcategories that sold more than twice the average.

Once you master *CALCULATE* and filter contexts, you will be able to author the same calculations with a shorter and more efficient syntax. Nevertheless, in this example you can already appreciate how combining table functions can produce powerful results, which are useful for dashboards and reports.

Understanding *VALUES*, *DISTINCT*, and the blank row

In the previous section, you saw that *ALL* used with one column returns a table with all its unique values. DAX provides two other similar functions that return a list of unique values for a column: *VALUES* and *DISTINCT*. These two functions look almost identical, the only difference being in how they handle the blank row that might exist in a table. You will learn about the optional blank row later in this section; for now let us focus on what these two functions perform.

ALL always returns all the distinct values of a column. On the other hand, *VALUES* returns only the distinct visible values. You can appreciate the difference between the two behaviors by looking at the two following measures:

```
NumOfAllColors := COUNTROWS ( ALL ( 'Product'[Color] ) )
NumOfColors := COUNTROWS ( VALUES ( 'Product'[Color] ) )
```

NumOfAllColors counts all the colors of the *Product* table, whereas *NumOfColors* counts only the ones that—given the filter in the report—are visible. The result of these two measures, sliced by category, is visible in Figure 3-8.

Category	NumOfColors	NumOfAllColors
Audio	10	16
Cameras and camcorders	14	16
Cell phones	8	16
Computers	12	16
Games and Toys	11	16
Home Appliances	13	16
Music, Movies and Audio Books	8	16
TV and Video	4	16
Total	**16**	**16**

FIGURE 3-8 For a given category, only a subset of the colors is returned by *VALUES*.

Because the report slices by category, each given category contains products with some, but not all, the colors. *VALUES* returns the distinct values of a column evaluated in the current filter. If we use *VALUES* or *DISTINCT* in a calculated column or in a calculated table, then their behavior is identical to that of *ALL* because there is no active filter. On the other hand, when used in a measure, these two functions compute their result considering the existing filters, whereas *ALL* ignores any filter.

As you read earlier, the two functions are nearly identical. It is now important to understand why *VALUES* and *DISTINCT* are two variations of the same behavior. The difference is the way they consider the presence of a blank row in the table. First, we need to understand how come a blank row might appear in our table if we did not explicitly create a blank row.

The fact is that the engine automatically creates a blank row in any table that is on the one-side of a relationship in case the relationship is invalid. To demonstrate the behavior, we removed all the silver-colored products from the *Product* table. Since there were 16 distinct colors initially and we removed one color, one would expect the total number of colors to be 15. Instead, the report in Figure 3-9 shows something unexpected: *NumOfAllColors* is still 16 and the report shows a new row at the top, with no name.

Category	NumOfColors	NumOfAllColors
	1	16
Audio	9	16
Cameras and camcorders	13	16
Cell phones	7	16
Computers	11	16
Games and Toys	10	16
Home Appliances	12	16
Music, Movies and Audio Books	7	16
TV and Video	3	16
Total	**16**	**16**

FIGURE 3-9 The first rows shows a blank for the category, and the total number of colors is 16 instead of 15.

Because *Product* is on the one-side of a relationship with *Sales,* for each row in the *Sales* table there is a related row in the *Product* table. Nevertheless, because we deliberately removed all the products with one color, there are now many rows in *Sales* that no longer have a valid relationship with the *Product* table. Be mindful, we did not remove any row from *Sales*; we removed a color with the intent of breaking the relationship.

To guarantee that these rows are considered in all the calculations, the engine automatically added to the *Product* table a row containing blank in all its columns. All the orphaned rows in *Sales* are linked to this newly introduced blank row.

Important Only one blank row is added to the *Product* table, despite the fact that multiple different products referenced in the *Sales* table no longer have a corresponding *ProductKey* in the *Product* table.

Indeed, in Figure 3-9 you can see that the first row shows a blank for the *Category* and accounts for one color. The number comes from a row containing blank in the category, blank in the color, and blank in all the columns of the table. You will not see the row if you inspect the table because it is an automatic row created during the loading of the data model. If, at some point, the relationship becomes valid again—if you were to add the silver products back—then the blank row will disappear from the table.

Certain functions in DAX consider the blank row as part of their result, whereas others do not. Specifically, *VALUES* considers the blank row as a valid row, and it returns it. On the other hand, *DISTINCT* does not return it. You can appreciate the difference by looking at the following new measure, which counts the *DISTINCT* colors instead of *VALUES*:

```
NumOfDistinctColors := COUNTROWS ( DISTINCT ( 'Product'[Color] ) )
```

The result is visible in Figure 3-10.

Category	NumOfColors	NumOfDistinctColors	NumOfAllColors
	1		16
Audio	9	9	16
Cameras and camcorders	13	13	16
Cell phones	7	7	16
Computers	11	11	16
Games and Toys	10	10	16
Home Appliances	12	12	16
Music, Movies and Audio Books	7	7	16
TV and Video	3	3	16
Total	**16**	**15**	**16**

FIGURE 3-10 *NumOfDistinctColors* shows a blank for the blank row, and its total shows 15 instead of 16.

A well-designed model should not present any invalid relationships. Thus, if your model is perfect, then the two functions always return the same values. Nevertheless, when dealing with invalid relationships, you need to be aware of this behavior because otherwise you might end up writing incorrect calculations. For example, imagine that we want to compute the average sales per product. A possible solution is to compute the total sales and divide that by the number of products, by using this code:

```
AvgSalesPerProduct :=
DIVIDE (
    SUMX (
        Sales,
        Sales[Quantity] * Sales[Net Price]
    ),
    COUNTROWS (
        VALUES ( 'Product'[Product Code] )
    )
)
```

The result is visible in Figure 3-11. It is obviously wrong because the first row is a huge, meaningless number.

Category	AvgSalesPerProduct
	6,798,560.86
Audio	2,959.80
Cameras and camcorders	18,954.27
Cell phones	5,522.99
Computers	9,903.37
Games and Toys	2,242.14
Home Appliances	14,611.76
Music, Movies and Audio Books	3,337.06
TV and Video	14,698.67
Total	**14,560.37**

FIGURE 3-11 The first row shows a huge value accounted for a category with no name.

The number shown in the first row, where *Category* is blank, corresponds to the sales of all the silver products—which no longer exist in the *Product* table. This blank row associates all the products that were silver and are no longer in the *Product* table. The numerator of *DIVIDE* considers all the sales of silver products. The denominator of *DIVIDE* counts a single blank row returned by *VALUES*. Thus, a single non-existing product (the blank row) is cumulating the sales of many other products referenced in *Sales* and not available in the *Product* table, leading to a huge number. Here, the problem is the invalid relationship, not the formula by itself. Indeed, no matter what formula we create, there are many sales of products in the *Sales* table for which the database has no information. Nevertheless, it is useful to look at how different formulations of the same calculation return different results. Consider these two other variations:

```
AvgSalesPerDistinctProduct :=
DIVIDE (
    SUMX ( Sales, Sales[Quantity] * Sales[Net Price] ),
    COUNTROWS ( DISTINCT ( 'Product'[Product Code] ) )
)

AvgSalesPerDistinctKey :=
DIVIDE (
    SUMX ( Sales, Sales[Quantity] * Sales[Net Price] ),
    COUNTROWS ( VALUES ( Sales[ProductKey] ) )
)
```

In the first variation, we used *DISTINCT* instead of *VALUES*. As a result, *COUNTROWS* returns a blank and the result will be a blank. In the second variation, we still used *VALUES*, but this time we are counting the number of *Sales[ProductKey]*. Keep in mind that there are many different *Sales[ProductKey]* values, all related to the same blank row. The result is visible in Figure 3-12.

Category	AvgSalesPerProduct	AvgSalesPerDistinctProduct	AvgSalesPerDistinctKey
	6,798,560.86		18,474.35
Audio	2,959.80	2,959.80	3,634.18
Cameras and camcorders	18,954.27	18,954.27	20,786.51
Cell phones	5,522.99	5,522.99	6,163.00
Computers	9,903.37	9,903.37	11,416.98
Games and Toys	2,242.14	2,242.14	2,386.79
Home Appliances	14,611.76	14,611.76	16,238.64
Music, Movies and Audio Books	3,337.06	3,337.06	3,883.12
TV and Video	14,698.67	14,698.67	16,687.96
Total	**14,560.37**	**14,567.31**	**13,687.40**

FIGURE 3-12 In the presence of invalid relationships, the measures are most likely wrong—each in their own way.

It is interesting to note that *AvgSalesPerDistinctKey* is the only correct calculation. Since we sliced by *Category*, each category had a different number of invalid product keys—all of which collapsed to the single blank row.

However, the correct approach should be to fix the relationship so that no sale is orphaned of its product. The golden rule is to not have any invalid relationships in the model. If, for any reason, you have invalid relationships, then you need to be extremely cautious in how you handle the blank row, as well as how its presence might affect your calculations.

As a final note, consider that the *ALL* function always returns the blank row, if present. In case you need to remove the blank row from the result, then *ALLNOBLANKROW* is the function you will want to use.

VALUES of multiple columns

The functions *VALUES* and *DISTINCT* only accept a single column as a parameter. There is no corresponding version for two or more columns, as there is for *ALL* and *ALLNO-BLANKROW*. In case we need to obtain the distinct, visible combinations of values from different columns, then *VALUES* is of no help. Later in Chapter 12 you will learn that:

```
VALUES ( 'Product'[Category], 'Product'[Subcategory] )
```

can be obtained by writing:

```
SUMMARIZE ( 'Product', 'Product'[Category], 'Product'[Subcategory] )
```

Later, you will see that *VALUES* and *DISTINCT* are often used as a parameter of iterator functions. There are no differences in their results whenever the relationships are valid. In such a case, when you iterate over the values of a column, you need to consider the blank row as a valid row, in order to make sure that you iterate all the possible values. As a rule of thumb, *VALUES* should be your default choice, only leaving *DISTINCT* to cases when you want to explicitly exclude the possible blank value. Later in this book, you will also learn how to leverage *DISTINCT* instead of *VALUES* to avoid circular dependencies. We will cover it in Chapter 15, "Advanced relationships handling."

VALUES and *DISTINCT* also accept a table as an argument. In that case, they exhibit different behaviors:

- *DISTINCT* returns the distinct values of the table, not considering the blank row. Thus, duplicated rows are removed from the result.

- *VALUES* returns all the rows of the table, without removing duplicates, plus the additional blank row if present. Duplicated rows, in this case, are kept untouched.

Using tables as scalar values

Although *VALUES* is a table function, we will often use it to compute scalar values because of a special feature in DAX: a table with a single row and a single column can be used as if it were a scalar value. Imagine we produce a report like the one in Figure 3-13, reporting the number of brands sliced by category and subcategory.

Category	NumOfBrands
Audio	**3**
Bluetooth Headphones	2
MP4&MP3	1
Recording Pen	1
Cameras and camcorders	**3**
Camcorders	1
Cameras & Camcorders Accessories	1
Digital Cameras	1
Digital SLR Cameras	3
Cell phones	**2**
Cell phones Accessories	1

FIGURE 3-13 The report shows the number of brands available for each category and subcategory.

One might also want to see the names of the brands beside their number. One possible solution is to use *VALUES* to retrieve the different brands and, instead of counting them, return their value. This is possible only in the special case when there is only one value for the brand. Indeed, in that case it is possible to return the result of *VALUES* and DAX automatically converts it into a scalar value. To make sure that there is only one brand, one needs to protect the code with an *IF* statement:

```
Brand Name :=
IF (
    COUNTROWS ( VALUES ( Product[Brand] ) ) = 1,
    VALUES ( Product[Brand] )
)
```

The result is visible in Figure 3-14. When the *Brand Name* column contains a blank, it means that there are two or more different brands.

Category	NumOfBrands	Brand Name
Audio	**3**	
Bluetooth Headphones	2	
MP4&MP3	1	Contoso
Recording Pen	1	Wide World Importers
Cameras and camcorders	**3**	
Camcorders	1	Fabrikam
Cameras & Camcorders Accessories	1	Contoso
Digital Cameras	1	A. Datum
Digital SLR Cameras	3	
Cell phones	**2**	
Cell phones Accessories	1	Contoso

FIGURE 3-14 When *VALUES* returns a single row, we can use it as a scalar value, as in the *Brand Name* measure.

The *Brand Name* measure uses *COUNTROWS* to check whether the *Color* column of the *Products* table only has one value selected. Because this pattern is frequently used in DAX code, there is a simpler function that checks whether a column only has one visible value: *HASONEVALUE*. The following is a better implementation of the *Brand Name* measure, based on *HASONEVALUE*:

```
Brand Name :=
IF (
    HASONEVALUE ( 'Product'[Brand] ),
    VALUES ( 'Product'[Brand] )
)
```

Moreover, to make the lives of developers easier, DAX also offers a function that automatically checks if a column contains a single value and, if so, it returns the value as a scalar. In case there are multiple values, it is also possible to define a default value to be returned. That function is *SELECTEDVALUE*. The previous measure can also be defined as

```
Brand Name := SELECTEDVALUE ( 'Product'[Brand] )
```

By including the second optional argument, one can provide a message stating that the result contains multiple results:

```
Brand Name := SELECTEDVALUE ( 'Product'[Brand], "Multiple brands" )
```

The result of this latest measure is visible in Figure 3-15.

Category	NumOfBrands	Brand Name
Audio	**3**	**Multiple brands**
Bluetooth Headphones	2	Multiple brands
MP4&MP3	1	Contoso
Recording Pen	1	Wide World Importers
Cameras and camcorders	**3**	**Multiple brands**
Camcorders	1	Fabrikam
Cameras & Camcorders Accessories	1	Contoso
Digital Cameras	1	A. Datum
Digital SLR Cameras	3	Multiple brands
Cell phones	**2**	**Multiple brands**
Cell phones Accessories	1	Contoso

FIGURE 3-15 *SELECTEDVALUE* returns a default value in case there are multiple rows for the *Brand Name* column.

What if, instead of returning a message like "Multiple brands," one wants to list all the brands? In that case, an option is to iterate over the *VALUES* of *Product[Brand]* and use the *CONCATENATEX* function, which produces a good result even if there are multiple values:

```
[Brand Name] :=
CONCATENATEX (
    VALUES ( 'Product'[Brand] ),
    'Product'[Brand],
    ", "
)
```

Now the result contains the different brands separated by a comma instead of the generic message, as shown in Figure 3-16.

Category	NumOfBrands	Brand Name
Audio	**3**	**Contoso, Wide World Importers, Northwind Traders**
Bluetooth Headphones	2	Wide World Importers, Northwind Traders
MP4&MP3	1	Contoso
Recording Pen	1	Wide World Importers
Cameras and camcorders	**3**	**Contoso, Fabrikam, A. Datum**
Camcorders	1	Fabrikam
Cameras & Camcorders Accessories	1	Contoso
Digital Cameras	1	A. Datum
Digital SLR Cameras	3	Contoso, Fabrikam, A. Datum
Cell phones	**2**	**Contoso, The Phone Company**
Cell phones Accessories	1	Contoso

FIGURE 3-16 *CONCATENATEX* builds strings out of tables, concatenating expressions.

Introducing *ALLSELECTED*

The last table function that belongs to the set of basic table functions is *ALLSELECTED*. Actually, *ALLSELECTED* is a very complex table function—probably the most complex table function in DAX. In Chapter 14, we will uncover all the secrets of *ALLSELECTED*. Nevertheless, *ALLSELECTED* is useful even in its basic implementation. For that reason, it is worth mentioning in this introductory chapter.

ALLSELECTED is useful when retrieving the list of values of a table, or a column, as visible in the current report and considering all and only the filters outside of the current visual. To see when *ALLSELECTED* becomes useful, look at the report in Figure 3-17.

Category		Category	Sales Amount	Sales Pct
☐	Audio	Audio	384,518.16	1.26%
☐	Cameras and camcorders	Cameras and camcorders	7,192,581.95	23.51%
☐	Cell phones	Cell phones	1,604,610.26	5.25%
☐	Computers	Computers	6,741,548.73	22.04%
☐	Games and Toys	Games and Toys	360,652.81	1.18%
☐	Home Appliances	Home Appliances	9,600,457.04	31.38%
☐	Music, Movies and Audio Books	Music, Movies and Audio Books	314,206.74	1.03%
☐	TV and Video	TV and Video	4,392,768.29	14.36%
		Total	**30,591,343.98**	**100.00%**

FIGURE 3-17 The report contains a matrix and a slicer, on the same page.

The value of *Sales Pct* is computed by the following measure:

```
Sales Pct :=
DIVIDE (
    SUMX ( Sales, Sales[Quantity] * Sales[Net Price] ),
    SUMX ( ALL ( Sales ), Sales[Quantity] * Sales[Net Price] )
)
```

Because the denominator uses the *ALL* function, it always computes the grand total of all sales, regardless of any filter. As such, if one uses the slicer to reduce the number of categories shown, the report still computes the percentage against all the sales. For example, Figure 3-18 shows what happens if one selects some categories with the slicer.

Category		Category	Sales Amount	Sales Pct
☐	Audio			
■	Cameras and camcorders	Cameras and camcorders	7,192,581.95	23.51%
■	Cell phones	Cell phones	1,604,610.26	5.25%
■	Computers	Computers	6,741,548.73	22.04%
■	Games and Toys	Games and Toys	360,652.81	1.18%
■	Home Appliances	Home Appliances	9,600,457.04	31.38%
☐	Music, Movies and Audio Books	**Total**	**25,499,850.79**	**83.36%**
☐	TV and Video			

FIGURE 3-18 Using *ALL*, the percentage is still computed against the grand total of all sales.

Some rows disappeared as expected, but the amounts reported in the remaining rows are unchanged. Moreover, the grand total of the matrix no longer accounts for 100%. If this is not the expected result, meaning that you want the percentage to be computed not against the grand total of sales but rather only on the selected values, then *ALLSELECTED* becomes useful.

Indeed, by writing the code of *Sales Pct* using *ALLSELECTED* instead of *ALL*, the denominator computes the sales of all categories considering all and only the filters outside of the matrix. In other words, it returns the sales of all categories except Audio, Music, and TV.

```
Sales Pct :=
DIVIDE (
    SUMX ( Sales, Sales[Quantity] * Sales[Net Price] ),
    SUMX ( ALLSELECTED ( Sales ), Sales[Quantity] * Sales[Net Price] )
)
```

The result of this latter version is visible in Figure 3-19.

Category		Category	Sales Amount	Sales Pct
☐	Audio			
■	Cameras and camcorders	Cameras and camcorders	7,192,581.95	28.21%
■	Cell phones	Cell phones	1,604,610.26	6.29%
■	Computers	Computers	6,741,548.73	26.44%
■	Games and Toys	Games and Toys	360,652.81	1.41%
■	Home Appliances	Home Appliances	9,600,457.04	37.65%
☐	Music, Movies and Audio Books	**Total**	**25,499,850.79**	**100.00%**
☐	TV and Video			

FIGURE 3-19 Using *ALLSELECTED*, the percentage is computed against the sales only considering outer filters.

The total is now 100% and the numbers reported reflect the percentage against the visible total, not against the grand total of all sales. *ALLSELECTED* is a powerful and useful function. Unfortunately, to achieve this purpose, it ends up being an extraordinarily complex function too. Only much later in the book will we be able to explain it in full. Because of its complexity, *ALLSELECTED* sometimes returns unexpected results. By unexpected we do not mean wrong, but rather, ridiculously hard to understand even for seasoned DAX developers.

When used in simple formulas like the one we have shown here, *ALLSELECTED* proves to be particularly useful, anyway.

Conclusions

As you have seen in this chapter, basic table functions are already immensely powerful, and they allow you to start creating many useful calculations. *FILTER*, *ALL*, *VALUES* and *ALLSELECTED* are extremely common functions that appear in many DAX formulas.

Learning how to mix table functions to produce the result you want is particularly important because it will allow you to seamlessly achieve advanced calculations. Moreover, when mixed with the power of *CALCULATE* and of context transition, table functions produce compact, neat, and powerful calculations. In the next chapters, we introduce evaluation contexts and the *CALCULATE* function. After having learned *CALCULATE*, you will probably revisit this chapter to use table functions as parameters of *CALCULATE*, thus leveraging their full potential.

Understanding evaluation contexts

At this point in the book, you have learned the basics of the DAX language. You know how to create calculated columns and measures, and you have a good understanding of common functions used in DAX. This is the chapter where you move to the next level in this language: After learning a solid theoretical background of the DAX language, you become a real DAX champion.

With the knowledge you have gained so far, you can already create many interesting reports, but you need to learn evaluation contexts in order to create more complex formulas. Indeed, evaluation contexts are the basis of all the advanced features of DAX.

We want to give a few words of warning to our readers. The concept of evaluation contexts is simple, and you will learn and understand it soon. Nevertheless, you need to thoroughly understand several subtle considerations and details. Otherwise, you will feel lost at a certain point on your DAX learning path. We have been teaching DAX to thousands of users in public and private classes, so we know that this is normal. At a certain point, you have the feeling that formulas work like magic because they work, but you do not understand why. Do not worry: you will be in good company. Most DAX students reach that point, and many others will reach it in the future. It simply means that evaluation contexts are not clear enough to them. The solution, at that point, is easy: Come back to this chapter, read it again, and you will probably find something new that you missed during your first read.

Moreover, evaluation contexts play an important role when using the *CALCULATE* function—which is probably the most powerful and hard-to-learn DAX function. We introduce *CALCULATE* in Chapter 5, "Understanding *CALCULATE* and *CALCULATETABLE*," and then we use it throughout the rest of the book. Understanding *CALCULATE* without having a solid understanding of evaluation contexts is problematic. On the other hand, understanding the importance of evaluation contexts without having ever tried to use *CALCULATE* is nearly impossible. Thus, in our experience with previous books we have written, this chapter and the subsequent one are the two that are always marked up and have the corners of pages folded over.

In the rest of the book we will use these concepts. Then in Chapter 14, "Advanced DAX concepts," you will complete your learning of evaluation contexts with expanded tables. Beware that the content of this chapter is not the definitive description of evaluation contexts just yet. A more detailed description of evaluation contexts is the description based on expanded tables, but it would be too hard to learn about expanded tables before having a good understanding of the basics of evaluation contexts. Therefore, we introduce the whole theory in different steps.

Introducing evaluation contexts

There are two evaluation contexts: the filter context and the row context. In the next sections, you learn what they are and how to use them to write DAX code. Before learning what they are, it is important to state one point: They are different concepts, with different functionalities and a completely different usage.

The most common mistake of DAX newbies is that of confusing the two contexts as if the row context was a slight variation of a filter context. This is not the case. The filter context filters data, whereas the row context iterates tables. When DAX is iterating, it is not filtering; and when it is filtering, it is not iterating. Even though this is a simple concept, we know from experience that it is hard to imprint in the mind. Our brain seems to prefer a short path to learning—when it believes there are some similarities, it uses them by merging the two concepts into one. Do not be fooled. Whenever you have the feeling that the two evaluation contexts look the same, stop and repeat this sentence in your mind like a mantra: "The filter context filters, the row context iterates, they are not the same."

An evaluation context is the context under which a DAX expression is evaluated. In fact, any DAX expression can provide different values in different contexts. This behavior is intuitive, and this is the reason why one can write DAX code without learning about evaluation contexts in advance. You probably reached this point in the book having authored DAX code without learning about evaluation contexts. Because you want more, it is now time to be more precise, to set up the foundations of DAX the right way, and to prepare yourself to unleash the full power of DAX.

Understanding filter contexts

Let us begin by understanding what an evaluation context is. All DAX expressions are evaluated inside a context. The context is the "environment" within which the formula is evaluated. For example, consider a measure such as

```
Sales Amount := SUMX ( Sales, Sales[Quantity] * Sales[Net Price] )
```

This formula computes the sum of quantity multiplied by price in the *Sales* table. We can use this measure in a report and look at the results, as shown in Figure 4-1.

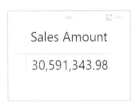

FIGURE 4-1 The measure *Sales Amount*, without a context, shows the grand total of sales.

This number alone does not look interesting. However, if you think carefully, the formula computes exactly what one would expect: the sum of all sales amounts. In a real report, one is likely to slice the value by a certain column. For example, we can select the product brand, use it on the rows, and the matrix report starts to reveal interesting business insights as shown in Figure 4-2.

Brand	Sales Amount
A. Datum	2,096,184.64
Adventure Works	4,011,112.28
Contoso	7,352,399.03
Fabrikam	5,554,015.73
Litware	3,255,704.03
Northwind Traders	1,040,552.13
Proseware	2,546,144.16
Southridge Video	1,384,413.85
Tailspin Toys	325,042.42
The Phone Company	1,123,819.07
Wide World Importers	1,901,956.66
Total	**30,591,343.98**

FIGURE 4-2 Sum of *Sales Amount*, sliced by brand, shows the sales of each brand in separate rows.

The grand total is still there, but now it is the sum of smaller values. Each value, together with all the others, provides more detailed insights. However, you should note that something weird is happening: The formula is not computing what we apparently asked. In fact, inside each cell of the report, the formula is no longer computing the sum of all sales. Instead, it computes the sales of a given brand. Finally, note that nowhere in the code does it say that it can (or should) work on subsets of data. This filtering happens outside of the formula.

Each cell computes a different value because of the *evaluation context* under which DAX executes the formula. You can think of the evaluation context of a formula as the surrounding area of the cell where DAX evaluates the formula.

> **DAX evaluates all formulas within a respective context. Even though the formula is the same, the result is different because DAX executes the same code against different subsets of data.**

This context is named *Filter Context* and, as the name suggests, it is a context that filters tables. Any formula ever authored will have a different value depending on the filter context used to perform its evaluation. This behavior, although intuitive, needs to be well understood because it hides many complexities.

Every cell of the report has a different filter context. You should consider that every cell has a different evaluation—as if it were a different query, independent from the other cells in the same report. The engine might perform some level of internal optimization to improve computation speed, but you should assume that every cell has an independent and autonomous evaluation of the underlying DAX expression. Therefore, the computation of the Total row in Figure 4-2 is not computed by summing the other rows of the report. It is computed by aggregating all the rows of the *Sales* table, although this means other iterations were already computed for the other rows in the same report. Consequently, depending on the DAX expression, the result in the Total row might display a different result, unrelated to the other rows in the same report.

 Note In these examples, we are using a matrix for the sake of simplicity. We can define an evaluation context with queries too, and you will learn more about it in future chapters. For now, it is better to keep it simple and only think of reports, to have a simplified and visual understanding of the concepts.

When *Brand* is on the rows, the filter context filters one brand for each cell. If we increase the complexity of the matrix by adding the year on the columns, we obtain the report in Figure 4-3.

Brand	CY 2007	CY 2008	CY 2009	**Total**
A. Datum	1,181,110.71	463,721.61	451,352.33	**2,096,184.64**
Adventure Works	2,249,988.11	892,674.52	868,449.65	**4,011,112.28**
Contoso	2,729,818.54	2,369,167.68	2,253,412.80	**7,352,399.03**
Fabrikam	1,652,751.34	1,993,123.48	1,908,140.91	**5,554,015.73**
Litware	647,385.82	1,487,846.74	1,120,471.47	**3,255,704.03**
Northwind Traders	372,199.93	469,827.70	198,524.49	**1,040,552.13**
Proseware	880,095.80	763,586.23	902,462.12	**2,546,144.16**
Southridge Video	688,107.56	294,635.04	401,671.25	**1,384,413.85**
Tailspin Toys	74,603.14	97,193.87	153,245.41	**325,042.42**
The Phone Company	362,444.46	355,629.36	405,745.25	**1,123,819.07**
Wide World Importers	471,440.71	740,176.76	690,339.18	**1,901,956.66**
Total	**11,309,946.12**	**9,927,582.99**	**9,353,814.87**	**30,591,343.98**

FIGURE 4-3 *Sales amount* is sliced by brand and year.

Now each cell shows a subset of data pertinent to one brand and one year. The reason for this is that the filter context of each cell now filters both the brand and the year. In the Total row, the filter is only on the brand, whereas in the Total column the filter is only on the year. The grand total is the only cell that computes the sum of all sales because—there—the filter context does not apply any filter to the model.

The rules of the game should be clear at this point: The more columns we use to slice and dice, the more columns are being filtered by the filter context in each cell of the matrix. If one adds the *Store[Continent]* column to the rows, the result is—again—different, as shown in Figure 4-4.

Brand	CY 2007	CY 2008	CY 2009	Total
A. Datum	**1,181,110.71**	**463,721.61**	**451,352.33**	**2,096,184.64**
Asia	281,936.73	125,055.80	145,386.55	**552,379.08**
Europe	395,159.31	165,924.22	146,867.73	**707,951.26**
North America	504,014.67	172,741.59	159,098.05	**835,854.31**
Adventure Works	**2,249,988.11**	**892,674.52**	**868,449.65**	**4,011,112.28**
Asia	620,545.52	347,150.65	414,507.89	**1,382,204.07**
Europe	662,553.70	275,126.51	264,973.65	**1,202,653.86**
North America	966,888.88	270,397.36	188,968.10	**1,426,254.35**
Contoso	**2,729,818.54**	**2,369,167.68**	**2,253,412.80**	**7,352,399.03**
Asia	838,967.94	998,113.24	753,146.22	**2,590,227.39**
Europe	905,295.91	529,596.05	694,250.12	**2,129,142.08**
North America	985,554.69	841,458.40	806,016.47	**2,633,029.56**
Fabrikam	**1,652,751.34**	**1,993,123.48**	**1,908,140.91**	**5,554,015.73**
Asia	640,664.16	727,025.63	783,871.11	**2,151,560.89**
Europe	503,428.83	383,827.59	454,944.80	**1,342,201.22**
Total	**11,309,946.12**	**9,927,582.99**	**9,353,814.87**	**30,591,343.98**

FIGURE 4-4 The context is defined by the set of fields on rows and on columns.

Now the filter context of each cell is filtering brand, country, and year. In other words, the filter context contains the complete set of fields that one uses on rows and columns of the report.

Note Whether a field is on the rows or on the columns of the visual, or on the slicer and/or page/report/visual filter, or in any other kind of filter we can create with a report—all this is irrelevant. All these filters contribute to define a single filter context, which DAX uses to evaluate the formula. Displaying a field on rows or columns is useful for aesthetic purposes, but nothing changes in the way DAX computes values.

Visual interactions in Power BI compose a filter context by combining different elements from a graphical interface. Indeed, the filter context of a cell is computed by merging together all the filters coming from rows, columns, slicers, and any other visual used for filtering. For example, look at Figure 4-5.

Brand	CY 2007	CY 2008	CY 2009	Total
A. Datum	57,276.00			57,276.00
Adventure Works	77,413.46		8,110.53	85,523.99
Contoso	125,596.01	2,638.18	14,156.95	142,391.14
Fabrikam	4,340.62	8,640.00	29,854.98	42,835.60
Litware	17,910.87		7,956.00	25,866.87
Northwind Traders	34,161.39	12,733.92	2,122.32	49,017.63
Proseware	13,183.70		10,647.00	23,830.70
Southridge Video	27,239.71	774.23	3,874.18	31,888.12
Tailspin Toys	4,581.53	3,976.38	5,886.67	14,444.57
The Phone Company	1,384.80	864.90		2,249.70
Wide World Importers	2,395.37			2,395.37
Total	**365,483.46**	**29,627.61**	**82,608.63**	**477,719.70**

(left panel: Sales Amount by Occupation — Clerical, Manual, Professional, Management, Skilled Manual; 0.0M to 0.5M. Continent: ☐ Asia, ■ Europe, ☐ North America)

FIGURE 4-5 In a typical report, the context is defined in many ways, including slicers, filters, and other visuals.

The filter context of the top-left cell (A.Datum, CY 2007, 57,276.00) not only filters the row and the column of the visual, but it also filters the occupation (Professional) and the continent (Europe), which are coming from different visuals. All these filters contribute to the definition of a single filter context valid for one cell, which DAX applies to the whole data model prior to evaluating the formula.

A more formal definition of a filter context is to say that a filter context is a set of filters. A filter, in turn, is a list of tuples, and a tuple is a set of values for some defined columns. Figure 4-6 shows a visual representation of the filter context under which the highlighted cell is evaluated. Each element of the report contributes to creating the filter context, and every cell in the report has a different filter context.

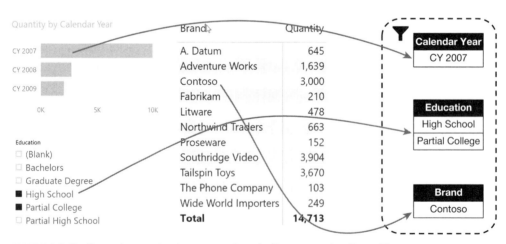

FIGURE 4-6 The figure shows a visual representation of a filter context in a Power BI report.

The filter context of Figure 4-6 contains three filters. The first filter contains a tuple for *Calendar Year* with the value CY 2007. The second filter contains two tuples for *Education* with the values High School and Partial College. The third filter contains a single tuple for *Brand*, with the value Contoso. You might notice that each filter contains tuples for one column only. You will learn how to create tuples with multiple columns later. Multi-column tuples are both powerful and complex tools in the hand of a DAX developer.

Before leaving this introduction, let us recall the measure used at the beginning of this section:

```
Sales Amount := SUMX ( Sales, Sales[Quantity] * Sales[Net Price] )
```

Here is the correct way of reading the previous measure: *The measure computes the sum of Quantity multiplied by Net Price for all the rows in Sales which are visible in the current filter context.*

The same applies to simpler aggregations. For example, consider this measure:

```
Total Quantity := SUM ( Sales[Quantity] )
```

It sums the *Quantity* column of all the rows in *Sales* that are visible in the current filter context. You can better understand its working by considering the corresponding *SUMX* version:

```
Total Quantity := SUMX ( Sales, Sales[Quantity] )
```

Looking at the *SUMX* definition, we might consider that the filter context affects the evaluation of the *Sales* expression, which only returns the rows of the *Sales* table that are visible in the current filter context. This is true, but you should consider that the filter context also applies to the following measures, which do not have a corresponding iterator:

```
Customers := DISTINCTCOUNT ( Sales[CustomerKey] )   -- Count customers in filter context

Colors :=
VAR ListColors = DISTINCT ( 'Product'[Color] )      -- Unique colors in filter context
RETURN COUNTROWS ( ListColors )                     -- Count unique colors
```

It might look pedantic, at this point, to spend so much time stressing the concept that a filter context is always active, and that it affects the formula result. Nevertheless, keep in mind that DAX requires you to be extremely precise. Most of the complexity of DAX is not in learning new functions. Instead, the complexity comes from the presence of many subtle concepts. When these concepts are mixed together, what emerges is a complex scenario. Right now, the filter context is defined by the report. As soon as you learn how to create filter contexts by yourself (a critical skill described in the next chapter), being able to understand which filter context is active in each part of your formula will be of paramount importance.

Understanding the row context

In the previous section, you learned about the filter context. In this section, you now learn the second type of evaluation context: the *row context*. Remember, although both the row context and the filter context are evaluation contexts, *they are not the same concept*. As you learned in the previous section, the purpose of the filter context is, as its name implies, to filter tables. On the other hand, the row context is not a tool to filter tables. Instead, it is used to iterate over tables and evaluate column values.

This time we use a different formula for our considerations, defining a calculated column to compute the gross margin:

```
Sales[Gross Margin] = Sales[Quantity] * ( Sales[Net Price] - Sales[Unit Cost] )
```

There is a different value for each row in the resulting calculated column, as shown in Figure 4-7.

Quantity	Unit Cost	Net Price	Gross Margin
1	915.08	1,989.90	1,074.82
1	960.82	2,464.99	1,504.17
1	1,060.22	2,559.99	1,499.77
1	1,060.22	2,719.99	1,659.77
1	1,060.22	2,879.99	1,819.77
1	1,060.22	3,199.99	2,139.77
2	0.48	0.76	0.56
2	0.48	0.88	0.81
2	1.01	1.79	1.56
2	1.01	1.85	1.68

FIGURE 4-7 There is a different value in each row of *Gross Margin*, depending on the value of other columns.

As expected, for each row of the table there is a different value in the calculated column. Indeed, because there are given values in each row for the three columns used in the expression, it comes as a natural consequence that the final expression computes different values. As it happened with the filter context, the reason is the presence of an evaluation context. This time, the context does not filter a table. Instead, it identifies the row for which the calculation happens.

Note The row context references a row in the result of a DAX table expression. It should not be confused with a row in the report. DAX does not have a way to directly reference a row or a column in the report. The values displayed in a matrix in Power BI and in a Pivot-Table in Excel are the result of DAX measures computed in a filter context, or are values stored in the table as native or calculated columns.

In other words, we know that a calculated column is computed row by row, but how does DAX know which row it is currently iterating? It knows the row because there is another evaluation context providing the row—it is the *row context*. When we create a calculated column over a table with one million rows, DAX creates a row context that evaluates the expression iterating over the table row by row, using the row context as the cursor.

When we create a calculated column, DAX creates a row context by default. In that case, there is no need to manually create a row context: A calculated column is always executed in a row context. You have already learned how to create a row context manually—by starting an iteration. In fact, one can write the gross margin as a measure, like in the following code:

```
Gross Margin :=
SUMX (
    Sales,
    Sales[Quantity] * ( Sales[Net Price] - Sales[Unit Cost] )
)
```

In this case, because the code is for a measure, there is no automatic row context. *SUMX*, being an iterator, creates a row context that starts iterating over the *Sales* table, row by row. During the iteration, it executes the second expression of *SUMX* inside the row context. Thus, during each step of the iteration, DAX knows which value to use for the three column names used in the expression.

The row context exists when we create a calculated column or when we are computing an expression inside an iteration. There is no other way of creating a row context. Moreover, it helps to think that a row context is needed whenever we want to obtain the value of a column for a certain row. For example, the following measure definition is invalid. Indeed, it tries to compute the value of *Sales[Net Price]* and there is no row context providing the row for which the calculation needs to be executed:

```
Gross Margin := Sales[Quantity] * ( Sales[Net Price] - Sales[Unit Cost] )
```

This same expression is valid when executed for a calculated column, and it is invalid if used in a measure. The reason is not that measures and calculated columns have different ways of using DAX. The reason is that a calculated column has an automatic row context, whereas a measure does not. If one wants to evaluate an expression row by row inside a measure, one needs to start an iteration to create a row context.

> **Note** A column reference requires a row context to return the value of the column from a table. A column reference can be also used as an argument for several DAX functions without a row context. For example, *DISTINCT* and *DISTINCTCOUNT* can have a column reference as a parameter, without defining a row context. Nonetheless, a column reference in a DAX expression requires a row context to be evaluated.

At this point, we need to repeat one important concept: A row context is not a special kind of filter context that filters one row. The row context is not filtering the model in any way; the row context only indicates to DAX which row to use out of a table. If one wants to apply a filter to the model, the tool to use is the filter context. On the other hand, if the user wants to evaluate an expression row by row, then the row context will do the job.

Testing your understanding of evaluation contexts

Before moving on to more complex descriptions about evaluation contexts, it is useful to test your understanding of contexts with a couple of examples. Please do not look at the explanation immediately; stop after the question and try to answer it. Then read the explanation to make sense of it. As a hint, try to remember, while thinking, *"The filter context filters; the row context iterates. This means that the row context does not filter, and the filter context does not iterate."*

Using *SUM* in a calculated column

The first test uses an aggregator inside a calculated column. What is the result of the following expression, used in a calculated column, in *Sales*?

```
Sales[SumOfSalesQuantity] = SUM ( Sales[Quantity] )
```

Remember, this internally corresponds to this equivalent syntax:

```
Sales[SumOfSalesQuantity] = SUMX ( Sales, Sales[Quantity] )
```

Because it is a calculated column, it is computed row by row in a row context. What number do you expect to see? Choose from these three answers:

- The value of *Quantity* for that row, that is, a different value for each row.

- The total of *Quantity* for all the rows, that is, the same value for all the rows.

- An error; we cannot use *SUM* inside a calculated column.

Stop reading, please, while we wait for your educated guess before moving on.

Here is the correct reasoning. You have learned that the formula means, *"the sum of quantity for all the rows visible in the current filter context."* Moreover, because the code is executed for a calculated column, DAX evaluates the formula row by row, in a row context. Nevertheless, the row context is not filtering the table. The only context that can filter the table is the filter context. This turns the question into a different one: What is the filter context, when the formula is evaluated? The answer is straightforward: The filter context is empty. Indeed, the filter context is created by visuals or by queries, and a calculated column is computed at data refresh time when no filtering is happening. Thus, *SUM* works on the whole *Sales* table, aggregating the value of *Sales[Quantity]* for all the rows of *Sales*.

The correct answer is the second answer. This calculated column computes the same value for each row, that is, the grand total of *Sales[Quantity]* repeated for all the rows. Figure 4-8 shows the result of the *SumOfSalesQuantity* calculated column.

Quantity	Unit Cost	Net Price	SumOfSalesQuantity
1	0.48	0.76	140,180.00
1	0.48	0.86	140,180.00
1	0.48	0.88	140,180.00
1	0.48	0.95	140,180.00
1	1.01	1.79	140,180.00
1	1.01	1.85	140,180.00
1	1.01	1.99	140,180.00
1	1.50	2.35	140,180.00
1	1.50	2.50	140,180.00
1	1.50	2.65	140,180.00
1	1.50	2.79	140,180.00
1	1.50	2.94	140,180.00

FIGURE 4-8 *SUM (Sales[Quantity])*, in a calculated column, is computed against the entire database.

This example shows that the two evaluation contexts exist at the same time, but they do not interact. The evaluation contexts both work on the result of a formula, but they do so in different ways. Aggregators like *SUM*, *MIN*, and *MAX* only use the filter context, and they ignore the row context. If you have chosen the first answer, as many students typically do, it is perfectly normal. The thing is that you are still confusing the filter context and the row context. Remember, the filter context filters; the row context iterates. The first answer is the most common, when using intuitive logic, but it is wrong— now you know why. However, if you chose the correct answer ... then we are glad this section helped you in learning the important difference between the two contexts.

Using columns in a measure

The second test is slightly different. Imagine we define the formula for the gross margin in a measure instead of in a calculated column. We have a column with the net price, another column for the product cost, and we write the following expression:

```
GrossMargin% := ( Sales[Net Price] - Sales[Unit Cost] ) / Sales[Unit Cost]
```

What will the result be? As it happened earlier, choose among the three possible answers:

- The expression works correctly, time to test the result in a report.

- An error, we should not even write this formula.

- We can define the formula, but it will return an error when used in a report.

As in the previous test, stop reading, think about the answer, and then read the following explanation.

The code references *Sales[Net Price]* and *Sales[Unit Cost]* without any aggregator. As such, DAX needs to retrieve the value of the columns for a certain row. DAX has no way of detecting which row the formula needs to be computed for because there is no iteration happening and the code is not in a calculated column. In other words, DAX is missing a row context that would make it possible to retrieve a value for the columns that are part of the expression. Remember that a measure does not have an automatic row context; only calculated columns do. If we need a row context in a measure, we should start an iteration.

Thus, the second answer is the correct one. We cannot write the formula because it is syntactically wrong, and we get an error when trying to enter the code.

Using the row context with iterators

You learned that DAX creates a row context whenever we define a calculated column or when we start an iteration with an X-function. When we use a calculated column, the presence of the row context is simple to use and understand. In fact, we can create simple calculated columns without even knowing about the presence of the row context. The reason is that the row context is created automatically by the engine. Therefore, we do not need to worry about the presence of the row context. On the other hand, when using iterators we are responsible for the creation and the handling of the row context. Moreover, by using iterators we can create multiple nested row contexts; this increases the complexity of the code. Therefore, it is important to understand more precisely the behavior of row contexts with iterators.

For example, look at the following DAX measure:

```
IncreasedSales := SUMX ( Sales, Sales[Net Price] * 1.1 )
```

Because *SUMX* is an iterator, *SUMX* creates a row context on the *Sales* table and uses it during the iteration. The row context iterates the *Sales* table (first parameter) and provides the current row to the second parameter during the iteration. In other words, DAX evaluates the inner expression (the second parameter of *SUMX*) in a row context containing the currently iterated row on the first parameter.

Please note that the two parameters of *SUMX* use different contexts. In fact, any piece of DAX code works in the context where it is called. Thus, when the expression is executed, there might already be a filter context and one or many row contexts active. Look at the same expression with comments:

```
SUMX (
    Sales,                   -- External filter and row contexts
    Sales[Net Price] * 1.1   -- External filter and row contexts + new row context
)
```

The first parameter, *Sales*, is evaluated using the contexts coming from the caller. The second parameter (the expression) is evaluated using both the external contexts plus the newly created row context.

All iterators behave the same way:

1. Evaluate the first parameter in the existing contexts to determine the rows to scan.

2. Create a new row context for each row of the table evaluated in the previous step.

3. Iterate the table and evaluate the second parameter in the existing evaluation context, including the newly created row context.

4. Aggregate the values computed during the previous step.

Be mindful that the original contexts are still valid inside the expression. Iterators add a new row context; they do not modify existing filter contexts. For example, if the outer filter context contains a filter for the color Red, that filter is still active during the whole iteration. Besides, remember that the row context iterates; it does not filter. Therefore, no matter what, we cannot override the outer filter context using an iterator.

This rule is always valid, but there is an important detail that is not trivial. If the previous contexts already contained a row context for the same table, then the newly created row context hides the previous existing row context on the same table. For DAX newbies, this is a possible source of mistakes. Therefore, we discuss row context hiding in more detail in the next two sections.

Nested row contexts on different tables

The expression evaluated by an iterator can be very complex. Moreover, the expression can, on its own, contain further iterations. At first sight, starting an iteration inside another iteration might look strange. Still, it is a common DAX practice because nesting iterators produce powerful expressions.

For example, the following code contains three nested iterators, and it scans three tables: *Categories, Products,* and *Sales.*

```
SUMX (
    'Product Category',                    -- Scans the Product Category table
    SUMX (                                 -- For each category
        RELATEDTABLE ( 'Product' ),        -- Scans the category products
        SUMX (                             -- For each product
            RELATEDTABLE ( Sales )         -- Scans the sales of that product
            Sales[Quantity]                --
                * 'Product'[Unit Price]    -- Computes the sales amount of that sale
                * 'Product Category'[Discount]
        )
    )
)
```

The innermost expression—the multiplication of three factors—references three tables. In fact, three row contexts are opened during that expression evaluation: one for each of the three tables that are currently being iterated. It is also worth noting that the two *RELATEDTABLE* functions return the rows of a related table starting from the current row context. Thus, *RELATEDTABLE (Product),* being executed in a row context from the Categories table, returns the products of the given category. The same reasoning applies to *RELATEDTABLE (Sales)*, which returns the sales of the given product.

The previous code is suboptimal in terms of both performance and readability. As a rule, it is fine to nest iterators provided that the number of rows to scan is not too large: hundreds is good, thousands is fine, millions is bad. Otherwise, we may easily hit performance issues. We used the previous code to demonstrate that it is possible to create multiple nested row contexts; we will see more useful examples of nested iterators later in the book. One can express the same calculation in a much faster and readable way by using the following code, which relies on one individual row context and the *RELATED* function:

```
SUMX (
    Sales,
    Sales[Quantity]
        * RELATED ( 'Product'[Unit Price] )
        * RELATED ( 'Product Category'[Discount] )
)
```

Whenever there are multiple row contexts on different tables, one can use them to reference the iterated tables in a single DAX expression. There is one scenario, however, which proves to be challenging. This happens when we nest multiple row contexts on the same table, which is the topic covered in the following section.

Nested row contexts on the same table

The scenario of having nested row contexts on the same table might seem rare. However, it does happen quite often, and more frequently in calculated columns. Imagine we want to rank products based on the list price. The most expensive product should be ranked 1, the second most expensive product should be ranked 2, and so on. We could solve the scenario using the *RANKX* function. But for educational purposes, we show how to solve it using simpler DAX functions.

To compute the ranking, for each product we can count the number of products whose price is higher than the current product's. If there is no product with a higher price than the current product price, then the current product is the most expensive and its ranking is 1. If there is only one product with a higher price, then the ranking is 2. In fact, what we are doing is computing the ranking of a product by counting the number of products with a higher price and adding 1 to the result.

Therefore, one can author a calculated column using this code, where we used **PriceOfCurrentProduct** as a placeholder to indicate the price of the current product.

```
1.  'Product'[UnitPriceRank] =
2.  COUNTROWS (
3.      FILTER (
4.          'Product',
5.          'Product'[Unit Price] > PriceOfCurrentProduct
6.      )
7.  ) + 1
```

FILTER returns the products with a price higher than the current products' price, and *COUNTROWS* counts the rows of the result of *FILTER*. The only remaining issue is finding a way to express the price of the current product, replacing **PriceOfCurrentProduct** with a valid DAX syntax. By "current," we mean the value of the column in the current row when DAX computes the column. It is harder than you might expect.

Focus your attention on line 5 of the previous code. There, the reference to *Product[Unit Price]* refers to the value of *Unit Price* in the current row context. What is the active row context when DAX executes row number 5? There are two row contexts. Because the code is written in a calculated column, there is a default row context automatically created by the engine that scans the *Product* table. Moreover, *FILTER* being an iterator, there is the row context generated by *FILTER* that scans the product table again. This is shown graphically in Figure 4-9.

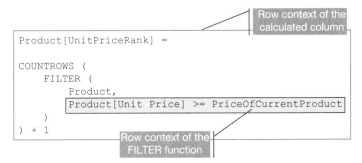

FIGURE 4-9 During the evaluation of the innermost expression, there are two row contexts on the same table.

The outer box includes the row context of the calculated column, which is iterating over *Product*. However, the inner box shows the row context of the *FILTER* function, which is iterating over *Product* too. The expression *Product[Unit Price]* depends on the context. Therefore, a reference to *Product[Unit Price]* in the inner box can only refer to the currently iterated row by *FILTER*. The problem is that, in that box, we need to evaluate the value of *Unit Price* that is referenced by the row context of the calculated column, which is now hidden.

Indeed, when one does not create a new row context using an iterator, the value of *Product[Unit Price]* is the desired value, which is the value in the current row context of the calculated column, as in this simple piece of code:

```
Product[Test] = Product[Unit Price]
```

To further demonstrate this, let us evaluate *Product[Unit Price]* in the two boxes, with some dummy code. What comes out are different results as shown in Figure 4-10, where we added the evaluation of *Product[Unit Price]* right before *COUNTROWS*, only for educational purposes.

```
Products[UnitPriceRank] =   This is the value of the current
                            product in the calculated column

Product[UnitPrice] +

COUNTROWS (
    FILTER (
        Product,
        Product[Unit Price] >= PriceOfCurrentProduct
    )
) + 1                              This is the value of the
                                   product iterated by FILTER
```

FIGURE 4-10 Outside of the iteration, *Product[Unit Price]* refers to the row context of the calculated column.

Here is a recap of the scenario so far:

- The inner row context, generated by *FILTER*, hides the outer row context.

- We need to compare the inner *Product[Unit Price]* with the value of the outer *Product[Unit Price]*.

- If we write the comparison in the inner expression, we are unable to access the outer *Product[Unit Price]*.

Because we can retrieve the current unit price, if we evaluate it outside of the row context of *FILTER*, the best approach to this problem is saving the value of the *Product[Unit Price]* inside a variable. Indeed, one can evaluate the variable in the row context of the calculated column using this code:

```
'Product'[UnitPriceRank] =
VAR
    PriceOfCurrentProduct = 'Product'[Unit Price]
RETURN
    COUNTROWS (
        FILTER (
            'Product',
            'Product'[Unit Price] > PriceOfCurrentProduct
        )
    ) + 1
```

Moreover, it is even better to write the code in a more descriptive way by using more variables to separate the different steps of the calculation. This way, the code is also easier to follow:

```
'Product'[UnitPriceRank] =
VAR PriceOfCurrentProduct = 'Product'[Unit Price]
VAR MoreExpensiveProducts =
    FILTER (
        'Product',
        'Product'[Unit Price] > PriceOfCurrentProduct
    )
RETURN
    COUNTROWS ( MoreExpensiveProducts ) + 1
```

Figure 4-11 shows a graphical representation of the row contexts of this latter formulation of the code, which makes it easier to understand which row context DAX computes each part of the formula in.

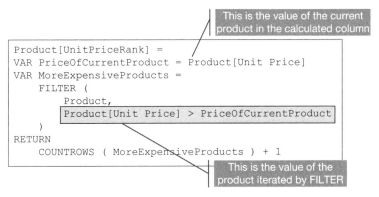

```
Product[UnitPriceRank] =
VAR PriceOfCurrentProduct = Product[Unit Price]
VAR MoreExpensiveProducts =
    FILTER (
        Product,
        Product[Unit Price] > PriceOfCurrentProduct
    )
RETURN
    COUNTROWS ( MoreExpensiveProducts ) + 1
```

This is the value of the current product in the calculated column

This is the value of the product iterated by FILTER

FIGURE 4-11 The value of *PriceOfCurrentProduct* is evaluated in the outer row context.

Figure 4-12 shows the result of this calculated column.

Product Name	Unit Price	UnitPriceRank
Fabrikam Refrigerator 24.7CuFt X9800 Blue	3,199.99	1
Fabrikam Refrigerator 24.7CuFt X9800 Brown	3,199.99	1
Fabrikam Refrigerator 24.7CuFt X9800 Green	3,199.99	1
Fabrikam Refrigerator 24.7CuFt X9800 Grey	3,199.99	1
Fabrikam Refrigerator 24.7CuFt X9800 Orange	3,199.99	1
Fabrikam Refrigerator 24.7CuFt X9800 Silver	3,199.99	1
Fabrikam Refrigerator 24.7CuFt X9800 White	3,199.99	1
Litware Refrigerator 24.7CuFt X980 Blue	3,199.99	1
Litware Refrigerator 24.7CuFt X980 Brown	3,199.99	1
Litware Refrigerator 24.7CuFt X980 Green	3,199.99	1
Litware Refrigerator 24.7CuFt X980 Grey	3,199.99	1
Litware Refrigerator 24.7CuFt X980 Silver	3,199.99	1
Litware Refrigerator 24.7CuFt X980 White	3,199.99	1
Litware Refrigerator L1200 Orange	3,199.99	1
Adventure Works 52" LCD HDTV X590 Black	2,899.99	15
Adventure Works 52" LCD HDTV X590 Brown	2,899.99	15
Adventure Works 52" LCD HDTV X590 Silver	2,899.99	15
Adventure Works 52" LCD HDTV X590 White	2,899.99	15
NT Washer & Dryer 27in L2700 Blue	2,652.90	19
NT Washer & Dryer 27in L2700 Green	2,652.90	19
NT Washer & Dryer 27in L2700 Silver	2,652.90	19

FIGURE 4-12 *UnitPriceRank* is a useful example of how to use variables to navigate within nested row contexts.

Because there are 14 products with the same unit price, their rank is always 1; the fifteenth product has a rank of 15, shared with other products with the same price. It would be great if we could rank 1, 2, 3 instead of 1, 15, 19 as is the case in the figure. We will fix this soon but, before that, it is important to make a small digression.

To solve a scenario like the one proposed, it is necessary to have a solid understanding of what a row context is, to be able to detect which row context is active in different parts of the formula and, most importantly, to conceive how the row context affects the value returned by a DAX expression. It is worth stressing that the same expression *Product[Unit Price]*, evaluated in two different parts of the formula, returns different values because of the different contexts under which it is evaluated. When one does not have a solid understanding of evaluation contexts, it is extremely hard to work on such complex code.

As you have seen, a simple ranking expression with two row contexts proves to be a challenge. Later in Chapter 5 you learn how to create multiple filter contexts. At that point, the complexity of the code increases a lot. However, if you understand evaluation contexts, these scenarios are simple. Before moving to the next level in DAX, you need to understand evaluation contexts well. This is the reason why we urge you to read this whole section again—and maybe the whole chapter so far—until these concepts are crystal clear. It will make reading the next chapters much easier and your learning experience much smoother.

Before leaving this example, we need to solve the last detail—that is, ranking using a sequence of 1, 2, 3 instead of the sequence obtained so far. The solution is easier than expected. In fact, in the previous code we focused on counting the products with a higher price. By doing that, the formula counted 14 products ranked 1 and assigned 15 to the second ranking level. However, counting products is not very useful. If the formula counted the prices higher than the current price, rather than the products, then all 14 products would be collapsed into a single price.

```
'Product'[UnitPriceRankDense] =
VAR PriceOfCurrentProduct = 'Product'[Unit Price]
VAR HigherPrices =
    FILTER (
        VALUES ( 'Product'[Unit Price] ),
        'Product'[Unit Price] > PriceOfCurrentProduct
    )
RETURN
    COUNTROWS ( HigherPrices ) + 1
```

Figure 4-13 shows the new calculated column, along with *UnitPriceRank*.

Product Name	Unit Price	UnitPriceRank	UnitPriceRankDense	^
Fabrikam Refrigerator 24.7CuFt X9800 Blue	3,199.99	1	1	
Fabrikam Refrigerator 24.7CuFt X9800 Brown	3,199.99	1	1	
Fabrikam Refrigerator 24.7CuFt X9800 Green	3,199.99	1	1	
Fabrikam Refrigerator 24.7CuFt X9800 Grey	3,199.99	1	1	
Fabrikam Refrigerator 24.7CuFt X9800 Orange	3,199.99	1	1	
Fabrikam Refrigerator 24.7CuFt X9800 Silver	3,199.99	1	1	
Fabrikam Refrigerator 24.7CuFt X9800 White	3,199.99	1	1	
Litware Refrigerator 24.7CuFt X980 Blue	3,199.99	1	1	
Litware Refrigerator 24.7CuFt X980 Brown	3,199.99	1	1	
Litware Refrigerator 24.7CuFt X980 Green	3,199.99	1	1	
Litware Refrigerator 24.7CuFt X980 Grey	3,199.99	1	1	
Litware Refrigerator 24.7CuFt X980 Silver	3,199.99	1	1	
Litware Refrigerator 24.7CuFt X980 White	3,199.99	1	1	
Litware Refrigerator L1200 Orange	3,199.99	1	1	
Adventure Works 52" LCD HDTV X590 Black	2,899.99	15	2	
Adventure Works 52" LCD HDTV X590 Brown	2,899.99	15	2	
Adventure Works 52" LCD HDTV X590 Silver	2,899.99	15	2	
Adventure Works 52" LCD HDTV X590 White	2,899.99	15	2	
NT Washer & Dryer 27in L2700 Blue	2,652.90	19	3	
NT Washer & Dryer 27in L2700 Green	2,652.90	19	3	
NT Washer & Dryer 27in L2700 Silver	2,652.90	19	3	
NT Washer & Dryer 27in L2700 White	2,652.90	19	3	v

FIGURE 4-13 *UnitPriceRankDense* returns a more useful ranking because it counts prices, not products.

This final small step is counting prices instead of counting products, and it might seem harder than expected. The more you work with DAX, the easier it will become to start thinking in terms of ad hoc temporary tables created for the purpose of a calculation.

In this example you learned that the best technique to handle multiple row contexts on the same table is by using variables. Keep in mind that variables were introduced in the DAX language as late as 2015. You might find existing DAX code—written before the age of variables—that uses another technique to access outer row contexts: the *EARLIER* function, which we describe in the next section.

Using the *EARLIER* function

DAX provides a function that accesses the outer row contexts: *EARLIER*. *EARLIER* retrieves the value of a column by using the previous row context instead of the last one. Therefore, we can express the value of **PriceOfCurrentProduct** using *EARLIER (Product[UnitPrice])*.

Many DAX newbies feel intimidated by *EARLIER* because they do not understand row contexts well enough and they do not realize that they can nest row contexts by creating multiple iterations over the same table. *EARLIER* is a simple function, once you understand the concept of row context and nesting. For example, the following code solves the previous scenario without using variables:

```
'Product'[UnitPriceRankDense] =
COUNTROWS (
    FILTER (
        VALUES ( 'Product'[Unit Price] ),
        'Product'[UnitPrice] > EARLIER ( 'Product'[UnitPrice] )
    )
) + 1
```

> **Note** *EARLIER* accepts a second parameter, which is the number of steps to skip, so that one can skip two or more row contexts. Moreover, there is also a function named *EARLIEST* that lets a developer access the outermost row context defined for a table. In the real world, neither *EARLIEST* nor the second parameter of *EARLIER* is used often. Though having two nested row contexts is a common scenario in calculated columns, having three or more of them is something that rarely happens. Besides, since the advent of variables, *EARLIER* has virtually become useless because variable usage superseded *EARLIER*.

The only reason to learn *EARLIER* is to be able to read existing DAX code. There are no further reasons to use *EARLIER* in newer DAX code because variables are a better way to save the required value when the right row context is accessible. Using variables for this purpose is a best practice and results in more readable code.

Understanding *FILTER*, *ALL*, and context interactions

In the preceding examples, we used *FILTER* as a convenient way of filtering a table. *FILTER* is a common function to use whenever one wants to apply a filter that further restricts the existing filter context.

Imagine that we want to create a measure that counts the number of red products. With the knowledge gained so far, the formula is easy:

```
NumOfRedProducts :=
VAR RedProducts =
    FILTER (
        'Product',
        'Product'[Color] = "Red"
    )
RETURN
    COUNTROWS ( RedProducts )
```

We can use this formula inside a report. For example, put the product brand on the rows to produce the report shown in Figure 4-14.

Brand	NumOfRedProducts
Adventure Works	6
Contoso	36
Fabrikam	12
Litware	12
Northwind Traders	3
Proseware	7
Southridge Video	13
Tailspin Toys	6
Wide World Importers	4
Total	**99**

FIGURE 4-14 We can count the number of red products using the *FILTER* function.

Before moving on with this example, stop for a moment and think carefully about how DAX computed these values. *Brand* is a column of the *Product* table. Inside each cell of the report, the filter context filters one given brand. Therefore, each cell shows the number of products of the given brand that are also red. The reason for this is that *FILTER* iterates the *Product* table as it is visible in the current filter context, which only contains products with that specific brand. It might seem trivial, but it is better to repeat this a few times than there being a chance of forgetting it.

This is more evident if we add a slicer to the report filtering the color. In Figure 4-15 there are two identical reports with two slicers filtering color, where each slicer only filters the report on its immediate right. The report on the left filters Red and the numbers are the same as in Figure 4-14, whereas the report on the right is empty because the slicer is filtering Azure.

Color	Brand	NumOfRedProducts	Color	Brand	NumOfRedProducts
☐ Azure			■ Azure		
☐ Black	Adventure Works	6	☐ Black	**Total**	
☐ Blue	Contoso	36	☐ Blue		
☐ Brown	Fabrikam	12	☐ Brown		
☐ Gold	Litware	12	☐ Gold		
☐ Green	Northwind Traders	3	☐ Green		
☐ Grey	Proseware	7	☐ Grey		
☐ Orange	Southridge Video	13	☐ Orange		
☐ Pink	Tailspin Toys	6	☐ Pink		
☐ Purple	Wide World Importers	4	☐ Purple		
■ Red	**Total**	**99**	☐ Red		
☐ Silver			☐ Silver		
☐ Silver Grey			☐ Silver Grey		
☐ Transparent			☐ Transparent		
☐ White			☐ White		

FIGURE 4-15 DAX evaluates *NumOfRedProducts* taking into account the outer context defined by the slicer.

In the report on the right, the *Product* table iterated by *FILTER* only contains Azure products, and, because *FILTER* can only return Red products, there are no products to return. As a result, the *NumOfRedProducts* measure always evaluates to blank.

The important part of this example is the fact that in the same formula, there are both a filter context coming from the outside—the cell in the report, which is affected by the slicer selection—and a row context introduced in the formula by the *FILTER* function. Both contexts work at the same time and modify the result. DAX uses the filter context to evaluate the *Product* table, and the row context to evaluate the filter condition row by row during the iteration made by *FILTER*.

We want to repeat this concept again: *FILTER* does not change the filter context. *FILTER* is an iterator that scans a table (already filtered by the filter context) and it returns a subset of that table, according to the filtering condition. In Figure 4-14, the filter context is filtering the brand and, after *FILTER* returned the result, it still only filtered the brand. Once we added the slicer on the color in Figure 4-15, the filter context contained both the brand and the color. For this reason, in the left-hand side report *FILTER* returned all the products iterated, and in the right-hand side report it did not return any product. In both reports, *FILTER* did not change the filter context. *FILTER* only scanned a table and returned a filtered result.

At this point, one might want to define another formula that returns the number of red products regardless of the selection done on the slicer. In other words, the code needs to ignore the selection made on the slicer and must always return the number of all the red products.

To accomplish this, the *ALL* function comes in handy. *ALL* returns the content of a table *ignoring the filter context*. We can define a new measure, named *NumOfAllRedProducts*, by using this expression:

```
NumOfAllRedProducts :=
VAR AllRedProducts =
    FILTER (
        ALL ( 'Product' ),
        'Product'[Color] = "Red"
    )
RETURN
    COUNTROWS ( AllRedProducts )
```

This time, *FILTER* does not iterate *Product*. Instead, it iterates *ALL (Product)*.

ALL ignores the filter context and always returns all the rows of the table, so that *FILTER* returns the red products even if products were previously filtered by another brand or color.

The result shown in Figure 4-16—although correct—might be surprising.

Color	Brand	NumOfAllRedProducts		Color	Brand	NumOfAllRedProducts
☐ Azure				■ Azure		
☐ Black	Adventure Works	99		☐ Black	A. Datum	99
☐ Blue	Contoso	99		☐ Blue	**Total**	**99**
☐ Brown				☐ Brown		
☐ Gold	Fabrikam	99		☐ Gold		
☐ Green	Litware	99		☐ Green		
☐ Grey	Northwind Traders	99		☐ Grey		
☐ Orange				☐ Orange		
☐ Pink	Proseware	99		☐ Pink		
☐ Purple	Southridge Video	99		☐ Purple		
■ Red	Tailspin Toys	99		☐ Red		
☐ Silver				☐ Silver		
☐ Silver Grey	Wide World Importers	99		☐ Silver Grey		
☐ Transparent	**Total**	**99**		☐ Transparent		
☐ White				☐ White		

FIGURE 4-16 *NumOfAllRedProducts* returns strange results.

There are a couple of interesting things to note here, and we want to describe both in more detail:

- The result is always 99, regardless of the brand selected on the rows.

- The brands in the left matrix are different from the brands in the right matrix.

First, 99 is the total number of red products, not the number of red products of any given brand. *ALL*—as expected—ignores the filters on the *Product* table. It not only ignores the filter on the color, but it also ignores the filter on the brand. This might be an undesired effect. Nonetheless, *ALL* is easy and powerful, but it is an all-or-nothing function. If used, *ALL* ignores all the filters applied to the table specified as its argument. With the knowledge you have gained so far, you cannot yet choose to only ignore part of the filter. In the example, it would have been better to only ignore the filter on the color. Only after the next chapter, with the introduction of *CALCULATE*, will you have better options to achieve the selective ignoring of filters.

Let us now describe the second point: The brands on the two reports are different. Because the slicer is filtering one color, the full matrix is computed with the filter on the color. On the left the color is Red, whereas on the right the color is Azure. This determines two different sets of products, and consequently, of brands. The list of brands used to populate the axis of the report is computed in the original filter context, which contains a filter on color. Once the axes have been computed, then DAX computes values for the measure, always returning 99 as a result regardless of the brand and color. Thus, the report on the left shows the brands of red products, whereas the report on the right shows the brands of azure products, although in both reports the measure shows the total of all the red products, regardless of their brand.

> **Note**   The behavior of the report is not specific to DAX, but rather to the *SUMMARIZE-COLUMNS* function used by Power BI. We cover *SUMMARIZECOLUMNS* in Chapter 13, "Authoring queries."

We do not want to further explore this scenario right now. The solution comes later when you learn *CALCULATE*, which offers a lot more power (and complexity) for the handling of filter contexts. As of now, we used this example to show that you might find unexpected results from relatively simple formulas because of context interactions and the coexistence, in the same expression, of filter and row contexts.

Working with several tables

Now that you have learned the basics of evaluation contexts, we can describe how the context behaves when it comes to relationships. In fact, few data models contain just one single table. There would most likely be several tables, linked by relationships. If there is a relationship between *Sales* and *Product*, does a filter context on *Product* filter *Sales*, too? And what about a filter on *Sales*, is it filtering *Product*? Because there are two types of evaluation contexts (the row context and the filter context) and relationships have two sides (a one-side and a many-side), there are four different scenarios to analyze.

The answer to these questions is already found in the mantra you are learning in this chapter, "*The filter context filters; the row context iterates*" and in its consequence, "*The filter context does not iterate; the row context does not filter.*"

To examine the scenario, we use a data model containing six tables, as shown in Figure 4-17.

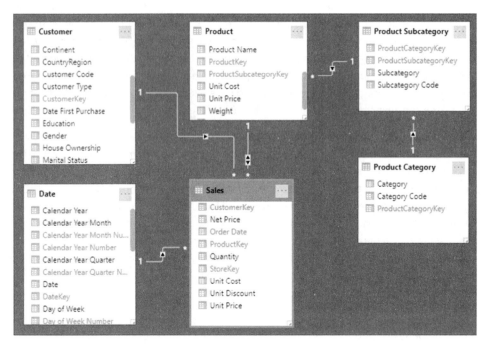

FIGURE 4-17 Data model used to learn the interaction between contexts and relationships.

The model presents a couple of noteworthy details:

- There is a chain of relationships starting from *Sales* and reaching *Product Category*, through *Product* and *Product Subcategory*.

- The only bidirectional relationship is between *Sales* and *Product*. All remaining relationships are set to be single cross-filter direction.

This model is going to be useful when looking at the details of evaluation contexts and relationships in the next sections.

Row contexts and relationships

The row context iterates; it does not filter. Iteration is the process of scanning a table row by row and of performing an operation in the meantime. Usually, one wants some kind of aggregation like sum or average. During an iteration, the row context is iterating an individual table, and it provides a value to all the columns of the table, and only that table. Other tables, although related to the iterated table, do not have a row context on them. In other words, the row context does not interact automatically with relationships.

Consider as an example a calculated column in the *Sales* table containing the difference between the unit price stored in the fact table and the unit price stored in the *Product* table. The following DAX code does not work because it uses the *Product[UnitPrice]* column and there is no row context on *Product*:

```
Sales[UnitPriceVariance] = Sales[Unit Price] - 'Product'[Unit Price]
```

This being a calculated column, DAX automatically generates a row context on the table containing the column, which is the *Sales* table. The row context on *Sales* provides a row-by-row evaluation of expressions using the columns in *Sales*. Even though *Product* is on the one-side of a one-to-many relationship with *Sales*, the iteration is happening on the *Sales* table only.

When we are iterating on the many-side of a relationship, we can access columns on the one-side of the relationship, but we must use the *RELATED* function. *RELATED* accepts a column reference as the parameter and retrieves the value of the column in the corresponding row in the target table. *RELATED* can only reference one column and multiple *RELATED* functions are required to access more than one column on the one-side of the relationship. The correct version of the previous code is the following:

```
Sales[UnitPriceVariance] = Sales[Unit Price] - RELATED ( 'Product'[Unit Price] )
```

RELATED requires a row context (that is, an iteration) on the table on the many-side of a relationship. If the row context were active on the one-side of a relationship, then *RELATED* would no longer be useful because *RELATED* would find multiple rows by following the relationship. In this case, that is, when iterating the one-side of a relationship, the function to use is *RELATEDTABLE*. *RELATEDTABLE* returns all the rows of the table on the many-side that are related with the currently iterated table. For example, if one wants to compute the number of sales of each product, the following formula defined as a calculated column on Product solves the problem:

```
Product[NumberOfSales] =
VAR SalesOfCurrentProduct = RELATEDTABLE ( Sales )
RETURN
    COUNTROWS ( SalesOfCurrentProduct )
```

This expression counts the number of rows in the *Sales* table that corresponds to the current product. The result is visible in Figure 4-18.

Product Name	NumberOfSales
A. Datum Advanced Digital Camera M300 Azure	13
A. Datum Advanced Digital Camera M300 Black	23
A. Datum Advanced Digital Camera M300 Green	32
A. Datum Advanced Digital Camera M300 Grey	32
A. Datum Advanced Digital Camera M300 Orange	3
A. Datum Advanced Digital Camera M300 Pink	41
A. Datum Advanced Digital Camera M300 Silver	18
A. Datum All in One Digital Camera M200 Azure	29
A. Datum All in One Digital Camera M200 Black	16
A. Datum All in One Digital Camera M200 Green	19
A. Datum All in One Digital Camera M200 Grey	51

FIGURE 4-18 *RELATEDTABLE* is useful in a row context on the one-side of the relationship.

Both *RELATED* and *RELATEDTABLE* can traverse a chain of relationships; they are not limited to a single hop. For example, one can create a column with the same code as before but, this time, in the *Product Category* table:

```
'Product Category'[NumberOfSales] =
VAR SalesOfCurrentProductCategory = RELATEDTABLE ( Sales )
RETURN
    COUNTROWS ( SalesOfCurrentProductCategory )
```

The result is the number of sales for the category, which traverses the chain of relationships from *Product Category* to *Product Subcategory*, then to *Product* to finally reach the *Sales* table.

In a similar way, one can create a calculated column in the *Product* table that copies the category name from the *Product Category* table.

```
'Product'[Category] = RELATED ( 'Product Category'[Category] )
```

In this case, a single *RELATED* function traverses the chain of relationships from *Product* to *Product Subcategory* to *Product Category*.

> **Note** The only exception to the general rule of *RELATED* and *RELATEDTABLE* is for one-to-one relationships. If two tables share a one-to-one relationship, then both *RELATED* and *RELATEDTABLE* work in both tables and they result either in a column value or in a table with a single row, depending on the function used.

Regarding chains of relationships, all the relationships need to be of the same type—that is, one-to-many or many-to-one. If the chain links two tables through a one-to-many relationship to a bridge table, followed by a many-to-one relationship to the second table, then neither *RELATED* nor *RELATED-TABLE* works with single-direction filter propagation. Only *RELATEDTABLE* can work using bidirectional filter propagation, as explained later. On the other hand, a one-to-one relationship behaves as a one-to-many and as a many-to-one relationship at the same time. Thus, there can be a one-to-one relationship in a chain of one-to-many (or many-to-one) without interrupting the chain.

For example, in the model we chose as a reference, *Customer* is related to *Sales* and *Sales* is related to *Product*. There is a one-to-many relationship between *Customer* and *Sales,* and then a many-to-one relationship between *Sales* and *Product*. Thus, a chain of relationships links *Customer* to *Product*. However, the two relationships are not in the same direction. This scenario is known as a many-to-many relationship. A customer is related to many products bought and a product is in turn related to many customers who bought that product. We cover many-to-many relationships later in Chapter 15, "Advanced relationships"; let us focus on row context, for the moment. If one uses *RELATEDTABLE* through a many-to-many relationship, the result would be wrong. Consider a calculated column in *Product* with this formula:

```
Product[NumOfBuyingCustomers] =
VAR CustomersOfCurrentProduct = RELATEDTABLE ( Customer )
RETURN
    COUNTROWS ( CustomersOfCurrentProduct )
```

The result of the previous code is not the number of customers who bought that product. Instead, the result is the total number of customers, as shown in Figure 4-19.

Product Name	NumOfBuyingCustomers
A. Datum Advanced Digital Camera M300 Azure	18869
A. Datum Advanced Digital Camera M300 Black	18869
A. Datum Advanced Digital Camera M300 Green	18869
A. Datum Advanced Digital Camera M300 Grey	18869
A. Datum Advanced Digital Camera M300 Orange	18869
A. Datum Advanced Digital Camera M300 Pink	18869
A. Datum Advanced Digital Camera M300 Silver	18869
A. Datum All in One Digital Camera M200 Azure	18869
A. Datum All in One Digital Camera M200 Black	18869
A. Datum All in One Digital Camera M200 Green	18869

FIGURE 4-19 *RELATEDTABLE* does not work over a many-to-many relationship.

RELATEDTABLE cannot follow the chain of relationships because they are not going in the same direction. The row context from *Product* does not reach *Customers*. It is worth noting that if we try the formula in the opposite direction, that is, if we count the number of products bought for each customer, the result is correct: a different number for each row representing the number of products bought by the customer. The reason for this behavior is not the propagation of a row context but, rather, the context transition generated by *RELATEDTABLE*. We added this final note for full disclosure. It is not time to elaborate on this just yet. You will have a better understanding of this after reading Chapter 5.

Filter context and relationships

In the previous section, you learned that the row context iterates and, as such, that it does not use relationships. The filter context, on the other hand, filters. A filter context is not applied to an individual table. Instead, it always works on the whole model. At this point, you can update the evaluation context mantra to its complete formulation:

The filter context filters the model; the row context iterates one table.

Because a filter context filters the model, it uses relationships. The filter context interacts with relationships automatically, and it behaves differently depending on how the cross-filter direction of the relationship is set. The cross-filter direction is represented with a small arrow in the middle of a relationship, as shown in Figure 4-20.

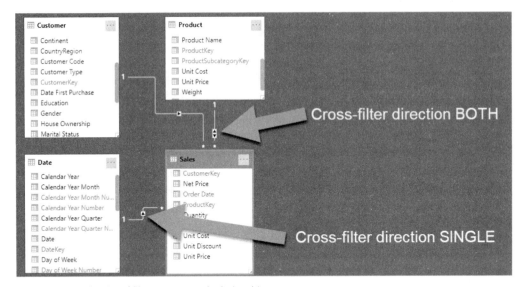

FIGURE 4-20 Behavior of filter context and relationships.

The filter context uses a relationship by going in the direction allowed by the arrow. In all relationships the arrow allows propagation from the one-side to the many-side, whereas when the cross-filter direction is *BOTH*, propagation is allowed from the many-side to the one-side too.

A relationship with a single cross-filter is a *unidirectional relationship*, whereas a relationship with *BOTH* cross-filter directions is a *bidirectional relationship*.

This behavior is intuitive. Although we have not explained this sooner, all the reports we have used so far relied on this behavior. Indeed, in a typical report filtering by *Product[Color]* and aggregating the *Sales[Quantity]*, one would expect the filter from *Product* to propagate to *Sales*. This is exactly what happens: *Product* is on the one-side of a relationship; thus a filter on *Product* propagates to *Sales*, regardless of the cross-filter direction.

Because our sample data model contains both a bidirectional relationship and many unidirectional relationships, we can demonstrate the filtering behavior by using three different measures that count the number of rows in the three tables: *Sales*, *Product*, and *Customer*.

```
[NumOfSales]     := COUNTROWS ( Sales )
[NumOfProducts]  := COUNTROWS ( Product )
[NumOfCustomers] := COUNTROWS ( Customer )
```

The report contains the *Product[Color]* on the rows. Therefore, each cell is evaluated in a filter context that filters the product color. Figure 4-21 shows the result.

Color	NumOfSales	NumOfProducts	NumOfCustomers
Azure	398	14	18,869
Black	24,048	602	18,869
Blue	6,277	200	18,869
Brown	1,840	77	18,869
Gold	988	50	18,869
Green	2,150	74	18,869
Grey	8,525	283	18,869
Orange	1,577	55	18,869
Pink	3,518	84	18,869
Purple	75	6	18,869
Red	5,802	99	18,869
Silver	19,735	417	18,869
Silver Grey	675	14	18,869
Transparent	896	1	18,869
White	21,854	505	18,869
Yellow	1,873	36	18,869
Total	**100,231**	**2,517**	**18,869**

FIGURE 4-21 This shows the behavior of filter context and relationships.

In this first example, the filter is always propagating from the one-side to the many-side of relationships. The filter starts from *Product[Color]*. From there, it reaches *Sales*, which is on the many-side of the relationship with *Product*, and *Product*, because it is the very same table. On the other hand, *NumOfCustomers* always shows the same value—the total number of customers. This is because the relationship between *Customer* and *Sales* does not allow propagation from *Sales* to *Customer*. The filter is moved from *Product* to *Sales*, but from there it does not reach *Customer*.

You might have noticed that the relationship between *Sales* and *Product* is a bidirectional relationship. Thus, a filter context on *Customer* also filters *Sales* and *Product*. We can prove it by changing the report, slicing by *Customer[Education]* instead of *Product[Color]*. The result is visible in Figure 4-22.

Education	NumOfSales	NumOfProducts	NumOfCustomers
	78,059	2,097	385
Bachelors	5,963	415	5,356
Graduate Degree	3,351	290	3,189
High School	4,721	392	3,294
Partial College	5,747	423	5,064
Partial High School	2,390	263	1,581
Total	**100,231**	**2,517**	**18,869**

FIGURE 4-22 Filtering by customer education, the *Product* table is filtered too.

This time the filter starts from *Customer*. It can reach the *Sales* table because *Sales* is on the many-side of the relationship. Furthermore, it propagates from *Sales* to *Product* because the relationship between *Sales* and *Product* is bidirectional—its cross-filter direction is *BOTH*.

Beware that a single bidirectional relationship in a chain does not make the whole chain bidirectional. In fact, a similar measure that counts the number of subcategories, such as the following one, demonstrates that the filter context starting from *Customer* does not reach *Product Subcategory*:

```
NumOfSubcategories := COUNTROWS ( 'Product Subcategory' )
```

Adding the measure to the previous report produces the results shown in Figure 4-23, where the number of subcategories is the same for all the rows.

Education	NumOfSales	NumOfProducts	NumOfCustomers	NumOfSubcategories
	78,059	2,097	385	44
Bachelors	5,963	415	5,356	44
Graduate Degree	3,351	290	3,189	44
High School	4,721	392	3,294	44
Partial College	5,747	423	5,064	44
Partial High School	2,390	263	1,581	44
Total	**100,231**	**2,517**	**18,869**	**44**

FIGURE 4-23 If the relationship is unidirectional, customers cannot filter subcategories.

Because the relationship between *Product* and *Product Subcategory* is unidirectional, the filter does not propagate to *Product Subcategory*. If we update the relationship, setting the cross-filter direction to *BOTH*, the result is different as shown in Figure 4-24.

Education	NumOfSales	NumOfProducts	NumOfCustomers	NumOfSubcategories
	78,059	2,097	385	32
Bachelors	5,963	415	5,356	32
Graduate Degree	3,351	290	3,189	32
High School	4,721	392	3,294	32
Partial College	5,747	423	5,064	32
Partial High School	2,390	263	1,581	31
Total	**100,231**	**2,517**	**18,869**	**44**

FIGURE 4-24 If the relationship is bidirectional, customers can filter subcategories too.

With the row context, we use *RELATED* and *RELATEDTABLE* to propagate the row context through relationships. On the other hand, with the filter context, no functions are needed to propagate the filter. The filter context filters the model, not a table. As such, once one applies a filter context, the entire model is subject to the filter according to the relationships.

Important   From the examples, it may look like enabling bidirectional filtering on all the relationships is a good option to let the filter context propagate to the whole model. **This is definitely not the case.** We will cover advanced relationships in depth later, in Chapter 15. Bidirectional filters come with a lot more complexity than what we can share with this introductory chapter, and you should not use them unless you have a clear idea of the consequences. As a rule, you should enable bidirectional filters in specific measures by using the *CROSSFILTER* function, and only when strictly required.

Using *DISTINCT* and *SUMMARIZE* in filter contexts

Now that you have a solid understanding of evaluation contexts, we can use this knowledge to solve a scenario step-by-step. In the meantime, we provide the analysis of a few details that—hopefully—will shed more light on the fundamental concepts of row context and filter context. Besides, in this example we also further describe the *SUMMARIZE* function, briefly introduced in Chapter 3, "Using basic table functions."

Before going into more details, please note that this example shows several inaccurate calculations before reaching the correct solution. The purpose is educational because we want to teach the process of writing DAX code rather than give a solution. In the process of authoring a measure, it is likely you will make several initial errors. In this guided example, we describe the correct way of reasoning, which helps you solve similar errors by yourself.

The requirement is to compute the average age of customers of Contoso. Even though this looks like a legitimate requirement, it is not complete. Are we speaking about their current age or their age at the time of the sale? If a customer buys three times, should it count as one event or as three events in the average? What if they buy three times at different ages? We need to be more precise. Here is the more complete requirement: *"Compute the average age of customers at the time of sale, counting each customer only once if they made multiple purchases at the same age."*

The solution can be split into two steps:

- Computing the age of the customer when the sale happened

- Averaging it

The age of the customer changes for every sale. Thus, the age needs to be stored in the *Sales* table. For each row in *Sales*, one can compute the age of the customer at the time when the sale happened. A calculated column perfectly fits this need:

```
Sales[Customer Age] =
DATEDIFF (                             -- Compute the difference between
    RELATED ( Customer[Birth Date] ), -- the customer's birth date
    Sales[Order Date],                -- and the date of the sale
    YEAR                              -- in years
)
```

Because *Customer Age* is a calculated column, it is evaluated in a row context that iterates *Sales*. The formula needs to access *Customer[Birth Date]*, which is a column in *Customer*, on the one-side of a relationship with *Sales*. In this case, *RELATED* is needed to let DAX access the target table. In the sample database Contoso, there are many customers for whom the birth date is blank. *DATEDIFF* returns blank if the first parameter is blank.

Because the requirement is to provide the average, a first—and inaccurate—solution might be a measure that averages this column:

```
Avg Customer Age Wrong := AVERAGE ( Sales[Customer Age] )
```

The result is incorrect because *Sales[Customer Age]* contains multiple rows with the same age if a customer made multiple purchases at a certain age. The requirement is to compute each customer only once, and this formula is not following such a requirement. Figure 4-25 shows the result of this last measure side-by-side with the expected result.

Color	Avg Customer Age Wrong	Correct Average
Azure	46.44	46.44
Black	46.59	46.67
Blue	45.87	45.91
Brown	45.48	45.48
Gold	45.26	45.26
Green	47.26	47.26
Grey	46.44	46.44
Orange	37.27	37.27
Pink	46.18	46.17
Purple	50.09	50.09
Red	45.42	45.45
Silver	45.87	45.82
Silver Grey	49.93	49.93
White	46.00	46.25
Yellow	47.76	47.76
Total	**46.18**	**46.20**

FIGURE 4-25 A simple average computes the wrong result for the customer's age.

Here is the problem: The age of each customer must be counted only once. A possible solution—still inaccurate—would be to perform a *DISTINCT* of the customer ages and then average it, with the following measure:

```
Avg Customer Age Wrong Distinct :=
AVERAGEX (                              -- Iterate on the distinct values of
    DISTINCT ( Sales[Customer Age] ),   -- Sales[Customer Age] and compute the
    Sales[Customer Age]                 -- average of the customer's age
)
```

This solution is not the correct one yet. In fact, *DISTINCT* returns the distinct values of the customer age. Two customers with the same age would be counted only once by this formula. The requirement is to count each customer once, whereas this formula is counting each age once. In fact, Figure 4-26 shows the report with the new formulation of *Avg Customer Age*. You see that this solution is still inaccurate.

Color	Avg Customer Age Wrong Distinct	Correct Average
Azure	50.92	46.44
Black	58.38	46.67
Blue	55.33	45.91
Brown	50.15	45.48
Gold	45.14	45.26
Green	50.92	47.26
Grey	54.33	46.44
Orange	38.33	37.27
Pink	53.45	46.17
Purple	53.74	50.09
Red	56.10	45.45
Silver	61.67	45.82
Silver Grey	47.93	49.93
White	58.57	46.25
Yellow	55.83	47.76
Total	**62.00**	**46.20**

FIGURE 4-26 The average of the distinct customer ages still provides a wrong result.

In the last formula, one might try to replace *Customer Age* with *CustomerKey* as the parameter of *DISTINCT*, as in the following code:

```
Avg Customer Age Invalid Syntax :=
AVERAGEX (                              -- Iterate on the distinct values of
    DISTINCT ( Sales[CustomerKey] ),    -- Sales[CustomerKey] and compute the
    Sales[Customer Age]                 -- average of the customer's age
)
```

This code contains an error and DAX will not accept it. Can you spot the reason, without reading the solution we provide in the next paragraph?

AVERAGEX generates a row context that iterates a table. The table provided as the first parameter to *AVERAGEX* is *DISTINCT (Sales[CustomerKey])*. *DISTINCT* returns a table with one column only, and all the unique values of the customer key. Therefore, the row context generated by *AVERAGEX* only contains one column, namely *Sales[CustomerKey]*. DAX cannot evaluate *Sales[Customer Age]* in a row context that only contains *Sales[CustomerKey]*.

What is needed is a row context that has the granularity of *Sales[CustomerKey]* but that also contains *Sales[Customer Age]*. *SUMMARIZE*, introduced in Chapter 3, can generate the existing unique combinations of two columns. Now we can finally show a version of this code that implements all the requirements:

```
Correct Average :=
AVERAGEX (                        -- Iterate on
    SUMMARIZE (                   -- all the existing combinations
        Sales,                    -- that exist in Sales
        Sales[CustomerKey],       -- of the customer key and
        Sales[Customer Age]       -- the customer age
    ),                            --
    Sales[Customer Age]           -- and average the customer's age
)
```

As usual, it is possible to use a variable to split the calculation in multiple steps. Note that the access to the *Customer Age* column still requires a reference to the *Sales* table name in the second argument of the *AVERAGEX* function. A variable can contain a table, but it cannot be used as a table reference.

```
Correct Average :=
VAR CustomersAge =
    SUMMARIZE (                   -- Existing combinations
        Sales,                    -- that exist in Sales
        Sales[CustomerKey],       -- of the customer key and
        Sales[Customer Age]       -- the customer age
    )
RETURN
AVERAGEX (                        -- Iterate on list of
    CustomersAge,                 -- Customers/age in Sales
    Sales[Customer Age]           -- and average the customer's age
)
```

SUMMARIZE generates all the combinations of customer and age available in the current filter context. Thus, multiple customers with the same age will duplicate the age, once per customer. *AVERAGEX* ignores the presence of *CustomerKey* in the table; it only uses the customer age. *CustomerKey* is only needed to count the correct number of occurrences of each age.

It is worth stressing that the full measure is executed in the filter context generated by the report. Thus, only the customers who bought something are evaluated and returned by *SUMMARIZE*. Every cell of the report has a different filter context, only considering the customers who purchased at least one product of the color displayed in the report.

Conclusions

It is time to recap the most relevant topics you learned in this chapter about evaluation contexts.

- There are two evaluation contexts: the filter context and the row context. The two evaluation contexts are not variations of the same concept: *the filter context filters the model*; *the row context iterates one table*.

- To understand a formula's behavior, you always need to consider both evaluation contexts because they operate at the same time.

- DAX creates a row context automatically for a calculated column. One can also create a row context programmatically by using an iterator. Every iterator defines a row context.

- You can nest row contexts and, in case they are on the same table, the innermost row context hides the previous row contexts on the same table. Variables are useful to store values retrieved when the required row context is accessible. In earlier versions of DAX where variables were not available, the *EARLIER* function was used to get access to the previous row context. As of today, using *EARLIER* is discouraged.

- When iterating over a table that is the result of a table expression, the row context only contains the columns returned by the table expression.

- Client tools like Power BI create a filter context when you use fields on rows, columns, slicers, and filters. A filter context can also be created programmatically by using *CALCULATE*, which we introduce in the next chapter.

- The row context does not propagate through relationships automatically. One needs to force the propagation by using *RELATED* and *RELATEDTABLE*. You need to use these functions in a row context on the correct side of a one-to-many relationship: *RELATED* on the many-side, *RELATEDTABLE* on the one-side.

- The filter context filters the model, and it uses relationships according to their cross-filter direction. It always propagates from the one-side to the many-side. In addition, if you use the cross-filtering direction *BOTH*, then the propagation also happens from the many-side to the one-side.

At this point, you have learned the most complex conceptual topics of the DAX language. These points rule all the evaluation flows of your formulas, and they are the pillars of the DAX language. Whenever you encounter an expression that does not compute what you want, there is a huge chance that was because you have not fully understood these rules.

As we said in the introduction, at first glance all these topics look simple. In fact, they are. What makes them complex is the fact that in a DAX expression you might have several evaluation contexts active in different parts of the formula. Mastering evaluation contexts is a skill that you will gain with experience, and we will try to help you on this by showing many examples in the next chapters. After writing some DAX formulas of your own, you will intuitively know which contexts are used and which functions they require, and you will finally master the DAX language.

Understanding *CALCULATE* and *CALCULATETABLE*

In this chapter we continue our journey in discovering the power of the DAX language with a detailed explanation of a single function: *CALCULATE*. The same considerations apply for *CALCULATETABLE*, which evaluates and returns a table instead of a scalar value. For simplicity's sake, we will refer to *CALCULATE* in the examples, but remember that *CALCULATETABLE* displays the same behavior.

CALCULATE is the most important, useful, and complex function in DAX, so it deserves a full chapter. The function itself is simple to learn; it only performs a few tasks. Complexity comes from the fact that *CALCULATE* and *CALCULATETABLE* are the only functions in DAX that can create new filter contexts. Thus, although they are simple functions, using *CALCULATE* or *CALCULATETABLE* in a formula instantly increases its complexity.

This chapter is as tough as the previous chapter was. We suggest you carefully read it once, get a general feeling for *CALCULATE,* and move on to the remaining part of the book. Then, as soon as you feel lost in a specific formula, come back to this chapter and read it again from the beginning. You will probably discover new information each time you read it.

Introducing *CALCULATE* and *CALCULATETABLE*

The previous chapter described the two evaluation contexts: the row context and the filter context. The row context automatically exists for a calculated column, and one can create a row context programmatically by using an iterator. The filter context, on the other hand, is created by the report, and we have not described yet how to programmatically create a filter context. *CALCULATE* and *CALCU-LATETABLE* are the only functions required to operate on the filter context. Indeed, *CALCULATE* and *CALCULATETABLE* are the only functions that can create a new filter context by manipulating the existing one. From here onwards, we will show examples based on *CALCULATE* only, but remember that *CALCULATETABLE* performs the same operation for DAX expressions returning a table. Later in the book there are more examples using *CALCULATETABLE*, as in Chapter 12, "Working with tables," and in Chapter 13, "Authoring queries."

Creating filter contexts

Here we will introduce the reason why one would want to create new filter contexts with a practical example. As described in the next sections, writing code without being able to create new filter contexts results in verbose and unreadable code. What follows is an example of how creating a new filter context can drastically improve code that, at first, looked rather complex.

Contoso is a company that sells electronic products all around the world. Some products are branded Contoso, whereas others have different brands. One of the reports requires a comparison of the gross margins, both as an amount and as a percentage, of Contoso-branded products against their competitors. The first part of the report requires the following calculations:

```
Sales Amount := SUMX ( Sales, Sales[Quantity] * Sales[Net Price] )
Gross Margin := SUMX ( Sales, Sales[Quantity] * ( Sales[Net Price] - Sales[Unit Cost] ) )
GM % := DIVIDE ( [Gross Margin], [Sales Amount] )
```

One beautiful aspect of DAX is that you can build more complex calculations on top of existing measures. In fact, you can appreciate this in the definition of *GM %*, the measure that computes the percentage of the gross margin against the sales. *GM %* simply invokes the two original measures as it divides them. If you already have a measure that computes a value, you can call the measure instead of rewriting the full code.

Using the three measures defined above, one can build the first report, as shown in Figure 5-1.

Category	Sales Amount	Gross Margin	GM %
Audio	384,518.16	196,713.38	51.16%
Cameras and camcorders	7,192,581.95	4,162,105.17	57.87%
Cell phones	1,604,610.26	821,136.57	51.17%
Computers	6,741,548.73	3,594,082.52	53.31%
Games and Toys	360,652.81	174,283.26	48.32%
Home Appliances	9,600,457.04	4,939,739.79	51.45%
Music, Movies and Audio Books	314,206.74	180,968.34	57.60%
TV and Video	4,392,768.29	2,173,609.72	49.48%
Total	**30,591,343.98**	**16,242,638.75**	**53.10%**

FIGURE 5-1 The three measures provide quick insights in the margin of different categories.

The next step in building the report is more intricate. In fact, the final report we want is the one in Figure 5-2 that shows two additional columns: the gross margin for Contoso-branded products, both as amount and as percentage.

Category	Sales Amount	Gross Margin	GM %	Contoso GM	Contoso GM %
Audio	384,518.16	196,713.38	51.16%	87,279.45	51.28%
Cameras and camcorders	7,192,581.95	4,162,105.17	57.87%	807,222.16	60.79%
Cell phones	1,604,610.26	821,136.57	51.17%	228,309.82	47.49%
Computers	6,741,548.73	3,594,082.52	53.31%	579,245.67	54.95%
Games and Toys	360,652.81	174,283.26	48.32%		
Home Appliances	9,600,457.04	4,939,739.79	51.45%	1,660,590.09	50.40%
Music, Movies and Audio Books	314,206.74	180,968.34	57.60%	92,994.17	57.84%
TV and Video	4,392,768.29	2,173,609.72	49.48%	421,429.28	48.79%
Total	**30,591,343.98**	**16,242,638.75**	**53.10%**	**3,877,070.65**	**52.73%**

FIGURE 5-2 The last two columns of the report show gross margin amount and gross margin percentage for Contoso-branded products.

With the knowledge acquired so far, you are already capable of authoring the code for these two measures. Indeed, because the requirement is to restrict the calculation to only one brand, a solution is to use *FILTER* to restrict the calculation of the gross margin to Contoso products only:

```
Contoso GM :=
VAR ContosoSales =              -- Saves the rows of Sales which are related
    FILTER (                    -- to Contoso-branded products into a variable
        Sales,
        RELATED ( 'Product'[Brand] ) = "Contoso"
    )
VAR ContosoMargin =             -- Iterates over ContosoSales
    SUMX (                      -- to only compute the margin for Contoso
        ContosoSales,
        Sales[Quantity] * ( Sales[Net Price] - Sales[Unit Cost] )
    )
RETURN
    ContosoMargin
```

The *ContosoSales* variable contains the rows of *Sales* related to all the Contoso-branded products. Once the variable is computed, *SUMX* iterates on *ContosoSales* to compute the margin. Because the iteration is on the *Sales* table and the filter is on the *Product* table, one needs to use *RELATED* to retrieve the related product for each row in *Sales*. In a similar way, one can compute the gross margin of Contoso by iterating the *ContosoSales* variable twice:

```
Contoso GM % :=
VAR ContosoSales =              -- Saves the rows of Sales which are related
    FILTER (                    -- to Contoso-branded products into a variable
        Sales,
        RELATED ( 'Product'[Brand] ) = "Contoso"
    )
VAR ContosoMargin =             -- Iterates over ContosoSales
    SUMX (                      -- to only compute the margin for Contoso
        ContosoSales,
        Sales[Quantity] * ( Sales[Net Price] - Sales[Unit Cost] )
    )
VAR ContosoSalesAmount =        -- Iterates over ContosoSales
    SUMX (                      -- to only compute the sales amount for Contoso
        ContosoSales,
        Sales[Quantity] * Sales[Net Price]
    )
VAR Ratio =
    DIVIDE ( ContosoMargin, ContosoSalesAmount )
RETURN
    Ratio
```

The code for *Contoso GM %* is a bit longer but, from a logical point of view, it follows the same pattern as *Contoso GM*. Although these measures work, it is easy to note that the initial elegance of DAX is lost. Indeed, the model already contains one measure to compute the gross margin and another measure to compute the gross margin percentage. However, because the new measures needed to be filtered, we had to rewrite the expression to add the condition.

It is worth stressing that the basic measures *Gross Margin* and *GM %* can already compute the values for Contoso. In fact, from Figure 5-2 you can note that the gross margin for Contoso is equal to 3,877,070.65 and the percentage is equal to 52.73%. One can obtain the very same numbers by slicing the base measures *Gross Margin* and *GM %* by *Brand*, as shown in Figure 5-3.

Brand	Sales Amount	Gross Margin	GM %
A. Datum	2,096,184.64	1,231,215.46	58.74%
Adventure Works	4,011,112.28	2,041,254.77	50.89%
Contoso	7,352,399.03	3,877,070.65	52.73%
Fabrikam	5,554,015.73	3,063,160.86	55.15%
Litware	3,255,704.03	1,687,426.65	51.83%
Northwind Traders	1,040,552.13	537,637.20	51.67%
Proseware	2,546,144.16	1,392,412.47	54.69%
Southridge Video	1,384,413.85	685,143.25	49.49%
Tailspin Toys	325,042.42	155,099.09	47.72%
The Phone Company	1,123,819.07	592,826.75	52.75%
Wide World Importers	1,901,956.66	979,391.62	51.49%
Total	**30,591,343.98**	**16,242,638.75**	**53.10%**

FIGURE 5-3 When sliced by brand, the base measures compute the value of *Gross Margin* and *GM %* for Contoso.

In the highlighted cells, the filter context created by the report is filtering the Contoso brand. The filter context filters the model. Therefore, a filter context placed on the *Product[Brand]* column filters the *Sales* table because of the relationship linking *Sales* to *Product*. Using the filter context, one can filter a table indirectly because the filter context operates on the whole model.

Thus, if we could make DAX compute the *Gross Margin* measure by creating a filter context programmatically, which only filters the Contoso-branded products, then our implementation of the last two measures would be much easier. This is possible by using *CALCULATE*.

The complete description of *CALCULATE* comes later in this chapter. First, we examine the syntax of *CALCULATE*:

```
CALCULATE ( Expression, Condition1, … ConditionN )
```

CALCULATE can accept any number of parameters. The only mandatory parameter is the first one, that is, the expression to evaluate. The conditions following the first parameter are called *filter arguments*. *CALCULATE* creates a new filter context based on the set of filter arguments. Once the new filter context is computed, CALCULATE applies it to the model, and it proceeds with the evaluation of the expression. Thus, by leveraging *CALCULATE*, the code for *Contoso Margin* and *Contoso GM %* becomes much simpler:

```
Contoso GM :=
CALCULATE (
    [Gross Margin],                    -- Computes the gross margin
```

```
      'Product'[Brand] = "Contoso"    -- In a filter context where brand = Contoso
)

Contoso GM % :=
CALCULATE (
    [GM %],                          -- Computes the gross margin percentage
    'Product'[Brand] = "Contoso"     -- In a filter context where brand = Contoso
)
```

Welcome back, simplicity and elegance! By creating a filter context that forces the brand to be Contoso, one can rely on existing measures and change their behavior without having to rewrite the code of the measures.

CALCULATE lets you create new filter contexts by manipulating the filters in the current context. As you have seen, this leads to simple and elegant code. In the next sections we provide a complete and more formal definition of the behavior of *CALCULATE*, describing in detail what *CALCULATE* does and how to take advantage of its features. Indeed, so far we have kept the example rather high-level when, in fact, the initial definition of the Contoso measures is not semantically equivalent to the final definition. There are some differences that one needs to understand well.

Introducing *CALCULATE*

Now that you have had an initial exposure to *CALCULATE*, it is time to start learning the details of this function. As introduced earlier, *CALCULATE* is the only DAX function that can modify the filter context; and remember, when we mention *CALCULATE*, we also include *CALCULATETABLE*. *CALCULATE* does not modify a filter context: It creates a new filter context by merging its filter parameters with the existing filter context. Once *CALCULATE* ends, its filter context is discarded and the previous filter context becomes effective again.

We have introduced the syntax of *CALCULATE* as

```
CALCULATE ( Expression, Condition1, … ConditionN )
```

The first parameter is the expression that *CALCULATE* will evaluate. Before evaluating the expression, *CALCULATE* computes the filter arguments and uses them to manipulate the filter context.

The first important thing to note about *CALCULATE* is that the filter arguments are not Boolean conditions: The filter arguments are tables. Whenever you use a Boolean condition as a filter argument of *CALCULATE*, DAX translates it into a table of values.

In the previous section we used this code:

```
Contoso GM :=
CALCULATE (
    [Gross Margin],                  -- Computes the gross margin
    'Product'[Brand] = "Contoso"     -- In a filter context where brand = Contoso
)
```

Using a Boolean condition is only a shortcut for the complete *CALCULATE* syntax. This is known as syntax sugar. It reads this way:

```
Contoso GM :=
CALCULATE (
    [Gross Margin],                -- Computes the gross margin
    FILTER (                       -- Using as valid values for Product[Brand]
        ALL ( 'Product'[Brand] ),  -- any value for Product[Brand]
        'Product'[Brand] = "Contoso"  -- which is equal to "Contoso"
    )
)
```

The two syntaxes are equivalent, and there are no performance or semantic differences between them. That being said, particularly when you are learning *CALCULATE* for the first time, it is useful to always read filter arguments as tables. This makes the behavior of *CALCULATE* more apparent. Once you get used to *CALCULATE* semantics, the compact version of the syntax is more convenient. It is shorter and easier to read.

A filter argument is a table, that is, a list of values. The table provided as a filter argument defines the list of values that will be visible—for the column—during the evaluation of the expression. In the previous example, *FILTER* returns a table with one row only, containing a value for *Product[Brand]* that equals "Contoso". In other words, "Contoso" is the only value that *CALCULATE* will make visible for the *Product[Brand]* column. Therefore, *CALCULATE* filters the model including only products of the Contoso brand. Consider these two definitions:

```
Sales Amount :=
    SUMX (
        Sales,
        Sales[Quantity] * Sales[Net Price]
    )

Contoso Sales :=
CALCULATE (
    [Sales Amount],
    FILTER (
        ALL ( 'Product'[Brand] ),
        'Product'[Brand] = "Contoso"
    )
)
```

The filter parameter of *FILTER* in the *CALCULATE* of *Contoso Sales* scans *ALL(Product[Brand])*; therefore, any previously existing filter on the product brand is overwritten by the new filter. This is more evident when you use the measures in a report that slices by brand. You can see in Figure 5-4 that *Contoso Sales* reports on all the rows/brands the same value as *Sales Amount* did for Contoso specifically.

In every row, the report creates a filter context containing the relevant brand. For example, in the row for Litware the original filter context created by the report contains a filter that only shows Litware products. Then, *CALCULATE* evaluates its filter argument, which returns a table containing only Contoso. The newly created filter overwrites the previously existing filter on the same column. You can see a graphic representation of the process in Figure 5-5.

Brand	Sales Amount	Contoso Sales
A. Datum	2,096,184.64	7,352,399.03
Adventure Works	4,011,112.28	7,352,399.03
Contoso	7,352,399.03	7,352,399.03
Fabrikam	5,554,015.73	7,352,399.03
Litware	3,255,704.03	7,352,399.03
Northwind Traders	1,040,552.13	7,352,399.03
Proseware	2,546,144.16	7,352,399.03
Southridge Video	1,384,413.85	7,352,399.03
Tailspin Toys	325,042.42	7,352,399.03
The Phone Company	1,123,819.07	7,352,399.03
Wide World Importers	1,901,956.66	7,352,399.03
Total	**30,591,343.98**	**7,352,399.03**

FIGURE 5-4 *Contoso Sales* overwrites the existing filter with the new filter for Contoso.

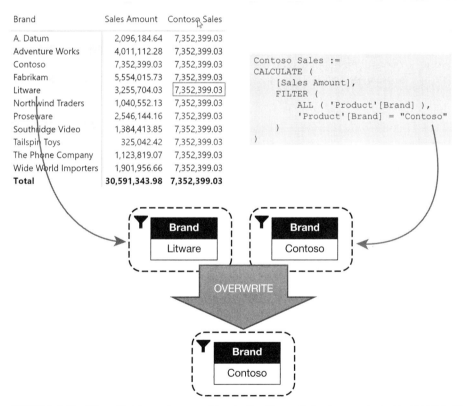

FIGURE 5-5 The filter with Litware is overwritten by the filter with Contoso evaluated by *CALCULATE*.

CALCULATE does not overwrite the whole original filter context. It only replaces previously existing filters on the columns contained in the filter argument. In fact, if one changes the report to now slice by *Product[Category]*, the result is different, as shown in Figure 5-6.

Category	Sales Amount	Contoso Sales
Audio	384,518.16	170,194.00
Cameras and camcorders	7,192,581.95	1,327,792.74
Cell phones	1,604,610.26	480,791.19
Computers	6,741,548.73	1,054,179.83
Games and Toys	360,652.81	
Home Appliances	9,600,457.04	3,294,849.09
Music, Movies and Audio Books	314,206.74	160,764.56
TV and Video	4,392,768.29	863,827.61
Total	**30,591,343.98**	**7,352,399.03**

FIGURE 5-6 If the report filters by Category, the filter on Brand will be merged and no overwrite happens.

Now the report is filtering *Product[Category]*, whereas *CALCULATE* applies a filter on *Product[Brand]* to evaluate the *Contoso Sales* measure. The two filters do not work on the same column of the *Product* table. Therefore, no overwriting happens, and the two filters work together as a new filter context. As a result, each cell is showing the sales of Contoso for the given category. The scenario is depicted in Figure 5-7.

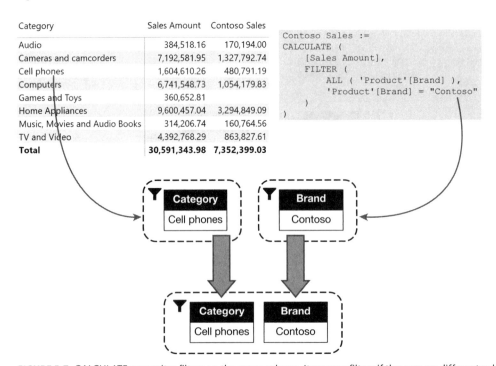

FIGURE 5-7 *CALCULATE* overwrites filters on the same column. It merges filters if they are on different columns.

Now that you have seen the basics of *CALCULATE*, we can summarize its semantics:

■ *CALCULATE* makes a copy of the current filter context.

■ *CALCULATE* evaluates each filter argument and produces, for each condition, the list of valid values for the specified columns.

■ If two or more filter arguments affect the same column, they are merged together using an *AND* operator (or using the set intersection in mathematical terms).

■ *CALCULATE* uses the new condition to replace existing filters on the columns in the model. If a column already has a filter, then the new filter replaces the existing one. On the other hand, if the column does not have a filter, then *CALCULATE* adds the new filter to the filter context.

■ Once the new filter context is ready, *CALCULATE* applies the filter context to the model, and it computes the first argument: the expression. In the end, *CALCULATE* restores the original filter context, returning the computed result.

> **Note** *CALCULATE* does another very important task: It transforms any existing row context into an equivalent filter context. You find a more detailed discussion on this topic later in this chapter, under "Understanding context transition." Should you do a second reading of this section, do remember: *CALCULATE* creates a filter context out of the existing row contexts.

CALCULATE accepts filters of two types:

■ **Lists of values**, in the form of a table expression. In that case, you provide the exact list of values you want to make visible in the new filter context. The filter can be a table with any number of columns. Only the existing combinations of values in different columns will be considered in the filter.

■ **Boolean conditions**, such as *Product[Color] = "White"*. These filters need to work on a single column because the result needs to be a list of values for a single column. This type of filter argument is also known as *predicate*.

If you use the syntax with a Boolean condition, DAX transforms it into a list of values. Thus, whenever you write this code:

```
Sales Amount Red Products :=
CALCULATE (
    [Sales Amount],
    'Product'[Color] = "Red"
)
```

DAX transforms the expression into this:

```
Sales Amount Red Products :=
CALCULATE (
    [Sales Amount],
    FILTER (
        ALL ( 'Product'[Color] ),
        'Product'[Color] = "Red"
    )
)
```

For this reason, you can only reference one column in a filter argument with a Boolean condition. DAX needs to detect the column to iterate in the *FILTER* function, which is generated in the background automatically. If the Boolean expression references two or more columns, then you must explicitly write the *FILTER* iteration, as you learn later in this chapter.

Using *CALCULATE* to compute percentages

Now that we have introduced *CALCULATE*, we can use it to define several calculations. The goal of this section is to bring your attention to some details about *CALCULATE* that are not obvious at first sight. Later in this chapter, we will cover more advanced aspects of *CALCULATE*. For now, we focus on some of the issues you might encounter when you start using *CALCULATE*.

A pattern that appears often is that of percentages. When working with percentages, it is very important to define exactly the calculation required. In this set of examples, you learn how different uses of *CALCULATE* and *ALL* functions provide different results.

We can start with a simple percentage calculation. We want to build the following report showing the sales amount along with the percentage over the grand total. You can see in Figure 5-8 the result we want to obtain.

Category	Sales Amount	Sales Pct
Audio	384,518.16	1.26%
Cameras and camcorders	7,192,581.95	23.51%
Cell phones	1,604,610.26	5.25%
Computers	6,741,548.73	22.04%
Games and Toys	360,652.81	1.18%
Home Appliances	9,600,457.04	31.38%
Music, Movies and Audio Books	314,206.74	1.03%
TV and Video	4,392,768.29	14.36%
Total	**30,591,343.98**	**100.00%**

FIGURE 5-8 *Sales Pct* shows the percentage of the current category against the grand total.

To compute the percentage, one needs to divide the value of *Sales Amount* in the current filter context by the value of *Sales Amount* in a filter context that ignores the existing filter on Category. In fact, the value of 1.26% for Audio is computed as 384,518.16 divided by 30,591,343.98.

In each row of the report, the filter context already contains the current category. Thus, for *Sales Amount*, the result is automatically filtered by the given category. The denominator of the ratio needs to ignore the current filter context, so that it evaluates the grand total. Because the filter arguments of *CALCULATE* are tables, it is enough to provide a table function that ignores the current filter context on the category and always returns all the categories—regardless of any filter. You previously learned that this function is *ALL*. Look at the following measure definition:

```
All Category Sales :=
CALCULATE (                    -- Changes the filter context of
    [Sales Amount],            -- the sales amount
    ALL ( 'Product'[Category] )  -- making ALL categories visible
)
```

ALL removes the filter on the *Product[Category]* column from the filter context. Thus, in any cell of the report, it ignores any filter existing on the categories. The effect is that the filter on the category applied by the row of the report is removed. Look at the result in Figure 5-9. You can see that each row of the report for the *All Category Sales* measure returns the same value all the way through—the grand total of *Sales Amount*.

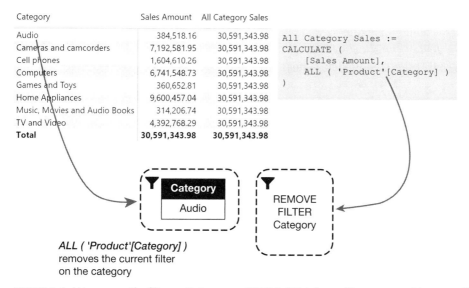

Category	Sales Amount	All Category Sales
Audio	384,518.16	30,591,343.98
Cameras and camcorders	7,192,581.95	30,591,343.98
Cell phones	1,604,610.26	30,591,343.98
Computers	6,741,548.73	30,591,343.98
Games and Toys	360,652.81	30,591,343.98
Home Appliances	9,600,457.04	30,591,343.98
Music, Movies and Audio Books	314,206.74	30,591,343.98
TV and Video	4,392,768.29	30,591,343.98
Total	**30,591,343.98**	**30,591,343.98**

```
All Category Sales :=
CALCULATE (
    [Sales Amount],
    ALL ( 'Product'[Category] )
)
```

Category
Audio

REMOVE
FILTER
Category

ALL ('Product'[Category])
removes the current filter
on the category

FIGURE 5-9 *ALL* removes the filter on *Category*, so *CALCULATE* defines a filter context without any filter on *Category*.

The *All Category Sales* measure is not useful by itself. It is unlikely a user would want to create a report that shows the same value on all the rows. However, that value is perfect as the denominator of the percentage we are looking to compute. In fact, the formula computing the percentage can be written this way:

```
Sales Pct :=
VAR CurrentCategorySales =          -- CurrentCategorySales contains
    [Sales Amount]                  -- the sales in the current context
VAR AllCategoriesSales =            -- AllCategoriesSales contains
    CALCULATE (                     -- the sales amount in a filter context
        [Sales Amount],             -- where all the product categories
        ALL ( 'Product'[Category] ) -- are visible
    )
VAR Ratio =
    DIVIDE (
        CurrentCategorySales,
        AllCategoriesSales
    )
RETURN
    Ratio
```

As you have seen in this example, mixing table functions and *CALCULATE* makes it possible to author useful measures easily. We use this technique a lot in the book because it is the primary calculation tool in DAX.

> **Note** *ALL* has specific semantics when used as a filter argument of *CALCULATE*. In fact, it does not replace the filter context with all the values. Instead, *CALCULATE* uses *ALL* to remove the filter on the category column from the filter context. The side effects of this behavior are somewhat complex to follow and do not belong in this introductory section. We will cover them in more detail later in this chapter.

As we said in the introduction of this section, it is important to pay attention to small details when authoring percentages like the one we are currently writing. In fact, the percentage works fine if the report is slicing by category. The code removes the filter from the category, but it does not touch any other existing filter. Therefore, if the report adds other filters, the result might not be exactly what one wants to achieve. For example, look at the report in Figure 5-10 where we added the *Product[Color]* column as a second level of detail in the rows of the report.

Category	Color	Sales Amount	Sales Pct
Audio	Black	61,823.15	1.05%
	Blue	66,799.65	2.74%
	Green	30,731.27	2.19%
	Orange	3,965.88	0.46%
	Pink	21,544.69	2.60%
	Purple	499.95	8.37%
	Red	33,123.82	2.98%
	Silver	97,417.78	1.43%
	White	54,806.65	0.94%
	Yellow	13,805.31	15.39%
	Total	**384,518.16**	**1.26%**
Cameras and camcorders	Azure	97,389.89	100.00%
	Black	1,005,267.83	17.15%
	Blue	698,711.40	28.69%

FIGURE 5-10 Adding the color to the report produces unexpected results at the color level.

Looking at percentages, the value at the category level is correct, whereas the value at the color level looks wrong. In fact, the color percentages do not add up—neither to the category level nor to 100%. To understand the meaning of these values and how they are evaluated, it is always of great help to focus on one cell and understand exactly what happened to the filter context. Focus on Figure 5-11.

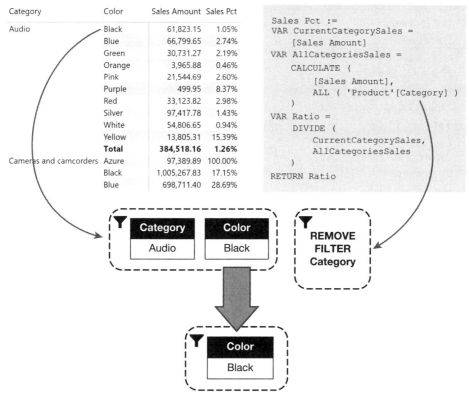

FIGURE 5-11 *ALL* on *Product[Category]* removes the filter on category, but it leaves the filter on color intact.

The original filter context created by the report contained both a filter on category and a filter on color. The filter on *Product[Color]* is not overwritten by *CALCULATE*, which only removes the filter from *Product[Category]*. As a result, the final filter context only contains the color. Therefore, the denominator of the ratio contains the sales of all the products of the given color—Black—and of any category.

The calculation being wrong is not an unexpected behavior of *CALCULATE*. The problem here is that the formula has been designed to specifically work with a filter on a category, leaving any other filter untouched. The same formula makes perfect sense in a different report. Look at what happens if one switches the order of the columns, building a report that slices by color first and category second, as in Figure 5-12.

Color	Category	Sales Amount	Sales Pct
Azure	Cameras and camcorders	97,389.89	100.00%
	Total	**97,389.89**	**100.00%**
Black	Audio	61,823.15	1.05%
	Cameras and camcorders	1,005,267.83	17.15%
	Cell phones	556,308.72	9.49%
	Computers	2,195,921.21	37.47%
	Games and Toys	82,000.86	1.40%
	Home Appliances	706,021.60	12.05%
	Music, Movies and Audio Books	102,542.26	1.75%
	TV and Video	1,150,180.50	19.63%
	Total	**5,860,066.14**	**100.00%**
Blue	Audio	66,799.65	2.74%
	Cameras and camcorders	698,711.40	28.69%
	Computers	172,083.09	7.07%
	Games and Toys	85,788.39	3.52%
	Home Appliances	1,411,124.43	57.94%
	Music, Movies and Audio Books	937.66	0.04%
	Total	**2,435,444.62**	**100.00%**

FIGURE 5-12 The result looks more reasonable once color and category are interchanged.

The report in Figure 5-12 makes a lot more sense. The measure computes the same result, but it is more intuitive thanks to the layout of the report. The percentage shown is the percentage of the category inside the given color. Color by color, the percentage always adds up to 100%.

In other words, when the user is required to compute a percentage, they should pay special attention in determining the denominator of the percentage. *CALCULATE* and *ALL* are the primary tools to use, but the specification of the formula depends on the business requirements.

Back to the example: The goal is to fix the calculation so that it computes the percentage against a filter on either the category or the color. There are multiple ways of performing the operation, all leading to slightly different results that are worth examining deeper.

One possible solution is to let *CALCULATE* remove the filter from both the category and the color. Adding multiple filter arguments to *CALCULATE* accomplishes this goal:

```
Sales Pct :=
VAR CurrentCategorySales =
    [Sales Amount]
VAR AllCategoriesAndColorSales =
    CALCULATE (
        [Sales Amount],
        ALL ( 'Product'[Category] ), -- The two ALL conditions could also be replaced
        ALL ( 'Product'[Color] )     -- by ALL ( 'Product'[Category], 'Product'[Color] )
    )
```

```
VAR Ratio =
    DIVIDE (
        CurrentCategorySales,
        AllCategoriesAndColorSales
    )
RETURN
    Ratio
```

This latter version of *Sales Pct* works fine with the report containing the color and the category, but it still suffers from limitations similar to the previous versions. In fact, it produces the right percentage with color and category—as you can see in Figure 5-13—but it will fail as soon as one adds other columns to the report.

Category	Color	Sales Amount	Sales Pct
Audio	Black	61,823.15	0.20%
	Blue	66,799.65	0.22%
	Green	30,731.27	0.10%
	Orange	3,965.88	0.01%
	Pink	21,544.69	0.07%
	Purple	499.95	0.00%
	Red	33,123.82	0.11%
	Silver	97,417.78	0.32%
	White	54,806.65	0.18%
	Yellow	13,805.31	0.05%
	Total	**384,518.16**	**1.26%**

FIGURE 5-13 With *ALL* on product category and color, the percentages now sum up correctly.

Adding another column to the report would create the same inconsistency noticed so far. If the user wants to create a percentage that removes all the filters on the *Product* table, they could still use the *ALL* function passing a whole table as an argument:

```
Sales Pct All Products :=
VAR CurrentCategorySales =
    [Sales Amount]
VAR AllProductSales =
    CALCULATE (
        [Sales Amount],
        ALL ( 'Product' )
    )
VAR Ratio =
    DIVIDE (
        CurrentCategorySales,
        AllProductSales
    )
RETURN
    Ratio
```

ALL on the *Product* table removes any filter on any column of the *Product* table. In Figure 5-14 you can see the result of that calculation.

Category	Color	Brand	Sales Amount	Sales Pct All Products
Audio	Black	Contoso	22,696.16	0.07%
		Northwind Traders	8,623.52	0.03%
		Wide World Importers	30,503.47	0.10%
		Total	**61,823.15**	**0.20%**
	Blue	Contoso	19,780.93	0.06%
		Northwind Traders	29,053.82	0.09%
		Wide World Importers	17,964.91	0.06%
		Total	**66,799.65**	**0.22%**
	Green	Contoso	23,475.45	0.08%
		Northwind Traders	1,619.84	0.01%
		Wide World Importers	5,635.99	0.02%
		Total	**30,731.27**	**0.10%**

FIGURE 5-14 *ALL* used on the product table removes the filters from all the columns of the *Product* table.

So far, you have seen that by using *CALCULATE* and *ALL* together, you can remove filters—from a column, from multiple columns, or from a whole table. The real power of *CALCULATE* is that it offers many options to manipulate a filter context, and its capabilities do not end there. In fact, one might want to analyze the percentages by also slicing columns from different tables. For example, if the report is sliced by product category and customer continent, the last measure we created is not perfect yet, as you can see in Figure 5-15.

Category	Continent	Sales Amount	Sales Pct All Products
Audio	Asia	110,501.26	1.03%
	Europe	132,735.79	1.53%
	North America	141,281.10	1.26%
	Total	**384,518.16**	**1.26%**
Cameras and camcorders	Asia	2,288,813.15	21.34%
	Europe	2,182,339.59	25.18%
	North America	2,721,429.21	24.30%
	Total	**7,192,581.95**	**23.51%**
Cell phones	Asia	557,888.46	5.20%
	Europe	507,813.97	5.86%
	North America	538,907.83	4.81%
	Total	**1,604,610.26**	**5.25%**

FIGURE 5-15 Slicing with columns of multiple tables still shows unexpected results.

At this point, the problem might be evident to you. The measure at the denominator removes any filter from the *Product* table, but it leaves the filter on *Customer[Continent]* intact. Therefore, the denominator computes the total sales of all products in the given continent.

As in the previous scenario, the filter can be removed from multiple tables by putting several filters as arguments of *CALCULATE:*

```
Sales Pct All Products and Customers :=
VAR CurrentCategorySales =
    [Sales Amount]
VAR AllProductAndCustomersSales =
    CALCULATE (
        [Sales Amount],
        ALL ( 'Product' ),
        ALL ( Customer )
    )
VAR Ratio =
    DIVIDE (
        CurrentCategorySales,
        AllProductAndCustomersSales
    )
RETURN
    Ratio
```

By using *ALL* on two tables, now *CALCULATE* removes the filters from both tables. The result, as expected, is a percentage that adds up correctly, as you can appreciate in Figure 5-16.

Category	Continent	Sales Amount	Sales Pct All Products and Customers
Audio	Asia	110,501.26	0.36%
	Europe	132,735.79	0.43%
	North America	141,281.10	0.46%
	Total	**384,518.16**	**1.26%**
Cameras and camcorders	Asia	2,288,813.15	7.48%
	Europe	2,182,339.59	7.13%
	North America	2,721,429.21	8.90%
	Total	**7,192,581.95**	**23.51%**
Cell phones	Asia	557,888.46	1.82%
	Europe	507,813.97	1.66%
	North America	538,907.83	1.76%
	Total	**1,604,610.26**	**5.25%**

FIGURE 5-16 Using *ALL* on two tables removes the filter context on both tables at the same time.

As with two columns, the same challenge comes up with two tables. If a user adds another column from a third table to the context, the measure will not remove the filter from the third table. One possible solution when they want to remove the filter from any table that might affect the calculation is to remove any filter from the fact table itself. In our model the fact table is *Sales*. Here is a measure that computes an additive percentage no matter what filter is interacting with the *Sales* table:

```
Pct All Sales :=
VAR CurrentCategorySales =
    [Sales Amount]
VAR AllSales =
    CALCULATE (
        [Sales Amount],
        ALL ( Sales )
    )
```

```
VAR Ratio =
    DIVIDE (
        CurrentCategorySales,
        AllSales
    )
RETURN
    Ratio
```

This measure leverages relationships to remove the filter from any table that might filter *Sales*. At this stage, we cannot explain the details of how it works because it leverages expanded tables, which we introduce in Chapter 14, "Advanced DAX concepts." You can appreciate its behavior by inspecting Figure 5-17, where we removed the amount from the report and added the calendar year on the columns. Please note that the *Calendar Year* belongs to the *Date* table, which is not used in the measure. Nevertheless, the filter on *Date* is removed as part of the removal of filters from *Sales*.

Category	CY 2007	CY 2008	CY 2009	Total
Audio	0.34%	0.34%	0.58%	**1.26%**
Cameras and camcorders	10.71%	7.14%	5.67%	**23.51%**
Cell phones	1.56%	1.51%	2.17%	**5.25%**
Computers	8.70%	6.75%	6.59%	**22.04%**
Games and Toys	0.29%	0.35%	0.54%	**1.18%**
Home Appliances	7.67%	12.95%	10.76%	**31.38%**
Music, Movies and Audio Books	0.29%	0.39%	0.35%	**1.03%**
TV and Video	7.42%	3.01%	3.93%	**14.36%**
Total	**36.97%**	**32.45%**	**30.58%**	**100.00%**

FIGURE 5-17 *ALL* on the fact table removes any filter from related tables as well.

Before leaving this long exercise with percentages, we want to show another final example of filter context manipulation. As you can see in Figure 5-17, the percentage is always against the grand total, exactly as expected. What if the goal is to compute a percentage over the grand total of only the current year? In that case, the new filter context created by *CALCULATE* needs to be prepared carefully. Indeed, the denominator needs to compute the total of sales regardless of any filter apart from the current year. This requires two actions:

- Removing all filters from the fact table

- Restoring the filter for the year

Beware that the two conditions are applied at the same time, although it might look like the two steps come one after the other. You have already learned how to remove all the filters from the fact table. The last step is learning how to restore an existing filter.

Note The goal of this section is to explain basic techniques for manipulating the filter context. Later in this chapter you see another easier approach to solve this specific requirement—percentage over the visible grand total—by using *ALLSELECTED*.

In Chapter 3, "Using basic table functions," you learned the *VALUES* function. *VALUES* returns the list of values of a column in the current filter context. Because the result of *VALUES* is a table, it can be used as a filter argument for *CALCULATE*. As a result, *CALCULATE* applies a filter on the given column, restricting its values to those returned by *VALUES*. Look at the following code:

```
Pct All Sales CY :=
VAR CurrentCategorySales =
    [Sales Amount]
VAR AllSalesInCurrentYear =
    CALCULATE (
        [Sales Amount],
        ALL ( Sales ),
        VALUES ( 'Date'[Calendar Year] )
    )
VAR Ratio =
    DIVIDE (
        CurrentCategorySales,
        AllSalesInCurrentYear
    )
RETURN
    Ratio
```

Once used in the report the measure accounts for 100% for every year, still computing the percentage against any other filter apart from the year. You see this in Figure 5-18.

Category	CY 2007	CY 2008	CY 2009	Total
Audio	0.91%	1.06%	1.89%	**1.26%**
Cameras and camcorders	28.96%	22.00%	18.53%	**23.51%**
Cell phones	4.22%	4.66%	7.10%	**5.25%**
Computers	23.52%	20.81%	21.54%	**22.04%**
Games and Toys	0.79%	1.07%	1.76%	**1.18%**
Home Appliances	20.75%	39.91%	35.18%	**31.38%**
Music, Movies and Audio Books	0.78%	1.22%	1.13%	**1.03%**
TV and Video	20.07%	9.27%	12.86%	**14.36%**
Total	**100.00%**	**100.00%**	**100.00%**	**100.00%**

FIGURE 5-18 By using *VALUES*, you can restore part of the filter context, reading it from the original filter context.

Figure 5-19 depicts the full behavior of this complex formula.

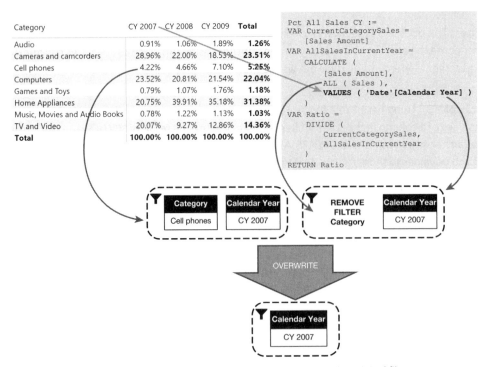

Category	CY 2007	CY 2008	CY 2009	Total
Audio	0.91%	1.06%	1.89%	1.26%
Cameras and camcorders	28.96%	22.00%	18.53%	23.51%
Cell phones	4.22%	4.66%	7.10%	5.25%
Computers	23.52%	20.81%	21.54%	22.04%
Games and Toys	0.79%	1.07%	1.76%	1.18%
Home Appliances	20.75%	39.91%	35.18%	31.38%
Music, Movies and Audio Books	0.78%	1.22%	1.13%	1.03%
TV and Video	20.07%	9.27%	12.86%	14.36%
Total	100.00%	100.00%	100.00%	100.00%

```
Pct All Sales CY :=
VAR CurrentCategorySales =
    [Sales Amount]
VAR AllSalesInCurrentYear =
    CALCULATE (
        [Sales Amount],
        ALL ( Sales ),
        VALUES ( 'Date'[Calendar Year] )
    )
VAR Ratio =
    DIVIDE (
        CurrentCategorySales,
        AllSalesInCurrentYear
    )
RETURN Ratio
```

FIGURE 5-19 The key of this diagram is that *VALUES* is still evaluated in the original filter context.

Here is a review of the diagram:

- The cell containing 4.22% (sales of Cell Phones for Calendar Year 2007) has a filter context that filters Cell phones for CY 2007.

- *CALCULATE* has two filter arguments: *ALL (Sales)* and *VALUES (Date[Calendar Year])*.

  - *ALL (Sales)* removes the filter from the *Sales* table.
  - *VALUES (Date[Calendar Year])* evaluates the *VALUES* function in the original filter context, still affected by the presence of CY 2007 on the columns. As such, it returns the only year visible in the current filter context—that is, CY 2007.

The two filter arguments of *CALCULATE* are applied to the current filter context, resulting in a filter context that only contains a filter on *Calendar Year*. The denominator computes the total sales in a filter context with CY 2007 only.

It is of paramount importance to understand clearly that the filter arguments of *CALCULATE* are evaluated in the original filter context where *CALCULATE* is called. In fact, *CALCULATE* changes the filter context, but this only happens after the filter arguments are evaluated.

Using *ALL* over a table followed by *VALUES* over a column is a technique used to replace the filter context with a filter over that same column.

> **Note** The previous example could also have been obtained by using *ALLEXCEPT*. The semantics of *ALL/VALUES* is different from *ALLEXCEPT*. In Chapter 10, "Working with the filter context," you will see a complete description of the differences between the *ALLEXCEPT* and the *ALL/VALUES* techniques.

As you have seen in these examples, *CALCULATE*, in itself, is not a complex function. Its behavior is simple to describe. At the same time, as soon as you start using *CALCULATE*, the complexity of the code becomes much higher. Indeed, you need to focus on the filter context and understand exactly how *CALCULATE* generates the new filter context. A simple percentage hides a lot of complexity, and that complexity is all in the details. Before one really masters the handling of evaluation contexts, DAX is a bit of a mystery. The key to unlocking the full power of the language is all in mastering evaluation contexts. Moreover, in all these examples we only had to manage one *CALCULATE*. In a complex formula, having four or five different contexts in the same code is not unusual because of the presence of many instances of *CALCULATE*.

It is a good idea to read this whole section about percentages at least twice. In our experience, a second read is much easier and lets you focus on the important aspects of the code. We wanted to show this example to stress the importance of theory, when it comes to *CALCULATE*. A small change in the code has an important effect on the numbers computed by the formula. After your second read, proceed with the next sections where we focus more on theory than on practical examples.

Introducing *KEEPFILTERS*

You learned in the previous sections that the filter arguments of *CALCULATE* overwrite any previously existing filter on the same column. Thus, the following measure returns the sales of Audio regardless of any previously existing filter on *Product[Category]*:

```
Audio Sales :=
CALCULATE (
    [Sales Amount],
    'Product'[Category] = "Audio"
)
```

As you can see in Figure 5-20, the value of Audio is repeated on all the rows of the report.

Category	Sales Amount	Audio Sales
Audio	384,518.16	384,518.16
Cameras and camcorders	7,192,581.95	384,518.16
Cell phones	1,604,610.26	384,518.16
Computers	6,741,548.73	384,518.16
Games and Toys	360,652.81	384,518.16
Home Appliances	9,600,457.04	384,518.16
Music, Movies and Audio Books	314,206.74	384,518.16
TV and Video	4,392,768.29	384,518.16
Total	**30,591,343.98**	**384,518.16**

FIGURE 5-20 *Audio Sales* always shows the sales of Audio products, regardless of the current filter context.

CALCULATE overwrites the existing filters on the columns where a new filter is applied. All the remaining columns of the filter context are left intact. In case you do not want to overwrite existing filters, you can wrap the filter argument with *KEEPFILTERS*. For example, if you want to show the amount of Audio sales when Audio is present in the filter context and a blank value if Audio is not present in the filter context, you can write the following measure:

```
Audio Sales KeepFilters :=
CALCULATE (
    [Sales Amount],
    KEEPFILTERS ( 'Product'[Category] = "Audio" )
)
```

KEEPFILTERS is the second *CALCULATE* modifier that you learn—the first one was *ALL*. We further cover *CALCULATE* modifiers later in this chapter. *KEEPFILTERS* alters the way *CALCULATE* applies a filter to the new filter context. Instead of overwriting an existing filter over the same column, it adds the new filter to the existing ones. Therefore, only the cells where the filtered category was already included in the filter context will produce a visible result. You see this in Figure 5-21.

Category	Sales Amount	Audio Sales	Audio Sales KeepFilters
Audio	384,518.16	384,518.16	384,518.16
Cameras and camcorders	7,192,581.95	384,518.16	
Cell phones	1,604,610.26	384,518.16	
Computers	6,741,548.73	384,518.16	
Games and Toys	360,652.81	384,518.16	
Home Appliances	9,600,457.04	384,518.16	
Music, Movies and Audio Books	314,206.74	384,518.16	
TV and Video	4,392,768.29	384,518.16	
Total	**30,591,343.98**	**384,518.16**	**384,518.16**

FIGURE 5-21 *Audio Sales KeepFilters* shows the sales of Audio products only for the Audio row and for the Grand Total.

KEEPFILTERS does exactly what its name implies. Instead of overwriting the existing filter, it keeps the existing filter and adds the new filter to the filter context. We can depict the behavior with Figure 5-22.

Because *KEEPFILTERS* avoids overwriting, the new filter generated by the filter argument of *CALCULATE* is added to the context. If we look at the cell for the *Audio Sales KeepFilters* measure in the Cell Phones row, there the resulting filter context contains two filters: one filters Cell Phones; the other filters Audio. The intersection of the two conditions results in an empty set, which produces a blank result.

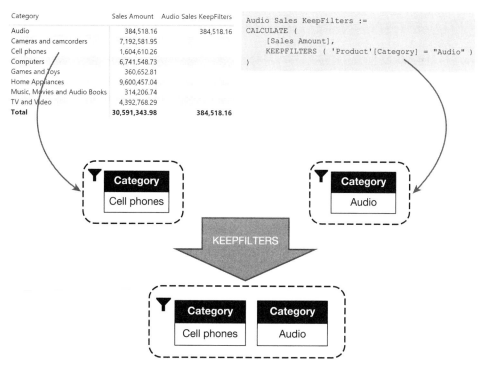

Category	Sales Amount	Audio Sales KeepFilters
Audio	384,518.16	384,518.16
Cameras and camcorders	7,192,581.95	
Cell phones	1,604,610.26	
Computers	6,741,548.73	
Games and Toys	360,652.81	
Home Appliances	9,600,457.04	
Music, Movies and Audio Books	314,206.74	
TV and Video	4,392,768.29	
Total	**30,591,343.98**	**384,518.16**

```
Audio Sales KeepFilters :=
CALCULATE (
    [Sales Amount],
    KEEPFILTERS ( 'Product'[Category] = "Audio" )
)
```

FIGURE 5-22 The filter context generated with *KEEPFILTERS* filters at the same time as both Cell phones and Audio.

The behavior of *KEEPFILTERS* is clearer when there are multiple elements selected in a column. For example, consider the following measures; they filter Audio and Computers with and without *KEEPFILTERS*:

```
Always Audio-Computers :=
CALCULATE (
    [Sales Amount],
    'Product'[Category] IN { "Audio", "Computers" }
)

KeepFilters Audio-Computers :=
CALCULATE (
    [Sales Amount],
    KEEPFILTERS ( 'Product'[Category] IN { "Audio", "Computers" } )
)
```

The report in Figure 5-23 shows that the version with *KEEPFILTERS* only computes the sales amount values for Audio and for Computers, leaving all other categories blank. The Total row only takes Audio and Computers into account.

Category	Sales Amount	Always Audio-Computers	KeepFilters Audio-Computers
Audio	384,518.16	7,126,066.89	384,518.16
Cameras and camcorders	7,192,581.95	7,126,066.89	
Cell phones	1,604,610.26	7,126,066.89	
Computers	6,741,548.73	7,126,066.89	6,741,548.73
Games and Toys	360,652.81	7,126,066.89	
Home Appliances	9,600,457.04	7,126,066.89	
Music, Movies and Audio Books	314,206.74	7,126,066.89	
TV and Video	4,392,768.29	7,126,066.89	
Total	**30,591,343.98**	**7,126,066.89**	**7,126,066.89**

FIGURE 5-23 Using *KEEPFILTERS*, the original and the new filter contexts are merged together.

KEEPFILTERS can be used either with a predicate or with a table. Indeed, the previous code could also be written in a more verbose way:

```
KeepFilters Audio-Computers :=
CALCULATE (
    [Sales Amount],
    KEEPFILTERS (
        FILTER (
            ALL ( 'Product'[Category] ),
            'Product'[Category] IN { "Audio", "Computers" }
        )
    )
)
```

This is just an example for educational purposes. You should use the simplest predicate syntax available for a filter argument. When filtering a single column, you can avoid writing the *FILTER* explicitly. Later however, you will see that more complex filter conditions require an explicit *FILTER*. In those cases, the *KEEPFILTERS* modifier can be used around the explicit *FILTER* function, as you see in the next section.

Filtering a single column

In the previous section, we introduced filter arguments referencing a single column in *CALCULATE*. It is important to note that you can have multiple references to the same column in one expression. For example, the following is a valid syntax because it references the same column (*Sales[Net Price]*) twice.

```
Sales 10-100 :=
CALCULATE (
    [Sales Amount],
    Sales[Net Price] >= 10 && Sales[Net Price] <= 100
)
```

In fact, this is converted into the following syntax:

```
Sales 10-100 :=
CALCULATE (
    [Sales Amount],
    FILTER (
        ALL ( Sales[Net Price] ),
        Sales[Net Price] >= 10 && Sales[Net Price] <= 100
    )
)
```

The resulting filter context produced by *CALCULATE* only adds one filter over the *Sales[Net Price]* column. One important note about predicates as filter arguments in *CALCULATE* is that although they look like conditions, they are tables. If you read the first of the last two code snippets, it looks as though *CALCULATE* evaluates a condition. Instead, *CALCULATE* evaluates the list of all the values of *Sales[Net Price]* that satisfy the condition. Then, *CALCULATE* uses this table of values to apply a filter to the model.

When two conditions are in a logical *AND*, they can be represented as two separate filters. Indeed, the previous expression is equivalent to the following one:

```
Sales 10-100 :=
CALCULATE (
    [Sales Amount],
    Sales[Net Price] >= 10,
    Sales[Net Price] <= 100
)
```

However, keep in mind that the multiple filter arguments of *CALCULATE* are always merged with a logical *AND*. Thus, you must use a single filter in case of a logical *OR* statement, such as in the following measure:

```
Sales Blue+Red :=
CALCULATE (
    [Sales Amount],
    'Product'[Color] = "Red" || 'Product'[Color] = "Blue"
)
```

By writing multiple filters, you would combine two independent filters in a single filter context. The following measure always produces a blank result because there are no products that are both Blue and Red at the same time:

```
Sales Blue and Red :=
CALCULATE (
    [Sales Amount],
    'Product'[Color] = "Red",
    'Product'[Color] = "Blue"
)
```

In fact, the previous measure corresponds to the following measure with a single filter:

```
Sales Blue and Red :=
CALCULATE (
    [Sales Amount],
    'Product'[Color] = "Red" && 'Product'[Color] = "Blue"
)
```

The filter argument always returns an empty list of colors allowed in the filter context. Therefore, the measure always returns a blank value.

Whenever a filter argument refers to a single column, you can use a predicate. We suggest you do so because the resulting code is much easier to read. You should do so for logical *AND* conditions too. Nevertheless, never forget that you are relying on syntax-sugaring only. *CALCULATE* always works with tables, although the compact syntax might suggest otherwise.

On the other hand, whenever there are two or more different column references in a filter argument, it is necessary to write the *FILTER* condition as a table expression. You learn this in the following section.

Filtering with complex conditions

A filter argument referencing multiple columns requires an explicit table expression. It is important to understand the different techniques available to write such filters. Remember that creating a filter with the minimum number of columns required by the predicate is usually a best practice.

Consider a measure that sums the sales for only the transactions with an amount greater than or equal to 1,000. Getting the amount of each transaction requires the multiplication of the *Quantity* and *Net Price* columns. This is because you do not have a column that stores that amount for each row of the *Sales* table in the sample Contoso database. You might be tempted to write something like the following expression, which unfortunately will not work:

```
Sales Large Amount :=
CALCULATE (
    [Sales Amount],
    Sales[Quantity] * Sales[Net Price] >= 1000
)
```

This code is not valid because the filter argument references two different columns in the same expression. As such, it cannot be converted automatically by DAX into a suitable *FILTER* condition. The best way to write the required filter is by using a table that only has the existing combinations of the columns referenced in the predicate:

```
Sales Large Amount :=
CALCULATE (
    [Sales Amount],
    FILTER (
        ALL ( Sales[Quantity], Sales[Net Price] ),
        Sales[Quantity] * Sales[Net Price] >= 1000
    )
)
```

This results in a filter context that has a filter with two columns and a number of rows that correspond to the unique combinations of *Quantity* and *Net Price* that satisfy the filter condition. This is shown in Figure 5-24.

Quantity	Net Price
1	1000.00
1	1001.00
1	1199.00
...	...
2	500.00
2	500.05
...	...
3	333.34
...	

FIGURE 5-24 The multi-column filter only includes combinations of *Quantity* and *Net Price* producing a result greater than or equal to 1,000.

This filter produces the result in Figure 5-25.

Net Price $0.76 — $3,199.99	Category	Sales Amount	Sales Large Amount
	Audio	384,518.16	7,803.95
	Cameras and camcorders	7,192,581.95	3,078,829.16
	Cell phones	1,604,610.26	150,687.21
	Computers	6,741,548.73	3,036,735.73
	Games and Toys	360,652.81	
	Home Appliances	9,600,457.04	5,390,769.53
	Music, Movies and Audio Books	314,206.74	11,873.57
	TV and Video	4,392,768.29	1,256,714.63
	Total	**30,591,343.98**	**12,933,413.78**

FIGURE 5-25 *Sales Large Amount* only shows sales of transactions with a large amount.

Be mindful that the slicer in Figure 5-25 is not filtering any value: The two displayed values are the minimum and the maximum values of *Net Price*. The next step is showing how the measure is interacting with the slicer. In a measure like *Sales Large Amount*, you need to pay attention when you overwrite existing filters over *Quantity* or *Net Price*. Indeed, because the filter argument uses *ALL* on the two columns, it ignores any previously existing filter on the same columns including, in this example, the filter of the slicer. The report in Figure 5-26 is the same as Figure 5-25 but, this time, the slicer filters for net prices between 500 and 3,000. The result is surprising.

Net Price	Category	Sales Amount	Sales Large Amount
$500.00 $3,000.00	Audio		7,803.95
	Cameras and camcorders	4,786,139.80	3,078,829.16
	Cell phones	47,152.49	150,687.21
	Computers	3,717,785.81	3,036,735.73
	Home Appliances	5,839,778.70	5,390,769.53
	Music, Movies and Audio Books		11,873.57
	TV and Video	987,758.58	1,256,714.63
	Total	**15,378,615.38**	**12,933,413.78**

FIGURE 5-26 There are no sales for Audio in the current price range; still *Sales Large Amount* is showing a result.

The presence of value of *Sales Large Amount* for Audio and Music, Movies and Audio Books is unexpected. Indeed, for these two categories there are no sales in the net price range between 500 and 3,000, which is the filter context generated by the slicer. Still, the *Sales Large Amount* measure is showing a result.

The reason is that the filter context of *Net Price* created by the slicer is ignored by the *Sales Large Amount* measure, which overwrites the existing filter over both *Quantity* and *Net Price*. If you carefully compare figures 5-25 and 5-26, you will notice that the value of *Sales Large Amount* is identical, as if the slicer was not added to the report. Indeed, *Sales Large Amount* is completely ignoring the slicer.

If you focus on a cell, like the value of *Sales Large Amount* for Audio, the code executed to compute its value is the following:

```
Sales Large Amount :=
CALCULATE (
    CALCULATE (
        [Sales Amount],
        FILTER (
            ALL ( Sales[Quantity], Sales[Net Price] ),
            Sales[Quantity] * Sales[Net Price] >= 1000
        )
    ),
    'Product'[Category] = "Audio",
    Sales[Net Price] >= 500
)
```

From the code, you can see that the innermost *ALL* ignores the filter on *Sales[Net Price]* set by the outer *CALCULATE*. In that scenario, you can use *KEEPFILTERS* to avoid the overwrite of existing filters:

```
Sales Large Amount KeepFilter :=
CALCULATE (
    [Sales Amount],
    KEEPFILTERS (
        FILTER (
            ALL ( Sales[Quantity], Sales[Net Price] ),
            Sales[Quantity] * Sales[Net Price] >= 1000
        )
    )
)
```

The new *Sales Large Amount KeepFilter* measure produces the result shown in Figure 5-27.

Net Price

$500.00 $3,000.00

Category	Sales Amount	Sales Large Amount	Sales Large Amount KeepFilter
Audio		7,803.95	
Cameras and camcorders	4,786,139.80	3,078,829.16	2,683,625.23
Cell phones	47,152.49	150,687.21	21,034.71
Computers	3,717,785.81	3,036,735.73	2,656,140.41
Home Appliances	5,839,778.70	5,390,769.53	4,560,035.33
Music, Movies and Audio Books		11,873.57	
TV and Video	987,758.58	1,256,714.63	490,518.59
Total	**15,378,615.38**	**12,933,413.78**	**10,411,354.27**

FIGURE 5-27 Using *KEEPFILTERS*, the calculation takes into account the outer slicer too.

Another way of specifying a complex filter is by using a table filter instead of a column filter. This is one of the preferred techniques of DAX newbies, although it is very dangerous to use. In fact, the previous measure can be written using a table filter:

```
Sales Large Amount Table :=
CALCULATE (
    [Sales Amount],
    FILTER (
        Sales,
        Sales[Quantity] * Sales[Net Price] >= 1000
    )
)
```

As you may remember, all the filter arguments of *CALCULATE* are evaluated in the filter context that exists outside of the *CALCULATE* itself. Thus, the iteration over *Sales* only considers the rows filtered in the existing filter context, which contains a filter on *Net Price*. Therefore, the semantic of the *Sales Large Amount Table* measure corresponds to the *Sales Large Amount KeepFilter* measure.

Although this technique looks easy, you should be careful in using it because it could have serious consequences on performance and on result accuracy. We will cover the details of these issues in Chapter 14. For now, just remember that the best practice is to always use a filter with the smallest possible number of columns.

Moreover, you should avoid table filters because they usually are more expensive. The *Sales* table might be very large, and scanning it row by row to evaluate a predicate can be a time-consuming operation. The filter in *Sales Large Amount KeepFilter*, on the other hand, only iterates the number of unique combinations of *Quantity* and *Net Price*. That number is usually much smaller than the number of rows of the entire *Sales* table.

Evaluation order in *CALCULATE*

Whenever you look at DAX code, the natural order of evaluation is innermost first. For example, look at the following expression:

```
Sales Amount Large :=
SUMX (
    FILTER ( Sales, Sales[Quantity] >= 100 ),
    Sales[Quantity] * Sales[Net Price]
)
```

DAX needs to evaluate the result of *FILTER* before starting the evaluation of *SUMX*. In fact, *SUMX* iterates a table. Because that table is the result of *FILTER*, *SUMX* cannot start executing before *FILTER* has finished its job. This rule is true for all DAX functions, except for *CALCULATE* and *CALCULATETABLE*. Indeed, *CALCULATE* evaluates its filter arguments first and only at the end does it evaluate the first parameter, which is the expression to evaluate to provide the *CALCULATE* result.

Moreover, things are a bit more intricate because *CALCULATE* changes the filter context. All the filter arguments are executed in the filter context outside of *CALCULATE,* and each filter is evaluated independently. The order of filters within the same *CALCULATE* does not matter. Consequently, all the following measures are completely equivalent:

```
Sales Red Contoso :=
CALCULATE (
    [Sales Amount],
    'Product'[Color] = "Red",
    KEEPFILTERS ( 'Product'[Brand] = "Contoso" )
)

Sales Red Contoso :=
CALCULATE (
    [Sales Amount],
    KEEPFILTERS ( 'Product'[Brand] = "Contoso" ),
    'Product'[Color] = "Red"
)

Sales Red Contoso :=
VAR ColorRed =
        FILTER (
            ALL ( 'Product'[Color] ),
            'Product'[Color] = "Red"
        )
VAR BrandContoso =
        FILTER (
            ALL ( 'Product'[Brand] ),
            'Product'[Brand] = "Contoso"
        )
```

```
VAR SalesRedContoso =
    CALCULATE (
        [Sales Amount],
        ColorRed,
        KEEPFILTERS ( BrandContoso )
    )
RETURN
    SalesRedContoso
```

The version of *Sales Red Contoso* defined using variables is more verbose than the other versions, but you might want to use it in case the filters are complex expressions with explicit filters. This way, it is easier to understand that the filter is evaluated "before" *CALCULATE*.

This rule becomes more important in case of nested *CALCULATE* statements. In fact, the outermost filters are applied first, and the innermost are applied later. Understanding the behavior of nested *CALCULATE* statements is important, because you encounter this situation every time you nest measures calls. For example, consider the following measures, where *Sales Green* calls *Sales Red*:

```
Sales Red :=
CALCULATE (
    [Sales Amount],
    'Product'[Color] = "Red"
)

Green calling Red :=
CALCULATE (
    [Sales Red],
    'Product'[Color] = "Green"
)
```

To make the nested measure call more evident, we can expand *Sales Green* this way:

```
Green calling Red Exp :=
CALCULATE (
    CALCULATE (
        [Sales Amount],
        'Product'[Color] = "Red"
    ),
    'Product'[Color] = "Green"
)
```

The order of evaluation is the following:

1. First, the outer *CALCULATE* applies the filter, *Product[Color] = "Green"*.

2. Second, the inner *CALCULATE* applies the filter, *Product[Color] = "Red"*. This filter overwrites the previous filter.

3. Last, DAX computes *[Sales Amount]* with a filter for *Product[Color] = "Red"*.

Therefore, the result of both *Red* and *Green calling Red* is still Red, as shown in Figure 5-28.

Category	Sales Amount	Sales Red	Green calling Red	Green calling Red Exp
Audio	384,518.16	33,123.82	33,123.82	33,123.82
Cameras and camcorders	7,192,581.95	1,514.39	1,514.39	1,514.39
Cell phones	1,604,610.26	38,227.47	38,227.47	38,227.47
Computers	6,741,548.73	240,222.29	240,222.29	240,222.29
Games and Toys	360,652.81	19,938.31	19,938.31	19,938.31
Home Appliances	9,600,457.04	770,373.33	770,373.33	770,373.33
Music, Movies and Audio Books	314,206.74	6,702.49	6,702.49	6,702.49
TV and Video	4,392,768.29			
Total	**30,591,343.98**	**1,110,102.10**	**1,110,102.10**	**1,110,102.10**

FIGURE 5-28 The last three measures return the same result, which is always the sales of red products.

> **Note** The description we provided is for educational purposes only. In reality the engine uses lazy evaluation for the filter context. So, in the presence of filter argument overwrites such as the previous code, the outer filter might never be evaluated because it would have been useless. Nevertheless, this behavior is for optimization only. It does not change the semantics of *CALCULATE* in any way.

We can review the order of the evaluation and how the filter context is evaluated with another example. Consider the following measure:

```
Sales YB :=
CALCULATE (
    CALCULATE (
        [Sales Amount],
        'Product'[Color] IN { "Yellow", "Black" }
    ),
    'Product'[Color] IN { "Black", "Blue" }
)
```

The evaluation of the filter context produced by *Sales YB* is visible in Figure 5-29.

As seen before, the innermost filter over *Product[Color]* overwrites the outermost filters. Therefore, the result of the measure shows the sum of products that are Yellow or Black. By using *KEEPFILTERS* in the innermost *CALCULATE*, the filter context is built by keeping the two filters instead of overwriting the existing filter:

```
Sales YB KeepFilters :=
CALCULATE (
    CALCULATE (
        [Sales Amount],
        KEEPFILTERS ( 'Product'[Color] IN { "Yellow", "Black" } )
    ),
    'Product'[Color] IN { "Black", "Blue" }
)
```

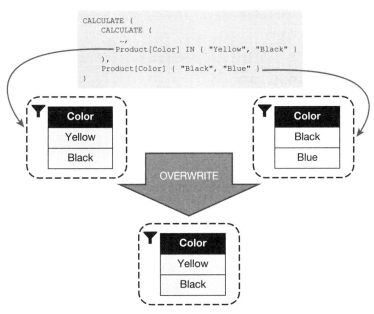

FIGURE 5-29 The innermost filter overwrites the outer filter.

The evaluation of the filter context produced by *Sales YB KeepFilters* is visible in Figure 5-30.

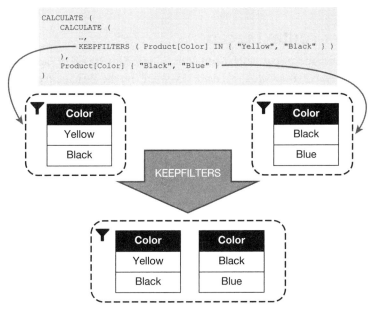

FIGURE 5-30 By using *KEEPFILTERS*, *CALCULATE* does not overwrite the previous filter context.

Because the two filters are kept together, they are intersected. Therefore, in the new filter context the only visible color is Black because it is the only value present in both filters.

However, the order of the filter arguments within the same *CALCULATE* is irrelevant because they are applied to the filter context independently.

Understanding context transition

In Chapter 4, "Understanding evaluation contexts," we evoked multiple times that the row context and the filter context are different concepts. This still holds true. However, there is one operation performed by *CALCULATE* that can transform a row context into a filter context. It is the operation of *context transition*, defined as follows:

> *CALCULATE invalidates any row context. It automatically adds as filter arguments all the columns that are currently being iterated in any row context—filtering their actual value in the row being iterated.*

Context transition is hard to understand at the beginning, and even seasoned DAX coders find it complex to follow all the implications of context transition. We are more than confident that the previous definition does not suffice to fully understand context transition.

Therefore, we are going to describe context transition through several examples of increasing complexity. But before discussing such a delicate concept, let us make sure we thoroughly understand row context and filter context.

Row context and filter context recap

We can recap some important facts about row context and filter context with the aid of Figure 5-31, which shows a report with the *Brand* on the rows and a diagram describing the evaluation process. *Products* and *Sales* in the diagram are not displaying real data. They only contain a few rows to make the points clearer.

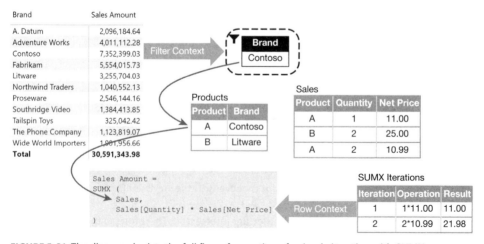

FIGURE 5-31 The diagram depicts the full flow of execution of a simple iteration with *SUMX*.

The following comments on Figure 5-31 are helpful to monitor your understanding of the whole process for evaluating the *Sales Amount* measure for the Contoso row:

- The report creates a filter context containing a filter for *Product[Brand]* = *"Contoso"*.

- The filter works on the entire model, filtering both the *Product* and the *Sales* tables.

- The filter context reduces the number of rows iterated by *SUMX* while scanning *Sales*. *SUMX* only iterates the *Sales* rows that are related to a Contoso product.

- In the figure there are two rows in *Sales* with product A, which is branded Contoso.

- Consequently, *SUMX* iterates two rows. In the first row it computes 1*11.00 with a partial result of 11.00. In the second row it computes 2*10.99 with a partial result of 21.98.

- *SUMX* returns the sum of the partial results gathered during the iteration.

- During the iteration of *Sales*, *SUMX* only scans the visible portion of the *Sales* table, generating a row context for each visible row.

- When *SUMX* iterates the first row, *Sales[Quantity]* equals 1, whereas *Sales[Net Price]* equals 11. On the second row, the values are different. Columns have a current value that depends on the iterated row. Potentially, each row iterated has a different value for all the columns.

- During the iteration, there is a row context and a filter context. The filter context is still the same that filters Contoso because no *CALCULATE* has been executed to modify it.

Speaking about context transition, the last statement is the most important. During the iteration the filter context is still active, and it filters Contoso. The row context, on the other hand, is currently iterating the *Sales* table. Each column of *Sales* has a given value. The row context is providing the value via the current row. Remember that the row context iterates; the filter context does not.

This is an important detail. We invite you to double-check your understanding in the following scenario. Imagine you create a measure that simply counts the number of rows in the *Sales* table, with the following code:

```
NumOfSales := COUNTROWS ( Sales )
```

Once used in the report, the measure counts the number of *Sales* rows that are visible in the current filter context. The result shown in Figure 5-32 is as expected: a different number for each brand.

Brand	NumOfSales
A. Datum	4,921
Adventure Works	7,819
Contoso	37,984
Fabrikam	7,861
Litware	7,214
Northwind Traders	1,636
Proseware	6,673
Southridge Video	10,658
Tailspin Toys	7,571
The Phone Company	3,106
Wide World Importers	4,788
Total	**100,231**

FIGURE 5-32 *NumOfSales* counts the number of rows visible in the current filter context in the *Sales* table.

Because there are 37,984 rows in *Sales* for the Contoso brand, this means that an iteration over *Sales* for Contoso will iterate exactly 37,984 rows. The *Sales Amount* measure we used so far would complete its execution after 37,984 multiplications.

With the understanding you have obtained so far, can you guess the result of the following measure on the Contoso row?

```
Sum Num Of Sales := SUMX ( Sales, COUNTROWS ( Sales ) )
```

Do not rush in deciding your answer. Take your time, study this simple code carefully, and make an educated guess. In the following paragraph we provide the correct answer.

The filter context is filtering Contoso. From the previous examples, it is understood that *SUMX* iterates 37,984 times. For each of these 37,984 rows, *SUMX* computes the number of rows visible in *Sales* in the current filter context. The filter context is still the same, so for each row the result of *COUNTROWS* is always 37,984. Consequently, *SUMX* sums the value of 37,984 for 37,984 times. The result is 37,984 squared. You can confirm this by looking at Figure 5-33, where the measure is displayed in the report.

Brand	NumOfSales	Sum Num Of Sales
A. Datum	4,921	24,216,241
Adventure Works	7,819	61,136,761
Contoso	37,984	1,442,784,256
Fabrikam	7,861	61,795,321
Litware	7,214	52,041,796
Northwind Traders	1,636	2,676,496
Proseware	6,673	44,528,929
Southridge Video	10,658	113,592,964
Tailspin Toys	7,571	57,320,041
The Phone Company	3,106	9,647,236
Wide World Importers	4,788	22,924,944
Total	**100,231**	**10,046,253,361**

FIGURE 5-33 *Sum Num Of Sales* computes *NumOfSales* squared because it counts all the rows for each iteration.

Now that we have refreshed the main ideas about row context and filter context, we can further discuss the impact of context transition.

Introducing context transition

A row context exists whenever an iteration is happening on a table. Inside an iteration are expressions that depend on the row context itself. The following expression, which you have studied multiple times by now, comes in handy:

```
Sales Amount :=
SUMX (
    Sales,
    Sales[Quantity] * Sales[Unit Price]
)
```

The two columns *Quantity* and *Unit Price* have a value in the current row context. In the previous section we showed that if the expression used inside an iteration is not strictly bound to the row context, then it is evaluated in the filter context. As such the results are surprising, at least for beginners. Nevertheless, one is completely free to use any function inside a row context. Among the many functions available, one appears to be more special: *CALCULATE*.

If executed in a row context, *CALCULATE* invalidates the row context before evaluating its expression. Inside the expression evaluated by *CALCULATE*, all the previous row contexts will no longer be valid. Thus, the following code produces a syntax error:

```
Sales Amount :=
SUMX (
    Sales,
    CALCULATE ( Sales[Quantity] )    -- No row context inside CALCULATE, ERROR !
)
```

The reason is that the value of the *Sales[Quantity]* column cannot be retrieved inside *CALCULATE* because *CALCULATE* invalidates the row context that exists outside of *CALCULATE* itself. Nevertheless, this is only part of what context transition performs. The second—and most relevant—operation is that *CALCULATE* adds as filter arguments all the columns of the current row context with their current value. For example, look at the following code:

```
Sales Amount :=
SUMX (
    Sales,
    CALCULATE ( SUM ( Sales[Quantity] ) ) -- SUM does not require a row context
)
```

There are no filter arguments in *CALCULATE*. The only *CALCULATE* argument is the expression to evaluate. Thus, it looks like *CALCULATE* will not overwrite the existing filter context. The point is that *CALCULATE*, because of context transition, is silently creating many filter arguments. It creates a filter for each column in the iterated table. You can use Figure 5-34 to obtain a first look at the behavior of context transition. We used a reduced set of columns for visual purposes.

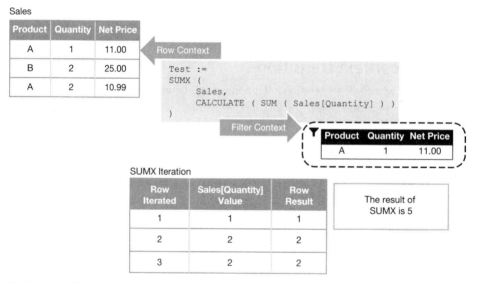

FIGURE 5-34 When *CALCULATE* is executed in a row context, it creates a filter context with a filter for each of the columns in the currently iterated table.

During the iteration *CALCULATE* starts on the first row, and it computes *SUM (Sales[Quantity])*. Even though there are no filter arguments, *CALCULATE* adds one filter argument for each of the columns of the iterated table. Namely, there are three columns in the example: *Product*, *Quantity*, and *Net Price*. As a result, the filter context generated by the context transition contains the current value (A, 1, 11.00) for each of the columns (*Product*, *Quantity*, *Net Price*). The process, of course, continues for each one of the three rows during the iteration made by *SUMX*.

In other words, the execution of the previous *SUMX* results in these three *CALCULATE* executions:

```
CALCULATE (
    SUM ( Sales[Quantity] ),
    Sales[Product] = "A",
    Sales[Quantity] = 1,
    Sales[Net Price] = 11
) +
CALCULATE (
    SUM ( Sales[Quantity] ),
    Sales[Product] = "B",
    Sales[Quantity] = 2,
    Sales[Net Price] = 25
) +
CALCULATE (
    SUM ( Sales[Quantity] ),
    Sales[Product] = "A",
    Sales[Quantity] = 2,
    Sales[Net Price] = 10.99
)
```

These filter arguments are hidden. They are added by the engine automatically, and there is no way to avoid them. In the beginning, context transition seems very strange. Nevertheless, once one gets used to context transition, it is an extremely powerful feature. Hard to master, but extremely powerful.

We summarize the considerations presented earlier, before we further discuss a few of them specifically:

- **Context transition is expensive.** If context transition is used during an iteration on a table with 10 columns and one million rows, then *CALCULATE* needs to apply 10 filters, one million times. No matter what, it will be a slow operation. This is not to say that relying on context transition should be avoided. However, it does make *CALCULATE* a feature that needs to be used carefully.

- **Context transition does not only filter one row.** The original row context existing outside of *CALCULATE* always only points to one row. The row context iterates on a row-by-row basis. When the row context is moved to a filter context through context transition, the newly created filter context filters all the rows with the same set of values. Thus, you should not assume that the context transition creates a filter context with one row only. This is very important, and we will return to this topic in the next sections.

- **Context transition uses columns that are not present in the formula.** Although the columns used in the filter are hidden, they are part of the expression. This makes any formula with *CALCULATE* much more complex than it first seems. If a context transition is used, then all the columns of the table are part of the expression as hidden filter arguments. This behavior might create unexpected dependencies. This topic is also described later in this section.

- **Context transition creates a filter context out of a row context.** You might remember the evaluation context mantra, "the row context iterates a table, whereas the filter context filters the model." Once context transition transforms a row context into a filter context, it changes the nature of the filter. Instead of iterating a single row, DAX filters the whole model; relationships become part of the equation. In other words, context transition happening on one table might propagate its filtering effects far from the table the row context originated from.

- **Context transition is invoked whenever there is a row context.** For example, if one uses *CALCULATE* in a calculated column, context transition occurs. There is an automatic row context inside a calculated column, and this is enough for context transition to occur.

- **Context transition transforms all the row contexts.** When nested iterations are being performed on multiple tables, context transition considers all the row contexts. It invalidates all of them and adds filter arguments for all the columns that are currently being iterated by all the active row contexts.

- **Context transition invalidates the row contexts.** Though we have repeated this concept multiple times, it is worth bringing to your attention again. None of the outer row contexts are valid inside the expression evaluated by *CALCULATE*. All the outer row contexts are transformed into equivalent filter contexts.

As anticipated earlier in this section, most of these considerations require further explanation. In the remaining part of this section about context transition, we provide a deeper analysis of these main points. Although all these considerations are shown as warnings, in reality they are important features. Being ignorant of certain behaviors can ensure surprising results. Nevertheless, once you master the behavior, you start leveraging it as you see fit. The only difference between a strange behavior and a useful feature—at least in DAX—is your level of knowledge.

Context transition in calculated columns

A calculated column is evaluated in a row context. Therefore, using *CALCULATE* in a calculated column triggers a context transition. We use this feature to create a calculated column in *Product* that marks as "High Performance" all the products that—alone—sold more than 1% of the total sales of all the products.

To produce this calculated column, we need two values: the sales of the current product and the total sales of all the products. The former requires filtering the *Sales* table so that it only computes sales amount for the current product, whereas the latter requires scanning the *Sales* table with no active filters. Here is the code:

```
'Product'[Performance] =
VAR TotalSales =                          -- Sales of all the products
    SUMX (
        Sales,                            -- Sales is not filtered
        Sales[Quantity] * Sales[Net Price]    -- thus here we compute all sales
    )
```

```
VAR CurrentSales =
    CALCULATE (                                   -- Performs context transition
        SUMX (
            Sales,                                -- Sales of the current product only
            Sales[Quantity] * Sales[Net Price]    -- thus here we compute sales of the
        )                                         -- current product only
    )
VAR Ratio = 0.01                                  -- 1% expressed as a real number
VAR Result =
    IF (
        CurrentSales >= TotalSales * Ratio,
        "High Performance product",
        "Regular product"
    )
RETURN
    Result
```

You note that there is only one difference between the two variables: *TotalSales* is executed as a regular iteration, whereas *CurrentSales* computes the same DAX code within a *CALCULATE* function. Because this is a calculated column, the row context is transformed into a filter context. The filter context propagates through the model and it reaches *Sales*, only filtering the sales of the current product.

Thus, even though the two variables look similar, their content is completely different. *TotalSales* computes the sales of all the products because the filter context in a calculated column is empty and does not filter anything. *CurrentSales* computes the sales of the current product only thanks to the context transition performed by *CALCULATE*.

The remaining part of the code is a simple *IF* statement that checks whether the condition is met and marks the product appropriately. One can use the resulting calculated column in a report like the one visible in Figure 5-35.

Performance	Sales Amount	NumOfProducts
High Performance product	3,078,318.10	4
A. Datum SLR Camera X137 Grey	725,840.28	1
Adventure Works 26" 720p LCD HDTV M140 Silver	1,303,983.46	1
Contoso Telephoto Conversion Lens X400 Silver	683,779.95	1
SV 16xDVD M360 Black	364,714.41	1
Regular product	27,513,025.88	2513
A. Datum Advanced Digital Camera M300 Azure	2,723.83	1
A. Datum Advanced Digital Camera M300 Black	5,313.82	1
A. Datum Advanced Digital Camera M300 Green	8,244.99	1
A. Datum Advanced Digital Camera M300 Grey	7,624.83	1
A. Datum Advanced Digital Camera M300 Orange	754.00	1
Total	**30,591,343.98**	**2517**

FIGURE 5-35 Only four products are marked High Performance.

In the code of the *Performance* calculated column, we used *CALCULATE* and context transition as a feature. Before moving on, we must check that we considered all the implications. The *Product* table is small, containing just a few thousand rows. Thus, performance is not an issue. The filter context generated by *CALCULATE* filters all the columns. Do we have a guarantee that *CurrentSales* only contains the sales of the current product? In this special case, the answer is yes. The reason is that each row of *Product* is unique because *Product* contains a column with a different value for each row—*ProductKey*. Consequently, the filter context generated by the context transition is guaranteed to only filter one product.

In this case, we could rely on context transition because each row of the iterated table is unique. Beware that this is not always true. We want to demonstrate that with an example that is purposely wrong. We create a calculated column, in *Sales*, containing this code:

```
Sales[Wrong Amt] =
CALCULATE (
    SUMX (
        Sales,
        Sales[Quantity] * Sales[Net Price]
    )
)
```

Being a calculated column, it runs in a row context. *CALCULATE* performs the context transition, so *SUMX* iterates all the rows in *Sales* with an identical set of values corresponding to the current row in *Sales*. The problem is that the *Sales* table does not have any column with unique values. Therefore, there is a chance that multiple identical rows exist and, if they exist, they will be filtered together. In other words, there is no guarantee that *SUMX* always iterates only one row in the *Wrong Amt* column.

If you are lucky, there are many duplicated rows, and the value computed by this calculated column is totally wrong. This way, the problem would be clearly visible and immediately recognized. In many real-world scenarios, the number of duplicated rows in tables is tiny, making these inaccurate calculations hard to spot and debug. The sample database we use in this book is no exception. Look at the report in Figure 5-36 showing the correct value for *Sales Amount* and the wrong value computed by summing the *Wrong Amt* calculated column.

Brand	Sales Amount	Wrong Amt
A. Datum	2,096,184.64	2,096,184.64
Adventure Works	4,011,112.28	4,011,112.28
Contoso	7,352,399.03	7,352,399.03
Fabrikam	5,554,015.73	5,558,757.73
Litware	3,255,704.03	3,255,704.03
Northwind Traders	1,040,552.13	1,040,552.13
Proseware	2,546,144.16	2,546,144.16
Southridge Video	1,384,413.85	1,384,413.85
Tailspin Toys	325,042.42	325,042.42
The Phone Company	1,123,819.07	1,123,819.07
Wide World Importers	1,901,956.66	1,901,956.66
Total	**30,591,343.98**	**30,596,085.98**

FIGURE 5-36 Most results are correct; only two rows have different values.

You can see that the difference only exists at the total level and for the Fabrikam brand. There are some duplicates in the *Sales* table—related to some Fabrikam product—that perform the calculation twice. The presence of these rows might be legitimate: The same customer bought the same product in the same store on the same day in the morning and in the afternoon, but the *Sales* table only stores the date and not the time of the transaction. Because the number of duplicates is small, most numbers look correct. However, the calculation is wrong because it depends on the content of the table. Inaccurate numbers might appear at any time because of duplicated rows. The more duplicates there are, the worse the result turns out.

In this case, relying on context transition is the wrong choice. Because the table is not guaranteed to only have unique rows, context transition is not safe to use. An expert DAX coder should know this in advance. Besides, the *Sales* table might contain millions of rows; thus, this calculated column is not only wrong, it is also very slow.

Context transition with measures

Understanding context transition is very important because of another important aspect of DAX.

Every measure reference always has an implicit CALCULATE surrounding it.

Because of *CALCULATE*, a measure reference generates an implicit context transition if executed in the presence of any row context. This is why in DAX, it is important to use the correct naming convention when writing column references (always including the table name) and measure references (always without the table name). You want to be aware of any implicit context transition writing and reading a DAX expression.

This simple initial definition deserves a longer explanation with several examples. The first one is that translating a measure reference always requires wrapping the expression of the measure within a *CALCULATE* function. For example, consider the following definition of the *Sales Amount* measure and of the *Product Sales* calculated column in the *Product* table:

```
Sales Amount :=
SUMX (
    Sales,
    Sales[Quantity] * Sales[Net Price]
)

'Product'[Product Sales] = [Sales Amount]
```

The *Product Sales* column correctly computes the sum of *Sales Amount* only for the current product in the *Product* table. Indeed, expanding the *Sales Amount* measure in the definition of *Product Sales* requires the *CALCULATE* function that wraps the definition of *Sales Amount*:

```
'Product'[Product Sales] =
CALCULATE
    SUMX (
        Sales,
        Sales[Quantity] * Sales[Net Price]
    )
)
```

Without *CALCULATE*, the result of the calculated column would produce the same value for all the products. This would correspond to the sales amount of all the rows in *Sales* without any filtering by product. The presence of *CALCULATE* means that context transition occurs, producing in this case the desired result. A measure reference always calls *CALCULATE*. This is very important and can be used to write short and powerful DAX expressions. However, it could also lead to big mistakes if you forget that the context transition takes place every time the measure is called in a row context.

As a rule of thumb, you can always replace a measure reference with the expression that defines the measure wrapped inside *CALCULATE*. Consider the following definition of a measure called *Max Daily Sales*, which computes the maximum value of *Sales Amount* computed day by day:

```
Max Daily Sales :=
MAXX (
    'Date',
    [Sales Amount]
)
```

This formula is intuitive to read. However, *Sales Amount* must be computed for each date, only filtering the sales of that day. This is exactly what context transition performs. Internally, DAX replaced the *Sales Amount* measure reference with its definition wrapped by *CALCULATE*, as in the following example:

```
Max Daily Sales :=
MAXX (
    'Date',
    CALCULATE (
        SUMX (
            Sales,
            Sales[Quantity] * Sales[Net Price]
        )
    )
)
```

We will use this feature extensively in Chapter 7, "Working with iterators and *CALCULATE*," when we start writing complex DAX code to solve specific scenarios. This initial description just completes the explanation of context transition, which happens in these cases:

- When a *CALCULATE* or *CALCULATETABLE* function is called in the presence of any row context.

- When there is a measure reference in the presence of any row context because the measure reference internally executes its DAX code within a *CALCULATE* function.

This powerful behavior might lead to mistakes, mainly due to the incorrect assumption that you can replace a measure reference with the DAX code of its definition. You cannot. This could work when there are no row contexts, like in a measure, but this is not possible when the measure reference appears within a row context. It is easy to forget this rule, so we provide an example of what could happen by making an incorrect assumption.

You may have noticed that in the previous example, we wrote the code for a calculated column repeating the iteration over *Sales* twice. Here is the code we already presented in the previous example:

```
'Product'[Performance] =
VAR TotalSales =                           -- Sales of all the products
    SUMX (
        Sales,                             -- Sales is not filtered
        Sales[Quantity] * Sales[Net Price] -- thus here we compute all sales
    )
VAR CurrentSales =
    CALCULATE (                            -- Performs the context transition
        SUMX (
            Sales,                         -- Sales of the current product only
            Sales[Quantity] * Sales[Net Price] -- thus here we compute sales of the
        )                                  -- current product only
    )
VAR Ratio = 0.01                           -- 1% expressed as a real number
VAR Result =
    IF (
        CurrentSales >= TotalSales * Ratio,
        "High Performance product",
        "Regular product"
    )
RETURN
    Result
```

The iteration executed by *SUMX* is the same code for the two variables: One is surrounded by *CALCULATE*, whereas the other is not. It might seem like a good idea to rewrite the code and use a measure to host the code of the iteration. This could be even more relevant in case the expression is not a simple *SUMX* but, rather, some more complex code. Unfortunately, this approach will not work because the measure reference will always include a *CALCULATE* around the expression that the measure replaced.

Imagine creating a measure, *Sales Amount*, and then a calculated column that calls the measure surrounding it—once with *CALCULATE* and once without *CALCULATE*.

```
Sales Amount :=
SUMX (
    Sales,
    Sales[Quantity] * Sales[Net Price]
)

'Product'[Performance] =
VAR TotalSales = [Sales Amount]
VAR CurrentSales = CALCULATE ( [Sales Amount] )
VAR Ratio = 0.01
VAR Result =
    IF (
        CurrentSales >= TotalSales * Ratio,
        "High Performance product",
        "Regular product"
    )
RETURN
    Result
```

Though it looked like a good idea, this calculated column does not compute the expected result. The reason is that both measure references will have their own implicit *CALCULATE* around them. Thus, *TotalSales* does not compute the sales of all the products. Instead, it only computes the sales of the current product because the hidden *CALCULATE* performs a context transition. *CurrentSales* computes the same value. In *CurrentSales*, the extra *CALCULATE* is redundant. Indeed, *CALCULATE* is already there, only because it is referencing a measure. This is more evident by looking at the code resulting by expanding the *Sales Amount* measure:

```
'Product'[Performance] =
VAR TotalSales =
CALCULATE (
    SUMX (
        Sales,
        Sales[Quantity] * Sales[Net Price]
    )
)
VAR CurrentSales =
CALCULATE (
    CALCULATE (
        SUMX (
            Sales,
            Sales[Quantity] * Sales[Net Price]
        )
    )
)
VAR Ratio = 0.01
VAR Result =
    IF (
        CurrentSales >= TotalSales * Ratio,
        "High Performance product",
        "Regular product"
    )
RETURN
    Result
```

Whenever you read a measure call in DAX, you should always read it as if *CALCULATE* were there. Because it is there. We introduced a rule in Chapter 2, "Introducing DAX," where we said that it is a best practice to always use the table name in front of columns, and never use the table name in front of measures. The reason is what we are discussing now.

When reading DAX code, it is of paramount importance that the user be immediately able to understand whether the code is referencing a measure or a column. The de facto standard that nearly every DAX coder adopts is to omit the table name in front of measures.

The automatic *CALCULATE* makes it easy to author formulas that perform complex calculations with iterations. We will use this feature extensively in Chapter 7 when we start writing complex DAX code to solve specific scenarios.

Understanding circular dependencies

When you design a data model, you should pay attention to the complex topic of circular dependencies in formulas. In this section, you learn what circular dependencies are and how to avoid them in your model. Before introducing circular dependencies, it is worth discussing simple, linear dependencies with the aid of an example. Look at the following calculated column:

```
Sales[Margin] = Sales[Net Price] - Sales[Unit Cost]
```

The new calculated column depends on two columns: *Net Price* and *Unit Cost*. This means that to compute the value of *Margin*, DAX needs to know in advance the values of the two other columns. Dependencies are an important part of the DAX model because they drive the order in which calculated columns and calculated tables are processed. In the example, *Margin* can only be computed after *Net Price* and *Unit Cost* already have a value. The coder does not need to worry about dependencies. Indeed, DAX handles them gracefully, building a complex graph that drives the order of evaluation of all its internal objects. However, it is possible to write code in such a way that circular dependencies appear in the graph. Circular dependencies happen when DAX cannot determine the order of evaluation of an expression because there is a loop in the chain of dependencies.

For example, consider two calculated columns with the following formulas:

```
Sales[MarginPct] = DIVIDE ( Sales[Margin], Sales[Unit Cost] )
Sales[Margin] = Sales[MarginPct] * Sales[Unit Cost]
```

In this code, *MarginPct* depends on *Margin* and, at the same time, *Margin* depends on *MarginPct*. There is a loop in the chain of dependencies. In that scenario, DAX refuses to accept the last formula and raises the error, "A circular dependency was detected."

Circular dependencies do not happen frequently because as humans we understand the problem well. B cannot depend on A if, at the same time, A depends on B. Nevertheless, there is a scenario where circular dependency occurs—not because it is one's intention to do so, but only because one does not consider certain implications by reading DAX code. This scenario includes the use of *CALCULATE*.

Imagine a calculated column in *Sales* with the following code:

```
Sales[AllSalesQty] = CALCULATE ( SUM ( Sales[Quantity] ) )
```

The interesting question is, which columns does *AllSalesQty* depend on? Intuitively, one would answer that the new column depends solely on *Sales[Quantity]* because it is the only column used in the expression. However, it is all too easy to forget the real semantics of *CALCULATE* and context transition. Because *CALCULATE* runs in a row context, all current values of all the columns of the table are included in the expression, though hidden. Thus, the real expression evaluated by DAX is the following:

```
Sales[AllSalesQty] =
CALCULATE (
    SUM ( Sales[Quantity] ),
    Sales[ProductKey] = <CurrentValueOfProductKey>,
    Sales[StoreKey] = <CurrentValueOfStoreKey>,
    ...,
    Sales[Margin] = <CurrentValueOfMargin>
)
```

As you see, the list of columns *AllSalesQty* depends on is actually the full set of columns of the table. Once *CALCULATE* is being used in a row context, the calculation suddenly depends on all the columns of the iterated table. This is much more evident in calculated columns, where the row context is present by default.

If one authors a single calculated column using *CALCULATE*, everything still works fine. The problem appears if one tries to author two separate calculated columns in a table, with both columns using *CALCULATE*, thus firing context transition in both cases. In fact, the following new calculated column will fail:

```
Sales[NewAllSalesQty] = CALCULATE ( SUM ( Sales[Quantity] ) )
```

The reason for this is that *CALCULATE* adds all the columns of the table as filter arguments. Adding a new column to a table changes the definition of existing columns too. If one were able to create *NewAllSalesQty*, the code of the two calculated columns would look like this:

```
Sales[AllSalesQty] =
CALCULATE (
    SUM ( Sales[Quantity] ),
    Sales[ProductKey] = <CurrentValueOfProductKey>,
    ...,
    Sales[Margin] = <CurrentValueOfMargin>,
    Sales[NewAllSalesQty] = <CurrentValueOfNewAllSalesQty>
)

Sales[NewAllSalesQty] =
CALCULATE (
    SUM ( Sales[Quantity] ),
    Sales[ProductKey] = <CurrentValueOfProductKey>,
    ...,
    Sales[Margin] = <CurrentValueOfMargin>,
    Sales[AllSalesQty] = <CurrentValueOfAllSalesQty>
)
```

You can see that the two highlighted rows reference each other. *AllSalesQty* depends on the value of *NewAllSalesQty* and, at the same time, *NewAllSalesQty* depends on the value of *AllSalesQty*. Although very well hidden, a circular dependency does exist. DAX detects the circular dependency, preventing the code from being accepted.

The problem, although somewhat complex to detect, has a simple solution. If the table on which *CALCULATE* performs the context transition contains one column with unique values and DAX is aware of that, then the context transition only filters that column from a dependency point of view.

For example, consider a calculated column in the *Product* table with the following code:

```
'Product'[ProductSales] = CALCULATE ( SUM ( Sales[Quantity] ) )
```

In this case, there is no need to add all the columns as filter arguments. In fact, *Product* contains one column that has a unique value for each row of the *Product* table—that is *ProductKey*. This is well-known by the DAX engine because that column is on the one-side of a one-to-many relationship. Consequently, when the context transition occurs, the engine knows that it would be pointless to add a filter to each column. The code would be translated into the following:

```
'Product'[ProductSales] =
CALCULATE (
    SUM ( Sales[Quantity] ),
    'Product'[ProductKey] = <CurrentValueOfProductKey>
)
```

As you can see, the *ProductSales* calculated column in the *Product* table depends solely on *Product-Key*. Therefore, one could create many calculated columns using *CALCULATE* because all of them would only depend on the column with unique values.

> **Note** The last *CALCULATE* equivalent statement for the context transition is not totally accurate. We used it for educational purposes only. *CALCULATE* adds all the columns of the table as filter arguments, even if a row identifier is present. Nevertheless, the internal dependency is only created on the unique column. The presence of the unique column lets DAX evaluate multiple columns with *CALCULATE*. Still, the semantics of *CALCULATE* is the same with or without the unique column: All the columns of the iterated table are added as filter arguments.

We already discussed the fact that relying on context transition on a table that contains duplicates is a serious problem. The presence of circular dependencies is another very good reason why one should avoid using *CALCULATE* and context transition whenever the uniqueness of rows is not guaranteed.

Resorting to a column with unique values for each row is not enough to ensure that *CALCULATE* only depends on it for the context transition. The data model must be aware of that. How does DAX know that a column contains unique values? There are multiple ways to provide this information to the engine:

- When a table is the target (one-side) of a relationship, then the column used to build the relationship is marked as unique. This technique works in any tool.

- When a column is selected in the *Mark As Date Table* setting, then the column is implicitly unique—more on this in Chapter 8, "Time intelligence calculations."

- You can manually set the property of a row identifier for the unique column by using the Table Behavior properties. This technique only works in Power Pivot for Excel and Analysis Services Tabular; it is not available in Power BI at the time of writing.

Any one of these operations informs the DAX engine that the table has a row identifier, stopping the process of a table that does not respect that constraint. When a table has a row identifier, you can use *CALCULATE* without worrying about circular dependencies. The reason is that the context transition depends on the key column only.

> **Note** Though described as a feature, this behavior is actually a side effect of an optimization. The semantics of DAX require the dependency from all the columns. A specific optimization introduced very early in the engine only creates the dependency on the primary key of the table. Because many users rely on this behavior today, it has become part of the language. Still, it remains an optimization. In borderline scenarios—for example when using *USERELATIONSHIP* as part of the formula—the optimization does not kick in, thus recreating the circular dependency error.

CALCULATE modifiers

As you have learned in this chapter, *CALCULATE* is extremely powerful and produces complex DAX code. So far, we have only covered filter arguments and context transition. There is still one concept required to provide the set of rules to fully understand *CALCULATE*. It is the concept of *CALCULATE modifier*.

We introduced two modifiers earlier, when we talked about *ALL* and *KEEPFILTERS*. While *ALL* can be both a modifier and a table function, *KEEPFILTERS* is always a filter argument modifier—meaning that it changes the way one filter is merged with the original filter context. *CALCULATE* accepts several different modifiers that change how the new filter context is prepared. However, the most important of all these modifiers is a function that you already know very well: *ALL*. When *ALL* is directly used in a *CALCULATE* filter argument, it acts as a *CALCULATE* modifier instead of being a table function. Other important modifiers include *USERELATIONSHIP*, *CROSSFILTER*, and *ALLSELECTED*, which have separate descriptions. The *ALLEXCEPT*, *ALLSELECTED*, *ALLCROSSFILTERED* and *ALLNOBLANKROW* modifiers have the same precedence rules of *ALL*.

In this section we introduce these modifiers; then we will discuss the order of precedence of the different *CALCULATE* modifiers and filter arguments. At the end, we will present the final schema of *CALCULATE* rules.

Understanding *USERELATIONSHIP*

The first *CALCULATE* modifier you learn is *USERELATIONSHIP*. *CALCULATE* can activate a relationship during the evaluation of its expression by using this modifier. A data model might contain both active and inactive relationships. One might have inactive relationships in the model because there are several relationships between two tables, and only one of them can be active.

As an example, one might have order date and delivery date stored in the *Sales* table for each order. Typically, the requirement is to perform sales analysis based on the order date, but one might need to consider the delivery date for some specific measures. In that scenario, an option is to create two relationships between *Sales* and *Date*: one based on *Order Date* and another one based on *Delivery Date*. The model looks like the one in Figure 5-37.

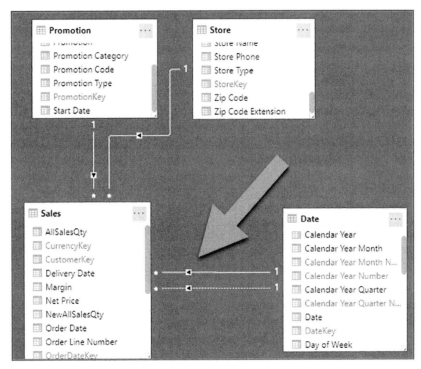

FIGURE 5-37 *Sales* and *Date* are linked through two relationships, although only one can be active.

Only one of the two relationships can be active at a time. For example, in this demo model the relationship with *Order Date* is active, whereas the one linked to *Delivery Date* is kept inactive. To author a measure that shows the delivered value in a given time period, the relationship with *Delivery Date* needs to be activated for the duration of the calculation. In this scenario, *USERELATIONSHIP* is of great help as in the following code:

```
Delivered Amount :=
CALCULATE (
    [Sales Amount],
    USERELATIONSHIP ( Sales[Delivery Date], 'Date'[Date] )
)
```

The relationship between *Delivery Date* and *Date* is activated during the evaluation of *Sales Amount*. In the meantime, the relationship with *Order Date* is deactivated. Keep in mind that at a given point in time, only one relationship can be active between any two tables. Thus, *USERELATIONSHIP* temporarily activates one relationship, deactivating the one active outside of *CALCULATE*.

Figure 5-38 shows the difference between *Sales Amount* based on the *Order Date,* and the new *Delivered Amount* measure.

Calendar Year	Sales Amount	Delivered Amount
CY 2007	**11,309,946.12**	**11,034,860.44**
January	794,248.24	624,650.61
February	891,135.91	790,981.53
March	961,289.24	992,760.62
April	1,128,104.82	1,140,575.75
May	936,192.74	839,658.92
June	982,304.46	991,050.56
July	922,542.98	1,078,819.68
August	952,834.59	776,586.75
September	1,009,868.98	1,082,690.27
October	914,273.54	901,968.98
November	825,601.87	872,217.70
December	991,548.75	942,899.08
Total	**30,591,343.98**	**30,591,343.98**

FIGURE 5-38 The figure illustrates the difference between ordered and delivered sales.

When using *USERELATIONSHIP* to activate a relationship, you need to be aware of an important aspect: Relationships are defined when a table reference is used, not when *RELATED* or other relational functions are invoked. We will cover the details of this in Chapter 14 by using expanded tables. For now, an example should suffice. To compute all amounts delivered in 2007, the following formula will not work:

```
Delivered Amount 2007 v1 :=
CALCULATE (
    [Sales Amount],
    FILTER (
        Sales,
        CALCULATE (
            RELATED ( 'Date'[Calendar Year] ),
            USERELATIONSHIP ( Sales[Delivery Date], 'Date'[Date] )
        ) = "CY 2007"
    )
)
```

In fact, *CALCULATE* would inactivate the row context generated by the *FILTER* iteration. Thus, inside the *CALCULATE* expression, one cannot use the *RELATED* function at all. One option to author the code would be the following:

```
Delivered Amount 2007 v2 :=
CALCULATE (
    [Sales Amount],
    CALCULATETABLE (
        FILTER (
            Sales,
            RELATED ( 'Date'[Calendar Year] ) = "CY 2007"
        ),
        USERELATIONSHIP (
            Sales[Delivery Date],
            'Date'[Date]
        )
    )
)
```

In this latter formulation, *Sales* is referenced after *CALCULATE* has activated the required relationship. Therefore, the use of *RELATED* inside *FILTER* happens with the relationship with *Delivery Date* active. The *Delivered Amount 2007 v2* measure works, but a much better formulation of the same measure relies on default filter context propagation rather than relying on *RELATED*:

```
Delivered Amount 2007 v3 :=
CALCULATE (
    [Sales Amount],
    'Date'[Calendar Year] = "CY 2007",
    USERELATIONSHIP (
        Sales[Delivery Date],
        'Date'[Date]
    )
)
```

When you use *USERELATIONSHIP* in a *CALCULATE* statement, all the filter arguments are evaluated using the relationship modifiers that appear in the same *CALCULATE* statement—regardless of their order. For example, in the *Delivered Amount 2007 v3* measure, the *USERELATIONSHIP* modifier affects the predicate filtering *Calendar Year*, although it is the previous parameter within the same *CALCULATE* function call.

This behavior makes the use of nondefault relationships a complex operation in calculated column expressions. The invocation of the table is implicit in a calculated column definition. Therefore, you do not have control over it, and you cannot change that behavior by using *CALCULATE* and *USERELATIONSHIP*.

One important note is the fact that *USERELATIONSHIP* does not introduce any filter by itself. Indeed, *USERELATIONSHIP* is not a filter argument. It is a *CALCULATE* modifier. It only changes the way other filters are applied to the model. If you carefully look at the definition of *Delivered Amount in 2007 v3*, you might notice that the filter argument applies a filter on the year 2007, but it does not indicate which relationship to use. Is it using *Order Date* or *Delivery Date*? The relationship to use is defined by *USERELATIONSHIP*.

Thus, *CALCULATE* first modifies the structure of the model by activating the relationship, and only later does it apply the filter argument. If that were not the case—that is, if the filter argument were always evaluated on the current relationship architecture—then the calculation would not work.

There are precedence rules in the application of filter arguments and of *CALCULATE* modifiers. The first rule is that *CALCULATE* modifiers are always applied before any filter argument, so that the effect of filter arguments is applied on the modified version of the model. We discuss precedence of *CALCULATE* arguments in more detail later.

Understanding *CROSSFILTER*

The next *CALCULATE* modifier you learn is *CROSSFILTER*. *CROSSFILTER* is somewhat similar to *USERELATIONSHIP* because it manipulates the architecture of the relationships in the model. Nevertheless, *CROSSFILTER* can perform two different operations:

- It can change the cross-filter direction of a relationship.

- It can disable a relationship.

USERELATIONSHIP lets you activate a relationship while disabling the active relationship, but it cannot disable a relationship without activating another one between the same tables. *CROSSFILTER* works in a different way. *CROSSFILTER* accepts two parameters, which are the columns involved in the relationship, and a third parameter that can be either *NONE*, *ONEWAY*, or *BOTH*. For example, the following measure computes the distinct count of product colors after activating the relationship between *Sales* and *Product* as a bidirectional one:

```
NumOfColors :=
CALCULATE (
    DISTINCTCOUNT ( 'Product'[Color] ),
    CROSSFILTER ( Sales[ProductKey], 'Product'[ProductKey], BOTH )
)
```

As is the case with *USERELATIONSHIP*, *CROSSFILTER* does not introduce filters by itself. It only changes the structure of the relationships, leaving to other filter arguments the task of applying filters. In the previous example, the effect of the relationship only affects the *DISTINCTCOUNT* function because *CALCULATE* has no further filter arguments.

Understanding *KEEPFILTERS*

We introduced *KEEPFILTERS* earlier in this chapter as a *CALCULATE* modifier. Technically, *KEEPFILTERS* is not a *CALCULATE* modifier, it is a filter argument modifier. Indeed, it does not change the entire evaluation of *CALCULATE*. Instead, it changes the way one individual filter argument is applied to the final filter context generated by *CALCULATE*.

We already discussed in depth the behavior of *CALCULATE* in the presence of calculations like the following one:

```
Contoso Sales :=
CALCULATE (
    [Sales Amount],
    KEEPFILTERS ( 'Product'[Brand] = "Contoso" )
)
```

The presence of *KEEPFILTERS* means that the filter on *Brand* does not overwrite a previously existing filter on the same column. Instead, the new filter is added to the filter context, leaving the previous one intact. *KEEPFILTERS* is applied to the individual filter argument where it is used, and it does not change the semantic of the whole *CALCULATE* function.

There is another way to use *KEEPFILTERS* that is less obvious. One can use *KEEPFILTERS* as a modifier for the table used for an iteration, like in the following code:

```
ColorBrandSales :=
SUMX (
    KEEPFILTERS ( ALL ( 'Product'[Color], 'Product'[Brand] ) ),
    [Sales Amount]
)
```

The presence of *KEEPFILTERS* as the top-level function used in an iteration forces DAX to use *KEEPFILTERS* on the implicit filter arguments added by *CALCULATE* during a context transition. In fact, during the iteration over the values of *Product[Color]* and *Product[Brand]*, *SUMX* invokes *CALCULATE* as part of the evaluation of the *Sales Amount* measure. At that point, the context transition occurs, and the row context becomes a filter context by adding a filter argument for *Color* and *Brand*.

Because the iteration started with *KEEPFILTERS*, context transition will not overwrite existing filters. It will intersect the existing filters instead. It is uncommon to use *KEEPFILTERS* as the top-level function in an iteration. We will cover some examples of this advanced use later in Chapter 10.

Understanding *ALL* in *CALCULATE*

ALL is a table function, as you learned in Chapter 3. Nevertheless, *ALL* acts as a *CALCULATE* modifier when used as a filter argument in *CALCULATE*. The function name is the same, but the semantics of *ALL* as a *CALCULATE* modifier is slightly different than what one would expect.

Looking at the following code, one might think that *ALL* returns all the years, and that it changes the filter context making all years visible:

```
All Years Sales :=
CALCULATE (
    [Sales Amount],
    ALL ( 'Date'[Year] )
)
```

However, this is not true. When used as a top-level function in a filter argument of *CALCULATE*, *ALL* removes an existing filter instead of creating a new one. A proper name for *ALL* would have been

REMOVEFILTER. For historical reasons, the name remained *ALL* and it is a good idea to know exactly how the function behaves.

If one considers *ALL* as a table function, they would interpret the *CALCULATE* behavior like in Figure 5-39.

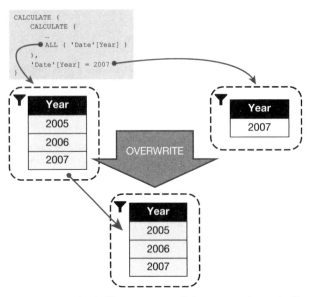

FIGURE 5-39 It looks like *ALL* returns all the years and uses the list to overwrite the previous filter context.

The innermost *ALL* over *Date[Year]* is a top-level *ALL* function call in *CALCULATE*. As such, it does not behave as a table function. It should really be read as *REMOVEFILTER*. In fact, instead of returning all the years, in that case *ALL* acts as a *CALCULATE* modifier that removes any filter from its argument. What really happens inside *CALCULATE* is the diagram of Figure 5-40.

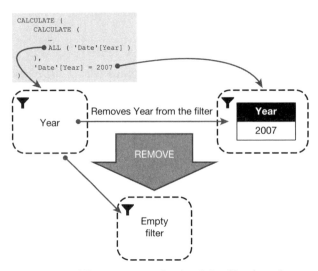

FIGURE 5-40 *ALL* removes a previously existing filter from the context, when used as *REMOVEFILTER*.

The difference between the two behaviors is subtle. In most calculations, the slight difference in semantics will go unnoticed. Nevertheless, when we start authoring more advanced code, this small difference will make a big impact. For now, the important detail is that when *ALL* is used as *REMOVE-FILTER*, it acts as a *CALCULATE* modifier instead of acting as a table function.

This is important because of the order of precedence of filters in *CALCULATE*. The *CALCULATE* modifiers are applied to the final filter context before explicit filter arguments. Thus, consider the presence of *ALL* on a column where *KEEPFILTERS* is being used on another explicit filter over that column; it produces the same result as a filter applied to that same column without *KEEPFILTERS*. In other words, the following definitions of the *Sales Red* measure produce the same result:

```
Sales Red :=
CALCULATE (
    [Sales Amount],
    'Product'[Color] = "Red"
)

Sales Red :=
CALCULATE (
    [Sales Amount],
    KEEPFILTERS ( 'Product'[Color] = "Red" ),
    ALL ( 'Product'[Color] )
)
```

The reason is that *ALL* is a *CALCULATE* modifier. Therefore, *ALL* is applied before *KEEPFILTERS*. Moreover, the same precedence rule of *ALL* is shared by other functions with the same *ALL* prefix: These are *ALL*, *ALLSELECTED*, *ALLNOBLANKROW*, *ALLCROSSFILTERED*, and *ALLEXCEPT*. We generally refer to these functions as the *ALL** functions. As a rule, *ALL** functions are *CALCULATE* modifiers when used as top-level functions in *CALCULATE* filter arguments.

Introducing *ALL* and *ALLSELECTED* with no parameters

We introduced *ALLSELECTED* in Chapter 3. We introduced it early on, mainly because of how useful it is. Like all the *ALL** functions, *ALLSELECTED* acts as a *CALCULATE* modifier when used as a top-level function in *CALCULATE*. Moreover, when introducing *ALLSELECTED,* we described it as a table function that can return the values of either a column or a table.

The following code computes a percentage over the total number of colors selected outside of the current visual. The reason is that *ALLSELECTED* restores the filter context outside of the current visual on the *Product[Color]* column.

```
SalesPct :=
DIVIDE (
    [Sales],
    CALCULATE (
        [Sales],
        ALLSELECTED ( 'Product'[Color] )
    )
)
```

One achieves a similar result using *ALLSELECTED (Product)*, which executes *ALLSELECTED* on top of a whole table. Nevertheless, when used as a *CALCULATE* modifier, both *ALL* and *ALLSELECTED* can also work without any parameter.

Thus, the following is a valid syntax:

```
SalesPct :=
DIVIDE (
    [Sales],
    CALCULATE (
        [Sales],
        ALLSELECTED ( )
    )
)
```

As you can easily notice, in this case *ALLSELECTED* cannot be a table function. It is a *CALCULATE* modifier that instructs *CALCULATE* to restore the filter context that was active outside of the current visual. The way this whole calculation works is rather complex. We will take the behavior of *ALL-SELECTED* to the next level in Chapter 14. Similarly, *ALL* with no parameters clears the filter context from all the tables in the model, restoring a filter context with no filters active.

Now that we have completed the overall structure of *CALCULATE*, we can finally discuss in detail the order of evaluation of all the elements involving *CALCULATE*.

CALCULATE rules

In this final section of a long and difficult chapter, we are now able to provide the definitive guide to *CALCULATE*. You might want to reference this section multiple times, while reading the remaining part of the book. Whenever you need to recall the complex behavior of *CALCULATE*, you will find the answer in this section.

Do not fear coming back here multiple times. We started working with DAX many years ago, and we must still remind ourselves of these rules for complex formulas. DAX is a clean and powerful language, but it is easy to forget small details here and there that are actually crucial in determining the calculation outcome of particular scenarios.

To recap, this is the overall picture of *CALCULATE*:

- *CALCULATE* is executed in an evaluation context, which contains a filter context and might contain one or more row contexts. This is the *original context*.

- *CALCULATE* creates a new filter context, in which it evaluates its first argument. This is the *new filter context*. The new filter context only contains a filter context. All the row contexts disappear in the new filter context because of the context transition.

- *CALCULATE* accepts three kinds of parameters:

  - One expression that will be evaluated in the new filter context. This is always the first argument.

  - A set of explicit filter arguments that manipulate the original filter context. Each filter argument might have a modifier, such as *KEEPFILTERS*.

  - A set of *CALCULATE* modifiers that can change the model and/or the structure of the original filter context, by removing some filters or by altering the relationships architecture.

- When the original context includes one or more row contexts, *CALCULATE* performs a context transition adding implicit and hidden filter arguments. The implicit filter arguments obtained by row contexts iterating table expressions marked as *KEEPFILTERS* are also modified by *KEEPFILTERS*.

When using all these parameters, *CALCULATE* follows a very precise algorithm. It needs to be well understood if the developer hopes to be able to make sense of certain complex calculations.

1. *CALCULATE* evaluates all the explicit filter arguments in the original evaluation context. This includes both the original row contexts (if any) and the original filter context. All explicit filter arguments are evaluated independently in the original evaluation context. Once this evaluation is finished, *CALCULATE* starts building the new filter context.

2. *CALCULATE* makes a copy of the original filter context to prepare the new filter context. It discards the original row contexts because the new evaluation context will not contain any row context.

3. *CALCULATE* performs the context transition. It uses the current value of columns in the original row contexts to provide a filter with a unique value for all the columns currently being iterated in the original row contexts. This filter may or may not contain one individual row. There is no guarantee that the new filter context contains a single row at this point. If there are no row contexts active, this step is skipped. Once all implicit filters created by the context transition are applied to the new filter context, *CALCULATE* moves on to the next step.

4. *CALCULATE* evaluates the *CALCULATE* modifiers *USERELATIONSHIP*, *CROSSFILTER*, and *ALL**. This step happens after step 3. This is very important because it means that one can remove the effects of the context transition by using *ALL*, as described in Chapter 10. The *CALCULATE* modifiers are applied after the context transition, so they can alter the effects of the context transition.

5. *CALCULATE* evaluates all the explicit filter arguments in the original filter context. It applies their result to the new filter context generated after step 4. These filter arguments are applied to the new filter context once the context transition has happened so they can overwrite it, after filter removal—their filter is not removed by any *ALL** modifier—and after the relationship architecture has been updated. However, the evaluation of filter arguments happens in the original filter context, and it is not affected by any other modifier or filter within the same *CALCULATE* function.

The filter context generated after point (5) is the new filter context used by *CALCULATE* in the evaluation of its expression.

Variables

Variables are important for at least two reasons: code readability and performance. In this chapter, we provide detailed information about variables and their usage, whereas considerations about performance and readability are found all around the book. Indeed, we use variables in almost all the code examples, sometimes showing the version with and without variables to let you appreciate how using variables improves readability.

Later in Chapter 20, "Optimizing DAX," we will also show how the use of variables can dramatically improve the performance of your code. In this chapter, we are mainly interested in providing all the useful information about variables in a single place.

Introducing *VAR* syntax

What introduces variables in an expression is first the keyword *VAR*, which defines the variable, followed by the *RETURN* part, which defines the result. You can see a typical expression containing a variable in the following code:

```
VAR SalesAmt =
    SUMX (
        Sales,
        Sales[Quantity] * Sales[Net Price]
    )
RETURN
    IF (
        SalesAmt > 100000,
        SalesAmt,
        SalesAmt * 1.2
    )
```

Adding more *VAR* definitions within the same block allows for the definition of multiple variables, whereas the *RETURN* block needs to be unique. It is important to note that the *VAR/RETURN* block is, indeed, an expression. As such, a variable definition makes sense wherever an expression can be used. This makes it possible to define variables during an iteration, or as part of more complex expressions, like in the following example:

```
VAR SalesAmt =
    SUMX (
        Sales,
```

```
        VAR Quantity = Sales[Quantity]
        VAR Price = Sales[Price]
        RETURN
            Quantity * Price
    )
RETURN
    ...
```

Variables are commonly defined at the beginning of a measure definition and then used through-out the measure code. Nevertheless, this is only a writing habit. In complex expressions, defining local variables deeply nested inside other function calls is common practice. In the previous code example, the *Quantity* and *Price* variables are assigned for every row of the *Sales* table iterated by *SUMX*. These variables are not available outside of the expression executed by *SUMX* for each row.

A variable can store either a scalar value or a table. The variables can be—and often are—of a different type than the expression returned after *RETURN*. Multiple variables in the same *VAR/RETURN* block can be of different types too—scalar values or tables.

A very frequent usage of variables is to divide the calculation of a complex formula into logical steps, by assigning the result of each step to a variable. For example, in the following code variables are used to store partial results of the calculation:

```
Margin% :=
VAR SalesAmount =
    SUMX ( Sales, Sales[Quantity] * Sales[Net Price] )
VAR TotalCost =
    SUMX ( Sales, Sales[Quantity] * Sales[Unit Cost] )
VAR Margin =
    SalesAmount - TotalCost
VAR MarginPerc =
    DIVIDE ( Margin, TotalCost )
RETURN
    MarginPerc
```

The same expression without variables takes a lot more attention to read:

```
Margin% :=
DIVIDE (
    SUMX (
        Sales,
        Sales[Quantity] * Sales[Net Price]
    ) - SUMX (
            Sales,
            Sales[Quantity] * Sales[Unit Cost]
        ),
    SUMX (
        Sales,
        Sales[Quantity] * Sales[Unit Cost]
    )
)
```

Moreover, the version with variables has the advantage that each variable is only evaluated once. For example, *TotalCost* is used in two different parts of the code but, because it is defined as a variable, DAX guarantees that its evaluation only happens once.

You can write any expression after *RETURN*. However, using a single variable for the *RETURN* part is considered best practice. For example, in the previous code, it would be possible to remove the *MarginPerc* variable definition by writing *DIVIDE* right after *RETURN*. However, using *RETURN* followed by a single variable (like in the example) allows for an easy change of the value returned by the measure. This is useful when inspecting the value of intermediate steps. In our example, if the total is not correct, it would be a good idea to check the value returned in each step, by using a report that includes the measure. This means replacing *MarginPerc* with *Margin*, then with *TotalCost,* and then with *SalesAmount* in the final *RETURN*. You would execute the report each time to see the result produced in the intermediate steps.

Understanding that variables are constant

Despite its name, a DAX variable is a constant. Once assigned a value, the variable cannot be modified. For example, if a variable is assigned within an iterator, it is created and assigned for every row iterated. Moreover, the value of the variable is only available within the expression of the iterator it is defined in.

```
Amount at Current Price :=
SUMX (
    Sales,
    VAR Quantity = Sales[Quantity]
    VAR CurrentPrice = RELATED ( 'Product'[Unit Price] )
    VAR AmountAtCurrentPrice = Quantity * CurrentPrice
    RETURN
        AmountAtCurrentPrice
)
-- Any reference to Quantity, CurrentPrice, or AmountAtCurrentPrice
-- would be invalid outside of SUMX
```

Variables are evaluated once in the scope of the definition (*VAR*) and not when their value is used. For example, the following measure always returns 100% because the *SalesAmount* variable is not affected by *CALCULATE*. Its value is only computed once. Any reference to the variable name returns the same value regardless of the filter context where the variable value is used.

```
% of Product :=
VAR SalesAmount = SUMX ( Sales, Sales[Quantity] * Sales[Net Price] )
RETURN
    DIVIDE (
        SalesAmount,
        CALCULATE (
            SalesAmount,
            ALL ( 'Product' )
        )
    )
```

In this latter example, we used a variable where we should have used a measure. Indeed, if the goal is to avoid the duplication of the code of *SalesAmount* in two parts of the expression, the right solution requires using a measure instead of a variable to obtain the expected result. In the following code, the correct percentage is obtained by defining two measures:

```
Sales Amount :=
SUMX ( Sales, Sales[Quantity] * Sales[Net Price] )

% of Product :=
DIVIDE (
    [Sales Amount],
    CALCULATE (
        [Sales Amount],
        ALL ( 'Product' )
    )
)
```

In this case the *Sales Amount* measure is evaluated twice, in two different filter contexts—leading as expected to two different results.

Understanding the scope of variables

Each variable definition can reference the variables previously defined within the same *VAR/RETURN* statement. All the variables already defined in outer *VAR* statements are also available.

A variable definition can access the variables defined in previous *VAR* statements, but not the variables defined in following statements. Thus, this code works fine:

```
Margin :=
VAR SalesAmount =
    SUMX ( Sales, Sales[Quantity] * Sales[Net Price] )
VAR TotalCost =
    SUMX ( Sales, Sales[Quantity] * Sales[Unit Cost] )
VAR Margin = SalesAmount - TotalCost
RETURN
    Margin
```

Whereas if one moves the definition of *Margin* at the beginning of the list, as in the following example, DAX will not accept the syntax. Indeed, *Margin* references two variables that are not yet defined—*SalesAmount* and *TotalCost*:

```
Margin :=
VAR Margin = SalesAmount - TotalCost -- Error: SalesAmount and TotalCost are not defined
VAR SalesAmount =
    SUMX ( Sales, Sales[Quantity] * Sales[Net Price] )
VAR TotalCost =
    SUMX ( Sales, Sales[Quantity] * Sales[Unit Cost] )
RETURN
    Margin
```

Because it is not possible to reference a variable before its definition, it is also impossible to create either a circular dependency between variables, or any sort of recursive definition.

It is possible to nest *VAR/RETURN* statements inside each other, or to have multiple *VAR/RETURN* blocks in the same expression. The scope of variables differs in the two scenarios. For example, in the following measure the two variables *LineAmount* and *LineCost* are defined in two different scopes that are not nested. Thus, at no point in the code can *LineAmount* and *LineCost* both be accessed within the same expression:

```
Margin :=
SUMX (
    Sales,
    (
        VAR LineAmount = Sales[Quantity] * Sales[Net Price]
        RETURN
            LineAmount
    ) -- The parenthesis closes the scope of LineAmount
      -- The LineAmount variable is not accessible from here on in

    _

    (
        VAR LineCost = Sales[Quantity] * Sales[Unit Cost]
        RETURN
            LineCost
    )
)
```

Clearly, this example is only for educational purposes. A better way of defining the two variables and of using them is the following definition of *Margin*:

```
Margin :=
SUMX (
    Sales,
    VAR LineAmount = Sales[Quantity] * Sales[Net Price]
    VAR LineCost = Sales[Quantity] * Sales[Unit Cost]
    RETURN
        LineAmount - LineCost
)
```

As a further educational example, it is interesting to consider the real scope where a variable is accessible when the parentheses are not used and an expression defines and reads several variables in separate *VAR/RETURN* statements. For example, consider the following code:

```
Margin :=
SUMX (
    Sales,
    VAR LineAmount = Sales[Quantity] * Sales[Net Price]
    RETURN LineAmount

        _

        VAR LineCost = Sales[Quantity] * Sales[Unit Cost]
        RETURN LineCost -- Here LineAmount is still accessible
)
```

The entire expression after the first *RETURN* is part of a single expression. Thus, the *LineCost* definition is nested within the *LineAmount* definition. Using the parentheses to delimit each *RETURN* expression and indenting the code appropriately makes this concept more visible:

```
Margin :=
SUMX (
    Sales,
    VAR LineAmount = Sales[Quantity] * Sales[Net Price]
    RETURN (
        LineAmount
        - VAR LineCost = Sales[Quantity] * Sales[Unit Cost]
          RETURN (
              LineCost
              -- Here LineAmount is still accessible
          )
    )
)
```

As shown in the previous example, because a variable can be defined for any expression, a variable can also be defined within the expression assigned to another variable. In other words, it is possible to define nested variables. Consider the following example:

```
Amount at Current Price :=
SUMX (
    'Product',
    VAR CurrentPrice = 'Product'[Unit Price]
    RETURN -- CurrentPrice is available within the inner SUMX
        SUMX (
            RELATEDTABLE ( Sales ),
            VAR Quantity = Sales[Quantity]
            VAR AmountAtCurrentPrice = Quantity * CurrentPrice
            RETURN
                AmountAtCurrentPrice
        )
        -- Any reference to Quantity, or AmountAtCurrentPrice
        -- would be invalid outside of the innermost SUMX
)
-- Any reference to CurrentPrice
-- would be invalid outside of the outermost SUMX
```

The rules pertaining to the scope of variables are the following:

- A variable is available in the *RETURN* part of its *VAR/RETURN* block. It is also available in all the variables defined after the variable itself, within that *VAR/RETURN* block. The *VAR/RETURN* block replaces any DAX expression, and in such expression the variable can be read. In other words, the variable is accessible from its declaration point until the end of the expression following the *RETURN* statement that is part of the same *VAR/RETURN* block.

- A variable is never available outside of its own *VAR/RETURN* block definition. After the expression following the *RETURN* statement, the variables declared within the *VAR/RETURN* block are no longer visible. Referencing them generates a syntax error.

Using table variables

A variable can store either a table or a scalar value. The type of the variable depends on its definition; for instance, if the expression used to define the variable is a table expression, then the variable contains a table. Consider the following code:

```
Amount :=
IF (
    HASONEVALUE ( Slicer[Factor] ),
    VAR
        Factor = VALUES ( Slicer[Factor] )
    RETURN
        DIVIDE (
            [Sales Amount],
            Factor
        )
)
```

If *Slicer[Factor]* is a column with a single value in the current filter context, then it can be used as a scalar expression. The *Factor* variable stores a table because it contains the result of *VALUES*, which is a table function. If the user does not check for the presence of a single row with *HASONEVALUE*, the variable assignment works fine; the line raising an error is the second parameter of *DIVIDE*, where the variable is used, and conversion fails.

When a variable contains a table, it is likely because one wants to iterate on it. It is important to note that, during such iteration, one should access the columns of a table variable by using their original names. In other words, a variable name is not an alias of the underlying table in column references:

```
Filtered Amount :=
VAR
    MultiSales = FILTER ( Sales, Sales[Quantity] > 1 )
RETURN
    SUMX (
        MultiSales,
        -- MultiSales is not a table name for column references
        -- Trying to access MultiSales[Quantity] would generate an error
        Sales[Quantity] * Sales[Net Price]
    )
```

Although *SUMX* iterates over *MultiSales*, you must use the *Sales* table name to access the *Quantity* and *Net Price* columns. A column reference such *as MultiSales[Quantity]* is invalid.

One current DAX limitation is that a variable cannot have the same name as any table in the data model. This prevents the possible confusion between a table reference and a variable reference. Consider the following code:

```
SUMX (
    LargeSales,
    Sales[Quantity] * Sales[NetPrice]
)
```

A human reader immediately understands that *LargeSales* should be a variable because the column references in the iterator reference another table name: *Sales*. However, DAX disambiguates at the language level through the distinctiveness of the name. A certain name can be either a table or a variable, but not both at the same time.

Although this looks like a convenient limitation because it reduces confusion, it might be problematic in the long run. Indeed, whenever you define the name of a variable, you should use a name that will never be used as a table name in the future. Otherwise, if at some point you create a new table whose name conflicts with variables used in any measure, you will obtain an error. Any syntax limitation that requires you to predict what will happen in the future—like choosing the name of a table—is an issue to say the least.

For this reason, when Power BI generates DAX queries, it uses variable names adopting a prefix with two underscores (__). The rationale is that a user is unlikely to use the same name in a data model.

 Note This behavior could change in the future, thus enabling a variable name to override the name of an existing table. When this change is implemented, there will no longer be a risk of breaking an existing DAX expression by giving a new table the name of a variable. When a variable name overrides a table name, the disambiguation will be possible by using the single quote to delimit the table identifier using the following syntax:

```
variableName
'tableName'
```

Should a developer design a DAX code generator to be injected in existing expressions, they can use the single quote to disambiguate table identifiers. This is not required in regular DAX code, if the code does not include ambiguous names between variables and tables.

Understanding lazy evaluation

As you have learned, DAX evaluates the variable within the evaluation context where it is defined, and not where it is being used. Still, the evaluation of the variable itself is delayed until its first use. This technique is known as *lazy evaluation*. Lazy evaluation is important for performance reasons: a variable that is never used in an expression will never be evaluated. Moreover, once a variable is computed for the first time, it will never be computed again in the same scope.

For example, consider the following code:

```
Sales Amount :=
VAR SalesAmount =
    SUMX ( Sales, Sales[Quantity] * Sales[Net Price] )
VAR DummyError =
    ERROR ( "This error will never be displayed" )
RETURN
    SalesAmount
```

The variable *DummyError* is never used, so its expression is never executed. Therefore, the error never happens and the measure works correctly.

Obviously, nobody would ever write code like this. The goal of the example is to show that DAX does not spend precious CPU time evaluating a variable if it is not useful to do so, and you can rely on this behavior when writing code.

If a sub-expression is used multiple times in a complex expression, then creating a variable to store its value is always a best practice. This guarantees that evaluation only happens once. Performance-wise, this is more important than you might think. We will discuss this in more detail in Chapter 20, but we cover the general idea here.

The DAX optimizer features a process called sub-formula detection. In a complex piece of code, sub-formula detection checks for repeating sub-expressions that should only be computed once. For example, look at the following code:

```
SalesAmount := SUMX ( Sales, Sales[Quantity] * Sales[Net Price] )
TotalCost   := SUMX ( Sales, Sales[Quantity] * Sales[Unit Cost] )
Margin      := [SalesAmount] – [TotalCost]
Margin%     := DIVIDE ( [Margin], [TotalCost] )
```

The *TotalCost* measure is called twice—once in *Margin* and once in *Margin%*. Depending on the quality of the optimizer, it might be able to detect that both measure calls refer to the same value, so it might be able to compute *TotalCost* only once. Nevertheless, the optimizer is not always able to detect that a sub-formula exists and that it can be evaluated only once. As a human, and being the author of your own code, you always have a much better understanding of when part of the code can be used in multiple parts of your formula.

If you get used to using variables whenever you can, defining sub-formulas as variables will come naturally. When you use their value multiple times, you will greatly help the optimizer in finding the best execution path for your code.

Common patterns using variables

In this section, you find practical uses of variables. It is not an exhaustive list of scenarios where variables become useful, and although there are many other situations where a variable would be a good fit, these are relevant and frequent uses.

The first and most relevant reason to use variables is to provide documentation in your code. A good example is when you need to use complex filters in a *CALCULATE* function. Using variables as *CALCULATE* filters only improves readability. It does not change semantics or performance. Filters would be executed outside of the context transition triggered by *CALCULATE* in any case, and DAX also uses lazy evaluation for filter contexts. Nevertheless, improving readability is an important task for any DAX developer. For example, consider the following measure definition:

```
Sales Large Customers :=
VAR LargeCustomers =
    FILTER (
        Customer,
        [Sales Amount] > 10000
    )
VAR WorkingDaysIn2008 =
    CALCULATETABLE (
        ALL ( 'Date'[IsWorkingDay], 'Date'[Calendar Year] ),
        'Date'[IsWorkingDay] = TRUE (),
        'Date'[Calendar Year] = "CY 2008"
    )
RETURN
    CALCULATE (
        [Sales Amount],
        LargeCustomers,
        WorkingDaysIn2008
    )
```

Using the two variables for the filtered customers and the filtered dates splits the full execution flow into three distinct parts: the definition of what a large customer is, the definition of the period one wants to consider, and the actual calculation of the measure with the two filters applied.

Although it might look like we are only talking about style, you should never forget that a more elegant and simple formula is more likely to also be an accurate formula. Writing a simpler formula, the author is more likely to have understood the code and fixed any possible flaws. Whenever an expression takes more than 10 lines of code, it is time to split its execution path with multiple variables. This allows the author to focus on smaller fragments of the full formula.

Another scenario where variables are important is when nesting multiple row contexts on the same table. In this scenario, variables let you save data from hidden row contexts and avoid the use of the *EARLIER* function:

```
'Product'[RankPrice] =
VAR CurrentProductPrice = 'Product'[Unit Price]
VAR MoreExpensiveProducts =
    FILTER (
        'Product',
        'Product'[Unit Price] > CurrentProductPrice
    )
RETURN
    COUNTROWS ( MoreExpensiveProducts ) + 1
```

Filter contexts can be nested too. Nesting multiple filter contexts does not create syntax problems as it does with multiple row contexts. One frequent scenario with nested filter contexts is needing to save the result of a calculation to use it later in the code when the filter context changes.

For example, if one needs to search for the customers who bought more than the average customer, this code is not going to work:

```
AverageSalesPerCustomer :=
AVERAGEX ( Customer, [Sales Amount] )

CustomersBuyingMoreThanAverage :=
COUNTROWS (
    FILTER (
        Customer,
        [Sales Amount] > [AverageSalesPerCustomer]
    )
)
```

The reason is that the *AverageSalesPerCustomer* measure is evaluated inside an iteration over *Customer*. As such, there is a hidden *CALCULATE* around the measure that performs a context transition. Thus, *AverageSalesPerCustomer* evaluates the sales of the current customer inside the iteration every time, instead of the average over all the customers in the filter context. There is no customer whose sales amount is strictly greater than the sales amount itself. The measure always returns blank.

To obtain the correct behavior, one needs to evaluate *AverageSalesPerCustomer* outside of the iteration. A variable fits this requirement perfectly:

```
AverageSalesPerCustomer :=
AVERAGEX ( Customer, [Sales Amount] )

CustomersBuyingMoreThanAverage :=
VAR AverageSales = [AverageSalesPerCustomer]
RETURN
    COUNTROWS (
        FILTER (
            Customer,
            [Sales Amount] > AverageSales
        )
    )
```

In this example DAX evaluates the variable outside of the iteration, computing the correct average sales for all the selected customers. Moreover, the optimizer knows that the variable can (and must) be evaluated only once, outside of the iteration. Thus, the code is likely to be faster than any other possible implementation.

Conclusions

Variables are useful for multiple reasons: readability, performance, and elegance of the code. Whenever you need to write a complex formula, split it into multiple variables. You will appreciate having done so the next time you review your code.

It is true that expressions using variables tend to be longer than the same expressions without variables. A longer expression is not a bad thing if it means that each part is easier to understand. Unfortunately, in several tools the user interface to author DAX code makes it hard to write expressions over 10 lines long. You might think that a shorter formulation of the same code without variables is preferable because it is easier to author in a specific tool—for example Power BI. That is incorrect.

We certainly need better tools to author longer DAX code that includes comments and many variables. These tools will come eventually. In the meantime, rather than authoring shorter and confusing code directly into a small text box, it is wiser to use external tools like DAX Studio to author longer DAX code. You would then copy and paste the resulting code into Power BI or Visual Studio.

Working with iterators and with *CALCULATE*

In previous chapters we provided the theoretical foundations of DAX: row context, filter context, and context transition. These are the pillars any DAX expression is built on. We already introduced iterators, and we used them in many different formulas. However, the real power of iterators starts to show when they are being used in conjunction with evaluation contexts and context transition.

In this chapter we take iterators to the next level, by describing the most common uses of iterators and by introducing many new iterators. Learning how to leverage iterators in your code is an important skill to acquire. Indeed, using iterators and context transition together is a feature that is unique to the DAX language. In our teaching experience, students usually struggle with learning the power of iterators. But that does not mean that the use of iterators is difficult to understand. The concept of iteration is simple, as is the usage of iterators in conjunction with context transition. What is hard is realizing that the solution to a complex calculation is resorting to an iteration. For this reason, we provide several examples of calculations that are simple to create with the help of iterators.

Using iterators

Most iterators accept at least two parameters: the table to iterate and an expression that the iterator evaluates on a row-by-row basis, in the row context generated during the iteration. A simple expression using *SUMX* will support our explanation:

```
Sales Amount :=
SUMX (
    Sales,                              -- Table to iterate
    Sales[Quantity] * Sales[Net Price]  -- Expression to evaluate row by row
)
```

SUMX iterates the *Sales* table, and for each row it computes the expression by multiplying quantity by net price. Iterators differ from one another in the use they make of the partial results gathered during the iteration. *SUMX* is a simple iterator that aggregates these results using sum.

It is important to understand the difference between the two parameters. The first argument is the value resulting from a table expression to iterate. Being a value parameter, it is evaluated before the iteration starts. The second parameter, on the other hand, is an expression that is not evaluated before the execution of *SUMX*. Instead, the iterator evaluates the expression in the row context of the iteration. The official Microsoft documentation does not provide an accurate classification of the iterator functions. More specifically, it does not indicate which parameters represent a value and which parameters represent an expression evaluated during the iteration. On https://dax.guide all the functions that evaluate an expression in a row context have a special marker (ROW CONTEXT) to identify the argument executed in a row context. Any function that has an argument marked with ROW CONTEXT is an iterator.

Several iterators accept additional arguments after the first two. For example, *RANKX* is an iterator that accepts many arguments, whereas *SUMX*, *AVERAGEX* and simple iterators only use two arguments. In this chapter we describe many iterators individually. But first, we go deeper on a few important aspects of iterators.

Understanding iterator cardinality

The first important concept to understand about iterators is the *iterator cardinality*. The cardinality of an iterator is the number of rows being iterated. For example, in the following iteration if *Sales* has one million rows, then the cardinality is one million:

```
Sales Amount :=
SUMX (
    Sales,                              -- Sales has 1M rows, as a consequence
    Sales[Quantity] * Sales[Net Price]  -- the expression is evaluated one million times
)
```

When speaking about cardinality, we seldom use numbers. In fact, the cardinality of the previous example depends on the number of rows of the *Sales* table. Thus, we prefer to say that the cardinality of the iterator is the same as the cardinality of *Sales*. The more rows in *Sales*, the higher the number of iterated rows.

In the presence of nested iterators, the resulting cardinality is a combination of the cardinality of the two iterators—up to the product of the two original tables. For example, consider the following formula:

```
Sales at List Price 1 :=
SUMX (
    'Product',
    SUMX (
        RELATEDTABLE ( Sales ),
        'Product'[Unit Price] * Sales[Quantity]
    )
)
```

In this example there are two iterators. The outer iterates *Product*. As such, its cardinality is the cardinality of *Product*. Then for each product the inner iteration scans the *Sales* table, limiting its iteration to the rows in *Sales* that have a relationship with the given product. In this case, because each row in *Sales* is pertinent to only one product, the full cardinality is the cardinality of *Sales*. If the inner table expression is not related to the outer table expression, then the cardinality becomes much higher.

For example, consider the following code. It computes the same value as the previous code, but instead of relying on relationships, it uses an *IF* function to filter the sales of the current product:

```
Sales at List Price High Cardinality :=
SUMX (
    VALUES ( 'Product' ),
    SUMX (
        Sales,
        IF (
            Sales[ProductKey] = 'Product'[ProductKey],
            'Product'[Unit Price] * Sales[Quantity],
            0
        )
    )
)
```

In this example the inner *SUMX* always iterates over the whole *Sales* table, relying on the internal IF statement to check whether the product should be considered or not for the calculation. In this case, the outer *SUMX* has the cardinality of *Product,* whereas the inner *SUMX* has the cardinality of *Sales.* The cardinality of the whole expression is *Product* times *Sales*; much higher than the first example. Be mindful that this example is for educational purposes only. It would result in bad performance if one ever used such a pattern in a DAX expression.

A better way to express this code is the following:

```
Sales at List Price 2 :=
SUMX (
    Sales,
    RELATED ( 'Product'[Unit Price] ) * Sales[Quantity]
)
```

The cardinality of the entire expression is the same as in the *Sales at List Price 1* measure, but the latter has a better execution plan. Indeed, it avoids nested iterators. Nested iterations mostly happen because of context transition. In fact, by looking at the following code, one might think that there are no nested iterators:

```
Sales at List Price 3 :=
SUMX (
    'Product',
    'Product'[Unit Price] * [Total Quantity]
)
```

However, inside the iteration there is a reference to a measure (*Total Quantity*) which we need to consider. In fact, here is the expanded definition of *Total Quantity*:

```
Total Quantity :=
SUM ( Sales[Quantity] )     -- Internally translated into SUMX ( Sales, Sales[Quantity] )

Sales at List Price 4 :=
SUMX (
    'Product',
```

```
    'Product'[Unit Price] *
        CALCULATE (
            SUMX (
                Sales,
                Sales[Quantity]
            )
        )
)
```

You can now see that there is a nested iteration—that is, a *SUMX* inside another *SUMX*. Moreover, the presence of *CALCULATE*, which performs a context transition, is also made visible.

From a performance point of view, when there are nested iterators, only the innermost iterator can be optimized with the more efficient query plan. The presence of outer iterators requires the creation of temporary tables in memory. These temporary tables store the intermediate result produced by the innermost iterator. This results in slower performance and higher memory consumption. As a consequence, nested iterators should be avoided if the cardinality of the outer iterators is very large—in the order of several million rows.

Please note that in the presence of context transition, unfolding nested iterations is not as easy as it might seem. In fact, a typical mistake is to obtain nested iterators by writing a measure that is supposed to reuse an existing measure. This could be dangerous when the existing logic of a measure is reused within an iterator. For example, consider the following calculation:

```
Sales at List Price 5 :=
SUMX (
    'Sales',
    RELATED ( 'Product'[Unit Price] ) * [Total Quantity]
)
```

The *Sales at List Price 5* measure seems identical to *Sales at List Price 3*. Unfortunately, *Sales at List Price 5* violates several of the rules of context transition outlined in Chapter 5, "Understanding *CALCULATE* and *CALCULATETABLE*": It performs context transition on a large table (*Sales*), and worse, it performs context transition on a table where the rows are not guaranteed to be unique. Consequently, the formula is slow and likely to produce incorrect results.

This is not to say that nested iterations are always bad. There are various scenarios where the use of nested iterations is convenient. In fact, in the rest of this chapter we show many examples where nested iterators are a powerful tool to use.

Leveraging context transition in iterators

A calculation might require nested iterators, usually when it needs to compute a measure in different contexts. These are the scenarios where using context transition is powerful and allows for the concise, efficient writing of complex calculations.

For example, consider a measure that computes the maximum daily sales in a time period. The definition of the measure is important because it defines the granularity right away. Indeed, one needs to first compute the daily sales in the given period, then find the maximum value in the list of computed values. Even though it would seem intuitive to create a table containing daily sales and then use *MAX* on it, in DAX you are not required to build such a table. Instead, iterators are a convenient way of obtaining the desired result without any additional table.

The idea of the algorithm is the following:

- Iterate over the *Date* table.

- Compute the sales amount for each day.

- Find the maximum of all the values computed in the previous step.

You can write this measure by using the following approach:

```
Max Daily Sales 1 :=
MAXX (
    'Date',
    VAR DailyTransactions =
        RELATEDTABLE ( Sales )
    VAR DailySales =
        SUMX (
            DailyTransactions,
            Sales[Quantity] * Sales[Net Price]
        )
    RETURN
        DailySales
)
```

However, a simpler approach is the following, which leverages the implicit context transition of the measure *Sales Amount*:

```
Sales Amount :=
SUMX (
    Sales,
    Sales[Quantity] * Sales[Net Price]
)

Max Daily Sales 2 :=
MAXX (
    'Date',
    [Sales Amount]
)
```

In both cases there are two nested iterators. The outer iteration happens on the *Date* table, which is expected to contain a few hundred rows. Moreover, each row in *Date* is unique. Thus, both calculations are safe and quick. The former version is more complete, as it outlines the full algorithm. On the other hand, the second version of *Max Daily Sales* hides many details and makes the code more readable, leveraging context transition to move the filter from *Date* over to *Sales*.

You can view the result of this measure in Figure 7-1 that shows the maximum daily sales for each month.

Calendar Year	Sales Amount	Max Daily Sales
CY 2007	**11,309,946.12**	**126,742.18**
January	794,248.24	92,244.07
February	891,135.91	108,923.95
March	961,289.24	122,503.54
April	1,128,104.82	126,742.18
May	936,192.74	102,857.58
June	982,304.46	77,082.30
July	922,542.98	124,176.88
August	952,834.59	85,114.89
September	1,009,868.98	102,588.78
October	914,273.54	81,926.23
November	825,601.87	71,959.23
December	991,548.75	101,708.68

FIGURE 7-1 The report shows the *Max Daily Sales* measure computed by month and year.

By leveraging context transition and an iteration, the code is usually more elegant and intuitive to write. The only issue you should be aware of is the cost involved in context transition: it is a good idea to avoid measure references in large iterators.

By looking at the report in Figure 7-1, a logical question is: When did sales hit their maximum? For example, the report is indicating that in one certain day in January 2007, Contoso sold 92,244.07 USD. But in which day did it happen? Iterators and context transition are powerful tools to answer this question. Look at the following code:

```
Date of Max =
VAR MaxDailySales = [Max Daily Sales]
VAR DatesWithMax =
    FILTER (
        VALUES ( 'Date'[Date] ),
        [Sales Amount] = MaxDailySales
    )
VAR Result =
    IF (
        COUNTROWS ( DatesWithMax ) = 1,
        DatesWithMax,
        BLANK ()
    )
RETURN
    Result
```

The formula first stores the value of the *Max Daily Sales* measure into a variable. Then, it creates a temporary table containing the dates where sales equals *MaxDailySales*. If there is only one date when this happened, then the result is the only row which passed the filter. If there are multiple dates, then the formula blanks its result, showing that a single date cannot be determined. You can look at the result of this code in Figure 7-2.

Calendar Year	Sales Amount	Max Daily Sales	Date of Max
CY 2007	**11,309,946.12**	**126,742.18**	**04/21/2007**
January	794,248.24	92,244.07	01/03/2007
February	891,135.91	108,923.95	02/03/2007
March	961,289.24	122,503.54	03/15/2007
April	1,128,104.82	126,742.18	04/21/2007
May	936,192.74	102,857.58	05/14/2007
June	982,304.46	77,082.30	06/27/2007
July	922,542.98	124,176.88	07/11/2007
August	952,834.59	85,114.89	08/11/2007
September	1,009,868.98	102,588.78	09/06/2007
October	914,273.54	81,926.23	10/12/2007
November	825,601.87	71,959.23	11/22/2007
December	991,548.75	101,708.68	12/01/2007

FIGURE 7-2 The *Date of Max* measures make it clear which unique date generated the maximum sales.

The use of iterators in DAX requires you to always define, in this order:

■ The granularity at which you want the calculation to happen,

■ The expression to evaluate at the given granularity,

■ The kind of aggregation to use.

In the previous example (*Max Daily Sales 2*) the granularity is the date, the expression is the amount of sales, and the aggregation to use is *MAX*. The result is the maximum daily sales.

There are several scenarios where the same pattern can be useful. Another example could be displaying the average customer sales. If you think about it in terms of iterators using the pattern described above, you obtain the following: Granularity is the individual customer, the expression to use is sales amount, and the aggregation is *AVERAGE*.

Once you follow this mental process, the formula is short and easy:

```
Avg Sales by Customer :=
AVERAGEX ( Customer, [Sales Amount] )
```

With this simple formula, one can easily build powerful reports like the one in Figure 7-3 that shows the average sales per customer by continent and year.

Continent	CY 2007	CY 2008	CY 2009	Total
Asia	2,503.71	3,647.64	7,732.60	**4,972.51**
Europe	1,306.95	2,458.10	1,836.57	**2,253.27**
North America	1,090.43	2,543.29	3,887.40	**2,223.02**
Total	**1,413.92**	**2,841.32**	**3,420.04**	**2,770.70**

FIGURE 7-3 The *Avg Sales by Customer* measure computed by year and by continent.

Context transition in iterators is a powerful tool. It can also be expensive, so always checking the cardinality of the outer iterator is a good practice. This will result in more efficient DAX code.

Using *CONCATENATEX*

In this section, we show a convenient usage of *CONCATENATEX* to display the filters applied to a report in a user-friendly way. Suppose you build a simple visual that shows sales sliced by year and continent, and you put it in a more complex report where the user has the option of filtering colors using a slicer. The slicer might be near the visual or it might be in a different page.

If the slicer is in a different page, then looking at the visual, it is not clear whether the numbers displayed are a subset of the whole dataset or not. In that case it would be useful to add a label to the report, showing the selection made by the user in textual form as in Figure 7-4.

Continent	CY 2007	CY 2008	CY 2009	Total
Asia	1,125,060.75	1,708,318.19	1,216,841.47	**4,050,220.41**
Europe	1,062,029.30	912,736.27	981,869.39	**2,956,634.96**
North America	1,148,462.69	1,321,175.78	1,251,710.25	**3,721,348.72**
Total	**3,335,552.74**	**3,942,230.25**	**3,450,421.10**	**10,728,204.09**

Showing Black, Blue, Brown, Green colors.

FIGURE 7-4 The label at the bottom of the visual indicates which filters are being applied.

One can inspect the values of the selected colors by querying the *VALUES* function. Nevertheless, *CONCATENATEX* is required to convert the resulting table into a string. Look at the definition of the *Selected Colors* measure, which we used to show the colors in Figure 7-4:

```
Selected Colors :=
"Showing " &
CONCATENATEX (
    VALUES ( 'Product'[Color] ),
    'Product'[Color],
    ", ",
```

```
    'Product'[Color],
    ASC
) & " colors."
```

CONCATENATEX iterates over the values of product color and creates a string containing the list of these colors separated by a comma. As you can see, *CONCATENATEX* accepts multiple parameters. As usual, the first two are the table to scan and the expression to evaluate. The third parameter is the string to use as the separator between expressions. The fourth and the fifth parameters indicate the sort order and its direction (*ASC* or *DESC*).

The only drawback of this measure is that if there is no selection on the color, it produces a long list with all the colors. Moreover, in the case where there are more than five colors, the list would be too long anyway and the user experience sub-optimal. Nevertheless, it is easy to fix both problems by making the code slightly more complex to detect these situations:

```
Selected Colors :=
VAR Colors =
    VALUES ( 'Product'[Color] )
VAR NumOfColors =
    COUNTROWS ( Colors )
VAR NumOfAllColors =
    COUNTROWS (
        ALL ( 'Product'[Color] )
    )
VAR AllColorsSelected = NumOfColors = NumOfAllColors
VAR SelectedColors =
    CONCATENATEX (
        Colors,
        'Product'[Color],
        ", ",
        'Product'[Color], ASC
    )
VAR Result =
    IF (
        AllColorsSelected,
        "Showing all colors.",
        IF (
            NumOfColors > 5,
            "More than 5 colors selected, see slicer page for details.",
            "Showing " & SelectedColors & " colors."
        )
    )
RETURN
    Result
```

In Figure 7-5 you can see two results for the same visual, with different selections for the colors. With this latter version, it is much clearer whether the user needs to look at more details or not about the color selection.

Continent	CY 2007	CY 2008	CY 2009	Total
Asia	1,156,160.73	1,738,396.65	1,274,148.22	**4,168,705.60**
Europe	1,138,376.83	973,048.39	1,023,358.17	**3,134,783.39**
North America	1,202,649.32	1,386,848.85	1,294,102.82	**3,883,600.99**
Total	**3,497,186.88**	**4,098,293.89**	**3,591,609.21**	**11,187,089.99**

More than 5 colors selected, see slicer page for details.

Continent	CY 2007	CY 2008	CY 2009	Total
Asia	3,532,732.93	3,713,296.91	3,479,670.07	**10,725,699.91**
Europe	3,582,341.75	2,391,726.88	2,694,249.12	**8,668,317.75**
North America	4,194,871.44	3,822,559.21	3,179,895.68	**11,197,326.32**
Total	**11,309,946.12**	**9,927,582.99**	**9,353,814.87**	**30,591,343.98**

Showing all colors

FIGURE 7-5 Depending on the filters, the label now shows user-friendly descriptions of the filtering.

This latter version of the measure is not perfect yet. In the case where the user selects five colors, but only four are present in the current selection because other filters hide some colors, then the measure does not report the complete list of colors. It only reports the existing list. In Chapter 10, "Working with the filter context," we describe a different version of this measure that addresses this last detail. In fact, to author the final version, we first need to describe a set of new functions that aim at investigating the content of the current filter context.

Iterators returning tables

So far, we have described iterators that aggregate an expression. There are also iterators that return a table produced by merging a source table with one or more expressions evaluated in the row context of the iteration. *ADDCOLUMNS* and *SELECTCOLUMNS* are the most interesting and useful. They are the topic of this section.

As its name implies, *ADDCOLUMNS* adds new columns to the table expression provided as the first parameter. For each added column, *ADDCOLUMNS* requires knowing the column name and the expression that defines it.

For example, you can add two columns to the list of colors, including for each color the number of products and the value of *Sales Amount* in two new columns:

```
Colors =
ADDCOLUMNS (
    VALUES ( 'Product'[Color] ),
    "Products", CALCULATE ( COUNTROWS ( 'Product' ) ),
    "Sales Amount", [Sales Amount]
)
```

The result of this code is a table with three columns: the product color, which is coming from the values of *Product[Color]*, and the two new columns added by *ADDCOLUMNS* as you can see in Figure 7-6.

Color	Sales Amount	Products
Azure	97,389.89	14
Black	5,860,066.14	602
Blue	2,435,444.62	200
Brown	1,029,508.95	77
Gold	361,496.01	50
Green	1,403,184.38	74
Grey	3,509,138.09	283
Orange	857,320.28	55
Pink	828,638.54	84
Purple	5,973.84	6
Red	1,110,102.10	99
Silver	6,798,560.86	417
Silver Grey	371,908.92	14
Transparent	3,295.89	1
White	5,829,599.91	505
Yellow	89,715.56	36

FIGURE 7-6 The *Sales Amount* and *Products* columns are computed by *ADDCOLUMNS*.

ADDCOLUMNS returns all the columns of the table expression it iterates, adding the requested columns. To keep only a subset of the columns of the original table expression, an option is to use *SELECTCOLUMNS*, which only returns the requested columns. For instance, you can rewrite the previous example of *ADDCOLUMNS* by using the following query:

```
Colors =
SELECTCOLUMNS (
    VALUES ( 'Product'[Color] ),
    "Color", 'Product'[Color],
    "Products", CALCULATE ( COUNTROWS ( 'Product' ) ),
    "Sales Amount", [Sales Amount]
)
```

The result is the same, but you need to explicitly include the *Color* column of the original table to obtain the same result. *SELECTCOLUMNS* is useful whenever you need to reduce the number of columns of a table, oftentimes resulting from some partial calculations.

ADDCOLUMNS and SELECTCOLUMNS are useful to create new tables, as you have seen in this first example. These functions are also often used when authoring measures to make the code easier and faster. As an example, look at the measure, defined earlier in this chapter, that aims at finding the date with the maximum daily sales:

```
Max Daily Sales :=
MAXX (
    'Date',
    [Sales Amount]
)

Date of Max :=
VAR MaxDailySales = [Max Daily Sales]
VAR DatesWithMax =
    FILTER (
        VALUES ( 'Date'[Date] ),
        [Sales Amount] = MaxDailySales
    )
VAR Result =
    IF (
        COUNTROWS ( DatesWithMax ) = 1,
        DatesWithMax,
        BLANK ()
    )
RETURN
    Result
```

If you look carefully at the code, you will notice that it is not optimal in terms of performance. In fact, as part of the calculation of the variable *MaxDailySales*, the engine needs to compute the daily sales to find the maximum value. Then, as part of the second variable evaluation, it needs to compute the daily sales again to find the dates when the maximum sales happened. Thus, the engine performs two iterations on the *Date* table, and each time it computes the sales amount for each date. The DAX optimizer might be smart enough to understand that it can compute the daily sales only once, and then use the previous result the second time you need it, but this is not guaranteed to happen. Nevertheless, by refactoring the code leveraging *ADDCOLUMNS*, one can write a faster version of the same measure. This is achieved by first preparing a table with the daily sales and storing it into a variable, then using this first—partial—result to compute both the maximum daily sales and the date with the maximum sales:

```
Date of Max :=
VAR DailySales =
    ADDCOLUMNS (
        VALUES ( 'Date'[Date] ),
        "Daily Sales", [Sales Amount]
    )
VAR MaxDailySales = MAXX ( DailySales, [Daily Sales] )
VAR DatesWithMax =
    SELECTCOLUMNS (
        FILTER (
            DailySales,
            [Daily Sales] = MaxDailySales
```

```
        ),
        "Date", 'Date'[Date]
    )
VAR Result =
IF (
    COUNTROWS ( DatesWithMax ) = 1,
    DatesWithMax,
    BLANK ()
)
RETURN
    Result
```

The algorithm is close to the previous one, with some noticeable differences:

■ The *DailySales* variable contains a table with date, and sales amount on each given date. This table is created by using *ADDCOLUMNS*.

■ *MaxDailySales* no longer computes the daily sales. It scans the precomputed *DailySales* variable, resulting in faster execution time.

■ The same happens with *DatesWithMax*, which scans the *DailySales* variable. Because after that point the code only needs the date and no longer the daily sales, we used *SELECTCOLUMNS* to remove the daily sales from the result.

This latter version of the code is more complex than the original version. This is often the price to pay when optimizing code: Worrying about performance means having to write more complex code.

You will see *ADDCOLUMNS* and *SELECTCOLUMNS* in more detail in Chapter 12, "Working with tables," and in Chapter 13, "Authoring queries." There are many details that are important there, especially if you want to use the result of *SELECTCOLUMNS* in other iterators that perform context transition.

Solving common scenarios with iterators

In this section we continue to show examples of known iterators and we also introduce a common and useful one: *RANKX*. You start learning how to compute moving averages and the difference between using an iterator or a straight calculation for the average. Later in this section, we provide a complete description of the *RANKX* function, which is extremely useful to compute ranking based on expressions.

Computing averages and moving averages

You can calculate the mean (arithmetic average) of a set of values by using one of the following DAX functions:

■ **AVERAGE**: returns the average of all the numbers in a numeric column.

■ **AVERAGEX**: calculates the average on an expression evaluated over a table.

Note DAX also provides the *AVERAGEA* function, which returns the average of all the numbers in a text column. However, you should not use it. *AVERAGEA* only exists in DAX for Excel compatibility. The main issue of *AVERAGEA* is that when you use a text column as an argument, it does not try to convert each text row to a number as Excel does. Instead, if you pass a string column as an argument, you always obtain 0 as a result. That is quite useless. On the other hand, *AVERAGE* would return an error, clearly indicating that it cannot average strings.

We discussed how to compute regular averages over a table earlier in this chapter. Here we want to show a more advanced usage, that is a moving average. For example, imagine that you want to analyze the daily sales of Contoso. If you just build a report that plots the sales amount sliced by day, the result is hard to analyze. As you can see in Figure 7-7, the value obtained has strong daily variations.

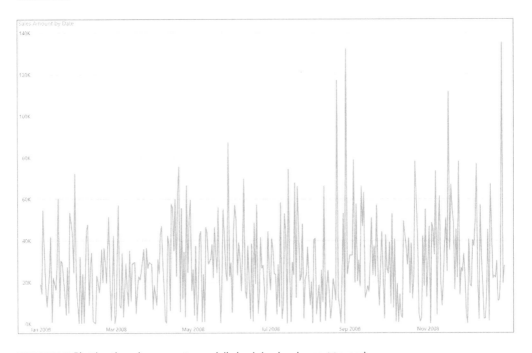

FIGURE 7-7 Plotting the sales amount on a daily basis is a hard report to read.

To smooth out the chart, a common technique is to compute the average over a certain period greater than just the day level. In our example, we decided to use 30 days as our period. Thus, on each day the chart shows the average over the last 30 days. This technique helps in removing peaks from the chart, making it easier to detect a trend.

The following calculation provides the average at the date cardinality, over the last 30 days:

```
AvgXSales30 :=
VAR LastVisibleDate = MAX ( 'Date'[Date] )
VAR NumberOfDays = 30
VAR PeriodToUse =
    FILTER (
        ALL ( 'Date' ),
        AND (
            'Date'[Date] > LastVisibleDate - NumberOfDays,
            'Date'[Date] <= LastVisibleDate
        )
    )
VAR Result =
    CALCULATE (
        AVERAGEX ( 'Date', [Sales Amount] ) ,
        PeriodToUse
    )
RETURN
    Result
```

The formula first determines the last visible date; in the chart, because the filter context set by the visual is at the date level, it returns the selected date. The formula then creates a set of all the dates between the last date and the last date minus 30 days. Finally, the last step is to use this period as a filter in *CALCULATE* so that the final *AVERAGEX* iterates over the 30-day period, computing the average of the daily sales.

The result of this calculation is visible in Figure 7-8. As you can see, the line is much smoother than the daily sales, making it possible to analyze trends.

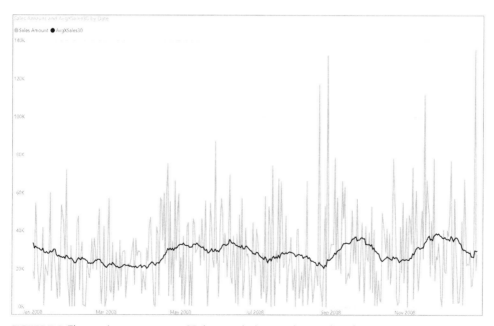

FIGURE 7-8 The moving average over 30 days results in a much smoother chart.

When the user relies on average functions like *AVERAGEX*, they need to pay special attention to the desired result. In fact, when computing an average, DAX ignores blank values. If on a given day there are no sales, then that day will not be considered as part of the average. Beware that this is a correct behavior. *AVERAGEX* cannot assume that if there are no sales in a day then we might want to use zero instead. This behavior might not be desirable when averaging over dates.

If the requirement is to compute the average over dates counting days with no sales as zeroes, then the formula to use is almost always a simple division instead of *AVERAGEX*. A simple division is also faster because the context transition within *AVERAGEX* requires more memory and increased execution time. Look at the following variation of the moving average, where the only difference from the previous formula is the expression inside *CALCULATE*:

```
AvgSales30 :=
VAR LastVisibleDate = MAX ( 'Date'[Date] )
VAR NumberOfDays = 30
VAR PeriodToUse =
    FILTER (
        ALL ( 'Date' ),
        'Date'[Date] > LastVisibleDate - NumberOfDays &&
        'Date'[Date] <= LastVisibleDate
    )
VAR Result =
CALCULATE (
    DIVIDE ( [Sales Amount], COUNTROWS ( 'Date' ) ),
    PeriodToUse
)
RETURN
    Result
```

Not leveraging *AVERAGEX*, this latter version of the code considers a day with no sales as a zero. This is reflected in the resulting value whose behavior is similar to the previous one, though slightly different. Moreover, the result of this latter calculation is always a bit smaller than the previous one because the denominator is nearly always a higher value, as you can appreciate in Figure 7-9.

As is often the case with business calculations, it is not that one is better than the other. It all depends on your specific requirements. DAX offers different ways of obtaining the result. It is up to you to choose the right one. For example, by using *COUNTROWS* the formula now accounts for days with no sales considering them as zeroes, but it also counts holidays and weekends as days with no sales. Whether this is correct or not depends on the specific requirements and the formula needs to be updated in order to reflect the correct average.

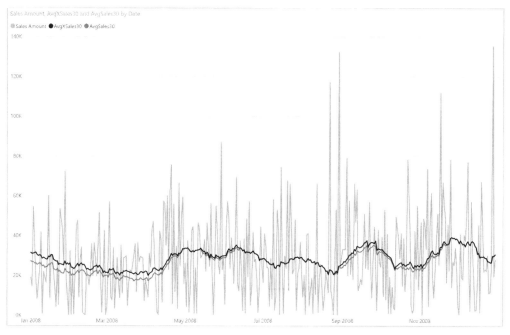

FIGURE 7-9 Different moving average calculations lead to slightly different results.

Using *RANKX*

The *RANKX* function is used to show the ranking value of an element according to a specific sort order. For example, a typical use of *RANKX* is to provide a ranking of products or customers based on their sales volumes. *RANKX* accepts several parameters, though most frequently only the first two are used. All the others are optional and seldom used.

For example, imagine wanting to build the report in Figure 7-10 that shows the ranking of a category against all others based on respective sales amounts.

Category	Sales Amount	Rank Cat on Sales
Audio	384,518.16	6
Cameras and camcorders	7,192,581.95	2
Cell phones	1,604,610.26	5
Computers	6,741,548.73	3
Games and Toys	360,652.81	7
Home Appliances	9,600,457.04	1
Music, Movies and Audio Books	314,206.74	8
TV and Video	4,392,768.29	4
Total	**30,591,343.98**	**1**

FIGURE 7-10 *Rank Cat on Sales* provides the ranking of the category based on the sales amount.

In this scenario, *RANKX* is the function to use. *RANKX* is an iterator and it is a simple function. Nevertheless, its use hides some complexities that are worth a deeper explanation.

The code of *Rank Cat on Sales* is the following:

```
Rank Cat on Sales :=
RANKX (
    ALL ( 'Product'[Category] ),
    [Sales Amount]
)
```

RANKX operates in three steps:

1. *RANKX* builds a lookup table by iterating over the table provided as the first parameter. During the iteration it evaluates its second parameter in the row context of the iteration. At the end, it sorts the lookup table.

2. *RANKX* evaluates its second parameter in the original evaluation context.

3. *RANKX* returns the position of the value computed in the second step by searching its place in the sorted lookup table.

The algorithm is outlined in Figure 7-11, where we show the steps needed to compute the value of 2, the ranking of Cameras and camcorders according to *Sales Amount*.

Category	Sales Amount	Rank Cat on Sales		Step 1 Lookup table	Step 2 Value
Audio	384,518.16	6		9,600,457.04	7,192,581.95
Cameras and camcorders	7,192,581.95	2	⇒	7,192,581.95	
Cell phones	1,604,610.26	5		6,741,548.73	
Computers	6,741,548.73	3		4,392,768.29	
Games and Toys	360,652.81	7		1,604,610.26	Step 3
Home Appliances	9,600,457.04	1		384,518.16	Position
Music, Movies and Audio Books	314,206.74	8		360,652.81	Result is
TV and Video	4,392,768.29	4		314,206.74	
Total	**30,591,343.98**	**1**			**2**

FIGURE 7-11 *RANKX* requires three steps to determine the ranking of Cameras and camcorders.

Here is a more detailed description of the behavior of *RANKX* in our example:

■   The lookup table is built during the iteration. In the code, we had to use *ALL* on the product category to ignore the current filter context that would otherwise filter the only category visible, producing a lookup table with only one row.

■   The value of *Sales Amount* is a different one for each category because of context transition. Indeed, during the iteration there is a row context. Because the expression to evaluate is a measure that contains a hidden *CALCULATE*, context transition makes DAX compute the value of *Sales Amount* only for the given category.

- The lookup table only contains values. Any reference to the category is lost: Ranking takes place only on values, once they are sorted correctly.

- The value determined in step 2 comes from the evaluation of the *Sales Amount* measure outside of the iteration, in the original evaluation context. The original filter context is filtering Cameras and camcorders. Therefore, the result is the amount of sales of cameras and camcorders.

- The value of 2 is the result of finding the place of *Sales Amount* of cameras and camcorders in the sorted lookup table.

You might have noticed that at the grand total, *RANKX* shows 1. This value does not make any sense from a human point of view because a ranking should not have any total at all. Nevertheless, this value is the result of the same process of evaluation, which at the grand total always shows a meaningless value. In Figure 7-12 you can see the evaluation process at the grand total.

Category	Sales Amount	Rank Cat on Sales	Step 1 Lookup table	Step 2 Value
				30,591,343.98
Audio	384,518.16	6	9,600,457.04	
Cameras and camcorders	7,192,581.95	2	7,192,581.95	
Cell phones	1,604,610.26	5	6,741,548.73	
Computers	6,741,548.73	3	4,392,768.29	
Games and Toys	360,652.81	7	1,604,610.26	Step 3
Home Appliances	9,600,457.04	1	384,518.16	Position
Music, Movies and Audio Books	314,206.74	8	360,652.81	Result is
TV and Video	4,392,768.29	4	314,206.74	
Total	**30,591,343.98**	**1**		**1**

FIGURE 7-12 The grand total always shows 1 if sorting of the lookup table is descending.

The value computed during step 2 is the grand total of sales, which is always greater than the sum of individual categories. Thus, the value shown at the grand total is not a bug or a defect; it is the standard *RANKX* behavior that loses its intended meaning at the grand total level. The correct way of handling the total is to hide it by using DAX code. Indeed, the ranking of a category against all other categories has meaning if (and only if) the current filter context only filters one category. Consequently, a better formulation of the measure relies on *HASONEVALUE* in order to avoid computing the ranking in a filter context that produces a meaningless result:

```
Rank Cat on Sales :=
IF (
    HASONEVALUE ( 'Product'[Category] ),
    RANKX (
        ALL ( 'Product'[Category] ),
        [Sales Amount]
    )
)
```

This code produces a blank whenever there are multiple categories in the current filter context, removing the total row. Whenever one uses *RANKX* or, in more general terms, whenever the measure computed depends on specific characteristics of the filter context, one should protect the measure with a conditional expression that ensures that the calculation only happens when it should, providing a blank or an error message in any other case. This is exactly what the previous measure does.

As we mentioned earlier *RANKX* accepts many arguments, not only the first two. There are three remaining arguments, which we introduce here. We describe them later in this section.

- The third parameter is the value expression, which might be useful when different expressions are being used to evaluate respectively the lookup table and the value to use for the ranking.

- The fourth parameter is the sort order of the lookup table. It can be *ASC* or *DESC*. The default is *DESC*, with the highest values on top—that is, higher value results in lower ranking.

- The fifth parameter defines how to compute values in case of ties. It can be *DENSE* or *SKIP*. If it is *DENSE*, then ties are removed from the lookup table; otherwise they are kept.

Let us describe the remaining parameters with some examples.

The third parameter is useful whenever one needs to use a different expression respectively to build the lookup table and to compute the value to rank. For example, consider the requirement of a custom table for the ranking, like the one depicted in Figure 7-13.

Sales
0
100,000
500,000
1,000,000
2,000,000
5,000,000
10,000,000

FIGURE 7-13 Instead of building a dynamic lookup table, one might need to use a fixed lookup table.

If one wants to use this table to compute the lookup table, then the expression used to build it should be different from the *Sales Amount* measure. In such a case, the third parameter becomes useful. To rank the sales amount against this specific lookup table—which is named *Sales Ranking*—the code is the following:

```
Rank On Fixed Table :=
RANKX (
    'Sales Ranking',
    'Sales Ranking'[Sales],
    [Sales Amount]
)
```

In this case, the lookup table is built by getting the value of *'Sales Ranking'[Sale]* in the row context of *Sales Ranking*. Once the lookup table is built, *RANKX* evaluates *[Sales Amount]* in the original evaluation context.

The result of this calculation is visible in Figure 7-14.

Category	Sales Amount	Rank On Fixed Table
Audio	384,518.16	6
Cameras and camcorders	7,192,581.95	2
Cell phones	1,604,610.26	4
Computers	6,741,548.73	2
Games and Toys	360,652.81	6
Home Appliances	9,600,457.04	2
Music, Movies and Audio Books	314,206.74	6
TV and Video	4,392,768.29	3
Total	**30,591,343.98**	**1**

FIGURE 7-14 *Rank On Fixed Table* ranks *Sales Amount* against the fixed *Sales Ranking* table.

The full process is depicted in Figure 7-15, where you can also appreciate that the lookup table is sorted before being used.

FIGURE 7-15 When using a fixed lookup table, the expression used to build the lookup table is different from the expression used for step 2.

The fourth parameter can be *ASC* or *DESC*. It changes the sort order of the lookup table. By default it is *DESC*, meaning that a lower ranking is assigned to the highest value. If one uses *ASC*, then the lower value will be assigned the lower ranking because the lookup table is sorted the opposite way.

The fifth parameter, on the other hand, is useful in the presence of ties. To introduce ties in the calculation, we use a different measure—*Rounded Sales*. *Rounded Sales* rounds values to the nearest multiple of one million, and we will slice it by brand:

```
Rounded Sales := MROUND ( [Sales Amount], 1000000 )
```

Then, we define two different rankings: One uses the default ranking (which is *SKIP*), whereas the other one uses *DENSE* for the ranking:

```
Rank On Rounded Sales :=
RANKX (
    ALL ( 'Product'[Brand] ),
    [Rounded Sales]
)

Rank On Rounded Sales Dense :=
RANKX (
    ALL ( 'Product'[Brand] ),
    [Rounded Sales],
    ,
    ,
    DENSE
)
```

The result of the two measures is different. In fact, the default behavior considers the number of ties and it increases the ranking accordingly. When using *DENSE*, the ranking increases by one regardless of ties. You can appreciate the different result in Figure 7-16.

Brand	Rounded Sales	Rank On Rounded Sales	Rank On Rounded Sales Dense
Contoso	7,000,000.00	1	1
Fabrikam	6,000,000.00	2	2
Adventure Works	4,000,000.00	3	3
Litware	3,000,000.00	4	4
Proseware	3,000,000.00	4	4
A. Datum	2,000,000.00	6	5
Wide World Importers	2,000,000.00	6	5
Northwind Traders	1,000,000.00	8	6
Southridge Video	1,000,000.00	8	6
The Phone Company	1,000,000.00	8	6
Tailspin Toys	0.00	11	7

FIGURE 7-16 Using *DENSE* or *SKIP* produces different ranking values in the presence of ties in the lookup table.

Basically, *DENSE* performs a *DISTINCT* on the lookup table before using it. *SKIP* does not, and it uses the lookup table as it is generated during the iteration.

When using *RANKX*, it is important to consider which table to use as the first parameter to obtain the desired result. In the previous queries, it was necessary to specify *ALL (Product[Brand])* because we wanted to obtain the ranking of each brand. For brevity, we omitted the usual test with *HASONEVALUE*. In practice you should never skip it; otherwise the measure is at risk of computing unexpected results. For example, a measure like the following one produces an error if not used in a report that slices by Brand:

```
Rank On Sales :=
RANKX (
    ALL ( 'Product'[Brand] ),
    [Sales Amount]
)
```

In Figure 7-17 we slice the measure by product color and the result is always 1.

Color	Sales Amount	Rank On Sales
Azure	97,389.89	1
Black	5,860,066.14	1
Blue	2,435,444.62	1
Brown	1,029,508.95	1
Gold	361,496.01	1
Green	1,403,184.38	1
Grey	3,509,138.09	1
Orange	857,320.28	1
Pink	828,638.54	1
Purple	5,973.84	1

FIGURE 7-17 A ranking by brand produces unexpected results if sliced by *Color*.

The reason is that the lookup table contains the sales amount sliced by brand and by color, whereas the values to search in the lookup table contain the total only by color. As such, the total by color will always be larger than any of its subsets by brand, resulting in a ranking of 1. Adding the protection code with *IF HASONEVALUE* ensures that—if the evaluation context does not filter a single brand—the result will be blank.

Finally, *ALLSELECTED* is oftentimes used with *RANKX*. If a user performs a selection of some brands out of the entire set of brands, ranking over *ALL* might produce gaps in the ranking. This is because *ALL* returns all the brands, regardless of the filter coming from the slicer. For example, consider the following measures:

```
Rank On Selected Brands :=
RANKX (
    ALLSELECTED ( 'Product'[Brand] ),
    [Sales Amount]
)

Rank On All Brands :=
RANKX (
    ALL ( 'Product'[Brand] ),
    [Sales Amount]
)
```

In Figure 7-18, you can see the comparison between the two measures in the presence of a slicer filtering certain brands.

Brand
- ■ A. Datum
- ■ Adventure Works
- ■ Contoso
- ■ Fabrikam
- ☐ Litware
- ■ Northwind Traders
- ■ Proseware
- ■ Southridge Video
- ■ Tailspin Toys
- ☐ The Phone Company
- ☐ Wide World Importers

Brand	Sales Amount	Rank On All Brands	Rank On Selected Brands
Contoso	7,352,399.03	1	1
Fabrikam	5,554,015.73	2	2
Adventure Works	4,011,112.28	3	3
Proseware	2,546,144.16	5	4
A. Datum	2,096,184.64	6	5
Southridge Video	1,384,413.85	8	6
Northwind Traders	1,040,552.13	10	7
Tailspin Toys	325,042.42	11	8

FIGURE 7-18 Using *ALLSELECTED* removes gaps in the ranking generated by using *ALL*.

Using RANK.EQ

The *RANK.EQ* function in DAX is like the Excel function of the same name. It returns the ranking of a number within a list of numbers, offering a subset of the features available with *RANKX*. You rarely use it in DAX unless you are migrating an Excel formula. It has the following syntax:

```
RANK.EQ ( <value>, <column> [, <order>] )
```

The <value> argument can be a DAX expression that has to be evaluated, and <column> is the name of an existing column against which rank will be determined. The order is optional and can be 0 for descending order and 1 for ascending order. In Excel, the same function can accept a range of cells as a column argument. However, in DAX, often the same column is used for value expression, meaning that you want to calculate the ranking of a column over itself. One scenario in which you might want to use a different column is when you have two tables: one table with elements that you want to rank, for example a specific group of products; and another table with the entire set of elements to use for ranking, for example the list of all the products. However, because of the limitations applied to the column parameter (it cannot be an expression or a column created by using *ADDCOLUMNS*, *SELECTCOLUMNS*, or other table functions), *RANK.EQ* is commonly used by passing the same column for value and column parameters in a calculated column expression, referring to columns of the same table as in the following example:

```
Product[Price Rank] =
RANK.EQ ( Product[Unit Price], Product[Unit Price] )
```

RANKX is much more powerful than *RANK.EQ*. Thus, once you learn *RANKX*, it is likely you will not spend too much time learning a less powerful version of the same function.

Changing calculation granularity

There are several scenarios where a formula cannot be easily computed at the total level. Instead, the same calculation could be performed at a higher granularity and then aggregated later.

Imagine needing to compute the sales amount per working day. The number of working days in every month is different because of the number of Saturdays and Sundays or because of the holidays in a month. For the sake of simplicity, in this example we only consider Saturdays and Sundays, but our readers can easily extend the concept to also considering holidays.

The *Date* table contains an *IsWorkingDay* column that contains 1 or 0 depending on whether that day is a working day or not. It is useful to store the information as an integer because it makes the calculation of days and working days very simple. Indeed, the two following measures compute the number of days in the current filter context and the corresponding number of working days:

```
NumOfDays := COUNTROWS ( 'Date' )
NumOfWorkingDays := SUM ( 'Date'[IsWorkingDay] )
```

In Figure 7-19 you can see a report with the two measures.

Calendar Year	Sales Amount	NumOfDays	NumOfWorkingDays
CY 2007	**4,694,127.73**	**365**	**261**
January		31	23
February		28	20
March		31	22
April		30	21
May		31	23
June		30	21
July		31	22
August	952,834.59	31	23
September	1,009,868.98	30	20
October	914,273.54	31	23
November	825,601.87	30	22
December	991,548.75	31	21
CY 2008	**9,927,582.99**	**366**	**262**
January	656,766.69	31	23
February	600,080.00	29	21
Total	**20,844,079.45**	**1,096**	**784**

FIGURE 7-19 The number of working days is different in each month, depending on weekends.

Based on these measures, we might want to compute the sales per working day. That is a simple division of the sales amount by the number of working days. This calculation is useful to produce a performance indicator for each month, considering both the gross amount of sales and the number of days in which sales were possible. Though the calculation looks simple, it hides some complexity that we solve by leveraging iterators. As we sometimes do in this book, we show this solution step-by-step, highlighting possible errors in the writing process. The goal of this demo is not to show a pattern. Instead, it is a showcase of different mistakes that a developer might make when authoring a DAX expression.

As anticipated, a simple division of *Sales Amount* by the number of working days produces correct results only at the month level. At the grand total, the result is surprisingly lower than any other month:

```
SalesPerWorkingDay := DIVIDE ( [Sales Amount], [NumOfWorkingDays] )
```

In Figure 7-20 you can look at the result.

Calendar Year	Sales Amount	NumOfDays	NumOfWorkingDays	SalesPerWorkingDay
CY 2007	**4,694,127.73**	**365**	**261**	**17,985.16**
January		31	23	
February		28	20	
March		31	22	
April		30	21	
May		31	23	
June		30	21	
July		31	22	
August	952,834.59	31	23	41,427.59
September	1,009,868.98	30	20	50,493.45
October	914,273.54	31	23	39,751.02
November	825,601.87	30	22	37,527.36
December	991,548.75	31	21	47,216.61
CY 2008	**9,927,582.99**	**366**	**262**	**37,891.54**
January	656,766.69	31	23	28,555.07
February	600,080.00	29	21	28,575.24
Total	**20,844,079.45**	**1,096**	**784**	**26,586.84**

FIGURE 7-20 Although monthly values look fine, the annual subtotal is definitely wrong.

If you focus your attention to the total of 2007, it shows 17,985.16. It is surprisingly low considering that all monthly values are above 37,000.00. The reason is that the number of working days at the year level is 261, including the months where there are no sales at all. In this model, sales started in August 2007 so it would be wrong to consider previous months where there cannot be other sales. The same issue also happens in the period containing the last day with data. For example, the total of the working days in the current year will likely consider future months as working days.

There are multiple ways of fixing the formula. We choose a simple one: if there are no sales in a month, then the formula should not consider the days in that month. This formula assumes that all the months between the oldest transaction and the last transaction available have transactions associated.

Because the calculation must work on a month-by-month basis, it needs to iterate over months and check if there are sales in each month. If there are sales, then it adds the number of working days. If there are no sales in the given month, then it skips it. *SUMX* can implement this algorithm:

```
SalesPerWorkingDay :=
VAR WorkingDays =
    SUMX (
        VALUES ( 'Date'[Month] ),
        IF (
            [Sales Amount] > 0,
            [NumOfWorkingDays]
        )
    )
VAR Result =
    DIVIDE (
        [Sales Amount],
        WorkingDays
    )
RETURN
    Result
```

This new version of the code provides an accurate result at the year level, as shown in Figure 7-21, though it is still not perfect.

Calendar Year	Sales Amount	NumOfDays	NumOfWorkingDays	SalesPerWorkingDay
CY 2007	**4,694,127.73**	**365**	**261**	**43,065.39**
January		31	23	
February		28	20	
March		31	22	
April		30	21	
May		31	23	
June		30	21	
July		31	22	
August	952,834.59	31	23	41,427.59
September	1,009,868.98	30	20	50,493.45
October	914,273.54	31	23	39,751.02
November	825,601.87	30	22	37,527.36
December	991,548.75	31	21	47,216.61
CY 2008	**9,927,582.99**	**366**	**262**	**37,891.54**
January	656,766.69	31	23	28,555.07
February	600,080.00	29	21	28,575.24
Total	**20,844,079.45**	**1,096**	**784**	**26,586.84**

FIGURE 7-21 Using an iterator the total at the year level is now accurate.

When performing the calculation at a different granularity, one needs to ensure the correct level of granularity. The iteration started by *SUMX* iterates the values of the month column, which are January through December. At the year level everything is working correctly, but the value is still incorrect at the grand total. You can observe this behavior in Figure 7-22.

Calendar Year	Sales Amount	NumOfDays	NumOfWorkingDays	SalesPerWorkingDay
CY 2007	4,694,127.73	365	261	43,065.39
CY 2008	9,927,582.99	366	262	37,891.54
CY 2009	6,222,368.73	365	261	35,967.45
Total	**20,844,079.45**	**1,096**	**784**	**26,586.84**

FIGURE 7-22 Every yearly total is above 35,000 and the grand total is—again—surprisingly low.

When the filter context contains the year, an iteration of months works fine because—after the context transition—the new filter context contains both a year and a month. However, at the grand total level, the year is no longer part of the filter context. Consequently, the filter context only contains the currently iterated month, and the formula does not check if there are sales in that year and month. Instead, it checks if there are sales in that month for any year.

The problem of this formula is the iteration over the month column. The correct granularity of the iteration is not the month; it is the pair of year and month together. The best solution is to iterate over a column containing a different value for each year and month. It turns out that we have such a column in the data model: the *Calendar Year Month* column. To fix the code, it is enough to iterate over the *Calendar Year Month* column instead of over *Month*:

```
SalesPerWorkingDay :=
VAR WorkingDays =
    SUMX (
        VALUES ( 'Date'[Calendar Year Month] ),
        IF (
            [Sales Amount] > 0,
            [NumOfWorkingDays]
        )
    )
VAR Result =
    DIVIDE (
        [Sales Amount],
        WorkingDays
    )
RETURN
    Result
```

This final version of the code works fine because it computes the total using an iteration at the correct level of granularity. You can see the result in Figure 7-23.

Calendar Year	Sales Amount	NumOfDays	NumOfWorkingDays	SalesPerWorkingDay
CY 2007	4,694,127.73	365	261	43,065.39
CY 2008	9,927,582.99	366	262	37,891.54
CY 2009	6,222,368.73	365	261	35,967.45
Total	**20,844,079.45**	**1,096**	**784**	**38,316.32**

FIGURE 7-23 Applying the calculation at the correct level of granularity returns accurate values also at the Total level.

Conclusions

As usual, let us conclude this chapter with a recap of the important concepts you learned here:

- Iterators are an important part of DAX, and you will find yourself using them more, the more you use DAX.

- There are mainly two kinds of iterations in DAX: iterations to perform simple calculations on a row-by-row basis and iterations that leverage context transition. The definition of *Sales Amount* we used so far in the book uses an iteration to compute the quantity multiplied by the net price, on a row-by-row basis. In this chapter, we introduced iterators with a context transition, a powerful tool to compute more complex expressions.

- Whenever using an iterator with context transition, you must check the cardinality the iteration should happen at—it should be quite small. You also need to check that the rows in the table are guaranteed to be unique. Otherwise, the code is at risk of being slow or of computing bad results.

- When computing averages over time, you always should check whether an iterator is the correct solution or not. *AVERAGEX* does not consider blanks as part of its calculation and, when using time, this could be wrong. Nevertheless, always double-check the formula requirements; each scenario is unique.

- Iterators are useful to compute values at a different granularity, as you learned in the last example. When dealing with calculations at different granularities, it is of paramount importance to check the correct granularity to avoid errors in the code.

You will see many more examples of iterators in the remaining part of the book. Starting from the next chapter, when dealing with time intelligence calculations, you will see different calculations, most of which rely on iterations.

Time intelligence calculations

Almost any data model includes some sort of calculation related to dates. DAX offers several functions to simplify these calculations, which are useful if the underlying data model follows certain specific requirements. On the other hand, if the model contains peculiarities in the handling of time that would prevent the use of standard time intelligence functions, then writing custom calculations is always an option.

In this chapter, you learn how to implement common date-related calculations such as year-to-date, year-over-year, and other calculations over time including nonadditive and semi-additive measures. You learn both how to use specific time intelligence functions and how to rely on custom DAX code for nonstandard calendars and week-based calculations.

Introducing time intelligence

Typically, a data model contains a date table. In fact, when slicing data by year and month, it is preferable to use the columns of a table specifically designed to slice dates. Extracting the date parts from a single column of type *Date* or *DateTime* in calculated columns is a less desirable approach.

There are several reasons for this choice. By using a date table, the model becomes easier to browse, and you can use specific DAX functions that perform time intelligence calculations. In fact, in order to work properly, most of the time intelligence functions in DAX require a separate date table.

If a model contains multiple dates, like the order date and the delivery date, then one can either create multiple relationships with a single date table or duplicate the date table. The resulting models are different, and so are the calculations. Later in this chapter, we will discuss these two alternatives in more detail.

In any case, one should always create at least one date table whenever there are one or more date columns in the data. Power BI and Power Pivot for Excel offer embedded features to automatically create tables or columns to manage dates in the model, whereas Analysis Services has no specific feature for the handling of time intelligence. However, the implementation of these features does not always follow the best practice of keeping a single date table in the data model. Also, because these features come with several restrictions, it is usually better to use your own date table. The next sections expand on this last statement.

Automatic Date/Time in Power BI

Power BI has a feature called Auto Date/Time, which can be configured through the options in the Data Load section (see Figure 8-1).

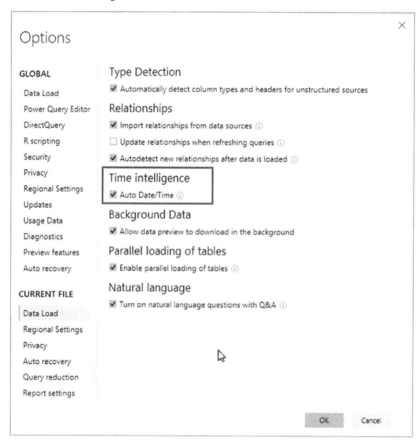

FIGURE 8-1 The Auto Date/Time setting is enabled by default in a new model.

When the setting is enabled—it is by default—Power BI automatically creates a date table for each *Date* or *DateTime* column in the model. We will call it a "date column" from here on. This makes it possible to slice each date by year, quarter, month, and day. These automatically created tables are hidden to the user and cannot be modified. Connecting to the Power BI Desktop file with DAX Studio makes them visible to any developers curious about their structure.

The Auto Date/Time feature comes with two major drawbacks:

■ Power BI Desktop generates one table per date column. This creates an unnecessarily high number of date tables in the model, unrelated to one another. Building a simple report presenting the amount ordered and the amount sold in the same matrix proves to be a real challenge.

■ The tables are hidden and cannot be modified by the developer. Consequently, if one needs to add a column for the weekday, they cannot.

Building a proper date table for complete freedom is a skill that you learn in the next few pages, and it only requires a few lines of DAX code. Forcing your model to follow bad practices in data modeling just to save a couple of minutes when building the model for the first time is definitely a bad choice.

Automatic date columns in Power Pivot for Excel

Power Pivot for Excel also has a feature to handle the automatic creation of data structures, making it easier to browse dates. However, it uses a different technique that is even worse than that of Power BI. In fact, when one uses a date column in a pivot table, Power Pivot automatically creates a set of calculated columns in the same table that contains the date column. Thus, it creates one calculated column for the year, one for the month name, one for the quarter, and one for the month number—required for sorting. In total, it adds four columns to your table.

As a bad practice, it shares all the bad features of Power BI and it adds a new one. In fact, if there are multiple date columns in a single table, then the number of these calculated columns will start to increase. There is no way to use the same set of columns to slice different dates, as is the case with Power BI. Finally, if the date column is in a table with millions of rows—as is often the case—these calculated columns increase the file size and the memory footprint of the model.

This feature can be disabled in the Excel options, as you can see in Figure 8-2.

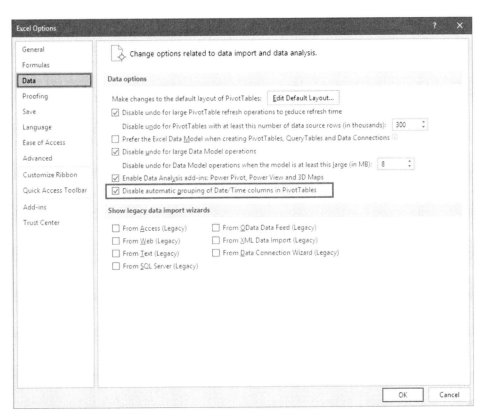

FIGURE 8-2 The Excel options contain a setting to disable automatic grouping of *DateTime* columns.

Date table template in Power Pivot for Excel

Excel offers another feature that works much better than the previous feature. Indeed, since 2017 there is an option in Power Pivot for Excel to create a date table, which can be activated through the Power Pivot window, as shown in Figure 8-3.

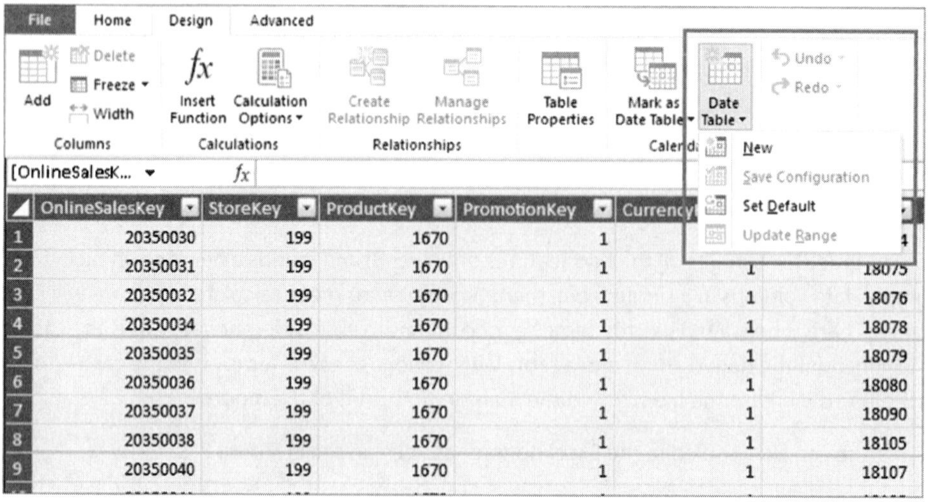

FIGURE 8-3 Power Pivot for Excel lets you create a new date table through a menu option.

In Power Pivot, clicking on New creates a new table in the model with a set of calculated columns that include year, month, and weekday. It is up to the developer to create the correct set of relationships in the model. Also, if needed, one has the option to modify the names and the formulas of the calculated columns, as well as adding new ones.

There is also the option of saving the current table as a new template, which will be used in the future for newly created date tables. Overall, this technique works well. The table generated by Power Pivot is a regular date table that fulfills all the requirements of a good date table. This, in conjunction with the fact that Power Pivot for Excel does not support calculated tables, makes the feature useful.

Building a date table

As you have learned, the first step for handling date calculations in DAX is to create a date table. Because of its relevance, one should pay attention to some details when creating the date table. In this section, we provide the best practices regarding the creation of a date table. There are two different aspects to consider: a technical aspect and a data modeling aspect.

From a technical point of view, the date table must follow these guidelines:

- The date table contains all dates included in the period to analyze. For example, if the minimum and maximum dates contained in *Sales* are July 3, 2016, and July 27, 2019, respectively, the range of dates of the table is between January 1, 2016, and December 31, 2019. In other words, the date table needs to contain all the days for all the years containing sales data. There can be no gaps in the sequence of dates. All dates need to be present, regardless of whether there are transactions or not on each date.

- The date table contains one column of *DateTime* type, with unique values. The *Date* data type is a better choice because it guarantees that the time part is empty. If the *DateTime* column also contains a time part, then all the times of the day need to be identical throughout the table.

- It is not necessary that the relationship between *Sales* and the date table be based on the *DateTime* column. One can use an integer to relate the two tables, yet the *DateTime* column needs to be present.

- The table should be marked as a *Date* table. Though this is not a strictly mandatory step, it greatly helps in writing correct code. We will cover the details of this feature later in this chapter.

> **Important** It is common for newbies to create a huge date table with many more years than needed. That is a mistake. For example, one might create a date table with two hundred years ranging from 1900 to 2100, just in case. Technically the date table works fine, but there will be serious performance issues whenever it is used in calculations. Using a table with only the relevant years is a best practice.

From the technical point of view, a table containing a single date column with all the required dates is enough. Nevertheless, a user typically wants to analyze information slicing by year, month, quarter, weekday, and many other attributes. Consequently, a good date table should include a rich set of columns that—although not used by the engine—greatly improve the user experience.

If you are loading the date table from an existing data source, then it is likely that all the columns describing a date are already present in the source date table. If necessary, additional columns can be created as calculated columns or by changing the source query. Performing simple calculations in the data source is preferable whenever possible—reducing the use of calculated columns to when they are strictly required. Alternatively, you can create the date table by using a DAX calculated table. We describe the calculated table technique along with the *CALENDAR* and *CALENDARAUTO* functions in the next sections.

> **Note** The term "Date" is a reserved keyword in DAX; it corresponds to the *DATE* function. Therefore, you should embed the *Date* name in quotes when referring to the table name, despite the fact that there are no spaces or special characters in that name. You might prefer using *Dates* instead of *Date* as the name of the table to avoid this requirement. However, it is better to be consistent in table names, so if you use the singular form for all the other table names, it is better to keep it singular for the date table too.

Using *CALENDAR* and *CALENDARAUTO*

If you do not have a date table in your data source, you can create the date table by using either *CALENDAR* or *CALENDARAUTO*. These functions return a table of one column, of *DateTime* data type. *CALENDAR* requires you to provide the upper and lower boundaries of the set of dates. *CALENDARAUTO* scans all the date columns across the entire data model, finds the minimum and maximum years referenced, and finally generates the set of dates between these years.

For example, a simple calendar table containing all the dates in the *Sales* table can be created using the following code:

```
Date =
CALENDAR (
    DATE ( YEAR ( MIN ( Sales[Order Date] ) ), 1, 1 ),
    DATE ( YEAR ( MAX ( Sales[Order Date] ) ), 12, 31 )
)
```

In order to force all dates from the first of January up to the end of December, the code only extracts the minimum and maximum years, forcing day and month to be the first and last of the year. A similar result can be obtained by using the simpler *CALENDARAUTO*:

```
Date = CALENDARAUTO ( )
```

CALENDARAUTO scans all the date columns, except for calculated columns. For example, if one uses *CALENDARAUTO* to create a *Date* table in a model that contains sales between 2007 and 2011 and has an *AvailableForSaleDate* column in the *Product* table starting in 2004, the result is the set of all the days between January 1, 2004, and December 31, 2011. However, if the data model contains other date columns, they affect the date range considered by *CALENDARAUTO*. Storing dates that are not useful to slice and dice is very common. For example, if among the many dates a model also contains the customers' birthdates, then the result of *CALENDARAUTO* starts from the oldest year of birth of any customer. This produces a large date table, which in turn negatively affects performance.

CALENDARAUTO accepts an optional parameter that represents the final month number of a fiscal year. If provided, *CALENDARAUTO* generates dates from the first day of the following month to the last day of the month indicated as an argument. This is useful when you have a fiscal year that ends in a month other than December. For example, the following expression generates a *Date* table for fiscal years starting on July 1 and ending on June 30:

```
Date = CALENDARAUTO ( 6 )
```

CALENDARAUTO is slightly easier to use than *CALENDAR* because it automatically determines the boundaries of the set of dates. However, it might extend this set by considering unwanted columns. One can obtain the best of both worlds by restricting the result of *CALENDARAUTO* to only the desired set of dates, as follows:

```
Date =
VAR MinYear = YEAR ( MIN ( Sales[Order Date] ) )
VAR MaxYear = YEAR ( MAX ( Sales[Order Date] ) )
RETURN
```

```
FILTER (
    CALENDARAUTO ( ),
    YEAR ( [Date] ) >= MinYear &&
    YEAR ( [Date] ) <= MaxYear
)
```

The resulting table only contains the useful dates. Finding the first and last day of the year is not that important because *CALENDARAUTO* handles this internally.

Once the developer has obtained the correct list of dates, they still must create additional columns using DAX expressions. Following is a list of commonly used expressions for this scope, with an example of their results in Figure 8-4:

```
Date =
VAR MinYear = YEAR ( MIN ( Sales[Order Date] ) )
VAR MaxYear = YEAR ( MAX ( Sales[Order Date] ) )
RETURN
ADDCOLUMNS (
    FILTER (
        CALENDARAUTO ( ),
        YEAR ( [Date] ) >= MinYear &&
        YEAR ( [Date] ) <= MaxYear
    ),
    "Year", YEAR ( [Date] ),
    "Quarter Number", INT ( FORMAT ( [Date], "q" ) ),
    "Quarter", "Q" & INT ( FORMAT ( [Date], "q" ) ),
    "Month Number", MONTH ( [Date] ),
    "Month", FORMAT ( [Date], "mmmm" ),
    "Week Day Number", WEEKDAY ( [Date] ),
    "Week Day", FORMAT ( [Date], "dddd" ),
    "Year Month Number", YEAR ( [Date] ) * 100 + MONTH ( [Date] ),
    "Year Month", FORMAT ( [Date], "mmmm" ) & " " & YEAR ( [Date] ),
    "Year Quarter Number", YEAR ( [Date] ) * 100 + INT ( FORMAT ( [Date], "q" ) ),
    "Year Quarter", "Q" & FORMAT ( [Date], "q" ) & "-" & YEAR ( [Date] )
)
```

Date	Year	Month	Month Number	Quarter	Quarter Number	Week Day	Week Day Number	Year Month	Year Month Number
01/01/07	2007	January	1	Q1	1	Monday	2	January 2007	200701
01/02/07	2007	January	1	Q1	1	Tuesday	3	January 2007	200701
01/03/07	2007	January	1	Q1	1	Wednesday	4	January 2007	200701
01/04/07	2007	January	1	Q1	1	Thursday	5	January 2007	200701
01/05/07	2007	January	1	Q1	1	Friday	6	January 2007	200701
01/06/07	2007	January	1	Q1	1	Saturday	7	January 2007	200701
01/07/07	2007	January	1	Q1	1	Sunday	1	January 2007	200701
01/08/07	2007	January	1	Q1	1	Monday	2	January 2007	200701
01/09/07	2007	January	1	Q1	1	Tuesday	3	January 2007	200701
01/10/07	2007	January	1	Q1	1	Wednesday	4	January 2007	200701
01/11/07	2007	January	1	Q1	1	Thursday	5	January 2007	200701
01/12/07	2007	January	1	Q1	1	Friday	6	January 2007	200701
01/13/07	2007	January	1	Q1	1	Saturday	7	January 2007	200701
01/14/07	2007	January	1	Q1	1	Sunday	1	January 2007	200701
01/15/07	2007	January	1	Q1	1	Monday	2	January 2007	200701
01/16/07	2007	January	1	Q1	1	Tuesday	3	January 2007	200701
01/17/07	2007	January	1	Q1	1	Wednesday	4	January 2007	200701

FIGURE 8-4 Using *ADDCOLUMNS* allows for the creation of a complete date table with a single expression.

Instead of using a single *ADDCOLUMNS* function, one could achieve the same result by creating several calculated columns through the user interface. The main advantage of using *ADDCOLUMNS* is the ability to reuse the same DAX expression to create a date table in other projects.

Using DAX Date Template

The code provided is an example for educational purposes, where we limited the number of columns in the date table to make the code fit the book. There are several examples of date templates available on the web. For example, we created a date table template as a Power BI template file, available at https://www.sqlbi.com/tools/dax-date-template/. You can also extract the same DAX code and implement it in an Analysis Services project.

Working with multiple dates

When there are multiple date columns in the model, you should consider two design options: creating multiple relationships to the same date table or creating multiple date tables. Choosing between the two options is an important decision because it affects the required DAX code and also the kind of analysis that is possible later on.

Consider a *Sales* table with the following three dates for every sales transaction:

- *Order Date*: the date when an order was received.

- *Due Date*: the date when the order is expected to be delivered.

- *Delivery Date*: the actual delivery date.

The developer can relate the three dates to the same date table, knowing that only one of the three relationships can be active. Or, they can create three date tables in order to be able to slice by any of the three freely. Besides, it is likely that other tables contain other dates. For example, a *Purchase* table might contain other dates about the purchase process, a *Budget* table contains other dates in turn, and so on. In the end, every data model typically contains several dates, and one needs to understand the best way to handle all these dates.

In the next sections, we show two design options to handle this scenario and how this affects the DAX code.

Handling multiple relationships to the *Date* table

One can create multiple relationships between two tables. Nevertheless, only one relationship can be active. The other relationships need to be kept inactive. Inactive relationships can be activated in *CALCULATE* through the *USERELATIONSHIP* modifier introduced in Chapter 5, "Understanding *CALCULATE* and *CALCULATETABLE*."

For example, consider the data model shown in Figure 8-5. There are two different relationships between *Sales* and *Date*, but only one can be active. In the example, the active relationship is the one between *Sales[Order Date]* and *Date[Date]*.

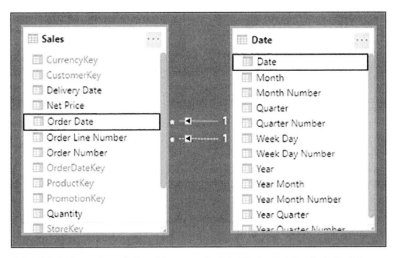

FIGURE 8-5 The active relationship connects *Sales[Order Date]* to *Date[Date]*.

You can create two measures for the sales amount based on a different relationship to the *Date* table:

```
Ordered Amount :=
SUMX ( Sales, Sales[Net Price] * Sales[Quantity] )

Delivered Amount :=
CALCULATE (
    SUMX ( Sales, Sales[Net Price] * Sales[Quantity] ),
    USERELATIONSHIP ( Sales[Delivery Date], 'Date'[Date] )
)
```

The first measure, *Ordered Amount*, uses the active relationship between *Sales* and *Date*, based on *Sales[Order Date]*. The second measure, *Delivered Amount*, executes the same DAX expression using the relationship based on *Sales[Delivery Date]*. *USERELATIONSHIP* changes the active relationship between *Sales* and *Date* in the filter context defined by *CALCULATE*. You can see in Figure 8-6 an example of a report using these measures.

Year	Ordered Amount	Delivered Amount
2007	**11,309,946.12**	**11,034,860.44**
January	794,248.24	624,650.61
February	891,135.91	790,981.53
March	961,289.24	992,760.62
April	1,128,104.82	1,140,575.75
May	936,192.74	839,658.92
June	982,304.46	991,050.56
July	922,542.98	1,078,819.68
August	952,834.59	776,586.75
September	1,009,868.98	1,082,690.27
October	914,273.54	901,968.98
November	825,601.87	872,217.70
December	991,548.75	942,899.08
2008	**9,927,582.99**	**9,901,407.94**

FIGURE 8-6 The *Ordered Amount* and *Delivered Amount* measures are different for each month because the date of delivery might be in the following month.

Using multiple relationships with a single date table increases the number of measures in the data model. Generally, one only defines the measures that are meaningful with certain dates. If you do not want to handle a large number of measures, or if you want complete freedom of using any measure with any date, then you might consider implementing calculation groups as explained in the following chapter.

Handling multiple date tables

Instead of duplicating every measure, an alternative approach is to create different date tables—one for each date in the model—so that every measure aggregates data according to the date selected in the report. From a maintenance point of view, this might seem like a better solution because it lowers the number of measures, and it allows for the selecting of sales that intersect between two months, but it produces a model that is harder to use. For example, one can easily produce a report with the total number of orders received in January and delivered in February of the same year—but it is harder to show in the same chart the amounts ordered and delivered by month.

This approach is also known as the role-playing dimension approach. The date table is a dimension that you duplicate once for each relationship—that is, once for each of its roles. These two options (using inactive relationships and duplicating the date table) are complementary to each other.

To create a *Delivery Date* table and an *Order Date* table, you add the same table twice in the data model. You must at least modify the table name when doing so. You can see in Figure 8-7 the data model containing two different date tables related to *Sales*.

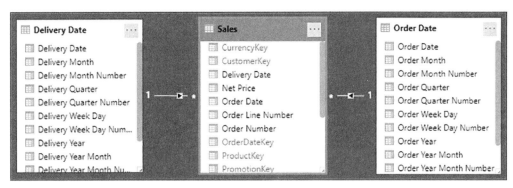

FIGURE 8-7 Each date column in *Sales* has a relationship with a different date table.

Important You must physically duplicate the *Date* table. Therefore, it is a best practice to create different views in the data source, one for each role dimension, so that each date table has different column names and different content. For example, instead of having the same *Year* column in all the date tables, it is better if you use *Order Year* and *Delivery Year*. Navigating the report will be easier this way. This is also visible in Figure 8-7. Furthermore, it is also a good practice to change the content of columns; for instance, by placing a prefix for the year depending on the role of the date. As an example, one might use the *CY* prefix for the content of the *Order Year* column and the *DY* prefix for the content of the *Delivery Year* column.

Figure 8-8 shows an example of a matrix using multiple date tables. Such a report cannot be created using multiple relationships with a single *Date* table. You can see that renaming column names and content is important to produce a readable result. In order to avoid confusion between order and delivery dates, we used *CY* as a prefix for order years and *DY* as a prefix for delivery years.

Order Year	DY 2007	DY 2008	DY 2009	DY 2010	**Total**
CY 2007	11,034,860.44	275,085.69			**11,309,946.12**
CY 2008		9,626,322.26	301,260.73		**9,927,582.99**
CY 2009			9,141,025.36	212,789.51	**9,353,814.87**
Total	**11,034,860.44**	**9,901,407.94**	**9,442,286.09**	**212,789.51**	**30,591,343.98**

FIGURE 8-8 The different prefixes for Year help the user see which is the order year (*CY*) and which is the delivery year (*DY*).

Using multiple date tables, the same measure displays different results depending on the columns used to slice and dice. However, it would be wrong to choose multiple date tables just to reduce the number of measures because this makes it impossible to create a report with the same measures grouped by two dates. For example, consider a single line chart showing *Sales Amount* by *Order Date* and *Delivery Date*. One needs a single *Date* table in the date axis of the chart, and this would be extremely complex to achieve with the multiple date tables pattern.

If your first priority is to reduce the number of measures in a model, enabling the user to browse any measure by any date, you should consider using the calculation groups described in Chapter 9, "Calculation groups," implementing a single date table in the model. The main scenario where multiple date tables are useful is to intersect the same measure by different dates in the same visualization, as demonstrated in Figure 8-8. In most other scenarios, a single date table with multiple relationships is a better choice.

Understanding basic time intelligence calculations

In the previous sections you learned how to correctly build a date table. The date table is useful to perform any time intelligence calculation. DAX provides several time intelligence functions that simplify such calculations. It is easy to use those functions and build useful calculations. Nevertheless, it is all too easy to start using those functions without a good understanding of their inner details. For educational purposes, in this section we demonstrate how to author any time intelligence calculation by using standard DAX functions such as *CALCULATE*, *CALCULATETABLE*, *FILTER*, and *VALUES*. Then, later in this chapter, you learn how the time intelligence functions in DAX help you shorten your code and make it more readable.

There are multiple reasons why we decided to use this approach. The main driver is that, when it comes to time intelligence, there are many different calculations that cannot be expressed by simply using standard DAX functions. At some point in your DAX career, you will need to author a measure more complex than a simple year-to-date (YTD) discovering that DAX has no predefined functions for your requirements. If you learned to code time intelligence the hard way, this will not be a problem. You will roll up your sleeves and write the correct filter function without the help of DAX predefined calculations. If, on the other hand, you simply leverage standard DAX functions, then complex time intelligence will be problematic to solve.

Here is a general explanation of how time intelligence calculations work. Consider a simple measure; its evaluation happens in the current filter context:

```
Sales Amount :=
SUMX ( Sales, Sales[Net Price] * Sales[Quantity] )
```

Because *Sales* has a relationship with *Date*, the current selection on *Date* determines the filter over *Sales*. To perform the calculation over *Sales* in a different period, the programmer needs to modify the existing filter on *Date*. For example, to compute a YTD when the filter context is filtering February 2007, they would need to change the filter context to include January and February 2007, before performing the iteration over *Sales*.

A solution for this is to use a filter argument in a *CALCULATE* function, which returns the year-to-date up to February 2007:

```
Sales Amount Jan-Feb 2007 :=
CALCULATE (
    SUMX ( Sales, Sales[Net Price]  * Sales[Quantity] ),
    FILTER (
```

```
            ALL ( 'Date' ),
            AND (
                'Date'[Date] >= DATE ( 2007, 1, 1 ),
                'Date'[Date] <= DATE ( 2007, 2, 28 )
            )
        )
    )
)
```

The result is visible in Figure 8-9.

Year	Sales Amount	Sales Amount Jan-Feb 2007
2007	**11,309,946.12**	**1,685,384.15**
January	794,248.24	1,685,384.15
February	891,135.91	1,685,384.15
March	961,289.24	1,685,384.15
April	1,128,104.82	1,685,384.15
May	936,192.74	1,685,384.15
June	982,304.46	1,685,384.15
July	922,542.98	1,685,384.15
August	952,834.59	1,685,384.15
September	1,009,868.98	1,685,384.15
October	914,273.54	1,685,384.15

FIGURE 8-9 The result is the sum of January and February 2007, regardless of the date range selection on rows.

The *FILTER* function used as a filter argument of *CALCULATE* returns a set of dates that replaces the selection of the *Date* table. In other words, even though the original filter context coming from the rows of the matrix filters an individual month, the measure computes the value on a different set of dates.

Obviously, a measure that returns the sum of two months is not useful. Nevertheless, once you understand the basic mechanism, you can use it to write a different calculation that computes the year-to-date such as the following code:

```
Sales Amount YTD :=
VAR LastVisibleDate = MAX ( 'Date'[Date] )
VAR CurrentYear = YEAR ( LastVisibleDate )
VAR SetOfDatesYtd =
    FILTER (
        ALL ( 'Date' ),
        AND (
            'Date'[Date] <= LastVisibleDate,
            YEAR ( 'Date'[Date] ) = CurrentYear
        )
    )
VAR Result =
    CALCULATE (
```

```
        SUMX ( Sales, Sales[Net Price]  * Sales[Quantity] ),
        SetOfDatesYtd
    )
RETURN
    Result
```

Though this code is a bit more complex than the previous code, the pattern is the same. In fact, this measure first retrieves in *LastVisibleDate* the last date selected in the current filter context. Once the date is known, it extracts its year and saves it in the *CurrentYear* variable. The third variable *SetOfDatesYtd* contains all the dates in the current year, before the end of the current period. This set is used to replace the filter context on the date to compute the year-to-date, as you can see in Figure 8-10.

Year	Sales Amount	Sales Amount YTD
2007	**11,309,946.12**	**11,309,946.12**
January	794,248.24	794,248.24
February	891,135.91	1,685,384.15
March	961,289.24	2,646,673.39
April	1,128,104.82	3,774,778.20
May	936,192.74	4,710,970.95
June	982,304.46	5,693,275.41
July	922,542.98	6,615,818.39
August	952,834.59	7,568,652.98
September	1,009,868.98	8,578,521.96
October	914,273.54	9,492,795.50
November	825,601.87	10,318,397.37
December	991,548.75	11,309,946.12

FIGURE 8-10 *Sales Amount YTD* computes the year-to-date with a simple *FILTER* function.

As explained earlier, one could write a time intelligence calculation without using time intelligence functions. The important concept here is that time intelligence calculations are not different from any other calculation involving filter context manipulation. Because the measure needs to aggregate values from a different set of dates, the calculation happens in two steps. First, it determines the new filter for the date. Second, it applies the new filter context before computing the actual measure. All time intelligence calculations behave the same way. Once you understand the basic concept, then time intelligence calculations will have no secrets for you.

Before moving further with more time intelligence calculations, it is important to describe a special behavior of DAX when handling relationships that are based on a date. Look at this slightly different formulation of the same code, where instead of filtering the entire date table, we only filter the *Date[Date]* column:

```
Sales Amount YTD :=
VAR LastVisibleDate = MAX ( 'Date'[Date] )
VAR CurrentYear = YEAR ( LastVisibleDate )
VAR SetOfDatesYtd =
    FILTER (
        ALL ( 'Date'[Date] ),
        AND (
            'Date'[Date] <= LastVisibleDate,
            YEAR ( 'Date'[Date] ) = CurrentYear
        )
    )
VAR Result =
    CALCULATE (
        SUMX ( Sales, Sales[Net Price]  * Sales[Quantity] ),
        SetOfDatesYtd
    )
RETURN
    Result
```

If someone uses this measure in a report instead of the previous measure, they will see no changes. In fact, the two versions of this measure compute exactly the same value, but they should not. Let us examine in detail one specific cell—for example, April 2007.

The filter context of the cell is Year 2007, Month April. As a consequence, *LastVisibleDate* contains the 30th of April 2007, whereas *CurrentYear* contains 2007. Then because of its formulation, *SetOfDatesYtd* contains all the dates between January 1, 2007, up to April 30, 2007. In other words, in the cell of April 2007, the code executed is equivalent to this:

```
CALCULATE (
    CALCULATE (
        [Sales Amount],
        AND (                                    -- This filter is equivalent
            'Date'[Date] >= DATE ( 2007, 1, 1),  -- to the result of the FILTER
            'Date'[Date] <= DATE ( 2007, 04, 30 ) -- function
        )
    ),
    'Date'[Year] = 2007,                         -- These are coming from the rows
    'Date'[Month] = "April"                      -- of the matrix in April 2007
)
```

If you recall what you learned about filter contexts and the *CALCULATE* behavior, you should verify that this code should not compute a correct year-to-date. Indeed, the inner *CALCULATE* filter argument returns a table containing the *Date[Date]* column. As such, it should overwrite any existing filter on *Date[Date]*, keeping other filters on other columns untouched. Because the outer *CALCULATE* applies a filter to *Date[Year]* and to *Date[Month]*, the final filter context where *[Sales Amount]* is computed should only contain April 2007. Nevertheless, the measure actually computes a correct result including the other months since January 2007.

The reason is a special behavior of DAX when the relationship between two tables is based on a date column, as it happens for the relationship with *Date* in the demo model we are using here. Whenever a filter is applied to a column of type *Date* or *DateTime* that is used in a relationship between two tables, DAX automatically adds an *ALL* to the entire *Date* table as an additional filter argument to *CALCULATE*. In other words, the previous code should read this way:

```
CALCULATE (
    CALCULATE (
        [Sales Amount],
        AND (                                   -- This filter is equivalent
            'Date'[Date] >= DATE ( 2007, 1, 1), -- to the result of the FILTER
            'Date'[Date] <= DATE ( 2007, 04, 30 ) -- function
        ),
        ALL ( 'Date' )    -- This is automatically added by the engine
    ),
    'Date'[Year] = 2007,                        -- These are coming from the rows
    'Date'[Month] = "April"                     -- of the matrix in April 2007
)
```

Every time a filter is applied on the column that defines a one-to-many relationship with another table, and the column has a *Date* or *DateTime* data type, DAX automatically propagates the filter to the other table and overrides any other filter on other columns of the same lookup table.

The reason for this behavior is to make time intelligence calculations work more simply in the case where the relationship between the date table and the sales table is based on a date column. In the next section, we describe the behavior of the Mark as Date Table feature, which introduces a similar behavior for relationships not based on a date column.

Using Mark as Date Table

Applying a filter on the date column of a calendar table works fine if the date column also defines the relationship. However, one might have a relationship based on another column. Many existing date tables use an integer column—typically in the format YYYYMMDD—to create the relationship with other tables.

In order to demonstrate the behavior, we created the *DateKey* column in both the *Date* and *Sales* tables. We then linked the two using the *DateKey* column instead of the date column. The resulting model is visible in Figure 8-11.

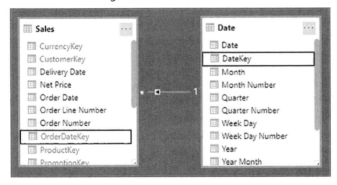

FIGURE 8-11 The relationship between *Sales* and *Date* uses the *DateKey* column, with an *Integer* data type.

Using the same code that worked in previous examples to compute the YTD in Figure 8-11 would result in an incorrect calculation. You see this in Figure 8-12.

Year	Sales Amount	Sales Amount YTD
2007	**11,309,946.12**	**11,309,946.12**
January	794,248.24	794,248.24
February	891,135.91	891,135.91
March	961,289.24	961,289.24
April	1,128,104.82	1,128,104.82
May	936,192.74	936,192.74
June	982,304.46	982,304.46
July	922,542.98	922,542.98
August	952,834.59	952,834.59
September	1,009,868.98	1,009,868.98
October	914,273.54	914,273.54
November	825,601.87	825,601.87
December	991,548.75	991,548.75

FIGURE 8-12 Using an integer for the relationship makes the previous code stop working.

As you can see, now the report shows the same value for *Sales Amount* and for *Sales Amount YTD*. Indeed, since the relationship is no longer based on a *DateTime* column, DAX does not add the automatic *ALL* function to the date table. As such, the filter with the date is intersecting with the previous filter, vanishing the effect of the measure.

In such cases there are two possible solutions: one is to manually add *ALL* to all the time intelligence calculations. This solution is somewhat cumbersome because it requires the DAX coder to always remember to add *ALL* to all of the calculations. The other possible solution is much more convenient: mark the *Date* table as a date table.

If the date table is marked as such, then DAX will automatically add *ALL* to the table even if the relationship was not based on a date column. Be mindful that once the table is marked as a date table, the automatic *ALL* on the table is always added whenever one modifies the filter context on the date column. There are scenarios where this effect is undesirable, and in such cases, one would need to write complex code to build the correct filter. We cover this later in this chapter.

Introducing basic time intelligence functions

Now that you have learned the basic mechanism that runs time intelligence calculations, it is time to simplify the code. Indeed, if DAX developers had to write complex *FILTER* expressions every time they need a simple year-to-date calculation, their life would be troublesome.

To simplify the authoring of time intelligence calculations, DAX offers a rich set of functions that automatically perform the same filtering we wrote manually in the previous examples. For example, this is the version of *Sales Amount YTD* measure we wrote earlier:

```
Sales Amount YTD :=
VAR LastVisibleDate = MAX ( 'Date'[Date] )
VAR CurrentYear = YEAR ( LastVisibleDate )
VAR SetOfDatesYTD =
    FILTER (
        ALL ( 'Date'[Date] ),
        AND (
            'Date'[Date] <= LastVisibleDate,
            YEAR ( 'Date'[Date] ) = CurrentYear
        )
    )
VAR Result =
    CALCULATE (
        SUMX ( Sales, Sales[Net Price]  * Sales[Quantity] ),
        SetOfDatesYTD
    )
RETURN
    Result
```

The same behavior can be expressed by a much simpler code using the *DATESYTD* function:

```
Sales Amount YTD :=
CALCULATE (
    SUMX ( Sales, Sales[Net Price]  * Sales[Quantity] ),
    DATESYTD ( 'Date'[Date] )
)
```

Be mindful that *DATESYTD* does exactly what the more complex code performs. The gain is neither in performance nor in behavior of the code. However, because it is so much easier to write, you see that learning the many time intelligence functions in DAX is worth your time.

Simple calculations like year-to-date, quarter-to-date, month-to-date, or the comparison of sales in the current year versus the previous year can be authored with simpler code as they all rely on basic time intelligence functions. More complex calculations can oftentimes be expressed by mixing standard time intelligence functions. The only scenario where the developer will really need to author complex code is when they need nonstandard calendars, like a weekly calendar, or for complex time intelligence calculations when the standard functions will not meet the requirements.

 Note   All time intelligence functions in DAX apply a filter condition on the date column of a *Date* table. You can find some examples of how to write these calculations in DAX later in this book and a complete list of all the time intelligence features rewritten in plain DAX at http://www.daxpatterns.com/time-patterns/.

In the next sections, we introduce the basic time intelligence calculations authored with the standard time intelligence functions in DAX. Later in this chapter, we will cover more advanced calculations.

Using year-to-date, quarter-to-date, and month-to-date

The calculations of year-to-date (YTD), quarter-to-date (QTD), and month-to-date (MTD) are all very similar. Month-to-date is meaningful only when you are looking at data at the day level, whereas year-to-date and quarter-to-date calculations are often used to look at data at the month level.

You can calculate the year-to-date value of sales for each month by modifying the filter context on dates for a range that starts on January 1 and ends on the month corresponding to the calculated cell. You see this in the following DAX formula:

```
Sales Amount YTD :=
CALCULATE (
    [Sales Amount],
    DATESYTD ( 'Date'[Date] )
)
```

DATESYTD is a function that returns a table with all the dates from the beginning of the year until the last date included in the current filter context. This table is used as a filter argument in *CALCULATE* to set the new filter for the *Sales Amount* calculation. Similar to *DATESYTD*, there are another two functions that return the month-to-date (*DATESMTD*) and quarter-to-date (*DATESQTD*) sets. For example, you can see measures based on *DATESYTD* and *DATESQTD* in Figure 8-13.

Year	Sales Amount	Sales Amount YTD	Sales Amount QTD
2007	**11,309,946.12**	**11,309,946.12**	**2,731,424.16**
January	794,248.24	794,248.24	794,248.24
February	891,135.91	1,685,384.15	1,685,384.15
March	961,289.24	2,646,673.39	2,646,673.39
April	1,128,104.82	3,774,778.20	1,128,104.82
May	936,192.74	4,710,970.95	2,064,297.56
June	982,304.46	5,693,275.41	3,046,602.02
July	922,542.98	6,615,818.39	922,542.98
August	952,834.59	7,568,652.98	1,875,377.57
September	1,009,868.98	8,578,521.96	2,885,246.55
October	914,273.54	9,492,795.50	914,273.54
November	825,601.87	10,318,397.37	1,739,875.41
December	991,548.75	11,309,946.12	2,731,424.16

FIGURE 8-13 The *Sales Amount YTD* and *Sales Amount QTD* measures are side by side with the regular *Sales Amount* measure.

This approach requires the use of *CALCULATE*. DAX also offers a set of functions to simplify the syntax of to-date calculations: *TOTALYTD*, *TOTALQTD*, and *TOTALMTD*. In the following code, you can see the year-to-date calculation expressed using *TOTALYTD*:

```
YTD Sales :=
TOTALYTD (
    [Sales Amount],
    'Date'[Date]
)
```

The syntax is somewhat different, as *TOTALYTD* requires the expression to aggregate as its first parameter and the date column as its second parameter. Nevertheless, the behavior is identical to the original measure. The name *TOTALYTD* hides the underlying *CALCULATE* function, which is a good reason to limit its use. In fact, whenever *CALCULATE* is present in the code, making it evident is always a good practice—for example, for the context transition it implies.

Similar to year-to-date, you can also define quarter-to-date and month-to-date with built-in functions, as in these measures:

```
QTD Sales := TOTALQTD ( [Sales Amount], 'Date'[Date] )
QTD Sales := CALCULATE ( [Sales Amount], DATESQTD ( 'Date'[Date] ) )
MTD Sales := TOTALMTD ( [Sales Amount], 'Date'[Date] )
MTD Sales := CALCULATE ( [Sales Amount], DATESMTD ( 'Date'[Date] ) )
```

Calculating a year-to-date measure over a fiscal year that does not end on December 31 requires an optional third parameter that specifies the end day of the fiscal year. For example, both the following measures calculate the fiscal year-to-date for *Sales*:

```
Fiscal YTD Sales := TOTALYTD ( [Sales Amount], 'Date'[Date], "06-30" )
Fiscal YTD Sales := CALCULATE ( [Sales Amount], DATESYTD ( 'Date'Date], "06-30" ) )
```

The last parameter corresponds to June 30—that is, the end of the fiscal year. There are several time intelligence functions that have a last, optional year-end date parameter for this purpose: *STARTOF-YEAR*, *ENDOFYEAR*, *PREVIOUSYEAR*, *NEXTYEAR*, *DATESYTD*, *TOTALYTD*, *OPENINGBALANCEYEAR*, and *CLOSINGBALANCEYEAR*.

> **Important**   Depending on the culture settings, you might have to use the day number first. You can also consider using a string with the format YYYY-MM-DD to avoid any ambiguity caused by culture settings; in that case, the year does not matter for the purpose of determining the last day of the year to use for year-to-date calculation:
>
> ```
> Fiscal YTD Sales := TOTALYTD ( [Sales Amount], 'Date'[Date], "30-06" )
> Fiscal YTD Sales := CALCULATE ( [Sales Amount], DATESYTD ( 'Date'[Date], "30-06" ) )
> Fiscal YTD Sales := CALCULATE ( [Sales Amount], DATESYTD ( 'Date'[Date], "2018-06-30" ) )
> ```
>
> However, consider that as of June 2018 there is a bug in case the fiscal year starts in March and ends in February. More details and a workaround are described later in the "Advanced time intelligence" section of this chapter.

Computing time periods from prior periods

Several calculations are required to get a value from the same period in the prior year (PY). This can be useful for making comparisons of trends during a time period this year to the same time period last year. In that case *SAMEPERIODLASTYEAR* comes in handy:

```
PY Sales := CALCULATE ( [Sales Amount], SAMEPERIODLASTYEAR ( 'Date'[Date] ) )
```

SAMEPERIODLASTYEAR returns a set of dates shifted one year back in time. *SAMEPERIODLAST-YEAR* is a specialized version of the more generic *DATEADD* function, which accepts the number and type of period to shift. The types of periods supported are *YEAR*, *QUARTER*, *MONTH*, and *DAY*. For example, you can define the same *PY Sales* measure using this equivalent expression, which uses *DATEADD* to shift the current filter context one year back in time:

```
PY Sales := CALCULATE( [Sales Amount], DATEADD ( 'Date'[Date], -1, YEAR ) )
```

DATEADD is more powerful than *SAMEPERIODLASTYEAR* because, in a similar way, DATEADD can compute the value from a previous quarter (PQ), month (PM), or day (PD):

```
PQ Sales := CALCULATE ( [Sales Amount], DATEADD ( 'Date'[Date], -1, QUARTER ) )
PM Sales := CALCULATE ( [Sales Amount], DATEADD ( 'Date'[Date], -1, MONTH ) )
PD Sales := CALCULATE ( [Sales Amount], DATEADD ( 'Date'[Date], -1, DAY ) )
```

In Figure 8-14 you can see the result of some of these measures.

Year	Sales Amount	PY Sales	PQ Sales	PM Sales
2007	**11,309,946.12**		**8,578,521.96**	**10,318,397.37**
January	794,248.24			
February	891,135.91			794,248.24
March	961,289.24			891,135.91
April	1,128,104.82		794,248.24	961,289.24
May	936,192.74		891,135.91	1,128,104.82
June	982,304.46		961,289.24	936,192.74
July	922,542.98		1,128,104.82	982,304.46
August	952,834.59		936,192.74	922,542.98
September	1,009,868.98		982,304.46	952,834.59
October	914,273.54		922,542.98	1,009,868.98
November	825,601.87		952,834.59	914,273.54
December	991,548.75		1,009,868.98	825,601.87
2008	**9,927,582.99**	**11,309,946.12**	**9,861,395.69**	**9,997,422.60**
January	656,766.69	794,248.24	914,273.54	991,548.75
February	600,080.00	891,135.91	825,601.87	656,766.69
March	559,538.52	961,289.24	991,548.75	600,080.00

FIGURE 8-14 *DATEADD* lets you shift the current filter context to different periods.

Another useful function is *PARALLELPERIOD*, which is similar to *DATEADD*, but returns the full period specified in the third parameter instead of the partial period returned by *DATEADD*. Thus, although a single month is selected in the current filter context, the following measure using *PARALLEPERIOD* calculates the amount of sales for the whole previous year:

```
PY Total Sales :=
CALCULATE ( [Sales Amount], PARALLELPERIOD ( 'Date'[Date], -1, YEAR ) )
```

In a similar way, using different parameters, one can obtain different periods:

```
PQ Total Sales :=
CALCULATE ( [Sales Amount], PARALLELPERIOD ( 'Date'[Date], -1, QUARTER ) )
```

In Figure 8-15 you can see *PARALLELPERIOD* used to compute the previous year and quarter.

Year	Sales Amount	PY Total Sales	PQ Total Sales
2007	11,309,946.12		8,578,521.96
Q1	2,646,673.39		
January	794,248.24		
February	891,135.91		
March	961,289.24		
Q2	3,046,602.02		2,646,673.39
April	1,128,104.82		2,646,673.39
May	936,192.74		2,646,673.39
June	982,304.46		2,646,673.39
Q3	2,885,246.55		3,046,602.02
July	922,542.98		3,046,602.02
August	952,834.59		3,046,602.02
September	1,009,868.98		3,046,602.02
Q4	2,731,424.16		2,885,246.55
October	914,273.54		2,885,246.55
November	825,601.87		2,885,246.55
December	991,548.75		2,885,246.55
2008	9,927,582.99	11,309,946.12	9,861,395.69
Q1	1,816,385.21	11,309,946.12	2,731,424.16
January	656,766.69	11,309,946.12	2,731,424.16
February	600,080.00	11,309,946.12	2,731,424.16
March	559,538.52	11,309,946.12	2,731,424.16

FIGURE 8-15 *PARALLELPERIOD* returns the full period instead of the current period shifted in time.

There are functions similar but not identical to *PARALLELPERIOD*, which are *PREVIOUSYEAR*, *PREVIOUSQUARTER*, *PREVIOUSMONTH*, *PREVIOUSDAY*, *NEXTYEAR*, *NEXTQUARTER*, *NEXTMONTH*, and *NEXTDAY*. These functions behave like *PARALLELPERIOD* when the selection has a single element selected corresponding to the function name—year, quarter, month, and day. If multiple periods are selected, then *PARALLELPERIOD* returns a shifted result of all of them. On the other hand, the specific functions (year, quarter, month, and day, respectively) return a single element that is contiguous to the selected period regardless of length. For example, the following code returns March, April, and May 2008 in case the second quarter of 2008 (April, May, and June) is selected:

```
PM Total Sales :=
CALCULATE ( [Sales Amount], PARALLELPERIOD ( 'Date'[Date], -1, MONTH ) )
```

Conversely, the following code only returns March 2008 in case the second quarter of 2008 (April, May, and June) is selected.

```
Last PM Sales :=
CALCULATE ( [Sales Amount], PREVIOUSMONTH( 'Date'[Date] ) )
```

The difference between the two measures is visible in Figure 8-16. The *Last PM Sales* measure returns the value of December 2007 for both 2008 and Q1 2008, whereas *PM Total Sales* always returns the value for the number of months of the selection—three for a quarter and twelve for a year. This occurs even though the initial selection is shifted back one month.

Year	Sales Amount	Last PM Sales	PM Total Sales
Q4	**2,731,424.16**	**1,009,868.98**	**2,749,744.39**
October	914,273.54	1,009,868.98	1,009,868.98
November	825,601.87	914,273.54	914,273.54
December	991,548.75	825,601.87	825,601.87
2008	**9,927,582.99**	**991,548.75**	**9,997,422.60**
Q1	**1,816,385.21**	**991,548.75**	**2,248,395.44**
January	656,766.69	991,548.75	991,548.75
February	600,080.00	656,766.69	656,766.69
March	559,538.52	600,080.00	600,080.00
Q2	**2,738,040.73**	**559,538.52**	**2,452,437.65**
April	999,667.17	559,538.52	559,538.52
May	893,231.96	999,667.17	999,667.17
June	845,141.60	893,231.96	893,231.96
Q3	**2,575,545.59**	**845,141.60**	**2,457,249.97**
July	890,547.41	845,141.60	845,141.60

FIGURE 8-16 *PREVIOUSMONTH* returns a single month even when the selection includes a quarter or a year.

Mixing time intelligence functions

One useful feature of time intelligence functions is the capability of composing more complex formulas by using time intelligence functions together. The first parameter of most time intelligence functions is the date column in the date table. However, this is just syntax sugar for the complete syntax. In fact, the full syntax of time intelligence functions requires a table as its first parameter, as you can see in the following two equivalent versions of the same measure. When used, the date column referenced is translated into a table with the unique values active in the filter context after a context transition, if a row context exists:

```
PY Sales :=
CALCULATE (
    [Sales Amount],
    DATESYTD ( 'Date'[Date] )
)

-- is equivalent to

PY Sales :=
CALCULATE (
    [Sales Amount],
    DATESYTD ( CALCULATETABLE ( DISTINCT ( 'Date'[Date] ) ) )
)
```

Time intelligence functions accept a table as their first parameter, and they act as time shifters. These functions take the content of the table, and they shift it back and forth over time by any number of years, quarters, months, or days. Because time intelligence functions accept a table, any table expression can be used in place of the table—including another time intelligence function. This makes it possible to combine multiple time intelligence functions, by cascading their results one into the other.

For example, the following code compares the year-to-date with the corresponding value in the previous year. It does so by combining *SAMEPERIODLASTYEAR* and *DATESYTD*. It is interesting to note that exchanging the order of the function calls does not change the result:

```
PY YTD Sales :=
CALCULATE (
    [Sales Amount],
    SAMEPERIODLASTYEAR ( DATESYTD ( 'Date'[Date] ) )
)

-- is equivalent to

PY YTD Sales :=
CALCULATE (
    [Sales Amount],
    DATESYTD ( SAMEPERIODLASTYEAR ( 'Date'[Date] ) )
)
```

It is also possible to use *CALCULATE* to move the current filter context to a different time period and then invoke a function that, in turn, analyzes the filter context and moves it to a different time period. The following two definitions of *PY YTD Sales* are equivalent to the previous two; *YTD Sales* and *PY Sales* measures are defined earlier in this chapter:

```
PY YTD Sales :=
CALCULATE (
    [YTD Sales],
    SAMEPERIODLASTYEAR ( 'Date'[Date] )
)
```

```
-- is equivalent to

PY YTD Sales :=
CALCULATE (
    [PY Sales],
    DATESYTD ( 'Date'[Date] )
)
```

You can see the results of *PY YTD Sales* in Figure 8-17. The values of *YTD Sales* are reported for *PY YTD Sales*, shifted one year ahead.

Year	Sales Amount	YTD Sales	PY YTD Sales
2007	11,309,946.12	11,309,946.12	
January	794,248.24	794,248.24	
February	891,135.91	1,685,384.15	
March	961,289.24	2,646,673.39	
April	1,128,104.82	3,774,778.20	
May	936,192.74	4,710,970.95	
June	982,304.46	5,693,275.41	
July	922,542.98	6,615,818.39	
August	952,834.59	7,568,652.98	
September	1,009,868.98	8,578,521.96	
October	914,273.54	9,492,795.50	
November	825,601.87	10,318,397.37	
December	991,548.75	11,309,946.12	
2008	9,927,582.99	9,927,582.99	11,309,946.12
January	656,766.69	656,766.69	794,248.24
February	600,080.00	1,256,846.69	1,685,384.15
March	559,538.52	1,816,385.21	2,646,673.39
April	999,667.17	2,816,052.38	3,774,778.20
May	893,231.96	3,709,284.34	4,710,970.95
June	845,141.60	4,554,425.94	5,693,275.41
July	890,547.41	5,444,973.35	6,615,818.39

FIGURE 8-17 The prior year year-to-date calculation can be computed by composing time intelligence functions.

All the examples seen in this section can operate at the year, quarter, month, and day levels, but not at the week level. Time intelligence functions are not available for week-based calculations because there are too many variations of years/quarters/months based on weeks. For this reason, you must implement DAX expressions to handle week-based calculations. You can find more details and an example of this approach in the "Working with custom calendars" section, later in this chapter.

Computing a difference over previous periods

A common operation is calculating the difference between a measure and its value in the prior year. You can express that difference as an absolute value or as a percentage. You have already seen how to obtain the value for the prior year with the *PY Sales* measure:

```
PY Sales := CALCULATE ( [Sales Amount], SAMEPERIODLASTYEAR ( 'Date'[Date] ) )
```

For *Sales Amount,* the absolute difference over the previous year (year-over-year or YOY) is a simple subtraction. However, you need to add a failsafe if you want to only show the difference when both values are available. In that case, variables are important to avoid calculating the same measure twice. You can define a *YOY Sales* measure with the following expression:

```
YOY Sales :=
VAR CySales = [Sales Amount]
VAR PySales = [PY Sales]
VAR YoySales =
    IF (
        NOT ISBLANK ( CySales ) && NOT ISBLANK ( PySales ),
        CySales - PySales
    )
RETURN
    YoySales
```

The equivalent calculation for comparing the year-to-date measure with a corresponding value in the prior year is a simple subtraction of two measures, *YTD Sales* and *PY YTD Sales*. You learned those in the previous section:

```
YTD Sales := TOTALYTD ( [Sales Amount], 'Date'[Date] )

PY YTD Sales :=
CALCULATE (
    [Sales Amount],
    DATESYTD ( SAMEPERIODLASTYEAR ( 'Date'[Date] ) )
)

YOY YTD Sales :=
VAR CyYtdSales = [YTD Sales]
VAR PyYtdSales = [PY YTD Sales]
VAR YoyYtdSales =
    IF (
        NOT ISBLANK ( CyYtdSales ) && NOT ISBLANK ( PyYtdSales ),
        CyYtdSales - PyYtdSales
    )
RETURN
    YoyYtdSales
```

Often, the year-over-year difference is better expressed as a percentage in a report. You can define this calculation by dividing *YOY Sales* by *PY Sales*; this way, the difference uses the previous year value as a reference for the percentage difference (100 percent corresponds to a value that is doubled in one year). In the following expressions that define the *YOY Sales%* measure, the *DIVIDE* function avoids a divide-by-zero error if there is no corresponding data in the prior year:

```
YOY Sales% := DIVIDE ( [YOY Sales], [PY Sales] )
```

A similar calculation displays the percentage difference of a year-over-year comparison for the year-to-date aggregation. The following definition of *YOY YTD Sales%* implements this calculation:

```
YOY YTD Sales% := DIVIDE ( [YOY YTD Sales], [PY YTD Sales] )
```

In Figure 8-18, you can see the results of these measures in a report.

Year	Sales Amount	PY Sales	YOY Sales	YOY Sales%	YTD Sales	PY YTD Sales	YOY YTD Sales	YOY YTD Sales%
2007	11,309,946.12		11,309,946.12		11,309,946.12		11,309,946.12	
January	794,248.24		794,248.24		794,248.24		794,248.24	
February	891,135.91		891,135.91		1,685,384.15		1,685,384.15	
March	961,289.24		961,289.24		2,646,673.39		2,646,673.39	
April	1,128,104.82		1,128,104.82		3,774,778.20		3,774,778.20	
May	936,192.74		936,192.74		4,710,970.95		4,710,970.95	
June	982,304.46		982,304.46		5,693,275.41		5,693,275.41	
July	922,542.98		922,542.98		6,615,818.39		6,615,818.39	
August	952,834.59		952,834.59		7,568,652.98		7,568,652.98	
September	1,009,868.98		1,009,868.98		8,578,521.96		8,578,521.96	
October	914,273.54		914,273.54		9,492,795.50		9,492,795.50	
November	825,601.87		825,601.87		10,318,397.37		10,318,397.37	
December	991,548.75		991,548.75		11,309,946.12		11,309,946.12	
2008	9,927,582.99	11,309,946.12	-1,382,363.13	-12.22%	9,927,582.99	11,309,946.12	-1,382,363.13	-12.22%
January	656,766.69	794,248.24	-137,481.55	-17.31%	656,766.69	794,248.24	-137,481.55	-17.31%
February	600,080.00	891,135.91	-291,055.92	-32.66%	1,256,846.69	1,685,384.15	-428,537.46	-25.43%
March	559,538.52	961,289.24	-401,750.72	-41.79%	1,816,385.21	2,646,673.39	-830,288.18	-31.37%
April	999,667.17	1,128,104.82	-128,437.65	-11.39%	2,816,052.38	3,774,778.20	-958,725.82	-25.40%

FIGURE 8-18 The report shows all the year-over-year (YOY) measures used in the same matrix.

Computing a moving annual total

Another common calculation that eliminates seasonal changes in sales is the moving annual total (MAT), which considers the sales aggregation over the past 12 months. You learned a technique to compute a moving average in Chapter 7, "Working with iterators and with *CALCULATE*." Here we want to describe a formula to compute a similar average by using time intelligence functions.

For example, summing the range of dates from April 2007 to March 2008 calculates the value of *MAT Sales* for March 2008. The easiest approach is to use the *DATESINPERIOD* function. *DATESINPERIOD* returns all the dates included within a period that can be a number of years, quarters, months, or days.

```
MAT Sales :=
CALCULATE (                          -- Compute the sales amount in a new filter
    [Sales Amount],                  -- context modified by the next argument.
    DATESINPERIOD (                  -- Returns a table containing
        'Date'[Date],                -- Date[Date] values,
        MAX ( 'Date'[Date] ),        -- starting from the last visible date
        -1,                          -- and going back 1
        YEAR                         -- year.
    )
)
```

Using *DATESINPERIOD* is usually the best option for the moving annual total calculation. For educational purposes, it is useful to see other techniques to obtain the same filter. Consider this alternative *MAT Sales* definition, which calculates the moving annual total for sales:

```
MAT Sales :=
CALCULATE (
    [Sales Amount],
    DATESBETWEEN (
        'Date'[Date],
        NEXTDAY ( SAMEPERIODLASTYEAR ( LASTDATE ( 'Date'[Date] ) ) ),
        LASTDATE ( 'Date'[Date] )
    )
)
```

The implementation of this measure requires some attention. The formula uses the *DATESBETWEEN* function, which returns the dates from a column included between two specified dates. Because *DATESBETWEEN* works at the day level, even if the report is querying data at the month level, the code must calculate the first day and the last day of the required interval. A way to obtain the last day is by using the *LASTDATE* function. *LASTDATE* is like *MAX,* but instead of returning a value, it returns a table. Being a table, it can be used as a parameter to other time intelligence functions. Starting from that date, the first day of the interval is computed by requesting the following day (by calling *NEXTDAY*) of the corresponding date one year before (by using *SAMEPERIODLASTYEAR*).

One problem with moving annual totals is that they compute the aggregated value—the sum. Dividing this value by the number of months included in the period averages it over the time frame. This gives you a moving annual average (MAA):

```
MAA Sales :=
CALCULATE (
    DIVIDE ( [Sales Amount], DISTINCTCOUNT ( 'Date'[Year Month] ) ),
    DATESINPERIOD (
        'Date'[Date],
        MAX ( 'Date'[Date] ),
        -1,
        YEAR
    )
)
```

As you have seen, using time intelligence functions results in powerful measures. In Figure 8-19, you can see a report that includes the moving annual total and average calculations.

Year	Sales Amount	MAT Sales	MAA Sales
2007	**11,309,946.12**	**11,309,946.12**	**942,495.51**
January	794,248.24	794,248.24	794,248.24
February	891,135.91	1,685,384.15	842,692.08
March	961,289.24	2,646,673.39	882,224.46
April	1,128,104.82	3,774,778.20	943,694.55
May	936,192.74	4,710,970.95	942,194.19
June	982,304.46	5,693,275.41	948,879.23
July	922,542.98	6,615,818.39	945,116.91
August	952,834.59	7,568,652.98	946,081.62
September	1,009,868.98	8,578,521.96	953,169.11
October	914,273.54	9,492,795.50	949,279.55
November	825,601.87	10,318,397.37	938,036.12
December	991,548.75	11,309,946.12	942,495.51
2008	**9,927,582.99**	**9,927,582.99**	**827,298.58**
January	656,766.69	11,172,464.58	931,038.71
February	600,080.00	10,881,408.66	906,784.06
March	559,538.52	10,479,657.94	873,304.83

FIGURE 8-19 The *MAT Sales* and *MAA Sales* measures are simple to author by using time intelligence functions.

Using the right call order for nested time intelligence functions

When nesting time intelligence functions, it is important to pay attention to the order used in the nesting. In the previous example, we used the following DAX expression to retrieve the first day of the moving annual total:

```
NEXTDAY ( SAMEPERIODLASTYEAR ( LASTDATE ( 'Date'[Date] ) ) )
```

You would obtain the same behavior by inverting the call order between *NEXTDAY* and *SAMEPERIOD-LASTYEAR*, as in the following code:

```
SAMEPERIODLASTYEAR ( NEXTDAY ( LASTDATE ( 'Date'[Date] ) ) )
```

The result is almost always the same, but this order of evaluation presents a risk of producing incorrect results at the end of the period. In fact, authoring the MAT code using this order would result in this version, which is wrong:

```
MAT Sales Wrong :=
CALCULATE (
    [Sales Amount],
    DATESBETWEEN (
        'Date'[Date],
        SAMEPERIODLASTYEAR ( NEXTDAY ( LASTDATE ( 'Date'[Date] ) ) ),
        LASTDATE ( 'Date'[Date] )
    )
)
```

This version of the formula computes the wrong result at the upper boundary of the date range. You can see this happening in a report like the one in Figure 8-20.

Year	Sales Amount	MAT Sales Wrong
12/20/09	386.51	9,410,763.07
12/21/09	65,730.00	9,430,959.15
12/22/09	14,818.07	9,423,905.05
12/23/09	10,483.74	9,411,255.28
12/24/09	35,297.95	9,424,346.89
12/25/09	52,181.37	9,446,383.19
12/26/09	21,490.72	9,456,772.35
12/27/09	19,949.44	9,465,159.42
12/28/09	21,174.80	9,463,422.23
12/29/09	15,790.76	9,343,878.70
12/30/09	16,428.63	9,340,739.84
12/31/09	40,930.59	30,591,343.98
Total	**9,353,814.87**	**30,591,343.98**

FIGURE 8-20 The *MAT Sales Wrong* measure shows an incorrect result at the end of 2009.

The measure computes the correct value up to December 30, 2009. Then, on December 31 the result is surprisingly high. The reason for this is that on December 31, 2009 *NEXTDAY* should return a table containing January 1, 2010. Unfortunately, the date table does not contain a row with January 1, 2010; thus, *NEXTDAY* cannot build its result. Consequently, not being able to return a valid result, *NEXTDAY* returns an empty table. A similar behavior happens with the following function: *SAMEPERIODLAST-YEAR*. It receives an empty table, and as the result, it returns an empty table too. Because *DATESBE-TWEEN* requires a scalar value, the empty result of *SAMEPERIODLASTYEAR* is considered as a blank value. Blank—as a *DateTime* value—equals zero, which is December 30, 1899. Thus, on December 31, 2009, *DATESBETWEEN* returns the whole set of dates in the *Date* table; indeed, the blank as a starting date defines no boundaries for the initial date, and this results in an incorrect result.

The solution is straightforward. It simply involves using the correct order of evaluation. If *SAMEPERI-ODLASTYEAR* is the first function called, then on December 31, 2009, it will return a valid date, which is December 31, 2008. Then, *NEXTDAY* returns January 1, 2009, that this time does exist in the *Date* table.

In general, all time intelligence functions return sets of existing dates. If a date does not belong to the *Date* table, then these functions return an empty table that corresponds to a blank scalar value. In some scenarios this behavior might produce unexpected results, as explained in this section. For the specific example of the moving annual total, using *DATESINPERIOD* is simpler and safer, but this concept is important in case time intelligence functions are combined for other custom calculations.

Understanding semi-additive calculations

The techniques you have learned so far to aggregate values from different time periods work fine with regular additive measures. An additive measure is a calculation that aggregates values using a regular sum when sliced by any attribute. As an example, think about the sales amount. The sales amount of all the customers is the sum of the sales amount of each individual customer. At the same time, the sales amount of a full year is the sum of the sales amount of all the days in the year. There is nothing special about additive measures; they are intuitive and easy to use and to understand.

However, not all calculations are additive. Some measures are non-additive. An example would be a distinct count of the gender of the customers. For each individual customer, the result is 1. But when computed over a set of customers including different genders, the result will never be greater than the number of genders (three in case of Contoso—blank, M, and F). Thus, the result over a set of customers, dates, or any other column cannot be computed by summing individual values. Nonadditive measures are frequent in reports, oftentimes associated with distinct counts calculations. Nonadditive measures are more difficult to use and to understand than regular additive measures. However, regarding additivity, they are not the hardest ones. Indeed, there is a third kind of measure, the semi-additive measure, that proves to be challenging.

A semi-additive measure uses one kind of aggregation (typically a sum) when sliced by certain columns and a different kind of aggregation (usually the last date) when sliced by other columns. A great example is the balance of a bank account. The balance of all the customers is the sum of each individual balance. However, the balance over a full year is not the sum of monthly balances. Instead it is the balance on the last date of the year. Slicing the balance by customer results in a regular calculation, whereas slicing by date means the calculation follows a different path. As an example, look at the data in Figure 8-21.

Name	Date ▲	Balance
Katie Jordan	1/31/2010	1,687.00
Luis Bonifaz	1/31/2010	1,470.00
Maurizio Macagno	1/31/2010	1,500.00
Katie Jordan	2/28/2010	2,812.00
Luis Bonifaz	2/28/2010	2,450.00
Maurizio Macagno	2/28/2010	2,500.00
Katie Jordan	3/31/2010	3,737.00
Luis Bonifaz	3/31/2010	3,430.00
Maurizio Macagno	3/31/2010	3,500.00

FIGURE 8-21 The figure shows an excerpt of the sample data used for semi-additive calculations.

The sample data shows that the balance of Katie Jordan at the end of January was 1,687.00, whereas at the end of February the balance was 2,812.00. When we look at January and February together, her balance is not the sum of the two values. Instead, it is the last balance available. On the other hand, the overall balance of all customers in January is the sum of the three customers together.

If one uses a simple sum to aggregate values, the result of the calculation would be a sum over all the attributes as you can see in Figure 8-22.

Year	Katie Jordan	Luis Bonifaz	Maurizio Macagno	Total
CY 2010	17,742.00	15,631.00	15,650.00	49,023.00
Q1	8,236.00	7,350.00	7,500.00	23,086.00
January	1,687.00	1,470.00	1,500.00	4,657.00
February	2,812.00	2,450.00	2,500.00	7,762.00
March	3,737.00	3,430.00	3,500.00	10,667.00
Q2	6,975.00	6,076.00	6,200.00	19,251.00
April	2,250.00	1,960.00	2,000.00	6,210.00
May	2,025.00	1,764.00	1,800.00	5,589.00
June	2,700.00	2,352.00	2,400.00	7,452.00
Q3	2,531.00	2,205.00	1,950.00	6,686.00
July	2,531.00	2,205.00	1,950.00	6,686.00
Total	17,742.00	15,631.00	15,650.00	49,023.00

FIGURE 8-22 The figure shows two types of totals; totals over time for each customer and totals over all customers for different time periods.

As you can note, the individual month values are correct. But at the aggregated levels—both at the quarter level and at the year level—the result is still a sum, making no sense. The correct result is visible in Figure 8-23, where—at each aggregate level—the report shows the last known value.

Year	Katie Jordan	Luis Bonifaz	Maurizio Macagno	Total
CY 2010	**2,531.00**	**2,205.00**	**1,950.00**	**6,686.00**
Q1	**3,737.00**	**3,430.00**	**3,500.00**	**10,667.00**
January	1,687.00	1,470.00	1,500.00	**4,657.00**
February	2,812.00	2,450.00	2,500.00	**7,762.00**
March	3,737.00	3,430.00	3,500.00	**10,667.00**
Q2	**2,700.00**	**2,352.00**	**2,400.00**	**7,452.00**
April	2,250.00	1,960.00	2,000.00	**6,210.00**
May	2,025.00	1,764.00	1,800.00	**5,589.00**
June	2,700.00	2,352.00	2,400.00	**7,452.00**
Q3	**2,531.00**	**2,205.00**	**1,950.00**	**6,686.00**
July	2,531.00	2,205.00	1,950.00	**6,686.00**
Total	**2,531.00**	**2,205.00**	**1,950.00**	**6,686.00**

FIGURE 8-23 The figure shows the numbers one would expect to see.

The handling of semi-additive measures is a complex topic, both because of the different possible calculations and because of the need to pay attention to several details. In the next sections we describe the basic techniques to handle semi-additive calculations.

Using *LASTDATE* and *LASTNONBLANK*

DAX offers several functions to handle semi-additive calculations. However, writing the correct code to handle semi-additive calculations is not just a matter of finding the correct function to use. Many subtle details might break a calculation if the author is not paying attention. In this section, we demonstrate different versions of the same code, which will or will not work depending on the data. The purpose of showing "wrong" solutions is educational because the "right" solution depends on the data present in the data model. Also, the solution of more complex scenarios requires some step-by-step reasoning.

The first function we describe is *LASTDATE*. We used the *LASTDATE* function earlier, when describing how to compute the moving annual total. *LASTDATE* returns a table only containing one row, which represents the last date visible in the current filter context. When used as a filter argument of *CALCU-LATE*, *LASTDATE* overrides the filter context on the date table so that only the last day of the selected period remains visible. The following code computes the last balance by using *LASTDATE* to overwrite the filter context on *Date*:

```
LastBalance :=
CALCULATE (
    SUM ( Balances[Balance] ),
    LASTDATE ( 'Date'[Date] )
)
```

LASTDATE is simple to use; unfortunately, *LASTDATE* is not the correct solution for many semi-additive calculations. In fact, *LASTDATE* scans the date table always returning the last date in the date table. For example, at the month level it always returns the last day of the month, and at the quarter level it returns the last date of the quarter. If the data is not available on the specific date returned by *LASTDATE*, the result of the calculation is blank. You see this in Figure 8-24 where the total of Q3 and the grand total are not visible. Because the total of Q3 is empty, the report does not even show Q3, resulting in a confusing result.

Year	Katie Jordan	Luis Bonifaz	Maurizio Macagno	Total
CY 2010				
Q1	**3,737.00**	**3,430.00**	**3,500.00**	**10,667.00**
January	1,687.00	1,470.00	1,500.00	**4,657.00**
February	2,812.00	2,450.00	2,500.00	**7,762.00**
March	3,737.00	3,430.00	3,500.00	**10,667.00**
Q2	**2,700.00**	**2,352.00**	**2,400.00**	**7,452.00**
April	2,250.00	1,960.00	2,000.00	**6,210.00**
May	2,025.00	1,764.00	1,800.00	**5,589.00**
June	2,700.00	2,352.00	2,400.00	**7,452.00**
Total				

FIGURE 8-24 The result, with *LASTDATE*, is confusing if data is not available on the last date of the month.

If, instead of using the month to slice data at the lowest level, we use the date, then the problem of *LASTDATE* becomes even more evident, as you can see in Figure 8-25. The Q3 row now is visible, even though its result is still blank.

Year	Katie Jordan	Luis Bonifaz	Maurizio Macagno	Total
CY 2010				
Q1	**3,737.00**	**3,430.00**	**3,500.00**	**10,667.00**
01/31/2010	1,687.00	1,470.00	1,500.00	**4,657.00**
02/28/2010	2,812.00	2,450.00	2,500.00	**7,762.00**
03/31/2010	3,737.00	3,430.00	3,500.00	**10,667.00**
Q2	**2,700.00**	**2,352.00**	**2,400.00**	**7,452.00**
04/30/2010	2,250.00	1,960.00	2,000.00	**6,210.00**
05/31/2010	2,025.00	1,764.00	1,800.00	**5,589.00**
06/30/2010	2,700.00	2,352.00	2,400.00	**7,452.00**
Q3				
07/15/2010	2,531.00	2,205.00		**4,736.00**
07/18/2010			1,950.00	**1,950.00**
Total				

FIGURE 8-25 Slicing by date, you can appreciate that data is available at the day level but not at the aggregate level.

If there are values on dates prior to the last day of the *Date* table, and that last day has no data available, then a better solution is to use the *LASTNONBLANK* function. *LASTNONBLANK* is an iterator that scans a table and returns the last value of the table for which the second parameter does not evaluate to *BLANK*. In our example, we use *LASTNONBLANK* to scan the *Date* table searching for the last date for which there are rows in the *Balances* table:

```
LastBalanceNonBlank :=
CALCULATE (
    SUM ( Balances[Balance] ),
    LASTNONBLANK (
        'Date'[Date],
        COUNTROWS ( RELATEDTABLE ( Balances ) )
    )
)
```

When used at the month level, *LASTNONBLANK* iterates over each date in the month, and for each date it checks whether the related table with the balances is empty. The innermost *RELATEDTABLE* function is executed in the row context of the *LASTNONBLANK* iterator, so that *RELATEDTABLE* only returns the balances of the given date. If there is no data, then *RELATEDTABLE* returns an empty table and *COUNTROWS* returns a blank. At the end of the iteration, *LASTNONBLANK* returns the last date that computed a nonblank result.

If all customer balances are gathered on the same date, then *LASTNONBLANK* solves the problem. In our example, we have different dates for different customers within the same month and this creates another issue. As we anticipated at the beginning of this section, with semi-additive calculations the devil is in the details. With our sample data *LASTNONBLANK* works much better than *LASTDATE* because it actively searches for the last date. However, it fails in computing correct totals, as you can see in Figure 8-26.

Year	Katie Jordan	Luis Bonifaz	Maurizio Macagno	Total
CY 2010	2,531.00	2,205.00	1,950.00	1,950.00
Q1	3,737.00	3,430.00	3,500.00	10,667.00
01/31/2010	1,687.00	1,470.00	1,500.00	4,657.00
02/28/2010	2,812.00	2,450.00	2,500.00	7,762.00
03/31/2010	3,737.00	3,430.00	3,500.00	10,667.00
Q2	2,700.00	2,352.00	2,400.00	7,452.00
04/30/2010	2,250.00	1,960.00	2,000.00	6,210.00
05/31/2010	2,025.00	1,764.00	1,800.00	5,589.00
06/30/2010	2,700.00	2,352.00	2,400.00	7,452.00
Q3	2,531.00	2,205.00	1,950.00	1,950.00
07/15/2010	2,531.00	2,205.00		4,736.00
07/18/2010			1,950.00	1,950.00
Total	2,531.00	2,205.00	1,950.00	1,950.00

FIGURE 8-26 This report is almost correct. The only unexpected results are at the year level and at the quarter level for Q3.

The result for each individual customer looks correct. Indeed, the last known balance for Katie Jordan is 2,531.00, which the formula correctly reports as her total. The same behavior produces correct results for Luis Bonifaz and Maurizio Macagno. Nevertheless, the grand total seems wrong. Indeed, the grand total is 1,950.00, which is the value of Maurizio Macagno only. It is confusing for a report to show a total composed in theory of three values (2,531.00, 2,205.00, 1,950.00) that only sums up the last value.

The reason is not hard to explain. When the filter context filters Katie Jordan, the last date with some values is July 15. When the filter context filters Maurizio Macagno, the last date becomes July 18. Nevertheless, when the filter context no longer filters the customer name, then the last date is Maurizio Macagno's, which is July 18. Neither Katie Jordan nor Luis Bonifaz have any data on July 18. Therefore, for the month of July the formula only reports the value of Maurizio Macagno.

As it often happens, there is nothing wrong with the behavior of DAX. The problem is that our code is not complete yet because it does not consider the fact that different customers might have different last dates in our data model.

Depending on the requirements, the formula can be corrected in different ways. Indeed, one needs to define exactly what to show at the total level. Given the fact that there is some data on July 18, the idea is to either

- Consider July 18 the last date to use for all the customers, regardless of their individual last date. Therefore, the customers not reported at a certain date have a zero balance at that date.

- Consider each customer's own last date, then aggregate the grand total using as the last date, the last date of each customer. Thus, the balance account of a customer is always the last balance available for that customer.

Both these definitions are correct, and it all depends on the requirements of the report. Because both are interesting to learn, we demonstrate how to write the code for both. The easier of the two is considering the last date for which there is some data regardless of the customer. The correct formula only requires changing the way *LASTNONBLANK* computes its result:

```
LastBalanceAllCustomers :=
VAR LastDateAllCustomers =
    CALCULATETABLE (
        LASTNONBLANK (
            'Date'[Date],
            COUNTROWS ( RELATEDTABLE ( Balances ) )
        ),
        ALL ( Balances[Name] )
    )
VAR Result =
    CALCULATE (
        SUM( Balances[Balance] ),
        LastDateAllCustomers
    )
RETURN
    Result
```

In this code we used *CALCULATETABLE* to remove the filter from the customer name during the evaluation of *LASTNONBLANK*. In this case, at the grand total *LASTNONBLANK* always returns July 18 regardless of the customer in the filter context. As a result, now the grand total adds up correctly, and the end balance of Katie Jordan and Luis Bonifaz is blank, as you can see in Figure 8-27.

Year	Katie Jordan	Luis Bonifaz	Maurizio Macagno	Total
CY 2010			1,950.00	1,950.00
Q1	3,737.00	3,430.00	3,500.00	10,667.00
01/31/2010	1,687.00	1,470.00	1,500.00	4,657.00
02/28/2010	2,812.00	2,450.00	2,500.00	7,762.00
03/31/2010	3,737.00	3,430.00	3,500.00	10,667.00
Q2	2,700.00	2,352.00	2,400.00	7,452.00
04/30/2010	2,250.00	1,960.00	2,000.00	6,210.00
05/31/2010	2,025.00	1,764.00	1,800.00	5,589.00
06/30/2010	2,700.00	2,352.00	2,400.00	7,452.00
Q3			1,950.00	1,950.00
07/15/2010	2,531.00	2,205.00		4,736.00
07/18/2010			1,950.00	1,950.00
Total			1,950.00	1,950.00

FIGURE 8-27 Using the last date for all the customers provides a different column total result.

The second option requires more complex reasoning. When using a different date for each customer, the grand total cannot be computed by simply using the filter context at the grand total. The formula needs to compute the subtotal of each customer and then aggregate the results. This is one of the scenarios where iterators are a simple and effective solution. Indeed, the following measure uses an outer *SUMX* to produce the total by summing the individual values of each customer:

```
LastBalanceIndividualCustomer :=
SUMX (
    VALUES ( Balances[Name] ),
    CALCULATE (
        SUM ( Balances[Balance] ),
        LASTNONBLANK (
            'Date'[Date],
            COUNTROWS ( RELATEDTABLE ( Balances ) )
        )
    )
)
```

The result of this latter measure computes for each customer the value on their own last date. It then aggregates the grand total by summing individual values. You see the result in Figure 8-28.

Year	Katie Jordan	Luis Bonifaz	Maurizio Macagno	Total
CY 2010	2,531.00	2,205.00	1,950.00	6,686.00
Q1	3,737.00	3,430.00	3,500.00	10,667.00
01/31/2010	1,687.00	1,470.00	1,500.00	4,657.00
02/28/2010	2,812.00	2,450.00	2,500.00	7,762.00
03/31/2010	3,737.00	3,430.00	3,500.00	10,667.00
Q2	2,700.00	2,352.00	2,400.00	7,452.00
04/30/2010	2,250.00	1,960.00	2,000.00	6,210.00
05/31/2010	2,025.00	1,764.00	1,800.00	5,589.00
06/30/2010	2,700.00	2,352.00	2,400.00	7,452.00
Q3	2,531.00	2,205.00	1,950.00	6,686.00
07/15/2010	2,531.00	2,205.00		4,736.00
07/18/2010			1,950.00	1,950.00
Total	2,531.00	2,205.00	1,950.00	6,686.00

FIGURE 8-28 The matrix now shows the subtotal of each customer on their own last date.

Note With a large number of customers, the *LastBalanceIndividualCustomer* measure might have performance issues. The reason is that the formula includes two nested iterators, and the outer iterator has a large granularity. A faster approach to this same requirement is included in Chapter 10, "Working with the filter context," leveraging functions like *TREATAS* that will be discussed in later chapters.

As you have learned, the complexity of semi-additive calculations is not in the code, but rather in the definition of its desired behavior. Once the behavior is clear, the choice between one pattern and the other is simple.

In this section we showed the most commonly used *LASTDATE* and *LASTNONBLANK* functions. There are two similar functions available to obtain the first date instead of the last date within a time period. These functions are *FIRSTDATE* and *FIRSTNONBLANK*. Moreover, there are further functions whose goal is to simplify calculations like the one demonstrated so far. We discuss them in the next section.

Working with opening and closing balances

DAX offers many functions like *LASTDATE* that simplify calculations retrieving the value of a measure at the opening or closing date of a time period. Although useful, these additional functions suffer from the same limitations as *LASTDATE*. That is, they work well if and only if the dataset contains values for all the dates.

These functions are *STARTOFYEAR*, *STARTOFQUARTER*, *STARTOFMONTH*, and the corresponding closing functions: *ENDOFYEAR*, *ENDOFQUARTER*, *ENDOFMONTH*. Intuitively, *STARTOFYEAR* always returns January 1 of the currently selected year in the filter context. In a similar way *STARTOFQUARTER* and *STARTOFMONTH* return the beginning of the quarter or of the month, respectively.

As an example, we prepared a different dataset that is aimed at resolving a different scenario where semi-additive calculations are useful. The demo file contains the prices of the Microsoft stock between 2013 and 2018. The value is well known at the day level. But what should a report show at an aggregated level—for example, at the quarter level? In this case, the most commonly used value is the last value of the stock price. In other words, stock prices are another example where the semi-additive pattern becomes useful.

A simple implementation of the last value of a stock works well for simple reports. The following formula computes the last value of the Microsoft stock, considering an average of the prices in case there are multiple rows for the same day:

```
Last Value :=
CALCULATE (
    AVERAGE ( MSFT[Value] ),
    LASTDATE ( 'Date'[Date] )
)
```

The result is correct when used in a daily chart like Figure 8-29.

However, this nice result is not due to the DAX code working well. The chart looks correct because we used the date level in the x axis, and the client tool—Power BI in this example—works hard to ignore all the empty values in our dataset. This results in a continuous line. But using the same measure in a matrix sliced by year and month would make the gaps in the calculation become much more evident. This shows in Figure 8-30.

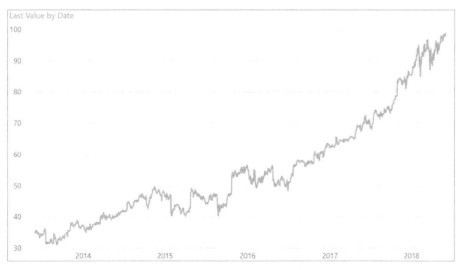

FIGURE 8-29 A line chart showing the price by day looks perfectly fine.

Month	CY 2013	CY 2014	CY 2015	CY 2016	CY 2017	CY 2018	**Total**
January		37.84			64.65	95.01	**95.01**
February		38.31		50.88	63.98	93.77	**93.77**
March		40.99	40.66	55.23	65.86		
April		40.40	48.64			93.52	**93.52**
May	34.90			53.00	69.84		
June		41.70	44.15	51.17	68.93		
July	31.84	43.16	46.70		72.70		
August			43.52	57.46	74.77		
September	33.28	46.36	44.26	57.60			
October	35.41	46.95		59.92	83.18		
November			54.35	60.26	84.17		
December	37.41	46.45	55.48				
Total	**37.41**	**46.45**	**55.48**				

FIGURE 8-30 The matrix showing years and months contains several blank values.

Using *LASTDATE* means you can expect empty values whenever there is no value on the exact last day of the month. That day might be either a weekend or a holiday. The correct version of *Last Value* is the following:

```
Last Value :=
CALCULATE (
    AVERAGE ( MSFT[Value] ),
    LASTNONBLANK (
        'Date'[Date],
        COUNTROWS ( RELATEDTABLE ( MSFT ) )
    )
)
```

Being mindful with these functions can prevent unexpected results. For example, imagine computing the Microsoft stock increase from the beginning of the quarter. One option, which again proves to be wrong, is the following code:

```
SOQ :=
CALCULATE (
    AVERAGE ( MSFT[Value] ),
    STARTOFQUARTER ( 'Date'[Date] )
)

SOQ% :=
DIVIDE (
    [Last Value] - [SOQ],
    [SOQ]
)
```

STARTOFQUARTER returns the date when the current quarter started, regardless the presence of data on that specific date. For example, January 1, which is the start of the first quarter, is also New Year's Day. Consequently, there is never a price for a stock on that date, and the previous measures produce the result visible in Figure 8-31.

Year	Last Value	SOQ	SOQ%
CY 2016	**62.14**		
Q1	**55.23**		
January	55.09		
February	50.88		
March	55.23		
Q2	**51.17**	**55.57**	**-7.92%**
April	49.87	55.57	-10.26%
May	53.00	55.57	-4.62%
June	51.17	55.57	-7.92%
Q3	**57.60**	**51.16**	**12.59%**
July	56.68	51.16	10.79%
August	57.46	51.16	12.31%
September	57.60	51.16	12.59%
Q4	**62.14**		
October	59.92		
November	60.26		
December	62.14		

FIGURE 8-31 *STARTOFQUARTER* returns a date whether it is a holiday or not.

You can note that there are no values for *SOQ* in the first quarter. Besides, the issue is present for any quarter that starts on a day for which there is no data. To compute the start or the end of a time period, only taking into account dates with data available, the functions to use are *FIRSTNONBLANK* and *LASTNONBLANK* mixed with other time intelligence functions like, for example, *DATESINPERIOD*.

A much better implementation of the *SOQ* calculation is the following:

```
SOQ :=
VAR FirstDateInQuarter =
    CALCULATETABLE (
        FIRSTNONBLANK (
            'Date'[Date],
            COUNTROWS ( RELATEDTABLE( MSFT ) )
        ),
        PARALLELPERIOD ( 'Date'[Date], 0, QUARTER )
    )
VAR Result =
    CALCULATE (
        AVERAGE ( MSFT[Value] ),
        FirstDateInQuarter
    )
RETURN
    Result
```

This latter version is much more complex both to author and to understand. However, it works in any scenario by only considering dates with data available. You can see the result of the matrix with the new implementation of *SOQ* in Figure 8-32.

Year	Last Value	SOQ	SOQ%
CY 2016	**62.14**	**54.80**	**13.39%**
Q1	**55.23**	**54.80**	**0.78%**
January	55.09	54.80	0.53%
February	50.88	54.80	-7.15%
March	55.23	54.80	0.78%
Q2	**51.17**	**55.57**	**-7.92%**
April	49.87	55.57	-10.26%
May	53.00	55.57	-4.62%
June	51.17	55.57	-7.92%
Q3	**57.60**	**51.16**	**12.59%**
July	56.68	51.16	10.79%
August	57.46	51.16	12.31%
September	57.60	51.16	12.59%
Q4	**62.14**	**57.42**	**8.22%**
October	59.92	57.42	4.35%
November	60.26	57.42	4.95%
December	62.14	57.42	8.22%

FIGURE 8-32 The new version of *SOQ* reports correct numbers regardless of weekends and holidays.

At the risk of seeming pedantic, it is worth repeating the same concept used when introducing the topic of semi-additive measures. The devil is in the details. DAX offers several functions that work for models with data for all the dates. Unfortunately, not all models contain data for all the dates. In those latter scenarios, it is always extremely important to consider all the possible implications of using these simple functions. One should consider time intelligence functions as building blocks for more complex calculations. Combining different time intelligence functions enables the accurate computing of different time periods, although there is no predefined function solving the problem in a single step.

This is why instead of just showing you a smooth example for each time intelligence function, we preferred walking them through different trial-and-error scenarios. The goal of this section—and of the whole book—is not to just show you how to use functions. The goal is to empower you to think in DAX, to identify which details you should take care of, and to build your own calculations whenever the basic functionalities of the language are not enough for your needs.

In the next section we move one step forward in that same direction, by showing how most time intelligence calculations can be computed without the aid of any time intelligence functions. The goal is not purely educational. When working with custom calendars, such as weekly calendars, time intelligence functions are not useful. You need to be prepared to author some complex DAX code to obtain the desired result.

Understanding advanced time intelligence calculations

This section describes many important details about time intelligence functions. To showcase these details, we write time intelligence calculations by using simpler DAX functions such as *FILTER*, *ALL*, *VALUES*, *MIN*, and *MAX*. The goal of this section is not to suggest you avoid standard time intelligence functions in favor of simpler functions. Instead, the goal is to help you understand the exact behavior of time intelligence functions even in particular side cases. This knowledge enables you to then write custom calculations whenever the available functions do not provide the exact calculation you need. You will also notice that the translation to simpler DAX sometimes requires more code than expected because of certain hidden functionalities in time intelligence calculations.

Your reason for rewriting a time intelligence calculation in DAX could be that you are dealing with a nonstandard calendar, where the first day of the year is not always the same for all the years. This is the case, for example, for ISO calendars based on weeks. Here the assumption made by the time intelligence function that year, month, and quarter can always be extracted from the date value is no longer true. You can write a different logic by changing the DAX code in the filter conditions; or you can simply take advantage of other columns in the date table, so you do not have a complex DAX expression to maintain. You will find more examples of this latter approach under "Working with custom calendars" later in this chapter.

Understanding periods to date

Earlier, we described the DAX functions that calculate month-to-date, quarter-to-date, and year-to-date: they are *DATESMTD*, *DATESQTD*, and *DATESYTD*. Each of these filter functions is like the result of a *FILTER* statement that can be written in DAX. For example, consider the following *DATESYTD* function:

```
DATESYTD ( 'Date'[Date] )
```

It corresponds to a filter over the date column using *FILTER* called by *CALCULATETABLE*, as in the following code:

```
CALCULATETABLE (
    VAR LastDateInSelection = MAX ( 'Date'[Date] )
    RETURN
        FILTER (
            ALL ( 'Date'[Date] ),
            'Date'[Date] <= LastDateInSelection
                && YEAR ( 'Date'[Date] ) = YEAR ( LastDateInSelection )
        )
)
```

In a similar way, the *DATESMTD* function:

```
DATESMTD ( 'Date'[Date] )
```

corresponds to the following code:

```
CALCULATETABLE (
    VAR LastDateInSelection = MAX ( 'Date'[Date] )
    RETURN
        FILTER (
            ALL ( 'Date'[Date] ),
            'Date'[Date] <= LastDateInSelection
                && YEAR ( 'Date'[Date] ) = YEAR ( LastDateInSelection )
                && MONTH ( 'Date'[Date] ) = MONTH ( LastDateInSelection )
        )
)
```

The *DATESQTD* function follows the same pattern. All these alternative implementations have a common characteristic: They extract the information about year, month, and quarter from the last day available in the current selection. Then, they use this date to create a suitable filter.

Context transition in time intelligence functions

You might have noticed that in the previous expressions we always use an outer *CALCULATETABLE* surrounding the whole code. The reason for the presence of *CALCULATETABLE* is to perform a context transition, which is required when a date column is specified as a column reference. Previously in this chapter you saw that a column reference in the first argument of a time intelligence function is translated into a table obtained by calling *CALCULATETABLE* and *DISTINCT*:

```
DATESYTD ( 'Date'[Date] )

-- corresponds to

DATESYTD ( CALCULATETABLE ( DISTINCT ( 'Date'[Date] ) ) )
```

Thus, the context transition only takes place to translate the column reference into a table. It does not happen when a table is used as an argument of a time intelligence function instead of a date column reference. A more accurate translation of *DATESYTD* is the following:

```
DATESYTD ( 'Date'[Date] )

-- corresponds to

VAR LastDateInSelection =
    MAXX ( CALCULATETABLE ( DISTINCT ( 'Date'[Date] ) ), [Date] )
RETURN
    FILTER (
        ALL ( 'Date'[Date] ),
        'Date'[Date] <= LastDateInSelection
            && YEAR ( 'Date'[Date] ) = YEAR ( LastDateInSelection )
    )
```

The context transition does not happen when the argument of a time intelligence function is a table.

The *CALCULATETABLE* generated for the column reference used in time intelligence functions is important when you have a row context. Look at the following two calculated columns, both created in the *Date* table:

```
'Date'[CountDatesYTD] = COUNTROWS ( DATESYTD ( 'Date'[Date] ) )

'Date'[CountFilter] =
COUNTROWS (
    VAR LastDateInSelection =
        MAX ( 'Date'[Date] )
    RETURN
        FILTER (
            ALL ( 'Date'[Date] ),
            'Date'[Date] <= LastDateInSelection
                && YEAR ( 'Date'[Date] ) = YEAR ( LastDateInSelection )
        )
)
```

Though they look similar, they are not. Indeed, you can see the result in Figure 8-33.

Date	CountDatesYTD	CountFilter
01/01/07	1	365
01/02/07	2	365
01/03/07	3	365
01/04/07	4	365
01/05/07	5	365
01/06/07	6	365
01/07/07	7	365
01/08/07	8	365
01/09/07	9	365
01/10/07	10	365
01/11/07	11	365
01/12/07	12	365
01/13/07	13	365

FIGURE 8-33 *CountFilter* does not perform context transition, whereas *CountDatesYTD* does.

CountDatesYTD returns the number of days from the beginning of the year, up to the date in the current row. To achieve this result, *DATESYTD* should inspect the current filter context and extract the selected period from the filter context. However, being computed in a calculated column, there is no filter context. The behavior of *CountFilter* is simpler to explain: When *CountFilter* computes the maximum date, it always retrieves the last date of the entire date table because there are no filters in the filter context. *CountDatesYTD* behaves differently because *DATESYTD* performs a context transition being called with a date column reference. Thus, it creates a filter context that only contains the currently iterated date.

If you rewrite *DATESYTD* and you know that the code will not be executed inside a row context, you can remove the outer *CALCULATETABLE,* which would otherwise be a useless operation. This is usually the case for a filter argument in a *CALCULATE* call not called within an iterator—a place where *DATESYTD* is often used. In these cases, instead of *DATESYTD,* you can write:

```
VAR LastDateInSelection = MAX ( 'Date'[Date] )
RETURN
    FILTER (
        ALL ( 'Date'[Date] ),
        'Date'[Date] <= LastDateInSelection
            && YEAR ( 'Date'[Date] ) = YEAR ( LastDateInSelection )
    )
```

On the other hand, to retrieve the date from the row context—for example, in a calculated column—it is easier to retrieve the date value of the current row in a variable instead of using *MAX*:

```
VAR CurrentDate = 'Date'[Date]
RETURN
    FILTER (
        ALL ( 'Date'[Date] ),
        'Date'[Date] <= CurrentDate
            && YEAR ( 'Date'[Date] ) = YEAR ( CurrentDate )
    )
```

DATESYTD allows the specifying of a year-end date, which is useful to compute YTD on fiscal years. For example, for a fiscal year starting on July 1, June 30 needs to be specified in the second argument by using one of the following versions:

```
DATESYTD ( 'Date'[Date], "06-30" )
DATESYTD ( 'Date'[Date], "30-06" )
```

Regardless of the local culture, let us assume that the programmer has specified the *<month>* and *<day>*. The corresponding *FILTER* of *DATESYTD* using these placeholders is the following:

```
VAR LastDateInSelection = MAX ( 'Date'[Date] )
RETURN
    FILTER (
        ALL ( 'Date'[Date] ),
        'Date'[Date] > DATE ( YEAR ( LastDateInSelection ) - 1, <month>, <day> )
            && 'Date'[Date] <= LastDateInSelection
    )
```

> **Important** It is important to note that *DATESYTD* always starts from the day after the specified end of the fiscal year. This causes a problem in the special case where a company has a fiscal year starting on March 1. In fact, the end of the fiscal year can be either February 28 or 29, depending on whether the calculation is happening in a leap year or not. As of April 2019, this special scenario is not supported by *DATESYTD*. Thus, if one needs to author code and they have to start the fiscal calendar on March 1, then *DATESYTD* cannot be used. A workaround is available at http://sql.bi/fymarch.

Understanding *DATEADD*

DATEADD retrieves a set of dates shifted in time by a certain offset. When *DATEADD* analyzes the current filter context, it includes special handling to detect whether the current selection is one month or a special period, like the beginning or the end of a month. For example, when *DATEADD* retrieves an entire month shifted back one quarter, it oftentimes returns a different number of days than the current selection. This happens because *DATEADD* understands that the current selection is a month, and it retrieves a full corresponding month regardless of the number of days.

These special behaviors are expressed in three rules that we describe in this section. These rules make it hard to rewrite *DATEADD* on a generic date table. The code would be painfully difficult to write and nearly impossible to manage over time. *DATEADD* only uses the values of the date column, extracting the information needed—such as year, quarter, and month—from the available date value. The same logic would be hard to reproduce in plain DAX. On the other hand, by using additional columns in the *Date* table, one can author an alternative version of *DATEADD*. We will elaborate on this technique later in this chapter, in the section about custom calendars.

Consider the following formula:

```
DATEADD ( 'Date'[Date], -1, MONTH )
```

The closest—but not totally equivalent—DAX formula is the following:

```
VAR OffsetMonth = -1
RETURN TREATAS (
    SELECTCOLUMNS (
        CALCULATETABLE ( DISTINCT ( 'Date'[Date] ) ),
        "Date", DATE (
            YEAR ( 'Date'[Date] ),
            MONTH ( 'Date'[Date] ) + OffsetMonth,
            DAY ( 'Date'[Date] )
        )
    ),
    'Date'[Date]
)
```

> **Note** In the previous example and in other formulas in this chapter, we use the *TREATAS* function, which applies a table expression to the filter context on the columns specified by the second and following arguments. You can read a more complete description of this function in Chapter 10.

The formula also works in January because a value lower than 1 for the month parameter is considered an offset to go into a previous year. However, this implementation only works properly if the destination month has the same number of days as the current month. If you move from February to January, the formula misses two or three days, depending on the year. In a similar way, if you move from March to February, the result might include days in March.

On the other hand, *DATEADD* does not have a similar problem and returns the entire month with the offset applied, in case an entire month was selected before the offset was applied. In order to achieve this, *DATEADD* uses three rules:

1. *DATEADD* only returns days that exist in the date column. If some expected dates are missing, then *DATEADD* returns only those dates that are not missing in the date column.

2. If a day does not exist in the corresponding month after the shifting operation, then the result of *DATEADD* includes the last day of the corresponding month.

3. If the selection includes the last two days of a month, then the result of *DATEADD* includes all the days between the corresponding days in the shifted month and the end of the shifted month.

A few examples are helpful to understand the effects of these behaviors. Consider the following measures: *Day count* counts the number of selected days; *PM Day count* counts the number of days shifted back in the previous month; *PM Range* returns the date range selected by *DATEADD*.

```
Day count :=
COUNTROWS ( 'Date' )

PM Day count :=
CALCULATE ( [Day count], DATEADD ( 'Date'[Date], -1, MONTH ) )

PM Range :=
CALCULATE (
    VAR MinDate = MIN ( 'Date'[Date] )
    VAR MaxDate = MAX ( 'Date'[Date] )
    VAR Result =
        FORMAT ( MinDate, "MM/DD/YYYY - " ) & FORMAT ( MaxDate, "MM/DD/YYYY" )
    RETURN
        Result,
    DATEADD ( 'Date'[Date], -1, MONTH )
)
```

■ **Rule 1** is in effect when the selection is near the boundaries of the range of dates included in the date column. For example, Figure 8-34 shows the *PM Day count* and *PM Range* measures returning valid values in February 2007 because dates in January 2007 exist in the date column, whereas the same measures return blanks in January 2007 because dates in December 2006 are not present in the date column.

Year	Day count	PM Day count	PM Range
01/27/07	1		
01/28/07	1		
01/29/07	1		
01/30/07	1		
01/31/07	1		
February	28	31	01/01/2007 - 01/31/2007
02/01/07	1	1	01/01/2007 - 01/01/2007
02/02/07	1	1	01/02/2007 - 01/02/2007
02/03/07	1	1	01/03/2007 - 01/03/2007
02/04/07	1	1	01/04/2007 - 01/04/2007
02/05/07	1	1	01/05/2007 - 01/05/2007
02/06/07	1	1	01/06/2007 - 01/06/2007

FIGURE 8-34 The dates selected are shifted back one month.

The main reason why the *Date* table should include all the days within one year is because of the behavior *of DATEADD*. Be mindful that several time intelligence functions in DAX internally use *DATEADD*. Therefore, having a complete date table is of paramount importance for DAX time intelligence functions to behave as expected.

■ **Rule 2** is relevant because months have different numbers of days. The 31st day does not exist for all months. If it is selected, it is moved to the last day of the month in the shifted period. For example, in Figure 8-35 the last days of March are all moved to the last day of February because February 29 to 31 do not exist in 2007.

Year	Day count	PM Day count	PM Range
03/22/07	1	1	02/22/2007 - 02/22/2007
03/23/07	1	1	02/23/2007 - 02/23/2007
03/24/07	1	1	02/24/2007 - 02/24/2007
03/25/07	1	1	02/25/2007 - 02/25/2007
03/26/07	1	1	02/26/2007 - 02/26/2007
03/27/07	1	1	02/27/2007 - 02/27/2007
03/28/07	1	1	02/28/2007 - 02/28/2007
03/29/07	1	1	02/28/2007 - 02/28/2007
03/30/07	1	1	02/28/2007 - 02/28/2007
03/31/07	1	1	02/28/2007 - 02/28/2007

FIGURE 8-35 A date that does not exist in the destination month is replaced by the last day of the destination month.

The consequence of this rule is that you might obtain a lower number of days than the initial selection. This is intuitive when the selection of 31 days in March should result in a corresponding selection of 28 or 29 days in February. However, when the selection includes a reduced number of days, the result might not be what is expected. For example, in Figure 8-36 you can see that a selection of 5 days in March 2007 results in only 2 days in February 2007.

Year	Day count	PM Day count	PM Range
2007	**5**	**2**	**02/27/2007 - 02/28/2007**
March	**5**	**2**	**02/27/2007 - 02/28/2007**
03/27/07	1	1	02/27/2007 - 02/27/2007
03/28/07	1	1	02/28/2007 - 02/28/2007
03/29/07	1	1	02/28/2007 - 02/28/2007
03/30/07	1	1	02/28/2007 - 02/28/2007
03/31/07	1	1	02/28/2007 - 02/28/2007
Total	**5**	**2**	**02/27/2007 - 02/28/2007**

FIGURE 8-36 Several days in the starting selection might result in the same day in the *DATEADD* result.

- **Rule 3** generates a special handling type when the last day of a month is included within a range of dates. For example, consider the initial selection of three days from June 29, 2007, to July 1, 2007. The selection only includes three days, but among those is the last day of June, which is June 30. When *DATEADD* shifts the dates back, it includes the last day of May (May 31). Figure 8-37 shows this behavior and it is worth a deeper look. Indeed, you can note that June 30 is moved to May 30. Only if the selection contains both June 29 and 30 does the result then include the last day of the previous month (May 31). In this case, the number of days in the previous month is greater than the number of days originally selected: 2 days selected in June 2017 return 3 days in the previous month (May 2007).

Year	Day count	PM Day count	PM Range
2007	**3**	**4**	**05/29/2007 - 06/01/2007**
June	2	3	**05/29/2007 - 05/31/2007**
06/29/07	1	1	05/29/2007 - 05/29/2007
06/30/07	1	1	05/30/2007 - 05/30/2007
July	1	**1**	**06/01/2007 - 06/01/2007**
07/01/07	1	1	06/01/2007 - 06/01/2007
Total	**3**	**4**	**05/29/2007 - 06/01/2007**

FIGURE 8-37 The result of *DATEADD* includes all days between the first and the last day of the selection after the shift operation.

The reason for these rules is to provide an intuitive behavior when a formula operates at the month level. As you can see in Figure 8-38, when you compare the selections at the month level, the result is intuitive and expected. It shows the complete range of days of the previous month.

Year	Day count	PM Day count	PM Range
2007	**365**	**334**	**01/01/2007 - 11/30/2007**
January	31		
February	28	31	01/01/2007 - 01/31/2007
March	31	28	02/01/2007 - 02/28/2007
April	30	31	03/01/2007 - 03/31/2007
May	31	30	04/01/2007 - 04/30/2007
June	30	31	05/01/2007 - 05/31/2007
July	31	30	06/01/2007 - 06/30/2007
August	31	31	07/01/2007 - 07/31/2007
September	30	31	08/01/2007 - 08/31/2007
October	31	30	09/01/2007 - 09/30/2007
November	30	31	10/01/2007 - 10/31/2007
December	31	30	11/01/2007 - 11/30/2007
2008	**366**	**366**	**12/01/2007 - 11/30/2008**
January	31	31	12/01/2007 - 12/31/2007
February	29	31	01/01/2008 - 01/31/2008
March	31	29	02/01/2008 - 02/29/2008
April	30	31	03/01/2008 - 03/31/2008

FIGURE 8-38 The *PM Day count measure* shows the number of days in the previous month.

Understanding the rules described in this section is important to handle side conditions that might happen with partial selections of days in months. For example, consider a filter over weekdays in a report. That filter might not include the last days of a month, which would guarantee that the entire previous month is selected. Moreover, the shift of dates performed by *DATEADD* only considers the number of days within the month and not the week days. The application of a filter to the date column of the *Date* table also generates an implicit *ALL* over the *Date* table itself, removing any existing filter over other columns of the *Date* table including weekdays. Thus, a slicer that filters weekdays is not compatible with the use of *DATEADD* because it does not produce the expected result.

For example, consider the following definition of *PM Sales DateAdd* displaying the *Sales Amount* of the previous month, as shown in Figure 8-39:

```
PM Sales DateAdd :=
CALCULATE (
    [Sales Amount],
    DATEADD ( 'Date'[Date], -1, MONTH )
)
```

Year	Sales Amount	PM Sales DateAdd
2007	**8,522,387.91**	**7,577,161.01**
January	512,658.97	
February	733,016.32	525,255.79
March	812,661.96	735,642.52
April	938,504.90	718,494.01
May	764,664.76	961,369.32
June	614,322.15	565,356.50
July	623,356.94	619,184.77
August	760,652.04	777,717.96
September	755,777.34	638,583.64
October	565,028.19	890,962.06
November	641,518.91	599,002.38
December	800,225.43	538,999.02
Total	**8,522,387.91**	**7,577,161.01**

Week Day
- ☐ Friday
- ☑ Monday
- ☑ Saturday
- ☑ Sunday
- ☑ Thursday
- ☑ Tuesday
- ☐ Wednesday

FIGURE 8-39 The *PM Sales DateAdd* measure does not correspond to *Sales Amount* of the previous month.

PM Sales DateAdd creates a filter of days that does not correspond to the full month. It translates the days of the month selected, including additional days at the end of the month according to Rule 3. This filter overrides and ignores the *Day of Week* selection for the value of the previous month. The result produces different values, even bigger than *Sales Amount* as in March and May 2007, for example.

In this case, computing correctly requires a custom calculation like the one implemented in the *PM Sales Weekday* measure. It applies a filter over the *YearMonthNumber* column keeping the filter on *Day of Week*, and removing the filter from all the other columns of the *Date* table using *ALLEXCEPT*. The *YearMonthNumber* calculated column is a sequential number over months and years:

```
Date[YearMonthNumber] =
'Date'[Year] * 12 + 'Date'[Month Number] - 1

PM Sales Weekday :=
VAR CurrentMonths = DISTINCT ( 'Date'[YearMonthNumber] )
VAR PreviousMonths =
    TREATAS (
        SELECTCOLUMNS (
            CurrentMonths,
            "YearMonthNumber", 'Date'[YearMonthNumber] - 1
        ),
        'Date'[YearMonthNumber]
    )
VAR Result =
    CALCULATE (
        [Sales Amount],
        ALLEXCEPT ( 'Date', 'Date'[Week Day] ),
        PreviousMonths
    )
RETURN
    Result
```

The result is visible in Figure 8-40.

Year	Sales Amount	PM Sales Weekday	Week Day
2007	**8,522,387.91**	**7,722,162.48**	☐ Friday
January	512,658.97		■ Monday
February	733,016.32	512,658.97	■ Saturday
March	812,661.96	733,016.32	■ Sunday
April	938,504.90	812,661.96	■ Thursday
May	764,664.76	938,504.90	■ Tuesday
June	614,322.15	764,664.76	☐ Wednesday
July	623,356.94	614,322.15	
August	760,652.04	623,356.94	
September	755,777.34	760,652.04	
October	565,028.19	755,777.34	
November	641,518.91	565,028.19	
December	800,225.43	641,518.91	
Total	**8,522,387.91**	**7,722,162.48**	

FIGURE 8-40 The *PM Sales Weekday* measure corresponds to *Sales Amount* of the previous month.

However, this solution works specifically for this report. If the selection of days were made based on other criteria like the first 6 days of the month, then the result produced by *PM Sales Weekday* would get the entire month, whereas the result produced by *PM Sales DateAdd* would work in this case. Depending on the columns visible to the user, one might implement different calculations based on the selection made. For example, the following *PM Sales* measure uses the *ISFILTERED* function to check whether a filter is active on the *Day of Week* column. A more detailed explanation of *ISFILTERED* is included in Chapter 10.

```
PM Sales :=
IF (
    ISFILTERED ( 'Date'[Day of Week] ),
    [PM Sales Weekday],
    [PM Sales DateAdd]
)
```

Understanding *FIRSTDATE, LASTDATE, FIRSTNONBLANK,* and *LASTNONBLANK*

In the "Understanding semi-additive calculations" section earlier in this chapter, you learned two functions that seem alike: *LASTDATE* and *LASTNONBLANK*. In fact, these functions exhibit distinctive behaviors, and so do the two companions *FIRSTDATE* and *FIRSTNONBLANK*.

FIRSTDATE and *LASTDATE* only operate on a date column. They return, respectively, the first and the last date in the active filter context, ignoring any data existing in other related tables:

```
FIRSTDATE ( 'Date'[Date] )
LASTDATE ( 'Date'[Date] )
```

FIRSTDATE returns the minimum value of the column received in the current filter context, whereas *LASTDATE* returns the maximum value. *FIRSTDATE* and *LASTDATE* behave somewhat like *MIN* and *MAX*, with one important difference: *FIRSTDATE* and *LASTDATE* return a table and perform a context transition, whereas *MIN* and *MAX* return a scalar value without doing any context transition.

For example, consider the following expression:

```
CALCULATE (
    SUM ( Inventory[Quantity] ),
    LASTDATE ( 'Date'[Date] )
)
```

You can rewrite the formula using *MAX* instead of *LASTDATE*, but this would result in unnecessary longer code:

```
CALCULATE (
    SUM ( Inventory[Quantity] ),
    FILTER (
        ALL ( 'Date'[Date] ),
        'Date'[Date] = MAX ( 'Date'[Date] )
    )
)
```

Besides, *LASTDATE* also performs a context transition. Consequently, the exact equivalent of *LAST-DATE* in plain DAX is as follows:

```
CALCULATE (
    SUM ( Inventory[Quantity] ),
    VAR LastDateInSelection =
        MAXX ( CALCULATETABLE ( DISTINCT ( 'Date'[Date] ) ), 'Date'[Date] )
    RETURN
        FILTER (
            ALL ( 'Date'[Date] ),
            'Date'[Date] = LastDateInSelection
        )
)
```

The context transition is relevant when you execute *FIRSTDATE/LASTDATE* in a row context. The best practice is to use *FIRSTDATE/LASTDATE* when you write a filter expression because a table expression is expected, whereas *MIN/MAX* functions are better when you are writing a logical expression in a row context that usually requires a scalar value. Indeed, *LASTDATE* with a column reference implies a context transition that hides the external filter context.

For example, you will favor *FIRSTDATE/LASTDATE* over *MIN/MAX* in a filter argument of *CALCULATE/CALCULATETABLE* functions because the syntax is simpler. However, you should use *MIN/MAX* when the context transition implied by *FIRSTDATE/LASTDATE* would modify the result. This is the case of the condition in a *FILTER* function. The following expression filters the dates for computing a running total:

```
FILTER (
    ALL ( 'Date'[Date] ),
    'Date'[Date] <= MAX ( 'Date'[Date] )
)
```

MAX is the right function to use. In fact, the result of using *LASTDATE* instead of *MAX* would always contain all the dates, regardless of the current selection because of the unwanted context transition. Thus, the following expression returns all dates, no matter what. The reason is that *LASTDATE*—because of context transition—returns the value of *Date[Date]* in each row of the *FILTER* iteration:

```
FILTER (
    ALL ( 'Date'[Date] ),
    'Date'[Date] <= LASTDATE ( 'Date'[Date] ) -- this condition is always true
)
```

LASTNONBLANK and *FIRSTNONBLANK* are different from *FIRSTDATE* and *LASTDATE*. In fact, *LASTNONBLANK* and *FIRSTNONBLANK* are iterators, meaning that they scan a table row by row in a row context and that they return the last (or first) of the values for which the second parameter is not a blank. Usually, the second parameter of these functions is either a measure or an expression including *CALCULATE*, so to rely on context transition.

To obtain the right value for the last non-blank date for a given measure/table, you use an expression like this:

```
LASTNONBLANK ( 'Date'[Date], CALCULATE ( COUNTROWS ( Inventory ) ) )
```

It returns the last date (in the current filter context) for which there are rows in the *Inventory* table. You can also use an equivalent formula:

```
LASTNONBLANK ( 'Date'[Date], COUNTROWS ( RELATEDTABLE ( Inventory ) ) )
```

That last expression returns the last date (in the current filter context) for which there is a related row in the *Inventory* table.

It is worth noting that *FIRSTNONBLANK/LASTNONBLANK* functions accept any data type as their first argument, whereas the *FIRSTDATE/LASTDATE* functions require a column of *DateTime* or *Date* data type. Thus, and though it is not a commonly used practice, *FIRSTNONBLANK* and *LASTNON-BLANK* can also be used with different tables like customers, products, or any other table.

Using drillthrough with time intelligence

A *drillthrough* operation is a request for the data source rows corresponding to the filter context used in a certain calculation. Every time you use a time intelligence function, you change the filter context on the *Date* table. This produces a different result for the measure from the result obtained with the initial filter context. When you use a client that performs a drillthrough action over a report, such as a pivot table in Excel, you could observe a behavior that is not what you might expect. In fact, the drillthrough operation made in MDX does not consider the changes in the filter context defined by the measure itself. Instead, it only considers the filter context defined by the rows, columns, filters, and slicers of the pivot table.

For example, by default the drillthrough on March 2007 always returns the same rows, regardless of the time intelligence function applied in the measure. By using *TOTALYTD,* one would expect all the days from January to March 2007; by using *SAMEPERIODLASTYEAR,* one would expect March 2006; and by using *LASTDATE,* one would only expect the rows for March 31, 2007. Indeed, in the default drillthrough any of these filters always returns all the rows for March 2007. This behavior can be controlled by the *Detail Rows* property in the Tabular model. At the time of writing (April 2019), the *Detail Rows* property can be set in an Analysis Services 2017 or Azure Analysis Services data model, but it is not available either in Power BI or in Power Pivot for Excel.

The *Detail Rows* property must apply the same filter used for the corresponding time intelligence measure. For example, consider the following year-to-date measure:

```
CALCULATE (
    [Sales Amount],
    DATESYTD ( 'Date'[Date] )
)
```

Its *Detail Rows* property should be set to

```
CALCULATETABLE (
    Sales,                      -- This expression also controls the columns returned
    DATESYTD ( 'Date'[Date] )
)
```

Working with custom calendars

As you have seen so far, the standard time intelligence functions in DAX only support standard Gregorian calendars. These are based on a solar calendar divided into 12 months, each one with a different number of days. These functions work well to analyze data by year, quarter, month, and day. However, there are models that have a different definition of time periods, like week-based calendars such as the ISO week date system. If someone needs a custom calendar, they need to rewrite the time intelligence logic in DAX because the standard time intelligence calculation would be of no use.

When it comes to nonstandard calendars, there are so many variations that it would be impossible to cover them all. Therefore, we show examples of how to implement time intelligence calculations in DAX when you cannot use standard functions.

In order to simplify the formulas, a common technique is to move part of the business logic in the date table through the use of dedicated columns. The standard DAX time intelligence functions do not use any information from the date table other than the date column. This is a design choice of DAX because this way the behavior of the language does not depend on the presence of additional metadata to identify columns to determine year, quarter, and month of a date—as was the case with MDX and Analysis Services Multidimensional. Being the owner of your model and of your DAX code, you can make more assumptions, and this helps in simplifying the code to handle custom time-related calculations.

This final section shows a few examples of the formulas for custom calendars. If needed, you can find more information, examples, and ready-to-use DAX formulas in the following articles:

- Time Patterns: http://www.daxpatterns.com/time-patterns/
- Week-Based Time Intelligence in DAX: http://sql.bi/isoweeks/

Working with weeks

DAX does not provide any time intelligence functions that handle weeks. The reason is that there are many different standards and techniques to define weeks within a year, and to define the notion of calculation over weeks. Oftentimes a single week crosses the boundaries of years, quarters, and months. You need to write the code to handle your own definition of a week-based calendar. For example, in ISO a week-date system of January 1 and January 2 in 2011 belongs to week 52 of year 2010, and the first week of 2011 starts on January 3.

Although there are different standards, you can learn a generic approach that should work in most cases. The approach involves the creation of additional columns in the *Date* table to store the relationship between weeks and their month/quarter/year. Changing the association rules will just require changing the content of the *Date* table, without modifying the DAX code of the measures.

For example, you can extend a *Date* table to support ISO weeks by using the following calculated columns:

```
'Date'[Calendar Week Number] = WEEKNUM ( 'Date'[Date], 1 )

'Date'[ISO Week Number] = WEEKNUM ( 'Date'[Date], 21 )

'Date'[ISO Year Number] = YEAR ( 'Date'[Date] + ( 3 - WEEKDAY ( 'Date'[Date], 3 ) ) )

'Date'[ISO Week] = "W" & 'Date'[ISO Week Number] & "-" & 'Date'[ISO Year Number]

'Date'[ISO Week Sequential] = INT ( ( 'Date'[Date] - 2 ) / 7 )

'Date'[ISO Year Day Number] =
VAR CurrentIsoYearNumber = 'Date'[ISO Year Number]
VAR CurrentDate = 'Date'[Date]
VAR DateFirstJanuary = DATE ( CurrentIsoYearNumber, 1, 1 )
VAR DayOfFirstJanuary = WEEKDAY ( DateFirstJanuary, 3 )
VAR OffsetStartIsoYear = - DayOfFirstJanuary + ( 7 * ( DayOfFirstJanuary > 3 ) )
VAR StartOfIsoYear = DateFirstJanuary + OffsetStartIsoYear
VAR Result = CurrentDate - StartOfIsoYear
RETURN
    Result
```

You can see in Figure 8-41 the result of these columns. The *ISO Week* column will be visible to users, whereas the *ISO Week Sequential Number* is for internal use only. *ISO Year Day Number* is the number of days since the beginning of the ISO year. These additional columns make it easy to compare different periods.

Date	ISO Week Number	Calendar Week Number	ISO Year Number	ISO Week	ISO Week Sequential	ISO Year Day Number
12/27/07	52	52	2007	W52-2007	5634	361
12/28/07	52	52	2007	W52-2007	5634	362
12/29/07	52	52	2007	W52-2007	5634	363
12/30/07	52	53	2007	W52-2007	5634	364
12/31/07	1	53	2008	W1-2008	5635	1
01/01/08	1	1	2008	W1-2008	5635	2
01/02/08	1	1	2008	W1-2008	5635	3
01/03/08	1	1	2008	W1-2008	5635	4
01/04/08	1	1	2008	W1-2008	5635	5
01/05/08	1	1	2008	W1-2008	5635	6
01/06/08	1	2	2008	W1-2008	5635	7
01/07/08	2	2	2008	W2-2008	5636	8
01/08/08	2	2	2008	W2-2008	5636	9
01/09/08	2	2	2008	W2-2008	5636	10

FIGURE 8-41 The calculated columns extend the *Date* table to support ISO weeks.

Using the new columns, a developer can write year-to-date aggregation by using the *ISO Year Number* column instead of extracting the year number from the date. This technique is the same as the one you learned in the "Understanding periods to date" section earlier in this chapter. We just added an additional check to make sure that only one *ISO Year* is selected, prior to invoking the *VALUES* function:

```
ISO YTD Sales :=
IF (
    HASONEVALUE ( 'Date'[ISO Year Number] ),
    VAR LastDateInSelection = MAX ( 'Date'[Date] )
    VAR YearSelected = VALUES ( 'Date'[ISO Year Number] )
    VAR Result =
        CALCULATE (
            [Sales Amount],
            'Date'[Date] <= LastDateInSelection,
            'Date'[ISO Year Number] = YearSelected,
            ALL ( 'Date' )
        )
    RETURN
        Result
)
```

Figure 8-42 shows the result of the *ISO YTD Sales* measure at the beginning of 2008, compared with a standard YTD computed through *DATESYTD*. The ISO version accurately includes December 31, 2007, which belongs to ISO Year 2008.

ISO Year Number	Sales Amount	ISO YTD Sales	CAL YTD Sales
2008	9,751,677.59	9,751,677.59	9,744,825.64
W1-2008	121,701.75	121,701.75	114,849.81
12/31/07	6,851.94	6,851.94	11,309,946.12
01/01/08	19,143.33	25,995.27	19,143.33
01/02/08	14,731.14	40,726.41	33,874.46
01/03/08	54,558.58	95,284.98	88,433.04
01/04/08		95,284.98	88,433.04
01/05/08	18,047.97	113,332.96	106,481.01
01/06/08	8,368.80	121,701.75	114,849.81

FIGURE 8-42 *ISO YTD Sales* accurately includes December 31, 2007, in the first week of 2008.

The comparison with the prior year should compare the relative weeks of the year with the same weeks in the previous year. Since the dates might be different, it is simpler to use other columns in the date table to implement the comparison logic. The distribution of weeks within each year is regular because each week always has seven days, whereas calendar months have different lengths and cannot benefit from the same assumption. In week-based calendars, you can simplify the calculation by looking in the previous year for the same relative days that were selected in the current filter context.

The following *ISO PY Sales* measure filters the same selection of days in the previous year. This technique also works when the selection includes complete weeks because the days are selected using the *ISO Year Day Number* value and not the effective date.

```
ISO PY Sales :=
IF (
    HASONEVALUE ( 'Date'[ISO Year Number] ),
    VAR DatesInSelection = VALUES ( 'Date'[ISO Year Day Number] )
    VAR YearSelected = VALUES ( 'Date'[ISO Year Number] )
    VAR PrevYear = YearSelected - 1
    VAR Result =
        CALCULATE (
            [Sales Amount],
            DatesInSelection,
            'Date'[ISO Year Number] = PrevYear,
            ALL ( 'Date' )
        )
    RETURN
        Result
)
```

Figure 8-43 shows the result produced by the *ISO PY Sales* measure. On the right we added the sales amount of 2007, to make it easier to understand the source of *ISO PY Sales*.

ISO Year Number	Sales Amount	CAL PY Sales	ISO PY Sales	ISO Year Number	Sales Amount
2008	9,751,677.59	11,243,758.33	11,303,094.18	2007	11,303,094.18
W1-2008	121,701.75	216,891.21	240,196.84	W1-2007	240,196.84
12/31/07	6,851.94			01/02/07	48,646.02
01/01/08	19,143.33		48,646.02	01/03/07	92,244.07
01/02/08	14,731.14	48,646.02	92,244.07	01/04/07	13,950.29
01/03/08	54,558.58	92,244.07	13,950.29	01/05/07	62,050.83
01/04/08		13,950.29	62,050.83	01/07/07	23,305.63
01/05/08	18,047.97	62,050.83		W2-2007	77,368.65
01/06/08	8,368.80		23,305.63	01/09/07	20,543.35
W2-2008	121,345.28	100,674.28	77,368.65	01/10/07	6,565.56
01/07/08	16,425.61	23,305.63		01/11/07	22,693.05
01/08/08	23,523.00		20,543.35	01/12/07	16,251.63
01/09/08	41,778.21	20,543.35	6,565.56	01/13/07	11,315.05
01/10/08	942.56	6,565.56	22,693.05	W3-2007	281,655.20
01/11/08	22,059.58	22,693.05	16,251.63	01/15/07	58,224.87
01/12/08		16,251.63	11,315.05	01/16/07	45,595.65
01/13/08	16.616.33	11.315.05		01/17/07	29.600.55

FIGURE 8-43 The *ISO PY Sales* shows the value of the same weeks one year earlier.

Week-based calendars are simple to manage because of the assumption you can make about the symmetry between days in different years. This is usually not compatible with the calendar month, so if you want to use both hierarchies (months and weeks), you should create different time intelligence calculations for each hierarchy.

Custom year-to-date, quarter-to-date, and month-to-date

Earlier in this chapter, you learned how to rewrite *DATESYTD* and similar functions in the "Understanding periods to date" section. There, we could still extract date attributes—like the year—from the date column. With ISO calendars, this logic is no longer in the date column. Instead, we created additional columns just for this calculation. In this section we now demonstrate how to replace the logic that extracts information from the date value by using other columns of the *Date* table.

For example, consider the following *YTD Sales* measure:

```
YTD Sales :=
CALCULATE (
    [Sales Amount],
    DATESYTD ( 'Date'[Date] )
)
```

The corresponding syntax in DAX without time intelligence is the following:

```
YTD Sales :=
VAR LastDateInSelection = MAX ( 'Date'[Date] )
VAR Result =
    CALCULATE (
        [Sales Amount],
        'Date'[Date] <= LastDateInSelection
            && YEAR ( 'Date'[Date] ) = YEAR ( LastDateInSelection )
    )
RETURN
    Result
```

If you use a custom calendar, you must replace the *YEAR* function call with an access to the *Year* column, such as in the following *YTD Sales Custom* measure:

```
YTD Sales Custom :=
VAR LastDateInSelection = MAX ( 'Date'[Date] )
VAR LastYearInSelection = MAX ( 'Date'[Calendar Year Number] )
VAR Result =
    CALCULATE (
        [Sales Amount],
        'Date'[Date] <= LastDateInSelection,
        'Date'[Calendar Year Number] = LastYearInSelection,
        ALL ( 'Date' )
    )
RETURN
    Result
```

You can use the same template to implement quarter-to-date and month-to-date calculations. The only difference is the column used instead of *Calendar Year Number*:

```
QTD Sales Custom :=
VAR LastDateInSelection = MAX ( 'Date'[Date] )
VAR LastYearQuarterInSelection = MAX ( 'Date'[Calendar Year Quarter Number] )
VAR Result =
    CALCULATE (
        [Sales Amount],
        'Date'[Date] <= LastDateInSelection,
        'Date'[Calendar Year Quarter Number] = LastYearQuarterInSelection,
        ALL ( 'Date' )
    )
RETURN
    Result

MTD Sales Custom :=
VAR LastDateInSelection = MAX ( 'Date'[Date] )
VAR LastYearMonthInSelection = MAX ( 'Date'[Calendar Year Month Number] )
VAR Result =
    CALCULATE (
        [Sales Amount],
        'Date'[Date] <= LastDateInSelection,
        'Date'[Calendar Year Month Number] = LastYearMonthInSelection,
        ALL ( 'Date' )
    )
RETURN
    Result
```

You can use these formulas to implement calculations for both standard calendars (in case you want to improve performance using *DirectQuery*) and custom calendars (in case the time periods are not standard periods).

Conclusions

In this long chapter, you learned the basics of time intelligence calculations in DAX. These are the important points we covered:

- Both Power Pivot and Power BI have mechanisms to automate the creation of a date table. They are not worth using, unless your requirements are really simple. Having control over your date table is important and the existing tools do not let you modify the tables to follow your needs.

- Building a date table is easy by leveraging *CALENDARAUTO* and some simple DAX code. It is worth investing some time to build your own date table, as you will reuse the code in many different projects. You can also download DAX templates for a date table on the web.

- A data table should be marked as a date table to simplify the use of time intelligence calculations.

- There are several time intelligence functions. Most of them simply return a table that can be used as a filter argument of *CALCULATE*.

- You should learn to treat time intelligence functions as building blocks for more complex calculations. By mixing time intelligence functions, one can create several different and complex calculations.

- When the requirements are such that standard time intelligence calculations no longer work, it is time to roll up your sleeves and learn to author time intelligence calculations with simpler DAX functions.

- There are several examples of time intelligence calculations in this book. However, you can find many more at https://www.daxpatterns.com/time-patterns/.

Calculation groups

In 2019, DAX received a major update with the introduction of calculation groups. Calculation groups are a utility feature inspired from a similar feature available in MDX, known as calculated members. If you already know what calculated members in MDX are, then learning calculation groups should be somewhat easier. However, the DAX implementation differs from the MDX implementation. Therefore, regardless of your previous knowledge, in this chapter you will learn what calculation groups are, what they were designed for, and how they can help build awesome calculations.

Calculation groups are easy to use; however, designing a model with calculation groups correctly can be challenging when you create multiple calculation groups or when you use calculation items in measures. For this reason, we provide best practices to help you avoid any issues. Deviating from these best practices requires a deep understanding of how calculation groups are designed, if one wants to obtain a sound model.

Calculation groups are a new feature in DAX, which, as of April 2019, has not been completed and released. Along this chapter we highlight the parts that may change in the final version of this feature. Therefore, it is important to visit the web page https://www.sqlbi.com/calculation-groups, where you will find updated material and examples about calculation groups in DAX.

Introducing calculation groups

Before we provide a description of calculation groups, it is useful to spend some time analyzing the business requirement that led to the introduction of this feature. Because you just finished digesting the chapter about time intelligence, an example involving time-related calculations fits perfectly well.

In our sample model we defined calculations to compute the sales amount, the total cost, the margin, and the total quantity sold by using the following DAX code:

```
Sales Amount := SUMX ( Sales, Sales[Quantity] * Sales[Net Price] )
Total Cost := SUMX ( Sales, Sales[Quantity] * Sales[Unit Cost] )
Margin := [Sales Amount] - [Total Cost]
Sales Quantity := SUM ( Sales[Quantity] )
```

All four measures are useful, and they provide different insights into the business. Moreover, all four measures are good candidates for time intelligence calculations. A year-to-date over sales quantity can be as interesting as a year-to-date over sales amount and over margin. The same consideration is true for many other time intelligence calculations: same period last year, growth in percentage against the previous year, and many others.

Nevertheless, if one wants to build all the different time intelligence calculations for all the measures, the number of measures in the data model may grow very quickly. In the real world, managing a data model with hundreds of measures is intimidating for both users and developers. Finally, consider that all the different measures for time intelligence calculations are simple variations of a common pattern. For example, the year-to-date versions of the previous list of four measures would look like the following:

```
YTD Sales Amount :=
CALCULATE (
    [Sales Amount],
    DATESYTD ( 'Date'[Date] )
)

YTD Total Cost :=
CALCULATE (
    [Total Cost],
    DATESYTD ( 'Date'[Date] )
)

YTD Margin :=
CALCULATE (
    [Margin],
    DATESYTD ( 'Date'[Date] )
)

YTD Sales Quantity :=
CALCULATE (
    [Sales Quantity],
    DATESYTD ( 'Date'[Date] )
)
```

All the previous measures only differ in their base measure; they all apply the same *DATESYTD* filter context to different base measures. It would be great if a developer were given the opportunity to define a more generic calculation, using a placeholder for the measure:

```
YTD <Measure> :=
CALCULATE (
    <Measure>,
    DATESYTD ( 'Date'[Date] )
)
```

The previous code is not a valid DAX syntax, but it provides a very good description of what calculation items are. You can read the previous code as: *When you need to apply the YTD calculation to a measure, call the measure after applying DATESYTD to the Date[Date] column.* This is what a calculation item is: A calculation item is a DAX expression containing a special placeholder. The placeholder is replaced with a measure by the engine just before evaluating the result. In other words, a calculation item is a variation of an expression that can be applied to any measure.

Moreover, a developer will likely find themselves needing several time intelligence calculations. As we noted at the beginning of the section, year-to-date, quarter-to-date, and same period last year are all calculations that somehow belong to the same group of calculations. Therefore, DAX offers calculation items and calculation groups. A calculation group is a set of calculation items that are conveniently grouped together because they are variations on the same topic.

Let us continue with DAX pseudo-code:

```
CALCULATION GROUP "Time Intelligence"
    CALCULATION ITEM CY := <Measure>
    CALCULATION ITEM PY := CALCULATE ( <Measure>, SAMPEPERIODLASTYEAR ( 'Date'[Date] ) )
    CALCULATION ITEM QTD := CALCULATE ( <Measure>, DATESQTD ( 'Date'[Date] ) )
    CALCULATION ITEM YTD := CALCULATE ( <Measure>, DATESYTD ( 'Date'[Date] ) )
```

As you can see, we grouped four time-related calculations in a group named *Time Intelligence*. In only four lines, the code defines dozens of different measures because the calculation items apply their variation to any measure in the model. Thus, as soon as a developer creates a new measure, the CY, PY, QTD, and YTD variations will be available at no cost.

There are still several details missing in our understanding of calculation groups, but only one is required to start taking advantage of them and to define the first calculation group: How does the user choose one variation? As we said, a calculation item is not a measure; it is a variation of a measure. Therefore, a user needs a way to put in a report a specific measure with one or more variations of the measure itself. Because users have the habit of selecting columns from tables, calculation groups are implemented as if they were columns in tables, whereas calculation items are like values of the given columns. This way, the user can use the calculation group in the columns of a matrix to display different variations of a measure in the report. For example, the calculation items previously described are applied to the columns of the matrix in Figure 9-1, showing different variations of the *Sales Amount* measure.

Calendar Year	Month	CY	PY	QTD	YTD
☐ CY 2005					
☐ CY 2006	January	656,766.69	794,248.24	656,766.69	656,766.69
☐ CY 2007	February	600,080.00	891,135.91	1,256,846.69	1,256,846.69
■ CY 2008	March	559,538.52	961,289.24	1,816,385.21	1,816,385.21
☐ CY 2009	April	999,667.17	1,128,104.82	999,667.17	2,816,052.38
	May	893,231.96	936,192.74	1,892,899.13	3,709,284.34
	June	845,141.60	982,304.46	2,738,040.73	4,554,425.94
	July	890,547.41	922,542.98	890,547.41	5,444,973.35
	August	721,560.95	952,834.59	1,612,108.36	6,166,534.30
	September	963,437.23	1,009,868.98	2,575,545.59	7,129,971.53
	October	719,792.99	914,273.54	719,792.99	7,849,764.52
	November	1,156,109.32	825,601.87	1,875,902.31	9,005,873.85
	December	921,709.14	991,548.75	2,797,611.46	9,927,582.99
	Total	**9,927,582.99**	**11,309,946.12**	**2,797,611.46**	**9,927,582.99**

FIGURE 9-1 The user can use a calculation group as if it were a column of the model, applying it to matrix columns.

Creating calculation groups

The implementation of calculation groups in a Tabular model depends on the user interface of the editor tool. At the time of writing (April 2019), neither Power BI nor SQL Server Data Tools (SSDT) for Analysis Services have a user interface for this feature, which is only available at the API level of Tabular Object Model (TOM). The first tool providing an editor for this feature is Tabular Editor, an open source tool available for free at https://tabulareditor.github.io/.

In Tabular Editor, the Model / New Calculation Group menu item creates a new calculation group, which appears as a table in the model with a special icon. This is shown in Figure 9-2 where the calculation group has been renamed *Time Intelligence*.

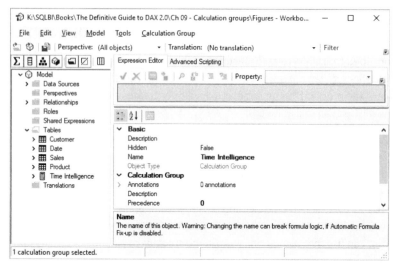

FIGURE 9-2 Tabular Editor displays the *Time Intelligence* calculation group as a special table.

A calculation group is a special table with a single column, named *Attribute* by default in Tabular Editor. In our sample model we renamed this column *Time calc*; then we added three items (**YTD**, **QTD**, and **SPLY** for same period last year) by using the New Calculation Item context menu item available by right-clicking on the *Time calc* column. Each calculation item has a DAX expression, as shown in Figure 9-3.

FIGURE 9-3 Every calculation item has a DAX expression that can be modified in Tabular Editor.

The *SELECTEDMEASURE* function is the DAX implementation of the <*Measure*> placeholder we used in the previous DAX pseudo-code. The DAX code for each calculation item is described in the following code. The comment preceding each DAX expression identifies the corresponding calculation item:

> **Note** It is best practice to always expose the business logic through measures in the model. When the model includes calculation groups, the Power BI client does not allow developers to aggregate columns because calculation groups can only be applied to measures, and they do not produce any effect on aggregation functions; they only operate on measures.

```
--
-- Calculation Item: YTD
--
    CALCULATE (
        SELECTEDMEASURE (),
        DATESYTD ( 'Date'[Date] )
    )


--
-- Calculation Item: QTD
--
    CALCULATE (
        SELECTEDMEASURE (),
        DATESQTD ( 'Date'[Date] )
    )


--
-- Calculation Item: SPLY
--
    CALCULATE (
        SELECTEDMEASURE (),
        SAMEPERIODLASTYEAR ( 'Date'[Date] )
    )
```

With this definition, the user will see a new table named *Time Intelligence*, with a column named *Time calc* containing three values: **YTD**, **QTD**, and **SPLY**. The user can create a slicer on that column, or use it on the rows and columns of visuals, as if it were a real column in the model. For example, when the user selects **YTD**, the engine applies the **YTD** calculation item to whatever measure is in the report. In Figure 9-4 you can see a matrix containing the *Sales Amount* measure. Because the slicer selects the **YTD** variation of the measure, the numbers shown are year-to-date values.

Time calc	Month	CY 2007	CY 2008	CY 2009
☐ QTD				
☐ SPLY	January	794,248.24	656,766.69	580,901.05
■ YTD	February	1,685,384.15	1,256,846.69	1,203,482.19
	March	2,646,673.39	1,816,385.21	1,699,620.05
	April	3,774,778.20	2,816,052.38	2,378,513.27
	May	4,710,970.95	3,709,284.34	3,445,678.50
	June	5,693,275.41	4,554,425.94	4,318,264.70
	July	6,615,818.39	5,444,973.35	5,386,661.27
	August	7,568,652.98	6,166,534.30	6,222,368.73
	September	8,578,521.96	7,129,971.53	6,931,979.13
	October	9,492,795.50	7,849,764.52	7,738,717.35
	November	10,318,397.37	9,005,873.85	8,606,881.36
	December	11,309,946.12	9,927,582.99	9,353,814.87
	Total	**11,309,946.12**	**9,927,582.99**	**9,353,814.87**

FIGURE 9-4 When the user selects **YTD**, the values in the matrix represent the **YTD** variation of the *Sales Amount* measure.

If on the same report the user selects **SPLY**, the result will be very different, as you can appreciate in Figure 9-5.

Time calc	Month	CY 2008	CY 2009	CY 2010
☐ QTD				
■ SPLY	January	794,248.24	656,766.69	580,901.05
☐ YTD	February	891,135.91	600,080.00	622,581.14
	March	961,289.24	559,538.52	496,137.87
	April	1,128,104.82	999,667.17	678,893.22
	May	936,192.74	893,231.96	1,067,165.23
	June	982,304.46	845,141.60	872,586.20
	July	922,542.98	890,547.41	1,068,396.58
	August	952,834.59	721,560.95	835,707.46
	September	1,009,868.98	963,437.23	709,610.40
	October	914,273.54	719,792.99	806,738.22
	November	825,601.87	1,156,109.32	868,164.01
	December	991,548.75	921,709.14	746,933.50
	Total	**11,309,946.12**	**9,927,582.99**	**9,353,814.87**

FIGURE 9-5 Selecting **SPLY** changes the results of the *Sales Amount* measure because it now uses a different variation. The values are the original *Sales Amount* values, shifted back one year.

If the user does not select one value or if the user selects multiple values together, then the engine does not apply any variation to the original measure. You can see this in Figure 9-6.

Time calc	Month	CY 2007	CY 2008	CY 2009
☐ QTD				
☐ SPLY	January	794,248.24	656,766.69	580,901.05
☐ YTD	February	891,135.91	600,080.00	622,581.14
	March	961,289.24	559,538.52	496,137.87
	April	1,128,104.82	999,667.17	678,893.22
	May	936,192.74	893,231.96	1,067,165.23
	June	982,304.46	845,141.60	872,586.20
	July	922,542.98	890,547.41	1,068,396.58
	August	952,834.59	721,560.95	835,707.46
	September	1,009,868.98	963,437.23	709,610.40
	October	914,273.54	719,792.99	806,738.22
	November	825,601.87	1,156,109.32	868,164.01
	December	991,548.75	921,709.14	746,933.50
	Total	**11,309,946.12**	**9,927,582.99**	**9,353,814.87**

FIGURE 9-6 When no calculation item is selected, the report shows the original measure.

> **Note** The behavior of calculation groups with no selection or with multiple items selected may change in the future. As of April 2019, when multiple calculation items are selected, the behavior is the same as if there were no selection on a calculation group. Nevertheless, this condition might return different results in future versions—for example, raising an error in case of a multiple selection.

Calculation groups can go further than that. At the beginning of this section we introduced four different measures: *Sales Amount*, *Total Cost*, *Margin*, and *Sales Quantity*. It would be extremely nice if the user could use a slicer in order to select the metric to show and not only the time intelligence calculation to apply. We would like to present a generic report that slices any of the four metrics by month and year, letting the user choose the desired metric. In other words, we want to obtain the report in Figure 9-7.

Time calc	Month	CY 2007	CY 2008	CY 2009
☐ QTD				
☐ SPLY	January	411,542.33	329,414.92	283,697.42
■ YTD	February	883,064.36	637,218.14	602,841.63
	March	1,387,425.09	925,460.26	855,248.48
	April	1,987,901.79	1,445,669.78	1,203,631.81
	May	2,514,206.64	1,930,431.61	1,811,248.06
Metric	June	3,055,699.88	2,393,304.49	2,299,080.65
■ Margin	July	3,579,035.50	2,879,436.96	2,902,951.43
☐ Sales Amount	August	4,111,793.71	3,277,582.86	3,360,057.10
☐ Sales Quantity	September	4,687,776.20	3,796,855.62	3,742,990.25
☐ Total Cost	October	5,189,581.59	4,187,403.58	4,198,974.31
	November	5,598,058.99	4,757,022.88	4,606,252.00
	December	6,075,652.35	5,212,190.14	4,954,796.26
	Total	**6,075,652.35**	**5,212,190.14**	**4,954,796.26**

FIGURE 9-7 The report shows the **YTD** time intelligence calculation applied to *Margin*, but the user can choose any other combination through the slicers.

In the example shown in Figure 9-7, the user is browsing the margin amount using a year-to-date variation. Nevertheless, the user can choose any combination of the slicers linked to the two calculation groups, *Metric* and *Time calc*.

In order to obtain this report, we created an additional calculation group named *Metric*, which includes the **Sales Amount**, **Total Cost**, **Margin**, and **Sales Quantity** calculation items. The expression for each calculation item just evaluates the corresponding measure, as shown in Figure 9-8 for the **Sales Amount** calculation item.

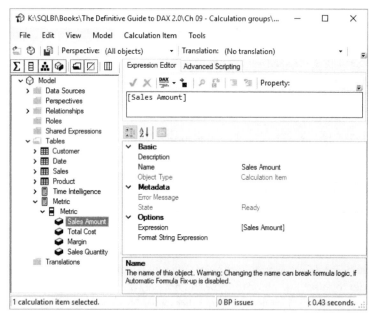

FIGURE 9-8 The *Metric* calculation group contains four calculation items; each one simply evaluates a corresponding measure.

When there are multiple calculation groups in the same data model, it is important to define in which order they should be applied by the DAX engine. The *Precedence* property of the calculation group defines the order of application: the first calculation group applied is the one with the larger value. In order to obtain the desired result, we increased the *Precedence* property of the *Time Intelligence* calculation group to 10, as shown in Figure 9-9. As a consequence, the engine applies the *Time Intelligence* calculation group before the *Metric* calculation group, which keeps the *Precedence* property at the default value of zero. We discuss the precedence of calculation groups in more detail later in this chapter.

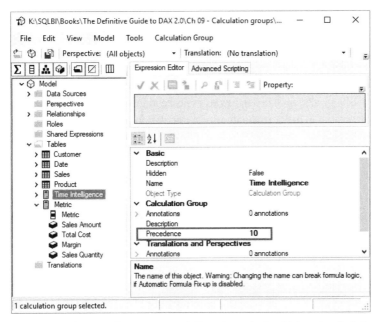

FIGURE 9-9 The *Precedence* property defines the order in which each calculation group is applied to a measure.

The following DAX code includes the definition of each calculation item in the *Metric* calculation group:

```
--
-- Calculation Item: Margin
--
    [Margin]


--
-- Calculation Item: Sales Amount
--
    [Sales Amount]


--
-- Calculation Item: Sales Quantity
--
    [Sales Quantity]


--
-- Calculation Item: Total Cost
--
    [Total Cost]
```

These calculation items are not modifiers of the original measure. Instead, they completely replace the original measure with a new one. To obtain this behavior, we omitted a reference to *SELECTED-MEASURE* in the expression. *SELECTEDMEASURE* is used very often in calculation items, but it is not mandatory.

This last example is useful to introduce the first of the many complexities that we will need to address with calculation groups. If the user selects **Quantity**, then the report shows the quantity, but it still uses the same format strings (with two decimals) as the other measures. Because the *Quantity* measure is an integer, it would be useful to remove the decimal places or, in general, to adopt a different format string. We discussed earlier the fact that the presence of multiple calculation groups in a calculation requires the definition of a precedence order, as was the case in the previous example. These are the first of several details to consider in order to create useful calculation groups.

 Note If you are using Analysis Services, be mindful that adding a calculation group to a model is an operation that requires a refresh of the table corresponding to the calculation group in order to make the calculation items visible to the client. This may prove to be counterintuitive because deploying measures does not require such an update—measures are visible to the clients just after the deployment. However, because calculation groups and items are presented to the client in tables and columns, after the deployment it is necessary to run a refresh operation to populate the internal structures of the tables and columns. In Power BI this operation will likely be handled automatically by the user interface—though this is pure speculation because calculation groups are not present in Power BI at the time of printing.

Understanding calculation groups

In the previous sections we focused on the use of calculation groups and how to implement them with Tabular Editor. In this section, we describe in more detail the properties and behavior of calculation groups and calculation items.

There are two entities: calculation groups and calculation items. A calculation group is a collection of calculation items, grouped together based on a user-defined criterion. For both calculation groups and calculation items, there are properties that the developer must set correctly. We introduce these entities and their properties here, providing more examples and details in the remaining part of this chapter.

A calculation group is a simple entity, defined by

- The calculation group **Name**. This is the name of the table that represents the calculation group on the client side.

- The calculation group **Precedence**. When there are multiple active calculation groups, a number that defines the precedence used to apply each calculation group to a measure reference.

- The calculation group attribute **Name**. This is the name of the column that includes the calculation items, displayed to the client as unique items available in the column.

A calculation item is a much more sophisticated entity, and here is the list of its properties:

- The calculation item **Name**. This becomes one value of the calculation group column. Indeed, a calculation item is like one row in the calculation group table.

- The calculation item **Expression**. A DAX expression that might contain special functions like *SELECTEDMEASURE*. This is the expression that defines how to apply the calculation item.

- The sort order of the calculation item is defined by the **Ordinal** value. This property defines how the different calculation items are sorted when presented to the user. It is very similar to the sort-by-column feature of the data model. *This feature is not available as of April 2019 but should be implemented before calculation groups are released.*

- **Format String**. If not specified, a calculation item inherits the format string of its base measure. Nevertheless, if the modifier changes the calculation, then it is possible to override the measure format string with the format of the calculation item.

The *Format String* property is important in order to obtain a consistent behavior of the measures in the model according to the calculation item being applied to them. For example, consider the following calculation group containing two calculation items for time intelligence: year-over-year (**YOY**) is the difference between a selected period and the same period in the previous year; year-over-year percentage (**YOY%**) is the percentage of **YOY** over the amount in the same period in the previous year:

```
--
-- Calculation Item: YOY
--
    VAR CurrYear =
        SELECTEDMEASURE ()
    VAR PrevYear =
        CALCULATE (
            SELECTEDMEASURE (),
            SAMEPERIODLASTYEAR ( 'Date'[Date] )
        )
    VAR Result =
        CurrYear - PrevYear
    RETURN Result


--
-- Calculation Item: YOY%
--
    VAR CurrYear =
        SELECTEDMEASURE ()
    VAR PrevYear =
        CALCULATE (
            SELECTEDMEASURE (),
            SAMEPERIODLASTYEAR ( 'Date'[Date] )
        )
    VAR Result =
        DIVIDE (
            CurrYear - PrevYear,
            PrevYear
        )
    RETURN Result
```

The result produced by these two calculation items in a report is correct, but if the *Format String* property does not override the default format string, then **YOY%** is displayed as a decimal number instead of as a percentage, as shown in Figure 9-10.

Calendar Year	Month	YOY	YOY%
☐ CY 2005			
☐ CY 2006	January	-75,865.64	-0.12
☐ CY 2007	February	22,501.14	0.04
☐ CY 2008	March	-63,400.65	-0.11
■ CY 2009	April	-320,773.95	-0.32
☐ CY 2010	May	173,933.27	0.19
☐ CY 2011	June	27,444.59	0.03
	July	177,849.17	0.20
	August	114,146.50	0.16
	September	-253,826.83	-0.26
	October	86,945.23	0.12
	November	-287,945.31	-0.25
	December	-174,775.64	-0.19
	Total	**-573,768.12**	**-0.06**

FIGURE 9-10 The two calculation items **YOY** and **YOY%** share the same format as the *Sales Amount* measure.

The example shown in Figure 9-10 displays the **YOY** evaluation of the *Sales Amount* measure using the same format string as the original *Sales Amount* measure. This is the correct behavior to display a difference. However, the **YOY%** calculation item displays the same amount as a percentage of the value of the previous year. The number shown is correct, but for January one would expect to see –12% instead of –0.12. In this case the expected format string should be a percentage, regardless of the format of the original measure. To obtain the desired behavior, set the *Format String* property of the **YOY%** calculation item to percentage, overriding the behavior of the underlying measure. You can see the result in Figure 9-11. If the *Format String* property is not assigned to a calculation item, the existing format string is used.

Calendar Year	Month	YOY	YOY%
☐ CY 2005			
☐ CY 2006	January	-75,865.64	-12%
☐ CY 2007	February	22,501.14	4%
☐ CY 2008	March	-63,400.65	-11%
■ CY 2009	April	-320,773.95	-32%
☐ CY 2010	May	173,933.27	19%
☐ CY 2011	June	27,444.59	3%
	July	177,849.17	20%
	August	114,146.50	16%
	September	-253,826.83	-26%
	October	86,945.23	12%
	November	-287,945.31	-25%
	December	-174,775.64	-19%
	Total	**-573,768.12**	**-6%**

FIGURE 9-11 The **YOY%** calculation item overrides the format of the *Sales Amount* measure displaying the value as a percentage.

The format string can be defined using a fixed format string or—in more complex scenarios—by using a DAX expression that returns the format string. When one is writing a DAX expression, it becomes possible to refer to the format string of the current measure using the *SELECTEDMEASURE-FORMATSTRING* function, which returns the format string currently defined for the measure. For example, if the model contains a measure that returns the currently selected currency and you want to include the currency symbol as part of the format string, you can use this code to append the currency symbol to the current format string:

```
SELECTEDMEASUREFORMATSTRING () & " " & [Selected Currency]
```

Customizing the format string of a calculation item is useful to preserve user experience consistency when browsing the model. However, a careful developer should consider that the format string operates on any measure used with the calculation item. When there are multiple calculation groups in a report, the result produced by these properties also depends on the calculation group precedence, as explained in a later section of this chapter.

Understanding calculation item application

So far, the description we gave of how a calculation item works has never been extremely precise. The reason is mainly educational: we wanted to introduce the concept of calculation items, without diving too deep into details that might be distracting. Indeed, we said that calculation items can be applied by the user using, for example, a slicer. A calculation item is applied by replacing measure references invoked when there is a calculation item active in the filter context. In this scenario, the calculation item rewrites the measure reference by applying the expression defined in the calculation item itself.

For example, consider the following calculation item:

```
--
-- Calculation Item: YTD
--
    CALCULATE (
        SELECTEDMEASURE (),
        DATESYTD ( 'Date'[Date] )
    )
```

In order to apply the calculation item in an expression, you need to filter the calculation group. You can create this filter using *CALCULATE*, like in the following example; this is the same technique used by the client tool when using slicers and visuals:

```
CALCULATE (
    [Sales Amount],
    'Time Intelligence'[Time calc] = "YTD"
)
```

There is nothing magical about calculation groups: They are tables, and as such they can be filtered by *CALCULATE* like any other table. When *CALCULATE* applies a filter to a calculation item, DAX uses the definition of the calculation item to rewrite the expression before evaluating it.

Therefore, based on the definition of the calculation item, the previous code is interpreted as follows:

```
CALCULATE (
    CALCULATE (
        [Sales Amount],
        DATESYTD ( 'Date'[Date] )
    )
)
```

 Note   Inside the inner *CALCULATE*, one can check with *ISFILTERED* whether the calculation item is filtered or not. In the example, we removed the outer filter on the calculation item for the sake of simplicity, to show that the calculation item has already been applied. Nevertheless, a calculation item retains its filters, and further sub-expressions might still perform the replacement of measures.

Despite being very intuitive in simple examples, this behavior hides some level of complexity. The application of a calculation item replaces a measure reference with the expression of the calculation item. Focus your attention on this last sentence: *A measure reference is replaced*. Without a measure reference, a calculation item does not apply any modification. For example, the following code is not affected by any calculation item because it does not contain any measure reference:

```
CALCULATE (
    SUMX ( Sales, Sales[Quantity] * Sales[Net Price] ),
    'Time Intelligence'[Time calc] = "YTD"
)
```

In this example, the calculation item does not perform any transformation because the code inside *CALCULATE* does not use any measure. The following code is the one executed after the application of the calculation item:

```
CALCULATE (
    SUMX ( Sales, Sales[Quantity] * Sales[Net Price] )
)
```

If the expression inside *CALCULATE* contains multiple measure references, all of them are replaced with the calculation item definition. For example, the expression in the following *Cost Ratio YTD* measure contains two measure references, *Total Cost* and *Sales Amount*:

```
CR YTD :=
CALCULATE (
    DIVIDE (
        [Total Cost],
        [Sales Amount]
    ),
    'Time Intelligence'[Time calc] = "YTD"
)
```

To obtain the actual code executed, replace the measure references with the expansion of the calculation item definition, as in the following *CR YTD Actual Code* measure:

```
CR YTD Actual Code :=
CALCULATE (
    DIVIDE (
        CALCULATE (
            [Total Cost],
            DATESYTD ( 'Date'[Date] )
        ),
        CALCULATE (
            [Sales Amount],
            DATESYTD ( 'Date'[Date] )
        )
    )
)
```

In this example, the code generated produces the same result as the next version in the *CR YTD Simplified* measure, which is more intuitive:

```
CR YTD Simplified :=
CALCULATE (
    CALCULATE (
        DIVIDE (
            [Total Cost],
            [Sales Amount]
        ),
        DATESYTD ( 'Date'[Date] )
    )
)
```

These three measures return the same result, as shown in Figure 9-12.

Calendar Year	Month	CR YTD	CR YTD Actual Code	CR YTD Simplified
☐ CY 2005				
☐ CY 2006	January	49.84 %	49.84 %	49.84 %
☐ CY 2007	February	49.30 %	49.30 %	49.30 %
☐ CY 2007	March	49.05 %	49.05 %	49.05 %
■ CY 2008	April	48.66 %	48.66 %	48.66 %
☐ CY 2009	May	47.96 %	47.96 %	47.96 %
☐ CY 2010	June	47.45 %	47.45 %	47.45 %
☐ CY 2011	July	47.12 %	47.12 %	47.12 %
	August	46.85 %	46.85 %	46.85 %
	September	46.75 %	46.75 %	46.75 %
	October	46.66 %	46.66 %	46.66 %
	November	47.18 %	47.18 %	47.18 %
	December	47.50 %	47.50 %	47.50 %
	Total	**47.50 %**	**47.50 %**	**47.50 %**

FIGURE 9-12 The *CR YTD*, *CR YTD Actual Code*, and *CR YTD Simplified* measures produce the same result.

Nevertheless, you must be very careful because the *CR YTD Simplified* measure does not correspond to the actual code generated by the calculation item, which is the code in *CR YTD Actual Code*. In this very special case, the two versions are equivalent. However, in more complex scenarios the difference is significant, and such a large difference can lead to unintended results that are extremely hard to follow and understand. Let us analyze a couple of examples. In the first example the *Sales YTD 2008 2009* measure has two nested *CALCULATE* functions: the outer *CALCULATE* sets a filter on the year 2008, whereas the inner *CALCULATE* sets a filter on the year 2009:

```
Sales YTD 2008 2009 :=
CALCULATE (
    CALCULATE (
        [Sales Amount],
        'Date'[Calendar Year] = "CY 2009"
    ),
    'Time Intelligence'[Time calc] = "YTD",
    'Date'[Calendar Year] = "CY 2008"
)
```

The outer *CALCULATE* filters the calculation item to the **YTD** value. Nevertheless, the application of the calculation item does not change the expression because the expression does not directly contain any measure. *CALCULATE* filters the calculation item, but its application does not lead to any modifications to the code.

Pay attention to the fact that the *Sales Amount* measure is within the scope of the inner *CALCULATE*. The application of a calculation item modifies the measures in the current scope of the filter context; it does not affect nested filter context scopes. Those are handled by their own *CALCULATE*—or equivalent code, such as *CALCULATETABLE* or context transitions—which may or may not retain the same filter on the calculation item.

When the inner *CALCULATE* applies its filter context, it does not change the filter status of the calculation item. Therefore, the engine finds that the calculation item is still filtered, and it remains filtered if no other *CALCULATE* changes it. Same as if it were a regular column. The inner *CALCULATE* contains a measure reference, and DAX performs the application of the calculation item. The resulting code corresponds to the definition of the *Sales YTD 2008 2009 Actual Code* measure:

```
Sales YTD 2008 2009 Actual Code :=
CALCULATE (
    CALCULATE (
        CALCULATE (
            [Sales Amount],
            DATESYTD ( 'Date'[Date] )
        ),
        'Date'[Calendar Year] = "CY 2009"
    ),
    'Date'[Calendar Year] = "CY 2008"
)
```

The result of these two measures is visible in Figure 9-13. The selection made by the slicer on the left applies to the matrix in the middle of the figure, which includes the *Sales YTD 2008 2009* and *Sales YTD*

2008 2009 Actual Code measures. However, the selection of the year CY 2008 is overridden by CY 2009. This can be verified by looking at the matrix on the right-hand side, which shows the *Sales Amount* measure transformed with the **YTD** calculation item for the CY 2008 and CY 2009 years. The numbers in the center matrix correspond to the *CY 2009* column of the matrix on the right.

Calendar Year	Month	Sales YTD 2008 2009	Sales YTD 2008 2009 Actual Code	Month	CY 2008	CY 2009
☐ CY 2005	January	580,901.05	580,901.05	January	656,766.69	580,901.05
☐ CY 2006	February	1,203,482.19	1,203,482.19	February	1,256,846.69	1,203,482.19
☐ CY 2007	March	1,699,620.05	1,699,620.05	March	1,816,385.21	1,699,620.05
■ CY 2008	April	2,378,513.27	2,378,513.27	April	2,816,052.38	2,378,513.27
☐ CY 2009	May	3,445,678.50	3,445,678.50	May	3,709,284.34	3,445,678.50
☐ CY 2010	June	4,318,264.70	4,318,264.70	June	4,554,425.94	4,318,264.70
☐ CY 2011	July	5,386,661.27	5,386,661.27	July	5,444,973.35	5,386,661.27
	August	6,222,368.73	6,222,368.73	August	6,166,534.30	6,222,368.73
	September	6,931,979.13	6,931,979.13	September	7,129,971.53	6,931,979.13
	October	7,738,717.35	7,738,717.35	October	7,849,764.52	7,738,717.35
	November	8,606,881.36	8,606,881.36	November	9,005,873.85	8,606,881.36
	December	9,353,814.87	9,353,814.87	December	9,927,582.99	9,353,814.87
	Total	**9,353,814.87**	**9,353,814.87**	**Total**	**9,927,582.99**	**9,353,814.87**

FIGURE 9-13 The *Sales YTD 2008 2009* and *Sales YTD 2008 2009 Actual Code* measures produce the same result.

The *DATESYTD* function is applied when the filter context is filtering the year 2009, not 2008. Despite the calculation item being filtered along with the filter for the year 2008, its actual application took place in a different filter context, namely the inner filter context. The behavior is counterintuitive to say the least. The more complex the expression used inside *CALCULATE*, the harder it becomes to understand how the application works.

The behavior of calculation items leads to one very important best practice: You need to use calculation items to modify an expression if and only if this expression is a single measure. The previous example was only useful to introduce the rule; let us now analyze the best practice with a more complex expression. The next expression computes the number of working days only for the months where there are sales:

```
SUMX (
    VALUES ( 'Date'[Calendar Year month] ),
    IF (
        [Sales Amount] > 0, -- Measure reference
        [# Working Days]    -- Measure reference
    )
)
```

This calculation is useful to compute *Sales Amount* per working day considering only the months with sales. The following example uses this calculation in a more complex expression:

```
DIVIDE (
    [Sales Amount],  -- Measure reference
    SUMX (
        VALUES ( 'Date'[Calendar Year month] ),
        IF (
```

```
        [Sales Amount] > 0, -- Measure reference
        [# Working Days]    -- Measure reference
      )
    )
  )
```

If this expression is executed within an outer *CALCULATE* that changes the calculation to a **YTD**, the result is the following new formula that produces an unexpected result:

```
Sales WD YTD 2008 :=
CALCULATE (
    DIVIDE (
        [Sales Amount],  -- Measure reference
        SUMX (
            VALUES ( 'Date'[Calendar Year month] ),
            IF (
                [Sales Amount] > 0, -- Measure reference
                [# Working Days]    -- Measure reference
            )
        )
    ),
    'Time Intelligence'[Time calc] = "YTD",
    'Date'[Calendar Year] = "CY 2008"
)
```

Intuitively, one would expect the previous expression to compute the *Sales Amount* measure per working days considering all the months before the current one. In other words, one would expect this code to be executed:

```
Sales WD YTD 2008 Expected Code :=
CALCULATE (
    CALCULATE (
        DIVIDE (
            [Sales Amount],  -- Measure reference
            SUMX (
                VALUES ( 'Date'[Calendar Year month] ),
                IF (
                    [Sales Amount] > 0, -- Measure reference
                    [# Working Days]    -- Measure reference
                )
            )
        ) ,
        DATESYTD ( 'Date'[Date] )
    ),
    'Date'[Calendar Year] = "CY 2008"
)
```

Nevertheless, you might have noticed that we have highlighted the three measure references with a few comments. This was not by chance. The application of a calculation item happens on the measure references, not on the entire expression. Therefore, the code executed by replacing the measure references with the calculation items active in the filter context is very different:

```
Sales WD YTD 2008 Actual Code :=
CALCULATE (
    DIVIDE (
        CALCULATE (
            [Sales Amount],
            DATESYTD ( 'Date'[Date] )
        ),
        SUMX (
            VALUES ( 'Date'[Calendar Year month] ),
            IF (
                CALCULATE (
                    [Sales Amount],
                    DATESYTD ( 'Date'[Date] )
                ) > 0,
                CALCULATE (
                    [# Working Days],
                    DATESYTD ( 'Date'[Date] )
                )
            )
        )
    ),
    'Date'[Calendar Year] = "CY 2008"
)
```

This latter version of the code produces an abnormal value for the number of working days because it sums the year-to-date of the number of working days for all the months visible in the current context. The chances of producing an inaccurate result are extremely high. When an individual month is selected, the result (by pure luck) is the right one, whereas at the quarter and at the year levels it is hilariously wrong. This is shown in Figure 9-14.

	Q1-2008	Q2-2008	Q3-2008	Q4-2008
Sales Amount	1,816,385.21	2,738,040.73	2,575,545.59	2,797,611.46
# Working Days	91	91	92	92
Sales WD YTD 2008	9,980.14	10,009.73	9,753.72	9,868.37
Sales WD YTD 2008 Expected Code	19,960.28	25,024.32	26,021.79	27,124.54
Sales WD YTD 2008 Actual Code	9,980.14	10,009.73	9,753.72	9,868.37
Sales WD YTD 2008 Fixed	19,960.28	25,024.32	26,021.79	27,124.54

FIGURE 9-14 Different versions of the *Sales WD* calculation computed for the all the quarters of 2008.

The *Sales WD YTD 2008 Expected Code* measure returns the correct number for every quarter, whereas the *Sales WD YTD 2008* and *Sales WD YTD 2008 Actual Code* measures return a smaller value. Indeed, the number of working days in the denominator of the ratio is computed as the sum of the year-to-date number of working days for each month in the period.

You can easily avoid this complexity by obeying the best practice: Use *CALCULATE* with calculation items only to invoke an individual measure. When one authors the *Sales WD YTD 2008 Fixed* measure that includes the full expression and uses the *Sales WD YTD 2008 Fixed* measure in a single *CALCULATE* function, the code is very different and easier to use:

```
--
-- Measure Sales WD
--
Sales WD :=
DIVIDE (
    [Sales Amount],
    SUMX (
        VALUES ( 'Date'[Calendar Year month] ),
        IF (
            [Sales Amount] > 0,
            [# Working Days]
        )
    )
)


--
-- Measure Sales WD YTD 2008 Fixed
-- New version of the Sales WD YTD 2008 measure that applies the YTD calculation item
--
Sales WD YTD 2008 Fixed :=
CALCULATE (
    [Sales WD],                              -- Measure reference
    'Time Intelligence'[Time calc] = "YTD",
    'Date'[Calendar Year] = "CY 2008"
)
```

In this case, the code generated by the application of the calculation item is much more intuitive:

```
Sales WD YTD 2008 Fixed Actual Code :=
CALCULATE (
    CALCULATE (
        [Sales WD],
        DATESYTD ( 'Date'[Date] )
    ),
    'Date'[Calendar Year] = "CY 2008"
)
```

In this latter example the filter provided by *DATESYTD* surrounds the entire expression, leading to the code that one intuitively expects from the application of the calculation item. The result of the *Sales WD YTD 2008 Fixed* and *Sales WD YTD 2008 Fixed Actual Code* measures is visible in Figure 9-14.

For very simple calculations containing simple expressions, it is possible to deviate from this best practice. However, when doing so, the developer must always think twice before creating any measure, because as soon as the complexity of the expression is no longer trivial, the chances of producing wrong calculations become very high.

When using client tools like Power BI, you never have to worry about these details. Indeed, these tools make sure that calculation items get applied the right way because they always invoke single measures as part of the query they execute. Nevertheless, as a DAX developer, you will end up using calculation items as filters in *CALCULATE*. When you do that, pay attention to the expression used in *CALCULATE*. If you want to stay on the safe side, use calculation items in *CALCULATE* to modify a single measure. Never apply calculation items to an expression.

Finally, we suggest you learn calculation items by rewriting the expression manually, applying the calculation item, and writing down the complete code that will be executed. It is a mental exercise that proves very useful in understanding exactly what is happening inside the engine.

Understanding calculation group precedence

In the previous section we described how to use *CALCULATE* to apply a calculation item to a measure. It is possible to apply multiple calculation items to the same measure. Even though each calculation group can only have one active calculation item, the presence of multiple calculation groups can activate multiple calculation items at the same time. This happens when a user uses multiple slicers over different calculation groups, or when a *CALCULATE* function filters calculation items in different calculation groups. For example, at the beginning of this chapter we defined two calculation groups: one to define the base measure and the other to define the time intelligence calculation to apply to the base measure.

If there are multiple calculation items active in the current filter context, it is important to define which calculation item is applied first, by defining a set of precedence rules. DAX enforces this by making it mandatory to set the *Precedence* property in a calculation group, in models that have more than one calculation group. This section describes how to correctly set the *Precedence* property of a calculation group through examples where the definition of the precedence changes the result of the calculations.

To prepare the demonstration, we created two different calculation groups, each one containing only one calculation item:

```
--------------------------------------------------------
-- Calculation Group: 'Time Intelligence'[Time calc]
--------------------------------------------------------


--
-- Calculation Item: YTD
--
    CALCULATE (
        SELECTEDMEASURE (),
        DATESYTD ( 'Date'[Date] )
    )
```

```
--------------------------------------------------------
-- Calculation Group: 'Averages'[Averages]
--------------------------------------------------------


--
-- Calculation Item: Daily AVG
--
    DIVIDE (
        SELECTEDMEASURE (),
        COUNTROWS ( 'Date' )
    )
```

YTD is a regular year-to-date calculation, whereas **Daily AVG** computes the daily average by dividing the selected measure by the number of days in the filter context. Both calculation items work just fine, as shown in Figure 9-15, where we use two measures to invoke the two calculation items individually:

```
YTD :=
CALCULATE (
    [Sales Amount],
    'Time Aggregation'[Aggregation] = "YTD"
)

Daily AVG :=
CALCULATE (
    [Sales Amount],
    'Averages'[Averages] = "Daily AVG"
)
```

Calendar Year	Month	Sales Amount	Daily AVG	YTD
☐ CY 2005	▲			
☐ CY 2006	January	580,901.05	18,738.74	580,901.05
☐ CY 2007	February	622,581.14	22,235.04	1,203,482.19
☐ CY 2008	March	496,137.87	16,004.45	1,699,620.05
■ CY 2009	April	678,893.22	22,629.77	2,378,513.27
☐ CY 2010	May	1,067,165.23	34,424.68	3,445,678.50
☐ CY 2011	June	872,586.20	29,086.21	4,318,264.70
	July	1,068,396.58	34,464.41	5,386,661.27
	August	835,707.46	26,958.31	6,222,368.73
	September	709,610.40	23,653.68	6,931,979.13
	October	806,738.22	26,023.81	7,738,717.35
	November	868,164.01	28,938.80	8,606,881.36
	December	746,933.50	24,094.63	9,353,814.87
	Total	**9,353,814.87**	**25,626.89**	**9,353,814.87**

FIGURE 9-15 Both *Daily AVG* and *YTD* calculation items work just fine when invoked individually in separate measures.

The scenario suddenly becomes more complex when both calculation items are used at the same time. Look at the following *Daily YTD AVG* measure definition:

```
Daily YTD AVG :=
CALCULATE (
    [Sales Amount],
    'Time Intelligence'[Time calc] = "YTD",
    'Averages'[Averages] = "Daily AVG"
)
```

The measure invokes both calculation items at the same time, but this raises the issue of precedence. Should the engine apply **YTD** first and **Daily AVG** later, or the other way around? In other words, which of these two expressions should be evaluated?

```
--
--  YTD is applied first, and then DIVIDE
--
DIVIDE (
    CALCULATE (
        [Sales Amount],
        DATESYTD ( 'Date'[Date] )
    ),
    COUNTROWS ( 'Date' )
)


--
--  DIVIDE is applied first, and then YTD
--
CALCULATE (
    DIVIDE (
        [Sales Amount],
        COUNTROWS ( 'Date' )
    ),
    DATESYTD ( 'Date'[Date] )
)
```

It is likely that the second expression is the correct one. Nevertheless, without further information, DAX cannot choose between the two. Therefore, the developer must define the correct order of application of the calculation groups.

The order of application depends on the *Precedence* property in the two calculation groups: The calculation group with the highest value is applied first; then the other calculation groups are applied according to their *Precedence* value in a descending order. Figure 9-16 shows the wrong result produced with the following settings:

- *Time Intelligence* calculation group—*Precedence*: 0

- *Averages* calculation group—*Precedence*: 10

Calendar Year	Month	Sales Amount	Daily AVG	YTD	Daily YTD AVG
☐ CY 2005	▲				
☐ CY 2006	January	580,901.05	18,738.74	580,901.05	18,738.74
☐ CY 2007	February	622,581.14	22,235.04	1,203,482.19	42,981.51
☐ CY 2008	March	496,137.87	16,004.45	1,699,620.05	54,826.45
■ CY 2009	April	678,893.22	22,629.77	2,378,513.27	79,283.78
☐ CY 2010	May	1,067,165.23	34,424.68	3,445,678.50	111,150.92
☐ CY 2011	June	872,586.20	29,086.21	4,318,264.70	143,942.16
	July	1,068,396.58	34,464.41	5,386,661.27	173,763.27
	August	835,707.46	26,958.31	6,222,368.73	200,721.57
	September	709,610.40	23,653.68	6,931,979.13	231,065.97
	October	806,738.22	26,023.81	7,738,717.35	249,636.04
	November	868,164.01	28,938.80	8,606,881.36	286,896.05
	December	746,933.50	24,094.63	9,353,814.87	301,735.96
	Total	**9,353,814.87**	**25,626.89**	**9,353,814.87**	**25,626.89**

FIGURE 9-16 The *Daily YTD AVG* measure does not produce an accurate result.

The value of the *Daily YTD AVG* is clearly wrong in all the months displayed but January. Let us analyze what happened in more depth. *Averages* has a precedence of 10; therefore, it is applied first. The application of the **Daily AVG** calculation item leads to this expression corresponding to the *Daily YTD AVG* measure reference:

```
CALCULATE (
    DIVIDE (
        [Sales Amount],
        COUNTROWS ( 'Date' )
    ),
    'Time Intelligence'[Time calc] = "YTD"
)
```

At this point, DAX activates the **YTD** calculation item from the *Time Intelligence* calculation group. The application of **YTD** rewrites the only measure reference in the formula, which is *Sales Amount*. Therefore, the final code corresponding to the *Daily YTD AVG* measure becomes the following:

```
DIVIDE (
    CALCULATE (
        [Sales Amount],
        DATESYTD ( 'Date'[Date] )
    ),
    COUNTROWS ( 'Date' )
)
```

Consequently, the number shown is obtained by dividing the *Sales Amount* measure computed using the **YTD** calculation item, by the number of days in the displayed month. For example, the value shown in December is obtained by dividing 9,353,814,87 (**YTD** of *Sales Amount*) by 31 (the number of days in December). The number should be much lower because the **YTD** variation should be applied to both the numerator and the denominator of the *DIVIDE* function used in the **Daily AVG** calculation item.

To solve the issue, the **YTD** calculation item must be applied before **Daily AVG**. This way, the transformation of the filter context for the *Date* column occurs before the evaluation of *COUNTROWS* over the *Date* table. In order to obtain this, we modify the *Precedence* property of the *Time Intelligence* calculation group to 20, obtaining the following settings:

- *Time Intelligence* calculation group—*Precedence*: 20

- *Averages* calculation group—*Precedence*: 10

Using these settings, the *Daily YTD AVG* measure returns the correct values, as shown in Figure 9-17.

Calendar Year	Month	Sales Amount	Daily AVG	YTD	Daily YTD AVG
☐ CY 2005	January	580,901.05	18,738.74	580,901.05	18,738.74
☐ CY 2006	February	622,581.14	22,235.04	1,203,482.19	20,398.00
☐ CY 2007	March	496,137.87	16,004.45	1,699,620.05	18,884.67
☐ CY 2008	April	678,893.22	22,629.77	2,378,513.27	19,820.94
■ CY 2009	May	1,067,165.23	34,424.68	3,445,678.50	22,819.06
☐ CY 2010	June	872,586.20	29,086.21	4,318,264.70	23,857.82
☐ CY 2011	July	1,068,396.58	34,464.41	5,386,661.27	25,408.78
	August	835,707.46	26,958.31	6,222,368.73	25,606.46
	September	709,610.40	23,653.68	6,931,979.13	25,391.87
	October	806,738.22	26,023.81	7,738,717.35	25,456.31
	November	868,164.01	28,938.80	8,606,881.36	25,769.11
	December	746,933.50	24,094.63	9,353,814.87	25,626.89
	Total	**9,353,814.87**	**25,626.89**	**9,353,814.87**	**25,626.89**

FIGURE 9-17 The *Daily YTD AVG* measure produces the right result.

This time, the two application steps are the following: DAX first applies the **YTD** calculation from the *Time Intelligence* calculation group, changing the expression to the following:

```
CALCULATE (
    CALCULATE (
        [Sales Amount],
        DATESYTD ( 'Date'[Date] )
    ),
    'Averages'[Averages] = "Daily AVG"
)
```

Then, DAX applies the **Daily AVG** calculation item from the *Averages* calculation group, replacing the measure reference with the *DIVIDE* function and obtaining the following expression:

```
CALCULATE (
    DIVIDE (
        [Sales Amount],
        COUNTROWS ( 'Date' )
    ),
    DATESYTD ( 'Date'[Date] )
)
```

The value displayed in December now considers 365 days in the denominator of *DIVIDE*, thus obtaining the correct number. Before moving further, please consider that, in this example, we followed the best practice of using calculation items with a single measure. Indeed, the first call comes from the visual of Power BI. However, one of the two calculation items rewrote the *Sales Amount* measure in such a way that the problem arose. In this scenario, following the best practices is not enough. It is mandatory that a developer understand and define the precedence of application of calculation groups very well.

All calculation items in a calculation group share the same precedence. It is impossible to define different precedence values for different calculation items within the same group.

The *Precedence* property is an integer value assigned to a calculation group. A higher value means a higher precedence of application; the calculation group with the higher precedence is applied first. In other words, DAX applies the calculation groups according to their *Precedence* value sorted in a descending order. The absolute value assigned to *Precedence* does not mean anything. What matters is how it compares with the *Precedence* of other calculation groups. There cannot be two calculation groups in a model with the same *Precedence*.

Because assigning different *Precedence* values to multiple calculation groups is mandatory, you must pay attention making this choice when you design a model. Choosing the right *Precedence* upfront is important because changing the *Precedence* of a calculation group might affect the existing reports of a model already deployed in production. When you have multiple calculation groups in a model, you should always spend time verifying that the results of the calculations are the results expected with any combination of calculation items. The chances of making mistakes in the definition of the precedence values is quite high without proper testing and validation.

Including and excluding measures from calculation items

There are scenarios where a calculation item implements a variation that does not make sense on all the measures. By default, a calculation item applies its effects on all the measures. Nevertheless, the developer might want to restrict which measures are affected by a calculation item.

One can write conditions in DAX that analyze the current measure evaluated in the model by using either *ISSELECTEDMEASURE* or *SELECTEDMEASURENAME*. For example, consider the requirement of restricting the measures affected by the **Daily AVG** calculation item so that a measure computing a percentage is not transformed into a daily average. The *ISSELECTEDMEASURE* function returns *True* if the measure evaluated by *SELECTEDMEASURE* is included in the list of measures specified in the arguments:

```
----------------------------------------------------------
-- Calculation Group: 'Averages'[Averages]
----------------------------------------------------------


--
-- Calculation Item: Daily AVG
--
```

```
IF (
    ISSELECTEDMEASURE (
        [Sales Amount],
        [Gross Amount],
        [Discount Amount],
        [Sales Quantity],
        [Total Cost],
        [Margin]
    ),
    DIVIDE (
        SELECTEDMEASURE (),
        COUNTROWS ( 'Date' )
    )
)
```

As you can see, the code specifies the measure on which to compute the daily average, returning blank when the **Daily AVG** calculation item is applied to any other measure. Now if the requirement is just to exclude specific measures, including any other measure by default, the code can be written this way:

```
---------------------------------------------------------
-- Calculation Group: 'Averages'[Averages]
---------------------------------------------------------


--
-- Calculation Item: Daily AVG
--
IF (
    NOT ISSELECTEDMEASURE ( [Margin %] ),
    DIVIDE (
        SELECTEDMEASURE (),
        COUNTROWS ( 'Date' )
    )
)
```

In both cases the **Daily AVG** calculation item excludes the calculation for the *Margin %* measure, as shown in Figure 9-18.

Calendar Year	Month	Sales Quantity	Sales Amount	Margin	Margin %
☐ CY 2005					
☐ CY 2006	January	50	9,363.67	4,721.91	
☐ CY 2007	February	54	10,729.93	5,575.99	
☐ CY 2008	March	48	9,294.77	4,815.71	
☐ CY 2009	April	56	13,365.07	6,995.57	
☐ CY 2010	May	58	13,348.34	7,459.37	
☐ CY 2011	June	55	12,857.30	7,105.71	
	July	61	13,278.74	7,434.74	
Averages	August	54	11,567.29	6,396.36	
■ Daily AVG	September	54	12,775.79	7,038.99	
	October	50	11,247.95	6,213.54	
	November	57	13,570.83	6,597.02	
	December	60	12,258.95	5,904.63	
	Total	**55**	**11,968.44**	**6,354.71**	

FIGURE 9-18 The **Daily AVG** calculation item is not applied to *Margin %*.

Another function that can be used to analyze the selected measure in a calculation item expression is *SELECTEDMEASURENAME*, which returns a string instead of a *Boolean* value. This function may be used instead of *ISSELECTEDMEASURE*, as in the following example:

```
--------------------------------------------------------
-- Calculation Group: 'Averages'[Averages]
--------------------------------------------------------


--
-- Calculation Item: Daily AVG
--
IF (
    NOT ( SELECTEDMEASURENAME () = "Margin %" ),
    DIVIDE (
        SELECTEDMEASURE (),
        COUNTROWS ( 'Date' )
    )
)
```

The result would be the same, but the *ISSELECTEDMEASURE* solution is preferable for several reasons:

- If the measure name is misspelled using a comparison with *SELECTEDMEASURENAME*, the DAX code simply return *False* without raising an error.

- If the measure name is misspelled using *ISSELECTEDMEASURE*, the expression fails with the error *Invalid input arguments for ISSELECTEDMEASURE*.

- If a measure is renamed in the model, all the expressions using *ISSELECTEDMEASURE* are automatically renamed in the model editor (formula fixup), whereas the strings compared to *SELECTEDMEASURENAME* must be updated manually.

The *SELECTEDMEASURENAME* function should be considered when the business logic of a calculation item must apply a transformation based on an external configuration. For example, the function might be useful when there is a table with a list of measures that should enable a behavior in a calculation item so that the model has an external configuration that can be modified without requiring an update of the DAX code.

Understanding sideways recursion

DAX calculation items do not provide full recursion. However, there is a limited form of recursion available, which is called sideways recursion. We describe this complex topic through examples. Let us start by understanding what recursion is and why it is important to discuss it. Recursion might occur when a calculation item refers to itself, leading to an infinite loop in the application of calculation items. Let us elaborate on this.

Consider a *Time Intelligence* calculation group with two calculation items defined as follows:

```
--------------------------------------------------------
-- Calculation Group: 'Time Intelligence'[Time calc]
--------------------------------------------------------


--
-- Calculation Item: YTD
--

    CALCULATE (
        SELECTEDMEASURE (),
        DATESYTD ( 'Date'[Date] )
    )


--
-- Calculation Item: SPLY
--

    CALCULATE (
        SELECTEDMEASURE (),
        SAMEPERIODLASTYEAR ( 'Date'[Date] )
    )
```

The requirement is to add a third calculation item that computes the year-to-date in the previous year (**PYTD**). As you learned in Chapter 8, "Time intelligence calculations," this can be obtained by mixing two time intelligence functions: *DATESYTD* and *SAMEPERIODLASTYEAR*. The following calculation item solves the scenario:

```
--
-- Calculation Item: PYTD
--

    CALCULATE (
        SELECTEDMEASURE (),
        DATESYTD ( SAMEPERIODLASTYEAR ( 'Date'[Date] ) )
    )
```

Given the simplicity of the calculation, this solution is already optimal. Nevertheless, as a mind challenge we can try to author the same code in a different way. Indeed, there already is a **YTD** calculation item that computes the year-to-date in place; therefore, one could think of using the calculation item instead of mixing time intelligence calculations within the same formula. Look at the following definition of the same **PYTD** calculation item:

```
--
-- Calculation Item: PYTD
--

    CALCULATE (
        SELECTEDMEASURE (),
        SAMEPERIODLASTYEAR ( 'Date'[Date] ),
        'Time Intelligence'[Time calc] = "YTD"
    )
```

The calculation item achieves the same result as the previous definition, but using a different technique. *SAMEPERIODLASTYEAR* moves the filter context back to the previous year, while the year-to-date calculation is obtained by applying an existing calculation item in the *Time calc* calculation group: **YTD**. As previously noted, in this example the code is less readable and needlessly more complex. That said, you can easily imagine that in a more complex scenario the ability to invoke previously defined calculation items might come very handy—to avoid repeating the same code multiple times in your measures.

This is a powerful mechanism to define complex calculations. It comes with some level of complexity that needs to be well understood: *recursion*. As you have seen in the **PYTD** calculation item, it is possible to define a calculation item based on another calculation item from the same calculation group. In other words, inside a calculation group certain items can be defined in terms of other items of the same calculation group. If the feature were available without any restriction, this would lead to extremely complex situations where calculation item A depends on B, which depends on C, which in turn can depend on A. The following fictitious example demonstrates the issue:

```
--------------------------------------------------------
-- Calculation Group: Infinite[Loop]
--------------------------------------------------------


--
-- Calculation Item: Loop A
--
    CALCULATE (
        SELECTEDMEASURE (),
        Infinite[Loop] = "Loop B"
    )


--
-- Calculation Item: Loop B
--
    CALCULATE (
        SELECTEDMEASURE (),
        Infinite[Loop] = "Loop A"
    )
```

If used in an expression like in the following example, DAX would not be able to apply the calculation items, because A requires the application of B, which in turn requires A, and so on:

```
CALCULATE (
    [Sales Amount],
    Infinite[Loop] = "Loop A"
)
```

Some programming languages allow similar circular dependencies to be used in the definition of expressions—typically in functions—leading to *recursive definitions*. A recursive function definition is a definition where the function is defined in terms of itself. Recursion is extremely powerful, but it is also extremely complex for developers writing code and for the optimizer looking for the best execution path.

For these reasons, DAX does not allow the definition of recursive calculation items. In DAX, a developer can reference another calculation item of the same calculation group, but without referencing the same calculation item twice. In other words, it is possible to use *CALCULATE* to invoke a calculation item, but the calculation item invoked cannot directly or indirectly invoke the original calculation item. This feature is called sideways recursion. Its goal is not to implement full recursion; Instead, it aims at reusing complex calculation items without providing the full power (and complexity) of recursion.

> **Note**   If you are familiar with the MDX language, you should be aware that MDX supports both sideways recursion and full recursion. These capabilities are part of the reasons MDX is more complex a language than DAX. Moreover, full recursion oftentimes leads to bad performance. For these reasons, DAX does not support full recursion by design.

Be mindful that recursion might also occur because a measure sets a filter on a calculation item, not only between calculation items. For example, consider the following definitions of measures (*Sales Amount*, *MA*, *MB*) and calculation items (**A** and **B**):

```
--
-- Measures definition
--
Sales Amount := SUMX ( Sales, Sales[Quantity] * Sales[Net Price] )
MA := CALCULATE ( [Sales Amount], Infinite[Loop] = "A" )
MB := CALCULATE ( [Sales Amount], Infinite[Loop] = "B" )


-------------------------------------------------------
-- Calculation Group: Infinite[Loop]
-------------------------------------------------------


--
-- Calculation Item: A
--
    [MB]


--
-- Calculation Item: B
--
    [MA]
```

The calculation items do not reference each other. Instead, they reference a measure that, in turn, references the calculation items, generating an infinite loop. We can see this happening by following the calculation item application step by step. Consider the following expression:

```
CALCULATE (
    [Sales Amount],
    Infinite[Loop] = "A"
)
```

The application of calculation item **A** produces the following result:

```
CALCULATE (
    CALCULATE ( [MB] )
)
```

However, the *MB* measure internally references both *Sales Amount* and calculation item **B**; it corresponds to the following code:

```
CALCULATE (
    CALCULATE (
        CALCULATE (
            [Sales Amount],
            Infinite[Loop] = "B"
        )
    )
)
```

At this point, the application of calculation item **B** produces the following result:

```
CALCULATE (
    CALCULATE (
        CALCULATE (
            CALCULATE ( [MA] )
        )
    )
)
```

Again, the *MA* measure internally references *Sales Amount* and calculation item **A**, and corresponds to the following code:

```
CALCULATE (
    CALCULATE (
        CALCULATE (
            CALCULATE (
                CALCULATE (
                    [Sales Amount],
                    Infinite[Loop] = "A"
                )
            )
        )
    )
)
```

Now we are back to the initial expression and we potentially enter into an infinite loop of calculation items applied to the expression—although the calculation items do not reference each other. Instead, they reference a measure that, in turn, references the calculation items. The engine is smart enough to detect that, in this case, an infinite loop is present. Therefore, DAX throws an error.

Sideways recursion can lead to very complex expressions that are hard to read and likely to produce unexpected results. Most of the complexity of calculation items with sideways recursion is seen when there are measures that internally apply calculation items with *CALCULATE*—all the while users change the calculation item through the user interface of the tool, like using a slicer in Power BI.

Our suggestion is to limit the use of sideways recursion in your code as much as you can, though this might mean repeating the same code in multiple places. Only in hidden calculation groups can you safely rely on sideways recursion, so that they can be managed by code but not by users. Keep in mind that Power BI users can define their own measures in a report, and, unaware of a complex topic like recursion, they might generate errors without properly understanding the reason.

Using the best practices

As we said in the introduction, there are only two best practices to follow to avoid encountering issues with calculation items:

- Use calculation items to modify the behavior of expressions consisting of one measure only. Never use calculation items to change the behavior of more complex expressions.

```
--
--   This is a BEST PRACTICE
--
SalesPerWd :=
CALCULATE (
    [Sales Amount],                        -- Single measure. This is good
    'Time Intelligence'[Time calc] = "YTD"
)


--
--   This is BAD PRACTICE - do not do this!
--
SalesPerWd :=
CALCULATE (
    SUMX ( Customer, [Sales Amount] ),     -- Complex expression, it is not a single
    'Time Intelligence'[Time calc] = "YTD" -- measure reference
)
```

- Avoid using sideways recursion in any calculation group that remains public and available to users. You can safely use sideways recursion in hidden calculation groups. Still, if you use sideways recursion, pay attention not to introduce full recursion, which would produce an error as a result.

Conclusions

Calculation groups are an extremely powerful tool to simplify the building of complex models. By letting the developer define variations of measures, calculation groups provide a very compact way of generating hundreds of measures without duplicating code. Moreover, users love calculation groups because they have the option of creating their own combination of calculations.

As a DAX developer, you should understand their power and their limitations. These are the lessons included in this chapter:

- Calculation groups are sets of calculation items.

- Calculation items are variations of a measure. By using the *SELECTEDMEASURE* function, calculation items have the option of changing the way a calculation goes.

- A calculation item can override the expression and the format string of the current measure.

- If multiple calculation groups are being used in a model, the developer must define the order of application of the calculation items to disambiguate their behavior.

- Calculation items are applied to measure references, not to expressions. Using a calculation item to change the behavior of an expression not consisting of a single measure reference is likely to produce unexpected results. Therefore, it is a best practice to only apply calculation items to expressions made up of a single measure reference.

- A developer can use sideways recursion in the definition of a calculation item, but this suddenly increases the complexity of the whole expression. The developer should limit the use of sideways recursion to hidden calculation groups and avoid sideways recursion in calculation groups that are visible to users.

- Following the best practices is the easiest way to avoid the complexity involved in calculation groups.

Finally, keep in mind that calculation groups are a very recent addition to the DAX language. This is a very powerful feature, and we just started discovering the many uses of calculation groups. We will update the web page mentioned in the introduction of this chapter with references to new articles and blog posts where you can continue to learn about calculation groups.

Working with the filter context

In the previous chapters you learned how to create filter contexts to perform advanced calculations. For example, in the time intelligence chapter, you learned how to mix time intelligence calculations to provide a comparison of different periods. In Chapter 9, "Calculation groups," you learned how to simplify the user experience and the DAX code using calculation groups. In this chapter, you learn many functions that read the state of the current filter context, in order to change the behavior of your formulas according to existing selections and filters. These functions, though powerful, are not frequently used. Nevertheless, a correct understanding of these functions is needed to create measures that work well in different reports rather than just in the report where they were used the first time.

A formula might work or not depending on how the filter context is set. For example, you might write a formula that works correctly at the month level but returns an inaccurate result at the year level. Another example would be the ranking of a customer against all other customers. That formula works if a single customer is selected in the filter context, but it would return an incorrect result if multiple customers were visible. Therefore, a measure designed to work in any report should inspect the filter context prior to returning a value. If the filter context satisfies the requirements of the formula, then it can return a meaningful value. Otherwise, if the filter context contains filters that are not compatible with the code, then returning a blank is a better choice.

Be mindful that no formula should ever return an incorrect value. It is always better to return no value than to compute an incorrect value. Users are expected to be able to browse your model without any previous knowledge of the internals of the code. As a DAX author, you are responsible for making sure your code works in any situation.

For each function introduced in this chapter, we show several scenarios where it might be useful and logical to use the function itself. But your scenario is surely different from any of our examples. Thus, when reading about these functions, try to figure out how they could improve the features of your model.

Besides, in this chapter we also introduce two important concepts: data lineage and the *TREATAS* function. Data lineage is an intuitive concept you have been using so far without a complete explanation. In this chapter we go deeper, describing its behavior and several scenarios where it is useful to consider it.

Using *HASONEVALUE* and *SELECTEDVALUE*

As outlined in the introduction, many calculations provide meaningful values based on the current selection. Nevertheless, the same calculation on a different selection provides incorrect figures. As an example, look at the following formula computing a simple quarter-to-date (QTD) of the sales amount:

```
QTD Sales :=
CALCULATE (
    [Sales Amount],
    DATESQTD ( 'Date'[Date] )
)
```

As you can see in Figure 10-1, the code works well for months and quarters, but at the year level (CY 2007) it produces a result stating that the QTD value of *Sales Amount* for 2017 is 2,731,424.16.

Calendar Year	Sales Amount	QTD Sales
CY 2007	**11,309,946.12**	**2,731,424.16**
Q1-2007	**2,646,673.39**	**2,646,673.39**
January	794,248.24	794,248.24
February	891,135.91	1,685,384.15
March	961,289.24	2,646,673.39
Q2-2007	**3,046,602.02**	**3,046,602.02**
April	1,128,104.82	1,128,104.82
May	936,192.74	2,064,297.56
June	982,304.46	3,046,602.02
Q3-2007	**2,885,246.55**	**2,885,246.55**
July	922,542.98	922,542.98
August	952,834.59	1,875,377.57
September	1,009,868.98	2,885,246.55
Q4-2007	**2,731,424.16**	**2,731,424.16**
October	914,273.54	914,273.54
November	825,601.87	1,739,875.41
December	991,548.75	2,731,424.16

FIGURE 10-1 *QTD Sales* reports values at the year level too, but the numbers might confuse some users.

Actually, the value reported by *QTD Sales* at the year level is the value of the last quarter of the year, which corresponds to the *QTD Sales* value of December. One might argue that—at the year level—the value of QTD does not make sense. To be correct, the value should not appear at the quarter level. Indeed, a QTD aggregation makes sense at the month level and below, but not starting at the quarter level and above. In other words, the formula should report the value of QTD at the month level and blank the value otherwise.

In such a scenario, the function *HASONEVALUE* becomes useful. For example, to remove the total at the quarter level and above, it is enough to detect multiple months selected. This is the case at the year and quarter levels, whereas at the month level there is only one month selected. Thus, protecting the code with an *IF* statement provides the desired behavior. The following code does the job:

```
QTD Sales :=
IF (
    HASONEVALUE ( 'Date'[Month] ),
    CALCULATE (
        [Sales Amount],
        DATESQTD ( 'Date'[Date] )
    )
)
```

The result of this new formula is visible in Figure 10-2.

Calendar Year	Sales Amount	QTD Sales
CY 2007	**11,309,946.12**	
Q1-2007	**2,646,673.39**	
January	794,248.24	794,248.24
February	891,135.91	1,685,384.15
March	961,289.24	2,646,673.39
Q2-2007	**3,046,602.02**	
April	1,128,104.82	1,128,104.82
May	936,192.74	2,064,297.56
June	982,304.46	3,046,602.02
Q3-2007	**2,885,246.55**	
July	922,542.98	922,542.98
August	952,834.59	1,875,377.57
September	1,009,868.98	2,885,246.55

FIGURE 10-2 Protecting *QTD Sales* with *HASONEVALUE* lets you blank undesired values.

This first example is already an important one. Instead of just leaving the calculation "as is," we decided to go one step further and question exactly "when" the calculation produces a value that makes sense. If it turns out that a certain formula does not produce accurate results in a filter context, it is better to verify whether the filter context satisfies the minimum requirements and operate accordingly.

In Chapter 7, "Working with iterators and with *CALCULATE*," you saw a similar scenario when you learned about the *RANKX* function. There, we had to produce a ranking of the current customer against all other customers, and we used *HASONEVALUE* to guarantee that such ranking is only produced when a single customer is selected in the current filter context.

Time intelligence is a scenario where *HASONEVALUE* is frequently used because many aggregations—like YTD, for example—only make sense when the filter context is filtering one quarter, one month, or one specific time period. In all other cases, the formula should avoid returning a value and should return *BLANK* instead.

Another common scenario where *HASONEVALUE* is useful is to extract one selected value from the filter context. There used to be many scenarios where this could be useful, but with the advent of calculation groups, their number is much lower. We will describe a scenario performing some sort of what-if analysis. In such a case, the developer typically builds a parameter table that lets the user select one value through a slicer; then, the code uses this parameter to adjust the calculation.

For example, consider evaluating the sales amount by adjusting the values of previous years based on the inflation rate. In order to perform the analysis, the report lets the user select a yearly inflation rate that should be used from each transaction date up to today. The inflation rate is a parameter of the algorithm. A solution to this scenario is to build a table with all the values that a user can select. In our example, we created a table with all the values from 0% to 20% with a step of 0.5%, obtaining the table you can partially see in Figure 10-3.

Inflation ▲
0.00%
0.50%
1.00%
1.50%
2.00%
2.50%
3.00%
3.50%
4.00%
4.50%

FIGURE 10-3 *Inflation* contains all the values between 0% and 20% with a step of 0.5%.

The user selects the desired value with a slicer; then the formula needs to apply the selected inflation rate for all the years from the transaction date up to the current date. If the user does not perform a selection or if they select multiple values, then the formula should use a default inflation rate of 0% to report the actual sales amount.

The final report looks like the one in Figure 10-4.

| Inflation | | Reporting year: 2009 | |
| 3.00% | ⌄ | | |

Calendar Year	Sales Amount	Inflation Adjusted Sales
CY 2007	**11,309,946.12**	**11,998,721.84**
Q1-2007	**2,646,673.39**	**2,807,855.80**
January	794,248.24	842,617.96
February	891,135.91	945,406.09
March	961,289.24	1,019,831.75
Q2-2007	**3,046,602.02**	**3,232,140.08**
April	1,128,104.82	1,196,806.40
May	936,192.74	993,206.88
June	982,304.46	1,042,126.80
Q3-2007	**2,885,246.55**	**3,060,958.07**
July	922,542.98	978,725.85
August	952,834.59	1,010,862.21
September	1,009,868.98	1,071,370.00
Q4-2007	**2,731,424.16**	**2,897,767.89**
October	914,273.54	969,952.80
November	825,601.87	875,881.02
December	991,548.75	1,051,934.07
CY 2008	**9,927,582.99**	**10,225,410.48**
Total	**30,591,343.98**	**31,577,947.19**

FIGURE 10-4 The *Inflation* parameter controls the multiplier of previous years.

> **Note** The What-If parameter feature in Power BI generates a table and a slicer using the same technique described here.

There are several interesting notes about this report:

- A user can select the inflation rate to apply through the top-left slicer.

- The report shows the year used to perform the adjustment, reporting the year of the last sale in the data model in the top-right label.

- *Inflation Adjusted Sales* multiplies the sales amount of the given year by a factor that depends on the user-selected inflation.

- At the grand total level, the calculation needs to apply a different multiplier to each year.

The code for the reporting year label is the simplest calculation in the report; it only needs to retrieve the year of the maximum order date from the *Sales* table:

```
Reporting year := "Reporting year: " & YEAR ( MAX ( Sales[Order Date] ) )
```

Similarly, one could retrieve the selected user inflation by using *MIN* or *MAX*, because when the user filters one value with the slicer, both *MIN* and *MAX* return the same value—that is, the only value selected. Nevertheless, a user might make an invalid selection by filtering multiple values or by applying no filter at all. In that case, the formula needs to behave correctly and still provide a default value.

Thus, a better option is to check with *HASONEVALUE* whether the user has actively filtered a single value with the slicer, and have the code behave accordingly to the *HASONEVALUE* result:

```
User Selected Inflation :=
IF (
    HASONEVALUE ( 'Inflation Rate'[Inflation] ),
    VALUES ( 'Inflation Rate'[Inflation] ),
    0
)
```

Because this pattern is very common, DAX also offers an additional choice. The *SELECTEDVALUE* function provides the behavior of the previous code in a single function call:

```
User Selected Inflation := SELECTEDVALUE ( 'Inflation Rate'[Inflation], 0 )
```

SELECTEDVALUE has two arguments. The second argument is the default returned in case there is more than one element selected in the column passed as the first argument.

Once the *User Selected Inflation* measure is in the model, one needs to compute the multiplier for the selected year. If the last year in the model is considered the year to use for the adjustment, then the multiplier needs to iterate over all the years between the last year and the selected year performing the multiplication of *1+Inflation* for each year:

```
Inflation Multiplier :=
VAR ReportingYear =
    YEAR ( CALCULATE ( MAX ( Sales[Order Date] ), ALL ( Sales ) ) )
VAR CurrentYear =
    SELECTEDVALUE ( 'Date'[Calendar Year Number] )
VAR Inflation = [User Selected Inflation]
VAR Years =
    FILTER (
        ALL ( 'Date'[Calendar Year Number] ),
        AND (
            'Date'[Calendar Year Number] >= CurrentYear,
            'Date'[Calendar Year Number] < ReportingYear
        )
    )
VAR Multiplier =
    MAX ( PRODUCTX ( Years, 1 + Inflation ), 1 )
RETURN
    Multiplier
```

The last step is to use the multiplier on a year-by-year basis. Here is the code of *Inflation Adjusted Sales*:

```
Inflation Adjusted Sales :=
SUMX (
    VALUES ( 'Date'[Calendar Year] ),
    [Sales Amount] * [Inflation Multiplier]
)
```

Introducing *ISFILTERED* and *ISCROSSFILTERED*

Sometimes the goal is not to gather a single value from the filter context; instead, the goal is to check whether a column or a table has an active filter on it. The reason one might want to check for the presence of a filter is usually to verify that all the values of a column are currently visible. In the presence of a filter, some values might be hidden and the number—at that point—might be inaccurate.

A column might be filtered because there is a filter applied to it or because some other column is being filtered, and therefore there is an indirect filter on the column. We can elaborate on this with a simple example:

```
RedColors :=
CALCULATE (
    [Sales Amount],
    'Product'[Color] = "Red"
)
```

During the evaluation of *Sales Amount*, the outer *CALCULATE* applies a filter on the *Product[Color]* column. Consequently, *Product[Color]* is filtered. There is a specific function in DAX that checks whether a column is filtered or not: *ISFILTERED*. *ISFILTERED* returns *TRUE* or *FALSE*, depending on whether the column passed as an argument has a direct filter on it or not. When *ISFILTERED* receives a table as an argument, it returns *TRUE* if any columns of the table are being filtered directly; otherwise, it returns *FALSE*.

Although the filter is on *Product[Color]*, all the columns of the *Product* table are indirectly filtered. For example, the *Brand* column only shows the brands that have at least one red product. Any brand with no red products will not be visible because of the filter on the color column. Apart from *Product[Color]*, all the other columns of the *Product* table have no direct filter. Nevertheless, their visible values are limited. Indeed, all the columns of *Product* are cross-filtered. A column is cross-filtered if there is a filter that may reduce its set of visible values, either a direct or an indirect filter. The function to use to check whether a column is cross-filtered or not is *ISCROSSFILTERED*.

It is important to note that if a column is filtered, it is also cross-filtered. The opposite does not hold true: A column can be cross-filtered even though it is not filtered. Moreover, *ISCROSSFILTERED* works either with a column or with a table. Indeed, whenever any column of a table is cross-filtered, all the remaining columns of the table are cross-filtered too. Therefore, *ISCROSSFILTERED* should be used with a table rather than with a column. You might still find *ISCROSSFILTERED* used with a column because—originally—*ISCROSSFILTERED* used to only work with columns. Only later was *ISCROSSFILTERED* introduced for tables. Thus, some old code might still only use *ISCROSSFILTERED* with a column.

Because filters work over the entire data model, a filter on the *Product* table also affects the related tables. Thus, the filter on *Product[Color]* applies its effect to the *Sales* table too. Therefore, any column in the *Sales* table is cross-filtered by the filter on *Product[Color]*.

To demonstrate the behavior of these functions, we used a slightly different model than the usual model used in the rest of the book. We removed some tables, and we upgraded the relationship between *Sales* and *Product* using bidirectional cross-filtering. You can see the resulting model in Figure 10-5.

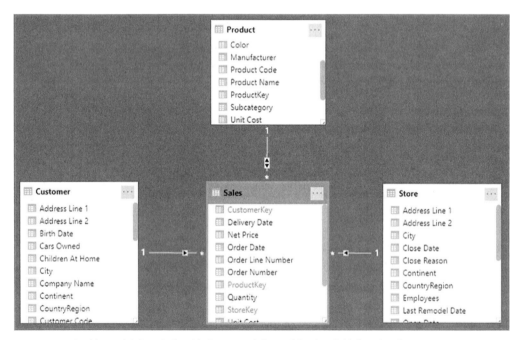

FIGURE 10-5 In this model the relationship between *Sales* and *Product* is bidirectional.

In this model, we authored this set of measures:

```
Filter Gender := ISFILTERED ( Customer[Gender] )
Cross Filter Customer := ISCROSSFILTERED ( Customer )
Cross Filter Sales := ISCROSSFILTERED ( Sales )
Cross Filter Product := ISCROSSFILTERED ( 'Product' )
Cross Filter Store := ISCROSSFILTERED ( Store )
```

Finally, we projected all the measures in a matrix with *Customer[Continent]* and *Customer[Gender]* on the rows. You can see the result in Figure 10-6.

Continent	Filter Gender	Cross Filter Customer	Cross Filter Sales	Cross Filter Store	Cross Filter Product
Asia	**False**	**True**	**True**	**False**	**True**
	True	True	True	False	True
F	True	True	True	False	True
M	True	True	True	False	True
Europe	**False**	**True**	**True**	**False**	**True**
	True	True	True	False	True
F	True	True	True	False	True
M	True	True	True	False	True
North America	**False**	**True**	**True**	**False**	**True**
	True	True	True	False	True
F	True	True	True	False	True
M	True	True	True	False	True
Total	**False**	**False**	**False**	**False**	**False**

FIGURE 10-6 The matrix shows the behavior of *ISFILTERED* and *ISCROSSFILTERED*.

Here are a few considerations about the results:

- *Customer[Gender]* is only filtered on the rows where there is an active filter on *Customer[Gender]*. At the subtotal level—where the filter is only on *Customer[Continent]*—the column is not filtered.

- The entire *Customer* table is cross-filtered when there is a filter on either *Customer[Continent]* or *Customer[Gender]*.

- The same applies to the *Sales* table. The presence of a filter on any column of the *Customer* table applies a cross-filter on the *Sales* table because *Sales* is on the many-side of a many-to-one relationship with *Customer*.

- *Store* is not cross-filtered because the filter on *Sales* does not propagate to *Customer*. Indeed, the relationship between *Sales* and *Store* is unidirectional, so the filter does not propagate from *Sales* to *Store*.

- Because the relationship between *Sales* and *Product* is bidirectional, then the filter on *Sales* propagates to *Product*. Therefore, *Product* is cross-filtered by any filter in other tables of this data model.

ISFILTERED and *ISCROSSFILTERED* are not frequently used in DAX expressions. They are used when performing advanced optimization by checking the set of filters on a column—to make the code follow different paths depending on the filters. Another common scenario is when working with hierarchies, as we will show in Chapter 11, "Handling hierarchies."

Beware that one cannot rely on the presence of a filter to determine whether all the values of a column are visible. In fact, a column can be both filtered and cross-filtered but still show all the values. A simple measure demonstrates this:

```
Test :=
CALCULATE (
    ISFILTERED ( Customer[City] ),
    Customer[City] <> "DAX"
)
```

There is no city named DAX in the *Customer* table. Thus, the filter does not have any effect on the *Customer* table because it shows all the rows. Therefore, *Customer[City]* shows all the possible values of the column, even though a filter is active on the same column and the *Test* measure returns *TRUE*.

To check whether all the possible values are visible in a column or in a table, the best option is to count the rows under different contexts. In this case, there are some important details to learn, which we discuss in the following sections.

Understanding differences between *VALUES* and *FILTERS*

FILTERS is a function like *VALUES*, with one important difference. *VALUES* returns the values visible in the filter context; *FILTERS* returns the values that are currently being filtered by the filter context.

Although the two descriptions look the same, they are not. Indeed, one might filter four product colors with a slicer, say Black, Brown, Azure, and Blue. Imagine that because of other filters in the filter context, only two of them are visible in the data if the other two are not used in any product. In that scenario, *VALUES* returns two colors, whereas *FILTER* returns all the filtered four. An example is useful to clarify this concept.

For this example, we use an Excel file connected to a Power BI model. The reason is that—at the time of writing—*FILTERS* does not work as expected when used by *SUMMARIZECOLUMNS*, which is the function used by Power BI to query the model. Thus, the example would not work in Power BI.

 Note Microsoft is aware of the issue of using *FILTERS* in Power BI, and it is possible that this problem will be solved in the future. However, for illustrating the concept in this book, we had to use Excel as a client because Excel does not leverage *SUMMARIZECOLUMNS*.

In Chapter 7 we demonstrated how to use *CONCATENATEX* to show a label in a report indicating the colors selected through a slicer. There, we ended up with a complex formula useful to demonstrate the usage of iterators and variables. Here, we recall the simpler version of that code for your convenience:

```
Selected Colors :=
"Showing " &
CONCATENATEX (
    VALUES ( 'Product'[Color] ),
    'Product'[Color],
    ", ",
    'Product'[Color],
    ASC
) & " colors."
```

Consider a report with two slicers: one slicer filters only one category, and the other slicer filters several colors, as shown in Figure 10-7.

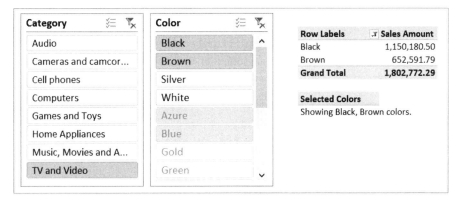

FIGURE 10-7 Although there are four colors selected, the *Selected Colors* measure only shows two of them.

Though there are four colors selected in the slicer, the *Selected Colors* measure only returns two of them. The reason is that *VALUES* returns the values of a column under the current filter context. There are no TV and Video products which are either blue or azure. Thus, even though the filter context is filtering four colors, *VALUES* only returns two of them.

If the measure is changed to use *FILTERS* instead of *VALUES*, then *FILTERS* returns the filtered values, regardless of whether there is any product in the current filter context representing those values:

```
Selected Colors :=
"Showing " &
CONCATENATEX (
    FILTERS ( 'Product'[Color] ),
    'Product'[Color],
    ", ",
    'Product'[Color],
    ASC
) & " colors."
```

With this new version of *Selected Colors*, now the report shows all four colors as the selected ones, as you can see in Figure 10-8.

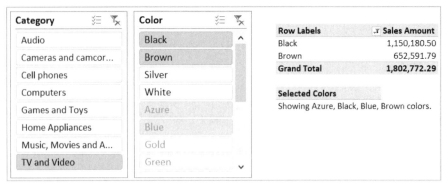

FIGURE 10-8 Using *FILTERS*, the *Selected Colors* measure now returns all four selected colors.

Similar to *HASONEVALUE*, DAX also offers a function to check whether a column only has one active filter: *HASONEFILTER*. Its use and syntax are similar to that of *HASONEVALUE*. The only difference is that *HASONEFILTER* might return *TRUE* when there is a single filter active, and at the same time *HASONEVALUE* returns *FALSE* because the value, although filtered, is not part of the visible values.

Understanding the difference between *ALLEXCEPT* and *ALL/VALUES*

In a previous section we introduced *ISFILTERED* and *ISCROSSFILTERED* to check for the presence of a filter. The presence of a filter is not enough to verify that all the values of a column—or of a table—are visible. A better option is to count the number of rows in the current filter context and check it against the count of all the rows without any filter.

As an example, look at Figure 10-9. The *Filtered Gender* measure checks for *ISFILTERED* on the *Customer[Gender]* column, whereas *NumOfCustomers* simply counts the number of rows in the *Customer* table:

```
NumOfCustomers := COUNTROWS ( Customer )
```

Customer Type	Filtered Gender	NumOfCustomers
Company	**False**	**385**
	True	385
Person	**False**	**18,484**
F	True	9,133
M	True	9,351
Total	**False**	**18,869**

FIGURE 10-9 Even though *Customer[Gender]* is filtered, all the customers are visible.

You can observe that whenever a customer is a company, as expected the gender is always a blank value. In the second row of the matrix, the filter on *Gender* is active; indeed, *Filtered Gender* returns *TRUE*. At the same time, the filter does not really filter anything because there is only one possible *Gender* value, and it is visible.

The presence of a filter does not imply that the table is actually filtered. It only states that a filter is active. To check whether all the customers are visible or not, it is better to rely on a simple count. Checking that the number of customers with and without the filter on *Gender* is the same helps identify that, although active, the filter is not effective.

When performing such calculations, one should pay attention to the details of the filter context and of the behavior of *CALCULATE*. There are two possible ways of checking the same condition:

■ Counting the customers of *ALL* genders.

■ Counting the customers with the same customer type (*Company* or *Person*).

Even though in the report of Figure 10-9 the two calculations return the same value, if one changes the columns used in the matrix, they compute different results. Besides, both calculations have pros and cons; these are worth learning because they might be useful in several scenarios. We start from the first and easiest one:

```
All Gender :=
CALCULATE (
    [NumOfCustomers],
    ALL ( Customer[Gender] )
)
```

ALL removes the filter on the *Gender* column, leaving all the remaining filters in place. As a result, it computes the number of customers in the current filter, regardless of the gender. In Figure 10-10 you can see the result, along with the *All customers visible* measure that compares the two counts.

Customer Type	Filtered Gender	NumOfCustomers	All Gender	All customers visible
Company	**False**	**385**	**385**	**True**
	True	385	385	True
Person	**False**	**18,484**	**18,484**	**True**
F	True	9,133	18,484	False
M	True	9,351	18,484	False
Total	**False**	**18,869**	**18,869**	**True**

FIGURE 10-10 On the second row, *All customers visible* returns *True*, even though *Gender* is filtered.

All Gender is a measure that works well. However, it has the disadvantage of hardcoding in the measure the fact that it only removes the filter from *Gender*. For example, using the same measure on a matrix that slices by *Continent*, the result is not the desired one. You see this in Figure 10-11 where the *All customers visible* measure is always *TRUE*.

Customer Type	Filtered Gender	NumOfCustomers	All Gender	All customers visible
Company	**False**	**385**	**385**	**True**
Asia	False	67	67	True
Europe	False	42	42	True
North America	False	276	276	True
Person	**False**	**18,484**	**18,484**	**True**
Asia	False	3,591	3,591	True
Europe	False	5,504	5,504	True
North America	False	9,389	9,389	True
Total	**False**	**18,869**	**18,869**	**True**

FIGURE 10-11 Filtering by continent, *All customers visible* returns incorrect results.

Beware that the measure is not incorrect. It computes the value correctly, but it only works if the report is slicing by gender. To obtain a measure that is independent from the *Gender*, then the path to follow is the other one: removing all the filters from the *Customer* table except for the *Customer Type* column.

Removing all the filters but one looks like a simple operation. However, it hides a trap that you should be aware of. As a matter of fact, the first function that comes to a student's mind is *ALLEXCEPT*. Unfortunately, *ALLEXCEPT* might return unexpected results in this scenario. Consider the following formula:

```
AllExcept Type :=
CALCULATE (
    [NumOfCustomers],
    ALLEXCEPT ( Customer, Customer[Customer Type] )
)
```

ALLEXCEPT removes all the existing filters from the *Customer* table except for the *Customer Type* column. When used in the previous report, it computes a correct result, as shown in Figure 10-12.

Customer Type	NumOfCustomers	AllExcept Type	All customers visible
Company	**385**	**385**	**True**
Asia	67	385	False
Europe	42	385	False
North America	276	385	False
Person	**18,484**	**18,484**	**True**
Asia	3,591	18,484	False
Europe	5,504	18,484	False
North America	9,389	18,484	False
Total	**18,869**	**18,869**	**True**

FIGURE 10-12 *ALLEXCEPT* removes the dependency from the gender; it works with any column.

The measure does not only work with the *Continent*. By replacing the continent with the gender in the report, it still produces a correct result, as shown in Figure 10-13.

Customer Type	NumOfCustomers	AllExcept Type	All customers visible
Company	385	385	True
	385	385	True
Person	18,484	18,484	True
F	9,133	18,484	False
M	9,351	18,484	False
Total	18,869	18,869	True

FIGURE 10-13 *ALLEXCEPT* works with the gender too.

Despite the report being accurate, there is a hidden trap in the formula. The *ALL** functions, when used as filter arguments in *CALCULATE*, act as *CALCULATE* modifiers. This is explained in Chapter 5, "Understanding *CALCULATE* and *CALCULATETABLE*." These modifiers do not return a table that is used as a filter. Instead, they only remove filters from the filter context.

Focus your attention on the row with a blank gender. There are 385 customers in this group: All of them are companies. If one removes the *Customer Type* column from the report, the only remaining column in the filter context is the gender. When the gender shows the blank row, we know that only companies are visible in the filter context. Nevertheless, Figure 10-14 is surprising because it shows the same value for all the rows in the report; this value is the total number of customers.

Gender	NumOfCustomers	AllExcept Type
	385	18,869
F	9,133	18,869
M	9,351	18,869
Total	18,869	18,869

FIGURE 10-14 *ALLEXCEPT* produces unexpected values if the customer type is not part of the report.

Here is a caveat: *ALLEXCEPT* removed all the filters from the *Customer* table apart from the filter on the customer type. However, there is no filter on the customer type to retain. Indeed, the only filter in the filter context is the filter on the *Gender*, which *ALLEXCEPT* removes.

Customer Type is cross-filtered, but it is not filtered. As a result, *ALLEXCEPT* has no filter to retain and its net effect is the same as an *ALL* on the customer table. The correct way of expressing this condition is by using a pair of *ALL* and *VALUES* instead of *ALLEXCEPT*. Look at the following formula:

```
All Values Type :=
CALCULATE (
    [NumOfCustomers],
    ALL ( Customer ),
    VALUES ( Customer[Customer Type] )
)
```

Though similar to the previous definition, its semantics are different. *ALL* removes any filter from the *Customer* table. *VALUES* evaluates the values of *Customer[Customer Type]* in the current filter context. There is no filter on the customer type, but customer type is cross-filtered. Therefore, *VALUES* only returns the values visible in the current filter context, regardless of which column is generating the filter that is cross-filtering the customer type. You can see the result in Figure 10-15.

Gender	NumOfCustomers	AllExcept Type	All Values Type
	385	18,869	385
F	9,133	18,869	18,484
M	9,351	18,869	18,484
Total	**18,869**	**18,869**	**18,869**

FIGURE 10-15 Using *ALL* and *VALUES* together produces the desired result.

The important lesson here is that there is a big difference between using *ALLEXCEPT* and using *ALL* and *VALUES* together as filter arguments in *CALCULATE*. The reason is that the semantic of an *ALL** function is always that of removing filters. *ALL** functions never add filters to the context; they can only remove them.

The difference between the two behaviors, adding filters or removing filters, is not relevant in many scenarios. Nevertheless, there are situations where this difference has a strong impact, like in the previous example.

This, along with many other examples in this book, shows that DAX requires you to be very precise in the definition of your code. Using a function like *ALLEXCEPT* without thinking carefully about all the implications might result in your code producing unexpected values. DAX hides a lot of its complexity by providing intuitive behaviors in most situations. Nevertheless, the complexity, although hidden, is still there. One should understand the behaviors of filter contexts and *CALCULATE* well in order to master DAX.

Using *ALL* to avoid context transition

By now, at this point in the book our readers have a solid understanding of context transition. It is an extremely powerful feature, and we have leveraged it many times to compute useful values. Nevertheless, sometimes it is useful to avoid it or at least to mitigate its effects. To avoid the effects of the context transition, the *ALL** functions are the tools to use.

It is important to remember that when *CALCULATE* performs its operations, it executes each step in a precise order: The filter arguments are evaluated first, then the context transition happens if there are row contexts, then the *CALCULATE* modifiers are applied, and finally *CALCULATE* applies the result of the filter arguments to the filter context. You can leverage this order of execution noting that

CALCULATE modifiers—among which we count the *ALL** functions—are applied after the context transition. Because of this, a filter modifier has the option of overriding the effect of the context transition.

For example, consider the following piece of code:

```
SUMX (
    Sales,
    CALCULATE (
        ...,
        ALL ( Sales )
    )
)
```

CALCULATE runs in the row context generated by *SUMX*, which is iterating over *Sales*. As such, it should perform a context transition. Because *CALCULATE* is invoked with a modifier—that is *ALL (Sales)*—the DAX engine knows that any filter on the *Sales* table should be removed.

When we described the behavior of *CALCULATE*, we said that *CALCULATE* first performs context transition (that is, it filters all the columns in *Sales*) and then uses *ALL* to remove those filters. Nevertheless, the DAX optimizer is smarter than that. Because it knows that *ALL* removes any filter from *Sales*, it also knows that it would be totally useless to apply a filter and then remove it straight after. Thus, the net effect is that **in this case *CALCULATE* does not perform any context transition**, even though it removes all the existing row contexts.

This behavior is important in many scenarios. It becomes particularly useful in calculated columns. In a calculated column there is always a row context. Therefore, whenever the code in a calculated column invokes a measure, it is always executed in a filter context only for the current row.

For example, imagine computing the percentage of sales of the current product against all products in a calculated column. Inside a calculated column one can easily compute the value of sales of the current product by just invoking the *Sales Amount* measure. The context transition makes sure that the value returned only represents the sales of the current product. Nevertheless, the denominator should compute the sales of all the products, but the context transition is a problem. So, one can avoid the context transition by using *ALL*, like in the following code:

```
'Product'[GlobalPct] =
VAR SalesProduct = [Sales Amount]
VAR SalesAllProducts =
    CALCULATE (
        [Sales Amount],
        ALL ( 'Product' )
    )
VAR Result =
    DIVIDE ( SalesProduct, SalesAllProducts )
RETURN
    Result
```

Remember: the reason why *ALL* is removing the effect of the context transition is because *ALL*—being a *CALCULATE* modifier—is executed after the context transition. For this reason, *ALL* can override the effects of the context transition.

Similarly, the percentage against all the products in the same category is a slight variation of the previous code:

```
'Product'[CategoryPct] =
VAR SalesProduct = [Sales Amount]
VAR SalesCategory =
    CALCULATE (
        [Sales Amount],
        ALLEXCEPT ( 'Product', 'Product'[Category] )
    )
VAR Result
    DIVIDE ( SalesProduct, SalesCategory )
RETURN
    Result
```

You can look at the result of these two calculated columns in Figure 10-16.

Product Name	GlobalPct ▼	CategoryPct
Adventure Works 26" 720p LCD HDTV M140 Silver	4.26%	29.68%
A. Datum SLR Camera X137 Grey	2.37%	10.09%
Contoso Telephoto Conversion Lens X400 Silver	2.24%	9.51%
SV 16xDVD M360 Black	1.19%	8.30%
Contoso Projector 1080p X980 White	0.84%	3.81%
Contoso Washer & Dryer 21in E210 Pink	0.60%	1.90%
Fabrikam Independent filmmaker 1/3" 8.5mm X200 White	0.54%	2.30%
Proseware Projector 1080p LCD86 Silver	0.53%	2.38%
NT Washer & Dryer 27in L2700 Blue	0.50%	1.58%
Contoso Washer & Dryer 21in E210 Green	0.49%	1.58%
Fabrikam Laptop19 M9000 Black	0.47%	2.14%
NT Washer & Dryer 27in L2700 Green	0.45%	1.43%

FIGURE 10-16 *GlocalPct* and *CategoryPct* use *ALL* and *ALLEXCEPT* to avoid the effect of the context transition.

Using *ISEMPTY*

ISEMPTY is a function used to test whether a table is empty, meaning that it has no values visible in the current filter context. Without *ISEMPTY*, the following expression would test that a table expression returns zero rows:

```
COUNTROWS ( VALUES ( 'Product'[Color] ) ) = 0
```

Using *ISEMPTY* makes the code easier:

```
ISEMPTY ( VALUES ( 'Product'[Color] ) )
```

From a performance point of view, using *ISEMPTY* is always a better choice because it informs the engine exactly what to check. *COUNTROWS* requires DAX to count the number of rows in the table, whereas *ISEMPTY* is more efficient and usually does not require a complete scan of the visible values of the target table.

For example, imagine computing the number of customers who never bought certain products. A solution to this requirement is the following measure, *NonBuyingCustomers*:

```
NonBuyingCustomers :=
VAR SelectedCustomers =
    CALCULATETABLE (
        DISTINCT ( Sales[CustomerKey] ),
        ALLSELECTED ()
    )
VAR CustomersWithoutSales =
    FILTER (
        SelectedCustomers,
        ISEMPTY ( RELATEDTABLE ( Sales ) )
    )
VAR Result =
    COUNTROWS ( CustomersWithoutSales )
RETURN
    Result
```

You can see in Figure 10-17 a report showing the number of customers and the number of nonbuying customers side-by-side.

Brand	Sales Amount	NumOfCustomers	NonBuyingCustomers
A. Datum	2,096,184.64	1,144	9,897
Adventure Works	4,011,112.28	2,587	8,454
Contoso	7,352,399.03	4,346	6,695
Fabrikam	5,554,015.73	526	10,515
Litware	3,255,704.03	994	10,047
Northwind Traders	1,040,552.13	1,002	10,039
Proseware	2,546,144.16	495	10,546
Southridge Video	1,384,413.85	5,200	5,841
Tailspin Toys	325,042.42	4,278	6,763
The Phone Company	1,123,819.07	318	10,723
Wide World Importers	1,901,956.66	517	10,524
Total	**30,591,343.98**	**11,041**	

FIGURE 10-17 *NonBuyingCustomers* counts the customers who never bought any of the selected products.

ISEMPTY is a simple function. Here we use it as an example to point the reader's attention to one detail. The previous code saved a list of customer keys in a variable, and later it iterated this list with *FILTER* to check whether the *RELATEDTABLE* result was empty or not.

If the content of the table in the *SelectedCustomer* variable were the list of customer keys, how could DAX know that those values have a relationship with *Sales*? A customer key, as a value, is not different from a product quantity. A number is a number. The difference is in the meaning of the number. As a customer key, 120 represents the customer with key 120, whereas as a quantity, it indicates the number of products sold.

Thus, a list of numbers has no clear meaning as a filter, unless one knows where these numbers come from. DAX maintains the knowledge about the source of column values through data lineage, which we explain in the next section.

Introducing data lineage and *TREATAS*

As we anticipated in the previous section, "Using *ISEMPTY*," a list of values is meaningless unless one knows what those values represent. For example, imagine a table of strings containing "Red" and "Blue" like the following anonymous table:

```
{ "Red", "Blue" }
```

As humans, we know these are colors. More likely, at this point in the book all our readers know that we are referencing product colors. But to DAX, this only represents a table containing two strings. Therefore, the following measure always produces the grand total of sales because the table containing two values cannot filter anything:

```
Test :=
CALCULATE (
    [Sales Amount],
    { "Red", "Blue" }
)
```

 Note The previous measure does not raise any error. The filter argument is applied to an anonymous table, without any effect on physical tables of the data model.

In Figure 10-18 you can see that the result is the same as *Sales Amount* because *CALCULATE* does not apply any further filtering.

Color	Sales Amount	Test
Azure	97,389.89	97,389.89
Black	5,860,066.14	5,860,066.14
Blue	2,435,444.62	2,435,444.62
Brown	1,029,508.95	1,029,508.95
Gold	361,496.01	361,496.01
Green	1,403,184.38	1,403,184.38
Grey	3,509,138.09	3,509,138.09
Orange	857,320.28	857,320.28
Pink	828,638.54	828,638.54
Purple	5,973.84	5,973.84
Red	1,110,102.10	1,110,102.10
Silver	6,798,560.86	6,798,560.86
Silver Grey	371,908.92	371,908.92
Transparent	3,295.89	3,295.89
White	5,829,599.91	5,829,599.91
Yellow	89,715.56	89,715.56
Total	**30,591,343.98**	**30,591,343.98**

FIGURE 10-18 Filtering with an anonymous table does not produce any filter.

For a value to filter the model, DAX needs to know the *data lineage* of the value itself. A value that represents a column in the data model holds the data lineage of that column. On the other hand, a value that is not linked to any column in the data model is an anonymous value. In the previous example, the *Test* measure used an anonymous table to filter the model and, as such, it did not filter any column of the data model.

The following is a correct way of applying a filter. Be mindful that we use the full syntax of the *CAL-CULATE* filter argument for educational purposes; a predicate to filter *Product[Color]* would be enough:

```
Test :=
CALCULATE (
    [Sales Amount],
    FILTER (
        ALL ( 'Product'[Color] ),
        'Product'[Color] IN { "Red", "Blue" }
    )
)
```

Data lineage flows this way: *ALL* returns a table that contains all product colors. The result contains the values from the original column, so DAX knows the meaning of each value. *FILTER* scans the table containing all the colors and checks whether each color is included in the anonymous table containing Red and Blue. As a result, *FILTER* returns a table containing the values of *Product[Color]*, so *CALCULATE* knows that the filter is applied to the *Product[Color]* column.

One can imagine data lineage as a special tag added to each column, identifying its position in the data model.

You typically do not have to worry about data lineage because DAX handles the complexity of data lineage by itself in a natural and intuitive way. For example, when a table value is assigned to a variable, the table contains data lineage information that is maintained through the whole DAX evaluation process using that variable.

The reason why it is important to learn data lineage is because one has the option of either maintaining or changing data lineage at will. In some scenarios it is important to keep the data lineage, whereas in other scenarios one might want to change the lineage of a column.

The function that can change the lineage of a column is *TREATAS*. *TREATAS* accepts a table as its first argument and then a set of column references. *TREATAS* updates the data lineage of the table tagging each column with the appropriate target column. For example, the previous *Test* measure can be rewritten this way:

```
Test :=
CALCULATE (
    [Sales Amount],
    TREATAS ( { "Red", "Blue" }, 'Product'[Color] )
)
```

TREATAS returns a table containing values tagged with the *Product[Color]* column. As such, this new version of the *Test* measure only filters the red and blue colors, as shown in Figure 10-19.

Color	Sales Amount	Test
Azure	97,389.89	3,545,546.72
Black	5,860,066.14	3,545,546.72
Blue	2,435,444.62	3,545,546.72
Brown	1,029,508.95	3,545,546.72
Gold	361,496.01	3,545,546.72
Green	1,403,184.38	3,545,546.72
Grey	3,509,138.09	3,545,546.72
Orange	857,320.28	3,545,546.72
Pink	828,638.54	3,545,546.72
Purple	5,973.84	3,545,546.72
Red	1,110,102.10	3,545,546.72
Silver	6,798,560.86	3,545,546.72
Silver Grey	371,908.92	3,545,546.72
Transparent	3,295.89	3,545,546.72
White	5,829,599.91	3,545,546.72
Yellow	89,715.56	3,545,546.72
Total	**30,591,343.98**	**3,545,546.72**

FIGURE 10-19 *TREATAS* updates the lineage of the anonymous table, so that filtering now works as expected.

The rules for data lineage are simple. A simple column reference maintains its data lineage, whereas an expression is always anonymous. Indeed, an expression generates a reference to an anonymous column. For example, the following expression returns a table with two columns that have the same content. The difference between the two columns is that the first one retains the data lineage information, whereas the second one does not because it is a new column:

```
ADDCOLUMNS (
    VALUES ( 'Product'[Color] ),
    "Color without lineage", 'Product'[Color] & ""
)
```

TREATAS is useful to update the data lineage of one or more columns in a table expression. The example shown so far was only for educational purposes. Now we show a better example related to time intelligence calculations. In Chapter 8, "Time intelligence calculations," we showed the following formula to compute the *LASTNONBLANK* date for semi-additive calculations:

```
LastBalanceIndividualCustomer :=
SUMX (
    VALUES ( Balances[Name] ),
    CALCULATE (
        SUM ( Balances[Balance] ),
        LASTNONBLANK (
            'Date'[Date],
            COUNTROWS ( RELATEDTABLE ( Balances ) )
        )
    )
)
```

This code works, but it suffers from a major drawback: It contains two iterations, and the optimizer is likely to use a suboptimal execution plan for the measure. It would be better to create a table containing the customer name and the date of the last balance, and then use that table as a filter argument in *CALCULATE* to filter the last date available for each customer. It turns out that this is possible by using *TREATAS*:

```
LastBalanceIndividualCustomer Optimized :=
VAR LastCustomerDate =
    ADDCOLUMNS (
        VALUES ( Balances[Name] ),
        "LastDate", CALCULATE (
            MAX ( Balances[Date] ),
            DATESBETWEEN ( 'Date'[Date], BLANK(), MAX ( Balances[Date] ) )
        )
    )
VAR FilterCustomerDate =
    TREATAS (
        LastCustomerDate,
        Balances[Name],
        'Date'[Date]
```

```
VAR SumLastBalance =
    CALCULATE (
        SUM ( Balances[Balance] ),
        FilterCustomerDate
    )
RETURN
    SumLastBalance
```

The measure performs the following operations:

- *LastCustomerDate* contains the last date for which there is data for each customer. The result is a table that contains two columns: the first is the *Balances[Name]* column, whereas the second is an anonymous column because it is the result of an expression.

- *FilterCustomerDate* has the same content as *LastCustomerDate*. By using *TREATAS*, both columns are now tagged with the desired data lineage. The first column targets *Balances[Name]*, whereas the second column targets *Date[Date]*.

- The last step is to use *FilterCustomerDate* as a filter argument of *CALCULATE*. Because the table is now correctly tagged with the data lineage, *CALCULATE* filters the model in such a way that only one date is selected for every customer. This date is the last date with data in the *Balances* table for the given customer.

Most of the time, *TREATAS* is applied to change the data lineage of a table with a single column. The previous example shows a more complex scenario where the data lineage is modified on a table containing two columns. The data lineage of a table resulting from a DAX expression can include columns of different tables. When this table is applied to the filter context, it often generates an arbitrarily shaped filter, discussed in the next section.

Understanding arbitrarily shaped filters

Filters in the filter context can have two different shapes: simple filters and arbitrarily shaped filters. All the filters we have used so far are simple filters. In this section, we describe arbitrarily shaped filters, and we briefly discuss the implications of using them in your code. Arbitrarily shaped filters can be created by using a PivotTable in Excel or by writing DAX code in a measure, whereas the Power BI user interface currently requires a custom visual to create arbitrarily shaped filters. This section describes what these filters are and how to manage them in DAX.

We can start by describing the difference between a simple filter and an arbitrarily shaped filter in the filter context.

- A **column filter** is a list of values for one column only. A list of three colors, like red, blue, and green, is a column filter. For example, the following *CALCULATE* generates a column filter in the filter context that only affects the *Product[Color]* column:

```
CALCULATE (
    [Sales Amount],
    'Product'[Color] IN { "Red", "Blue", "Green" }
)
```

- A **simple filter** is a filter over one or more columns that corresponds to a set of simple column filters. Almost all the filters used in this book so far are column filters. Column filters are created quite simply, by using multiple filter arguments in *CALCULATE*:

```
CALCULATE (
    [Sales Amount],
    'Product'[Color] IN { "Red", "Blue" },
    'Date'[Calendar Year Number] IN { 2007, 2008, 2009 }
)
```

The previous code could be written using a simple filter with two columns:

```
CALCULATE (
    [Sales Amount],
    TREATAS (
        {
            ( "Red", 2007 ),
            ( "Red", 2008 ),
            ( "Red", 2009 ),
            ( "Blue", 2007 ),
            ( "Blue", 2008 ),
            ( "Blue", 2009 )
        },
        'Product'[Color],
        'Date'[Calendar Year Number]
    )
)
```

Because a simple filter contains all the possible combinations of two columns, it is simpler to express it using two column filters.

- An **arbitrarily shaped filter** is any filter that cannot be expressed as a simple filter. For example, look at the following expression:

```
CALCULATE (
    [Sales Amount],
    TREATAS (
        {
            ( "CY 2007", "December" ),
            ( "CY 2008", "January" )
        },
        'Date'[Calendar Year],
        'Date'[Month]
    )
)
```

The filter on year and month is not a column filter because it involves two columns. Moreover, the filter does not include all the combinations of the two columns existing in the data model. In fact, one cannot filter year and month separately. Indeed, there are two year and two month references, and there are four existing combinations in the *Date* table for the values provided, whereas the filter only includes two of these combinations. In other words, using two column filters, the resulting filter context would also include January 2007 and December 2008, which are not included in the filter described by the previous code. Therefore, this is an arbitrarily shaped filter.

An arbitrarily shaped filter is not just a filter with multiple columns. Certainly, a filter with multiple columns could be an arbitrarily shaped filter, but one can build a filter with multiple columns retaining the shape of a simple filter. The following example is a simple filter, despite it involving multiple columns:

```
CALCULATE (
    [Sales Amount],
    TREATAS (
        {
            ( "CY 2007", "December" ),
            ( "CY 2008", "December" )
        },
        'Date'[Calendar Year],
        'Date'[Month]
    )
)
```

The previous expression can be rewritten as the combination of two column filters this way:

```
CALCULATE (
    [Sales Amount],
    'Date'[Calendar Year] IN { "CY 2007",  "CY 2008" },
    'Date'[Month] = "December"
)
```

Although they seem complex to author, arbitrarily shaped filters can easily be defined through the user interface of Excel and Power BI. At the time of writing, Power BI can only generate an arbitrarily shaped filter by using the Hierarchy Slicer custom visual, which defines filters based on a hierarchy with multiple columns. For example, in Figure 10-20 you can see the Hierarchy Slicer filtering different months in 2007 and 2008.

Calendar Year	Calendar Year	Sales Amount
☐ July		
☐ August	CY 2007	**3,741,293.14**
☑ September	September	1,009,868.98
☑ October	October	914,273.54
☑ November	November	825,601.87
☑ December	December	991,548.75
◢ ▣ CY 2008	CY 2008	**1,816,385.21**
☑ January	January	656,766.69
☑ February	February	600,080.00
☑ March	March	559,538.52
☐ April	**Total**	**5,557,678.35**
☐ May		
☐ June		
☐ July		
☐ August		

FIGURE 10-20 Filtering a hierarchy makes it possible to build an arbitrarily shaped filter.

In Microsoft Excel you find a native feature to build arbitrarily shaped sets out of hierarchies, as shown in Figure 10-21.

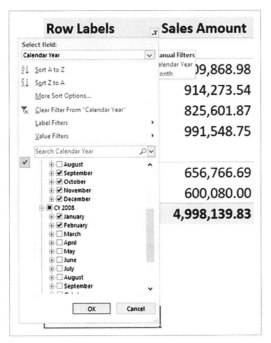

FIGURE 10-21 Microsoft Excel builds arbitrarily shaped filters using the native hierarchy filter.

Arbitrarily shaped filters are complex to use in DAX because of the way *CALCULATE* might change them in the filter context. In fact, when *CALCULATE* applies a filter on a column, it removes previous filters on that column only, replacing any previous filter with the new filter. The result is that typically, the original shape of the arbitrarily shaped filter is lost. This behavior leads to formulas that produce inaccurate results and that are hard to debug. Thus, to demonstrate the problem, we will increase the complexity of the code step-by-step, until the problem arises.

Imagine you define a simple measure that overwrites the year, forcing it to be 2007:

```
Sales Amount 2007 :=
CALCULATE (
    [Sales Amount],
    'Date'[Calendar Year] = "CY 2007"
)
```

CALCULATE overwrites the filter on the year but it does not change the filter on the month. When it is used in a report, the results of the measure might seem unusual, as shown in Figure 10-22.

Calendar Year	Sales Amount	Sales Amount 2007
CY 2007	**3,741,293.14**	**3,741,293.14**
September	1,009,868.98	1,009,868.98
October	914,273.54	914,273.54
November	825,601.87	825,601.87
December	991,548.75	991,548.75
CY 2008	**1,816,385.21**	**2,646,673.39**
January	656,766.69	794,248.24
February	600,080.00	891,135.91
March	559,538.52	961,289.24
Total	**5,557,678.35**	**6,387,966.53**

FIGURE 10-22 The year 2007 replaces the previous filter on the year.

When 2007 is selected, the results of the two measures are the same. However, when the year selected is 2008, it gets replaced with 2007, whereas months are left untouched. The result is that the value shown for January 2008 is the sales amount of January 2007. The same happens for February and March. The main thing to note is that the original filter did not contain the first three months of 2007, and by replacing the filter on the year, our formula shows their value. As anticipated, so far there is nothing special.

Things suddenly become much more intricate if one wants to compute the average monthly sales. A possible solution to this calculation is to iterate over the months and average the partial results using *AVERAGEX*:

```
Monthly Avg :=
AVERAGEX (
    VALUES ( 'Date'[Month] ),
    [Sales Amount]
)
```

You can see the result in Figure 10-23. This time, the grand total is surprisingly large.

Calendar Year			Calendar Year	Sales Amount	Monthly Avg
☐ July					
☐ August			CY 2007	**3,741,293.14**	**935,323.29**
☑ September			September	1,009,868.98	1,009,868.98
☑ October			October	914,273.54	914,273.54
☑ November			November	825,601.87	825,601.87
☑ December			December	991,548.75	991,548.75
◢ ◨ CY 2008			CY 2008	**1,816,385.21**	**605,461.74**
☑ January			January	656,766.69	656,766.69
☑ February			February	600,080.00	600,080.00
☑ March			March	559,538.52	559,538.52
☐ April			**Total**	**5,557,678.35**	**1,709,342.92**
☐ May					
☐ June					

FIGURE 10-23 The grand total is definitely not the average of months; it is too large.

Understanding the problem is much harder than fixing it. Focus your attention on the cell that computes the wrong value—the grand total of *Monthly Avg*. The filter context of the *Total* row of the report is the following:

```
TREATAS (
    {
        ( "CY 2007", "September" ),
        ( "CY 2007", "October" ),
        ( "CY 2007", "November" ),
        ( "CY 2007", "December" ),
        ( "CY 2008", "January" ),
        ( "CY 2008", "February" ),
        ( "CY 2008", "March" )
    },
    'Date'[Calendar Year],
    'Date'[Month]
)
```

In order to follow the execution of the DAX code, we expand the full calculation in that cell by defining the corresponding filter context in a *CALCULATE* statement that evaluates the *Monthly Avg* measure. Moreover, we expand the code of *Monthly Avg* to build a single formula that simulates the execution:

```
CALCULATE (
    AVERAGEX (
        VALUES ( 'Date'[Month] ),
        CALCULATE (
            SUMX (
                Sales,
                Sales[Quantity] * Sales[Net Price]
            )
        )
    ),
    TREATAS (
        {
            ( "CY 2007", "September" ),
            ( "CY 2007", "October" ),
            ( "CY 2007", "November" ),
            ( "CY 2007", "December" ),
            ( "CY 2008", "January" ),
            ( "CY 2008", "February" ),
            ( "CY 2008", "March" )
        },
        'Date'[Calendar Year],
        'Date'[Month]
    )
)
```

The key to fixing the problem is to understand what happens when the highlighted *CALCULATE* is executed. That *CALCULATE* is executed in a row context that is iterating over the *Date[Month]* column. Consequently, context transition takes place and the current value of the month is added to the filter context. On a given month, say January, *CALCULATE* adds January to the filter context, replacing the current filter on the month but leaving all the other filters untouched.

When *AVERAGEX* is iterating January, the resulting filter context is January in both 2007 and 2008; this is because the original filter context filters two years for the year column. Therefore, on each iteration DAX computes the sales amount of one month in two distinct years. This is the reason why the value is much higher than any monthly sales.

The original shape of the arbitrarily shaped filter is lost because *CALCULATE* overrides one of the columns involved in the arbitrarily shaped filter. The net result is that the calculation produces an incorrect result.

Fixing the problem is much easier than expected. Indeed, it is enough to iterate over a column that is guaranteed to have a unique value on every month. If, instead of iterating over the month name, which is not unique over different years, the formula iterates over the *Calendar Year Month* column, then the code produces the correct result:

```
Monthly Avg :=
AVERAGEX (
    VALUES ( 'Date'[Calendar Year Month] ),
    [Sales Amount]
)
```

Using this version of *Monthly Avg*, on each iteration the context transition overrides the filter on *Calendar Year Month*, which represents both year and month values in the same column. As a result, it is guaranteed to always return the sales of an individual month, producing the correct outcome shown in Figure 10-24.

Calendar Year	Sales Amount	Monthly Avg
CY 2007	3,741,293.14	935,323.29
September	1,009,868.98	1,009,868.98
October	914,273.54	914,273.54
November	825,601.87	825,601.87
December	991,548.75	991,548.75
CY 2008	1,816,385.21	605,461.74
January	656,766.69	656,766.69
February	600,080.00	600,080.00
March	559,538.52	559,538.52
Total	**5,557,678.35**	**793,954.05**

Calendar Year
- July
- ☐ August
- ☑ September
- ☑ October
- ☑ November
- ☑ December
- ◢ ☐ CY 2008
- ☑ January
- ☑ February
- ☑ March
- ☐ April
- ☐ May
- ☐ June

FIGURE 10-24 Iterating over a unique column makes the code compute the correct result.

If a unique column for the cardinality of the iterator is not available, another viable solution is to use *KEEPFILTERS*. The following alternative version of the code works correctly, because instead of replacing the previous filter, it adds the month filter to the previously existing arbitrarily shaped set; this maintains the format of the original filter:

```
Monthly Avg KeepFilters :=
AVERAGEX (
    KEEPFILTERS ( VALUES ( 'Date'[Month] ) ),
    [Sales Amount]
)
```

As anticipated, arbitrarily shaped sets are not commonly observed in real-world reports. Nevertheless, users have multiple and legitimate ways of generating them. In order to guarantee that a measure works correctly even in the presence of arbitrarily shaped sets, it is important to follow some best practices:

- When iterating over a column, make sure that the column has unique values at the granularity where the calculation is being performed. For example, if a *Date* table has more than 12 months, a *YearMonth* column should be used for monthly calculations.

- If the previous best practice cannot be applied, then protect the code using *KEEPFILTERS* to guarantee that the arbitrarily shaped filter is maintained in the filter context. Be mindful that *KEEPFILTERS* might change the semantics of the calculations. Indeed, it is important to double-check that *KEEPFILTERS* does not introduce errors in the measure.

Following these simple rules, your code will be safe even in the presence of arbitrarily shaped filters.

Conclusions

In this chapter we described several functions that are useful to inspect the content of the filter context and/or to modify the behavior of a measure depending on the context. We also introduced important techniques to manipulate the filter context with the increased knowledge of the possible states of the filter context. Here is a recap of the important concepts you learned in this chapter:

- A column can be either filtered or cross-filtered. It is filtered if there is a direct filter; it is cross-filtered if the filter is coming from a direct filter on another column or table. You can verify whether a column is filtered or not by using *ISFILTERED* and *ISCROSSFILTERED*.

- *HASONEVALUE* checks whether a column only has one value visible in the filter context. This is useful before retrieving that value using *VALUES*. The *SELECTEDVALUE* function simplifies the *HASONEVALUE/VALUES* pattern.

- Using *ALLEXCEPT* is not the same as using the pair *ALL* and *VALUES*. In the presence of cross-filtering, *ALL/VALUES* is safer because it also considers cross-filtering as part of its evaluation.

- *ALL* and all the *ALL** functions are useful to avoid the effect of context transition. Indeed, using *ALL* in a calculated column, or in general in a row context, informs DAX that the context transition is not needed.

- Each column in a table is tagged with data lineage. Data lineage lets DAX apply filters and relationships. Data lineage is maintained whenever one references a column, whereas it is lost when using expressions.

- Data lineage can be assigned to one or more columns by using *TREATAS*.

- Not all filters are simple filters. A user can build more complex filters either through the user interface or by code. The most complex kind of filter is the arbitrarily shaped filter, which could be complex to use because of its interaction with the *CALCULATE* function and the context transition.

You will likely not remember all the concepts and functions described in this chapter immediately after having read them. Regardless, it is crucial that you be exposed to these concepts in your learning of DAX. You will for sure run into one of the issues described here as you gain DAX experience. At that point, it will be useful to come back to this chapter and refresh your memory about the specific problem you are dealing with.

In the next chapter, we use many of the functions described here to apply calculations over hierarchies. As you will learn, working with hierarchies is mainly a matter of understanding the shape of the current filter context.

Handling hierarchies

Hierarchies are oftentimes present in data models to make it easier for the user to slice and dice using predefined exploration paths. Nevertheless, DAX does not have any built-in function providing a calculation over hierarchies. Computing a simple calculation like the ratio to parent requires complex DAX code, and the support for calculations over hierarchies proves to be a challenge in general.

However, it is worth learning the DAX code required to handle hierarchies because calculations over hierarchies are very common. In this chapter, we show how to create basic calculations over hierarchies and how to use DAX to transform a parent/child hierarchy into a regular hierarchy.

Computing percentages over hierarchies

A common requirement when dealing with hierarchies is to create a measure that behaves differently depending on the level of the item selected. An example is the ratio to parent calculation. Ratio to parent displays for each level the percentage of that level against its parent.

For instance, consider a hierarchy made of product category, subcategory, and product name. A ratio to parent calculation shows the percentage of a category against the grand total, of a subcategory against its category, and of a product against its subcategory. Thus, depending on the level of the hierarchy, it shows a different calculation.

An example of this report is visible in Figure 11-1.

In Excel, one might create this calculation by using the PivotTable feature Show Values As, so that the computation is performed by Excel. However, if you want to use the calculation regardless of specific features of the client, then it is better to create a new measure that performs the computation so that the value is computed in the data model. Moreover, learning the technique comes handy in many similar scenarios.

Unfortunately, computing the ratio to parent in DAX is not so easy. Here is the first big DAX limitation we face: There is no way of building a generic ratio to parent measure that works on any arbitrary combination of columns in a report. The reason is that inside DAX, there is no way of knowing how the report was created or how the hierarchy was used in the client tool. DAX has no knowledge of the way a user builds a report. It receives a DAX query; the query does not contain information about what is on the rows, what is on the columns, or what slicers were used to build the report.

Category	Sales Amount	PercOnParent
Audio	**21,544.69**	**2.60%**
Bluetooth Headphones	**4,444.69**	**20.63%**
NT Bluetooth Stereo Headphones E52 Pink	904.29	20.35%
NT Wireless Bluetooth Stereo Headphones E302 Pink	324.40	7.30%
WWI Wireless Bluetooth Stereo Headphones M170 Pink	1,560.00	35.10%
WWI Wireless Bluetooth Stereo Headphones M270 Pink	1,656.00	37.26%
MP4&MP3	**5,846.40**	**27.14%**
Contoso 16GB New Generation MP5 Player M1650 Pink	5,846.40	100.00%
Recording Pen	**11,253.60**	**52.23%**
WWI 1GB Digital Voice Recorder Pen E100 Pink	2,995.20	26.62%
WWI 4GB Video Recording Pen X200 Pink	8,258.40	73.38%
Cameras and camcorders	**364,444.58**	**43.98%**
Cameras & Camcorders Accessories	**3,940.47**	**1.08%**
Contoso Carrying Case E312 Pink	1,351.42	34.30%
Contoso Conversion Lens M550 Pink	184.50	4.68%
Contoso Cyber Shot Digital Cameras Adapter E306 Pink	1,937.52	49.17%
Contoso Lens Cap Keeper E314 Pink	467.04	11.85%

FIGURE 11-1 The *PercOnParent* measure is useful to better understand the values in a table.

Though a generic formula cannot be created, it is still possible to create a measure that computes the correct percentages when used properly. Because there are three levels in the hierarchy (category, subcategory, and product), we start with three different measures that compute three different percentages, one for each level:

```
PercOnSubcategory :=
DIVIDE (
    [Sales Amount],
    CALCULATE (
        [Sales Amount],
        ALLSELECTED ( Product[Product Name] )
    )
)

PercOnCategory :=
DIVIDE (
    [Sales Amount],
    CALCULATE (
        [Sales Amount],
        ALLSELECTED  ( Product[Subcategory] )
    )
)

PercOnTotal :=
DIVIDE (
    [Sales Amount],
    CALCULATE (
        [Sales Amount],
```

```
        ALLSELECTED ( Product[Category] )
    )
)
```

These three measures compute the percentages needed. Figure 11-2 shows the results in a report.

Category	Sales Amount	PercOnTotal	PercOnCategory	PercOnSubcategory
Audio	**21,544.69**	**2.60%**	**100.00%**	**100.00%**
Bluetooth Headphones	**4,444.69**	**100.00%**	**20.63%**	**100.00%**
NT Bluetooth Stereo Headphones E52 Pink	904.29	100.00%	100.00%	20.35%
NT Wireless Bluetooth Stereo Headphones E302 Pink	324.40	100.00%	100.00%	7.30%
WWI Wireless Bluetooth Stereo Headphones M170 Pink	1,560.00	100.00%	100.00%	35.10%
WWI Wireless Bluetooth Stereo Headphones M270 Pink	1,656.00	100.00%	100.00%	37.26%
MP4&MP3	**5,846.40**	**100.00%**	**27.14%**	**100.00%**
Contoso 16GB New Generation MP5 Player M1650 Pink	5,846.40	100.00%	100.00%	100.00%
Recording Pen	**11,253.60**	**100.00%**	**52.23%**	**100.00%**
WWI 1GB Digital Voice Recorder Pen E100 Pink	2,995.20	100.00%	100.00%	26.62%
WWI 4GB Video Recording Pen X200 Pink	8,258.40	100.00%	100.00%	73.38%
Cameras and camcorders	**364,444.58**	**43.98%**	**100.00%**	**100.00%**
Cameras & Camcorders Accessories	**3,940.47**	**100.00%**	**1.08%**	**100.00%**
Contoso Carrying Case E312 Pink	1,351.42	100.00%	100.00%	34.30%
Contoso Conversion Lens M550 Pink	184.50	100.00%	100.00%	4.68%
Contoso Cyber Shot Digital Cameras Adapter E306 Pink	1,937.52	100.00%	100.00%	49.17%

FIGURE 11-2 The three measures work well only at the level where they have meaning.

You can see that the measures only show the correct values where they are relevant. Otherwise, they return 100%, which is useless. Moreover, there are three different measures, but the goal is to only have one measure showing different percentages at different levels. This is the next step.

We start by clearing the 100% out of the *PercOnSubcategory* measure. We want to avoid performing the calculation if the hierarchy is not showing the *Product Name* column on the rows. This means checking if the *Product Name* is currently being filtered by the query that produces the matrix. There is a specific function for this purpose: *ISINSCOPE. ISINSCOPE* returns *TRUE* if the column passed as the argument is filtered and it is part of the columns used to perform the grouping. Thus, the formula can be updated to this new expression:

```
PercOnSubcategory :=
IF (
    ISINSCOPE ( Product[Product Name] ),
    DIVIDE (
        [Sales Amount],
        CALCULATE (
            [Sales Amount],
            ALLSELECTED ( Product[Product Name] )
        )
    )
)
```

Figure 11-3 shows the report using this new formula.

Category	Sales Amount	PercOnTotal	PercOnCategory	PercOnSubcategory
Audio	21,544.69	2.60%	100.00%	
Bluetooth Headphones	4,444.69	100.00%	20.63%	
NT Bluetooth Stereo Headphones E52 Pink	904.29	100.00%	100.00%	20.35%
NT Wireless Bluetooth Stereo Headphones E302 Pink	324.40	100.00%	100.00%	7.30%
WWI Wireless Bluetooth Stereo Headphones M170 Pink	1,560.00	100.00%	100.00%	35.10%
WWI Wireless Bluetooth Stereo Headphones M270 Pink	1,656.00	100.00%	100.00%	37.26%
MP4&MP3	5,846.40	100.00%	27.14%	
Contoso 16GB New Generation MP5 Player M1650 Pink	5,846.40	100.00%	100.00%	100.00%
Recording Pen	11,253.60	100.00%	52.23%	
WWI 1GB Digital Voice Recorder Pen E100 Pink	2,995.20	100.00%	100.00%	26.62%
WWI 4GB Video Recording Pen X200 Pink	8,258.40	100.00%	100.00%	73.38%
Cameras and camcorders	364,444.58	43.98%	100.00%	
Cameras & Camcorders Accessories	3,940.47	100.00%	1.08%	
Contoso Carrying Case E312 Pink	1,351.42	100.00%	100.00%	34.30%
Contoso Conversion Lens M550 Pink	184.50	100.00%	100.00%	4.68%
Contoso Cyber Shot Digital Cameras Adapter E306 Pink	1,937.52	100.00%	100.00%	49.17%

FIGURE 11-3 Using *ISINSCOPE*, we remove the useless 100% values from the *PercOnSubcategory* column.

The same technique can be used to remove the 100% from other measures. Be careful that in *PercOnCategory*, we must check that *Subcategory* is in scope and *Product Name* is not. This is because when the report is slicing by *Product Name* using the hierarchy, it is also slicing by *Subcategory*—displaying a product rather than a subcategory. In order to avoid duplicating code to check these conditions, a better option is to write a single measure that executes a different operation depending on the level of the hierarchy visible—based on the *ISINSCOPE* condition tested from the bottom to the top of the hierarchy levels. Here is the code for the *PercOnParent* measure:

```
PercOnParent :=
VAR CurrentSales = [Sales Amount]
VAR SubcategorySales =
    CALCULATE (
        [Sales Amount],
        ALLSELECTED ( Product[Product Name] )
    )
VAR CategorySales =
    CALCULATE (
        [Sales Amount],
        ALLSELECTED ( Product[Subcategory] )
    )
VAR TotalSales =
    CALCULATE (
        [Sales Amount],
        ALLSELECTED ( Product[Category] )
    )
VAR RatioToParent =
    IF (
        ISINSCOPE ( Product[Product Name] ),
        DIVIDE ( CurrentSales, SubcategorySales ),
        IF (
            ISINSCOPE  ( Product[Subcategory] ),
            DIVIDE ( CurrentSales, CategorySales ),
            IF (
```

```
                ISINSCOPE  ( Product[Category] ),
                DIVIDE ( CurrentSales, TotalSales )
            )
        )
    )
RETURN RatioToParent
```

Using the *PercOnParent* measure, the result is as expected, as you can see in Figure 11-4.

Category	Sales Amount	PercOnParent
Audio	21,544.69	2.60%
Bluetooth Headphones	4,444.69	20.63%
NT Bluetooth Stereo Headphones E52 Pink	904.29	20.35%
NT Wireless Bluetooth Stereo Headphones E302 Pink	324.40	7.30%
WWI Wireless Bluetooth Stereo Headphones M170 Pink	1,560.00	35.10%
WWI Wireless Bluetooth Stereo Headphones M270 Pink	1,656.00	37.26%
MP4&MP3	5,846.40	27.14%
Contoso 16GB New Generation MP5 Player M1650 Pink	5,846.40	100.00%
Recording Pen	11,253.60	52.23%
WWI 1GB Digital Voice Recorder Pen E100 Pink	2,995.20	26.62%
WWI 4GB Video Recording Pen X200 Pink	8,258.40	73.38%
Cameras and camcorders	364,444.58	43.98%
Cameras & Camcorders Accessories	3,940.47	1.08%
Contoso Carrying Case E312 Pink	1,351.42	34.30%
Contoso Conversion Lens M550 Pink	184.50	4.68%
Contoso Cyber Shot Digital Cameras Adapter E306 Pink	1,937.52	49.17%
Contoso Lens Cap Keeper E314 Pink	467.04	11.85%

FIGURE 11-4 The *PercOnParent* measure merges the three columns computed before into a single column.

The three measures created previously are no longer useful. A single measure computes everything needed, putting the right value into a single column by detecting the level the hierarchy is being browsed at.

Note The order of the *IF* conditions is important. We want to start by testing the innermost level of the hierarchy and then proceed one step at a time to check the outer levels. Otherwise, if we reverse the order of the conditions, the results will be incorrect. It is important to remember that when the subcategory is filtered through the hierarchy, the category is filtered too.

The *PercOnParent* measure written in DAX only works if the user puts the correct hierarchy on the rows. For example, if the user replaces the category hierarchy with the color, the numbers reported are hard to understand. Indeed, the measure always works considering the product hierarchy regardless of whether it is used or not in the report.

Handling parent/child hierarchies

The native data model used by DAX does not support true parent/child hierarchies, such as the ones found in a Multidimensional database in Analysis Services. However, several DAX functions are available to flatten parent/child hierarchies into regular, column-based hierarchies. This is good enough for most scenarios, though it means making an educated guess at design time about what the maximum depth of the hierarchy will be. In this section, you learn how to use DAX functions to create a parent/child hierarchy, often abbreviated as P/C.

You can see a classical P/C hierarchy in Figure 11-5.

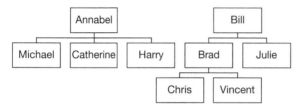

FIGURE 11-5 The chart shows a graphical representation of a P/C hierarchy.

P/C hierarchies present certain unique qualities:

- The number of levels is not always the same throughout the hierarchy. For example, the path from Annabel to Michael has a depth of two levels, whereas in the same hierarchy the path from Bill to Chris has a depth of three levels.

- The hierarchy is normally represented in a single table, storing a link to the parent for each row.

The canonical representation of P/C hierarchies is visible in Figure 11-6.

PersonKey	Name	ParentKey
1	Bill	
2	Brad	1
3	Julie	1
4	Chris	2
5	Vincent	2
6	Annabel	
7	Catherine	6
8	Harry	6
9	Michael	6

FIGURE 11-6 A table containing a P/C hierarchy.

It is easy to see that the *ParentKey* is the key of the parent of each node. For example, for Catherine it shows 6, which is the key of her parent, Annabel. The issue with this data model is that this time, the relationship is self-referenced; that is, the two tables involved in the relationship are really the same table.

A tabular data model does not support self-referencing relationships. Consequently, the data model itself has to be modified; the parent/child hierarchy needs to be turned into a regular hierarchy, based on one column for each level of the hierarchy.

Before we delve into the details of P/C hierarchies handling, it is worth noting one last point. Look at the table in Figure 11-7 containing the values we want to aggregate using the hierarchy.

PersonKey	Name	Amount
2	Brad	200
2	Brad	200
3	Julie	300
4	Chris	400
5	Vincent	500
6	Annabel	600
7	Catherine	600
7	Catherine	600
8	Harry	400
8	Harry	400
9	Michael	300
9	Michael	300

FIGURE 11-7 This table contains the data for the P/C hierarchy.

The rows in the fact table contain references to both leaf-level and middle nodes in the hierarchy. For example, the highlighted row references Annabel. Not only does Annabel have a value by herself, she also has three children nodes. Therefore, when summarizing all her data, the formula needs to aggregate both her numbers and her children's values.

Figure 11-8 displays the result we want to achieve.

Level1	FinalFormula
Annabel	**3,200**
Annabel	**600**
Catherine	**1,200**
Harry	**800**
Michael	**600**
Bill	**1,600**
Brad	**1,300**
Brad	400
Chris	400
Vincent	500
Julie	**300**
Total	**4,800**

FIGURE 11-8 This report shows the result of browsing a P/C with a matrix visual.

There are many steps to cover before reaching the final goal. Once the tables have been loaded in the data model, the first step is to create a calculated column that contains the path to reach each node, respectively. In fact, because we cannot use standard relationships, we will need to use a set of special functions available in DAX and designed for P/C hierarchies handling.

The new calculated column named *FullPath* uses the *PATH* function:

```
Persons[FullPath] = PATH ( Persons[PersonKey], Persons[ParentKey] )
```

PATH is a function that receives two parameters. The first parameter is the key of the table (in this case, *Persons[PersonKey]*), and the second parameter is the name of the column that holds the parent key. *PATH* performs a recursive traversal of the table, and for each node it builds the path as a list of keys separated by the pipe (|) character. In Figure 11-9, you can see the *FullPath* calculated column.

PersonKey	Name	FullPath
1	Bill	1
2	Brad	1|2
3	Julie	1|3
4	Chris	1|2|4
5	Vincent	1|2|5
6	Annabel	6
7	Catherine	6|7
8	Harry	6|8
9	Michael	6|9

FIGURE 11-9 The *FullPath* column contains the complete path to reach each node, respectively.

The *FullPath* column by itself is not useful. However, it is important because it acts as the basis for another set of calculated columns required to build the hierarchy. The next step is to build three calculated columns, one for each level of the hierarchy:

```
Persons[Level1] = LOOKUPVALUE(
    Persons[Name],
    Persons[PersonKey], PATHITEM ( Persons[FullPath], 1, INTEGER )
)

Persons[Level2] = LOOKUPVALUE(
    Persons[Name],
    Persons[PersonKey], PATHITEM ( Persons[FullPath], 2, INTEGER )
)

Persons[Level3] = LOOKUPVALUE(
    Persons[Name],
    Persons[PersonKey], PATHITEM ( Persons[FullPath], 3, INTEGER )
)
```

The three columns will be *Level1*, *Level2*, and *Level3* and the only change is in the second *PATHITEM* parameter, which is 1, 2, and 3. The calculated column uses *LOOKUPVALUE* to search a row where the *PersonKey* equals the result of *PATHITEM*. *PATHITEM* returns the nth item in a column built with *PATH*, or it returns blank if there is no such item when we request a number greater than the length of the path. The resulting table is shown in Figure 11-10.

PersonKey	Name	FullPath	Level1	Level2	Level3
1	Bill	1	Bill		
2	Brad	1|2	Bill	Brad	
3	Julie	1|3	Bill	Julie	
4	Chris	1|2|4	Bill	Brad	Chris
5	Vincent	1|2|5	Bill	Brad	Vincent
6	Annabel	6	Annabel		
7	Catherine	6|7	Annabel	Catherine	
8	Harry	6|8	Annabel	Harry	
9	Michael	6|9	Annabel	Michael	

FIGURE 11-10 The *Level* columns contain the values to show in the hierarchy.

In this example, we used three columns because the maximum depth of the hierarchy is three. In a real-world scenario, one needs to count the maximum number of levels of the hierarchy and to build a number of columns big enough to hold all the levels. Thus, although the number of levels in a P/C hierarchy should be flexible, in order to implement hierarchies in a data model, that maximum number needs to be set. It is a good practice to add a couple more levels to create space and enable any future growth of the hierarchy without needing to update the data model.

Now, we need to transform the set of level columns into a hierarchy. Also, because none of the other columns in the P/C is useful, we should hide everything else from the client tools. At this point, we can create a report using the hierarchy on the rows and the sum of amounts on the values—but the result is not yet as desired. Figure 11-11 displays the result in a matrix.

There are a couple problems with this report:

- Under Annabel, two blank rows contain the value of Annabel herself.

- Under Catherine, a blank row contains the value of Catherine herself. The same happens for many other rows.

The hierarchy always shows three levels, even for paths where the maximum depth should be two such as Harry, who has no children.

Level1	Amount
Annabel	**3200**
	600
	600
Catherine	**1200**
	1200
Harry	**800**
	800
Michael	**600**
	600
Bill	**1600**
Brad	**1300**
	400
Chris	400
Vincent	500
Julie	**300**
	300
Total	**4800**

FIGURE 11-11 The P/C hierarchy is not exactly what we want because it shows too many rows.

These issues pertain to the visualization of the results. Other than that, the hierarchy computes the correct values, because under Annabel's row, you can see the values of all of Annabel's children. The important aspect of this solution is that we were able to mimic a self-referencing relationship (also known as a recursive relationship) by using the *PATH* function to create a calculated column. The remaining part is solving the presentation issues, but at least things are moving toward the correct solution.

Our first challenge is the removal of all the blank values. For example, the second row of the matrix in the report accounts for an amount of 600 that should be visible for Annabel and not for blank. We can solve this by modifying the formula for the *Level* columns. First, we remove all the blanks, repeating the previous level if we reached the end of the path. Here, you see the pattern for *Level2*:

```
PC[Level2] =
IF ( PATHLENGTH ( Persons[FullPath] ) >= 2,
    LOOKUPVALUE (
        Persons[Name],
        Persons[PersonKey], PATHITEM ( Persons[FullPath], 2, INTEGER )
    ),
    Persons[Level1]
)
```

Level1 does not need to be modified because there is always a first level. Columns from *Level3* must follow the same pattern as *Level2*. With this new formula, the table looks like Figure 11-12.

PersonKey ▲	Name	FullPath	Level1	Level2	Level3
1	Bill	1	Bill	Bill	Bill
2	Brad	1|2	Bill	Brad	Brad
3	Julie	1|3	Bill	Julie	Julie
4	Chris	1|2|4	Bill	Brad	Chris
5	Vincent	1|2|5	Bill	Brad	Vincent
6	Annabel	6	Annabel	Annabel	Annabel
7	Catherine	6|7	Annabel	Catherine	Catherine
8	Harry	6|8	Annabel	Harry	Harry
9	Michael	6|9	Annabel	Michael	Michael

FIGURE 11-12 With the new formula, the *Level* columns never contain a blank.

At this point, if you look at the report, the blank rows are gone. Yet, there are still too many rows. In Figure 11-13, you can see the report with two rows highlighted.

Level1	Amount
Annabel	**3200**
Annabel	**600**
Annabel	600
Catherine	**1200**
Catherine	1200
Harry	**800**
Harry	800
Michael	**600**
Michael	600

FIGURE 11-13 The new report does not have blank rows.

Pay attention to the second and third rows of the report. In both cases, the matrix shows a single row of the hierarchy (that is, the row of Annabel). We might want to show the second row because it contains a relevant value for Annabel. However, we certainly do not want to see the third row because the hierarchy is browsing too deep and the path of Annabel is no longer helpful. As you see, the decision whether to show or hide a node of the hierarchy depends on the depth of the node. We can let a user expand Annabel up to the second level of the hierarchy, but we surely want to remove the third level of Annabel.

We can store the length of the path needed to reach the row into a calculated column. The length of the path shows that Annabel is a root node. Indeed, it is a node of level 1 with a path containing one value only. Catherine, on the other hand, is a node of level 2 because she is a daughter of Annabel and the path of Catherine is of length 2. Moreover, although it might not be so evident, Catherine is visible at level 1 because her value is aggregated under the first node of Annabel. In other words, even though the name of Catherine is not present in the report at level 1, her amount is aggregated under her parent, which is Annabel. The name of Catherine is visible because her row contains Annabel as *Level1*.

Once we know the level of each node in the hierarchy, we can define that each node be visible whenever the report browses the hierarchy up to its level. When the report shows a level that is too deep, then the node needs to be hidden. To implement this algorithm, two values are needed:

- The depth of each node; this is a fixed value for each row of the hierarchy, and as such, it can safely be stored in a calculated column.

- The current browsing depth of the report visual; this is a dynamic value that depends on the current filter context. It needs to be a measure because its value changes depending on the report and it has a different value for each row of the report. For example, Annabel is a node at level 1, but she appears in three rows because the current depth of the report has three different values.

The depth of each node is easy to compute. We can add a new calculated column to the *Persons* table with this simple expression:

```
Persons[NodeDepth] = PATHLENGTH ( Persons[FullPath] )
```

PATHLENGTH returns the length of a value computed by *PATH*. You can see the resulting calculated column in Figure 11-14.

PersonKey	Name	FullPath	Level1	Level2	Level3	NodeDepth
1	Bill	1	Bill	Bill	Bill	1
2	Brad	1|2	Bill	Brad	Brad	2
3	Julie	1|3	Bill	Julie	Julie	2
4	Chris	1|2|4	Bill	Brad	Chris	3
5	Vincent	1|2|5	Bill	Brad	Vincent	3
6	Annabel	6	Annabel	Annabel	Annabel	1
7	Catherine	6|7	Annabel	Catherine	Catherine	2
8	Harry	6|8	Annabel	Harry	Harry	2
9	Michael	6|9	Annabel	Michael	Michael	2

FIGURE 11-14 The *NodeDepth* column stores the depth of each node in a calculated column.

The *NodeDepth* column is easy to create. Computing the browsing depth is more difficult because it needs to be computed in a measure. Nevertheless, the logic behind it is not very complex, and it is similar to the technique you have already learned for standard hierarchies. The measure uses *ISIN-SCOPE* to discover which of the hierarchy columns is filtered versus not.

Moreover, the formula takes advantage of the fact that a *Boolean* value can be converted to a number, where *TRUE* has a value of 1 and *FALSE* has a value of 0:

```
BrowseDepth :=
ISINSCOPE ( Persons[Level1] ) +
ISINSCOPE ( Persons[Level2] ) +
ISINSCOPE ( Persons[Level3] )
```

Thus, if only *Level1* is filtered, then the result is 1. If both *Level1* and *Level2* are filtered, but not *Level3*, then the result is 2, and so on. You can see the result for the *BrowseDepth* measure in Figure 11-15.

Level1	Amount	BrowseDepth
Annabel	3200	1
Annabel	600	2
Annabel	600	3
Catherine	1200	2
Catherine	1200	3
Harry	800	2
Harry	800	3
Michael	600	2
Michael	600	3

FIGURE 11-15 The *BrowseDepth* measure computes the depth of browsing in the report.

We are nearing the resolution of the scenario. The last piece of information we need is that by default, a report will hide rows that result in a blank value for all the displayed measures. Specifically, we are going to use this behavior to hide the unwanted rows. By transforming the value of *Amount* into a blank when we do not want it to appear in the report, we will be able to hide rows from the matrix. Thus, the solution is going to use these elements:

- The depth of each node, in the *NodeDepth* calculated column,

- The depth of the current cell in the report, in the *BrowseDepth* measure,

- A way to hide unwanted rows, by means of blanking the value of the result.

It is time to merge all this information into a single measure, as follows:

```
PC Amount :=
IF (
    MAX (Persons[NodeDepth]) < [BrowseDepth],
    BLANK (),
    SUM(Sales[Amount])
)
```

To understand how this measure works, look at the report in Figure 11-16. It contains all the values that are useful to grasp the behavior of the formula.

Level1	Amount	BrowseDepth	MaxNodeDepth	PC Amount
Annabel	**3200**	**1**	**2**	**3,200**
Annabel	**600**	2	1	
Annabel	600	3	1	
Catherine	**1200**	2	**2**	**1,200**
Catherine	1200	3	2	
Harry	**800**	2	**2**	**800**
Harry	800	3	2	
Michael	**600**	2	**2**	**600**
Michael	600	3	2	
Bill	**1600**	**1**	**3**	**1,600**
Bill		2	1	
Bill		3	1	

FIGURE 11-16 This report shows the result and all the partial measures used by the formula.

If you look at Annabel in the first row, you see that *BrowseDepth* equals 1 because this is the root of the hierarchy. *MaxNodeDepth,* which is defined as *MAX (Persons[NodeDepth]),* has a value of 2—meaning that the current node is not only showing data at level 1, but also data for some children that are at level 2. Thus, the current node is showing data for some children too, and for this reason it needs to be visible. The second line of Annabel, on the other hand, has a *BrowseDepth* of 2 and a *MaxNodeDepth* of 1. The reason is that the filter context filters all the rows where *Level1* equals Annabel and *Level2* equals Annabel, and there is only one row in the hierarchy satisfying this condition—this is Annabel herself. But Annabel has a *NodeDepth* of 1, and because the report is browsing at level 2, we need to hide the node. Indeed, the *PC Amount* measure returns a blank.

It is useful to verify the behavior for other nodes by yourself. This way you can improve your understanding of how the formula is working. Although one can simply return to this part of the book and copy the formula whenever they need to, understanding it is a good exercise because it forces you to think in terms of how the filter context interacts with various parts of the formula.

To reach the result, the last step is to remove all the columns that are not needed from the report, leaving *PC Amount* alone. The visualization becomes the one we wanted, as you can see in Figure 11-17.

Level1	PC Amount
Annabel	**3,200**
Catherine	**1,200**
Harry	**800**
Michael	**600**
Bill	**1,600**
Brad	**1,300**
Chris	400
Vincent	500
Julie	**300**
Total	**4,800**

FIGURE 11-17 Once the measure is left alone in the report, all unwanted rows disappear.

The biggest drawback of this approach is that the same pattern has to be used for any measure a user may add to the report after the P/C hierarchy is in place. If a measure that does not have a blank for unwanted rows is being used as a value, then all the rows will suddenly appear and disrupt the pattern.

At this point, the result is already satisfactory. Yet there is still a small problem. Indeed, if you look at the total of Annabel, it is 3,200. Summed up, her children show a total of 2,600. There is a missing amount of 600, which is the value of Annabel herself. Some might already be satisfied by this visualization: The value of a node is easy to calculate, by simply looking at the difference between its total and the total of its children. However, if you compare this figure to the original goal, you see that in the final formula, the value of each node is clearly visible as a child of the node itself. The comparison is visible in Figure 11-18, which shows the current and the desired results together.

Level1	PC Amount	FinalFormula
Annabel	**3,200**	**3,200**
Annabel		**600**
Catherine	**1,200**	**1,200**
Harry	**800**	**800**
Michael	**600**	**600**
Bill	**1,600**	**1,600**
Brad	**1,300**	**1,300**
Brad		400
Chris	400	400
Vincent	500	500
Julie	**300**	**300**
Total	**4,800**	**4,800**

FIGURE 11-18 The original goal has not been reached yet. We still need to show some rows.

At this point, the technique should be clear enough. To show a value for Annabel, we need to find a condition that lets us identify it as a node that should be made visible. In this case, the condition is somewhat complex. The nodes that need to be made visible are non-leaf nodes—that is, they have children—that have values for themselves. The code will make those nodes visible for one additional level. All other nodes—that is, leaf nodes or nodes with no value associated—will follow the original rule and be hidden when the hierarchy is browsing over their depth.

First, we need to create a calculated column in the *PC* table that indicates whether a node is a leaf. The DAX expression is easy: leaves are nodes that are not parents of any other node. In order to check the condition, we can count the number of nodes that have the current node as their parent. If it equals zero, then we know that the current node is a leaf. The following code does this:

```
Persons[IsLeaf] =
VAR CurrentPersonKey = Persons[PersonKey]
VAR PersonsAtParentLevel =
    CALCULATE (
        COUNTROWS ( Persons ),
        ALL ( Persons ),
        Persons[ParentKey] = CurrentPersonKey
    )
VAR Result = ( PersonsAtParentLevel = 0 )
RETURN Result
```

In Figure 11-19, the *IsLeaf* column has been added to the data model.

PersonKey	Name	ParentKey	FullPath	Level1	Level2	Level3	NodeDepth	IsLeaf
1	Bill	1		Bill	Bill	Bill	1	False
2	Brad	1	1|2	Bill	Brad	Brad	2	False
3	Julie	1	1|3	Bill	Julie	Julie	2	True
4	Chris	2	1|2|4	Bill	Brad	Chris	3	True
5	Vincent	2	1|2|5	Bill	Brad	Vincent	3	True
6	Annabel	6		Annabel	Annabel	Annabel	1	False
7	Catherine	6	6|7	Annabel	Catherine	Catherine	2	True
8	Harry	6	6|8	Annabel	Harry	Harry	2	True
9	Michael	6	6|9	Annabel	Michael	Michael	2	True

FIGURE 11-19 The *IsLeaf* column indicates which nodes are leaves of the hierarchy.

Now that we can identify leaves, it is time to write the final formula for handling the P/C hierarchy:

```
FinalFormula =
VAR TooDeep = [MaxNodeDepth] + 1 < [BrowseDepth]
VAR AdditionalLevel = [MaxNodeDepth] + 1 = [BrowseDepth]
VAR Amount =
    SUM ( Sales[Amount] )
VAR HasData =
    NOT ISBLANK ( Amount )
VAR Leaf =
```

```
    SELECTEDVALUE (
        Persons[IsLeaf],
        FALSE
    )
VAR Result =
    IF (
        NOT TooDeep,
        IF (
            AdditionalLevel,
            IF (
                NOT Leaf && HasData,
                Amount
            ),
            Amount
        )
    )
RETURN
    Result
```

The use of variables makes the formula easier to read. Here are some comments about their usage:

- *TooDeep* checks if the browsing depth is greater than the maximum node depth plus one; that is, it checks whether the browsing of the report is over the additional level.

- *AdditionalLevel* checks if the current browsing level is the additional level for nodes that have values for themselves and that are not leaves.

- *HasData* checks if a node itself has a value.

- *Leaf* checks whether a node is a leaf or not.

- *Result* is the final result of the formula, making it easy to change the measure result to inspect intermediate steps during development.

The remaining part of the code is just a set of *IF* statements that check the various scenarios and behave accordingly.

It is clear that if the data model had the ability to handle P/C hierarchies natively, then all this hard work would have been avoided. After all, this is not an easy formula to digest because it requires a full understanding of evaluation contexts and data modeling.

> **Important**   If the model is in compatibility level 1400, you can enable the behavior of a special property called Hide Members. Hide Members automatically hides blank members. This property is unavailable in Power BI and in Power Pivot as of April 2019. A complete description of how to use this property in a Tabular model is available at https://docs.microsoft.com/en-us/sql/analysis-services/what-s-new-in-sql-server-analysis-services-2017?view=sql-server-2017. In case the tool you are using implements this important feature, then we strongly suggest using the Hide Members property instead of implementing the complex DAX code shown above to hide levels of an unbalanced hierarchy.

Conclusions

In this chapter you learned how to correctly handle calculations over hierarchies. As usual, we now recap the most relevant topics covered in the chapter:

- Hierarchies are not part of DAX. They can be built in the model, but from a DAX point of view there is no way to reference a hierarchy and use it inside an expression.

- In order to detect the level of a hierarchy, one needs to use *ISINSCOPE*. Although it is a simple workaround, *ISINSCOPE* does not actually detect the browsing level; rather, it detects the presence of a filter on a column.

- Computing simple percentages over the parent requires the ability to both analyze the current level of a hierarchy and create a suitable set of filters to recreate the filter of the parent.

- Parent/child hierarchies can be handled in DAX by using the predefined *PATH* function and by building a proper set of columns, one for each level of the hierarchy.

- Unary operators, often used in parent/child hierarchies, can prove to be a challenge; they can therefore be handled in their simpler version (only +/-) by authoring rather complex DAX code. Handling more complex scenarios requires even more complicated DAX code, which is beyond the scope of this chapter.

Working with tables

Tables are an important part of DAX formulas. In previous chapters you learned how to iterate over tables, how to create calculated tables, and how to perform several other calculation techniques that require a table as their starting point. Moreover, *CALCULATE* filter arguments are tables: When authoring complex formulas, an ability to build the correct filter table is of paramount importance. DAX offers a rich set of functions to manage tables. In this chapter we introduce many DAX functions that are helpful for creating and managing tables.

For most of the new functions, we provide some examples that are useful for two purposes: They show how to use the function, and they act as a good DAX exercise to understand how to write complex measures.

Using *CALCULATETABLE*

The first function to manipulate tables is *CALCULATETABLE*. We have already used *CALCULATETABLE* multiple times in the book prior to this point. In this section we provide a more complete reference to the function, along with some considerations about when to use it.

CALCULATETABLE performs the same operations as *CALCULATE*, the only difference being in their result. *CALCULATETABLE* returns a table, whereas *CALCULATE* returns a single value like an integer or a string. As an example, if one needs to produce a table containing only red products, then *CALCULATETABLE* is the function to use:

```
CALCULATETABLE (
    'Product',
    'Product'[Color] = "Red"
)
```

A common question is what the difference is between *CALCULATETABLE* and *FILTER*. Indeed, the previous expression can be written with *FILTER* too:

```
FILTER (
    'Product',
    'Product'[Color] = "Red"
)
```

Even though the only difference seems to be the function name, in reality the semantics of these two functions are very different. *CALCULATETABLE* operates by changing the filter context first and later evaluating the expression. *FILTER*, on the other hand, iterates the result of its first argument, retrieving the rows that satisfy the condition. In other words, *FILTER* does not change the filter context.

You can appreciate the difference by reviewing the following example:

```
Red Products CALCULATETABLE =
CALCULATETABLE (
    ADDCOLUMNS (
        VALUES ( 'Product'[Color] ),
        "Num of Products", COUNTROWS ( 'Product' )
    ),
    'Product'[Color] = "Red"
)
```

The result is in Figure 12-1.

Color	Num of Products
Red	99

FIGURE 12-1 There are 99 red products in the Contoso database.

By using *CALCULATETABLE*, the filter context where both *ADDCOLUMNS* and COUNTROWS are evaluated is filtering red products. Therefore, the result is one row only that contains red as color and 99 as number of products. In other words, *COUNTROWS* only counted the red products, without requiring a context transition from the row generated by the *VALUES* function.

If one replaces *CALCULATETABLE* with *FILTER*, the result is different. Look at the following table:

```
Red Products FILTER external =
FILTER (
    ADDCOLUMNS (
        VALUES ( 'Product'[Color] ),
        "Num of Products", COUNTROWS ( 'Product' )
    ),
    'Product'[Color] = "Red"
)
```

This time, the result is no longer 99; instead, it shows the total number of products, as shown in Figure 12-2.

Color	Num of Products
Red	2517

FIGURE 12-2 Although it shows a single line with Red, *Num of Products* counts all the products.

This table still contains Red for the product color, but now the number of products computes 2,517, which is the total number of products. The reason is that *FILTER* does not change the filter context. Moreover, *FILTER* is evaluated after *ADDCOLUMNS*. Consequently, *ADDCOLUMNS* iterates all the products, and *COUNTROWS* computes the total number of products because there is no context transition. Only later does *FILTER* select the Red row out of all the colors.

If one uses *FILTER* instead of *CALCULATETABLE*, the expression must be written differently, relying on *CALCULATE* to force the context transition:

```
Red Products FILTER internal =
ADDCOLUMNS (
    FILTER (
        VALUES ( 'Product'[Color] ),
        'Product'[Color] = "Red"
    ),
    "Num of Products", CALCULATE ( COUNTROWS ( 'Product' ) )
)
```

Now the result is back to 99. In order to obtain the same behavior as *CALCULATETABLE*, we needed to invert the execution order. This way *FILTER* runs first, and then the calculation of the number of rows relies on the context transition to force the row context of *ADDCOLUMNS* to become a filter context for *COUNTROWS*.

CALCULATETABLE works by modifying the filter context. It is powerful because it propagates its effect to multiple functions in a DAX expression. Its power comes with limitations in the type of filtering it can create. For example, *CALCULATETABLE* can only apply filters to columns that belong to the data model. If one only needs the customer whose sales amount is greater than one million, then *CALCULATE-TABLE* is not the right choice because *Sales Amount* is a measure. Therefore, *CALCULATETABLE* cannot apply a filter on a measure, whereas *FILTER* can. This is shown in the following expression; replacing *FILTER* with *CALCULATETABLE* is not an option, as it would lead to a syntax error:

```
Large Customers =
FILTER (
    Customer,
    [Sales Amount] > 1000000
)
```

CALCULATETABLE—like *CALCULATE*—performs a context transition and can have all the *CALCU-LATE* modifiers like *ALL*, *USERELATIONSHIPS*, *CROSSFILTER*, and many others. Consequently, it is much more powerful than *FILTER*. This is not to say that one should always try to use *CALCULATETABLE* and stop using *FILTER*. Each of the two functions has advantages and disadvantages, and the choice needs to be an educated one.

As a rule of thumb, one uses *CALCULATETABLE* whenever they need to apply a filter on a model column and/or there is the need for the other functionalities of *CALCULATETABLE*, like context transition and filter context modifiers.

Manipulating tables

DAX offers several functions to manipulate tables. These functions can be used to create new calculated tables, to create tables to iterate on, or to use their results as filter arguments in *CALCULATE*. In this section we provide a complete reference of those functions, along with examples. There are also other table functions that are mainly useful in queries. We show them in Chapter 13, "Authoring queries."

Using *ADDCOLUMNS*

ADDCOLUMNS is an iterator that returns all the rows and columns of its first argument, adding newly created columns to the output. For example, the following calculated table definition produces a table with all the colors and the value of sales amount for each color:

```
ColorsWithSales =
ADDCOLUMNS (
    VALUES ( 'Product'[Color] ),
    "Sales Amount", [Sales Amount]
)
```

You can see the result in Figure 12-3.

Color	Sales Amount
Silver	6,798,560.86
Blue	2,435,444.62
White	5,829,599.91
Red	1,110,102.10
Black	5,860,066.14
Green	1,403,184.38
Orange	857,320.28
Pink	828,638.54
Yellow	89,715.56
Purple	5,973.84
Brown	1,029,508.95
Grey	3,509,138.09
Gold	361,496.01
Azure	97,389.89
Silver Grey	371,908.92
Transparent	3,295.89

FIGURE 12-3 The result contains all the product colors and the sales amount for each color.

Being an iterator, *ADDCOLUMNS* evaluates the column expressions in a row context. In this example, it computes the sales of the given product color because the expression of *Sales Amount* uses a measure. Thus, there is an automatic *CALCULATE* surrounding *Sales Amount* that generates the context transition. If one uses a regular expression instead of a measure, then *CALCULATE* is frequently used to force the context transition.

ADDCOLUMNS is oftentimes used in conjunction with *FILTER* to obtain filters on temporary calculated columns. For example, to compute the products that sold more than 150,000.00 USD, a possible implementation is the following one:

```
HighSalesProducts =
VAR ProductsWithSales =
    ADDCOLUMNS (
```

```
        VALUES ( 'Product'[Product Name] ),
        "Product Sales", [Sales Amount]
    )
VAR Result =
    FILTER (
        ProductsWithSales,
        [Product Sales] >= 150000
    )
RETURN Result
```

You can see the result in Figure 12-4.

Product Name	Product Sales
Adventure Works 26" 720p LCD HDTV M140 Silver	1,303,983.46
SV 16xDVD M360 Black	364,714.41
Proseware Projector 1080p LCD86 Silver	160,627.05
Contoso Projector 1080p X980 White	257,154.75
A. Datum SLR Camera X137 Grey	725,840.28
Fabrikam Independent filmmaker 1/3" 8.5mm X200 White	165,594.00
Contoso Telephoto Conversion Lens X400 Silver	683,779.95
NT Washer & Dryer 27in L2700 Blue	151,427.53
Contoso Washer & Dryer 21in E210 Green	151,265.40
Contoso Washer & Dryer 21in E210 Pink	182,094.12

FIGURE 12-4 The result contains all the product names and the sales amount for each name.

The same expression can be written in several different ways, even without using *ADDCOLUMNS*. The following code, for example, ends up even simpler than the previous one, even though it does not add a *Product Sales* column to the output:

```
FILTER (
    VALUES ( 'Product'[Product Name] ),
    [Sales Amount] >= 150000
)
```

ADDCOLUMNS is useful to compute multiple columns or when further calculations are needed after this first step. For example, consider computing the set of products that together represent 15% of total sales. This calculation is no longer trivial because several steps are needed:

1. Computing the sales amount for each product.

2. Computing a running total of sales amount, by aggregating each product with all the products that sold more than the product itself.

3. Transforming the running total into a percentage against the grand total of sales.

4. Only returning the products whose percentage is less than or equal to 15%.

Authoring the full query in a single step is unnecessarily complex, whereas splitting the evaluation in four steps proves much easier:

```
Top Products =
VAR TotalSales = [Sales Amount]
VAR ProdsWithSales =
    ADDCOLUMNS (
        VALUES ( 'Product'[Product Name] ),
        "ProductSales", [Sales Amount]
    )
VAR ProdsWithRT =
    ADDCOLUMNS (
        ProdsWithSales,
        "RunningTotal",
        VAR SalesOfCurrentProduct = [ProductSales]
        RETURN
            SUMX (
                FILTER (
                    ProdsWithSales,
                    [ProductSales] >= SalesOfCurrentProduct
                ),
                [ProductSales]
            )
    )
VAR Top15Percent =
    FILTER (
        ProdsWithRT,
        [RunningTotal] / TotalSales <= 0.15
    )
RETURN Top15Percent
```

You can see the result in Figure 12-5.

Product Name	ProductSales	RunningTotal
Adventure Works 26" 720p LCD HDTV M140 Silver	1,303,983.46	1,303,983.46
SV 16xDVD M360 Black	364,714.41	3,078,318.10
Fabrikam Laptop19 M9000 Black	144,133.85	4,290,614.80
Proseware Projector 1080p LCD86 Silver	160,627.05	3,843,788.02
Contoso Projector 1080p X980 White	257,154.75	3,335,472.85
A. Datum SLR Camera X137 Grey	725,840.28	2,029,823.74
Fabrikam Independent filmmaker 1/3'' 8.5mm X200 White	165,594.00	3,683,160.97
Contoso Telephoto Conversion Lens X400 Silver	683,779.95	2,713,603.69
NT Washer & Dryer 27in L2700 Blue	151,427.53	3,995,215.55
NT Washer & Dryer 27in L2700 Green	137,605.92	4,428,220.72
Contoso Washer & Dryer 21in E210 Green	151,265.40	4,146,480.95
Contoso Washer & Dryer 21in E210 Pink	182,094.12	3,517,566.97
Litware Refrigerator 24.7CuFt X980 White	135,039.58	4,563,260.30

FIGURE 12-5 The result contains the top products that generate 15% of sales.

In the example, we implemented the result as a calculated table, but other uses are possible. For example, one could iterate the *Top15Percent* variable using *SUMX* to create a measure computing the sales of those products.

As with most other DAX functions, one should think of *ADDCOLUMNS* as one of the many building blocks of DAX. The real power of DAX unfolds when you learn how to leverage those building blocks and have them interact in more sophisticated calculations.

Using *SUMMARIZE*

SUMMARIZE is one of the most commonly used functions in DAX. It scans a table (its first argument), grouping columns of the same or other related tables in groups of one or more. The main use of *SUM-MARIZE* is to only retrieve an existing combination of values, rather than the full list of values.

An example would be computing the number of distinct colors sold, to produce a report that shows the number of colors available and the number of colors sold at least once. The following measures would produce the desired result:

```
Num of colors :=
COUNTROWS (
    VALUES ( 'Product'[Color] )
)

Num of colors sold :=
COUNTROWS (
    SUMMARIZE ( Sales, 'Product'[Color] )
)
```

You can see the result of these two measures by brand in the report in Figure 12-6.

Calendar Year Month February 2007		
Brand	**Num of colors**	**Num of colors sold**
A. Datum	10	7
Adventure Works	7	6
Contoso	15	9
Fabrikam	12	7
Litware	12	7
Northwind Traders	9	2
Proseware	7	6
Southridge Video	10	5
Tailspin Toys	11	3
The Phone Company	6	4
Wide World Importers	12	6
Total	**16**	**13**

FIGURE 12-6 *Num of colors sold* uses *SUMMARIZE* to compute the number of colors sold.

In this case we used *SUMMARIZE* to group the sales by *Product[Color]*, and then we counted the number of rows in the result. Because *SUMMARIZE* performs a group by, it only returns the colors referenced by *Sales*. On the other hand, *VALUES (Product[Color])* returns all the existing colors whether they have sales or not.

Using *SUMMARIZE*, one can group data by any number of columns, provided that the columns used as parameters are reachable from *Sales* only when following many-to-one or one-to-one relationships. For example, to compute the average quantity sold per product and per day, this is one possible implementation:

```
AvgDailyQty :=
VAR ProductsDatesWithSales =
    SUMMARIZE (
        Sales,
        'Product'[Product Name],
        'Date'[Date]
    )
VAR Result =
    AVERAGEX (
        ProductsDatesWithSales,
        CALCULATE (
            SUM ( Sales[Quantity] )
        )
    )
RETURN Result
```

You can see the result of this measure in Figure 12-7.

Brand	CY 2007	CY 2008	CY 2009	Total
A. Datum	17.68	13.76	15.78	**15.93**
Adventure Works	24.07	13.77	17.85	**18.93**
Contoso	19.88	20.41	31.37	**23.99**
Fabrikam	12.02	14.13	15.69	**13.91**
Litware	9.67	12.99	18.50	**13.99**
Northwind Traders	24.24	12.84	13.87	**16.99**
Proseware	10.28	13.38	16.70	**13.41**
Southridge Video	28.07	17.28	22.86	**23.56**
Tailspin Toys	12.33	20.24	35.85	**22.44**
The Phone Company	11.32	12.77	13.13	**12.37**
Wide World Importers	11.79	15.19	16.70	**14.78**
Total	**17.20**	**16.37**	**22.79**	**18.75**

FIGURE 12-7 The report shows the average daily sales quantity per year and per brand.

In this case, we used *SUMMARIZE* to scan *Sales* and to group it by product name and by date. The resulting table contains the product name and the date, only considering days with sales for that product. *AVERAGEX* takes care of computing the average over each row of the temporary table returned by

SUMMARIZE. If there are no sales for a certain product on any given day, then the resulting table will not contain that date.

SUMMARIZE can also be used like *ADDCOLUMNS* to add further columns to the result. For example, the previous measure could also be authored the following way:

```
AvgDailyQty :=
VAR ProductsDatesWithSalesAndQuantity =
    SUMMARIZE (
        Sales,
        'Product'[Product Name],
        'Date'[Date],
        "Daily qty", SUM ( Sales[Quantity] )
    )
VAR Result =
    AVERAGEX (
        ProductsDatesWithSalesAndQuantity,
        [Daily qty]
    )
RETURN Result
```

In this case *SUMMARIZE* returns a table that contains the product name, the date, and a newly introduced column named *Daily qty*. *Daily qty* is later averaged by *AVERAGEX*. Nevertheless, **the use of SUMMARIZE to create temporary columns is deprecated** because *SUMMARIZE* creates one row context and one filter context at the same time. For this reason, results are complex to understand when a context transition is generated in the expression by referencing either a measure or an explicit *CALCULATE* function. If one needs to compute additional columns after *SUMMARIZE* has performed the grouping operation, then it is better to use a pair of *ADDCOLUMNS* and *SUMMARIZE* together:

```
AvgDailyQty :=
VAR ProductsDatesWithSales =
    SUMMARIZE (
        Sales,
        'Product'[Product Name],
        'Date'[Date]
    )
VAR ProductsDatesWithSalesAndQuantity =
    ADDCOLUMNS (
        ProductsDatesWithSales,
        "Daily qty", CALCULATE ( SUM ( Sales[Quantity] ) )
    )
VAR Result =
    AVERAGEX (
        ProductsDatesWithSalesAndQuantity,
        [Daily qty]
    )
RETURN Result
```

Despite the code being more verbose, it is much easier to read and write because there is a single row context used in a context transition. This row context is introduced by *ADDCOLUMNS* while iterating over the result of *SUMMARIZE*. This pattern results in simpler (and most of the times faster) code.

It is possible to use more—optional—parameters with *SUMMARIZE*. They exist for the calculation of subtotals and to add columns to the result. We deliberately decided not to write about them to make the point even stronger: *SUMMARIZE works fine when grouping tables and should not be used to compute additional columns.* Although you can find code on the web that still uses *SUMMARIZE* to author new columns, consider it a very bad practice and always replace it with the pair *ADDCOLUMNS/ SUMMARIZE.*

Using *CROSSJOIN*

CROSSJOIN performs the cross-join of two tables, returning the cartesian product of the two input tables. In other words, it returns all possible combinations of the values in the input tables. For example, the following expression returns all the combinations of product names and years:

```
CROSSJOIN (
    ALL ( 'Product'[Product Name] ),
    ALL ( 'Date'[Calendar Year] )
)
```

If the model contains 1,000 product names and five years, the resulting table contains 5,000 rows. *CROSSJOIN* is more often used in queries than in measures. Nevertheless, there are some scenarios where the use of *CROSSJOIN* becomes relevant—mostly because of performance.

For example, consider the need for an *OR* condition between two different columns in a *CALCULATE* filter argument. Because *CALCULATE* merges its filter arguments with an intersection, implementing the *OR* condition requires closer attention. For example, this is a possible implementation of *CALCULATE* filtering all the products that belong to the Audio category or have a Black color:

```
AudioOrBlackSales :=
VAR CategoriesColors =
    SUMMARIZE (
        'Product',
        'Product'[Category],
        'Product'[Color]
    )
VAR AudioOrBlack =
    FILTER (
        CategoriesColors,
        OR (
            'Product'[Category] = "Audio",
            'Product'[Color] = "Black"
        )
    )
VAR Result =
    CALCULATE (
        [Sales Amount],
        AudioOrBlack
    )
RETURN Result
```

The previous code works well, and it is optimal also from a performance point of view. *SUMMARIZE* scans the *Product* table, which is expected to contain a small number of rows. Thus, the evaluation of the filter is very quick.

If the requirement is to filter columns from different tables like color and year, then things are different. Indeed, one could extend the previous example; but to summarize by columns from two separate tables, *SUMMARIZE* needs to scan the *Sales* table:

```
AudioOr2007 Sales :=
VAR CategoriesYears =
    SUMMARIZE (
        Sales,
        'Product'[Category],
        'Date'[Calendar Year]
    )
VAR Audio2007 =
    FILTER (
        CategoriesYears,
        OR (
            'Product'[Category] = "Audio",
            'Date'[Calendar Year] = "CY 2007"
        )
    )
VAR Result =
    CALCULATE (
        [Sales Amount],
        Audio2007
    )
RETURN Result
```

Sales is not a small table; it might contain hundreds of millions of rows. Scanning it to retrieve the existing combinations of category and years could result in an expensive operation. Regardless, the resulting filter is not going to be large because there are only a few categories and years, yet the engine needs to scan a large table to retrieve the filter.

In that scenario, we recommend you build all the combinations of category and year, producing a small table; you would then filter that table, as in the following code:

```
AudioOr2007 Sales :=
VAR CategoriesYears =
    CROSSJOIN (
        VALUES ( 'Product'[Category] ),
        VALUES ( 'Date'[Calendar Year] )
    )
VAR Audio2007 =
    FILTER (
        CategoriesYears,
        OR (
            'Product'[Category] = "Audio",
            'Date'[Calendar Year] = "CY 2007"
        )
    )
```

```
VAR Result =
    CALCULATE (
        [Sales Amount],
        Audio2007
    )
RETURN Result
```

The full *CROSSJOIN* of categories and years contains a few hundred rows and the execution of this last version of the measure is faster.

CROSSJOIN is not only useful to speed up calculations. Sometimes, one is interested in retrieving rows even when no event happened. For example, by using *SUMMARIZE* to scan sales by category and country, the result only contains the categories and countries with sales for certain products. This is the intended behavior of *SUMMARIZE*, so it is not surprising. However, sometimes the absence of an event is more important than its presence. For example, one might want to investigate which brands have no sales in certain regions. In that case, the measure needs to build a more complex expression involving a *CROSSJOIN*, so to be able to also retrieve nonexistent combinations of values. We will provide more examples of *CROSSJOIN* in the next chapter.

Using *UNION*

UNION is a set function that performs the union of two tables. The ability to combine different tables into a single table can be important in certain circumstances. It is mainly used in calculated tables, much less frequently in measures. For example, the following table contains all the countries from both the *Customer* and the *Store* tables:

```
AllCountryRegions =
UNION (
    ALL ( Customer[CountryRegion] ),
    ALL ( Store[CountryRegion] )
)
```

You can look at the result in Figure 12-8.

CountryRegion
Australia
Australia
United States
United States
Canada
Canada
Germany
Germany
United Kingdom
United Kingdom

FIGURE 12-8 *UNION* does not remove duplicates.

UNION does not remove duplicates before returning a result. Thus, if Australia belongs to the countries of both customers and stores, it appears twice in the resulting table. If needed, leveraging the DISTINCT function will remove duplicates.

We have described and used DISTINCT multiple times prior to this point, to obtain the distinct values of a column as visible in the current filter context. DISTINCT can also be used with a table expression as a parameter, and in that special case it returns the distinct rows of the table. Thus, the following is a good implementation removing potential duplicates from the CountryRegion column:

```
DistinctCountryRegions =
VAR CountryRegions =
    UNION (
        ALL ( Customer[CountryRegion] ),
        ALL ( Store[CountryRegion] )
    )
VAR UniqueCountryRegions =
    DISTINCT ( CountryRegions )
RETURN UniqueCountryRegions
```

You can see the resulting table in Figure 12-9.

CountryRegion
Australia
United States
Canada
Germany
United Kingdom
France
the Netherlands
Greece
Switzerland

FIGURE 12-9 DISTINCT removes duplicates from a table.

UNION maintains the data lineage of the input tables if the lineage of both tables is the same. In the previous formula, the result of DISTINCT has no lineage because the first table contains Customer[CountryRegion], and the second table contains Store[CountryRegion]. Because the data lineage of the input tables is different, the result has a new lineage not corresponding to any of the existing columns. Therefore, the following calculated table returns the same grand total of sales on all the rows:

```
DistinctCountryRegions =
VAR CountryRegions =
    UNION (
        ALL ( Customer[CountryRegion] ),
        ALL ( Store[CountryRegion] )
    )
```

```
VAR UniqueCountryRegions =
    DISTINCT ( CountryRegions )
VAR Result =
    ADDCOLUMNS (
        UniqueCountryRegions,
        "Sales Amount", [Sales Amount]
    )
RETURN Result
```

The result is presented in Figure 12-10.

CountryRegion	Sales Amount
Australia	30,591,343.98
United States	30,591,343.98
Canada	30,591,343.98
Germany	30,591,343.98
United Kingdom	30,591,343.98
France	30,591,343.98
the Netherlands	30,591,343.98
Greece	30,591,343.98

FIGURE 12-10 *CountryRegion* is not a column in the model. Therefore, it does not filter *Sales Amount*.

If the calculated table needs to contain both the sales amount and the number of stores, including all country regions of both customers and stores, then the filtering must be handled manually through a more complex expression:

```
DistinctCountryRegions =
VAR CountryRegions =
    UNION (
        ALL ( Customer[CountryRegion] ),
        ALL ( Store[CountryRegion] )
    )
VAR UniqueCountryRegions =
    DISTINCT ( CountryRegions )
VAR Result =
    ADDCOLUMNS (
        UniqueCountryRegions,
        "Customer Sales Amount",
            VAR CurrentRegion = [CountryRegion]
            RETURN
                CALCULATE (
                    [Sales Amount],
                    Customer[CountryRegion] = CurrentRegion
                ),
        "Number of stores",
            VAR CurrentRegion = [CountryRegion]
            RETURN
                CALCULATE (
                    COUNTROWS ( Store ),
```

```
                            Store[CountryRegion] = CurrentRegion
                )
        )
RETURN Result
```

You see the result in Figure 12-11.

CountryRegion	Customer Sales Amount	Number of stores
Australia	7,638,059.94	3
United States	10,312,118.25	198
Canada	885,208.07	11
Germany	2,519,890.80	12
United Kingdom	3,621,032.16	15
France	1,109,665.43	8
the Netherlands	191,358.54	1
Greece	162,284.00	1
Switzerland	174,910.99	1
Ireland	130,595.28	1
Portugal	184,888.06	1
Spain	107,124.20	1
Italy	115,086.61	5

FIGURE 12-11 By using more complex *CALCULATE* statements, one can move the filter on stores and sales.

In the previous example *CALCULATE* applies a filter on either the customer or the store country region, using the value currently iterated by *ADDCOLUMN* on the result of *UNION*. Another option to obtain the same result is to restore the lineage using *TREATAS* (see Chapter 10, "Working with the filter context," for more information about *TREATAS*), as in the following equivalent expression:

```
DistinctCountryRegions =
VAR CountryRegions =
    UNION (
        ALL ( Customer[CountryRegion] ),
        ALL ( Store[CountryRegion] )
    )
VAR UniqueCountryRegions =
    DISTINCT ( CountryRegions )
VAR Result =
    ADDCOLUMNS (
        UniqueCountryRegions,
        "Customer Sales Amount", CALCULATE (
            [Sales Amount],
            TREATAS (
                { [CountryRegion] },
                Customer[CountryRegion]
            )
        ),
        "Number of stores", CALCULATE (
            COUNTROWS ( Store ),
            TREATAS (
                { [CountryRegion] },
```

```
                 Store[CountryRegion]
            )
        )
    )
RETURN Result
```

The result of our last two examples is the same; what differs is the technique used to move the filter from a new column to one that is part of the model. Moreover, in this last example you may notice the use of a table constructor: The curly braces transform *CountryRegion* into a table that can be used as a parameter of *TREATAS*.

Because *UNION* loses the data lineage if values come from different columns, *TREATAS* is a convenient function to control the data lineage of the result. It is worth noting that *TREATAS* ignores values that do not exist in the target columns.

Using *INTERSECT*

INTERSECT is a set function much like *UNION*. However, instead of appending one table to another, it returns the intersection of the two tables—that is, only the rows that appear in both tables. It was popular before the *TREATAS* function was introduced because it allows one to apply the result of a table expression as a filter to other tables and columns. Since the introduction of *TREATAS*, the number of use cases of *INTERSECT* was greatly reduced.

For example, if one needs to retrieve the customers who bought in both 2007 and 2008, a possible implementation is the following:

```
CustomersBuyingInTwoYears =
VAR Customers2007 =
    CALCULATETABLE (
        SUMMARIZE ( Sales, Customer[Customer Code] ),
        'Date'[Calendar Year] = "CY 2007"
    )
VAR Customers2008 =
    CALCULATETABLE (
        SUMMARIZE ( Sales, Customer[Customer Code] ),
        'Date'[Calendar Year] = "CY 2008"
    )
VAR Result =
    INTERSECT ( Customers2007, Customers2008 )
RETURN Result
```

From the lineage point of view, *INTERSECT* retains the data lineage of the first table. In the previous example, both tables have the same data lineage. If one builds a table with different data lineages, then only the lineage of the first table is kept. For example, the countries where there are both customers and stores can be expressed as follows:

```
INTERSECT (
    ALL ( Store[CountryRegion] ),
    ALL ( Customer[CountryRegion] )
)
```

In this latter example, the lineage is that of *Store[CountryRegion]*. Consequently, a more complex expression like the following returns the sales filtered by *Store[CountryRegion]*, not *Customer[CountryRegion]*:

```
SalesStoresInCustomersCountries =
VAR CountriesWithStoresAndCustomers =
    INTERSECT (
        ALL ( Store[CountryRegion] ),
        ALL ( Customer[CountryRegion] )
    )
VAR Result =
    ADDCOLUMNS (
        CountriesWithStoresAndCustomers,
        "StoresSales", [Sales Amount]
    )
RETURN Result
```

You see the result of this expression in Figure 12-12.

CountryRegion	StoresSales
United States	11,195,063.06
United Kingdom	
France	
Australia	
Canada	
Germany	8,670,581.01
Turkmenistan	
Thailand	
China	10,725,699.91
Kyrgyzstan	

FIGURE 12-12 *StoresSales* contains the sales in the store country, not the sales in the customer country.

In this latter example, the *StoresSales* column contains the sales related to the country of the store.

Using *EXCEPT*

EXCEPT is the last of the set functions introduced in this section. *EXCEPT* removes the rows present in the second table from the first table. As such, it implements set subtraction with two tables. For example, if one is interested in customers who bought a product in 2007 but not in 2008, one possible implementation is the following:

```
CustomersBuyingIn2007butNotIn2008 =
VAR Customers2007 =
    CALCULATETABLE (
        SUMMARIZE ( Sales, Customer[Customer Code] ),
```

```
            'Date'[Calendar Year] = "CY 2007"
    )
VAR Customers2008 =
    CALCULATETABLE (
        SUMMARIZE ( Sales, Customer[Customer Code] ),
        'Date'[Calendar Year] = "CY 2008"
    )
VAR Result =
    EXCEPT ( Customers2007, Customers2008 )
RETURN Result
```

The first rows of the calculated table are visible in Figure 12-13.

Customer Code
11005
11006
11007
11008

FIGURE 12-13 Partial list of customers that bought a product in 2007 but not in 2008.

As usual, one could use the previous calculation as a filter argument of *CALCULATE* to obtain the sales amount of those customers. *EXCEPT* is frequently used when analyzing customer behavior. For example, a common calculation for many businesses is establishing the number of new customers, returning customers, and lost customers.

There are several possible implementations of the same calculations, each one targeted to a specific data model. The following implementation is not always the most optimal, but it is flexible and easy to understand. To compute the number of customers who did not buy anything last year but bought something this year, the following measure removes customers who bought a product in the previous year from the set of current customers:

```
SalesOfNewCustomers :=
VAR CurrentCustomers =
    VALUES ( Sales[CustomerKey] )
VAR CustomersLastYear =
    CALCULATETABLE (
        VALUES ( Sales[CustomerKey] ),
        DATESINPERIOD ( 'Date'[Date], MIN ( 'Date'[Date] ) - 1, -1, YEAR )
    )
VAR CustomersNotInLastYear =
    EXCEPT ( CurrentCustomers, CustomersLastYear )
VAR Result =
    CALCULATE ( [Sales Amount], CustomersNotInLastYear )
RETURN Result
```

The implementation of this code as a measure works with any filter and provides a flexible way to slice by any column. Please be mindful that this implementation of new customers is not the best in terms of performance. We used it here to demonstrate a possible usage of *EXCEPT*. Later in this chapter we show a much faster version of the same calculation, although a bit more complex to learn.

From the lineage point of view, *EXCEPT* retains the data lineage of the first table, as was the case with *INTERSECT*. For example, the following expression computes the sales made to customers living in countries where there are no stores:

```
SalesInCountriesWithNoStores :=
VAR CountriesWithActiveStores =
    CALCULATETABLE (
        SUMMARIZE ( Sales, Store[CountryRegion] ),
        ALL ( Sales )
    )
VAR CountriesWithSales =
    SUMMARIZE ( Sales, Customer[CountryRegion] )
VAR CountriesWithNoStores =
    EXCEPT ( CountriesWithSales, CountriesWithActiveStores )
VAR Result =
    CALCULATE (
        [Sales Amount],
        CountriesWithNoStores
    )
RETURN Result
```

The result of *EXCEPT* filters the *Customer[CountryRegion]* column because it is the column used by the table taken as the first argument of *EXCEPT*.

Using tables as filters

Functions manipulating tables are oftentimes used to build complex filters for *CALCULATE* parameters. In this section, we provide further examples, always leading you one step further in your understanding of DAX.

Implementing *OR* conditions

A first example where manipulating tables proves to be a useful skill is the following. Imagine having to implement an *OR* condition between the selections made in different slicers, instead of the default *AND* behavior provided by client tools like Excel and Power BI.

The report in Figure 12-14 contains two slicers. The default behavior of Power BI is to intersect the two conditions. As a consequence, the numbers shown represent the sales of Home Appliances to customers with a High School education.

Category	⌄	Month	CY 2007	CY 2008	CY 2009	Total
☐ Audio		January	9,948.27	30,973.91		40,922.18
☐ Cameras and camcorders		February	6,155.43	4,639.68		10,795.11
☐ Cell phones		March	19,947.99	5,508.77	1,858.14	27,314.90
☐ Computers		April	37,120.39	73,178.22		110,298.61
☐ Games and Toys		May	13,040.21	12,076.70	18,901.77	44,018.68
■ Home Appliances		June	2,373.00	1,790.10	21,341.58	25,504.68
☐ Music, Movies and Audio Books		July	11,822.85	1,998.00	1,331.88	15,152.73
☐ TV and Video		August	28,309.82		3,596.40	31,906.22
Education		September	11,695.95	23,922.27		35,618.22
☐ (Blank)		October	17,096.80	24,700.44	7,959.60	49,756.84
☐ Bachelors		November	17,617.44	10,077.12	336.00	28,030.56
☐ Graduate Degree		December	29,998.16	10,101.60	9,943.68	50,043.44
■ High School		**Total**	**205,126.31**	**198,966.81**	**65,269.05**	**469,362.16**
☐ Partial College						
☐ Partial High School						

FIGURE 12-14 By default, slicer conditions are intersected so that all the conditions are applied together.

Instead of intersecting the two conditions, one might want to merge them. In other words, the numbers shown in the report need to be the sales of products sold to customers with a High School education or the sales of Home Appliances. Because Power BI does not support "or" conditions between slicers, one can solve the problem by using DAX.

Remember that each cell of the report has a filter context containing both a filter on the category and a filter on the education. Both filters need to be replaced. There are several possible solutions to the same pattern; we demonstrate the use of three different formulas.

The first, and probably the easiest expression of that filter, is the following:

```
OR 1 :=
VAR CategoriesEducations =
    CROSSJOIN (
        ALL ( 'Product'[Category] ),
        ALL ( Customer[Education] )
    )
VAR CategoriesEducationsSelected =
    FILTER (
        CategoriesEducations,
        OR (
            'Product'[Category] IN VALUES ( 'Product'[Category] ),
            Customer[Education] IN VALUES ( Customer[Education] )
        )
    )
VAR Result =
    CALCULATE (
        [Sales Amount],
        CategoriesEducationsSelected
    )
RETURN Result
```

The measure first builds the cross-join of all the categories and education levels. Once the table is prepared, it filters out the rows that do not satisfy the condition, and finally it uses the resulting table as a filter argument for *CALCULATE*. *CALCULATE* overrides the current filter on both the category and the education, resulting in the report in Figure 12-15.

Category ⌄	Month	CY 2007	CY 2008	CY 2009	**Total**
☐ Audio	January	262,512.08	260,921.71	262,686.39	**786,120.18**
☐ Cameras and camcorders	February	225,024.45	181,594.36	203,901.13	**610,519.94**
☐ Cell phones	March	242,516.02	235,588.38	155,285.26	**633,389.66**
☐ Computers	April	432,992.41	510,691.71	237,981.77	**1,181,665.89**
☐ Games and Toys	May	258,641.80	406,915.71	481,154.70	**1,146,712.21**
■ Home Appliances	June	201,855.29	350,851.26	339,850.92	**892,557.47**
☐ Music, Movies and Audio Books	July	251,993.38	407,779.81	361,962.95	**1,021,736.13**
☐ TV and Video	August	287,874.68	338,909.58	245,665.31	**872,449.58**
Education ⌄	September	186,553.63	342,886.85	224,487.70	**753,928.18**
☐ (Blank)	October	306,477.40	307,138.26	370,054.52	**983,670.18**
☐ Bachelors	November	235,081.21	306,800.23	178,155.71	**720,037.15**
☐ Graduate Degree	December	330,435.87	385,719.06	262,530.19	**978,685.13**
■ High School	**Total**	**3,221,958.21**	**4,035,796.92**	**3,323,716.54**	**10,581,471.68**
☐ Partial College					
☐ Partial High School					

FIGURE 12-15 The report now shows sales volumes for the Home Appliances category *OR* the High School education level.

The first implementation of the measure is already simple—both to use and to understand. In case there is a large number of rows in the columns used to filter the *OR* condition, or when there are more than just two conditions, the resulting temporary table would quickly become huge. In such a case, one can limit its size by removing the *CROSSJOIN* in favor of *SUMMARIZE*, as in this second implementation of the same measure:

```
OR 2 :=
VAR CategoriesEducations =
    CALCULATETABLE (
        SUMMARIZE (
            Sales,
            'Product'[Category],
            Customer[Education]
        ),
        ALL ( 'Product'[Category] ),
        ALL ( Customer[Education] )
    )
VAR CategoriesEducationsSelected =
    FILTER (
        CategoriesEducations,
        OR (
            'Product'[Category] IN VALUES ( 'Product'[Category] ),
            Customer[Education] IN VALUES ( Customer[Education] )
        )
    )
VAR Result =
    CALCULATE (
```

```
        [Sales Amount],
        CategoriesEducationsSelected
    )
RETURN Result
```

The logic of this second implementation is close to the first one, the only noticeably difference being the presence of *SUMMARIZE* instead of *CROSSJOIN*. Moreover, it is worth pointing out that *SUMMARIZE* needs to be executed in a filter context without the filter on *Category* and *Education*. Otherwise, the slicer would affect the calculation executed by *SUMMARIZE*, destroying the effort of the filter.

There is at least a third solution to the same scenario, potentially faster though harder to understand at first sight. Indeed, the same table filter can be expressed thinking that if the category is in the selected values for the categories, then any value for the education level is fine. The same happens for the education level: As long as the education level is in the selected values for the education level, then any category is fine. This reasoning leads to the third formulation of the same expression:

```
OR 3 :=
VAR Categories =
    CROSSJOIN (
        VALUES ( 'Product'[Category] ),
        ALL ( Customer[Education] )
    )
VAR Educations =
    CROSSJOIN (
        ALL ( 'Product'[Category] ),
        VALUES ( Customer[Education] )
    )
VAR CategoriesEducationsSelected =
    UNION ( Categories, Educations )
VAR Result =
    CALCULATE (
        [Sales Amount],
        CategoriesEducationsSelected
    )
RETURN Result
```

As you can see, one can author the same formula in several ways. The difference is in both readability and performance. Being able to write the same formula using different methods is a skill that will prove extremely useful in the final optimization chapters, where you learn to evaluate the performance of different versions of the same code, seeking the most optimal.

Narrowing sales computation to the first year's customers

As another example of a useful calculation involving the manipulation of tables, we demonstrate how to analyze sales over time but only considering customers who made a purchase during the first year of a selected time period. In other words, we consider the first year with sales in the visual, evaluate the customers who bought during that first year, and then we only analyze the sales of those customers over the following years, ignoring those who became customers afterwards.

The code needs to perform three steps:

1. Checking what is the first year with sales on any product.

2. Storing the set of customers of that first year into a variable, ignoring any other filter.

3. Computing the sales of the customers determined in step 2 in the current period.

The following code implements this algorithm by using variables to store temporary results:

```
SalesOfFirstYearCustomers :=
VAR FirstYearWithSales =
    CALCULATETABLE (
        FIRSTNONBLANK (
            'Date'[Calendar Year],
            [Sales Amount]
        ),
        ALLSELECTED ()
    )
VAR CustomersFirstYear =
    CALCULATETABLE (
        VALUES ( Sales[CustomerKey] ),
        FirstYearWithSales,
        ALLSELECTED ()
    )
VAR Result =
    CALCULATE (
        [Sales Amount],
        KEEPFILTERS ( CustomersFirstYear )
    )
RETURN Result
```

The *FirstYearWithSales* variable stores the first year with sales. Please note that *FIRSTNONBLANK* returns a table as a result, with the data lineage of *Date[Calendar Year]*. The *CustomersFirstYear* variable retrieves the list of all customers in that first year. The last step is the easiest because it only applies the filter on the customer; in each cell of the report, the value of *Sales Amount* is restricted to only the customers found during the second step. The *KEEPFILTERS* modifier makes it possible to filter these customers by country, for example.

The result is visible in Figure 12-16, indicating that—after the first year—sales made to those customers are decreasing over time.

Category	CY 2007	CY 2008	CY 2009	Total
Audio	102,722.07	61,558.94	27,853.52	**192,134.53**
Cameras and camcorders	3,274,847.26	481,456.84	733.10	**3,757,037.20**
Cell phones	477,451.74	105,582.66	7,268.40	**590,302.81**
Computers	2,660,318.87	397,317.15	6,258.20	**3,063,894.22**
Games and Toys	89,860.07	53,309.30	43,023.91	**186,193.27**
Home Appliances	2,347,281.80	975,860.25	177,173.74	**3,500,315.79**
Music, Movies and Audio Books	87,874.44	26,083.81	700.80	**114,659.05**
TV and Video	2,269,589.88	248,960.74	38,640.26	**2,557,190.88**
Total	**11,309,946.12**	**2,350,129.69**	**301,651.93**	**13,961,727.74**

FIGURE 12-16 The report shows sales over the years, focusing only on customers acquired in 2007.

This latter example is important to learn. Indeed, there are several scenarios where one needs to place a filter over time, compute a set, and finally analyze the behavior of this set (of customers, products, stores) over different years. With this pattern one can easily implement same-store analyses or any other calculation with similar requirements.

Computing new customers

In a previous section of this chapter about *EXCEPT*, we showed how to compute new customers. In this section we provide a much better implementation of the same calculation that—again—makes heavy use of table functions.

The idea in this new algorithm is the following: First we determine the earliest day when each customer made a purchase. Once this table is available, the formula checks if the first sale to the customer falls within the current time period. If that holds true, it means that the customer—in the current period—is a new customer.

Here is the code of the measure:

```
New Customers :=
VAR CustomersFirstSale =
    CALCULATETABLE (
        ADDCOLUMNS (
            VALUES ( Sales[CustomerKey] ),
            "FirstSale", CALCULATE (
                MIN ( Sales[Order Date] )
            )
        ),
        ALL ( 'Date' )
    )
VAR CustomersWith1stSaleInCurrentPeriod =
    FILTER (
        CustomersFirstSale,
        [FirstSale] IN VALUES ( 'Date'[Date] )
```

```
    )
VAR Result =
    COUNTROWS ( CustomersWith1stSaleInCurrentPeriod )
RETURN Result
```

The *CustomersFirstSale* variable needs to use *ALL* on the *Date* table to first compute sales that happened before the current time period. You can see the resulting report in Figure 12-17.

Calendar Year	Num of Customers	New Customers
CY 2007	**7,999**	**7,999**
January	1,375	1,375
February	1,153	1,037
March	1,038	900
April	1,197	960
May	1,049	774
June	643	436
July	823	592
August	630	423
September	675	436
October	489	268
November	693	397
December	689	401

FIGURE 12-17 The report shows the number of customers and new customers over the year 2007.

The way it is written now, if a user further filters other tables like the product category, a customer will be considered new when they buy the selected category for the first time. Thus, one individual customer might be considered new multiple times, depending on the filters applied. By adding further *CALCULATE* modifiers to the computation of the first variable, it is possible to implement several different variations of the same code. For example, by adding *ALL (Product)*, then customers are only considered new when they buy any product. By adding *ALL (Store)*, customers are only new the first time they buy in any store.

Using *IN, CONTAINSROW,* and *CONTAINS*

In the previous example, as in many others, we used the *IN* keyword to check whether a value is present in a table. Internally, *IN* is translated into a *CONTAINSROW* function call, so there are no differences in performance between the two syntaxes. The two following expressions are equivalent:

```
Product[Color] IN { "Red", "Blue", "Yellow" }
CONTAINSROW ( { "Red", "Blue", "Yellow" }, Product[Color] )
```

The syntax also works with tables containing multiple columns:

```
( 'Date'[Year], 'Date'[MonthNumber] ) IN { ( 2018, 12 ), ( 2019, 1 ) }
CONTAINSROW ( { ( 2018, 12 ), ( 2019, 1 ) }, 'Date'[Year], 'Date'[MonthNumber] )
```

IN and *CONTAINSROW* are not available in older versions of DAX. An alternative to these functions is *CONTAINS*, which requires us to provide pairs of columns and values to search for the presence of a row in a table. However, *CONTAINS* is less efficient than *IN* and *CONTAINSROW*. Because the syntax of table constructors is not available in versions of DAX without *IN* and *CONTAINSROW*, using *CONTAINS* requires a much more verbose syntax:

```
VAR Colors =
    UNION (
        ROW ( "Color", "Red" ),
        ROW ( "Color", "Blue" ),
        ROW ( "Color", "Yellow" )
    )
RETURN
    CONTAINS ( Colors, [Color], Product[Color] )
```

At the time of writing, *IN* is the most convenient way of searching for a value in a table; it is much easier to read than any other function of its category, and it provides the same performance as *CONTAINSROW*.

Reusing table expressions with *DETAILROWS*

The PivotTable in Excel offers a feature to retrieve the underlying data used to compute a cell. That feature is called "Show Details" in the Excel user interface, and its more technical name is "drillthrough." This name could be confusing because in Power BI the term "drillthrough" refers to a feature that allows the user to move from one report page to another, in a manner controlled by the report author. For this reason, a feature that allows control over the "Show Details" result was called "Detail Rows Expression" in the Tabular model and was introduced in SQL Server Analysis Services 2017. As of April 2019, it is not available in Power BI, but it should be planned for a future release.

The Detail Rows Expression is a DAX table expression associated with a measure and invoked to retrieve the table for the Show Details feature. This expression is executed in the filter context of the measure. The idea is that if a measure changes the filter context to compute a variable, the Detail Rows Expression should apply a similar transformation to the filter context.

For example, consider *Sales YTD* that computes the year-to-date value of *Sales Amount*:

```
Sales YTD :=
CALCULATE (
    [Sales Amount],
    DATESYTD ( 'Date'[Date] )
)
```

The corresponding Detail Rows Expression should be a *CALCULATETABLE* that applies the same filter context transformation as the one made by the corresponding measure. For example, the following expression returns all the columns of the *Sales* table from the beginning of the year considered in the calculation:

```
CALCULATETABLE (
    Sales,
    DATESYTD ( 'Date'[Date] )
)
```

A DAX client tool executes this measure by invoking a specific DAX function called *DETAILROWS*, specifying the measure that the Detail Rows Expression belongs to:

```
DETAILROWS ( [Sales YTD] )
```

The *DETAILROWS* function invokes a table expression stored in a measure. Therefore, one can define hidden measures just to store long table expressions often used as filter arguments of many other DAX measures. For example, consider a *Cumulative Total* measure with a Detail Rows Expression that retrieves any dates less than or equal to the maximum date available in the filter context:

```
-- Detail Rows Expression for Cumulative Total measure
VAR LastDateSelected = MAX ( 'Date'[Date] )
RETURN
    FILTER (
        ALL ( 'Date'[Date] ),
        'Date'[Date] <= LastDateSelected
    )
```

One can reference this table expression in different measures by using the *DETAILROWS* function:

```
Cumulative Sales Amount :=
CALCULATE (
    [Sales Amount],
    DETAILROWS ( [Cumulative Total] )
)

Cumulative Total Cost :=
CALCULATE (
    [Total Cost],
    DETAILROWS ( [Cumulative Total] )
)
```

More detailed examples of this technique are available at https://www.sqlbi.com/articles/creating-table-functions-in-dax-using-detailrows/. However, reusing table expressions with *DETAILROWS* is just a workaround for the lack of custom-defined functions in DAX, and it may have performance implications. Many use cases for *DETAILROWS* can be solved by using calculation groups, and this technique will become obsolete once DAX introduces measures returning tables or custom-defined DAX functions.

Creating calculated tables

All the table functions shown in the previous sections can be used either as table filters in *CALCULATE* or to create calculated tables and queries. Earlier on, we described the ones more likely to be used as table filters, whereas in this section we describe some additional functions that are mostly used when creating calculated tables. There are other table functions whose main usage is in authoring queries; we will describe them in the next chapter. Nevertheless, be mindful that there are no limits in the use of table functions. Nothing is preventing anyone from using *DATATABLE*, *SELECTCOLUMNS*, or *GENERATE-SERIES* (some of the functions described later) in a measure or as a table filter. It is only a matter of convenience: Some functions better fit certain specific needs.

Using *SELECTCOLUMNS*

SELECTCOLUMNS is useful to reduce the number of columns in a table, and it also provides the capability to add new columns like *ADDCOLUMNS* does. In practice, *SELECTCOLUMNS* implements projection of columns like the SQL *SELECT* statement.

The most common usage of *SELECTCOLUMNS* is to scan a table and only return some of the columns. For example, the following expression only returns the customer education and gender, that is, two columns:

```
SELECTCOLUMNS (
    Customer,
    "Education", Customer[Education],
    "Gender", Customer[Gender]
)
```

The result contains a lot of duplicates, as you can see in Figure 12-18.

Education	Gender
Partial College	M
Partial College	F
Partial College	F
Partial College	M
Partial College	F
Partial College	M
Partial College	M
Partial College	M

FIGURE 12-18 *SELECTCOLUMNS* returns duplicate values.

SELECTCOLUMNS is very different from *SUMMARIZE*. *SUMMARIZE* performs a grouping of the result, whereas *SELECTCOLUMNS* only reduces the number of columns. Therefore, the output of *SELECTCOLUMNS* might contain duplicates, whereas the output of *SUMMARIZE* does not. One needs to provide *SELECTCOLUMNS* with pairs of names and expressions for each column in the resulting set.

The resulting columns can also be new ones. For example, the following formula returns a new column named *Customer* containing the name followed by its code in parentheses:

```
SELECTCOLUMNS (
    Customer,
    "Education", Customer[Education],
    "Gender", Customer[Gender],
    "Customer", Customer[Name] & " (" & Customer[Customer Code] & ")"
)
```

You can see the result in Figure 12-19.

Education	Gender	Customer
Partial College	M	Xie, Russell (11024)
Partial College	F	Russell, Jennifer (11036)
Partial College	F	Carter, Amanda (11041)
Partial College	M	Simmons, Nathan (11043)
Partial College	F	Morris, Isabella (11928)
Partial College	M	Alexander, Seth (11938)
Partial College	M	Garcia, Joseph (11954)
Partial College	M	Green, Gabriel (11955)

FIGURE 12-19 *SELECTCOLUMNS* can also compute new columns, like *ADDCOLUMNS* does.

SELECTCOLUMNS maintains the data lineage if the expression is a single column reference, whereas it generates a new data lineage whenever one uses an expression. Consequently, the following result contains two columns: The first column has the data lineage of *Customer[Name]*, whereas the second column has a different data lineage that cannot filter the original columns, even though the content of the two columns is the same:

```
SELECTCOLUMNS (
    Customer,
    "Customer Name with lineage", Customer[Name],
    "Customer Name without lineage", Customer[Name] & ""
)
```

Creating static tables with *ROW*

ROW is a simple function that returns a table with only one row. *ROW* requires pairs of name and expression, and the result is a table with one row and a suitable number of columns. For example, the following expression is a table with one row and two columns, containing the sales amount and the quantity sold:

```
ROW (
    "Sales", [Sales Amount],
    "Quantity", SUM ( Sales[Quantity] )
)
```

The result is a table with one row and two columns, as you can see in Figure 12-20.

Sales	Quantity
30,591,343.98	140,180

FIGURE 12-20 *ROW* creates a table with one single row.

ROW is no longer commonly used since the table constructor syntax was introduced. Indeed, the previous expression can be written as:

```
{
    ( [Sales Amount], SUM ( Sales[Quantity] ) )
}
```

The column names are generated automatically by the table constructor syntax, as shown in Figure 12-21.

Value1	Value2
30,591,343.98	140,180

FIGURE 12-21 The table constructor generates column names automatically.

When using the table constructor syntax, commas separate rows. To include multiple columns, one needs to use parentheses to encapsulate multiple columns in a single row. The main difference between the *ROW* function and the curly braces syntax is that *ROW* specifies names for the columns, whereas the curly braces automatically generate names for the columns. The latter makes it harder to later reference column values.

Creating static tables with *DATATABLE*

ROW is useful when wanting to create a table with a single row. On the other hand, to create multiple rows, one would use *DATATABLE*. *DATATABLE* creates a table specifying not only the column names, but also the data type of each column and its content. For example, if one needs a table with three rows to cluster prices, an easy way to build the table is the following expression:

```
DATATABLE (
    "Segment", STRING,
    "Min", DOUBLE,
    "Max", DOUBLE,
    {
        { "LOW", 0, 20 },
        { "MEDIUM", 20, 50 },
        { "HIGH", 50, 99 }
    }
)
```

You can see the result in Figure 12-22.

Segment	Min	Max
LOW	0.00	20.00
MEDIUM	20.00	50.00
HIGH	50.00	99.00

FIGURE 12-22 The figure shows the resulting table generated with *DATATABLE*.

The data type of columns can be any of the following values: *INTEGER, DOUBLE, STRING, BOOLEAN, CURRENCY,* and *DATETIME*. The syntax is somewhat inconsistent with the new table constructor using curly braces. Indeed, *DATATABLE* uses curly braces to delimit rows, whereas the anonymous table constructor uses regular parentheses leaving the curly braces only to delimit the entire table.

A strong limitation of *DATATABLE* is that the contents of the table need to be constant values. Using any DAX expression would result in an error. This makes *DATATABLE* a function that is not used much. The table constructor syntax gives developers much more flexibility in terms of expressivity.

One can use *DATATABLE* to define simple, constant calculated tables. In SQL Server Data Tools (SSDT) for Analysis Services Tabular, a calculated table using *DATATABLE* is generated when a developer pastes the content of the clipboard into the model, whereas Power BI uses Power Query to define constant tables. This is another reason why *DATATABLE* is not common among Power BI users.

Using *GENERATESERIES*

GENERATESERIES is a utility function that generates series of values once the developer provides a lower boundary, an upper boundary, and a step. For example, the following expression produces a table containing 20 values, from 1 to 20:

```
GENERATESERIES ( 1, 20, 1 )
```

The resulting data type depends on the input; that can be either a number or a *DateTime*. For example, if the developer needs a table containing the time of the day, this expression provides a quick way of generating an 86,400-row table (one row per second):

```
Time =
GENERATESERIES (
    TIME ( 0, 0, 0 ),        -- Start value
    TIME ( 23, 59, 59 ),     -- End value
    TIME ( 0, 0, 1 )         -- Step: 1 second
)
```

By changing the step and adding new columns, one could create a smaller table that acts as a suitable dimension—for example, to slice sales by time:

```
Time =
SELECTCOLUMNS (
    GENERATESERIES (
        TIME ( 0, 0, 0 ),
        TIME ( 23, 59, 59 ),
        TIME ( 0, 30, 0 )
```

```
    ),
    "Time", [Value],
    "HH:MM AMPM", FORMAT ( [Value], "HH:MM AM/PM" ),
    "HH:MM", FORMAT ( [Value], "HH:MM" ),
    "Hour", HOUR ( [Value] ),
    "Minute", MINUTE ( [Value] )
)
```

You can see the result in Figure 12-23.

Time	HH:MM AMPM	HH:MM	Hour	Minute
12:00:00 AM	12:00 AM	00:00	0	0
12:30:00 AM	12:30 AM	00:30	0	30
01:00:00 AM	01:00 AM	01:00	1	0
01:30:00 AM	01:30 AM	01:30	1	30
02:00:00 AM	02:00 AM	02:00	2	0
02:30:00 AM	02:30 AM	02:30	2	30
03:00:00 AM	03:00 AM	03:00	3	0
03:30:00 AM	03:30 AM	03:30	3	30

FIGURE 12-23 Using *GENERATESERIES* and *SELECTCOLUMNS*, one can easily create a time table.

Using *GENERATESERIES* in a measure is uncommon, whereas that function is called upon to create simple tables that become useful as slicers, so the user can select different parameters. For example, Power BI uses *GENERATESERIES* to add parameters for the what-if analysis.

Conclusions

In this chapter, we introduced many new table functions. Still, many have yet to come in the next chapter. Here we focused the attention on the set of table functions that are commonly used to create calculated tables or to implement complex filter arguments for *CALCULATE* and *CALCULATETABLE*. Always remember that the code we provide is an example of what is possible with DAX; we leave it up to the reader's imagination to find practical scenarios calling for the code in a specific model.

The main functions you learned in this chapter are:

- *ADDCOLUMNS*, to add new columns to the input table.

- *SUMMARIZE*, to perform grouping after the scan of a table.

- *CROSSJOIN*, to perform the cartesian product of two tables.

- *UNION, INTERSECT*, and *EXCEPT*, to compute the basic set of operations on tables.

- *SELECTCOLUMNS*, to select certain columns of a table.

- *ROW, DATATABLE*, and *GENERATESERIES*, to generate mostly constant tables as calculated tables.

In the next chapter, we will describe other table functions focusing more on complex queries or complex calculated tables.

Authoring queries

In this chapter we continue our journey, discovering new table functions in DAX. Here, the focus is on functions that are more useful when preparing queries and calculated tables, rather than in measures. Keep in mind that most of the functions you learn in this chapter can be used in measures too, although some have limitations that we outline.

For each function, we provide examples of queries using them. The chapter has two goals: learning new functions and presenting useful patterns that you can implement in your data model.

All the demo files in this chapter are provided as a text file, containing the query executed with DAX Studio connected to a common Power BI file. The Power BI file contains the usual Contoso data model used through the entire book.

Introducing DAX Studio

DAX Studio is a free tool available at www.daxstudio.org that provides help in authoring queries, debugging code, and measuring the performance of queries.

DAX Studio is a live project with new features continuously being added to it. Here are a few of the most relevant features:

- Connectivity to Analysis Services, Power BI, or Power Pivot for Excel.

- Full text editor to author queries and code.

- Automatic formatting of the code through the daxformatter.com service.

- Automatic measure definition to debug or fine-tune performance.

- Detailed performance information about your queries.

Though other tools are available to test and write queries in DAX, we strongly encourage the reader to download, install and learn DAX Studio. If you are unsure, just think that we wrote all the DAX code in this book using that tool. We work with DAX all day long, and we like to be productive. A complete documentation of DAX Studio is available at http://daxstudio.org/documentation/.

Understanding *EVALUATE*

EVALUATE is a DAX statement that is needed to execute a query. *EVALUATE* followed by any table expression returns the result of the table expression. Moreover, one or more *EVALUATE* statements can be preceded by special definitions like local tables, columns, measures, and variables that have the scope of the entire batch of *EVALUATE* statements executed together.

For example, the following query returns the red products by using *EVALUATE,* followed by a simple *CALCULATETABLE* function:

```
EVALUATE
CALCULATETABLE (
    'Product',
    'Product'[Color] = "Red"
)
```

Before diving deeper into the description of more advanced table functions, we must introduce the syntax and the options available in *EVALUATE*, which we will use when writing complex queries.

Introducing the *EVALUATE* syntax

An *EVALUATE* statement is divided in three parts:

- **Definition section:** Introduced by the *DEFINE* keyword, it includes the definition of local entities like tables, columns, variables, and measures. There can be a single definition section for the entire query, even though the query can contain multiple *EVALUATE* statements.

- **Query expression:** Introduced by the *EVALUATE* keyword, it contains the table expression to evaluate and return as the result. There might be multiple query expressions, each introduced by *EVALUATE* and each with its own set of result modifiers.

- **Result modifiers:** An optional additional section to *EVALUATE*, which is introduced by the keyword *ORDER BY*. It includes the sort order of the result and the optional definition of which rows to return, by providing a starting point with *START AT*.

The first and the third part of the statement are optional. Thus, one can just use *EVALUATE* followed by any table expression to produce a query. Nevertheless, by doing so, the developer cannot use many useful features of *EVALUATE*. Therefore, time spent learning the whole syntax is time well spent.

Here is an example of a query:

```
DEFINE
    VAR MinimumAmount = 2000000
    VAR MaximumAmount = 8000000
EVALUATE
FILTER (
    ADDCOLUMNS (
        SUMMARIZE ( Sales, 'Product'[Category] ),
        "CategoryAmount", [Sales Amount]
    ),
```

```
      AND (
          [CategoryAmount] >= MinimumAmount,
          [CategoryAmount] <= MaximumAmount
      )
)
ORDER BY [CategoryAmount]
```

The previous query returns the result shown in Figure 13-1.

Category	CategoryAmount
TV and Video	4,392,768.29
Computers	6,741,548.73
Cameras and camcorders	7,192,581.95

FIGURE 13-1 The result only includes the category amount included between 2,000,000 and 8,000,000.

The example defines two variables storing the upper and lower boundary of the sales amount. The query then retrieves all the categories whose total sales fall in between the boundaries defined by the variables. Finally, it sorts the result by sales amount. As simple as it is, the syntax is powerful, and in the next sections, we provide some important considerations about the usage of each part of the *EVALU-ATE* syntax.

One important detail is that the definition section and the result modifiers are only available in conjunction with *EVALUATE*. Thus, these features are only available when authoring queries. If writing a query that will later be used as a calculated table, a careful developer should avoid relying on the *DEFINE* and *ORDER BY* sections, only focusing on the query expression. A calculated table is defined by a table expression, not by a DAX query.

Using *VAR* in *DEFINE*

In the definition section, it is possible to use the *VAR* keyword to define variables. Each variable is as simple as a name followed by an expression. Variables introduced in queries do not need the *RETURN* part required when variables are used as part of an expression. Indeed, the result is defined by the *EVALUATE* section. We distinguish between regular variables (variables used in expressions) and variables defined in the *DEFINE* section by naming the former *expression variables,* and the latter *query variables.*

As is the case with expression variables, query variables can contain both values and tables without restriction. For example, the query shown in the previous section can also be authored with a query table variable:

```
DEFINE
    VAR MinimumAmount = 2000000
    VAR MaximumAmount = 8000000
    VAR CategoriesSales =
        ADDCOLUMNS (
            SUMMARIZE ( Sales, 'Product'[Category] ),
            "CategoryAmount", [Sales Amount]
```

```
        )
EVALUATE
FILTER (
    CategoriesSales,
    AND (
        [CategoryAmount] >= MinimumAmount,
        [CategoryAmount] <= MaximumAmount
    )
)
ORDER BY [CategoryAmount]
```

A query variable has the scope of the entire batch of *EVALUATE* statements executed together. This means that after it has been defined, the variable can be used anywhere in the following queries. The one limitation is that a variable can only be referenced after it has been defined. In the previous query, if you define *CategoriesSales* before *MinimumAmount* or *MaximumAmount*, the result is a syntax error: The expression of *CategoriesSales* references two variables not yet defined. This is useful to prevent circular dependencies. Besides, the very same limitation exists for expression variables; therefore, query variables follow the same limitations as expression variables.

If the query contains multiple *EVALUATE* sections, query variables are available through all of them. For example, queries generated by Power BI use the *DEFINE* part to store slicer filters in query variables and then include multiple *EVALUATE* statements to compute the various parts of the visual.

Variables can also be defined in the *EVALUATE* section; in that case, being expression variables, they are local to the table expression. The previous query can be equivalently defined this way:

```
EVALUATE
VAR MinimumAmount = 2000000
VAR MaximumAmount = 8000000
VAR CategoriesSales =
    ADDCOLUMNS (
        SUMMARIZE ( Sales, 'Product'[Category] ),
        "CategoryAmount", [Sales Amount]
    )
RETURN
    FILTER (
        CategoriesSales,
        AND (
            [CategoryAmount] >= MinimumAmount,
            [CategoryAmount] <= MaximumAmount
        )
    )
ORDER BY [CategoryAmount]
```

As you can see, the variables are now defined as part of the table expression, and the *RETURN* keyword is needed to define the result of the expression. The scope of the expression variables, in this case, is the *RETURN* section.

Choosing between using a query variable or an expression variable comes with advantages and disadvantages. If the variable is needed in further table or column definitions, then you need to use a query variable. On the other hand, if the variable is not required in other definitions (or in multiple

EVALUATE sections), then it is better to use an expression variable. Indeed, if the variable is part of the expression, then it will be much easier to use the expression to compute a calculated table or to embed it into a measure. Otherwise, there will always be the need to update the syntax of the query to transform it into an expression.

The rule of thumb for choosing between query variables and expression variables is simple. Use expression variables whenever possible and use query variables when strictly necessary; indeed, query variables require additional work to re-use the code in a different formula.

Using *MEASURE* in *DEFINE*

Another entity that one can define locally to a query is a measure. This is achieved by using the keyword *MEASURE*. A query measure behaves in all respects like a regular measure, but it exists only for the lifetime of the query. In the definition of the measure it is mandatory to specify the table that hosts the measure. The following is an example of a query measure:

```
DEFINE
    MEASURE Sales[LargeSales] =
        CALCULATE (
            [Sales Amount],
            Sales[Net Price] >= 200
        )
EVALUATE
ADDCOLUMNS (
    VALUES ( 'Product'[Category] ),
    "Large Sales", [LargeSales]
)
```

The result of the query is visible in Figure 13-2.

Category	Large Sales
Audio	85,029.32
Cameras and camcorders	6,424,083.52
Cell phones	1,110,860.57
Computers	5,571,044.77
Games and Toys	
Home Appliances	8,167,467.64

FIGURE 13-2 The *LargeSales* query measure is evaluated for every *Category* in the *Large Sales* column of the result.

Query measures are useful for two purposes: the first, more obvious, is to write complex expressions that can be called multiple times inside the query. The other reason is that query measures are extremely useful for debugging and for performance tuning. Indeed, if a query measure has the same name as a model measure, it gains precedence in the query. In other words, references to the measure name in the query will use the query measure and not the model measure. However, any other model measures that reference the redefined measure still use the original measure. Therefore, you should include all the dependent measures as query measures to evaluate the impact of changing a measure in the model.

Thus, when testing the behavior of a measure, the best strategy is to write a query that uses the measure, add the local definition of the measure, and then perform various tests to either debug or optimize the code. Once the process is done, the code of the measure can be updated in the model with the new version. DAX Studio offers a specific feature for this purpose: It lets a developer automatically add the *DEFINE MEASURE* statement to a query to speed up these steps.

Implementing common DAX query patterns

Now that we have described the syntax of *EVALUATE*, we introduce many functions that are common in authoring queries. For the most commonly used functions, we also provide sample queries that allow further elaborating on their use.

Using *ROW* to test measures

Introduced in the previous chapter, *ROW* is typically used to obtain the value of a measure or to perform an investigation on the measure query plan. *EVALUATE* requires a table as an argument, and it returns a table as a result. If all you need is the value of a measure, *EVALUATE* will not accept it as an argument. It will require a table instead. So, by using *ROW*, you can transform any value into a table, like in the following example:

```
EVALUATE
ROW ( "Result", [Sales Amount] )
```

The result is visible in Figure 13-3.

Result
30,591,343.98

FIGURE 13-3 The *ROW* function returns a table with a single row.

Be mindful that the same behavior can be obtained by using the table constructor syntax:

```
EVALUATE
{ [Sales Amount] }
```

Figure 13-4 displays the result of the preceding example.

Value
30,591,343.98

FIGURE 13-4 The table constructor returns a row with a column named *Value*.

ROW provides the developer with control over the resulting column's name, which on the other hand is generated automatically with the table constructor. *ROW* allows the developer to generate a table with more than one column, where they can provide for each column a column name and its corresponding expression. In case one needs to simulate the presence of a slicer, *CALCULATETABLE* comes in handy:

```
EVALUATE
CALCULATETABLE (
    ROW (
        "Sales", [Sales Amount],
        "Cost", [Total Cost]
    ),
    'Product'[Color] = "Red"
)
```

The result is visible in Figure 13-5.

Sales	Cost
1,110,102.10	545,018.43

FIGURE 13-5 The *ROW* function can return multiple columns, and values provided are computed in a filter context.

Using *SUMMARIZE*

We introduced and used *SUMMARIZE* in previous chapters of the book. We mentioned that *SUMMARIZE* performs two operations: grouping by columns and adding values. Using *SUMMARIZE* to group tables is a safe operation, whereas using *SUMMARIZE* to add new columns might lead to unexpected results that are hard to debug.

Though adding columns with *SUMMARIZE* is a bad idea, at this point we introduce two additional features of *SUMMARIZE* used in order to add columns. Our intention is to support our reader in understanding code they might run into, written by someone else. However, we reiterate here that **using SUMMARIZE to add columns aggregating values should be avoided**.

In case one uses *SUMMARIZE* to compute values, the option is there to let *SUMMARIZE* compute additional rows that represent subtotals. There is a *SUMMARIZE* modifier named *ROLLUP* that changes the aggregation function of columns requiring for the subtotals to be added to the result. Look at the following query:

```
EVALUATE
SUMMARIZE (
    Sales,
    ROLLUP (
        'Product'[Category],
        'Date'[Calendar Year]
    ),
    "Sales", [Sales Amount]
)
ORDER BY
```

```
'Product'[Category],
'Date'[Calendar Year]
```

ROLLUP instructs *SUMMARIZE* to not only compute the value of *Sales* for each category and year, but also to add additional rows that contain a blank in the year and that represent the subtotal at the category level. Because the category is also marked as *ROLLUP*, one row in the set contains a blank in both category and year along with the grand total for *Sales*. This is shown in Figure 13-6.

Category	Calendar Year	Sales
		30,591,343.98
Audio		384,518.16
Audio	CY 2007	102,722.07
Audio	CY 2008	105,363.42
Audio	CY 2009	176,432.67
Cameras and camcorders		7,192,581.95
Cameras and camcorders	CY 2007	3,274,847.26

FIGURE 13-6 The *ROLLUP* function creates additional total rows in the *SUMMARIZE* result.

The rows added by *ROLLUP* contain a blank instead of the value of the column they are summing up. In case there are blanks in the column, then the output contains two rows with a blank category: one with the value for the blank category and one with the total by category. To distinguish between the two, and to make it easier to mark subtotal rows, one can add a new column using the *ISSUBTOTAL* function:

```
EVALUATE
SUMMARIZE (
    Sales,
    ROLLUP (
        'Product'[Category],
        'Date'[Calendar Year]
    ),
    "Sales", [Sales Amount],
    "SubtotalCategory", ISSUBTOTAL ( 'Product'[Category] ),
    "SubtotalYear", ISSUBTOTAL ( 'Date'[Calendar Year] )
)
ORDER BY
    'Product'[Category],
    'Date'[Calendar Year]
```

The last two columns of the previous query contain a *Boolean* value that is set to *TRUE* when the row contains a subtotal (on category or on year) and *FALSE* otherwise, as shown in Figure 13-7.

Category	Calendar Year	Sales	SubtotalCategory	SubtotalYear
		30,591,343.98	True	True
Audio		384,518.16	False	True
Audio	CY 2007	102,722.07	False	False
Audio	CY 2008	105,363.42	False	False
Audio	CY 2009	176,432.67	False	False
Cameras and camcorders		7,192,581.95	False	True
Cameras and camcorders	CY 2007	3,274,847.26	False	False

FIGURE 13-7 The *ISSUBTOTAL* function returns *True* whenever a column is a subtotal in the *SUMMARIZE* result.

By adding these additional columns using *ISSUBTOTAL*, it is possible to clearly distinguish between rows containing actual data and rows containing subtotals.

> **Important** *SUMMARIZE* should not be used to add new columns. Therefore, we mention the syntax of *ROLLUP* and *ISSUBTOTAL* just to be able to read existing code. You should never use *SUMMARIZE* this way, but prefer *SUMMARIZECOLUMNS* instead, or use *ADD-COLUMNS* and *SUMMARIZE* when the use of *SUMMARIZECOLUMNS* is not possible.

Using *SUMMARIZECOLUMNS*

SUMMARIZECOLUMNS is an extremely powerful query function that is intended to be the "one function fits all" to run queries. In a single function, *SUMMARIZECOLUMNS* contains all the features needed to execute a query. *SUMMARIZECOLUMNS* lets you specify:

- A set of columns used to perform the group-by, like in *SUMMARIZE*, with the option of producing subtotals.

- A set of new columns to add to the result, like both *SUMMARIZE* and *ADDCOLUMNS*.

- A set of filters to apply to the model prior to performing the group-by, like *CALCULATETABLE*.

Finally, *SUMMARIZECOLUMNS* automatically removes from the output any row for which all the added columns produce a blank value. It does not come as a surprise that Power BI uses *SUMMARIZE-COLUMNS* for nearly all the queries it runs.

The following is a first, simple query using *SUMMARIZECOLUMNS*:

```
EVALUATE
SUMMARIZECOLUMNS (
    'Product'[Category],
    'Date'[Calendar Year],
    "Amount", [Sales Amount]
)
ORDER BY
    'Product'[Category],
    'Date'[Calendar Year]
```

The previous query groups data by category and year, computing the sales amount in a filter context containing the given category and year for every row of the result. The result is visible in Figure 13-8.

Category	Calendar Year	Amount
Audio	CY 2007	102,722.07
Audio	CY 2008	105,363.42
Audio	CY 2009	176,432.67
Cameras and camcorders	CY 2007	3,274,847.26
Cameras and camcorders	CY 2008	2,184,189.54
Cameras and camcorders	CY 2009	1,733,545.15
Cell phones	CY 2007	477,451.74
Cell phones	CY 2008	462,713.47
Cell phones	CY 2009	664,445.05

FIGURE 13-8 The result contains the category, year, and the amount of the given category and year.

Years with no sales (like 2005) do not appear in the result. The reason is that, for that specific row of the result, the new Amount column returned a blank, so *SUMMARIZECOLUMNS* removed the row from the result. If the developer needs to ignore this behavior for certain columns, they can use the *IGNORE* modifier like in the following variation of the same query:

```
EVALUATE
SUMMARIZECOLUMNS (
    'Product'[Category],
    'Date'[Calendar Year],
    "Amount", IGNORE ( [Sales Amount] )
)
ORDER BY
    'Product'[Category],
    'Date'[Calendar Year]
```

As a result, *SUMMARIZECOLUMNS* ignores the fact that *Sales Amount* returns a blank; the result also contains sales for Audio in 2005 and 2006, as you can see in Figure 13-9.

Category	Calendar Year	Amount
Audio	CY 2005	
Audio	CY 2006	
Audio	CY 2007	102,722.07
Audio	CY 2008	105,363.42
Audio	CY 2009	176,432.67
Audio	CY 2010	
Audio	CY 2011	
Cameras and camcorders	CY 2005	
Cameras and camcorders	CY 2006	
Cameras and camcorders	CY 2007	3,274,847.26
Cameras and camcorders	CY 2008	2,184,189.54
Cameras and camcorders	CY 2009	1,733,545.15

FIGURE 13-9 Using *IGNORE*, combinations producing blank results in a measure are still returned.

In case multiple columns are added by *SUMMARIZECOLUMNS*, it is possible to choose which one to tag with *IGNORE* and which one to use for blank checks. The common practice is that of removing blanks anyway, to avoid empty results.

SUMMARIZECOLUMNS offers the option of computing subtotals too, using both *ROLLUPADDSUB-TOTAL* and *ROLLUPGROUP*. In the previous query, if you need the yearly subtotal, you should mark the *Date[Calendar Year]* column with *ROLLUPADDISSUBTOTAL*, also specifying the name of a column that indicates whether a given row is a subtotal or not:

```
EVALUATE
SUMMARIZECOLUMNS (
    'Product'[Category],
    ROLLUPADDISSUBTOTAL (
        'Date'[Calendar Year],
        "YearTotal"
    ),
    "Amount", [Sales Amount]
)
ORDER BY
    'Product'[Category],
    'Date'[Calendar Year]
```

The result now contains additional rows representing the subtotal at the year level, with an additional column named *YearTotal* containing *TRUE* only for the subtotal rows. You see this in Figure 13-10 where the subtotal rows are highlighted.

Category	Calendar Year	YearTotal	Amount
Audio		True	384,518.16
Audio	CY 2007	False	102,722.07
Audio	CY 2008	False	105,363.42
Audio	CY 2009	False	176,432.67
Cameras and camcorders		True	7,192,581.95
Cameras and camcorders	CY 2007	False	3,274,847.26
Cameras and camcorders	CY 2008	False	2,184,189.54
Cameras and camcorders	CY 2009	False	1,733,545.15
Cell phones		True	1,604,610.26
Cell phones	CY 2007	False	477,451.74
Cell phones	CY 2008	False	462,713.47
Cell phones	CY 2009	False	664,445.05

FIGURE 13-10 *ROLLUPADDISSUBTOTAL* creates a Boolean column indicating the presence of a subtotal, and new rows with the subtotal amounts.

When summarizing by multiple columns, you can mark several columns with *ROLLUPADDISSUB-TOTAL*. This produces several total groups. For example, the following query produces both the subtotal of a category for all years and a subtotal of a year over all categories:

```
EVALUATE
SUMMARIZECOLUMNS (
    ROLLUPADDISSUBTOTAL (
        'Product'[Category],
        "CategoryTotal"
    ),
    ROLLUPADDISSUBTOTAL (
        'Date'[Calendar Year],
        "YearTotal"
    ),
    "Amount", [Sales Amount]
)
ORDER BY
    'Product'[Category],
    'Date'[Calendar Year]
```

The subtotal of a year over all categories and an example of a subtotal of a category for all years are highlighted in that order, in Figure 13-11.

Category	Calendar Year	CategoryTotal	YearTotal	Amount
		True	True	30,591,343.98
	CY 2007	True	False	11,309,946.12
	CY 2008	True	False	9,927,582.99
	CY 2009	True	False	9,353,814.87
Audio		False	True	384,518.16
Audio	CY 2007	False	False	102,722.07
Audio	CY 2008	False	False	105,363.42
Audio	CY 2009	False	False	176,432.67
Cameras and camcorders		False	True	7,192,581.95
Cameras and camcorders	CY 2007	False	False	3,274,847.26
Cameras and camcorders	CY 2008	False	False	2,184,189.54
Cameras and camcorders	CY 2009	False	False	1,733,545.15

FIGURE 13-11 *ROLLUPADDISSUBTOTAL* can group multiple columns.

If you need subtotals for a group of columns instead of just one column, then the modifier *ROLLUP-GROUP* becomes useful. The following query produces only one subtotal for both category and year, adding only one extra row to the result:

```
EVALUATE
SUMMARIZECOLUMNS (
    ROLLUPADDISSUBTOTAL (
        ROLLUPGROUP (
            'Product'[Category],
            'Date'[Calendar Year]
        ),
        "CategoryYearTotal"
    ),
    "Amount", [Sales Amount]
)
ORDER BY
```

```
'Product'[Category],
'Date'[Calendar Year]
```

You can see the result with only one total row in Figure 13-12.

Category	Calendar Year	CategoryYearTotal	Amount
		True	30,591,343.98
Audio	CY 2007	False	102,722.07
Audio	CY 2008	False	105,363.42
Audio	CY 2009	False	176,432.67
Cameras and camcorders	CY 2007	False	3,274,847.26
Cameras and camcorders	CY 2008	False	2,184,189.54
Cameras and camcorders	CY 2009	False	1,733,545.15
Cell phones	CY 2007	False	477,451.74
Cell phones	CY 2008	False	462,713.47

FIGURE 13-12 *ROLLUPADDISSUBTOTAL* creates both new rows and one new column with the subtotals.

The last feature of *SUMMARIZECOLUMNS* is the ability to filter the result, like *CALCULATETABLE* does. One can specify one or more filters by using tables as additional arguments. For example, the following query only retrieves the sales of customers with a high school education; the result is similar to Figure 13-13, but with smaller amounts:

```
EVALUATE
SUMMARIZECOLUMNS (
    ROLLUPADDISSUBTOTAL (
        ROLLUPGROUP (
            'Product'[Category],
            'Date'[Calendar Year]
        ),
        "CategoryYearTotal"
    ),
    FILTER (
        ALL ( Customer[Education] ),
        Customer[Education] = "High School"
    ),
    "Amount", [Sales Amount]
)
```

Please note that with *SUMMARIZECOLUMNS*, the compact syntax of filter arguments using predicates in *CALCULATE* and *CALCULATETABLE* is not available. Thus, the following query generates a syntax error:

```
EVALUATE
SUMMARIZECOLUMNS (
    ROLLUPADDISSUBTOTAL (
        ROLLUPGROUP (
            'Product'[Category],
```

```
            'Date'[Calendar Year]
        ),
        "CategoryYearTotal"
    ),
    Customer[Education] = "High School",    -- This syntax is not available
    "Amount", [Sales Amount]
)
```

The reason is that the filter arguments of *SUMMARIZECOLUMNS* need to be tables, and there are no shortcuts in this case. An easy and compact way of expressing a filter with *SUMMARIZECOLUMNS* is to use *TREATAS*:

```
EVALUATE
SUMMARIZECOLUMNS (
    ROLLUPADDISSUBTOTAL (
        ROLLUPGROUP (
            'Product'[Category],
            'Date'[Calendar Year]
        ),
        "CategoryYearTotal"
    ),
    TREATAS ( { "High School" }, Customer[Education] ),
    "Amount", [Sales Amount]
)
```

SUMMARIZECOLUMNS is extremely powerful, but it comes with a strong limitation: It cannot be called if the external filter context has performed a context transition. For this reason, *SUMMARIZE-COLUMNS* is useful when authoring queries; however, it is not available as a replacement for *ADD-COLUMNS* and *SUMMARIZE* in measures because it will not work in most reports. Indeed, a measure is often used in a visual like a matrix or a chart, which internally executes the measure in a row context for each value displayed in the report.

As a further example of *SUMMARIZECOLUMNS* limitations in a row context, consider the following query that returns the total sales of all products using an inefficient but still valid approach:

```
EVALUATE
{
    SUMX (
        VALUES ( 'Product'[Category] ),
        CALCULATE (
            SUMX (
                ADDCOLUMNS (
                    VALUES ( 'Product'[Subcategory] ),
                    "SubcategoryTotal", [Sales Amount]
                ),
                [SubcategoryTotal]
            )
        )
    )
}
```

If you replace the innermost *ADDCOLUMNS* with *SUMMARIZECOLUMNS*, then the query fails because *SUMMARIZECOLUMNS* is being called in a context where *CALCULATE* forced context transition. Therefore, the following query is not valid:

```
EVALUATE
{
    SUMX (
        VALUES ( 'Product'[Category] ),
        CALCULATE (
            SUMX (
                SUMMARIZECOLUMNS (
                    'Product'[Subcategory],
                    "SubcategoryTotal", [Sales Amount]
                ),
                [SubcategoryTotal]
            )
        )
    )
}
```

In general, *SUMMARIZECOLUMNS* is not suitable in measures because the measure will be called inside a much more complex query generated by the client tool. That query is likely to contain context transitions, making *SUMMARIZECOLUMNS* fail.

Using *TOPN*

TOPN is a function that sorts a table and then returns a subset of the first rows only. It is useful whenever one needs to reduce the number of rows of a set. For example, when Power BI shows the result of a table, it does not retrieve the full result from the database. Instead, it only retrieves the first few rows that are needed to produce the page on the screen. The remaining part of the result is retrieved only on demand, when the user scrolls down the visual. Another scenario where *TOPN* is useful is to retrieve top performers, like top products, top customers, and so on.

The top three products based on sales can be computed with the following query, which evaluates the *Sales Amount* measure for each row of the *Product* table:

```
EVALUATE
TOPN (
    3,
    'Product',
    [Sales Amount]
)
```

The resulting table contains all the columns of the source table. When a table is used in a query, one is seldom interested in all the columns, so the input table of *TOPN* should reduce the columns to merely the ones needed. The following variation produces fewer columns than are available in the entire *Product* table. This is shown in Figure 13-13:

```
EVALUATE
VAR ProductsBrands =
```

```
      SUMMARIZE (
          Sales,
          'Product'[Product Name],
          'Product'[Brand]
      )
VAR Result =
      TOPN (
          3,
          ProductsBrands,
          [Sales Amount]
      )
RETURN Result
ORDER BY 'Product'[Product Name]
```

Product Name	Brand
A. Datum SLR Camera X137 Grey	A. Datum
Adventure Works 26" 720p LCD HDTV M140 Silver	Adventure Works
Contoso Telephoto Conversion Lens X400 Silver	Contoso

FIGURE 13-13 *TOPN* filters the rows of a table expression based on the value of the Sales Amount measure.

It is likely that one also needs the value of *Sales Amount* in the result, in order to correctly sort the resulting three rows. In such a case, the best option is to precompute the value inside the parameter of *SUMMARIZE* and then reference it in *TOPN*. Thus, the most frequently used pattern of *TOPN* is the following:

```
EVALUATE
VAR ProductsBrands =
      SUMMARIZE (
          Sales,
          'Product'[Product Name],
          'Product'[Brand]
      )
VAR ProductsBrandsSales =
      ADDCOLUMNS (
          ProductsBrands,
          "Product Sales", [Sales Amount]
      )
VAR Result =
      TOPN (
          3,
          ProductsBrandsSales,
          [Product Sales]
      )
RETURN Result
ORDER BY [Product Sales] DESC
```

You can see the result of this query in Figure 13-14.

Product Name	Brand	Product Sales
Adventure Works 26" 720p LCD HDTV M140 Silver	Adventure Works	1,303,983.46
A. Datum SLR Camera X137 Grey	A. Datum	725,840.28
Contoso Telephoto Conversion Lens X400 Silver	Contoso	683,779.95

FIGURE 13-14 *TOPN* returns the top N rows of a table sorted by an expression.

The table can be sorted ascending or descending order to apply the top filter. By default, it is sorted in descending order so that it returns the rows with the largest values first. The third, optional parameter can change the sort order. The values can be 0 or *FALSE* for the default descending order, or 1 or *TRUE* for the ascending order.

> **Important** Do not confuse the sort order of *TOPN* with the sort order of the result of the query; the latter is managed by the *ORDER BY* condition of the *EVALUATE* statement. The third parameter of *TOPN* only affects how to sort the table generated internally by *TOPN* itself.

In the presence of ties, *TOPN* is not guaranteed to return the exact number of rows requested. Instead, it returns all the rows with the same value. For example, in the following query we request the top four brands, and we introduced a modified calculation that uses *MROUND* to fictitiously introduce ties:

```
EVALUATE
VAR SalesByBrand =
    ADDCOLUMNS (
        VALUES ( 'Product'[Brand] ),
        "Product Sales", MROUND ( [Sales Amount], 1000000 )
    )
VAR Result =
    TOPN (
        4,
        SalesByBrand,
        [Product Sales]
    )
RETURN Result
ORDER BY [Product Sales] DESC
```

The result contains five rows, not just four, because both Litware and Proseware produce a result of 3,000,000. Finding ties and not knowing how to differentiate between the two, *TOPN* returns both, as you can see in Figure 13-15.

Brand	Product Sales
Contoso	7,000,000.00
Fabrikam	6,000,000.00
Adventure Works	4,000,000.00
Litware	3,000,000.00
Proseware	3,000,000.00

FIGURE 13-15 In the presence of ties, *TOPN* might return more values than requested.

A common technique to avoid this problem is to add extra columns to the expression of *TOPN*. Indeed, in the third parameter, multiple columns can be used to sort the result of *TOPN*. For example, to retrieve the top four brands and to choose the first brand in alphabetical order in case of a tie, you can use additional sort orders:

```
EVALUATE
VAR SalesByBrand =
    ADDCOLUMNS (
        VALUES ( 'Product'[Brand] ),
        "Product Sales", MROUND ( [Sales Amount], 1000000 )
    )
VAR Result =
    TOPN (
        4,
        SalesByBrand,
        [Product Sales], 0,
        'Product'[Brand], 1
    )
RETURN Result
ORDER BY [Product Sales] DESC
```

The result shown in Figure 13-16 removes Proseware because alphabetically it comes after Litware. Please note that in the query, we used a descending order for the sales and an ascending order for the brand.

Brand	Product Sales
Contoso	7,000,000.00
Fabrikam	6,000,000.00
Adventure Works	4,000,000.00
Litware	3,000,000.00

FIGURE 13-16 Using additional sort orders, one can remove ties in the table.

Be mindful that adding columns to the sort order does not guarantee that only the right number of rows will be returned. *TOPN* can always return multiple rows in the presence of ties. Adding columns to the sort order only mitigates the problem by reducing the number of ties. If one needs a guarantee to retrieve an exact number of rows, then a column with unique values should be added to the sort order, removing any possible ties.

Consider a more complex example where *TOPN* is mixed with set functions and variables. The requirement is a report showing the sales of the top 10 products plus an additional "Others" row showing the sales of all other products combined. A possible implementation is the following:

```
EVALUATE
VAR NumOfTopProducts = 10
VAR ProdsWithSales =
    ADDCOLUMNS (
```

```
        VALUES ( 'Product'[Product Name] ),
        "Product Sales", [Sales Amount]
    )
VAR TopNProducts =
    TOPN (
        NumOfTopProducts,
        ProdsWithSales,
        [Product Sales]
    )
VAR RemainingProducts =
    EXCEPT ( ProdsWithSales, TopNProducts )
VAR OtherRow =
    ROW (
        "Product Name", "Others",
        "Product Sales", SUMX (
            RemainingProducts,
            [Product Sales]
        )
    )
VAR Result =
    UNION ( TopNProducts, OtherRow )
RETURN Result
ORDER BY [Product Sales] DESC
```

The *ProdsWithSales* variable computes a table with products and sales. Then *TopNProducts* only computes the top 10 products. The *RemainingProducts* variable uses *EXCEPT* to compute the products that are not in the top 10. Once the code has split the products into two sets (*TopNProducts* and *RemainingProducts*), it builds a single-row table containing the string "Others"; it also aggregates all the products in the *RemainingProducts* variable, summing all the remaining products. The result is then the *UNION* of the top 10 products with the additional row, computed in the formula. The result is visible in Figure 13-17.

Product Name	Product Sales
Others	26,444,863.03
Adventure Works 26" 720p LCD HDTV M140 Silver	1,303,983.46
A. Datum SLR Camera X137 Grey	725,840.28
Contoso Telephoto Conversion Lens X400 Silver	683,779.95
SV 16xDVD M360 Black	364,714.41
Contoso Projector 1080p X980 White	257,154.75
Contoso Washer & Dryer 21in E210 Pink	182,094.12
Fabrikam Independent filmmaker 1/3" 8.5mm X200 White	165,594.00
Proseware Projector 1080p LCD86 Silver	160,627.05
NT Washer & Dryer 27in L2700 Blue	151,427.53
Contoso Washer & Dryer 21in E210 Green	151,265.40

FIGURE 13-17 The additional row containing Others is created by the query.

Although correct, this result is not perfect yet. Indeed, the Others row appears at the beginning of the report, but it could actually appear in any position depending on its value. One might want to sort the rows in such a way that the Others row is always at the end of the report, while the top products are sorted by their sales, with the top performer being first.

The result can be achieved by introducing a sort column that moves the Others row to the end by using a ranking based on *Product Sales* for the top rows:

```
EVALUATE
VAR NumOfTopProducts = 10
VAR ProdsWithSales =
    ADDCOLUMNS (
        VALUES ( 'Product'[Product Name] ),
        "Product Sales", [Sales Amount]
    )
VAR TopNProducts =
    TOPN (
        NumOfTopProducts,
        ProdsWithSales,
        [Product Sales]
    )
VAR RemainingProducts =
    EXCEPT ( ProdsWithSales, TopNProducts )
VAR RankedTopProducts =
    ADDCOLUMNS(
        TopNProducts,
        "SortColumn", RANKX ( TopNProducts, [Product Sales] )
    )
VAR OtherRow =
    ROW (
        "Product Name", "Others",
        "Product Sales", SUMX (
            RemainingProducts,
            [Product Sales]
        ),
        "SortColumn", NumOfTopProducts + 1
    )
VAR Result =
    UNION ( RankedTopProducts, OtherRow )
RETURN
    Result
ORDER BY [SortColumn]
```

The result visible in Figure 13-18 is now sorted better.

Product Name	Product Sales	SortColumn
Adventure Works 26" 720p LCD HDTV M140 Silver	1,303,983.46	1
A. Datum SLR Camera X137 Grey	725,840.28	2
Contoso Telephoto Conversion Lens X400 Silver	683,779.95	3
SV 16xDVD M360 Black	364,714.41	4
Contoso Projector 1080p X980 White	257,154.75	5
Contoso Washer & Dryer 21in E210 Pink	182,094.12	6
Fabrikam Independent filmmaker 1/3'' 8.5mm X200 White	165,594.00	7
Proseware Projector 1080p LCD86 Silver	160,627.05	8
NT Washer & Dryer 27in L2700 Blue	151,427.53	9
Contoso Washer & Dryer 21in E210 Green	151,265.40	10
Others	26,444,863.03	11

FIGURE 13-18 The *SortColumn* index is how a developer can sort the results as desired.

Using *GENERATE* and *GENERATEALL*

GENERATE is a powerful function that implements the OUTER APPLY logic from the SQL language. *GENERATE* takes two arguments: a table and an expression. It iterates the table, evaluates the expression in the row context of the iteration, and then joins the row of the iteration with the rows returned by the table expression. Its behavior is like a regular join, but instead of joining with a table, it joins with an expression evaluated for each row. It is an extremely versatile function.

To demonstrate its behavior, we extend the previous *TOPN* example. Instead of computing the top products of all time, the requirement is to compute the top three products by year. We can split this problem into two steps: first, computing the top three products, and then repeating this calculation for every year. One possible solution for the top three products is the following:

```
EVALUATE
VAR ProductsSold =
    SUMMARIZE (
        Sales,
        'Product'[Product Name]
    )
VAR ProductsSales =
    ADDCOLUMNS (
        ProductsSold,
        "Product Sales", [Sales Amount]
    )
VAR Top3Products =
    TOPN (
        3,
        ProductsSales,
        [Product Sales]
    )
RETURN
    Top3Products
ORDER BY [Product Sales] DESC
```

The result shown in Figure 13-19 contains just three products.

Product Name	Product Sales
Adventure Works 26" 720p LCD HDTV M140 Silver	1,303,983.46
A. Datum SLR Camera X137 Grey	725,840.28
Contoso Telephoto Conversion Lens X400 Silver	683,779.95

FIGURE 13-19 *TOPN* returns the top three products of all time.

If the previous query is evaluated in a filter context that filters the year, the result is different: It returns the top three products of the given year. Here is where *GENERATE* comes in handy: We use *GENERATE* to iterate the years, and for each year we compute the *TOPN* expression. During each iteration, *TOPN* returns the top three products of the selected year. Finally, *GENERATE* joins the years with the result of the expression at each iteration. This is the complete query:

```
EVALUATE
GENERATE (
    VALUES ( 'Date'[Calendar Year] ),
    CALCULATETABLE (
        VAR ProductsSold =
            SUMMARIZE ( Sales, 'Product'[Product Name] )
        VAR ProductsSales =
            ADDCOLUMNS ( ProductsSold, "Product Sales", [Sales Amount] )
        VAR Top3Products =
            TOPN ( 3, ProductsSales, [Product Sales] )
        RETURN Top3Products
    )
)
ORDER BY
    'Date'[Calendar Year],
    [Product Sales] DESC
```

The result of the query is visible in Figure 13-20.

Calendar Year	Product Name	Product Sales
CY 2007	Adventure Works 26" 720p LCD HDTV M140 Silver	1,289,602.38
CY 2007	A. Datum SLR Camera X137 Grey	716,435.28
CY 2007	Contoso Telephoto Conversion Lens X400 Silver	675,449.95
CY 2008	Litware Refrigerator 24.7CuFt X980 White	135,039.58
CY 2008	Litware Refrigerator 24.7CuFt X980 Blue	100,479.69
CY 2008	Litware Refrigerator 24.7CuFt X980 Grey	93,759.71
CY 2009	Fabrikam Refrigerator 24.7CuFt X9800 White	109,759.66
CY 2009	Fabrikam Refrigerator 24.7CuFt X9800 Grey	89,599.72
CY 2009	Contoso Projector 1080p X980 White	71,374.50

FIGURE 13-20 *GENERATE* joins the years with the top three products by year.

If one needs to compute the top products by category, the only thing that needs to be updated in the formula is the table iterated by *GENERATE*. The following produces the top three products by category:

```
EVALUATE
GENERATE (
    VALUES ( 'Product'[Category] ),
    CALCULATETABLE (
        VAR ProductsSold =
            SUMMARIZE ( Sales, 'Product'[Product Name] )
        VAR ProductsSales =
            ADDCOLUMNS ( ProductsSold, "Product Sales", [Sales Amount] )
        VAR Top3Products =
            TOPN ( 3, ProductsSales, [Product Sales] )
        RETURN Top3Products
    )
)
ORDER BY
    'Product'[Category],
    [Product Sales] DESC
```

As shown in Figure 13-21, the result now contains three products for each category.

Category	Product Name	Product Sales
Audio	Contoso 4G MP3 Player E400 Silver	47,952.41
Audio	NT Bluetooth Stereo Headphones E52 Blue	22,820.17
Audio	WWI 2GB Pulse Smart pen M100 Silver	17,655.59
Cameras and camcorders	A. Datum SLR Camera X137 Grey	725,840.28
Cameras and camcorders	Contoso Telephoto Conversion Lens X400 Silver	683,779.95
Cameras and camcorders	Fabrikam Independent filmmaker 1/3" 8.5mm X200 White	165,594.00
Cell phones	The Phone Company Touch Screen Phone 1600 TFT-1.4" L250 Grey	32,400.89
Cell phones	The Phone Company PDA Handheld 4.7 inch L650 Silver	29,953.00
Cell phones	The Phone Company PDA Phone 4.7 inches L360 White	29,888.70

FIGURE 13-21 Iterating over the categories, the result shows the top three products by category.

If the expression provided as the second argument of *GENERATE* produces an empty table, then *GENERATE* skips the row from the result. If one needs to also retrieve rows of the first table producing an empty result, then *GENERATEALL* is needed. For example, there are no sales in 2005, so there are no top three products in 2005; *GENERATE* does not return any row for 2005. The following query leverages *GENERATEALL* and returns 2005 and 2006:

```
EVALUATE
GENERATEALL (
    VALUES ( 'Date'[Calendar Year] ),
    CALCULATETABLE (
        VAR ProductsSold =
            SUMMARIZE ( Sales, 'Product'[Product Name] )
        VAR ProductsSales =
            ADDCOLUMNS ( ProductsSold, "Product Sales", [Sales Amount] )
```

```
        VAR Top3Products =
            TOPN ( 3, ProductsSales, [Product Sales] )
        RETURN Top3Products
    )
)
ORDER BY
    'Date'[Calendar Year],
    [Product Sales] DESC
```

The result of this query is visible in Figure 13-22.

Calendar Year	Product Name	Product Sales
CY 2005		
CY 2006		
CY 2007	Adventure Works 26" 720p LCD HDTV M140 Silver	1,289,602.38
CY 2007	A. Datum SLR Camera X137 Grey	716,435.28
CY 2007	Contoso Telephoto Conversion Lens X400 Silver	675,449.95
CY 2008	Litware Refrigerator 24.7CuFt X980 White	135,039.58
CY 2008	Litware Refrigerator 24.7CuFt X980 Blue	100,479.69
CY 2008	Litware Refrigerator 24.7CuFt X980 Grey	93,759.71
CY 2009	Fabrikam Refrigerator 24.7CuFt X9800 White	109,759.66
CY 2009	Fabrikam Refrigerator 24.7CuFt X9800 Grey	89,599.72
CY 2009	Contoso Projector 1080p X980 White	71,374.50
CY 2010		
CY 2011		

FIGURE 13-22 *GENERATEALL* returns years for which there are no sales, whereas *GENERATE* did not.

Using *ISONORAFTER*

ISONORAFTER is a utility function. It is heavily used by Power BI and reporting tools to provide pagi-nation, and it is seldom used by developers in queries and measures. When a user browses a report in Power BI, the engine only retrieves the rows needed for the current page from the data model. To obtain this, it always uses a *TOPN* function.

If a user is browsing a products table, they might reach a certain point during the scanning. For example, in Figure 13-23 the last row shown is Stereo Bluetooth Headphones New Gen, and the arrow shows the relative position in the list.

Category	Color	Product Name	Sales Amount
Audio	White	WWI 2GB Pulse Smart pen M100 White	13,206.70
Audio	White	WWI 2GB Spy Video Recorder Pen M300 White	
Audio	White	WWI Stereo Bluetooth Headphones E1000 W…	2,217.46
Audio	White	WWI Wireless Bluetooth Stereo Headphones …	612.00
Audio	White	WWI Wireless Bluetooth Stereo Headphones …	1,012.00
Audio	White	WWI Wireless Transmitter and Bluetooth Hea…	9,112.14
Audio	Yellow	Contoso 4GB Portable MP3 Player M450 Yellow	1,247.35
Audio	Yellow	Contoso 8GB MP3 Player new model M820 Ye…	1,782.20
Audio	Yellow	NT Bluetooth Stereo Headphones E52 Yellow	385.35
Audio	Yellow	NT Wireless Bluetooth Stereo Headphones E3…	1,986.95
Audio	Yellow	WWI 4GB Video Recording Pen X200 Yellow	6,541.60
Audio	Yellow	WWI Stereo Bluetooth Headphones New Gen…	1,861.86
Total			**30,591,343.98**

FIGURE 13-23 The user is browsing the *Product* table and has reached a certain point in the list.

When the user scrolls down, they might reach the bottom of the rows retrieved previously; at this point, Power BI needs to retrieve the next rows. The query that retrieves the next rows will still be a *TOPN* because Power BI always retrieves a subset of the whole data. Moreover, it needs to be the next *TOPN*. This is where *ISONORAFTER* comes in. This is the full query executed by Power BI when scrolling down, and its result is shown in Figure 13-24:

```
EVALUATE
TOPN (
    501,
    FILTER (
        KEEPFILTERS (
            SUMMARIZECOLUMNS (
                'Product'[Category],
                'Product'[Color],
                'Product'[Product Name],
                "Sales_Amount", 'Sales'[Sales Amount]
            )
        ),
        ISONORAFTER (
            'Product'[Category], "Audio", ASC,
            'Product'[Color], "Yellow", ASC,
            'Product'[Product Name],
                "WWI Stereo Bluetooth Headphones New Generation M370 Yellow", ASC
        )
    ),
    'Product'[Category], 1,
    'Product'[Color], 1,
    'Product'[Product Name], 1
)
ORDER BY
    'Product'[Category],
    'Product'[Color],
    'Product'[Product Name]
```

Category	Color	Product Name	Sales_Amount
Audio	Yellow	WWI Stereo Bluetooth Headphones New Generation M370 Yellow	1,861.86
Cameras and camcorders	Azure	A. Datum Advanced Digital Camera M300 Azure	2,723.83
Cameras and camcorders	Azure	A. Datum All in One Digital Camera M200 Azure	6,504.80
Cameras and camcorders	Azure	A. Datum Bridge Digital Camera M300 Azure	10,242.12
Cameras and camcorders	Azure	A. Datum Compact Digital Camera M200 Azure	7,301.40
Cameras and camcorders	Azure	A. Datum Consumer Digital Camera E100 Azure	6,406.80
Cameras and camcorders	Azure	A. Datum Consumer Digital Camera M300 Azure	7,121.70

FIGURE 13-24 This is the next set of rows starting from the last row in the previous figure.

The code executes a *TOPN 501* of a *FILTER*. *FILTER* is used to remove previously retrieved rows, and in order to obtain the scope, it leverages *ISONORAFTER*. That same condition of *ISONORAFTER* could have been expressed with standard Boolean logic. Indeed, the whole preceding *ISONORAFTER* expression could be written this way:

```
'Product'[Category] > "Audio"
|| ( 'Product'[Category] = "Audio" && 'Product'[Color] > "Yellow" )
|| ( 'Product'[Category] = "Audio"
        && 'Product'[Color] = "Yellow"
        && 'Product'[Product Name]
                >= "WWI Stereo Bluetooth Headphones New Generation M370 Yellow"
   )
```

The advantage of using *ISONORAFTER* is twofold: The code is easier to write, and the query plan is potentially better.

Using *ADDMISSINGITEMS*

ADDMISSINGITEMS is another function frequently used by Power BI and seldom used in authoring data models. Its purpose is to add rows that might have been skipped by *SUMMARIZECOLUMNS*. For example, the following query uses *SUMMARIZECOLUMNS* grouping by year; its result is visible in Figure 13-25.

```
EVALUATE
SUMMARIZECOLUMNS (
    'Date'[Calendar Year],
    "Amt", [Sales Amount]
)
ORDER BY 'Date'[Calendar Year]
```

Calendar Year	Amt
CY 2007	11,309,946.12
CY 2008	9,927,582.99
CY 2009	9,353,814.87

FIGURE 13-25 *SUMMARIZECOLUMNS* does not include years without sales where *Amt* column would be blank.

Years with no sales are not returned by *SUMMARIZECOLUMNS*. To retrieve the rows removed by *SUMMARIZECOLUMNS*, one option is to use *ADDMISSINGITEMS*:

```
EVALUATE
ADDMISSINGITEMS (
    'Date'[Calendar Year],
    SUMMARIZECOLUMNS (
        'Date'[Calendar Year],
        "Amt", [Sales Amount]
    ),
    'Date'[Calendar Year]
)
ORDER BY 'Date'[Calendar Year]
```

The result of this query is visible in Figure 13-26, where we highlighted the rows returned by *SUMMARIZECOLUMNS*. The rows with a blank in the *Amt* column were added by *ADDMISSINGITEMS*.

Calendar Year	Amt
CY 2005	
CY 2006	
CY 2007	11,309,946.12
CY 2008	9,927,582.99
CY 2009	9,353,814.87
CY 2010	
CY 2011	

FIGURE 13-26 *ADDMISSINGITEMS* added the rows with a blank value for *Amt*.

ADDMISSINGITEMS accepts several modifiers and parameters to better control the result for subtotals and other filters.

Using *TOPNSKIP*

The *TOPNSKIP* function is used extensively by Power BI to send just a few rows of a large raw dataset to the Data View of Power BI. Other tools, such as Power Pivot and SQL Server Data Tools, use other techniques to quickly browse and filter the raw data of a table. The reason for using them is to quickly browse over a large table without having to wait for the materialization of the entire set of rows. Both *TOPNSKIP* and other techniques are described in the article at http://www.sqlbi.com/articles/querying-raw-data-to-tabular/.

Using *GROUPBY*

GROUPBY is a function used to group a table by one or more columns, aggregating other data similarly to what is possible using *ADDCOLUMNS* and *SUMMARIZE*. The main difference between *SUMMARIZE* and *GROUPBY* is that *GROUPBY* can group columns whose data lineage does not correspond to columns in the data model, whereas *SUMMARIZE* can only use columns defined in the data model.

In addition, columns added by *GROUPBY* need to use an iterator that aggregates data such as *SUMX*, *AVERAGEX*, or other "X" aggregation functions.

For example, consider the requirement to group sales by year and month and compute the sales amount. This is a possible solution using *GROUPBY*; the query result is visible in Figure 13-27:

```
EVALUATE
GROUPBY (
    Sales,
    'Date'[Calendar Year],
    'Date'[Month],
    'Date'[Month Number],
    "Amt", AVERAGEX (
        CURRENTGROUP (),
        Sales[Quantity] * Sales[Net Price]
    )
)
ORDER BY
    'Date'[Calendar Year],
    'Date'[Month Number]
```

Calendar Year	Month	Month Number	Amt
CY 2007	January	1	285.19
CY 2007	February	2	329.44
CY 2007	March	3	355.51
CY 2007	April	4	394.44
CY 2007	May	5	327.68
CY 2007	June	6	398.66

FIGURE 13-27 *GROUPBY* in this example aggregates the average of the line amount by year and month.

Performance-wise, *GROUPBY* can be slow in handling larger datasets—tens of thousands of rows or more. Indeed, GROUPBY performs the grouping after having materialized the table; it is thus not the suggested option to scan larger datasets. Besides, most queries can be expressed more easily by using the *ADDCOLUMNS* and *SUMMARIZE* pair. Indeed, the previous query is better written as:

```
EVALUATE
ADDCOLUMNS (
    SUMMARIZE (
        Sales,
        'Date'[Calendar Year],
        'Date'[Month],
        'Date'[Month Number],
    ),
    "Amt", AVERAGEX (
        RELATEDTABLE ( Sales ),
        Sales[Quantity] * Sales[Net Price]
    )
)
ORDER BY
```

```
'Date'[Calendar Year],
'Date'[Month Number]
```

> **Note**   In the previous query, it is worthwhile to note that the result of *SUMMARIZE* is a table containing columns from the *Date* table. Therefore, when *AVERAGEX* later iterates over the result of *RELATEDTABLE*, the table returned by *RELATEDTABLE* is the table of the year and month currently iterated by *ADDCOLUMNS* over the result of *SUMMARIZE*. Remember that data lineage is kept; therefore, the result of *SUMMARIZE* is a table along with its data lineage.

One advantage of *GROUPBY* is its option to group by columns added to the query by *ADDCOLUMNS* or *SUMMARIZE*. The following is an example where *SUMMARIZE* would not be an alternative:

```
EVALUATE
VAR AvgCustomerSales =
    AVERAGEX (
        Customer,
        [Sales Amount]
    )
VAR ClassifiedCustomers =
    ADDCOLUMNS (
        VALUES ( Customer[Customer Code] ),
        "Customer Category", IF (
            [Sales Amount] >= AvgCustomerSales,
            "Above Average",
            "Below Average"
        )
    )
VAR GroupedResult =
    GROUPBY (
        ClassifiedCustomers,
        [Customer Category],
        "Number of Customers", SUMX (
            CURRENTGROUP (),
            1
        )
    )
RETURN GroupedResult
ORDER BY [Customer Category]
```

You can see the result in Figure 13-28.

Customer Category	Number of Customers
Above Average	807
Below Average	18,062

FIGURE 13-28 *GROUPBY* can group columns computed during the query.

The previous formula shows both the advantages and the disadvantages of *GROUPBY* at the same time. Indeed, the code first creates a new column in the customer table that checks if the customer sales are above or below the average sales. It then groups by this temporary column, and it returns the number of customers.

Grouping by a temporary column is a useful feature; however, to compute the number of customers, the code needs to use a *SUMX* over a *CURRENTGROUP* using a constant expression of 1. The reason is that columns added by *GROUPBY* need to be iterations over *CURRENTGROUP*. A simple function like *COUNTROWS (CURRENTGROUP ())* would not work here.

There are only a few scenarios where *GROUPBY* is useful. In general, *GROUPBY* can be used when there is the need to group by a column added in the query, but be mindful that the column used to group by should have a small cardinality. Otherwise, you might face performance and memory consumption issues.

Using *NATURALINNERJOIN* and *NATURALLEFTOUTERJOIN*

DAX uses model relationships automatically whenever a developer runs a query. Still, it might be useful to join two tables that have no relationships. For example, one might define a variable containing a table and then join a calculated table with that variable.

Consider the requirement to compute the average sales per category and to then build a report showing the categories below, around, and above the average. This column is easy to compute with a simple *SWITCH* function. However, if the results need to be sorted in a particular way, then it is necessary to compute both the category description and the sort order (as a new column) at the same time, using a similar piece of code.

Another approach would be to compute only one of the two values and then use a temporary table with a temporary relationship to retrieve the description. This is exactly what the following query does:

```
EVALUATE
VAR AvgSales =
    AVERAGEX (
        VALUES ( 'Product'[Brand] ),
        [Sales Amount]
    )
VAR LowerBoundary = AvgSales * 0.8
VAR UpperBoundary = AvgSales * 1.2
VAR Categories =
    DATATABLE (
        "Cat Sort", INTEGER,
        "Category", STRING,
        {
            { 0, "Below Average" },
            { 1, "Around Average" },
            { 2, "Above Average" }
        }
    )
VAR BrandsClassified =
```

```
    ADDCOLUMNS (
        VALUES ( 'Product'[Brand] ),
        "Sales Amt", [Sales Amount],
        "Cat Sort", SWITCH (
            TRUE (),
            [Sales Amount] <= LowerBoundary, 0,
            [Sales Amount] >= UpperBoundary, 2,
            1
        )
    )
VAR JoinedResult =
    NATURALINNERJOIN (
        Categories,
        BrandsClassified
    )
RETURN JoinedResult
ORDER BY
    [Cat Sort],
    'Product'[Brand]
```

It is useful to look at the result of the query shown in Figure 13-29 before commenting on it.

Cat Sort	Category	Brand	Sales Amt
0	Below Average	A. Datum	2,096,184.64
0	Below Average	Northwind Traders	1,040,552.13
0	Below Average	Southridge Video	1,384,413.85
0	Below Average	Tailspin Toys	325,042.42
0	Below Average	The Phone Company	1,123,819.07
0	Below Average	Wide World Importers	1,901,956.66
1	Around Average	Litware	3,255,704.03
1	Around Average	Proseware	2,546,144.16
2	Above Average	Adventure Works	4,011,112.28
2	Above Average	Contoso	7,352,399.03
2	Above Average	Fabrikam	5,554,015.73

FIGURE 13-29 The *Cat Sort* column must be used as the "sort by column" argument on *Category*.

The query first builds a table containing the brands, the sales amounts, and a column with values between 0 and 2. The value will be used as a key in the *Categories* variable to retrieve the category description. This final join between the temporary table and the variable is performed by *NATURAL-INNERJOIN*, which joins the two tables based on the *Cat Sort* column.

NATURALINNERJOIN performs the join between two tables based on columns that have the same name in both tables. *NATURALLEFTOUTERJOIN* performs the same operation, but instead of an inner join, it uses a left outer join. By using a left outer join, *NATURALLEFTOUTERJOIN* keeps rows in the first table even if there are no matches in the second table.

In case the two tables are physically defined in the data model, they can only be joined using a relationship. This can be useful to obtain the result of the join between two tables—similarly to what is possible in a SQL query. Both *NATURALINNERJOIN* and *NATURALLEFTOUTERJOIN* use the relationship between the tables if it exists. Otherwise, they need the same data lineage to perform the join.

For example, this query returns all the rows in *Sales* that have corresponding rows in *Product*, only including all the columns of the two tables once:

```
EVALUATE
NATURALINNERJOIN ( Sales, Product )
```

The following query returns all the rows in *Product*, also showing the products that have no *Sales*:

```
EVALUATE
NATURALLEFTOUTERJOIN ( Product, Sales )
```

In both cases, the column that defines the relationship is only present once in the result, which includes all the other columns of the two tables.

However, one important limitation of these join functions is that they do not match two columns of the data model with different data lineage and no relationship. In practice, two tables of the data model that have one or more columns with the same name and no relationship cannot be joined together. As a workaround, one can use *TREATAS* to change the data lineage of a column so that the join becomes possible. The article at https://www.sqlbi.com/articles/from-sql-to-dax-joining-tables/ describes this limitation and a possible workaround in detail.

NATURALINNERJOIN or *NATURALLEFTOUTERJOIN* are useful in a limited number of cases; in DAX, they are not as frequent as the equivalent join function in the SQL language.

 Important   *NATURALINNERJOIN* and *NATURALLEFTOUTERJOIN* are useful to join the result of temporary tables, where the data lineage of certain columns does not point to physical columns of the data model. In order to join tables in the model that do not have a proper relationship, it is necessary to use *TREATAS* to change the data lineage of the columns to use in the join operation.

Using *SUBSTITUTEWITHINDEX*

The *SUBSTITUTEWITHINDEX* function can replace the columns in a row set corresponding to the column headers of a matrix, with indexes representing their positions. *SUBSTITUTEWITHINDEX* is not a function a developer would use in a regular query because its behavior is quite intricate. One possible usage might be when creating a dynamic user interface for querying DAX. Indeed, Power BI internally uses *SUBSTITUTEWITHINDEX* for matrix charts.

For example, consider the Power BI matrix in Figure 13-30.

Category	CY 2007	CY 2008	CY 2009
Audio	102,722.07	105,363.42	176,432.67
Cameras and camcorders	3,274,847.26	2,184,189.54	1,733,545.15
Cell phones	477,451.74	462,713.47	664,445.05
Computers	2,660,318.87	2,066,341.75	2,014,888.11
Games and Toys	89,860.07	105,738.23	165,054.51
Home Appliances	2,347,281.80	3,962,572.24	3,290,603.00
Music, Movies and Audio Books	87,874.44	120,717.83	105,614.47
TV and Video	2,269,589.88	919,946.50	1,203,231.91

FIGURE 13-30 A matrix in Power BI is populated using a query with *SUBSTITUTEWITHINDEX*.

The result of a DAX query is always a table. Each cell of the matrix in the report corresponds to a single row of the table returned by the DAX query. In order to correctly display the data in the report, Power BI uses *SUBSTITUTEWITHINDEX* to translate the column names of the matrix (CY 2007, CY 2008, and CY 2009) into sequential numbers, making it easier to populate the matrix when reading the result. The following is a simplified version of the DAX request generated for the previous matrix:

```
DEFINE
    VAR SalesYearCategory =
        SUMMARIZECOLUMNS (
            'Product'[Category],
            'Date'[Calendar Year],
            "Sales_Amount", [Sales Amount]
        )
    VAR MatrixRows =
        SUMMARIZE (
            SalesYearCategory,
            'Product'[Category]
        )
    VAR MatrixColumns =
        SUMMARIZE (
            SalesYearCategory,
            'Date'[Calendar Year]
        )
    VAR SalesYearCategoryIndexed =
        SUBSTITUTEWITHINDEX (
            SalesYearCategory,
            "ColumnIndex", MatrixColumns,
            'Date'[Calendar Year], ASC
        )

-- First result: matrix column headers
EVALUATE
MatrixColumns
ORDER BY 'Date'[Calendar Year]

-- Second result: matrix rows and content
EVALUATE
NATURALLEFTOUTERJOIN (
```

```
      MatrixRows,
      SalesYearCategoryIndexed
)
ORDER BY
    'Product'[Category],
    [ColumnIndex]
```

The request contains two *EVALUATE* statements. The first *EVALUATE* returns the content of the column headers, as shown in Figure 13-31.

Calendar Year
CY 2007
CY 2008
CY 2009

FIGURE 13-31 Result of the column headers of a matrix in Power BI.

The second *EVALUATE* returns the remaining content of the matrix, providing one row for each cell of the matrix content. Every row in the result has the columns required to populate the row header of the matrix followed by the numbers to display, and one column containing the column index computed by using the *SUBSTITUTEWITHINDEX* function. This is shown in Figure 13-32.

Category	Sales_Amount	ColumnIndex
Audio	102,722.07	0
Audio	105,363.42	1
Audio	176,432.67	2
Cameras and camcorders	3,274,847.26	0
Cameras and camcorders	2,184,189.54	1
Cameras and camcorders	1,733,545.15	2
Cell phones	477,451.74	0
Cell phones	462,713.47	1

FIGURE 13-32 Result of the rows' content of a matrix in Power BI generated using *SUBSTITUTEWITHINDEX*.

SUBSTITUTEWITHINDEX is mainly used to build visuals like the matrix in Power BI.

Using *SAMPLE*

SAMPLE returns a sample of rows from a table. Its arguments are the number of rows to be returned, the table name, and a sort order. *SAMPLE* returns the first and the last rows of the table, plus additional rows up to exactly the number of rows requested. *SAMPLE* picks evenly distributed rows from the source table.

For example, the following query returns exactly 10 products after having sorted the input table by *Product Name*:

```
EVALUATE
SAMPLE (
    10,
    ADDCOLUMNS (
        VALUES ( 'Product'[Product Name] ),
        "Sales", [Sales Amount]
    ),
    'Product'[Product Name]
)
ORDER BY 'Product'[Product Name]
```

The result of the previous query is visible in Figure 13-33.

Product Name	Sales
A. Datum Advanced Digital Camera M300 Azure	2,723.83
Adventure Works Laptop16 M1601 Red	25,445.52
Contoso DVD 9-Inch Player Portable M300 White	1,119.93
Contoso Rubberized Skin BlackBerry E100 Black	8,152.01
Fabrikam Independent Filmmaker 1/3" 8.5mm X200 Blue	69,156.00
Litware Home Theater System 2.1 Channel E212 Silver	18,866.71
MGS Rise of Nations: Gold Edition 2009 E143	3,311.00
Proseware Projector 720p LCD56 Black	14,189.70
The Phone Company PDA Phone Unlocked 3.7 inches M510 Black	8,175.30
WWI Wireless Transmitter and Bluetooth Headphones X250 White	9,112.14

FIGURE 13-33 *SAMPLE* returns a subset of a table by choosing evenly distributed rows.

SAMPLE is useful for a DAX client tool to generate values for the axis of a chart. Another scenario is an analysis where the user needs a sample of a table to perform a statistical calculation.

Understanding the auto-exists behavior in DAX queries

Many DAX functions use a behavior known as *auto-exists*. Auto-exists is a mechanism used when a function joins two tables. It is important when authoring queries because, although it is usually intuitive, it might produce unexpected results.

Consider the following expression:

```
EVALUATE
SUMMARIZECOLUMNS (
    'Product'[Category],
```

```
        'Product'[Subcategory]
)
ORDER BY
    'Product'[Category],
    'Product'[Subcategory]
```

The result can be either the full cross-join of categories and subcategories, or only the existing combinations of categories and subcategories. Indeed, each category contains just a subset of subcategories. Thus, the list of existing combinations is smaller than the full cross-join.

The most intuitive answer would be that *SUMMARIZECOLUMNS* only returns the existing combination. This is exactly what happens because of the auto-exists feature. The result in Figure 13-34 shows no more than three subcategories for the Audio category, and not a list of all the subcategories.

Category	Subcategory
Audio	Bluetooth Headphones
Audio	MP4&MP3
Audio	Recording Pen
Cameras and camcorders	Camcorders
Cameras and camcorders	Cameras & Camcorders Accessories
Cameras and camcorders	Digital Cameras
Cameras and camcorders	Digital SLR Cameras
Cell phones	Cell phones Accessories

FIGURE 13-34 *SUMMARIZECOLUMNS* only returns the existing combinations of values.

Auto-exists kicks in whenever the query groups by columns coming from the same table. When the auto-exists logic is used, existing combinations of values are generated exclusively. This reduces the number of rows to evaluate, generating better query plans. On the other hand, if one uses columns coming from different tables, then the result is different. If the columns used in *SUMMARIZECOLUMNS* are from different tables, then the result is the full cross-join of the two tables. This is made visible by the following query whose result is shown in Figure 13-35:

```
EVALUATE
SUMMARIZECOLUMNS (
    'Product'[Category],
    'Date'[Calendar Year]
)
ORDER BY
    'Product'[Category],
    'Date'[Calendar Year]
```

Though the two tables are linked to the *Sales* table through relationships and there are years without transactions, the auto-exists logic is not used when the columns do not come from the same table.

Category	Calendar Year
Audio	CY 2005
Audio	CY 2006
Audio	CY 2007
Audio	CY 2008
Audio	CY 2009
Audio	CY 2010
Audio	CY 2011
Cameras and camcorders	CY 2005
Cameras and camcorders	CY 2006
Cameras and camcorders	CY 2007
Cameras and camcorders	CY 2008
Cameras and camcorders	CY 2009
Cameras and camcorders	CY 2010
Cameras and camcorders	CY 2011
Cell phones	CY 2005

FIGURE 13-35 Columns coming from different tables generate the full cross-join.

Be mindful that *SUMMARIZECOLUMNS* removes the columns if all the additional columns computing aggregation expressions are blank. Thus, if the previous query also includes the *Sales Amount* measure, *SUMMARIZECOLUMNS* removes the years and categories without sales, as shown in Figure 13-36:

```
DEFINE
    MEASURE Sales[Sales Amount] =
        SUMX (
            Sales,
            Sales[Quantity] * Sales[Net Price]
        )
EVALUATE
SUMMARIZECOLUMNS (
    'Product'[Category],
    'Date'[Calendar Year],
    "Sales", [Sales Amount]
)
ORDER BY
    'Product'[Category],
    'Date'[Calendar Year]
```

Category	Calendar Year	Sales
Audio	CY 2007	102,722.07
Audio	CY 2008	105,363.42
Audio	CY 2009	176,432.67
Cameras and camcorders	CY 2007	3,274,847.26
Cameras and camcorders	CY 2008	2,184,189.54
Cameras and camcorders	CY 2009	1,733,545.15
Cell phones	CY 2007	477,451.74

FIGURE 13-36 The presence of an aggregation expression removes the rows with a blank result.

The behavior of the previous query does not correspond to an auto-exists logic because it is based on the result of an expression that includes an aggregation. Constant expressions are ignored on this basis. For example, the presence of a 0 instead of a blank generates a list with all the years and categories. The result of the following query is visible in Figure 13-37:

```
DEFINE
    MEASURE Sales[Sales Amount] =
        SUMX (
            Sales,
            Sales[Quantity] * Sales[Net Price]
        )
EVALUATE
SUMMARIZECOLUMNS (
    'Product'[Category],
    'Date'[Calendar Year],
    "Sales", [Sales Amount] + 0 -- Returns 0 instead of blank
)
ORDER BY
    'Product'[Category],
    'Date'[Calendar Year]
```

Category	Calendar Year	Sales
Audio	CY 2005	0.00
Audio	CY 2006	0.00
Audio	CY 2007	102,722.07
Audio	CY 2008	105,363.42
Audio	CY 2009	176,432.67
Audio	CY 2010	0.00
Audio	CY 2011	0.00
Cameras and camcorders	CY 2005	0.00
Cameras and camcorders	CY 2006	0.00
Cameras and camcorders	CY 2007	3,274,847.26
Cameras and camcorders	CY 2008	2,184,189.54
Cameras and camcorders	CY 2009	1,733,545.15
Cameras and camcorders	CY 2010	0.00
Cameras and camcorders	CY 2011	0.00
Cell phones	CY 2005	0.00

FIGURE 13-37 An aggregation expression resulting in 0 instead of blank maintains the rows in the *SUMMARIZE-COLUMNS* results.

However, the same approach does not produce additional combinations for columns coming from the same table. The auto-exists behavior is always applied to columns of the same table. The following query solely generates existing combinations of *Category* and *Subcategory* values, despite the measure expression returning 0 instead of blank:

```
DEFINE
    MEASURE Sales[Sales Amount] =
        SUMX (
            Sales,
            Sales[Quantity] * Sales[Net Price]
        )
EVALUATE
SUMMARIZECOLUMNS (
    'Product'[Category],
    'Product'[Subcategory],
    "Sales", [Sales Amount] + 0
)
ORDER BY
    'Product'[Category],
    'Product'[Subcategory]
```

The result is visible in Figure 13-38.

Category	Subcategory	Sales
Audio	Bluetooth Headphones	124,450.79
Audio	MP4&MP3	170,194.00
Audio	Recording Pen	89,873.37
Cameras and camcorders	Camcorders	3,157,075.19
Cameras and camcorders	Cameras & Camcorders Accessories	800,534.42
Cameras and camcorders	Digital Cameras	784,935.68
Cameras and camcorders	Digital SLR Cameras	2,450,036.66
Cell phones	Cell phones Accessories	274,049.03

FIGURE 13-38 *SUMMARIZECOLUMNS* applies the auto-exists to columns from the same table even when aggregation expressions return 0.

It is important to consider the auto-exists logic when using *ADDMISSINGITEMS*. Indeed, *ADDMISSINGITEMS* only adds rows that are removed because of blank results in *SUMMARIZECOLUMNS*. *ADDMISSINGITEMS* does not add rows removed by auto-exists for columns of the same table. The following query thus returns the same result as the one shown in Figure 13-38:

```
DEFINE
    MEASURE Sales[Sales Amount] =
        SUMX (
            Sales,
            Sales[Quantity] * Sales[Net Price]
        )
EVALUATE
ADDMISSINGITEMS (
    'Product'[Category],
    'Product'[Subcategory],
    SUMMARIZECOLUMNS (
        'Product'[Category],
        'Product'[Subcategory],
        "Sales", [Sales Amount] + 0
    ),
```

```
        'Product'[Category],
        'Product'[Subcategory]
)
ORDER BY
        'Product'[Category],
        'Product'[Subcategory]
```

Auto-exists is an important aspect to consider when using *SUMMARIZECOLUMNS*. On the other hand, the behavior of *SUMMARIZE* is different. *SUMMARIZE* always requires a table to use as a bridge between the columns, acting as an auto-exists between different tables. For example, the following *SUMMARIZE* produces just the combinations of category and year where there are corresponding rows in the *Sales* table, as shown by the result in Figure 13-39:

```
EVALUATE
SUMMARIZE (
    Sales,
    'Product'[Category],
    'Date'[Calendar Year]
)
```

Category	Calendar Year
Audio	CY 2007
Audio	CY 2008
Audio	CY 2009
TV and Video	CY 2007
TV and Video	CY 2008
TV and Video	CY 2009
Computers	CY 2007
Computers	CY 2008
Computers	CY 2009

FIGURE 13-39 *SUMMARIZE* only returns combinations between categories and year where there are matching rows in *Sales*.

The reason why nonexisting combinations are not returned is because *SUMMARIZE* uses the *Sales* table as the starting point to perform the grouping. Thus, any value in category or year not referenced in *Sales* is not part of the result. Even though the result is identical, *SUMMARIZE* and *SUMMARIZE-COLUMNS* achieve the same result through different techniques.

Be mindful that the user experience might be different when using a specific client tool. Indeed, if a user puts the category and the year in a Power BI report without including any measure, the result only shows the existing combinations in the *Sales* table. The reason is not that auto-exists is in place. The reason is that Power BI adds its own business rules to the auto-exists logic of DAX. A simple report with just *Year* and *Category* in a table produces a complex query like the following one:

```
EVALUATE
TOPN (
    501,
    SELECTCOLUMNS (
        KEEPFILTERS (
            FILTER (
                KEEPFILTERS (
                    SUMMARIZECOLUMNS (
                        'Date'[Calendar Year],
                        'Product'[Category],
                        "CountRowsSales", CALCULATE ( COUNTROWS ( 'Sales' ) )
                    )
                ),
                OR (
                    NOT ( ISBLANK ( 'Date'[Calendar Year] ) ),
                    NOT ( ISBLANK ( 'Product'[Category] ) )
                )
            )
        ),
        "'Date'[Calendar Year]", 'Date'[Calendar Year],
        "'Product'[Category]", 'Product'[Category]
    ),
    'Date'[Calendar Year], 1,
    'Product'[Category], 1
)
```

The highlighted row shows that Power BI adds a hidden calculation that computes the number of rows in *Sales*. Because *SUMMARIZECOLUMNS* removes all the rows where the aggregation expression is blank, this results in a behavior similar to the auto-exists obtained by combining columns of the same table.

Power BI only adds this calculation if there are no measures in the report, including a table that has a many-to-one relationship with all the tables used in *SUMMARIZECOLUMNS*. As soon as one adds a calculation by using a measure, Power BI stops this behavior and checks for the measure value instead of the number of rows in *Sales*.

Overall, the behavior of *SUMMARIZECOLUMNS* and *SUMMARIZE* is intuitive most of the time. However, in complex scenarios like many-to-many relationships, the results might be surprising. In this short section we only introduced auto-exists. A more detailed explanation of how these functions work in complex scenarios is available in the article "Understanding DAX Auto-Exist," available at https://www.sqlbi.com/articles/understanding-dax-auto-exist/. The article also shows how this behavior might produce reports with unexpected—or just counterintuitive—results.

Conclusions

This chapter presented several functions that are useful to author queries. Always remember that any of these functions (apart from *SUMMARIZECOLUMNS* and *ADDMISSINGITEMS*) can be used in measures too. Some experience is needed to learn how to mix these functions together to build more complex queries.

Here is the list of the most relevant topics covered in the chapter:

- Some functions are more useful in queries. Others are so technical and specialized that their purpose is more to serve client tools generating queries, rather than data modelers writing DAX expressions manually. Regardless, it is important to read about all of them; at some point, it could become necessary to read somebody else's code, so basic knowledge of all the functions is important.

- *EVALUATE* introduces a query. Using *EVALUATE,* you can define variables and measures that only exist for the duration of the query.

- *EVALUATE* cannot be used to create calculated tables. A calculated table comes from an expression. Thus, when creating a query for a calculated table, you cannot create local measures or columns.

- *SUMMARIZE* is useful to perform grouping, and it is usually side-by-side with *ADDCOLUMNS.*

- *SUMMARIZECOLUMNS* is one-function-fits-all. It is useful and powerful to generate complex queries, and it is used extensively by Power BI. However, *SUMMARIZECOLUMNS* cannot be used in a filter context that contains a context transition. This usually prevents the use of *SUMMARIZECOLUMNS* in measures.

- *TOPN* is extremely useful to retrieve the top (or the bottom) performers out of a category.

- *GENERATE* implements the OUTER APPLY logic of SQL. It becomes handy whenever you need to produce a table with a first set of columns that act as a filter and a second set of columns that depends on the values of the first set.

- Many other functions are mostly useful for query generators.

Finally, remember that all the table functions described in previous chapters can be used to author queries. The options available to produce queries are not limited to the functions demonstrated in this chapter.

Advanced DAX concepts

So far in the book, we have provided a complete description of the pillars of DAX: row context, filter context and context transition. In previous chapters, we made several references to this chapter as the chapter where we would uncover all the secrets of DAX. You might want to read this chapter multiple times, for a complete understanding of certain concepts. In our experience, the first read can make a developer wonder, "Why should it be so complicated?" However, after learning the concepts outlined here for the first time, readers start to realize that many of the concepts they struggled in learning have a common denominator; once they grasp it, everything becomes clear.

We introduced several chapters saying that the goal of the chapter was to move the reader to the next level. If each chapter is a level, this is the boss level! Indeed, the concepts of expanded tables and of shadow filter contexts are hard to learn. Once learned, they shed a completely different light upon everything described so far. It is fair to say that—after finishing this chapter—a second read of the whole book is strongly suggested. A second read will likely uncover many details that did not seem helpful at first read. We realize that a full second read of the book takes a lot of effort. But then we did promise that reading *The Definitive Guide to DAX* would transform the reader into a DAX guru. We never said it would be an easy task.

Introducing expanded tables

The first—and most important—concept to learn is that of *expanded tables*. In DAX, every table has a matching expanded version. The expanded version of a table contains all the columns of the original table, plus all the columns of the tables that are on the one-side of a chain of many-to-one relationships starting from the source table.

Consider the model in Figure 14-1.

Table expansion goes towards the one-side. Therefore, to expand a table, one starts from the base table and adds to the base table all the columns of the related tables that are on the one-side of any relationships. For example, *Sales* has a many-to-one relationship with *Product*, so the expanded version of *Sales* contains also all the columns of *Product*. On the other hand, the expanded version of *Product Category* only contains the base table. Indeed, the only table with a relationship with *Product Category* is *Product Subcategory*, but it is on the many-side of the relationship. Thus, table expansion goes from *Product Subcategory* to *Product Category*, but not the other way around.

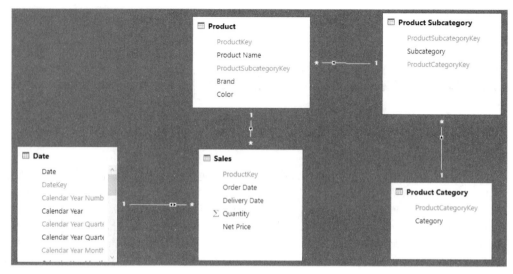

FIGURE 14-1 The figure shows the model used to describe the concept of expanded tables.

Table expansion does not stop at the first level. For example, from *Sales* one can reach *Product Category* following only many-to-one relationships. Thus, the expanded version of *Sales* contains *Product, Product Subcategory,* and *Product Category* columns. Moreover, because *Sales* is on the many side of a many-to-one relationship with *Date*, the expanded version of *Sales* contains *Date* too. In other words, the expanded version of *Sales* contains the entire data model.

The *Date* table requires a bit more attention. In fact, it can be filtered by *Sales* because the relationship that links *Sales* and *Date* has a bidirectional filter direction. Though this relationship is bidirectional, it is not a many-to-one: It is a one-to-many. The expanded version of *Date* only contains *Date* itself, even though *Date* can be filtered by *Sales, Product, Product Subcategory,* and *Product Category.* When filtering occurs because a relationship is bidirectional, the mechanism that applies the filtering is not that of expanded tables. Instead, filters are injected by the DAX code using a different mechanism, which is out of the scope of this chapter. Bidirectional filter propagation is discussed in Chapter 15, "Advanced relationships."

When repeating the same exercise for the other tables in the data model, we create the expanded tables described in Table 14-1.

TABLE 14-1 Expanded versions of the tables

Table	Expanded Version
Date	Date
Sales	All the tables in the entire model
Product	Product, Product Subcategory, Product Category
Product Subcategory	Product Subcategory, Product Category
Product Category	Product Category

There might be different kinds of relationships in a data model: one-to-one relationships, one-to-many relationships, and many-to-many relationships. The rule is always the same: Expansion goes towards the one-side of a relationship. Nevertheless, some examples might help in understanding the concept better. For example, consider the data model in Figure 14-2, which does not follow best practices in data modeling but is useful for educational purposes.

FIGURE 14-2 In this model both relationships have a bidirectional filter. One relationship is one-to-one, and the other is many-to-many.

We purposely used complex kinds of relationships in this model, where the *Product Category* table has one row for each value in *Subcategory*, so there are multiple rows for each category in such a table, and the *ProductCategoryKey* column does not contain unique values. Both relationships have a bidirectional filter. The relationship between *Product* and *Product Details* is a one-to-one relationship, whereas the one between *Product* and *Product Category* is a weak relationship where both sides are the many-side. The rule is always the same: Expansion goes towards the one-side of a relationship, regardless of the side it starts from.

Consequently, *Product Details* expands to *Product,* and *Product* expands to *Product Details* at the same time. The expanded version of the two tables, *Product* and *Product Details*, is indeed the same. Moreover, *Product Category* does not expand to *Product*, nor does *Product* expand to *Product Category*. The reason is that both tables are on the many-side of a weak relationship. When both sides of a relationship are the many-side, expansion does not happen. When both sides of a relationship are set as the many-side, the relationship becomes automatically a *weak relationship*. Not that they have any kind of weakness—weak relationships, like bidirectional filtering, work with a different goal than that of table expansion.

Expanded tables are a useful concept because they provide a clear explanation of how filter context propagation works within a DAX formula. Once a filter is being applied to a column, all the expanded tables containing that column are filtered. This statement deserves further explanation.

We present the expanded tables of the model used in Figure 14-1 on a diagram, which is shown in Figure 14-3.

	Product Category	Product Subcategory	Product	Sales	Date
Category					
ProductCategoryKey					
ProductCategoryKey					
Subcategory					
ProductSubcategoryKey					
ProductSubcategoryKey					
Product Name					
Manufacturer					
Color					
ProductKey					
ProductKey					
Unit Price					
Quantity					
Orde rDate					
Date					
Date Key					
Calendar Year					
Month					
Legend	Native Columns		Related Columns		

FIGURE 14-3 Presenting the data model on a diagram makes it easier to visualize expanded tables.

The chart in Figure 14-3 lists all the columns of the model on the horizontal lines and each table name on the vertical lines. Please note that some column names appear multiple times. Duplicate column names come from the fact that different tables may have column names in common. We colored the cells to distinguish between the columns of the base table and the columns belonging to the expanded table. There are two types of columns:

- **Native columns** are the columns that originally belong to the base table, colored in a slightly darker grey.

- **Related columns** are the columns added to the expanded table by following the existing relationships. These columns are light grey in the diagram.

The diagram helps in finding which tables are filtered by a column. For example, the following measure uses *CALCULATE* to apply a filter on the *Product[Color]* column:

```
RedSales :=
CALCULATE (
    SUM ( Sales[Quantity] ),
    'Product'[Color] = "Red"
)
```

We can use the diagram to highlight the tables containing the *Product[Color]* column. Looking at Figure 14-4, we can immediately conclude that both *Product* and *Sales* are the affected tables.

	Product Category	Product Subcategory	Product	Sales	Date
Category					
ProductCategoryKey					
ProductCategoryKey					
Subcategory					
ProductSubcategoryKey					
ProductSubcategoryKey					
Product Name					
Manufacturer					
Color					
ProductKey					
ProductKey					
Unit Price					
Quantity					
Order Date					
Date					
Date Key					
Calendar Year					
Month					
Legend	Native Columns		Related Columns		

FIGURE 14-4 Coloring the line corresponding to a column makes it evident which tables are filtered.

We can use the same diagram to check how the filter context propagates through relationships. Once DAX filters any column on the one-side of a relationship, it filters all the tables that contain that column in their expanded version. This includes all the tables that are on the many-side of the relationships.

Thinking in terms of expanded tables makes the whole filter context propagation much easier. Indeed, a *filter context operates on all the expanded tables containing the filtered columns*. When speaking in terms of expanded tables, one no longer needs to consider relationships as part of the discussion. Table expansion uses relationships. Once a table has been expanded, the relationships have been included in the expanded tables. They no longer need to be taken into account.

Note Please note that the filter on *Color* propagates to *Date* too, though technically, *Color* does not belong to the expanded version of *Date*. This is the effect of bidirectional filtering at work. It is important to note that the filter on *Color* reaches *Date* through a completely different process, not through expanded tables. Internally, DAX injects a specific filtering code to make bidirectional relationships work, whereas filtering on expanded tables occurs automatically. The difference is only internal, yet it is important to point it out. The same applies for weak relationships: They do not use expanded tables. Weak relationships use filter injection instead.

Understanding *RELATED*

Whenever one references a table in DAX, it is always the expanded table. From a semantic point of view, the *RELATED* keyword does not execute any operation. Instead, it gives a developer access to the related columns of an expanded table. Thus, in the following code the *Unit Price* column belongs to the expanded table of *Sales*, and *RELATED* permits access to it through the row context pointing to the *Sales* table:

```
SUMX (
    Sales,
    Sales[Quantity] * RELATED ( 'Product'[Unit Price] )
)
```

One important aspect of table expansion is that it takes place when a table is defined, not when it is being used. For example, consider the following query:

```
EVALUATE
VAR SalesA =
    CALCULATETABLE (
        Sales,
        USERELATIONSHIP ( Sales[Order Date], 'Date'[Date] )
    )
VAR SalesB =
    CALCULATETABLE (
        Sales,
        USERELATIONSHIP ( Sales[Delivery Date], 'Date'[Date] )
    )
RETURN
    GENERATE (
        VALUES ( 'Date'[Calendar Year] ),
        VAR CurrentYear = 'Date'[Calendar Year]
        RETURN
            ROW (
                "Sales From A", COUNTROWS (
                    FILTER (
                        SalesA,
                        RELATED ( 'Date'[Calendar Year] ) = CurrentYear
                    )
                ),
                "Sales From B", COUNTROWS (
                    FILTER (
                        SalesB,
                        RELATED ( 'Date'[Calendar Year] ) = CurrentYear
                    )
                )
            )
    )
```

SalesA and SalesB are two copies of the Sales table, evaluated in a filter context where two different relationships are active: SalesA uses the relationship between Order Date and Date, whereas SalesB activates the relationship between Delivery Date and Date.

Once the two variables are evaluated, GENERATE iterates over the years; it then creates two additional columns. The two additional columns contain the count of SalesA and SalesB, applying a further filter for the rows where RELATED ('Date'[Calendar Year]) equals the current year. Please note that we had to write rather convoluted code in order to avoid any context transition. Indeed, no context transitions are taking place in the whole GENERATE function call.

The question here is understanding what happens when the two highlighted RELATED functions are called. Unless one thinks in terms of expanded tables, the answer is problematic. When RELATED is executed, the active relationship is the one between *Sales[Order Date]* and *Date[Date]* because the two variables have already been computed earlier and both *USERELATIONSHIP* modifiers have finished their job. Nevertheless, both *SalesA* and *SalesB* are expanded tables, and the expansion occurred when there were two different relationships active. Because *RELATED* only gives access to an expanded column, the consequence is that when iterating over *SalesA*, *RELATED* returns the order year, whereas while iterating over *SalesB*, *RELATED* returns the delivery year.

We can appreciate the difference by looking at the result in Figure 14-5. Without the expanded table, we would have expected the same number of rows for each order year in both columns.

Calendar Year	Sales From A	Sales From B
CY 2005		
CY 2006		
CY 2007	31,682	30,918
CY 2008	28,756	28,759
CY 2009	39,793	39,580
CY 2010		974
CY 2011		

FIGURE 14-5 The two calculations filter different years.

Using *RELATED* in calculated columns

The *RELATED* function accesses the expanded columns of a table. The table expansion occurs when the table is defined, not when it is used. Because of these facts, changing the relationships in a calculated column turns out to be problematic.

As an example, look at the model in Figure 14-6, with two relationships between *Sales* and *Date*.

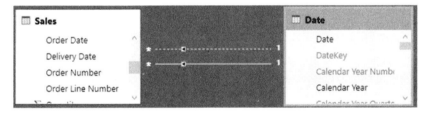

FIGURE 14-6 There are two relationships between *Sales* and *Date*, but only one can be active.

A developer might be interested in adding a calculated column in *Sales* that checks whether the delivery happened in the same quarter as the order. The *Date* table contains a column—*Date[Calendar Year Quarter]*—that can be used for the comparison. Unfortunately, it is easy to obtain the quarter of the order date, whereas retrieving the quarter of the delivery proves to be more challenging.

Indeed, *RELATED ('Date'[Calendar Year Quarter])* returns the quarter of the order date by using the default active relationship. Nevertheless, writing an expression like the following will not change the relationship used for *RELATED*:

```
Sales[DeliveryQuarter] =
CALCULATE (
    RELATED ( 'Date'[Calendar Year Quarter] ),
    USERELATIONSHIP (
        Sales[Delivery Date],
        'Date'[Date]
    )
)
```

There are several problems here. The first is that *CALCULATE* removes the row context, but *CALCULATE* is needed to change the active relationship for *RELATED*. Thus, *RELATED* cannot be used inside the formula argument of *CALCULATE* because *RELATED* requires a row context. There is a second sneaky problem: Even if it were possible to do that, *RELATED* would not work because the row context of a calculated column is created when the table is defined. The row context of a calculated column is generated automatically, so the table is always expanded using the default relationship.

There is no perfect solution to this problem. The best option is to rely on *LOOKUPVALUE*. *LOOKUPVALUE* is a search function that retrieves a value from a table, searching for columns that are equal to certain values provided. The delivery quarter can be computed using the following code:

```
Sales[DeliveryQuarter] =
LOOKUPVALUE (
    'Date'[Calendar Year Quarter],    -- Returns the Calendar Year quarter
    'Date'[Date],                     -- where the Date[Date] column is equal
    Sales[Delivery Date]              -- to the value of Sales[Delivery Date]
)
```

LOOKUPVALUE searches for values that are equal. One cannot add more complex conditions. If needed, then a more complex expression using *CALCULATE* would be required. Moreover, in this case we used *LOOKUPVALUE* in a calculated column, so the filter context is empty. But even in cases where the filter context is actively filtering the model, *LOOKUPVALUE* would ignore it. *LOOKUPVALUE* always searches for a row in a table ignoring any filter context. Finally, *LOOKUPVALUE* accepts a last argument, if provided alone, that is the default value in case there is no match.

Understanding the difference between table filters and column filters

In DAX there is a huge difference between filtering a table and filtering a column. Table filters are powerful tools in the hands of an experienced DAX developer, but they can get quite confusing if used improperly. We will start by looking at a scenario where table filters produce an incorrect result. Later in this section, we will demonstrate how to leverage table filters properly in complex scenarios.

Often a novice DAX developer makes the mistake of thinking that the two following expressions compute the same value:

```
CALCULATE (
    [Sales Amount],
    Sales[Quantity] > 1
)

CALCULATE (
    [Sales Amount],
    FILTER (
        Sales,
        Sales[Quantity] > 1
    )
)
```

The two definitions are actually very different. One is filtering a column; the other is filtering a table. Even though the two versions of the code provide the same result in several scenarios, they are, in fact, computing a completely different expression. To demonstrate their behavior, we included the two definitions in a query:

```
EVALUATE
ADDCOLUMNS (
    VALUES ( 'Product'[Brand] ),
    "FilterCol", CALCULATE (
        [Sales Amount],
        Sales[Quantity] > 1
    ),
    "FilterTab", CALCULATE (
        [Sales Amount],
        FILTER (
            Sales,
            Sales[Quantity] > 1
        )
    )
)
```

The result is surprising to say the least, as we can see in Figure 14-7.

FilterCol returns the expected values, whereas *FilterTab* always returns the same number that corresponds to the grand total of all the brands. Expanded tables play an important role in understanding the reason for this result.

We can examine the behavior of the *FilterTab* calculation in detail. The filter argument of *CALCULATE* iterates over *Sales* and returns all the rows of *Sales* with a quantity greater than 1. The result of *FILTER* is a subset of rows of the *Sales* table. Remember: In DAX a table reference always references the expanded table. Because *Sales* has a relationship with *Product*, the expanded table of *Sales* contains the whole *Product* table too. Among the many columns, it also contains *Product[Brand]*.

Brand	FilterCol	FilterTab
Contoso	3,149,599.81	13,021,408.33
Wide World Importers	814,205.21	13,021,408.33
Northwind Traders	403,528.07	13,021,408.33
Adventure Works	1,706,002.29	13,021,408.33
Southridge Video	598,872.55	13,021,408.33
Litware	1,380,558.35	13,021,408.33
Fabrikam	2,365,917.61	13,021,408.33
Proseware	1,078,439.49	13,021,408.33
A. Datum	906,209.66	13,021,408.33
The Phone Company	479,841.37	13,021,408.33
Tailspin Toys	138,233.93	13,021,408.33

FIGURE 14-7 The first column computes the correct results, whereas the second column always shows a higher number corresponding to the grand total.

The filter arguments of *CALCULATE* are evaluated in the original filter context, ignoring the context transition. The filter on *Brand* comes into effect after *CALCULATE* has performed the context transition. Consequently, the result of *FILTER* contains the values of all the brands related to rows with a quantity greater than 1. Indeed, there are no filters on *Product[Brand]* during the iteration made by *FILTER*.

When generating the new filter context, *CALCULATE* performs two consecutive steps:

1. It operates the context transition.

2. It applies the filter arguments.

Therefore, filter arguments might override the effects of context transition. Because *ADDCOLUMNS* is iterating over the product brand, the effects of context transition on each row should be that of filtering an individual brand. Nevertheless, because the result of *FILTER* also contains the product brand, it overrides the effects of the context transition. The net result is that the value shown is always the total of *Sales Amount* for all the transactions whose quantity is greater than 1, regardless of the product brand.

Using table filters is always challenging because of table expansion. Whenever one applies a filter to a table, the filter is really applied to the expanded table, and this can cause several side effects. The golden rule is simple: Try to avoid using table filters whenever possible. Working with columns leads to simpler calculations, whereas working with tables is much more problematic.

Note The example shown in this section might not be easily applied to a measure defined in a data model. This is because the measure is always executed in an implicit *CALCULATE* to produce the context transition. For example, consider the following measure:

```
Multiple Sales :=
CALCULATE (
    [Sales Amount],
    FILTER (
        Sales,
        Sales[Quantity] > 1
    )
)
```

When executed in a report, a possible DAX query could be:

```
EVALUATE
ADDCOLUMNS (
    VALUES ( 'Product'[Brand] ),
    "FilterTabMeasure", [Multiple Sales]
)
```

The expansion of the table drives the execution of this corresponding query:

```
EVALUATE
ADDCOLUMNS (
    VALUES ( 'Product'[Brand] ),
    "FilterTabMeasure", CALCULATE (
        CALCULATE (
            [Sales Amount],
            FILTER (
                Sales,
                Sales[Quantity] > 1
            )
        )
    )
)
```

The first *CALCULATE* performs the context transition that affects both arguments of the second *CALCULATE*, including the *FILTER* argument. Even though this produces the same result as *FilterCol*, the use of a table filter has a negative impact on performance. Therefore, it is always better to use column filters whenever possible.

Using table filters in measures

In the previous section, we showed a first example where being familiar with expanded tables helped make sense of a result. However, there are several other scenarios where expanded tables prove to be useful. Besides, in previous chapters we used the concept of expanded tables multiple times, although we could not describe what was happening in detail just yet.

For example in Chapter 5, "Understanding *CALCULATE* and *CALCULATETABLE*," while explaining how to remove all the filters applied to the model, we used the following code in a report that was slicing measures by category:

```
Pct All Sales :=
VAR CurrentCategorySales =
    [Sales Amount]
VAR AllSales =
    CALCULATE (
        [Sales Amount],
        ALL ( Sales )
    )
VAR Result =
    DIVIDE (
        CurrentCategorySales,
        AllSales
    )
RETURN
    Result
```

Why does *ALL (Sales)* remove any filter? If one does not think in terms of expanded tables, *ALL* should only remove filters from the *Sales* table, keeping any other filter untouched. In fact, using *ALL* on the *Sales* table means removing any filter from the expanded *Sales* table. Because *Sales* expands to all the related tables, including *Product, Customer, Date, Store,* and any other related tables, using *ALL (Sales)* removes any filter from the entire data model used by that example.

Most of the time this behavior is the one desired and it works intuitively. Still, understanding the internal behavior of expanded tables is of paramount importance; failing to gain that understanding might be a root cause for inaccurate calculations. In the next example, we demonstrate how a simple calculation can fail simply due to a subtlety of expanded tables. We will see why it is better to avoid using table filters in *CALCULATE* statements, unless the developer is purposely looking to take advantage of the side effects of expanded tables. The latter are described in the following sections.

Consider the requirements of a report like the one in Figure 14-8. The report contains a slicer that filters the *Category,* and a matrix showing the sales of subcategories and their respective percentage against the total.

Category	Subcategory	Sales Amount	Pct
☐ Audio	Computers Accessories	341,362.15	5.06%
☐ Cameras and camcorders	Desktops	1,017,127.27	15.09%
☐ Cell phones			
■ Computers	Laptops	1,925,105.28	28.56%
☐ Games and Toys	Monitors	604,386.23	8.97%
☐ Home Appliances	Printers, Scanners & Fax	505,519.67	7.50%
☐ Music, Movies and Audio Books	Projectors & Screens	2,348,048.13	34.83%
☐ TV and Video	**Total**	**6,741,548.73**	**100.00%**

FIGURE 14-8 The *Pct* column shows the percentage of a subcategory against the total sales.

Because the percentage needs to divide the current *Sales Amount* by the corresponding *Sales Amount* for all the subcategories of the selected category, a first (inaccurate) solution might be the following:

```
Pct :=
DIVIDE (
    [Sales Amount],
    CALCULATE (
        [Sales Amount],
        ALL ( 'Product Subcategory' )
    )
)
```

The idea is that by removing the filter on *Product Subcategory*, DAX retains the filter on *Category* and produces the correct result. However, the result is wrong, as we can see in Figure 14-9.

Category	Subcategory	Sales Amount	Pct
☐ Audio	Computers Accessories	341,362.15	1.12%
☐ Cameras and camcorders	Desktops	1,017,127.27	3.32%
☐ Cell phones	Laptops	1,925,105.28	6.29%
■ Computers	Monitors	604,386.23	1.98%
☐ Games and Toys	Printers, Scanners & Fax	505,519.67	1.65%
☐ Home Appliances	Projectors & Screens	2,348,048.13	7.68%
☐ Music, Movies and Audio Books	**Total**	**6,741,548.73**	**22.04%**
☐ TV and Video			

FIGURE 14-9 The first implementation of *Pct* produces the wrong result.

The problem with this formula is that *ALL ('Product Subcategory')* refers to the expanded *Product Subcategory* table. *Product Subcategory* expands to *Product Category*. Consequently, *ALL* removes the filter not only from the *Product Subcategory* table, but also from the *Product Category* table. Therefore, the denominator returns the grand total of all the categories, in turn calculating the wrong percentage.

There are multiple solutions available. In the current report, they all compute the same value, even though they use slightly different approaches. For example, the following *Pct Of Categories* measure computes the percentage of the selected subcategories compared to the total of the related categories. After removing the filter from the expanded table of *Product Subcategory*, *VALUES* restores the filter of the *Product Category* table:

```
Pct Of Categories :=
DIVIDE (
    [Sales Amount],
    CALCULATE (
        [Sales Amount],
        ALL ( 'Product Subcategory' ),
        VALUES ( 'Product Category' )
    )
)
```

Another possible solution is the *Pct Of Visual Total* measure, which uses *ALLSELECTED* without an argument. *ALLSELECTED* restores the filter context of the slicers outside the visual, without the developer having to worry about expanded tables:

```
Pct Of Visual Total :=
DIVIDE (
    [Sales Amount],
    CALCULATE (
        [Sales Amount],
        ALLSELECTED ()
    )
)
```

ALLSELECTED is attractive because of its simplicity. However, in a later section of this chapter we introduce shadow filter contexts. These will provide the reader with a fuller understanding of *ALLSELECTED*. *ALLSELECTED* can be powerful, but it is also a complex function that must be used carefully in convoluted expressions.

Finally, another solution is available using *ALLEXCEPT*, thus comparing the selected subcategories with the categories selected in the slicer:

```
Pct :=
DIVIDE (
    [Sales Amount],
    CALCULATE (
        [Sales Amount],
        ALLEXCEPT ( 'Product Subcategory', 'Product Category' )
    )
)
```

This last formula leverages a particular *ALLEXCEPT* syntax that we have never used so far in the book: *ALLEXCEPT* with two tables, instead of a table and a list of columns.

ALLEXCEPT removes filters from the source table, with the exception of any columns provided as further arguments. That list of columns can include any column (or table) belonging to the expanded table of the first argument. Because the expanded table of *Product Subcategory* contains the whole *Product Category* table, the code provided is a valid syntax. It removes any filter from the whole expanded table of *Product Subcategory*, except for the columns of the expanded table of *Product Category*.

It is worth noting that expanded tables tend to cause more issues when the data model is not correctly denormalized. As a matter of fact, in most of this book we use a version of Contoso where *Category* and *Subcategory* are stored as columns in the *Product* table, instead of being tables by themselves. In other words, we denormalized the category and subcategory tables as attributes of the *Product* table. In a correctly denormalized model, table expansion takes place between *Sales* and *Product* in a more natural way. So as it often happens, putting some thought into the model makes the DAX code easier to author.

Understanding active relationships

When working with expanded tables, another important aspect to consider is the concept of active relationships. It is easy to get confused in a model with multiple relationships. In this section, we want to share an example where the presence of multiple relationships proves to be a real challenge.

Imagine needing to compute *Sales Amount* and *Delivered Amount*. These two measures can be computed by activating the correct relationship with *USERELATIONSHIP*. The following two measures work:

```
Sales Amount :=
SUMX (
    Sales,
    Sales[Quantity] * Sales[Net Price]
)

Delivered Amount :=
CALCULATE (
    [Sales Amount],
    USERELATIONSHIP ( Sales[Delivery Date], 'Date'[Date] )
)
```

The result is visible in Figure 14-10.

Calendar Year	Sales Amount	Delivered Amount
CY 2007	11,309,946	11,034,860
CY 2008	9,927,583	9,901,408
CY 2009	9,353,815	9,442,286
CY 2010		212,790
Total	**30,591,344**	**30,591,344**

FIGURE 14-10 *Sales Amount* and *Delivered Amount* use different relationships.

It is interesting to see a variation of the *Delivered Amount* measure that does not work because it uses a table filter:

```
Delivered Amount =
CALCULATE (
    [Sales Amount],
    CALCULATETABLE (
        Sales,
        USERELATIONSHIP ( Sales[Delivery Date], 'Date'[Date] )
    )
)
```

This new—and unfortunate—formulation of the measure produces a blank result, as we can see in Figure 14-11.

Calendar Year	Sales Amount	Delivered Amount
CY 2007	11,309,946	
CY 2008	9,927,583	
CY 2009	9,353,815	
Total	**30,591,344**	

FIGURE 14-11 Using a table filter, *Delivered Amount* only produces a blank value.

We now investigate why the result is a blank. This requires paying a lot of attention to expanded tables. The result of *CALCULATETABLE* is the expanded version of *Sales*, and among other tables it contains the *Date* table. When *Sales* is evaluated by *CALCULATETABLE,* the active relationship is the one with *Sales[Delivery Date]*. *CALCULATETABLE* therefore returns all the sales delivered in a given year, as an expanded table.

When *CALCULATETABLE* is used as a filter argument by the outer *CALCULATE*, the result of *CALCULATETABLE* filters *Sales* and *Date* through the *Sales* expanded table, which uses the relationship between *Sales[Delivery Date]* and *Date[Date]*. Nevertheless, once *CALCULATETABLE* ends its execution, the default relationship between *Sales[Order Date]* and *Date[Date]* becomes the active relationship again. Therefore, the dates being filtered are now the order dates, not the delivery dates any more. In other words, a table containing delivery dates is used to filter order dates. At this point, the only rows that remain visible are the ones where *Sales[Order Date]* equals *Sales[Delivery Date]*. There are no rows in the model that satisfy this condition; consequently, the result is blank.

To further clarify the concept, imagine that the *Sales* table contains just a few rows, like the ones in Table 14-2.

TABLE 14-2 Example of *Sales* table with only two rows

Order Date	Delivery Date	Quantity
12/31/2007	01/07/2008	100
01/05/2008	01/10/2008	200

If the year 2008 is selected, the inner *CALCULATETABLE* returns the expanded version of *Sales*, containing, among many others, the columns shown in Table 14-3.

TABLE 14-3 The result of *CALCULATETABLE* is the expanded *Sales* table, including *Date[Date]* using the *Sales[Delivery Date]* relationship

Order Date	Delivery Date	Quantity	Date
12/31/2007	01/07/2008	100	01/07/2008
01/05/2008	01/10/2008	200	01/10/2008

When this table is used as a filter, the *Date[Date]* column uses the active relationship, which is the one between *Date[Date]* and *Sales[Order Date]*. At this point, the expanded table of *Sales* appears as in Table 14-4.

TABLE 14-4 The expanded *Sales* table using the default active relationship using the *Sales[Order Date]* column

Order Date	Delivery Date	Quantity	Date
12/31/2007	01/07/2008	100	12/31/2007
01/05/2008	01/10/2008	200	01/05/2008

The rows visible in Table 14-3 try to filter the rows visible in Table 14-4. However, the *Date* column is always different in the two tables, for each corresponding row. Because they do not have the same value, the first row will be removed from the active set of rows. Following the same reasoning, the second row is excluded too.

At the end, only the rows where *Sales[Order Date]* equals *Sales[Delivery Date]* survive the filter; they produce the same value in the *Date[Date]* column of the two expanded tables generated for the different relationships. This time, the complex filtering effect comes from the active relationship. Changing the active relationship inside a *CALCULATE* statement only affects the computation inside *CALCULATE,* but when the result is used outside of *CALCULATE,* the relationship goes back to the default.

As usual, it is worth pointing out that this behavior is the correct one. It is complex, but it is correct. There are good reasons to avoid table filters as much as possible. Using table filters might result in the correct behavior, or it might turn into an extremely complex and unpredictable scenario. Moreover, the measure with a column filter instead of a table filter works fine and it is easier to read.

The golden rule with table filters is to avoid them. The price to pay for developers who do not follow this simple suggestion is twofold: A significant amount of time will be spent understanding the filtering behavior, and performance becomes the worst it could possibly be.

Difference between table expansion and filtering

As explained earlier, table expansion solely takes place from the many-side to the one-side of a relationship. Consider the model in Figure 14-12, where we enabled bidirectional filtering in all the relationships of the data model.

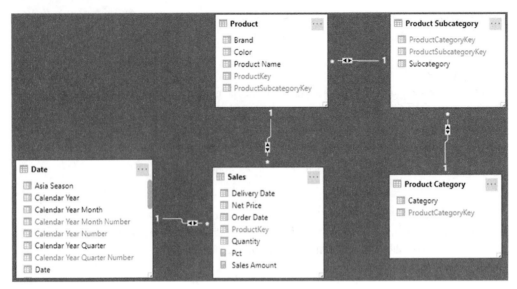

FIGURE 14-12 All the relationships in this model are set with bidirectional cross-filter.

Though the relationship between *Product* and *Product Subcategory* is set with bidirectional filtering, the expanded *Product* table contains subcategories, whereas the expanded *Product Subcategory* table does not contain *Product*.

The DAX engine injects filtering code in the expressions to make bidirectional filtering work as if the expansion went both ways. A similar behavior happens when using the *CROSSFILTER* function. Therefore, in most cases a measure works just as if table expansion took place in both directions. However, be mindful that table expansion actually does not go in the many-side direction.

The difference becomes important with the use of *SUMMARIZE* or *RELATED*. If a developer uses *SUMMARIZE* to perform a grouping of a table based on another table, they have to use one of the columns of the expanded table. For example, the following *SUMMARIZE* statement works well:

```
EVALUATE
SUMMARIZE (
    'Product',
    'Product Subcategory'[Subcategory]
)
```

Whereas the next one—which tries to summarize subcategories based on product color—does not work:

```
EVALUATE
SUMMARIZE (
    'Product Subcategory',
    'Product'[Color]
)
```

The error is "The column *'Color'* specified in the *'SUMMARIZE'* function was not found in the input table," meaning that the expanded version of *Product Subcategory* does not contain *Product[Color]*. Like *SUMMARIZE*, *RELATED* also works with columns that belong to the expanded table exclusively.

Similarly, one cannot group the *Date* table by using columns from other tables, even when these tables are linked by a chain of bidirectional relationships:

```
EVALUATE
SUMMARIZE ( 'Date', 'Product'[Color] )
```

There is only one special case where table expansion goes in both directions, which is the case of a relationship defined as one-to-one. If a relationship is a one-to-one relationship, then both tables are expanded one into the other. This is because a one-to-one relationship makes the two tables semantically identical: Each row in one table has a direct relationship with a single row in the other table. Therefore, it is fair to think of the two tables as being one, split into two sets of columns.

Context transition in expanded tables

The expanded table also influences context transition. The row context converts into an equivalent filter context for all the columns that are part of the expanded table. For example, consider the following query returning the category of a product using two techniques: the *RELATED* function in a row context and the *SELECTEDVALUE* function with a context transition:

```
EVALUATE
SELECTCOLUMNS (
    'Product',
    "Product Key", 'Product'[ProductKey],
    "Product Name", 'Product'[Product Name],
    "Category RELATED", RELATED ( 'Product Category'[Category] ),
    "Category Context Transition", CALCULATE (
        SELECTEDVALUE ( 'Product Category'[Category] )
    )
)
ORDER BY [Product Key]
```

The result of the query includes two identical columns, *Category RELATED* and *Category Context Transition*, as shown in Figure 14-13.

Product Key	Product Name	Category RELATED	Category Context Transition
113	WWI Wireless Transmitter and Bluetooth Headphones X250 White	Audio	Audio
114	WWI Wireless Transmitter and Bluetooth Headphones X250 Red	Audio	Audio
115	WWI Wireless Transmitter and Bluetooth Headphones X250 Silver	Audio	Audio
116	Adventure Works 20" CRT TV E15 Silver	TV and Video	TV and Video
117	Adventure Works 20" CRT TV E15 Black	TV and Video	TV and Video
118	Adventure Works 20" CRT TV E15 White	TV and Video	TV and Video

FIGURE 14-13 The category of each product is displayed in two columns computed with different techniques.

The *Category RELATED* column shows the category corresponding to the product displayed on the same line of the report. This value is retrieved by using *RELATED* when the row context on *Product* is available. The *Category Context Transition* column uses a different approach, generating a context transition by invoking *CALCULATE*. The context transition filters just one row in the *Product* table; this filter is also applied to *Product Subcategory* and *Product Category*, filtering the corresponding rows for the product. Because at this point the filter context only filters one row in *Product Category*, *SELECTEDVALUE* returns the value of the *Product Category* column in the only row filtered in the *Product Category* table.

While this side effect is well known, it is not efficient to rely on this behavior when wanting to retrieve a value from a related table. Even though the result is identical, performance could be very different. The solution using a context transition is particularly expensive if used for many rows in *Product*. Context transition comes at a significant computational cost. Thus, as we will see later in the book, reducing the number of context transitions is important in order to improve performance. Therefore, *RELATED* is a better solution to this specific problem; it avoids the context transition required for *SELECTEDVALUE* to work.

Understanding *ALLSELECTED* and shadow filter contexts

ALLSELECTED is a handy function that hides a giant trap. In our opinion, *ALLSELECTED* is the most complex function in the whole DAX language, even though it looks harmless. In this section we provide an exhaustive technical description of the *ALLSELECTED* internals, along with a few suggestions on when to use and when not to use *ALLSELECTED*.

ALLSELECTED, as any other *ALL** function, can be used in two different ways: as a table function or as a *CALCULATE* modifier. Its behavior differs in these two scenarios. Moreover, *ALLSELECTED* is the only DAX function that leverages *shadow filter contexts*. In this section, we first examine the behavior of *ALLSELECTED*, then we introduce shadow filter contexts, and finally we provide a few tips on using *ALLSELECTED* optimally.

ALLSELECTED can be used quite intuitively. For example, consider the requirements for the report in Figure 14-14.

Brand		Brand	Sales Amount	Pct
☐	A. Datum			
■	Adventure Works	Adventure Works	4,011,112.28	16.88%
■	Contoso	Contoso	7,352,399.03	30.94%
■	Fabrikam	Fabrikam	5,554,015.73	23.38%
■	Litware	Litware	3,255,704.03	13.70%
■	Northwind Traders	Northwind Traders	1,040,552.13	4.38%
■	Proseware	Proseware	2,546,144.16	10.72%
☐	Southridge Video	**Total**	**23,759,927.34**	**100.00%**
☐	Tailspin Toys			
☐	The Phone Company			
☐	Wide World Importers			

FIGURE 14-14 The report shows the sales amount of a few selected brands, along with their percentages.

The report uses a slicer to filter certain brands. It shows the sales amount of each brand, along with the percentage of each given brand over the total of all selected brands. The percentage formula is simple:

```
Pct :=
DIVIDE (
    [Sales Amount],
    CALCULATE (
        [Sales Amount],
        ALLSELECTED ( 'Product'[Brand] )
    )
)
```

Intuitively, our reader likely knows that *ALLSELECTED* returns the values of the brands selected outside of the current visual—that is, the brands selected between Adventure Works and Proseware. But what Power BI sends to the DAX engine is a single DAX query that does not have any concept of "current visual."

How does DAX know about what is selected in the slicer and what is selected in the matrix? The answer is that it does not know these. *ALLSELECTED* does not return the values of a column (or table) filtered outside a visual. What it does is a totally different task, which as a side effect returns the same result most of the time. The correct definition of *ALLSELECTED* consists of the two following statements:

- When used as a table function, *ALLSELECTED* returns the set of values as visible in the last shadow filter context.

- When used as a *CALCULATE* modifier, *ALLSELECTED* restores the last shadow filter context on its parameter.

These last two sentences deserve a much longer explanation.

Introducing shadow filter contexts

In order to introduce shadow filter contexts, it is useful to look at the query that is executed by Power BI to produce the result shown in Figure 14-14:

```
DEFINE
    VAR __DS0FilterTable =
        TREATAS (
            {
                "Adventure Works",
                "Contoso",
                "Fabrikam",
                "Litware",
                "Northwind Traders",
                "Proseware"
            },
            'Product'[Brand]
        )
```

```
EVALUATE
TOPN (
    502,
    SUMMARIZECOLUMNS (
        ROLLUPADDISSUBTOTAL (
            'Product'[Brand],
            "IsGrandTotalRowTotal"
        ),
        __DSOFilterTable,
        "Sales_Amount", 'Sales'[Sales Amount],
        "Pct", 'Sales'[Pct]
    ),
    [IsGrandTotalRowTotal], 0,
    'Product'[Brand], 1
)
ORDER BY
    [IsGrandTotalRowTotal] DESC,
    'Product'[Brand]
```

The query is a bit too complex to analyze—not because of its inherent complexity but because it is generated by an engine and is thus not designed to be human-readable. The following is a version of the formula that is close enough to the original, but easier to understand and describe:

```
EVALUATE
VAR Brands =
    FILTER (
        ALL ( 'Product'[Brand] ),
        'Product'[Brand]
            IN {
                "Adventure Works",
                "Contoso",
                "Fabrikam",
                "Litware",
                "Northwind Traders",
                "Proseware"
            }
    )
RETURN
    CALCULATETABLE (
        ADDCOLUMNS (
            VALUES ( 'Product'[Brand] ),
            "Sales_Amount", [Sales Amount],
            "Pct", [Pct]
        ),
        Brands
    )
```

The result of this latter query is nearly the same as the report we examined earlier, with the noticeable difference that it is missing the total. We see this in Figure 14-15.

Brand	Sales_Amount	Pct
Contoso	7,352,399.03	30.94%
Northwind Traders	1,040,552.13	4.38%
Adventure Works	4,011,112.28	16.88%
Litware	3,255,704.03	13.70%
Fabrikam	5,554,015.73	23.38%
Proseware	2,546,144.16	10.72%

FIGURE 14-15 The query provides almost the same result as the prior report. The only missing part is the total.

Here are some useful notes about the query:

- The outer *CALCULATETABLE* creates a filter context containing six brands.

- *ADDCOLUMNS* iterates over the six brands visible inside the *CALCULATETABLE*.

- Both *Sales Amount* and *Pct* are measures executed inside an iteration. Therefore, a context transition is taking place before the execution of both measures, and the filter context of each of the two measures only contains the currently iterated brand.

- *Sales Amount* does not change the filter context, whereas *Pct* uses *ALLSELECTED* to modify the filter context.

- After *ALLSELECTED* modifies the filter context inside *Pct*, the updated filter context shows all six brands instead of the currently iterated brand.

The last point is the most helpful point in order to understand what a shadow filter context is and how DAX uses it in *ALLSELECTED*. Indeed, the key is that *ADDCOLUMNS* iterates over six brands, the context transition makes only one of them visible, and *ALLSELECTED* needs a way to restore a filter context containing the six iterated brands.

Here is a more detailed description of the query execution, where we introduce shadow filter contexts in step 3:

1. The outer *CALCULATETABLE* creates a filter context with six brands.

2. *VALUES* returns the six visible brands and returns the result to *ADDCOLUMNS*.

3. Being an iterator, *ADDCOLUMNS* creates a *shadow filter context* containing the result of *VALUES*, right before starting the iteration.

   - The shadow filter context is like a filter context, but it remains dormant, not affecting the evaluation in any way.

   - A shadow filter context can only be activated by *ALLSELECTED*, as we are about to explain. For now, just remember that the shadow filter context contains the six iterated brands.

   - We distinguish between a shadow filter context and a regular filter context by calling the latter an *explicit filter context*.

4. During the iteration, the context transition occurs on one given row. Therefore, the context transition creates a new explicit filter context containing solely the iterated brand.

5. When *ALLSELECTED* is invoked during the evaluation of the *Pct* measure, *ALLSELECTED* does the following: **ALLSELECTED restores the last shadow filter context on the column or table passed as parameter, or on all the columns if ALLSELECTED has no arguments**. (The behavior of *ALLSELECTED* without parameters is explained in the following section.)

   • Because the last shadow filter context contained six brands, the selected brands become visible again.

This simple example allowed us to introduce the concept of shadow filter context. The previous query shows how *ALLSELECTED* takes advantage of shadow filter contexts to retrieve the filter context outside of the current visual. Please note that the description of the execution does not use the Power BI visuals anywhere. Indeed, the DAX engine is not cognizant of which visual it is helping to produce. All it receives is a DAX query.

Most of the time *ALLSELECTED* retrieves the correct filter context; indeed, all the visuals in Power BI and, in general, most of the visuals generated by any client tool all generate the same kind of query. Those auto-generated queries always include a top-level iterator that generates a shadow filter context on the items it is displaying. This is the reason why *ALLSELECTED* seems to restore the filter context outside of the visual.

Having taken our readers one step further in their understanding of *ALLSELECTED*, we now need to examine more closely the conditions required for *ALLSELECTED* to work properly:

■ The query needs to contain an iterator. If there is no iterator, then no shadow filter context is present, and *ALLSELECTED* does not perform any operation.

■ If there are multiple iterators before *ALLSELECTED* is executed, then *ALLSELECTED* restores the last shadow filter context. In other words, nesting *ALLSELECTED* inside an iteration in a measure will most likely produce unwanted results because the measure is almost always executed in another iteration of the DAX query produced by a client tool.

■ If the columns passed to *ALLSELECTED* are not filtered by a shadow filter context, then *ALLSELECTED* does not do anything.

At this point, our readers can see more clearly that the behavior of *ALLSELECTED* is quite complex. Developers predominantly use *ALLSELECTED* to retrieve the outer filter context of a visualization. We also used *ALLSELECTED* previously in the book for the very same purpose. In doing so, we always double-checked that *ALLSELECTED* was used in the correct environment, even though we did not explain in detail what was happening.

The fuller semantics of *ALLSELECTED* are related to shadow filter contexts, and merely by chance (or, to be honest, by careful and masterful design) does its effect entail the retrieving of the filter context outside of the current visual.

A good developer knows exactly what *ALLSELECTED* does and only uses it in the scenarios where *ALLSELECTED* works the right way. Overusing *ALLSELECTED* by relying on it in conditions where it is not expected to work can only produce unwanted results, at which point the developer is to blame, not *ALLSELECTED*....

The golden rule for *ALLSELECTED* is quite simple: **ALLSELECTED can be used to retrieve the outer filter context if and only if it is being used in a measure that is directly projected in a matrix or in a visual**. By no means should the developer expect to obtain correct results by using a measure containing *ALLSELECTED* inside an iteration, as we are going to demonstrate in the following sections. Because of this, we, as DAX developers, use a simple rule: If a measure contains *ALLSELECTED* anywhere in the code, then that measure cannot be called by any other measure. This is to avoid the risk that in the chain of measure calls, a developer could start an iteration that includes a call to a measure containing *ALLSELECTED*.

ALLSELECTED returns the iterated rows

To further demonstrate the behavior of *ALLSELECTED*, we make a small change to the previous query. Instead of iterating over *VALUES (Product[Brand])*, we make *ADDCOLUMNS* iterate over *ALL (Product[Brand])*:

```
EVALUATE
VAR Brands =
    FILTER (
        ALL ( 'Product'[Brand] ),
        'Product'[Brand]
            IN {
                "Adventure Works",
                "Contoso",
                "Fabrikam",
                "Litware",
                "Northwind Traders",
                "Proseware"
            }
    )
RETURN
    CALCULATETABLE (
        ADDCOLUMNS (
            ALL ( 'Product'[Brand] ),
            "Sales_Amount", [Sales Amount],
            "Pct", [Pct]
        ),
        Brands
    )
```

In this new scenario, the shadow filter context created by *ADDCOLUMNS* before the iteration contains all the brands—not simply the selected brands. Therefore, when called in the *Pct* measure, *ALLSELECTED* restores the shadow filter context, thus making all brands visible. The result shown in Figure 14-16 is different from that of the previous query shown in Figure 14-15.

Brand	Sales_Amount	Pct
Contoso	7,352,399.03	24.03%
Wide World Importers	1,901,956.66	6.22%
Northwind Traders	1,040,552.13	3.40%
Adventure Works	4,011,112.28	13.11%
Southridge Video	1,384,413.85	4.53%
Litware	3,255,704.03	10.64%
Fabrikam	5,554,015.73	18.16%
Proseware	2,546,144.16	8.32%
A. Datum	2,096,184.64	6.85%
The Phone Company	1,123,819.07	3.67%
Tailspin Toys	325,042.42	1.06%

FIGURE 14-16 *ALLSELECTED restores the currently iterated values, not the previous filter context.*

As you can see, all the brands are visible—and this is expected—but the numbers are different than before, even though the code computing them is the same. The behavior of *ALLSELECTED* in this scenario is correct. Developers might think that it behaves unexpectedly because the filter context defined by the *Brands* variable is ignored by the *Pct* measure; however, *ALLSELECTED* is indeed behaving as it was designed to. *ALLSELECTED* returns the last shadow filter context; In this latter version of the query, the last shadow filter context contains all brands, not only the filtered ones. Indeed, *ADDCOLUMNS* introduced a shadow filter context on the rows it is iterating, which includes all brands.

If one needs to retain the previous filter context, they cannot rely solely on *ALLSELECTED*. The *CALCULATE* modifier that retains the previous filter context is *KEEPFILTERS*. It is interesting to see the result when *KEEPFILTERS* comes into play:

```
EVALUATE
VAR Brands =
    FILTER (
        ALL ( 'Product'[Brand] ),
        'Product'[Brand]
            IN {
                "Adventure Works",
                "Contoso",
                "Fabrikam",
                "Litware",
                "Northwind Traders",
                "Proseware"
            }
    )
RETURN
    CALCULATETABLE (
        ADDCOLUMNS (
            KEEPFILTERS ( ALL ( 'Product'[Brand] ) ),
            "Sales_Amount", [Sales Amount],
            "Pct", [Pct]
        ),
        Brands
    )
```

When used as a modifier of an iterator, *KEEPFILTERS* does not change the result of the iterated table. Instead, it instructs the iterator to apply *KEEPFILTERS* as an implicit *CALCULATE* modifier whenever context transition occurs while iterating on the table. As a result, *ALL* returns all the brands and the shadow filter context also contains all the brands. When the context transition takes place, the previous filter applied by the outer *CALCULATETABLE* with the *Brands* variable is kept. Thus, the query returns all the brands, but values are computed considering only the selected brands, as we can see in Figure 14-17.

Brand	Sales_Amount	Pct
Contoso	7,352,399.03	30.94%
Wide World Importers		
Northwind Traders	1,040,552.13	4.38%
Adventure Works	4,011,112.28	16.88%
Southridge Video		
Litware	3,255,704.03	13.70%
Fabrikam	5,554,015.73	23.38%
Proseware	2,546,144.16	10.72%
A. Datum		
The Phone Company		
Tailspin Toys		

FIGURE 14-17 *ALLSELECTED* with *KEEPFILTERS* produces another result, containing many blanks.

ALLSELECTED without parameters

As the name suggests, *ALLSELECTED* belongs to the *ALL** family. As such, when used as a *CALCULATE* modifier, it acts as a filter remover. If the column used as a parameter is included in any shadow filter context, then it restores the last shadow filter context on that column only. Otherwise, if there is no shadow filter context then it does not do anything.

When used as a *CALCULATE* modifier, *ALLSELECTED,* like *ALL*, can also be used without any parameter. In that case, *ALLSELECTED* restores the last shadow filter context on any column. Remember that this happens if and only if the column is included in any shadow filter context. If a column is filtered through explicit filters only, then its filter remains untouched.

The *ALL** family of functions

Because of the complexity of the *ALL** family of functions, in this section we provide a summary of their behavior. Every *ALL** function behaves slightly differently, so mastering them takes time and experience. In this chapter about advanced DAX concepts, it is time to sum up the main concepts.

The *ALL** family includes the following functions: *ALL, ALLEXCEPT, ALLNOBLANKROW, ALLCROSSFILTERED,* and *ALLSELECTED*. All these functions can be used either as table functions or as *CALCULATE* modifiers. When used as table functions, they are much easier to understand than when used as

CALCULATE modifiers. Indeed, when used as *CALCULATE* modifiers, they might produce unexpected results because they act as filter removers.

Table 14-5 provides a summary of the *ALL** functions. In the remaining part of this section we provide a more complete description of each function.

TABLE 14-5 Summary of the *ALL** family of functions

Function	Table function	*CALCULATE* modifier
ALL	Returns all the distinct values of a column or of a table.	Removes any filter from columns or expanded tables. It never adds a filter; it only removes them if present.
ALLEXCEPT	Returns all the distinct values of a table, ignoring filters on some of the columns of the expanded table.	Removes filters from an expanded table, except from the columns (or tables) passed as further arguments.
ALLNOBLANKROW	Returns all the distinct values of a column or table, ignoring the blank row added for invalid relationships.	Removes any filter from columns or expanded tables; also adds a filter that only removes the blank row. Thus, even if there are no filters, it actively adds one filter to the context.
ALLSELECTED	Returns the distinct values of a column or a table, as they are visible in the last shadow filter context.	Restores the last shadow filter context on tables or columns, if a shadow filter context is present. Otherwise, it does not do anything. It always adds filters, even in the case where the filter shows all the values.
ALLCROSSFILTERED	Not available as a table function.	Removes any filter from an expanded table, including also the tables that can be reached directly or indirectly through bidirectional cross-filters. *ALLCROSSFILTERED* never adds a filter; it only removes filters if present.

The "Table function" column in Table 14-5 corresponds to the scenario where the *ALL** function is being used in a DAX expression, whereas the "*CALCULATE* modifier" column is the specific case when the *ALL** function is the top-level function of a filter argument in *CALCULATE*.

Another significant difference between the two usages is that when one retrieves the result of these *ALL** functions through an *EVALUATE* statement, the result contains only the base table columns and not the expanded table. Nevertheless, internal calculations like the context transition always use the corresponding expanded table. The following examples of DAX code show the different uses of the *ALL* function. The same concepts can be applied to any function of the *ALL** family.

In the following example, *ALL* is used as a simple table function.

```
SUMX (
    ALL ( Sales ),                              -- ALL is a table function
    Sales[Quantity] * Sales[Net Price]
)
```

In the next example there are two formulas, involving iterations. In both cases the *Sales Amount* measure reference generates the context transition, and the context transition happens on the expanded table. When used as a table function, *ALL* returns the whole expanded table.

```
FILTER (
    Sales,
    [Sales Amount] > 100                    -- The context transition takes place
                                            -- over the expanded table
)

FILTER (
    ALL ( Sales ),                          -- ALL is a table function
    [Sales Amount] > 100                    -- The context transition takes place
                                            -- over the expanded table anyway
)
```

In the next example we use *ALL* as a *CALCULATE* modifier to remove any filter from the expanded version of *Sales*:

```
CALCULATE (
    [Sales Amount],
    ALL ( Sales )                           -- ALL is a CALCULATE modifier
)
```

This latter example, although similar to the previous one, is indeed very different. *ALL* is not used as a *CALCULATE* modifier; instead, it is used as an argument of *FILTER*. In such a case, *ALL* behaves as a regular table function returning the entire expanded *Sales* table.

```
CALCULATE (
    [Sales Amount],
    FILTER ( ALL ( Sales ), Sales[Quantity] > 0 )   -- ALL is a table function
                                            -- The filter context receives the
                                            -- expanded table as a filter anyway
)
```

The following are more detailed descriptions of the functions included in the *ALL** family. These functions look simple, but they are rather complex. Most of the time, their behavior is exactly what is needed, but they might produce undesired effects in boundary cases. It is not easy to remember all these rules and all the specific behaviors. We hope our reader finds Table 14-5 useful when unsure about an *ALL** function.

ALL

When used as a table function, *ALL* is a simple function. It returns all the distinct values of one or more columns, or all the values of a table. When used as a *CALCULATE* modifier, it acts as a hypothetical *REMOVEFILTER* function. If a column is filtered, it removes the filter. It is important to note that if a column is cross-filtered, then the filter is not removed. Only direct filters are removed by *ALL*. Thus, using *ALL (Product[Color])* as a *CALCULATE* modifier might still leave *Product[Color]* cross-filtered in case there is a filter on another column of the *Product* table. *ALL* operates on the expanded table. This is why *ALL (Sales)* removes any filter from the tables in the sample model: the expanded *Sales* table includes all the tables of the entire model. *ALL* with no arguments removes any filter from the entire model.

ALLEXCEPT

When used as a table function, *ALLEXCEPT* returns all the distinct values of the columns in a table, except the columns listed. If used as a filter, the result includes the full expanded table. When used as a filter argument in *CALCULATE*, *ALLEXCEPT* acts exactly as an *ALL*, but it does not remove the filter from the columns provided as arguments. It is important to remember that using *ALL/VALUES* is not the same as *ALLEXCEPT*. *ALLEXCEPT* only removes filters, whereas *ALL* removes filters while *VALUES* retains cross-filtering by imposing a new filter. Though subtle, this difference is important.

ALLNOBLANKROW

When used as a table function, *ALLNOBLANKROW* behaves like *ALL*, but it does not return the blank row potentially added because of invalid relationships. *ALLNOBLANKROW* can still return a blank row, if blanks are present in the table. The only row that is never returned is the one added automatically by the engine to fix invalid relationships. When used as a *CALCULATE* modifier, *ALLNOBLANKROW* replaces all the filters with a new filter that only removes the blank row. Therefore, all the columns will only filter out the blank value.

ALLSELECTED

When used as a table function, *ALLSELECTED* returns the values of a table (or column) as filtered in the last shadow filter context. When used as a *CALCULATE* modifier, it restores the last shadow filter context on each column. If multiple columns are present in different shadow filter contexts, it uses the last shadow filter context for each column.

ALLCROSSFILTERED

ALLCROSSFILTERED can be used only as a *CALCULATE* modifier and cannot be used as a table function. *ALLCROSSFILTERED* has only one argument that must be a table. *ALLCROSSFILTERED* removes all the filters on an expanded table (like *ALL*) and on columns and tables that are cross-filtered because of bidirectional cross-filters set on relationships directly or indirectly connected to the expanded table.

Understanding data lineage

We introduced data lineage in Chapter 10, "Working with the filter context," and we have shown our readers how to control data lineage using *TREATAS*. In Chapter 12, "Working with tables," and Chapter 13, "Authoring queries," we described how certain table functions can manipulate the data lineage of the result. This section is a summary of the rules to remember about data lineage, with additional information we could not cover in previous chapters.

Here are the basic rules of data lineage:

- Each column of a table in a data model has a unique data lineage.

- When a filter context filters the model, it filters the model column with the same data lineage of the columns included in the filter context.

- Because a filter is the result of a table, it is important to know how a table function may affect the data lineage of the result:

  - In general, columns used to group data keep their data lineage in the result.

  - Columns containing the result of an aggregation always have a new data lineage.

  - Columns created by *ROW* and *ADDCOLUMNS* always have a new data lineage.

  - Columns created by *SELECTEDCOLUMNS* keep the data lineage of the original column whenever the expression is just a copy of a column in the data model; otherwise, they have a new data lineage.

For example, the following code seems to produce a table where each product color has a corresponding *Sales Amount* value summing all the sales for that color. Instead, because *C2* is a column created by *ADDCOLUMNS*, it does not have the same lineage as *Product[Color]*, even though it has the same content. Please note that we had to use several steps: first, we create the *C2* column; then we select that column only. If other columns remain in the same table, then the result would be very different.

```
DEFINE
    MEASURE Sales[Sales Amount] =
        SUMX ( Sales, Sales[Quantity] * Sales[Net Price] )
EVALUATE
VAR NonBlueColors =
    FILTER (
        ALL ( 'Product'[Color] ),
        'Product'[Color] <> "Blue"
    )
VAR AddC2 =
    ADDCOLUMNS (
        NonBlueColors,
        "[C2]", 'Product'[Color]
    )
VAR SelectOnlyC2 =
    SELECTCOLUMNS ( AddC2, "C2", [C2] )
VAR Result =
    ADDCOLUMNS ( SelectOnlyC2, "Sales Amount", [Sales Amount] )
RETURN Result
ORDER BY [C2]
```

The previous query produces a result where the *Sales Amount* column always has the same value, corresponding to the sum of all the rows in the *Sales* table. This is shown in Figure 14-18.

C2	Sales Amount
Azure	30,591,343.98
Black	30,591,343.98
Brown	30,591,343.98
Gold	30,591,343.98
Green	30,591,343.98
Grey	30,591,343.98
Orange	30,591,343.98
Pink	30,591,343.98
Purple	30,591,343.98
Red	30,591,343.98
Silver	30,591,343.98
Silver Grey	30,591,343.98
Transparent	30,591,343.98
White	30,591,343.98
Yellow	30,591,343.98

FIGURE 14-18 The *C2* column does not have the same data lineage as *Product[Color]*.

TREATAS can be used to transform the data lineage of a table. For example, the following code restores the data lineage to *Product[Color]* so that the last *ADDCOLUMNS* computes *Sales Amount* leveraging the context transition over the *Color* column:

```
DEFINE
    MEASURE Sales[Sales Amount] =
        SUMX ( Sales, Sales[Quantity] * Sales[Net Price] )
EVALUATE
VAR NonBlueColors =
    FILTER (
        ALL ( 'Product'[Color] ),
        'Product'[Color] <> "Blue"
    )
VAR AddC2 =
    ADDCOLUMNS (
        NonBlueColors,
        "[C2]", 'Product'[Color]
    )
VAR SelectOnlyC2 =
    SELECTCOLUMNS ( AddC2, "C2", [C2] )
VAR TreatAsColor =
    TREATAS ( SelectOnlyC2, 'Product'[Color] )
VAR Result =
    ADDCOLUMNS ( TreatAsColor, "Sales Amount", [Sales Amount] )
RETURN Result
ORDER BY 'Product'[Color]
```

As a side effect, *TREATAS* also changes the column name, which must be correctly referenced in the *ORDER BY* condition. The result is visible in Figure 14-19.

Color	Sales Amount
Azure	97,389.89
Black	5,860,066.14
Brown	1,029,508.95
Gold	361,496.01
Green	1,403,184.38
Grey	3,509,138.09
Orange	857,320.28
Pink	828,638.54
Purple	5,973.84
Red	1,110,102.10
Silver	6,798,560.86
Silver Grey	371,908.92
Transparent	3,295.89
White	5,829,599.91
Yellow	89,715.56

FIGURE 14-19 The *Color* column in the result has the same data lineage as *Product[Color]*.

Conclusions

In this chapter we introduced two complex concepts: expanded tables and shadow filter contexts.

Expanded tables are at the core of DAX. It takes some time before one gets used to thinking in terms of expanded tables. However, once the concept of expanded tables has become familiar, they are much simpler to work with than relationships. Only rarely does a developer have to deal with expanded tables, but knowing about them proves to be invaluable when they are the only way to make sense of a result.

In this regard, shadow filter contexts are like expanded tables: They are hard to see and understand, but when they come into play in the evaluation of a formula, they explain exactly how the numbers were computed. Making sense of a complex formula that uses *ALLSELECTED* without first mastering shadow filter contexts is nearly impossible.

However, both concepts are so complex that the best thing to do is to try to avoid them. We do show a few examples of expanded tables being useful in Chapter 15. Shadow filter contexts are useless in code; they are merely a technical means for DAX to let developers compute totals at the visual level.

Try to avoid using expanded tables by only using column filters and not table filters in *CALCULATE* filter arguments. Doing this, the code will be much easier to understand. Usually, it is possible to ignore expanded tables, as long as they are not required for some complex measure.

Try to avoid shadow filter context by never letting *ALLSELECTED* be called inside an iteration. The only iteration before *ALLSELECTED* needs to be the outermost iteration created by the query engine—mostly Power BI. Calling a measure containing *ALLSELECTED* from inside an iteration makes the calculation more complex.

When you follow these two pieces of advice, your DAX code will be correct and easy to understand. Remember that experts can appreciate complexity, but they also understand when it is better to stay away from complexity. Avoiding table filters and *ALLSELECTED* inside iterations does not make a developer look uneducated. Rather, it puts the developer in the category of experts that want their code to always work smoothly.

Advanced relationships

At this point in the book, there are no more DAX secrets to share. In previous chapters we covered all there is to know about the syntax and the functionalities of DAX. Still, there is a long way to go. There are another two chapters dedicated to DAX, and then we will talk about optimization. The next chapter is dedicated to advanced DAX calculations. In this chapter we describe how to leverage DAX to create advanced types of relationships. These include calculated physical relationships and virtual relationships. Then, while on the topic of relationships, we want to share a few considerations about different types of physical relationships: one-to-one, one-to-many, and many-to-many. Each of these types of relationships is worth describing in its peculiarities. Moreover, a topic that still needs some attention is ambiguity. A DAX model can be—or become—ambiguous; this is a serious problem you need to be aware of, in order to handle it well.

At the end of this chapter we cover a topic that is more relevant to data modeling than to DAX, which is relationships with different granularity. When a developer needs to analyze budget and sales, they are likely working with multiple tables with different granularity. Knowing how to manage them properly is a useful skill for DAX developers.

Implementing calculated physical relationships

The first set of relationships we describe is *calculated physical relationships*. In scenarios where the relationship cannot be set because a key is missing, or when one needs to compute the key with complex formulas, a good option is to leverage calculated columns to set the relationship. The result is still a physical relationship; the only difference with a standard relationship is that the relationship key is a calculated column instead of being a column from the data source.

Computing multiple-column relationships

A Tabular model allows the creation of relationships based on a single column only. It does not support relationships based on multiple columns. Nevertheless, relationships based on multiple columns are useful when they appear in data models that cannot be changed. Here are two methods to work with relationships based on multiple columns:

- Define a calculated column containing the composition of the keys; then use it as the new key for the relationship.

- Denormalize the columns of the target table—the one-side in a one-to-many relationship—using the *LOOKUPVALUE* function.

As an example, consider the case of Contoso offering a "Products of the Day" promotion. On certain days, a discount is offered on a set of products. The model is visible in Figure 15-1.

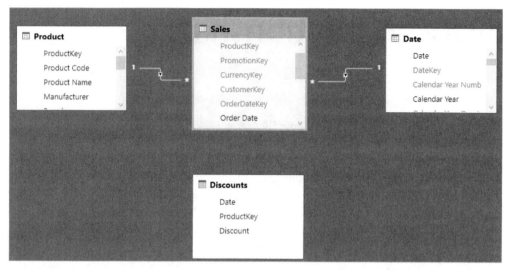

FIGURE 15-1 The *Discounts* table needs a relationship based on two columns with *Sales*.

The *Discounts* table contains three columns: *Date, ProductKey,* and *Discount.* If a developer needs this information in order to compute the amount of the discount, they are faced with a problem: for any given sale, the discount depends on *ProductKey* and *Order Date.* Thus, it is not possible to create the relationship between *Sales* and *Discounts*; it would involve two columns, and DAX only supports relationships based on a single column.

The first option is to create a new column in both *Discount* and *Sales,* containing the combination of the two columns:

```
Sales[DiscountKey] =
COMBINEVALUES (
    "-",
    Sales[Order Date],
    Sales[ProductKey]
)

Discounts[DiscountKey] =
COMBINEVALUES(
    "-",
    Discounts[Date],
    Discounts[ProductKey]
)
```

The calculated columns use the *COMBINEVALUES* function. *COMBINEVALUES* requires a separator and a set of expressions that are concatenated as strings, separated by the separator provided. One could obtain the same result in terms of column values by using a simpler string concatenation, but *COMBINEVALUES* offers a few advantages. Indeed, *COMBINEVALUES* is particularly useful when creating relationships based on calculated columns if the model uses DirectQuery. *COMBINEVALUES* assumes—but does not validate—that when the input values are different, the output strings are also different. Based on this assumption, when *COMBINEVALUES* is used to create calculated columns to build a relationship that joins multiple columns from two DirectQuery tables, an optimized join condition is generated at query time.

> **Note** More details about optimizations obtained by using *COMBINEVALUES* with Direct-Query are available at https://www.sqlbi.com/articles/using-combinevalues-to-optimize-directquery-performance/.

Once the two columns are in place, one can finally create the relationship between the two tables. Indeed, a relationship can be safely created on top of calculated columns.

This solution is straightforward and works well. Yet there are scenarios where this is not the best option because it requires the creation of two calculated columns with potentially many different values. As you learn in later chapters about optimization, this might have a negative impact on both model size and query speed.

The second option is to use the *LOOKUPVALUE* function. Using *LOOKUPVALUE,* one can denormalize the discount in the *Sales* table by defining a new calculated column containing the discount:

```
Sales[Discount] =
LOOKUPVALUE (
    Discounts[Discount],
    Discounts[ProductKey], Sales[ProductKey],
    Discounts[Date], Sales[Order Date]
)
```

Following this second pattern, no relationship is created. Instead, the *Discount* value is denormalized in the *Sales* table by performing a lookup.

Both options work well, and picking the right one depends on several factors. If *Discount* is the only column needed, then denormalization is the best option because it makes the code simple to author, and it reduces memory usage. Indeed, it requires a single calculated column with fewer distinct values compared to the two calculated columns required for a relationship.

On the other hand, if the *Discounts* table contains many columns needed in the code, then each of them should be denormalized in the *Sales* table. This results in a waste of memory and possibly in decreased processing performance. In that case, the calculated column with the new composite key might be preferable.

This simple first example is important because it demonstrates a common and important feature of DAX: the ability to create relationships based on calculated columns. This demonstrates that a user can create a new relationship, provided that they can compute and materialize the key in a calculated column. The next example demonstrates how to create relationships based on static ranges. By extending the concept, it is possible to create several kinds of relationships.

Implementing relationships based on ranges

In order to show why calculated physical relationships are a useful tool, we examine a scenario where one needs to perform a static segmentation of products based on their list price. The price of a product has many different values and performing an analysis slicing by price does not provide useful insights. In that case, a common technique is to partition the different prices into separate buckets, using a configuration table like the one in Figure 15-2.

PriceRangeKey	PriceRange	MinPrice	MaxPrice
1	Very low		10
2	Low	10	30
3	Medium	30	80
4	High	80	150
5	Very high	150	99,999

FIGURE 15-2 This is the *Configuration* table for the price ranges.

As was the case in the previous example, it is not possible to create a direct relationship between the *Sales* table and the *Configuration* table. The reason is that the key in the configuration table depends on a relationship based on a range of values (also known as a between condition), which is not supported by DAX. We could compute a key in the *Sales* table by using nested *IF* statements; however, this would require including the values of the configuration table in the formula like in the following example, which is not the suggested solution:

```
Sales[PriceRangeKey] =
SWITCH (
    TRUE (),
    Sales[Net Price] <=  10, 1,
    Sales[Net Price] <=  30, 2,
    Sales[Net Price] <=  80, 3,
    Sales[Net Price] <= 150, 4,
    5
)
```

A good solution should not include the boundaries in the formula. Instead, the code should be designed to adapt to the contents of the table, so that updating the configuration table updates the whole model.

In this case a better solution is to denormalize the price range directly in the *Sales* table by using a calculated column. The pattern of the code is quite similar to the previous one—the main difference being the formula, which, this time, cannot be a simple *LOOKUPVALUE*:

```
Sales[PriceRange] =
VAR FilterPriceRanges =
    FILTER (
        PriceRanges,
        AND (
            PriceRanges[MinPrice] <= Sales[Net Price],
```

```
        PriceRanges[MaxPrice] > Sales[Net Price]
        )
    )
VAR Result =
    CALCULATE (
        VALUES ( PriceRanges[PriceRange] ),
        FilterPriceRanges
    )
RETURN
    Result
```

It is interesting to note the usage of *VALUES* to retrieve a single value: *VALUES* returns a table, not a value. However, as explained in Chapter 3, "Using basic table functions," whenever a table contains a single row and a single column, the table is automatically converted into a scalar value if required by the expression.

Because of the way *FILTER* computes its result, it always returns a single row from the configuration table. Therefore, *VALUES* is guaranteed to always return a single row; the result of *CALCULATE* is thus the description of the price range containing the net price of the current row in the *Sales* table. This expression works well if the configuration table is well designed. But if the ranges contain holes or overlaps in range of values, then *VALUES* might return multiple rows, and the expression might result in an error.

The previous technique denormalizes values in the *Sales* table. Going one step further means denormalizing the key instead of the description and then building a physical relationship based on the new calculated column. This additional step requires some level of attention in the definition of the calculated column. A simple modification of the *PriceRange* column is enough to retrieve the key, but it is still not enough to create the relationship. The following is the code required to retrieve the key and blank the result in case of errors:

```
Sales[PriceRangeKey] =
VAR FilterPriceRanges =
    FILTER (
        PriceRanges,
        AND (
            PriceRanges[MinPrice] <= Sales[Net Price],
            PriceRanges[MaxPrice] > Sales[Net Price]
        )
    )
VAR Result =
    CALCULATE (
        IFERROR (
            VALUES ( PriceRanges[PriceRangeKey] ),
            BLANK ()
        ),
        FilterPriceRanges
    )
RETURN
    Result
```

The column computes the correct value. Unfortunately, trying to build the relationship between *PriceRanges* and *Sales* based on the newly created *PriceRangeKey* column results in an error because of a circular dependency. Circular dependencies frequently occur when creating relationships based on calculated columns or calculated tables.

In this example, the fix is indeed simple: you need to use *DISTINCT* instead of *VALUES* in the highlighted row of the formula. Once *DISTINCT* is in place, the relationship can be created. The result is visible in Figure 15-3.

PriceRange	Sales Amount
Very low	139,686.63
Low	495,522.26
Medium	855,390.66
High	2,130,309.01
Very high	26,970,435.41
Total	**30,591,343.98**

FIGURE 15-3 Slicing by price range is possible once the relationship is set correctly.

Prior to using *DISTINCT*, the presence of *VALUES* would generate a circular dependency. Replacing *VALUES* with *DISTINCT* works like magic. The underlying mechanisms are quite intricate. The next section provides a complete explanation of circular dependencies that might appear because of relationships with calculated columns or calculated tables, along with a complete explanation of why *DISTINCT* removes the problem.

Understanding circular dependency in calculated physical relationships

In the previous example, we created a calculated column and then used it in a relationship. This resulted in a circular dependency error. As soon as you start working with calculated physical relationships, this error can appear quite often. Therefore, it is useful to spend some time understanding exactly the source of the error. This way, you will also learn how to avoid it.

Let us recall the code of the calculated column in its shorter form:

```
Sales[PriceRangeKey] =
CALCULATE (
    VALUES ( PriceRanges[PriceRangeKey] ),
    FILTER (
        PriceRanges,
        AND (
            PriceRanges[MinPrice] <= Sales[Net Price],
            PriceRanges[MaxPrice] > Sales[Net Price]
        )
    )
)
```

The *PriceRangeKey* column depends on the *PriceRanges* table. If a change is detected in the *PriceRanges* table, then *Sales[PriceRangeKey]* must be recalculated. Because the formula contains several references to the *PriceRanges* table, the dependency is clear. What is less obvious is that creating a relationship between this column and the *PriceRanges* table creates a dependency the other way around.

In Chapter 3 we mentioned that the DAX engine creates a blank row on the one-side of a relationship if the relationship is invalid. Thus, when a table is on the one-side of a relationship, its content depends on the validity of the relationship. In turn, the validity of the relationship depends on the content of the column used to set the relationship.

In our scenario, if one could create a relationship between *Sales* and *PriceRanges* based on *Sales[PriceRangeKey]*, then *PriceRanges* might have a blank row or not, depending on the value of *Sales[PriceRangeKey]*. In other words, when the value of *Sales[PriceRangeKey]* changes, the content of the *PriceRanges* table might also change. But in turn, if the value of *PriceRanges* changes, then *Sales[PriceRangeKey]* might require an update—even though the added blank row should never be used. This is the reason why the engine detects a circular dependency. It is hard to spot for a human, but the DAX algorithm finds it immediately.

If the engineers who created DAX had not worked on the problem, it would have been impossible to create relationships based on calculated columns. Instead, they added some logic in DAX specifically to handle scenarios like this.

Instead of having only one kind of dependency, in DAX there are two types of dependencies: formula dependency and blank row dependency. In our example, this is the situation:

- *Sales[PriceRangeKey]* depends on *PriceRanges* both because of the formula (it references the *PriceRanges* table) and because of the blank row (it uses the *VALUES* function, which might return the additional blank row).

- *PriceRanges* depends on *Sales[PriceRangeKey]* only because of the blank row. A change in the value of *Sales[PriceRangeKey]* does not change the content of *PriceRanges*. It only affects the presence of the blank row.

To break the chain of the circular dependency, it is enough to break the dependency of *Sales[PriceRangeKey]* from the presence of the blank row in *PriceRanges*. This can be obtained by making sure that all the functions used in the formula do not depend on the blank row. *VALUES* includes the additional blank row if present. Therefore, *VALUES* depends on the blank row. *DISTINCT,* on the other hand, always has the same value, regardless of the presence of the additional blank row. Consequently, *DISTINCT* does not depend on the blank row.

If you use *DISTINCT* instead of *VALUES*, then *Sales[PriceRangeKey]* no longer depends on the blank row. The net effect is that the two entities—the table and the column—still depend on each other, but for different reasons. *PriceRanges* depends on *Sales[PriceRangeKey]* for the blank row, whereas *Sales[PriceRangeKey]* depends on *Sales* because of the formula. Being two unrelated dependencies, the circular dependency disappears and it is possible to create the relationship.

Whenever creating columns that might later be used to set relationships, you need to pay special attention to the following details:

- Using *DISTINCT* instead of *VALUES*.

- Using *ALLNOBLANKROW* instead of *ALL*.

- Beware of *CALCULATE* with filters using the compact syntax.

The first two points are quite clear. The following elaborates on the last point—paying attention to *CALCULATE*. For example, consider the following expression:

```
=
CALCULATE (
    MAX ( Customer[YearlyIncome] ),
    Customer[Education] = "High school"
)
```

At first sight, it looks like this formula does not depend on the blank row in *Customer*. But in fact, it does. The reason is that DAX expands the syntax of *CALCULATE* with the compact syntax of a filter argument, into a complete filter over a table corresponding to the following code:

```
=
CALCULATE (
    MAX ( Customer[YearlyIncome] ),
    FILTER (
        ALL ( Customer[Education] ),
        Customer[Education] = "High school"
    )
)
```

The highlighted row containing the *ALL* function creates a dependency on the blank row. In general, blank row dependencies might be hard to spot. But once you understand the basic principle of circular dependencies, they are not complex to remove. The previous example can easily be rewritten this way:

```
=
CALCULATE (
    MAX ( Customer[YearlyIncome] ),
    FILTER (
        ALLNOBLANKROW ( Customer[Education] ),
        Customer[Education] = "High school"
    )
)
```

By using *ALLNOBLANKROW* instead of *ALL*, the dependency on the additional blank row in *Customer* table disappears.

It is important to note that often, the presence of functions that rely on the blank row is hidden within the code. As an example, consider the code used in the previous section where we created the calculated physical relationship based on the price range. Here is the original code:

```
Sales[PriceRangeKey] =
CALCULATE (
    VALUES ( PriceRanges[PriceRangeKey] ),
    FILTER (
        PriceRanges,
        AND (
            PriceRanges[MinPrice] <= Sales[Net Price],
            PriceRanges[MaxPrice] > Sales[Net Price]
        )
    )
)
```

In the previous formula, the presence of *VALUES* is very clear. Yet, a different way to author the same code without using *VALUES* is to rely on *SELECTEDVALUE*, which does not return an error in case multiple rows are visible:

```
Sales[PriceRangeKey] =
VAR FilterPriceRanges =
    FILTER (
        PriceRanges,
        AND (
            PriceRanges[MinPrice] <= Sales[Net Price],
            PriceRanges[MaxPrice] > Sales[Net Price]
        )
    )
VAR Result =
    CALCULATE (
        SELECTEDVALUE ( PriceRanges[PriceRangeKey] ),
        FilterPriceRanges
    )
RETURN Result
```

Unfortunately, as soon as you try to create the relationship, this code raises a circular dependency error too, although it looks like *VALUES* is not present. Indeed, though hidden, *VALUES* is present. The reason is that *SELECTEDVALUE* internally implements the following logic:

```
Sales[PriceRangeKey] =
VAR FilterPriceRanges =
    FILTER (
        PriceRanges,
        AND (
            PriceRanges[MinPrice] <= Sales[Net Price],
            PriceRanges[MaxPrice] > Sales[Net Price]
        )
    )
VAR Result =
    CALCULATE (
        IF (
            HASONEVALUE ( PriceRanges[PriceRangeKey] ),
```

```
              VALUES ( PriceRanges[PriceRangeKey] ),
              BLANK ()
          ),
          FilterPriceRanges
      )
RETURN
    Result
```

By expanding the code of *SELECTEDVALUES*, now the presence of *VALUES* is more evident. Hence, so is the dependency on the blank row that generates the circular dependency.

Implementing virtual relationships

In the previous sections we discussed how to leverage calculated columns to create physical relationships. However, there are scenarios where a physical relationship is not the right solution and virtual relationships are a better approach. A virtual relationship mimics a real relationship. From a user point of view, a virtual relationship looks like a real relationship although there is no relationship in the physical model. Because there is no relationship, you need to author DAX code to transfer a filter from one table to another.

Transferring filters in DAX

One of the most powerful features of DAX is its ability to move a filter from one table to another by following relationships. Yet, there are scenarios where it is hard—if not impossible—to create a physical relationship between two entities. A DAX expression can mimic the relationship in multiple ways. This section shows a few techniques by using a somewhat elaborate scenario.

Contoso advertises in local newspapers and on the web, choosing one or more brands to promote each month. This information is stored in a table named *Advertised Brands* that contains the year, the month, and the brand—if any—on sale. You can see an excerpt of the table in Figure 15-4.

Calendar Year	Month	Brand
CY 2007	February	A. Datum
CY 2007	February	Tailspin Toys
CY 2007	March	A. Datum
CY 2007	March	Northwind Traders
CY 2007	March	Proseware
CY 2007	March	Southridge Video
CY 2007	March	Tailspin Toys
CY 2007	March	The Phone Company
CY 2007	March	Wide World Importers
CY 2007	April	A. Datum
CY 2007	April	Contoso
CY 2007	April	Proseware
CY 2007	May	Adventure Works

FIGURE 15-4 The table contains one row for each brand in the month where it was advertised.

It is important to note that there is no unique column in the table. Although all the rows are unique, each column has many duplicates. Therefore, the table cannot be on the one-side of a relationship. This fact becomes of higher importance as soon as we further outline the requirements.

The requirement is to create a measure that computes the sales amount of the products, only within the time period when they were being advertised. In order to solve that scenario, it is necessary to determine whether a brand is being advertised or not in a given month. If it were possible to create a relationship between *Sales* and the *Advertised Brands* table, the code would be simple to author. Unfortunately, the relationship is not easy to create (and this is by design for the purpose of this teaching).

One possible solution is to create a new calculated column in both tables containing the concatenation of year, month, and brand. This follows the technique outlined earlier in this chapter, to create a relationship between two tables based on multiple columns. Nevertheless, in this scenario there are other interesting alternatives worth exploring that avoid the creation of new calculated columns.

A first yet suboptimal solution is to rely on iterations. One could iterate the *Sales* table row by row, and on each row check if the brand of the product being sold was being advertised in that month. Thus, the following measure solves the scenario, but it is not the best solution:

```
Advertised Brand Sales :=
SUMX (
    FILTER (
        Sales,
        CONTAINS (
            'Advertised Brands',
            'Advertised Brands'[Brand], RELATED ( 'Product'[Brand] ),
            'Advertised Brands'[Calendar Year], RELATED ( 'Date'[Calendar Year] ),
            'Advertised Brands'[Month], RELATED ( 'Date'[Month] )
        )
    ),
    Sales[Quantity] * Sales[Net Price]
)
```

The measure uses the *CONTAINS* function, which searches for the presence of a row in a table. *CONTAINS* accepts the table to search in as its first parameter. Following are pairs of parameters: the first one being a column in the table to search and the second one being the value to search. In the example, *CONTAINS* returns *True* if in *Advertised Brands* there is at least one row where the brand is the current brand, the year is the current year, and the month is the current month—where "current" means the *Sales* row currently iterated by *FILTER*.

The measure computes a correct result, as shown in Figure 15-5, but there are several issues.

Calendar Year	Sales Amount	Advertised Brand Sales
CY 2007	**30,591,343.98**	**2,670,647.22**
Audio	384,518.16	22,607.34
Cameras and camcorders	7,192,581.95	1,031,119.78
Cell phones	1,604,610.26	133,897.59
Computers	6,741,548.73	499,697.11
Games and Toys	360,652.81	22,971.36
Home Appliances	9,600,457.04	561,845.41
Music, Movies and Audio Books	314,206.74	10,591.25
TV and Video	4,392,768.29	387,917.40
CY 2008	**30,591,343.98**	**2,861,643.84**
Audio	384,518.16	29,084.79
Cameras and camcorders	7,192,581.95	349,467.40

FIGURE 15-5 *Advertised Brand Sales* represents the sales of only the brands being advertised.

Here are the two most problematic issues of the previous code:

- *FILTER* iterates over *Sales*—which is a large table—and for each row it calls the *CONTAINS* function. Even though *CONTAINS* is a fast function, calling it millions of times results in poor performance.

- The measure does not take advantage of the presence of the *Sales Amount* measure, which already computes the sales amount. In this case the duplicated code is a simple multiplication, but if the measure to compute were more complex, this approach would not be the best. Indeed, it requires duplicating the expression to compute within the iteration.

A much better option to solve the scenario is to use *CALCULATE* to transfer the filter from the *Advertised Brands* table both to the *Product* table (using the brand as a filter) and to the *Date* table (using the year and the month). This can be accomplished in several ways, as shown in the next sections.

Transferring a filter using *TREATAS*

The first and best option is using *TREATAS* to move the filter from the *Advertised Brands* over to the other tables. As explained in Chapters 10, "Working with the filter context," 12, "Working with tables," and 13, "Authoring queries," *TREATAS* changes the data lineage of a table so that its content can be used as a filter on specific columns of the data model.

Advertised Brands has no relationships with any other table in the model. Thus, normally its content cannot be used as a filter. By using *TREATAS*, one can change the data lineage of *Advertised Brands* so that it can be used as a filter argument of *CALCULATE* and propagate its filter to the entire model. The following measure performs exactly this operation:

```
Advertised Brand Sales TreatAs :=
VAR AdvertisedBrands =
    SUMMARIZE (
        'Advertised Brands',
```

```
        'Advertised Brands'[Brand],
        'Advertised Brands'[Calendar Year],
        'Advertised Brands'[Month]
    )
VAR FilterAdvertisedBrands =
    TREATAS (
        AdvertisedBrands,
        'Product'[Brand],
        'Date'[Calendar Year],
        'Date'[Month]
    )
VAR Result =
    CALCULATE ( [Sales Amount], KEEPFILTERS ( FilterAdvertisedBrands ) )
RETURN
    Result
```

SUMMARIZE retrieves the brand, year, and month advertised. *TREATAS* receives this table and changes its lineage, so that it will filter the product brand and the year and month in *Date*. The resulting table in *FilterAdvertisedBrands* has the correct data lineage. Therefore, it filters the model showing only the brands in the year and month when they are being advertised.

It is important to note that *KEEPFILTERS* is required. Indeed, forgetting it means that *CALCULATE* will override the filter context on the brand, year, and month—and this is unwanted. The *Sales* table needs to receive both the filter coming from the visual (which might be filtering only one year or one brand) and the filter coming from the *Advertised Brands* table. Therefore, *KEEPFILTERS* is mandatory to obtain a correct result.

This version of the code is much better than the one using the iteration. It uses the *Sales Amount* measure, thus avoiding the need to rewrite its code, and it does not iterate over the *Sales* table to perform the lookup. This code only scans the *Advertised Brands* table, which is expected to be on the smaller side; it then applies the filter to the model prior to calling the *Sales Amount* measure. Even though this version might be less intuitive, it performs much better than the example based on *CON-TAINS* shown in the previous section.

Transferring a filter using *INTERSECT*

Another option to obtain the same result is to use the *INTERSECT* function. Compared to the previous example using *TREATAS*, the logic is similar; performance-wise there is a small difference in favor of the *TREATAS* version, which is still the best option. The following code implements the technique based on *INTERSECT*:

```
Advertised Brand Sales Intersect :=
VAR SelectedBrands =
    SUMMARIZE (
        Sales,
        'Product'[Brand],
        'Date'[Calendar Year],
        'Date'[Month]
    )
```

```
VAR AdvertisedBrands =
    SUMMARIZE (
        'Advertised Brands',
        'Advertised Brands'[Brand],
        'Advertised Brands'[Calendar Year],
        'Advertised Brands'[Month]
    )
VAR Result =
    CALCULATE (
        [Sales Amount],
        INTERSECT (
            SelectedBrands,
            AdvertisedBrands
        )
    )
RETURN
    Result
```

INTERSECT retains the data lineage of the first table it receives. Therefore, the resulting table is still a table that can filter *Product* and *Date*. This time, *KEEPFILTERS* is not needed because the first *SUMMA-RIZE* already only contains the visible brands and months; *INTERSECT* only removes from this list the ones that are not being advertised.

From a performance point of view, this code requires a scan of the *Sales* table to produce the list of existing brands and months, plus another scan to compute the sales amount. Therefore, it is slower than the version using *TREATAS*. But it is worth learning this technique because it might be useful in other scenarios involving other set functions, like *UNION* and *EXCEPT*. The set functions in DAX can be combined to create filters, authoring powerful measures in a relatively simple way.

Transferring a filter using *FILTER*

A third alternative is available to the DAX developer: using *FILTER* and *CONTAINS*. The code is similar to the first version with *SUMX*—the main differences being that it uses *CALCULATE* instead of *SUMX*, and it avoids iterating over the *Sales* table. The following code implements this alternative:

```
Advertised Brand Sales Contains :=
VAR SelectedBrands =
    SUMMARIZE (
        Sales,
        'Product'[Brand],
        'Date'[Calendar Year],
        'Date'[Month]
    )
VAR FilterAdvertisedBrands =
    FILTER (
        SelectedBrands,
        CONTAINS (
            'Advertised Brands',
            'Advertised Brands'[Brand], 'Product'[Brand],
            'Advertised Brands'[Calendar Year], 'Date'[Calendar Year],
            'Advertised Brands'[Month], 'Date'[Month]
```

```
        )
    )
VAR Result =
    CALCULATE (
        [Sales Amount],
        FilterAdvertisedBrands
    )
RETURN
    Result
```

The *FILTER* function used as a filter argument to *CALCULATE* uses the same *CONTAINS* technique used in the first example. This time, instead of iterating *Sales*, it iterates over the result of *SUMMARIZE*. As explained in Chapter 14, "Advanced DAX concepts," using the *Sales* table as a filter argument in *CALCULATE* would be wrong because of the expanded table. Therefore, filtering only three columns is a better approach. The result of *SUMMARIZE* already has the correct data lineage; moreover, *KEEPFILTERS* is not required because *SUMMARIZE* already only retains the existing values for brand, year, and month.

Performance-wise this is the worst solution among the last three, even though it is faster than the original code based on *SUMX*. Moreover, all the solutions based on *CALCULATE* share the significant advantage that they do not need to duplicate the business logic of the calculation included in the *Sales Amount* measure, as our first trial with *SUMX* did.

Implementing dynamic segmentation using virtual relationships

In all the variations demonstrated earlier, we used DAX code to compute values and transfer a filter in absence of a relationship, though it would have been possible to create a physical relationship modifying the data model. However, there are scenarios where the relationship cannot be created in any way, like the one described in this section.

The virtual relationship solves a variation of the static segmentation learned earlier in this chapter. In the static segmentation, we assigned each sale to a specific segment using a calculated column. In dynamic segmentation, the assignment occurs dynamically; also, it is not based on a column like the net price but rather on a calculation like the sales amount. The dynamic segmentation must have a filter target: In this example, the segmentation filters customers based on the *Sales Amount* measure.

The configuration table contains the segment names and their boundaries, as shown in Figure 15-6.

Segment	MinSale	MaxSale
Very Low	0	75
Low	75	100
Medium	100	500
High	500	1,000
Very High	1,000	99,999,999

FIGURE 15-6 Configuration table for dynamic segmentation.

If a customer spends between 75 and 100 USD in one sale, then they are assigned to the Low segment as per the configuration table. One important detail about dynamic segmentation is that the value of the measure depends on the user selection in the report. For example, if a user selects one color, then the assignment of a customer to a segment must be executed only considering the sales of products of that given color. Because of this dynamic calculation, using a relationship is not an option. Consider the following report in Figure 15-7 that shows how many customers belong to each segment every year, only filtering a selection of categories.

Category	Segment	CY 2007	CY 2008	CY 2009	Total
■ Audio					
☐ Cameras and camcorders	Very Low	210	1	3	**213**
■ Cell phones	Low	258	33	3	**289**
☐ Computers	Medium	427	133	88	**641**
☐ Games and Toys					
☐ Home Appliances	High	28	13	29	**63**
☐ Music, Movies and Audio Books	Very High	49	78	119	**231**
☐ TV and Video	**Total**	**972**	**258**	**242**	**1,437**

FIGURE 15-7 Each customer is assigned a segment, possibly a different one every year.

One customer might belong to different segments over the years. One customer can be in the Very Low segment in 2008 and then move to the Medium segment the next year. Moreover, by changing the selection on the categories, all the numbers must be updated accordingly.

In other words, a user browsing the model has the perception that a relationship is indeed present, meaning that each customer is uniquely assigned to one segment. However, this assignment cannot be made by using a physical relationship. The reason is that the same customer can be assigned to different segments in different cells of the report. In this scenario, DAX is the only way to solve the problem.

The measure to compute is the number of customers belonging to a specific segment. In other words, the measure counts how many customers belong to a segment considering all the filters in the current filter context. The formula looks simple, and yet its behavior requires a little clarification:

```
CustInSegment :=
SUMX (
    Segments,
    COUNTROWS (
        FILTER (
            Customer,
            VAR SalesOfCustomer = [Sales Amount]
            VAR IsCustomerInSegment =
                AND (
                    SalesOfCustomer > Segments[MinSale],
                    SalesOfCustomer <= Segments[MaxSale]
                )
            RETURN
                IsCustomerInSegment
        )
    )
)
```

Apart from the grand total, every row of the report in Figure 15-7 has a filter context filtering one segment only. Thus, *SUMX* iterates only one row. *SUMX* is useful to make it easy to retrieve the segment boundaries (*MinSale* and *MaxSale*) and to correctly compute the total in the presence of filters. Inside *SUMX*, *COUNTROWS* counts the number of customers whose sales (saved in the *SalesOfCustomer* variable for performance reasons) fall between the boundaries of the current segment.

The resulting measure is additive against segments and customers, and nonadditive against all other filters. You can note that in the first row of the report, the Total result 213 is lower than the sum of the three years, which is 214. The reason is that at the Total level, the formula counts the number of customers that are in the Very Low segment over the three years. It appears that one of those customers bought enough products in three years to be moved to the next segment at the total level.

Though it is somewhat counterintuitive, the nonadditive behavior over time is a good feature. Indeed, to make it additive over the years, one would need to update the formula to include the time as part of the calculation. For instance, the following version of the code is additive over time. Yet, it is less powerful because one can no longer produce meaningful results if the year is not part of the report:

```
CustInSegment Additive :=
SUMX (
    VALUES ( 'Date'[Calendar Year] ),
    SUMX (
        Segments,
        COUNTROWS (
            FILTER (
                Customer,
                VAR SalesOfCustomer = [Sales Amount]
                VAR IsCustomerInSegment =
                    AND (
                        SalesOfCustomer > Segments[MinSale],
                        SalesOfCustomer <= Segments[MaxSale]
                    )
                RETURN
                    IsCustomerInSegment
            )
        )
    )
)
```

As shown in Figure 15-8, the rows now sum up correctly in the Total column, even though the Grand Total—that is, the total of all years and segments—might be inaccurate.

Category	Segment	CY 2007	CY 2008	CY 2009	**Total**
■ Audio					
☐ Cameras and camcorders	Very Low	210	1	3	**214**
■ Cell phones	Low	258	33	3	**294**
☐ Computers	Medium	427	133	88	**648**
☐ Games and Toys					
☐ Home Appliances	High	28	13	29	**70**
☐ Music, Movies and Audio Books	Very High	49	78	119	**246**
☐ TV and Video	**Total**	**972**	**258**	**242**	**1,472**

FIGURE 15-8 Now the rows sum up correctly, but the column total might be inaccurate.

The problem is that by obtaining the correct sum for one segment, one needs to sacrifice the grand total cumulating multiple segments and years. For example, one customer might be in the Very Low cluster in 2009 and in the Very High cluster in 2008; therefore, in the Grand Total they would be counted twice. The Grand Total shown in Figure 15-8 is 1,472, whereas the total number of customers is 1,437 as reported accurately in Figure 15-7.

Unfortunately with these kinds of calculations, additivity is more of a problem than a feature. By nature these calculations are nonadditive. Trying to make them additive might be appealing at first sight, but it is likely to produce misleading results. Therefore, it is always important to pay attention to these details, and our suggestion is to not force a measure to be additive without carefully considering the implications of that choice.

Understanding physical relationships in DAX

A relationship can be *strong* or *weak*. In a *strong* relationship the engine knows that the one-side of the relationship contains unique values. If the engine cannot check that the one-side of the relationship contains unique values for the key, then the relationship is *weak*. A relationship can be weak because either the engine cannot ensure the uniqueness of the constraint, due to technical reasons we outline later in this section, or the developer defined it as such. A weak relationship is not used as part of table expansion described in Chapter 14.

Starting from 2018, Power BI allows composite models. In a composite model it is possible to create tables in a model containing data in both VertiPaq mode (a copy of data from the data source is preloaded and cached in memory) and in DirectQuery mode (the data source is accessed only at query time). DirectQuery and VertiPaq engines are explained in Chapter 17, "The DAX engines."

A single data model can contain some tables stored in VertiPaq and some others stored in Direct-Query. Moreover, tables in DirectQuery can originate from different data sources, generating several DirectQuery data islands.

In order to differentiate between data in VertiPaq and data in DirectQuery, we talk about data in the *continent* (VertiPaq) or in the *islands* (DirectQuery data sources), as depicted in Figure 15-9.

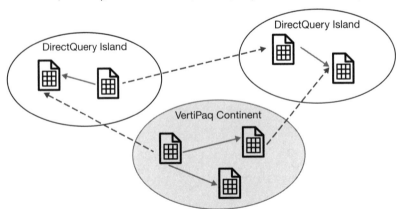

FIGURE 15-9 A composite model contains tables in different islands.

The VertiPaq store is nothing but another data island. We call it the continent only because it is the most frequently used data island.

A relationship links two tables. If both tables belong to the same island, then the relationship is an intra-island relationship. If the two tables belong to different islands, then it is a cross-island relationship. Cross-island relationships are always weak relationships. Therefore, table expansion never crosses islands.

Relationships have a cardinality, of which there are three types. The difference between them is both technical and semantical. Here we do not cover the reasoning behind those relationships because it would involve many data modeling digressions that are outside of the scope of the book. Instead, we need to cover the technical details of physical relationships and the impact they have on the DAX code.

These are the three types of relationship cardinality available:

- **One-to-many relationships:** This is the most common type of relationship cardinality. On the one-side of the relationship the column must have unique values; on the many-side the value can (and usually does) contain duplicates. Some client tools differentiate between one-to-many relationships and many-to-one relationships. Still, they are the same type of relationship. It all depends on the order of the tables: a one-to-many relationship between *Product* and *Sales* is the same as a many-to-one relationship between *Sales* and *Product*.

- **One-to-one relationships:** This is a rather uncommon type of relationship cardinality. On both sides of the relationship the columns need to have unique values. A more accurate name would be "zero-or-one"-to-"zero-or-one" relationship because the presence of a row in one table does not imply the presence of a corresponding row in the other table.

- **Many-to-many relationships:** On both sides of the relationship the columns can have duplicates. This feature was introduced in 2018, and unfortunately its name is somewhat confusing. Indeed, in common data modeling language "many-to-many" refers to a different kind of implementation, created by using pairs of one-to-many and many-to-one relationships. It is important to understand that in this scenario many-to-many does not refer to the many-to-many relationship but, instead, to the many-to-many cardinality of the relationship.

In order to avoid ambiguity between the canonical terminology, which uses many-to-many for a different kind of implementation, we use acronyms to describe the cardinality of a relationship:

- One-to-many relationship: We call them **SMR**, which stands for Single-Many-Relationship.

- One-to-one relationship : We use the acronym **SSR**, which stands for Single-Single-Relationship.

- Many-to-many relationship: We call them **MMR**, which stands for Many-Many-Relationship.

Another important detail is that an MMR relationship is always weak, regardless of whether the two tables belong to the same island or not. If the developer defines both sides of the relationship as the many-side, then the relationship is automatically treated as a weak relationship, with no table expansion happening.

In addition, each relationship has a cross-filter direction. The cross-filter direction is the direction used by the filter context to propagate its effect. The cross-filter can be set to one of two values:

- **Single:** The filter context is always propagated in one direction of the relationship and not the other way around. In a one-to-many relationship, the direction is always from the one-side of the relationship to the many-side. This is the standard and most desirable behavior.

- **Both:** The filter context is propagated in both directions of the relationship. This is also called a **bidirectional cross-filter** and sometimes just a bidirectional relationship. In a one-to-many relationship, the filter context still retains its feature of propagating from the one-side to the many-side, but it also propagates from the many-side to the one-side.

The cross-filter directions available depend on the type of relationship.

- In an **SMR** relationship one can always choose single or bidirectional.

- An **SSR** relationship always uses bidirectional filtering. Because both sides of the relationship are the one-side and there is no many-side, bidirectional filtering is the only option available.

- In an **MMR** relationship both sides are the many-side. This scenario is the opposite of the SSR relationship: Both sides can be the source and the target of a filter context propagation. Thus, one can choose the cross-filter direction to be bidirectional, in which case the propagation always goes both ways. Or if the developer chooses single propagation, they also must choose which table to start the filter propagation from. As with all other relationships, single propagation is the best practice. Later in this chapter we expand on this topic.

Table 15-1 summarizes the different types of relationships with the available cross-filter directions, their effect on the filter context propagation, and the options for weak/strong relationship.

TABLE 15-1 Different types of relationships

Type of Relationship	Cross-filter Direction	Filter Context Propagation	Weak / Strong Type
SMR	Single	From the one side to the many side	Weak if cross-island, strong otherwise
SMR	Both	Bidirectional	Weak if cross-island, strong otherwise
SSR	Both	Bidirectional	Weak if cross-island, strong otherwise
MMR	Single	Must choose the source table	Always weak
MMR	Both	Bidirectional	Always weak

When two tables are linked through a strong relationship, the table on the one-side might contain the additional blank row in case the relationship is invalid. Thus, if the many-side of a strong relationship contains values not present in the table on the one-side, then a blank row is appended to the one-side table. This was further explained in Chapter 3. The additional blank row is never added to a weak relationship.

As explained earlier, we are not going to discuss why one would choose one type of relationship over another. The choice between different types of relationships and filter propagation is in the hands of the data modeler; their decision flows from a deep reasoning on the semantics of the model itself. However, from a DAX point of view each relationship behaves differently, and it is important to understand the differences among the relationships and the impact they have on DAX code.

The next sections provide useful information about the differences between these types of relationships and several tips on which relationship to use in your models.

Using bidirectional cross-filters

Bidirectional cross-filters can be enabled in two ways: in the data model or by using the *CROSSFILTER* modifier in a *CALCULATE* function, as explained in Chapter 5, "Understanding *CALCULATE* and *CALCULATETABLE*." As a rule, a bidirectional cross-filter should not be enabled in the data model unless strictly needed. The reason is that bidirectional cross-filters quickly increase the complexity of the filter context propagation, up to a point where it is hard to predict and control how the filter context will propagate.

Nevertheless, there are scenarios where bidirectional cross-filtering is a useful feature. For example, look at the report in Figure 15-10; it is built on top of the usual Contoso model with all relationships set to single cross-filter propagation.

Brand	CountryRegion	CountryRegion	Sales Amount
☐ A. Datum	☐ Armenia		
☐ Adventure Works	☐ Australia	Australia	375,091.54
☐ Contoso	☐ Bhutan	Bhutan	13,598.64
☐ Fabrikam	☐ Canada	Canada	52,201.68
☐ Litware	☐ China	China	1,135.40
■ Northwind Traders	☐ France	France	29,783.07
☐ Proseware	☐ Germany	Germany	94,998.72
☐ Southridge Video	☐ Greece	Greece	5,551.82
☐ Tailspin Toys	☐ India	India	721.05
☐ The Phone Company	☐ Iran	Iran	9,519.41
☐ Wide World Importers	☐ Ireland		
	☐ Italy		

FIGURE 15-10 The *CountryRegion* slicer shows countries with no sales.

There are two slicers: *Brand*, which filters the *Product[Brand]* column; and *CountryRegion*, which filters the *Customer[CountryRegion]* column. Even though there are no sales for Northwind Traders in Armenia, the *CountryRegion* slicer shows Armenia as valid options to select.

The reason for this is that the filter context *on Product[Brand]* affects *Sales* because of the one-to-many relationship between *Product* and *Brand*. But then from *Sales*, the filter does not move to *Customer* because *Customer* is on the one-side of the one-to-many relationship between *Customer* and *Sales*. Therefore, the slicer shows all the possible values of *CountryRegion*. In other words, the two slicers are not in sync. The matrix does not show Armenia because the value of *Sales Amount* is a blank for this country, and by default a matrix does not show rows containing blank values from measures.

If slicer syncing is important, then it is possible to enable the bidirectional cross-filter between *Customer* and *Sales,* generating a model like the one in Figure 15-11.

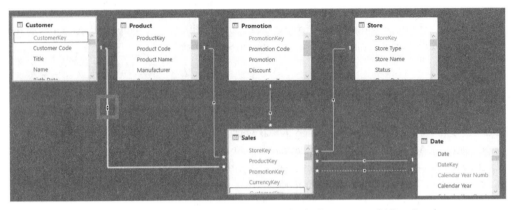

FIGURE 15-11 The cross-filter direction between *Customer* and *Sales* is now set to bidirectional.

Setting the cross-filter direction of the relationship to bidirectional ensures that the *CountryRegion* slicer only shows the rows that are referenced by *Sales.* Figure 15-12 shows that the slicers are now synced, improving user experience.

Brand	CountryRegion	CountryRegion	Sales Amount
☐ A. Datum	☐ Australia	Australia	375,091.54
☐ Adventure Works	☐ Bhutan	Bhutan	13,598.64
☐ Contoso	☐ Canada	Canada	52,201.68
☐ Fabrikam	☐ China	China	1,135.40
☐ Litware	☐ France	France	29,783.07
■ Northwind Traders	☐ Germany	Germany	94,998.72
☐ Proseware	☐ Greece	Greece	5,551.82
☐ Southridge Video	☐ India	India	721.05
☐ Tailspin Toys	☐ Iran	Iran	9,519.41
☐ The Phone Company	☐ Japan		
☐ Wide World Importers	☐ Kyrgyzstan		
	☐ Singapore		

FIGURE 15-12 By enabling bidirectional cross-filter, the slicers are now synced.

Bidirectional filtering is convenient, but it comes at a price. First, from a performance point of view, the bidirectional cross-filter slows down the model because the filter context must be propagated to both sides of the relationship. It is much faster to filter the many-side starting from the one-side rather than going in the opposite direction. Thus, with the goal of optimal performance in mind, bidirectional cross-filtering is one of the features to avoid. Moreover, bidirectional cross-filters increase chances to generate ambiguous data models. We discuss ambiguity later in this chapter.

Note Using visual level filters, it is possible to reduce the members visible in a Power BI visual without using the bidirectional filter in a relationship. Unfortunately, visual level filters are not supported for slicers in Power BI as of April 2019. Once visual level filters will also be available for slicers, using bidirectional filters will be no longer necessary to reduce the members visible in a slicer.

Understanding one-to-many relationships

One-to-many relationships are the most common and desirable type of relationships in a data model. For example, a one-to-many relationship relates *Product* with *Sales*. Given one product there can be many sales related to it, whereas for one given sale there is only one product. Consequently, *Product* is on the one-side and *Sales* is on the many-side.

Moreover, when analyzing data, users expect to be able to slice by a product attribute and compute values from *Sales*. Therefore, the default behavior is that a filter on *Product* (one-side) is propagated to *Sales* (many-side). If needed, one can change this behavior by enabling a bidirectional cross-filter in the relationship.

With strong one-to-many relationships, table expansion always goes towards the one-side. Moreover, in case the relationship is invalid, the table sitting on the one-side of the relationship might receive the blank row. Semantically, weak one-to-many relationships behave the same, except from the blank row. Performance-wise, weak one-to-many relationships generally generate slower queries.

Understanding one-to-one relationships

One-to-one relationships are quite uncommon in data models. Two tables linked through a one-to-one relationship are really just the same table split into two. In a well-designed model, these two tables would have been joined together before being loaded into the data model.

Therefore, the best way to handle one-to-one relationships is to avoid them by merging the two tables into a single table. One exception to this best practice is when data is going into one same business entity from different data sources that must be refreshed independently. In those cases, one might prefer to import two separate tables into the data model, avoiding complex and expensive transformations during the refresh operation. In any case, when handling one-to-one relationships, users need to pay attention to the following details:

- The cross-filter direction is always bidirectional. One cannot set the cross-filter direction to single on a one-to-one relationship. Thus, a filter on one of the two tables is always propagated to the other table, unless the relationship is deactivated—either by using *CROSSFILTER* or in the model.

- From a table expansion point of view, as described in Chapter 14 in a strong one-to-one relationship each table expands the other table that is part of that relationship. In other words, a strong one-to-one relationship produces two identical expanded tables.

- Because both sides of the relationship are on the one-side, if the relationship is both strong and invalid—that is, there are values for the key in one table that are not matched in the other—then both tables might contain the blank row. Moreover, the values of the column used for the relationship need to be unique in both tables.

Understanding many-to-many relationships

Many-to-many relationships are an extremely powerful modeling tool, and they appear much more often than one-to-one relationships. Handling them correctly is not trivial, yet it is useful to master them because of their analytical power.

A many-to-many relationship is present in a model whenever two entities cannot be related through a simple one-to-many relationship. There are two different types of many-to-many relationships, and several ways to solve the two scenarios. The next sections present several techniques to manage many-to-many relationships.

Implementing many-to-many using a bridge table

The following example comes from a banking scenario. The bank stores accounts in one table and customers in a different table. One account can be owned by multiple customers, while one customer may own multiple accounts. Therefore, it is not possible to store the customer name in the account, and at the same time it is not possible to store the account number in the customer table. This scenario cannot be modeled by using regular relationships between accounts and customers.

The canonical solution to this scenario is to build a table to store the relationship between customers and accounts. This is called a bridge table, and is shown in the model in Figure 15-13.

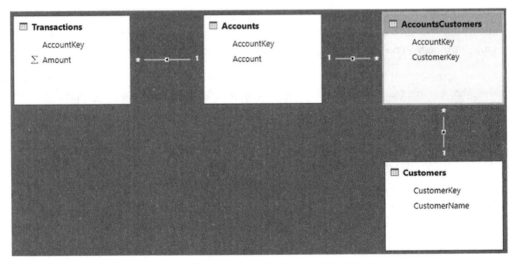

FIGURE 15-13 The *AccountsCustomers* table is related to both *Accounts* and *Customers*.

In this model, the many-to-many relationship between *Account* and *Customers* is implemented through the bridge table called *AccountsCustomers*. A row in the bridge table indicates that one account is owned by one customer.

As it is now, the model is not working yet. Indeed, a report slicing by *Account* works well because *Accounts* filters *Transactions*, *Accounts* being on the one-side of a one-to-many relationship. On the other hand, slicing by *Customers* does not work because *Customers* filters *Accounts-Customers*, but then *AccountsCustomers* does not propagate the filter to *Accounts* because the cross-filter goes in the other direction. Moreover, this last relationship must have its one-side on the *Accounts* table because *AccountKey* has unique values in *Accounts* and contains duplicates in *AccountsCustomers*.

Figure 15-14 shows that the *CustomerName* values do not apply any kind of filter to the sum of *Amount* displayed in the matrix.

Account	Luke	Mark	Paul	Robert	**Total**
Luke	800.00	800.00	800.00	800.00	**800.00**
Mark	800.00	800.00	800.00	800.00	**800.00**
Mark-Paul	1,000.00	1,000.00	1,000.00	1,000.00	**1,000.00**
Mark-Robert	1,000.00	1,000.00	1,000.00	1,000.00	**1,000.00**
Paul	700.00	700.00	700.00	700.00	**700.00**
Robert	700.00	700.00	700.00	700.00	**700.00**
Total	**5,000.00**	**5,000.00**	**5,000.00**	**5,000.00**	**5,000.00**

FIGURE 15-14 *Accounts* on rows filters the amount, whereas *Customers* on columns does not.

This scenario can be solved by enabling the bidirectional cross-filter in the relationship between *AccountsCustomers* and *Accounts*; this is achieved either by updating the data model or by using *CROSSFILTER* as in the following measure:

```
-- Version using CROSSFILTER
SumOfAmt CF :=
CALCULATE (
    SUM ( Transactions[Amount] ),
    CROSSFILTER (
        AccountsCustomers[AccountKey],
        Accounts[AccountKey],
        BOTH
    )
)
```

Either way, the formula will now produce the expected result, as shown in Figure 15-15.

Account	Luke	Mark	Paul	Robert	Total
Luke	800.00				**800.00**
Mark		800.00			**800.00**
Mark-Paul		1,000.00	1,000.00		**1,000.00**
Mark-Robert		1,000.00		1,000.00	**1,000.00**
Paul			700.00		**700.00**
Robert				700.00	**700.00**
Total	**800.00**	**2,800.00**	**1,700.00**	**1,700.00**	**5,000.00**

FIGURE 15-15 By enabling the bidirectional cross-filter, the measure now returns the correct result.

Setting the bidirectional cross-filter in the data model has the advantage of ensuring that it is automatically applied to any calculation—also working on implicit measures generated by client tools such as Excel or Power BI. However, the presence of bidirectional cross-filters in a data model increases the complexity of the filter propagation and might have a negative impact on the performance of measures that should not be affected by said filter. Moreover, if new tables are later added to the data model, the presence of the bidirectional cross-filter might generate ambiguities that require a change in the cross-filter. This could potentially break other, pre-existing reports. For these reasons, before enabling bidirectional cross-filters on a relationship, one should think twice and carefully check that the model is still sound.

You are of course free to use bidirectional cross-filter in your models. But for all the reasons described in the book, our personal attitude is to never enable bidirectional cross-filter on a relationship. Because we love simplicity and sound models, we strongly prefer the *CROSSFILTER* solution applied to every measure. Performance-wise, enabling the bidirectional cross-filter in the data model or using *CROSSFILTER* in DAX is identical.

Another way of achieving our goal is by using more complex DAX code. Despite its complexity, that code also brings an increased level of flexibility. One option to author the *SumOfAmt* measure without using *CROSSFILTER* is to rely on *SUMMARIZE* and use it as a *CALCULATE* filter argument:

```
-- Version using SUMMARIZE
SumOfAmt SU :=
CALCULATE (
    SUM ( Transactions[Amount] ),
    SUMMARIZE (
        AccountsCustomers,
        Accounts[AccountKey]
    )
)
```

SUMMARIZE returns a column with the data lineage of *Accounts[AccountKey]*, actively filtering the *Accounts* and then the *Transactions* table. Another way of obtaining a similar result is by using *TREATAS*:

```
-- Version using TREATAS
SumOfAmt TA :=
CALCULATE (
    SUM ( Transactions[Amount] ),
    TREATAS (
        VALUES ( AccountsCustomers[AccountKey] ),
        Accounts[AccountKey]
    )
)
```

Also in this case, *VALUES* returns the values of *AccountsCustomers[AccountKey]* filtered by the *Customers* table, and *TREATAS* changes the data lineage to make it filter the *Accounts* and then the *Transactions* table.

Lastly, an even simpler formulation of the same expression is to use table expansion. Noting that the bridge table expands to both the *Customers* and the *Accounts* tables, the following code produces almost the same result as the previous ones. It is, however, noticeably shorter:

```
-- Version using Expanded Table
SumOfAmt ET :=
CALCULATE (
    SUM ( Transactions[Amount] ),
    AccountsCustomers
)
```

Despite the many variations, all these solutions can be grouped into two options:

- Using the bidirectional cross-filter feature of DAX.

- Using a table as a filter argument in *CALCULATE*.

These two groups behave differently if the relationship between *Transactions* and *Accounts* is invalid. Indeed, if a relationship is invalid, the table on the one-side of the relationship contains an additional blank row. In case the *Transactions* table relates to accounts that are not available in the *Accounts* table, the relationship between *Transactions* and *Accounts* is invalid and the blank row is added to the *Accounts* table. This effect does not propagate to *Customers*. Therefore, in this case the *Customers* table has no blank row, and only the *Accounts* table has one blank row.

Consequently, slicing *Transactions* by *Account* shows the blank row, whereas slicing *Transactions* by *CustomerName* does not show transactions linked to the blank row. This behavior might be confusing; to demonstrate the behavior, we added a row to the *Transactions* table with an invalid *AccountKey* and a value of 10,000.00. The different results are visible in Figure 15-16, where the matrix on the left slices by *Account* and the matrix on the right slices by *CustomerName*. The measure shown is the one using *CROSSFILTER*.

Account	SumOfAmt CF		CustomerName	SumOfAmt CF
	10,000.00		Luke	800.00
Luke	800.00		Mark	2,800.00
Mark	800.00		Paul	1,700.00
Mark-Paul	1,000.00		Robert	1,700.00
Mark-Robert	1,000.00		**Total**	**15,000.00**
Paul	700.00			
Robert	700.00			
Total	**15,000.00**			

FIGURE 15-16 *CustomerName* does not contain a blank row; consequently, the total on the right looks wrong.

When the matrix is slicing by *Account*, the blank row is present and the value of 10,000.00 is visible. When the matrix is slicing by *CustomerName*, there is no blank row to show. The filter starts from the *CustomerName* column in the *Customers* table, but there are no values in *AccountsCustomers* that can include in the filter the blank row in *Accounts*. The value related to the blank row is only visible at the grand total because the filter on *CustomerName* is no longer present there. Consequently, at the grand total level the *Accounts* table is no longer cross-filtered; all the rows of *Accounts* become active, including the blank row, and 15,000.00 is displayed as a result.

Be mindful that we are using the blank row as an example, but the same scenario would happen whenever there are accounts that are not linked to any customer. Starting the filter from the customer, their value will not show up other than on the grand total. The reason is that the filter on the customer removes accounts not linked to any customer from any row. This consideration is important because the behavior observed in Figure 15-16 is not necessarily related to the presence of an invalid relationship. For example, if the transaction with the value of 10,000.00 were related to a Service account defined in the *Accounts* table but not related to any *Customer*, the *Account* name would be visible in the report—despite the fact that this value still would not be related to any single customer. This is shown in Figure 15-17.

Account	SumOfAmt CF		CustomerName	SumOfAmt CF
Luke	800.00		Luke	800.00
Mark	800.00		Mark	2,800.00
Mark-Paul	1,000.00		Paul	1,700.00
Mark-Robert	1,000.00		Robert	1,700.00
Paul	700.00		**Total**	**15,000.00**
Robert	700.00			
Service	10,000.00			
Total	**15,000.00**			

FIGURE 15-17 The value related to the Service account does not appear related to any single *CustomerName*.

Note The scenario depicted in Figure 15-17 does not violate any referential integrity constraints in a relational database, as was the case in Figure 15-16. Thus, validating data making sure that this condition is not present requires additional validation logic in the relational database.

If, instead of using the *CROSSFILTER* technique, we rely on table filtering in *CALCULATE*, then the behavior is different. The rows that are not reachable from the bridge table are always filtered out. Because the filter is always forced by *CALCULATE*, they will not show even at the grand total level. In other words, the filter is always forced to be active. You can look at the result in Figure 15-18.

Account	SumOfAmt ET	CustomerName	SumOfAmt ET
Luke	800.00	Luke	800.00
Mark	800.00	Mark	2,800.00
Mark-Paul	1,000.00	Paul	1,700.00
Mark-Robert	1,000.00	Robert	1,700.00
Paul	700.00	**Total**	**5,000.00**
Robert	700.00		
Total	**5,000.00**		

FIGURE 15-18 Using the table filter technique, the blank row disappears everywhere and is not included in the total.

Not only does the total now show a lower value; this time, even slicing by *Account* does not show the blank row anymore. The reason is that the blank row is filtered out by the table filter applied by *CALCULATE*.

Neither of these values is totally correct or totally wrong. Moreover, if the bridge table references all the rows in *Transactions* starting from *Customers*, then the two measures behave the same way. Developers should choose the technique that better fit their needs, paying attention to details and making sense of unexpected values, if any.

Note Performance-wise, the solutions based on using a table as a filter argument in *CALCULATE* always involve paying the price of scanning the bridge table (*AccountsCustomers*). This means that any report using the measure without a filter over *Customers* will pay the highest possible price, which is useless in case every account has at least one customer. Therefore, the solutions based on the bidirectional cross-filter should be the default choice whenever the data consistency guarantees the same result with both techniques. Moreover, remember that any solution involving table expansion works only with strong relationships. Therefore, the presence of weak relationships might force the solution in favor of the bidirectional cross-filter. More details about these considerations are available in the article at https://www.sqlbi.com/articles/many-to-many-relationships-in-power-bi-and-excel-2016/.

Implementing many-to-many using a common dimension

There is another scenario where many-to-many is a useful tool, even though from a technical point of view it is not a many-to-many relationship. This scenario defines a relationship between two entities at a granularity different from the primary key.

The example comes from a budgeting scenario, where the budget information is stored in a table containing the country, the brand, and the budget for the one year. The model is visible in Figure 15-19.

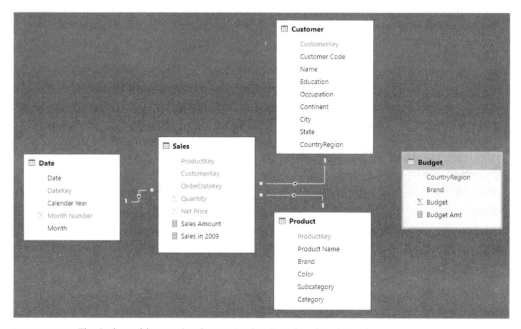

FIGURE 15-19 The *Budget* table contains *CountryRegion*, *Brand*, and *Budget* columns.

If the requirement is to produce a report that shows the sales and the budget values side-by-side, then it is necessary to filter both the *Budget* table and the *Sales* table at the same time. The *Budget* table contains *CountryRegion*, which is also a column in *Customer*. However, the *CountryRegion* column is not unique—neither in the *Customer* table nor in the *Budget* table. Similarly, *Brand* is a column in *Product*, but it is also not unique in either table. One could author a *Budget Amt* measure that simply sums the *Budget* column of the *Budget* table.

```
Budget Amt :=
SUM ( Budget[Budget] )
```

A matrix slicing by *Customer[CountryRegion]* with this data model produces the result visible in Figure 15-20. The *Budget Amt* measure always shows the same value, corresponding to the sum of all the rows in the *Budget* table.

CountryRegion	Sales in 2009	Budget Amt
China	4,606,828.52	39,004,512.00
Germany	3,715,974.54	39,004,512.00
United States	32,296,069.79	39,004,512.00
Total	**40,618,872.86**	**39,004,512.00**

FIGURE 15-20 *Budget Amt* is not filtered by *Customer[CountryRegion]* and always shows the same value.

There are several solutions to this scenario. One involves implementing a virtual relationship using one of the techniques previously shown in this chapter, moving the filter from one table to another. For example, by using *TREATAS*, one could move the filter from both the *Customer* and *Product* tables to the *Budget* table using this code:

```
Budget Amt :=
CALCULATE (
    SUM ( Budget[Budget] ),
    TREATAS (
        VALUES ( Customer[CountryRegion] ),
        Budget[CountryRegion]
    ),
    TREATAS (
        VALUES ( 'Product'[Brand] ),
        Budget[Brand]
    )
)
```

The *Budget Amt* measure now uses the filter coming from *Customer* and/or from *Product* properly, producing the correct result shown in Figure 15-21.

CountryRegion	Sales in 2009	Budget Amt
China	4,606,828.52	4,393,380.00
Germany	3,715,974.54	3,631,310.00
United States	32,296,069.79	30,979,822.00
Total	**40,618,872.86**	**39,004,512.00**

FIGURE 15-21 *Budget Amt* is now filtered by *Customer[CountryRegion]*.

This solution presents a couple of limitations:

- If a new brand exists in the *Budget* table and it is not present in the *Product* table, its value will always be filtered out. As a result, the figures of the budget will be inaccurate.

- Instead of using the most efficient technique of relying on physical relationships, the code is using DAX to move the filter. On large models, this might lead to bad performance.

A better solution to this scenario is to slightly change the data model, adding a new table that acts as a filter on both the *Budget* and the *Customer* tables. This can be easily accomplished with a DAX calculated table:

```
CountryRegions =
DISTINCT (
    UNION (
        DISTINCT ( Budget[CountryRegion] ),
        DISTINCT ( Customer[CountryRegion] )
    )
)
```

This formula retrieves all the values of *CountryRegion* from both *Customer* and *Budget*, then it merges them into a single table that contains duplicates. Finally, the formula removes duplicates from the table. As a result, this new table contains all the values of *CountryRegion*, whether they come from *Budget* or from *Customer*. In a similar way, a table that links to *Product* and *Budget* is needed, following the same process for *Product[Brand]* and for *Budget[Brand]*.

```
Brands =
DISTINCT (
    UNION (
        DISTINCT ( 'Product'[Brand] ),
        DISTINCT ( Budget[Brand] )
    )
)
```

Once the table is in the data model, one then needs to create the proper set of relationships. The resulting model is visible in Figure 15-22.

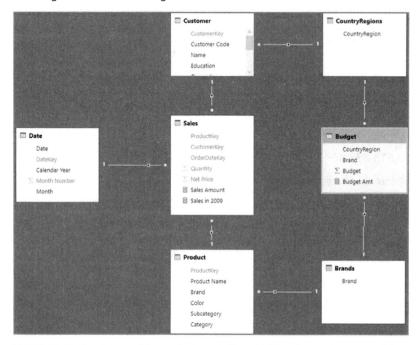

FIGURE 15-22 The data model contains two additional tables: *CountryRegions* and *Brands*.

With the new model in place, the *Brands* table filters both *Product* and *Budget*, whereas the new *CountryRegions* table filters both *Customer* and *Budget*. Thus, there is no need to use the *TREATAS* pattern shown in the previous example. A simple *SUM* computes the correct value from both *Budget* and *Sales* as shown in the following version of the *Budget Amt* measure. This does require using the columns from the *CountryRegions* and *Brands* tables in the report, which will appear as in Figure 15-21.

```
Budget Amt :=
SUM ( Budget[Budget] )
```

By leveraging the bidirectional cross-filter between *Customer* and *CountryRegions* and between *Product* and *Brands*, it is possible to hide the *CountryRegions* and *Brands* tables in report view, moving the filter from *Customer* and *Product* to *Budget* without writing any additional DAX code. The resulting model shown in Figure 15-23 creates a logical relationship between *Customer* and *Budget* at the granularity of the *CountryRegion* column. The same happens between *Product* and *Budget* at the granularity of the *Brand* column.

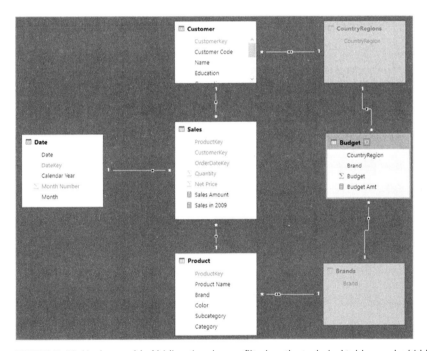

FIGURE 15-23 Having enabled bidirectional cross-filtering, the technical tables can be hidden.

The result of the report produced by this model is identical to Figure 15-21. The relationship between *Customer* and *Budget* is a sequence of a many-to-one and a one-to-many relationship. The bidirectional cross-filter between *Customer* and *CountryRegions* ultimately transfers the filter from *Customer* to *Budget* and not the other way around. If the bidirectional filter were also active between *CountryRegions* and *Budget*, the model would have involved some level of ambiguity that would stop the creation of a similar pattern between *Product* and *Budget*.

> **Note** The model in Figure 15-23 suffers from the same limitations as the model in Figure 15-19: If there are brands or countries in the budget that are not defined in the *Customer* and *Product* tables, that budget value might disappear in the report. This problem is described in more detail in the next section.

Be mindful that technically, this is not a many-to-many pattern. In this model we are linking *Product* to *Budget* (same for *Customer*) using a granularity that is not the individual product. Instead, we are linking the two tables at the granularity level of *Brand*. The same operation can be achieved in a simpler—though less effective—way by using weak relationships, as described in the next section. Moreover, linking tables at different granularity conceals several complex aspects that are discussed later in this chapter.

Implementing many-to-many using MMR weak relationships

In the previous example we linked *Products* to *Budget* by using an intermediate—ad hoc—table. DAX versions from after October 2018 introduced the feature of weak relationships, which addresses the same scenario in a more automated way.

One can create an MMR weak relationship between two tables in case the two columns involved in the relationship have duplicates in both tables. In other words, the same model shown in Figure 15-23 can be created by directly linking *Budget* to *Product* using the *Product[Brand]* column, avoiding the creation of the intermediate *Brands* table used in the previous section. The resulting model is visible in Figure 15-24.

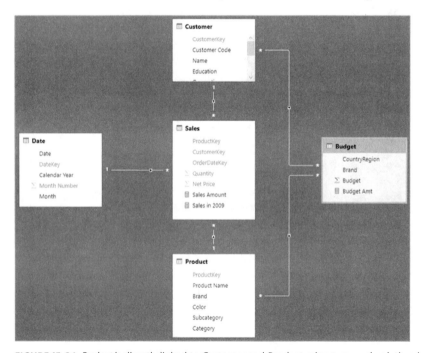

FIGURE 15-24 *Budget* is directly linked to *Customer* and *Product* using two weak relationships.

When creating an MMR weak relationship, one has the option of choosing the direction of the filter context propagation. It can be bidirectional or single, as is the case with a regular one-to-many relationship. The choice for this example is necessarily the single direction from *Customer* to *Budget* and from *Product* to *Budget*. Setting a bidirectional filter in both relationships would create a model ambiguity.

In MMR relationships, both sides of the relationship are the many-side. Therefore, the columns can contain duplicates in both tables. This model works exactly like the model shown in Figure 15-23, and it computes the correct values without the need for additional DAX code in measures or calculated tables.

Nevertheless, a trap lies in this model that our reader must be aware of. Because the relationship is weak, neither of the two tables will contain the blank row in case the relationship is invalid. In other words, if *Budget* contains a country or a brand that is not present in *Customer* or in *Product*, then its values will be hidden, as is the case for the model in Figure 15-24.

To demonstrate this behavior, we changed the content of the *Budget* table, replacing Germany with Italy. There are no customers whose country is Italy in the model used for this example. The result of this change is somewhat surprising, as shown in Figure 15-25.

CountryRegion	Sales in 2009	Budget Amt
China	4,606,828.52	4,393,380.00
Germany	3,715,974.54	
United States	32,296,069.79	30,979,822.00
Total	**40,618,872.86**	**39,004,512.00**

FIGURE 15-25 If the relationship between *Budget* and *Customer* is invalid, the missing blank row produces surprising results.

The row with Germany is empty. This is correct, because we moved the entire budget of Germany to Italy. But you should notice two details:

- There is no row showing the budget for Italy.

- The grand total of the budget is larger than the sum of the two visible rows.

When there is a filter on *Customer[CountryRegion]*, the filter is moved to the *Budget* table through the weak relationship. As a consequence, the *Budget* table only shows the values of the given country. Because Italy does not exist in *Customer[CountryRegion]*, no value is shown. That said, when there is no filter on *Customer[CountryRegion]*, *Budget* does not receive any filter. As such, it shows its grand total, which also includes Italy.

The result of *Budget Amt* thus depends on the presence of a filter on *Customer[CountryRegion]*; in the presence of invalid relationships, the numbers produced might be surprising.

Weak MMR relationships represent a powerful tool that greatly simplifies the creation of data models because it reduces the need to create additional tables. Nevertheless, the fact that no blank row is ever added to the tables might produce unexpected results if the feature is not used properly. We showed the more complex technique of creating additional tables before showing weak relationships because they are basically the same thing: The difference is that creating additional tables makes visible the values that exist in just one of the two related tables—something that is not possible using weak MMR relationships, but that might be required in particular scenarios.

Indeed, if we perform the same substitution of Germany with Italy in the data model with the *Brands* and *CountryRegions* table (Figure 15-23), the result is much clearer, as shown in Figure 15-26.

CountryRegion	Sales in 2009	Budget Amt
China	4,606,828.52	4,393,380.00
Germany	3,715,974.54	
Italy		3,631,310.00
United States	32,296,069.79	30,979,822.00
Total	**40,618,872.86**	**39,004,512.00**

FIGURE 15-26 Using the intermediate table, Italy and Germany both appear in the report with their correct values.

Choosing the right type of relationships

Complex relationships are a powerful way to generate advanced models. Working with complex scenarios, you face the choice between building a physical (maybe calculated) relationship and building a virtual relationship.

Physical and virtual relationships are similar because they fulfill the same goal: transferring a filter from one table to another. However, they have different performance and different implications at the data model level.

- **A physical relationship is defined in the data model; a virtual relationship only exists in DAX code.** The diagram view of a data model clearly shows the relationships between tables. Yet virtual relationships are not visible in the diagram view; locating them requires a detailed review of the DAX expression used in measures, calculated columns, and calculated tables. If a logical relationship is used in several measures, its code must be duplicated in every measure requiring it, unless the logical relationship is implemented in a calculation item of a calculation group. Physical relationships are easier to manage and less error-prone than virtual relationships.

- **A physical relationship defines a constraint on the one-side table of the relationship.** One-to-many and one-to-one relationships require that the column used on the one-side of a relationship have unique nonblank values. The refresh operation of a data model fails in case the new data would violate this constraint. From this point of view, there is a huge difference with the foreign key constraint defined in a relational database. A foreign key relationship defines a constraint on the many-side of a relationship, whose values can only be values that exist in the other table. A relationship in a Tabular model never enforces a foreign key constraint.

- **A physical relationship is faster than a virtual relationship.** The physical relationship defines an additional structure that accelerates the query execution, enabling the storage engine to execute part of the query involving two or more queries. A virtual relationship always requires additional work from the formula engine, which is slower than the storage engine. Differences between formula engine and storage engine are discussed in Chapter 17.

Generally, physical relationships are a better option. In terms of query performance there is no difference between a standard relationship (based on a column coming from the data source) and a calculated physical relationship (based on a calculated column). The engine computes calculated columns at process time (when data is refreshed), so it does not really matter how complex the expression is; the relationship is a physical relationship and the engine can take full advantage of it.

A virtual relationship is just an abstract concept. Technically, every time one transfers a filter from one table to another using DAX code, they are implementing a virtual relationship. Virtual relationships are resolved at query time, and the engine does not have the additional structures created for physical relationships to optimize the query execution. Thus, whenever you have the option of doing that, you should prefer a physical relationship to a virtual relationship.

The many-to-many relationships are in an intermediate position between physical and virtual relationships. One can define many-to-many relationships in the model by leveraging bidirectional relationships or table expansion. In general, the presence of a relationship is better than an approach based on table expansion because the engine has more chances to optimize the query plan by removing unnecessary filter propagations. Even so, table expansion and bidirectional cross-filters have a similar cost when a filter is active, even though technically they execute two different query plans with a similar cost.

Performance-wise the priority in relationships choice should be the following:

- Physical one-to-many relationships to get best performance and the best use of the VertiPaq engine. Calculated physical relationships have the same query performance as relationships on native columns.

- Bidirectional cross-filter relationships, many-to-many with table expansion, and weak relationships are a second option. They provide good performance and a good use of the engine, although not the best.

- Virtual relationships are the last choice because of the risk of bad performance. Note that being at risk does not mean you will experience performance issues, but only that you need to care about different aspects of the query, which you will learn in the next chapters about optimization.

Managing granularities

As described in earlier sections, by using intermediate tables or MMR weak relationships, one can link two tables using a relationship at a granularity level lower than the primary key of a table. In a previous example, we linked the *Budget* table to both *Product* and *Customer*. The relationship with *Product* is at the *Brand* level, whereas the relationship with *Customer* is at the *CountryRegion* level.

If a data model contains relationships at a lower granularity, special care needs to be taken whenever authoring measures that use that relationship. As an example, Figure 15-27 shows the starting model with two MMR weak relationships between *Customer*, *Product*, and *Budget*.

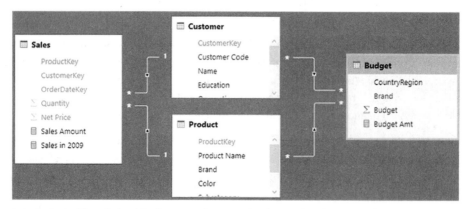

FIGURE 15-27 The relationships between *Customer*, *Product*, and *Budget* are weak relationships.

A weak relationship transfers the filter from one table to another following the granularity of the column. This statement is true for any relationship. Indeed, the relationship between *Customer* and *Sales* also transfers the filter at the granularity of the column involved in the relationship. Nevertheless, if the column used to create the relationship is the key of the table, the behavior is intuitive. When the relationship is set at a lower granularity—as in the case of weak relationships—it is all too easy to produce calculations that might be hard to understand.

For example, consider the *Product* table. The relationship with *Budget* is set at the *Brand* level. Thus, one can create a matrix that slices *Budget Amt* by *Brand* and obtain an accurate result, as shown in Figure 15-28.

Brand	Budget Amt
A. Datum	1,777,784.00
Adventure Works	4,985,172.00
Contoso	7,127,903.00
Fabrikam	8,667,819.00
Litware	4,284,028.00
Northwind Traders	911,918.00
Proseware	3,192,659.00
Southridge Video	1,643,555.00
Tailspin Toys	600,524.00
The Phone Company	2,233,721.00
Wide World Importers	3,579,429.00
Total	**39,004,512.00**

FIGURE 15-28 Slicing budget by brand, all calculations provide an accurate result.

Things suddenly become much more intricate if other columns from the *Product* table are involved in the analysis. In Figure 15-29 we added a slicer to filter a few colors, and we added the color on the columns of the matrix. The result is confusing.

Color	Brand	Black	Blue	Green	Total
	A. Datum	1,777,784.00	1,777,784.00	1,777,784.00	**1,777,784.00**
	Adventure Works	4,985,172.00	4,985,172.00		**4,985,172.00**
	Contoso	7,127,903.00	7,127,903.00	7,127,903.00	**7,127,903.00**
	Fabrikam	8,667,819.00	8,667,819.00	8,667,819.00	**8,667,819.00**
	Litware	4,284,028.00	4,284,028.00	4,284,028.00	**4,284,028.00**
	Northwind Traders	911,918.00	911,918.00	911,918.00	**911,918.00**
	Proseware	3,192,659.00	3,192,659.00	3,192,659.00	**3,192,659.00**
	Southridge Video	1,643,555.00	1,643,555.00		**1,643,555.00**
	Tailspin Toys	600,524.00	600,524.00	600,524.00	**600,524.00**
	The Phone Company	2,233,721.00			**2,233,721.00**
	Wide World Importers	3,579,429.00	3,579,429.00	3,579,429.00	**3,579,429.00**
	Total	**39,004,512.00**	**36,770,791.00**	**30,142,064.00**	**39,004,512.00**

Slicer (Color): (Blank), Azure, ■ Black, ■ Blue, Brown, Gold, ■ Green, Grey, Orange, Pink, Purple, Red, Silver, Silver Grey, Transparent, White, Yellow

FIGURE 15-29 Slicing budget by brand and color, the numbers reported are confusing.

Please note that given a *Brand*, its value—if present—is always the same, regardless of the filter on the color. The total of each color is different, but the grand total is clearly not the sum of individual colors.

To make sense of these numbers, we use a simplified version of the matrix where the brand is not present. In Figure 15-30, *Budget Amt* is sliced only by *Product[Color]*.

Color	Budget Amt
Black	39,004,512.00
Blue	36,770,791.00
Green	30,142,064.00
Total	**39,004,512.00**

FIGURE 15-30 Slicing only by color makes it easier to focus on individual cells.

Look at the Blue budget amount in Figure 15-30. When the evaluation starts, the filter context filters the *Product* table only showing blue products. Not all the brands produce blue products. For instance, The Phone Company does not have any product that is blue, as shown in Figure 15-29. Thus, the *Product[Brand]* column is cross-filtered by *Product[Color]*, and it shows all the brands except for The Phone Company. When the filter context is moved to the *Budget* table, the operation occurs at the *Brand* granularity. Consequently, the *Budget* table is filtered showing all brands but The Blue Company.

The value shown is the sum of all brands except for The Blue Company. While traversing the relationship, the information about the color has been lost. The relationship between *Color* and *Brand* is used when cross-filtering *Brand* by *Color*, but then, the filter on *Budget* is based on *Brand* alone. In other words, every cell shows the sum of all brands that have at least one product of the given color. This behavior is seldom desirable. There are few scenarios where this is exactly the calculation required; most of the times the numbers are just wrong.

The problem appears whenever a user browses an aggregation of values at a granularity that is not supported by the relationship. A good practice consists of hiding the value if the browsing granularity is not supported. This raises the problem of detecting when the report is or is not analyzing data at the correct granularity. To solve the problem, we create more measures.

We start with a matrix containing the brand (correct granularity) and the color (wrong granularity). In the report, we also added a new measure, *NumOfProducts* that just counts the number of rows in the *Product* table:

```
NumOfProducts :=
COUNTROWS ( 'Product' )
```

You can see the resulting report in Figure 15-31.

Brand	Budget Amt	NumOfProducts
A. Datum	1,777,784.00	132
Azure	1,777,784.00	14
Black	1,777,784.00	18
Blue	1,777,784.00	4
Gold	1,777,784.00	4
Green	1,777,784.00	14
Grey	1,777,784.00	18
Orange	1,777,784.00	18
Pink	1,777,784.00	18
Silver	1,777,784.00	18
Silver Grey	1,777,784.00	6
Adventure Works	4,985,172.00	192
Black	4,985,172.00	54
Blue	4,985,172.00	12
Brown	4,985,172.00	15

FIGURE 15-31 The value of *Budget Amt* is correct for the *Brand* and wrong for the individual colors.

The key to solve the scenario is the *NumOfProducts* measure. When the A. Datum brand is selected, there are 132 products visible, which are all A. Datum products. If the user further filters with the color (or any other column), the number of visible products is reduced. The values from *Budget* make sense if all 132 products are visible. They lose meaning if fewer products are selected. Thus, we hide the value of the *Budget Amt* measure when the number of visible products is not exactly the number of all the products within the selected brand.

A measure that computes the number of products at the brand granularity is the following:

```
NumOfProducts Budget Grain :=
CALCULATE (
    [NumOfProducts],
    ALL ( 'Product' ),
    VALUES ( 'Product'[Brand] )
)
```

In this case *ALL / VALUES* must be used instead of *ALLEXCEPT*; the reader can find more details about their differences in Chapter 10. With this new measure, it is now enough to use a simple *IF* statement to check if the two numbers are identical to show the *Budget Amt* measure; otherwise, a blank is returned and the row will be hidden in the report. The *Corrected Budget* measure implements this logic:

```
Corrected Budget :=
IF (
    [NumOfProducts] = [NumOfProducts Budget Grain],
    [Budget Amt]
)
```

Figure 15-32 shows the entire report with the newly introduced measures. The *Corrected Budget* value is hidden when the granularity of the report is not compatible with the granularity of the *Budget* table.

Brand	Budget Amt	NumOfProducts	NumOfProducts Budget Grain	Corrected Budget
A. Datum	**1,777,784.00**	**132**	**132**	**1,777,784.00**
Azure	1,777,784.00	14	132	
Black	1,777,784.00	18	132	
Blue	1,777,784.00	4	132	
Gold	1,777,784.00	4	132	
Green	1,777,784.00	14	132	
Grey	1,777,784.00	18	132	
Orange	1,777,784.00	18	132	
Pink	1,777,784.00	18	132	
Silver	1,777,784.00	18	132	
Silver Grey	1,777,784.00	6	132	
Adventure Works	**4,985,172.00**	**192**	**192**	**4,985,172.00**
Black	4,985,172.00	54	192	
Blue	4,985,172.00	12	192	
Brown	4,985,172.00	15	192	

FIGURE 15-32 The value of *Corrected Budget* is hidden whenever the report is browsing an incompatible granularity.

The same pattern must be applied to the *Customer* table too, where the granularity is set at the *CountryRegion* level. If needed, more information about this pattern is available at https://www.daxpatterns.com/budget-patterns/.

In general, whenever using relationships at a granularity different than the key of a table, one should always check the calculations and make sure any value is hidden if the granularity is not supported. Using MMR weak relationships always requires attention to these details.

Managing ambiguity in relationships

When we think about relationships, another important topic is ambiguity. Ambiguity might appear in a model if there are multiple paths linking two tables, and unfortunately, ambiguity could be hard to spot in a complex data model.

The simplest kind of ambiguity that one can introduce in a model is by creating two or more relationships between two tables. For example, the *Sales* table contains both the order date and the delivery date. When you try to create two relationships between *Date* and *Sales* based on the two columns, the second one is disabled. For example, Figure 15-33 shows that one of the two relationship between *Date* and *Sales* is represented by a dashed line because it is not active.

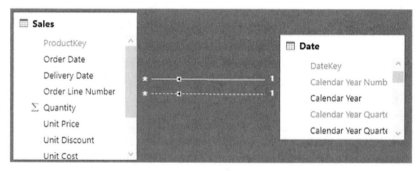

FIGURE 15-33 No more than one relationship can be active between any two tables.

If both relationships were active at the same time, then the model would be ambiguous. The engine would not know which path to follow to transfer a filter from *Date* to *Sales*.

Understanding ambiguity when working with two tables is easy. But as the number of tables increases, ambiguity is much harder to spot. The engine automatically detects ambiguity in a model and prevents developers from creating ambiguous models. However, the engine uses an algorithm that is complex, following rules that are not easy to grasp for humans. As a result, sometimes it does not consider as ambiguous a model that, in reality, contains ambiguity.

For example, consider the model in Figure 15-34. Before moving further, focus on the figure and answer this simple question: Is the model ambiguous?

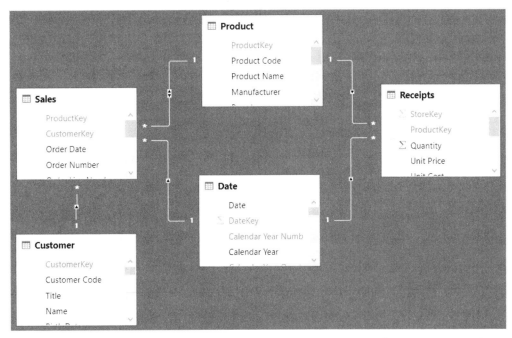

FIGURE 15-34 Is this model ambiguous? Will a developer be able to create it, or will it generate an error?

The answer to the question itself is ambiguous: The model is ambiguous for a human, but it is not ambiguous for DAX. Still, it is a bad data model because it is extremely complex to analyze. First, we analyze where the ambiguity is.

There is a bidirectional cross-filter in the relationship between *Product* and *Sales*, meaning that the filter context from *Sales* flows to *Product* and then to *Receipts*. Now, focus on *Date*. Starting from *Date*, the filter can go to *Sales*, then to *Product*, and finally to *Receipts*, following a legitimate path. At the same time, the filter could flow from *Date* to *Receipts*, simply using the relationship between the two tables. Thus, the model is ambiguous because there are multiple paths to propagate the filter from *Date* to *Receipts*.

Nevertheless, it is possible to create and use such models because the DAX engine implements special rules to reduce the number of ambiguous models detected. In this case, the rule is that only the shortest path propagates the filter. Therefore, the model is allowed, even though it is ambiguous. This is not to say that working with such models is a good idea in any way. Instead, it is a bad idea, and we strongly suggest our readers avoid ambiguity at all in their models.

Moreover, things are more intricate than this. Ambiguity can appear in a model because of the way relationships are designed. Ambiguity might also appear during the execution of DAX code because a DAX developer can change the relationship architecture using *CALCULATE* modifiers like *USERELA-TIONSHIP* and *CROSSFILTER*. For example, you write a measure that works perfectly fine, then you call the measure from inside another measure that uses *CROSSFILTER* to enable a relationship, and your measure starts computing wrong values because of ambiguity introduced in the model by *CROSSFIL-TER*. We do not want to scare our readers; we want them to be aware of the complexity that can arise in a model as soon as ambiguity comes into play.

Understanding ambiguity in active relationships

The first example is based on the model shown in Figure 15-34. The report projects *Sales Amount* and *Receipts Amount* (simple *SUMX* over the two tables) in a matrix that slices by year. The result is visible in Figure 15-35.

Calendar Year	Sales Amt	Receipts Amt
CY 2007	11,309,946.12	92,929,563.18
CY 2008	9,927,582.99	88,287,767.29
CY 2009	9,353,814.87	79,908,559.19
Total	**30,591,343.98**	**261,125,889.66**

FIGURE 15-35 *Calendar Year* is filtering *Receipts*, but through which path?

The filter from *Date* can reach *Receipts* through two paths:

- A direct path (*Date* to *Receipts*).

- A path traversing *Date* to *Sales*, then *Sales* to *Product*, and finally *Product* to *Receipts*.

The model is not considered ambiguous because the DAX engine chooses the shortest path between the two tables. Having the ability to move the filter from *Date* to *Receipts* directly, it ignores any other path. If the shortest path is not available, then the engine uses the longer one. Look at what happens by creating a new measure that calls *Receipts Amt* after having disabled the relationship between *Date* and *Receipts*:

```
Rec Amt Longer Path :=
CALCULATE (
    [Receipts Amt],
    CROSSFILTER ( 'Date'[Date], Receipts[Sale Date], NONE )
)
```

The *Rec Amt Longer Path* measure disables the relationship between *Date* and *Receipts*, so the engine must follow the longer path. The result is visible in Figure 15-36.

Calendar Year	Sales Amt	Receipts Amt	Rec Amt Longer Path
CY 2007	11,309,946.12	92,929,563.18	155,636,856.07
CY 2008	9,927,582.99	88,287,767.29	172,390,011.89
CY 2009	9,353,814.87	79,908,559.19	159,020,856.51
Total	**30,591,343.98**	**261,125,889.66**	**261,125,889.66**

FIGURE 15-36 *Rec Amt Longer Path* uses the longer path to filter *Receipts* starting from *Date*.

At this point, one interesting exercise for the reader is to describe exactly what the numbers reported by *Rec Amt Longer Path* mean. We encourage this effort be made before reading further, as the answer follows in the next paragraphs.

The filter starts from *Date*; then it reaches *Sales*. From *Sales*, it proceeds to *Product*. The products filtered are the ones that were sold in one of the selected dates. In other words, when the filter is 2007, *Product* only shows the products sold in 2007. Then, the filter moves one step forward and it reaches *Receipts*. In other words, the number is the total of *Receipts* for all the products sold in one given year. Not an intuitive value at all.

The most complex detail about the formula is that it uses *CROSSFILTER NONE*. Thus, a developer would tend to think that the code only deactivates a relationship. In reality, deactivating one path makes another path active. Thus, the measure does not really remove a relationship, it activates another one that is not cited anywhere in the code.

In this scenario, ambiguity is introduced by the bidirectional cross-filter between *Product* and *Sales*. A bidirectional cross-filter is a very dangerous feature because it might introduce ambiguities that are resolved by the engine but hard for a developer to find. After many years using DAX, we concluded that the bidirectional cross-filter should be avoided if not strictly necessary. Moreover, in the few scenarios where it makes sense to use a bidirectional cross-filter, one should double-check the whole model and then double-check it again to make sure no ambiguity is present. Obviously, as soon as another table or relationship is added to the model, the full checking process should start again. Doing this exercise on a model with 50 tables is a tedious exercise that can be easily avoided by staying away from bidirectional cross-filters defined in the data model.

Solving ambiguity in non-active relationships

Though bidirectional cross-filters are likely the most offending feature that generates ambiguity, they are not the only reason behind the appearance of ambiguity. Indeed, a developer could create a perfectly legitimate model, with no ambiguity, and still face the problem of ambiguity at query time.

As an example, look at the model in Figure 15-37. It is not ambiguous.

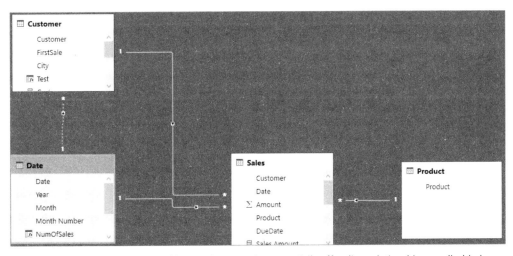

FIGURE 15-37 The model is not ambiguous, because the potentially offending relationships are disabled.

Focus on the *Date* table. *Date* filters *Sales* through the only active relationship (*Date[Date]* to *Sales[Date]*). There are two relationships between *Date* and *Sales*. One of them is inactive to avoid ambiguity. There is also a relationship between *Date* and *Customer*, based on *Customer[FirstSale]* that must be inactive. If this latter relationship were activated, then the filter from *Date* could reach *Sales* following two paths, making the model ambiguous. Thus, this model works just fine because it only uses the active relationships.

Now what happens if one activates one or more of the inactive relationships inside a *CALCULATE*? The model would suddenly become ambiguous. For example, the following measure activates the relationship between *Date* and *Customer*:

```
First Date Sales :=
CALCULATE (
    [Sales Amount],
    USERELATIONSHIP ( Customer[FirstSale], 'Date'[Date] )
)
```

Because *USERELATIONSHIP* makes the relationship active, inside *CALCULATE* the model becomes ambiguous. The engine cannot work on an ambiguous model, so it needs to deactivate other relationships. In this case, it does not use the shortest path. Indeed, the shortest path between *Date* and *Sales* is the direct relationship. A reasonable conclusion could be that—to disambiguate the model—the engine uses the direct relationship, as it did in the previous example. But because the developer explicitly asked to activate the relationship between *Customer* and *Date* by using *USERELATIONSHIP*, the engine decides to disable the relationship between *Date* and *Sale* instead.

As a result, because of *USERELATIONSHIP*, the filter will not propagate from *Date* to *Sales* using the direct relationship. Instead, it propagates the filter from *Date* to *Customer* and then from *Customer* to *Sales*. Therefore, given a customer and a date, the measure shows all the sales of that customer but only at the date of that customer's first purchase. You can see this behavior in Figure 15-38.

Customer	Sales Amount	First Date Sales
Alberto	**1,000**	**1,000**
02/01/2018	500	1,000
03/01/2018	500	
Daniele	**2,000**	**2,000**
03/01/2018	2,000	2,000
Marco	**300**	**300**
01/01/2018	100	300
02/01/2018	100	
03/01/2018	100	
Total	**3,300**	**3,300**

FIGURE 15-38 *First Date Sales* shows all the sales of a customer, but only on the day of their first purchase.

The *First Date Sales* measure always shows the total of the *Sales* of each customer, showing blank values on dates that do not correspond to the first date of purchase. From a business point of view, this measure shows the future value of a customer projected on the date when that customer was acquired. While this description makes sense, the chances that it be a real requirement are very low.

As it happened earlier, the goal here is not to understand exactly how the engine resolved the ambiguity. The disambiguation rules have never been documented; thus, they might change at some point. The real problem of such models is that ambiguity might appear in a valid model because of an inactive relationship being activated. Understanding which of the multiple paths the engine will follow to solve ambiguities is more of a guess than science.

With ambiguity and relationships, the golden rule is to just keep it simple. DAX might have some disambiguation algorithm that is powerful and can disambiguate nearly every model. Indeed, to raise an ambiguity error at runtime, one needs to use a set of USERELATIONSHIP functions that forces the model to be ambiguous. Only in such cases does the engine raise an error. For example, the following measure requests a clearly ambiguous model:

```
First Date Sales ERROR :=
CALCULATE (
    [Sales Amount],
    USERELATIONSHIP ( Customer[FirstSale], 'Date'[Date] ),
    USERELATIONSHIP ( 'Date'[Date], Sales[Date] )
)
```

At this point, DAX is not able to disambiguate a model with both relationships active, and it raises an error. Regardless, the measure can be defined in the data model without raising any exception; the error only appears when the measure is executed and filtered by date.

The goal of this section was not to describe the modeling options in Tabular. Instead, we wanted to bring your attention to issues that might happen when the data model is not correctly built. Building the correct model to perform an analysis is a complex task. Using bidirectional cross-filters and inactive relationships without a deep understanding of their implications is perhaps the quickest way to produce an unpredictable model.

Conclusions

Relationships are an important part of any data model. The Tabular mode offers different types of relationships, like one-to-many (SMR), one-to-one (SSR), and MMR weak relationships. MMR relationships are also called many-to-many relationships in some user interfaces, which is a misleading name that can be confused with a different data modeling concept. Every relationship can propagate the filter either in a single direction or bidirectionally, with the only exception of one-to-one relationships that are always bidirectional.

The available tools can be extended in a logical data model by implementing calculated physical relationships, or virtual relationships by using *TREATAS*, *SUMMARIZE*, or table expansion.

The many-to-many relationships between business entities can be implemented with a bridge table and rely on bidirectional cross-filters applied to the relationships in the chain.

All these features are extremely powerful, and being powerful they can be dangerous. Relationships must be handled with care. A developer should always double-check the models for ambiguity, also verifying that ambiguity will not be introduced by using *USERELATIONSHIP* or *CROSSFILTER*.

The larger the model, the higher the chances of making mistakes. If a model contains any inactive relationship, check the reason why the relationship is inactive and what would happen if it were activated. Remember that investing the time to properly design your model is foundational to successful DAX calculations, whereas a poorly designed model will usually give developers many headaches down the road.

Advanced calculations in DAX

In this last chapter about the features of the DAX language and before discussing optimization, we want to show several examples of calculations performed with DAX. The goal of this chapter is not to provide ready-to-use patterns that one can use out of the box; these patterns are available at https://www.daxpatterns.com. Instead, the goal is to show formulas of different levels of complexity to exercise your mind in the fascinating art of "thinking in DAX."

DAX does indeed require your brain to think creatively. Now that you have learned all the secrets of the language, it is time to put everything into practice. From the next chapter onwards, we will start to cover optimization. Therefore, in this chapter we start bringing up measure performance, providing the first clues as to how to measure the complexity of a formula.

Here, the goal is not to try to achieve the best performance because performance analysis requires knowledge that you will only learn in later chapters. Nevertheless, in this chapter we provide different formulations of the same measure, analyzing the complexity of each version. Being able to author several different versions of the same measure is a skill that will be of paramount importance in performance optimization.

Computing the working days between two dates

Given two dates, one can compute the difference in days by using a simple subtraction. In the *Sales* table there are two dates: the delivery date and the order date. The average number of days required for delivery can be obtained with the following measure:

```
Avg Delivery :=
AVERAGEX (
    Sales,
    INT ( Sales[Delivery Date] - Sales[Order Date] + 1)
)
```

Because of the internal format of a *DateTime*, this measure produces an accurate result. Yet it would be unfair to consider that an order received on Friday and shipped on Monday took three days to deliver, if Saturdays and Sundays are considered nonworking days. In fact, it only took one working day to ship the order—same as if the order had been received on Monday and shipped on Tuesday. Therefore, a more accurate calculation should consider the difference between the two dates expressed in working days. We provide several versions of the same calculation, seeking for the best in terms of performance and flexibility.

Excel provides a specific function to perform that calculation: *NETWORKDAYS*. However, DAX does not offer an equivalent feature. DAX offers the building blocks to author a complex expression that computes the equivalent of *NETWORKDAYS*, and much more. For example, a first way to compute the number of working days between two dates is to count the number of days between the two dates that are working days:

```
Avg Delivery WD :=
AVERAGEX (
    Sales,
    VAR RangeOfDates =
        DATESBETWEEN (
            'Date'[Date],
            Sales[Order Date],
            Sales[Delivery Date]
        )
    VAR WorkingDates =
        FILTER (
            RangeOfDates,
            NOT ( WEEKDAY ( 'Date'[Date] ) IN { 1, 7 } )
        )
    VAR NumberOfWorkingDays =
        COUNTROWS ( WorkingDates )
    RETURN
        NumberOfWorkingDays
)
```

For each row in *Sales*, the measure creates a temporary table in *RangeOfDates* with all the dates in between the order and delivery dates. Then, it filters out Saturdays and Sundays in *WorkingDates*, and finally it counts the number of rows that survived the filter in *NumberOfWorkingDays*. Figure 16-1 shows a line chart with the difference between the average delivery time in days and in working days.

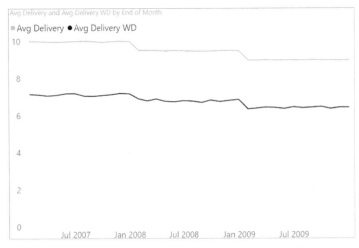

FIGURE 16-1 The average delivery days and working days are different.

The measure works well, with a few shortcomings. First, it does not consider holidays. For example, by removing Saturdays and Sundays, the first of January is considered a regular working day, provided it does not fall on a weekend. The same happens for any other holidays in the year. Second, the performance of the formula can be improved.

In order to handle holidays, one needs to store the information about whether a given day is a holiday or not in a table. The *Date* table is the perfect place for this, in a column named *Is Holiday*. Then, the formula should use other columns of the *Date* table instead of just using the *Date[Date]* column like the previous measure did:

```
Avg Delivery WD DT :=
AVERAGEX (
    Sales,
    VAR RangeOfDates =
        DATESBETWEEN (
            'Date'[Date],
            Sales[Order Date],
            Sales[Delivery Date]
        )
    VAR NumberOfWorkingDays =
        CALCULATE (
            COUNTROWS ( 'Date' ),
            RangeOfDates,
            NOT ( WEEKDAY ( 'Date'[Date] ) IN { 1, 7 } ),
            'Date'[Is Holiday] = 0
        )
    RETURN
        NumberOfWorkingDays
)
```

Now that the measure is more data-driven, one could also store the information about the weekend in the *Date* table, replacing the test with *WEEKDAY* with a new column containing *Workday* or *Weekend*. This reduces the complexity of the measure and moves most of the logic into the data, gaining in flexibility.

In terms of complexity, the measure performs two operations:

- An iteration over the *Sales* table.

- For each row in *Sales*, the creation of a temporary table with all the dates between the order and delivery dates.

If there are one million rows in *Sales* and the average for delivery days is seven, the complexity of the measure is around seven million. Indeed, the engine needs to build a temporary table with around seven rows, one million times.

It is possible to reduce the complexity of the formula by reducing either the number of iterations performed by *AVERAGEX* or the number of rows in the temporary table with the business days. An interesting point is that the calculation is not necessary at the individual sale level. Indeed, all the orders with the same *Order Date* and *Delivery Date* share the same duration. Thus, it is possible to first group all the orders by *Order Date* and *Delivery Date*, then compute the duration of these pairs of dates for a reduced number of rows. By doing so, we can reduce the number of iterations performed by *AVERAGEX,* but at the same time we lose information about how many orders each pair of dates was pertaining to. This can be resolved by transforming the simple average into a weighted average, using the number of orders as the weight for the average.

This idea is implemented in the following code:

```
Avg Delivery WD WA :=
VAR NumOfAllOrders =
    COUNTROWS ( Sales )
VAR CombinationsOrderDeliveryDates =
    SUMMARIZE (
        Sales,
        Sales[Order Date],
        Sales[Delivery Date]
    )
VAR DeliveryWeightedByNumOfOrders =
    SUMX (
        CombinationsOrderDeliveryDates,
        VAR RangeOfDates =
            DATESBETWEEN (
                'Date'[Date],
                Sales[Order Date],
                Sales[Delivery Date]
            )
        VAR NumOfOrders =
            CALCULATE (
                COUNTROWS ( Sales )
            )
        VAR WorkingDays =
            CALCULATE (
                COUNTROWS ( 'Date' ),
                RangeOfDates,
                NOT ( WEEKDAY ( 'Date'[Date] ) IN { 1, 7 } ),
                'Date'[Is Holiday] = 0
            )
        VAR NumberOfWorkingDays = NumOfOrders * WorkingDays
        RETURN
            NumberOfWorkingDays
    )
VAR AverageWorkingDays =
    DIVIDE (
        DeliveryWeightedByNumOfOrders,
        NumOfAllOrders
    )
RETURN
    AverageWorkingDays
```

The code is now much harder to read. An important question is: is it worth making the code more complex just to improve performance? As always, it depends. Before diving into this kind of optimization, it is always useful to perform some tests to check if the number of iterations is indeed reduced. In this case, one could evaluate the benefits by running the following query, which returns the total number of rows and the number of unique combinations of *Order Date* and *Delivery Date*:

```
EVALUATE
{ (
    COUNTROWS ( Sales ),
    COUNTROWS (
        SUMMARIZE (
            Sales,
            Sales[Order Date],
            Sales[Delivery Date]
        )
    )
) }

-- The result is:
--
-- Value1 |  Value2
-- -------------------
-- 100231 |    6073
```

In the demo database there are 100,231 rows in *Sales* and only 6,073 distinct combinations of order and delivery dates. The more complex code in the *Avg Delivery WD WA* measure reduces the number of iterations by a bit more than an order of magnitude. Therefore, in this case authoring more complex code is worth the effort. You will learn how to evaluate the impact on execution time in later chapters. For now, we focus on code complexity.

The complexity of the *Avg Delivery WD WA* measure depends on the number of combinations of order and delivery dates, and on the average duration of an order. If the average duration of an order is just a few days, then the formula runs very fast. If the average duration of an order is of several years, then performance might start to be an issue because the result of *DATESBETWEEN* starts to be a large table with hundreds of rows.

Because the number of nonworking days is usually smaller than the number of working days, an idea could be to count nonworking days instead of counting working days. Therefore, another algorithm might be the following:

1. Compute the difference between the two dates in days.

2. Compute the number of nonworking days in between the two dates.

3. Subtract the values computed in (1) and (2).

One can implement this with the following measure:

```
Avg Delivery WD NWD :=
VAR NonWorkingDays =
    CALCULATETABLE (
```

```
            VALUES ( 'Date'[Date] ),
            WEEKDAY ( 'Date'[Date] ) IN { 1, 7 },
            ALL ( 'Date' )
    )
VAR NumOfAllOrders =
    COUNTROWS ( Sales )
VAR CombinationsOrderDeliveryDates =
    SUMMARIZE (
        Sales,
        Sales[Order Date],
        Sales[Delivery Date]
    )
VAR DeliveryWeightedByNumOfOrders =
    CALCULATE (
        SUMX (
            CombinationsOrderDeliveryDates,
            VAR NumOfOrders =
                CALCULATE (
                    COUNTROWS ( Sales )
                )
            VAR NonWorkingDaysInPeriod =
                FILTER (
                    NonWorkingDays,
                    AND (
                        'Date'[Date] >= Sales[Order Date],
                        'Date'[Date] <= Sales[Delivery Date]
                    )
                )
            VAR NumberOfNonWorkingDays =
                COUNTROWS ( NonWorkingDaysInPeriod )
            VAR DeliveryWorkingDays =
                Sales[Delivery Date] - Sales[Order Date] - NumberOfNonWorkingDays + 1
            VAR NumberOfWorkingDays =
                NumOfOrders * DeliveryWorkingDays
            RETURN
                NumberOfWorkingDays
        )
    )
VAR AverageWorkingDays =
    DIVIDE (
        DeliveryWeightedByNumOfOrders,
        NumOfAllOrders
    )
RETURN
    AverageWorkingDays
```

This code runs more slowly than the previous code in the database used for this book. Regardless, this version of the same calculation might perform better on a different database where orders have a much larger duration. Only testing will point you in the right direction.

Why *ALL* is used in the *NonWorkingDays* variable

In the previous example, the *NonWorkingDays* variable calls an *ALL* on the *Date* table. This *ALL* function was not present in previous formulations of similar tables used as filters. The reason is that in previous versions of the measure, we used *DATESBETWEEN*, which is designed to ignore the filter context.

When used in a matrix, the *Date* table might be filtered to show a smaller time period. In that situation, orders having the order date outside of the selected time period would produce an incorrect result. Therefore, before building the table with nonworking days, one should get rid of the filter context on *Date*.

It is interesting to note that *ALL* might not be entirely necessary. Consider this expression of the variable:

```
VAR NonWorkingDays =
    CALCULATETABLE (
        VALUES ( 'Date'[Date] ),
        NOT ( WEEKDAY ( 'Date'[Date] ) IN { 1, 7 } )
    )
```

The filtering condition of *CALCULATE* does not seem to have an *ALL* anywhere. But *ALL* is indeed present, and it becomes evident by expanding the compact syntax of the filter predicate to the full syntax:

```
VAR NonWorkingDays =
    CALCULATETABLE (
        VALUES ( 'Date'[Date] ),
        FILTER (
            ALL ( 'Date'[Date] ),
            NOT ( WEEKDAY ( 'Date'[Date] ) IN { 1, 7 } )
        )
    )
```

Because *ALL* works on the *Date* column of the *Date* table, marked as a date table in the model, the engine automatically adds an *ALL* on the entire *Date* table.

Even though we could have authored the code that way, we do not want our measures to be cryptic and hard to read. Therefore, we preferred a more explicit formulation of the same code, making it easier to read.

Finally, be mindful that when seeking optimal performance, nothing beats precomputing the values. Indeed, no matter what, the difference in working days between two dates always leads to the same result. We already know that there are around 6,000 combinations of order and delivery dates in our demo data model. One could precompute the difference in working days between these 6,000 pairs of dates and store the result in a physical, hidden table. Therefore, at query time there is no need to compute the value. A simple lookup of the result provides the number needed.

Therefore, an option is to create a physical hidden table with the following code:

```
WD Delta =
ADDCOLUMNS (
    SUMMARIZE (
        Sales,
        Sales[Order Date],
        Sales[Delivery Date]
    ),
    "Duration", [Avg Delivery WD WA]
)
```

Once the table is in the model, we take advantage of the precomputed differences in working days by modifying the previous best formula with the following:

```
Avg Delivery WD WA Precomp :=
VAR NumOfAllOrders =
    COUNTROWS ( Sales )
VAR CombinationsOrderDeliveryDates =
    SUMMARIZE (
        Sales,
        Sales[Order Date],
        Sales[Delivery Date]
    )
VAR DeliveryWeightedByNumOfOrders =
    SUMX (
        CombinationsOrderDeliveryDates,
        VAR NumOfOrders =
            CALCULATE (
                COUNTROWS ( Sales )
            )
        VAR WorkingDays =
            LOOKUPVALUE (
                'WD Delta'[Duration],
                'WD Delta'[Order Date], Sales[Order Date],
                'WD Delta'[Delivery Date], Sales[Delivery Date]
            )
        VAR NumberOfWorkingDays = NumOfOrders * WorkingDays
        RETURN
            NumberOfWorkingDays
    )
VAR AverageWorkingDays =
    DIVIDE (
        DeliveryWeightedByNumOfOrders,
        NumOfAllOrders
    )
RETURN
    AverageWorkingDays
```

It is very unlikely that this level of optimization would be required for a simple calculation involving the number of working days between two dates. That said, we were not trying to demonstrate how to super-optimize a measure. Instead, we wanted to show several different ways of obtaining the same result, from the most intuitive version down to a very technical and optimized version that is unlikely to be useful in most scenarios.

Showing budget and sales together

Consider a data model that contains budget information for the current year, along with actual sales. At the beginning of the year, the only available information is the budget figures. As time goes by, there are actual sales, and it becomes interesting both to compare sales and budget, and to adjust the forecast until the end of the year by mixing budget and actual sales.

To simulate this scenario, we removed all the sales after August 15, 2009, and we created a *Budget* table containing the daily budget for the entire year 2009. The resulting data is visible in Figure 16-2.

Month	Budget Amt	Sales Amount
January	3,312,711.98	1,984,496.21
February	2,992,126.95	2,424,777.23
March	3,312,711.98	2,072,712.51
April	3,205,850.30	4,259,638.78
May	3,312,711.98	4,073,469.82
June	3,205,850.30	5,081,121.32
July	3,312,711.98	3,297,393.79
August	3,312,711.98	1,632,927.46
September	3,205,850.30	
October	3,312,711.98	
November	3,205,850.30	
December	3,312,711.98	
Total	**39,004,512.00**	**24,826,537.11**

FIGURE 16-2 Sales stop in August, whereas the budget goes until the end of the year.

The business question is: provided that on August 15, the *Sales Amount* is 24 million, what should be the adjusted forecast at the end of the year, using actuals for the past and budget for the future? Be mindful that because sales ended on the 15th, in August there should be a mix of sales and budget.

The first step is determining the date where sales stop. Using a simple function like *TODAY* would be misleading because data in the model are not necessarily updated to the current day. A better approach is to search for the last date with any data in the *Sales* table. A simple *MAX* works well, but it is important to note that user selection might have a negative effect on the result. For example, consider the following measure:

```
LastDateWithSales := MAX ( 'Sales'[OrderDateKey] )
```

Different brands, or in general different selections, might return different dates. This is shown in Figure 16-3.

Brand	LastDateWithSales
A. Datum	20090814
Adventure Works	20090815
Contoso	20090814
Fabrikam	20090814
Litware	20090814
Northwind Traders	20090809
Proseware	20090814
Southridge Video	20090814
Tailspin Toys	20090815
The Phone Company	20090814
Wide World Importers	20090814
Total	**20090815**

FIGURE 16-3 Not all brands have the same last date with sales.

An appropriate way to compute the last date with any sales is to remove all the filters before computing the maximum date. This way, August 15, 2009, is used for all the products. If any brand does not have any sales on August 15, the value to use is zero, not the budget of the last day with sales for that brand. Therefore, the correct formulation for *LastDateWithSales* is the following:

```
LastDateWithSales :=
CALCULATE (
    MAX ( 'Sales'[OrderDateKey] ),
    ALL ( Sales )
)
```

By removing the filter from *Sales* (which is the expanded *Sales* table), the code is ignoring any filter coming from the query, always returning August 15, 2009. At this point, one needs to write code that uses the value of *Sales Amount* for all the dates before the last date with any sales, and the value of *Budget Amt* for the dates after. One simple implementation is the following:

```
Adjusted Budget :=
VAR LastDateWithSales =
    CALCULATE (
        MAX ( Sales[OrderDateKey] ),
```

```
        ALL ( Sales )
    )
VAR AdjustedBudget =
    SUMX (
        'Date',
        IF (
            'Date'[DateKey] <= LastDateWithSales,
            [Sales Amount],
            [Budget Amt]
        )
    )
RETURN AdjustedBudget
```

Figure 16-4 shows the result of the new *Adjusted Budget* measure.

Month	Budget Amt	Sales Amount	Adjusted Budget
January	3,312,711.98	1,984,496.21	1,984,496.21
February	2,992,126.95	2,424,777.23	2,424,777.23
March	3,312,711.98	2,072,712.51	2,072,712.51
April	3,205,850.30	4,259,638.78	4,259,638.78
May	3,312,711.98	4,073,469.82	4,073,469.82
June	3,205,850.30	5,081,121.32	5,081,121.31
July	3,312,711.98	3,297,393.79	3,297,393.79
August	3,312,711.98	1,632,927.46	3,342,714.28
September	3,205,850.30		3,205,850.30
October	3,312,711.98		3,312,711.98
November	3,205,850.30		3,205,850.30
December	3,312,711.98		3,312,711.98
Total	**39,004,512.00**	**24,826,537.11**	**39,573,448.50**

FIGURE 16-4 *Adjusted Budget* uses actuals or budget, depending on the date.

At this point, we can investigate the measure's complexity. The outer iteration performed by *SUMX* iterates over the *Date* table. In a year, it iterates 365 times. At every iteration, depending on the value of the date, it scans either the *Sales* or the *Budget* table, performing a context transition. It would be good to reduce the number of iterations, thus reducing the number of context transitions and/or aggregations of the larger *Sales* and *Budget* tables.

Indeed, a good solution does not need to iterate over the dates. The only reason to perform the iteration is that the code is more intuitive to read. A slightly different algorithm is the following:

1. Split the current selection on *Date* in two sets: before and after the last date with sales.

2. Compute the sales for the previous period.

3. Compute the budget for the future.

4. Sum sales and budget computed earlier during (2) and (3).

Moreover, there is no need to compute sales just for the period before the last date. Indeed, there will be no sales in the future, so there is no need to filter dates when computing the amount of sales. The only measure that needs to be restricted is the budget. In other words, the formula can sum the entire amount of sales plus the budget of the dates after the last date with sales. This leads to a different formulation of the *Adjusted Budget* measure:

```
Adjusted Budget Optimized :=
VAR LastDateWithSales =
    CALCULATE (
        MAX ( Sales[OrderDateKey] ),
        ALL ( Sales )
    )
VAR SalesAmount = [Sales Amount]
VAR BudgetAmount =
    CALCULATE (
        [Budget Amt],
        KEEPFILTERS ( 'Date'[DateKey] > LastDateWithSales )
    )
VAR AdjustedBudget = SalesAmount + BudgetAmount
RETURN
    AdjustedBudget
```

The results from *Adjusted Budget Optimized* are identical to those of the *Adjusted Budget* measure, but the code complexity is much lower. Indeed, the code of *Adjusted Budget Optimized* only requires one scan of the *Sales* table and one scan of the *Budget* table, the latter with an additional filter on the *Date* table. Please note that *KEEPFILTERS* is required. Otherwise, the condition on the *Date* table would override the current context, providing incorrect figures. This final version of the code is slightly harder to read and to understand, but it is much better performance-wise.

As with previous examples, there are different ways of expressing the same algorithm. Finding the best way requires experience and a solid understanding of the internals of the engine. With that said, simple considerations about the cardinality required in a DAX expression already help a lot in optimizing the code.

Computing same-store sales

This scenario is one specific case of a much broader family of calculations. Contoso has several stores all around the world, and each store has different departments, each one selling specific product categories. Departments are continuously updated: Some are opened, others are closed or renewed. When analyzing sales performance, it is important to compare like-for-like—that is, analyze the sales behavior of comparable departments. Otherwise, one might erroneously conclude that a department performed very poorly, just because for some time in the selected period it had been closed down.

The like-for-like concept can be tailored to every business. In this example, the requirement is to exclusively compare stores and product categories that have sales in the years considered for the analysis. For each product category, a report should solely include stores that have sales in the same years. Variations to this requirement might use the month or the week as granularity in the like-for-like comparison, without changing the approach described as follows.

For example, consider the report in Figure 16-5, which analyzes the sales of one product category (Audio) in German stores over three calendar years.

| Category | | | | |
| Audio ⌄ | | | | |
Store Name	CY 2007	CY 2008	CY 2009	**Total**
Contoso Baumholder Store	3,920.40	539.20	2,589.64	**7,049.24**
Contoso Berlin Store		1,199.92	2,754.90	**3,954.82**
Contoso Dusseldorf Store	1,915.07		1,999.00	**3,914.07**
Contoso Giebelstadt Store	994.10	1,224.00	1,499.90	**3,718.00**
Contoso Hofheim Store	1,019.35		3,219.84	**4,239.19**
Contoso koln No.1 Store	1,179.49	1,340.00	2,960.00	**5,479.49**
Contoso koln No.2 Store	836.05		1,204.70	**2,040.75**
Contoso Landstuhl Store	478.77	421.96		**900.73**
Contoso Munich Store	377.44		310.61	**688.05**
Contoso obamberg Store	3,491.21	2,131.20	1,783.72	**7,406.13**
Contoso Ramstein Store	1,925.48	1,654.80		**3,580.28**
Total	**16,137.35**	**8,511.08**	**18,322.31**	**42,970.74**

FIGURE 16-5 Several stores were opened and closed over the years, polluting the analysis.

The Berlin store was closed in 2007. Out of the two stores in Koln, one was under maintenance in 2008; it was thus only open two out of the three years considered. In order to achieve a fair comparison of the values calculated, any analysis of sales trends needs to be restricted to stores within the selection that were always open.

Because the rules of a like-for-like comparison can be complex and require different types of adjustments, it is a good idea to store the status of the comparable elements in a separate table. This way, any complexity in the business logic will not affect the query performance but only the time required to refresh the status table. In this example, the *StoresStatus* table contains one row for each combination of year, category, and store, alongside with status, which can be Open or Closed. Figure 16-6 shows the status of the German stores, only showing the Open status and hiding the Closed status to improve readability.

Category

Audio

Store Name	CY 2007	CY 2008	CY 2009	**Total**
Contoso Baumholder Store	Open	Open	Open	**Open**
Contoso Berlin Store		Open	Open	
Contoso Dusseldorf Store	Open		Open	
Contoso Giebelstadt Store	Open	Open	Open	**Open**
Contoso Hofheim Store	Open		Open	
Contoso koln No.1 Store	Open	Open	Open	**Open**
Contoso koln No.2 Store	Open		Open	
Contoso Landstuhl Store	Open	Open		
Contoso Munich Store	Open		Open	
Contoso obamberg Store	Open	Open	Open	**Open**
Contoso Ramstein Store	Open	Open		

FIGURE 16-6 The *StoresStatus* table indicates whether a store is open in a given year and for a given product category.

The most interesting column is the last one: Just four stores have been open for all three years. A relevant trend analysis should consider these four stores exclusively, for Audio sales. Moreover, if one changes the selection on the years, the status changes too. Indeed, if one only selects two years (2007 and 2008), the status of the stores is different, as shown in Figure 16-7.

Category

Audio

Store Name	CY 2007	CY 2008	**Total**
Contoso Baumholder Store	Open	Open	**Open**
Contoso Berlin Store		Open	
Contoso Dusseldorf Store	Open		
Contoso Giebelstadt Store	Open	Open	**Open**
Contoso Hofheim Store	Open		
Contoso koln No.1 Store	Open	Open	**Open**
Contoso koln No.2 Store	Open		
Contoso Landstuhl Store	Open	Open	**Open**
Contoso Munich Store	Open		
Contoso obamberg Store	Open	Open	**Open**
Contoso Ramstein Store	Open	Open	**Open**

FIGURE 16-7 The *Total* column considers the status of the years included in the report.

The like-for-like measure must perform the following steps:

- Determine the stores open in all the years of the report for each product category.
- Use the result of the first step to filter the *Amount* measure, restricting the values to stores and product categories that have sales in all the years included in the report.

Before moving further with the example, a deeper analysis of the data model is required. The diagram view is represented in Figure 16-8.

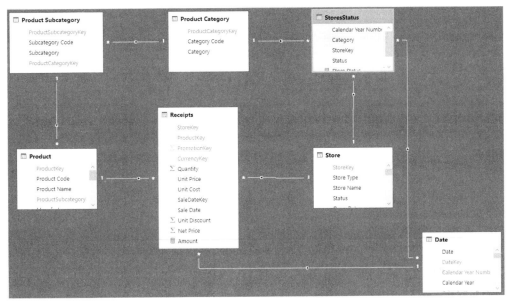

FIGURE 16-8 The *StoreStatus* table has the status of each store for any combination of year and product category.

Let us point out a few things about the model:

- The relationship between *Date* and *StoreStatus* is an MMR weak relationship based on *Year*, with the cross-filter direction going towards *StoreStatus*. *Date* filters *StoreStatus*, not the other way around.

- The relationship between *Product Category* and *StoreStatus* is a regular one-to-many relationship.

- All other relationships are regular one-to-many relationships, with a single cross-filter used in many other demos of this book.

- *StoreStatus* contains one row for each store, product category, and year combination. The status of each row is either Open or Closed. In other words, there are no gaps in the table. This is relevant to reduce the complexity of the formula.

The first step is determining which departments are open over all the years selected. To obtain this, the code must filter the *StoresStatus* table with a given product category and all the selected years. If after having performed this filter, all the filtered rows contain Open in the status, then the department has been open over the whole time period. Otherwise, if there are multiple values (some Open, some Closed), this means that the department was closed at some point. The following query performs this calculation:

```
EVALUATE
VAR StatusGranularity =
    SUMMARIZE (
        Receipts,
        Store[Store Name],
        'Product Category'[Category]
    )
VAR Result =
    FILTER (
        StatusGranularity,
        CALCULATE (
            SELECTEDVALUE ( StoresStatus[Status] ),
            ALLSELECTED ( 'Date'[Calendar Year] )
        ) = "Open"
    )
RETURN
    Result
```

The query iterates at the store/category cardinality, and for each of these pairs it checks if the value of the *Status* is Open for all selected years. In case there are multiple values for *StoreStatus[Status]*, the result of *SELECTEDVALUE* is blank preventing the pair from surviving the filter.

Once we can determine the set of departments open all of the years, the set obtained can be used as a filter to *CALCULATE* to obtain the result:

```
OpenStoresAmt :=
VAR StatusGranularity =
    SUMMARIZE (
        Receipts,
        Store[Store Name],
        'Product Category'[Category]
    )
VAR OpenStores =
    FILTER (
        StatusGranularity,
        CALCULATE (
            SELECTEDVALUE ( StoresStatus[Status] ),
            ALLSELECTED ( 'Date'[Calendar Year] )
        ) = "Open"
    )
VAR AmountLikeForLike =
    CALCULATE (
        [Amount],
        OpenStores
    )
RETURN
    AmountLikeForLike
```

Once projected in a matrix, the measure produces the report in Figure 16-9.

Category		CountryRegion		Store Type	
Audio	∨	Germany	∨	Store	∨

Store Name	CY 2007	CY 2008	CY 2009	Total
Contoso Baumholder Store	3,920.40	539.20	2,589.64	**7,049.24**
Contoso Giebelstadt Store	994.10	1,224.00	1,499.90	**3,718.00**
Contoso koln No.1 Store	1,179.49	1,340.00	2,960.00	**5,479.49**
Contoso obamberg Store	3,491.21	2,131.20	1,783.72	**7,406.13**
Total	**9,585.19**	**5,234.40**	**8,833.26**	**23,652.85**

FIGURE 16-9 *OpenStoreAmt* only returns a value if the store has been open in all selected years.

Stores that are not open all the time have disappeared from the report. It is important to learn this technique well because it is one of the most powerful and useful techniques in DAX. The ability to compute a table containing a filter and then use it to restrict the calculation is the foundation of several advanced calculations in DAX.

In this example, we used an additional table to store the information about whether a store is open or closed. We could have achieved a similar goal by inspecting the *Receipts* table alone, inferring whether a store was open or closed based on their sales. If there are sales, then the assumption is that the store was open. Unfortunately, the opposite is not quite true. The absence of sales does not imply that the store department selling that category was closed. In an unfortunate and borderline scenario, the absence of sales might simply mean that although the department was open, no sale took place.

This last consideration is more about data modeling than DAX, yet we felt it was important to mention it. In case one needs to retrieve the information about the store being open from the *Receipts* table, the formula requires more attention.

The following measure implements the *OpenStoresAmt* measure without using the *StoresStatus* table. For each pair of store and product category, the measure must check whether the number of years in which there are sales is the same as the number of years selected. If a store has sales for just two out of three years, this means that the considered department was closed for one year. The following code is a possible implementation:

```
OpenStoresAmt Dynamic :=
VAR SelectedYears =
    CALCULATE (
        DISTINCTCOUNT ( 'Date'[Calendar Year] ),
        CROSSFILTER ( Receipts[SaleDateKey], 'Date'[DateKey], BOTH ),
        ALLSELECTED ()
    )
VAR StatusGranularity =
    SUMMARIZE (
        Receipts,
        Store[Store Name],
        'Product Category'[Category]
    )
```

```
VAR OpenStores =
    FILTER (
        StatusGranularity,
        VAR YearsWithSales =
            CALCULATE (
                DISTINCTCOUNT ( 'Date'[Calendar Year] ),
                CROSSFILTER ( Receipts[SaleDateKey], 'Date'[DateKey], BOTH ),
                ALLSELECTED ( 'Date'[Calendar Year] )
            )
        RETURN
            YearsWithSales = SelectedYears
    )
VAR AmountLikeForLike =
    CALCULATE (
        [Amount],
        OpenStores
    )
RETURN
    AmountLikeForLike
```

The complexity of this latter version is much higher. Indeed, it requires moving the filter from the *Receipts* table to the *Date* table for every product category to compute the number of years with sales. Because—typically—the *Receipts* table is much larger than a table with only the status for the store, this code is slower than the previous solution based on the *StoresStatus* table. Nevertheless, it is useful to note that the only difference between the previous version and this one is in the condition inside *FILTER*. Instead of inspecting a dedicated table, the formula needs to scan the *Receipts* table. The pattern is still the same.

Another important detail of this code is the way it computes the *SelectedYears* variable. Here, a simple *DISTINCTCOUNT* of all the selected years would not fit. Indeed, the value to compute is not the number of all the selected years, but solely the selected years with sales. If there are 10 years in the *Date* table and just three of them have sales, using a simpler *DISTINCTCOUNT* would also consider the years with no sales, returning blank on every cell.

Numbering sequences of events

This section analyzes a surprisingly common pattern: the requirement to number sequences of events, to easily find the first, the last, and the previous event. In this example, the requirement is to number each order by customer in the Contoso database. The goal is to obtain a new calculated column that contains 1 for the first order of a customer, 2 for the second, and so on. Different customers will have the same number 1 for their first order.

 Warning We should start with a big warning: Some of these formulas are slow. We show samples of code to discuss their complexity while searching for a better solution. If you plan to try them on your model, be prepared for a very long calculation time. By "long," we mean hours of computation and tens of gigabytes of RAM used by the demo model provided. Otherwise, simply follow the description; we show a much better code at the end of the section.

The result to obtain is depicted in Figure 16-10.

Name	Order Number	Order Position
Hill, Wyatt	20080518711016	1
Hill, Wyatt	20080821711016	2
Hill, Wyatt	20081104711016	3
Murphy, Jesse	20070316811040	1
Murphy, Jesse	20080518711040	2
Murphy, Jesse	20080821711040	3
Murphy, Jesse	20081104711040	4
Young, Chloe	20070823711015	1
Young, Chloe	20080331711015	2
Young, Chloe	20080821711015	3
Young, Chloe	20081104711015	4

FIGURE 16-10 Within all the orders of a same customer, *Order Position* contains the relative position of each order.

A first way to compute the order position is the following: for one same customer, the code could count the number of orders that date prior to the current order. Unfortunately, using the date does not work because there are customers who placed multiple orders on the same day; this would generate an incorrect numbering sequence. Luckily, the order number is unique and its value increases for every order. Thus, the formula computes the correct value by counting for one same customer, the number of orders with an order number less than or equal to the current order number.

The following code implements this logic:

```
Sales[Order Position] =
VAR CurrentOrderNumber = Sales[Order Number]
VAR Position =
    CALCULATE (
        DISTINCTCOUNT ( Sales[Order Number] ),
        Sales[Order Number] <= CurrentOrderNumber,
        ALLEXCEPT (
            Sales,
            Sales[CustomerKey]
        )
    )
RETURN
    Position
```

Although it looks rather straightforward, this code is extremely complex. Indeed, in *CALCULATE* it uses a filter on the order number and the context transition generated by the calculated column. For each row in *Sales*, the engine must filter the *Sales* table itself. Therefore, its complexity is the size of *Sales* squared. Because *Sales* contains 100,000 rows, the total complexity is 100,000 multiplied by 100,000; that results in 10 billion. The net result is that this calculated column takes hours to compute. On a larger dataset, it would put any server on its knees.

We discussed the topic of using *CALCULATE* and context transition on large tables in Chapter 5, "Understanding *CALCULATE* and *CALCULATETABLE*." A good developer should try to avoid using context transition on large tables; otherwise, they run the risk of incurring poor performance.

A better implementation of the same idea is the following: Instead of using *CALCULATE* to apply a filter with the expensive context transition, the code could create a table containing all the combinations of *CustomerKey* and *Order Number*. Then, it could apply a similar logic to that table by counting the number of order numbers lower than the current one for that same customer. Here is the code:

```
Sales[Order Position] =
VAR CurrentCustomerKey = Sales[CustomerKey]
VAR CurrentOrderNumber = Sales[Order Number]
VAR CustomersOrders =
    ALL (
        Sales[CustomerKey],
        Sales[Order Number]
    )
VAR PreviousOrdersCurrentCustomer =
    FILTER (
        CustomersOrders,
        AND (
            Sales[CustomerKey] = CurrentCustomerKey,
            Sales[Order Number] <= CurrentOrderNumber
        )
    )
VAR Position =
    COUNTROWS ( PreviousOrdersCurrentCustomer )
RETURN
    Position
```

This new formulation is much quicker. First, the number of distinct combinations of *CustomerKey* and *Order Number* is 26,000 instead of 100,000. Moreover, by avoiding context transition the optimizer can generate a much better execution plan.

The complexity of this formula is still high, and the code is somewhat hard to follow. A much better implementation of the same logic uses the *RANKX* function. *RANKX* is useful to rank a value against a table, and doing that it can easily compute a sequence number. Indeed, the sequence number of an order is the same value as the ascending ranking of the order in the list of all the orders of the same customer.

The following is an implementation of the same calculation as the previous formula, this time using *RANKX*:

```
Sales[Order Position] =
VAR CurrentCustomerKey = Sales[CustomerKey]
VAR CustomersOrders =
    ALL (
        Sales[CustomerKey],
        Sales[Order Number]
    )
VAR OrdersCurrentCustomer =
    FILTER (
        CustomersOrders,
```

```
        Sales[CustomerKey] = CurrentCustomerKey
    )
VAR Position =
    RANKX (
        OrdersCurrentCustomer,
        Sales[Order Number],
        Sales[Order Number],
        ASC,
        DENSE
    )
RETURN
    Position
```

RANKX is very well optimized. It has an efficient internal sorting algorithm that lets it execute quickly even on large datasets. On the demo database the difference between the last two formulas is not very high, yet a deeper analysis of the query plan reveals that the version with *RANKX* is the most efficient. The analysis of query plans is a topic discussed in the next chapters of the book.

Also, in this example there are multiple ways of expressing the same code. Using *RANKX* to compute a sequence number might not be obvious to a DAX novice, which is the reason we included this example in the book. Showing different versions of the same code provides food for thought.

Computing previous year sales up to last date of sales

The following example extends time intelligence calculations with more business logic. The goal is to compute a year-over-year comparison accurately, ignoring in the previous year any sales that took place after a set date. To demonstrate the scenario, we removed from the demo database all sales after August 15, 2009. Therefore, the last year (2009) is incomplete, and so is the month of August 2009.

Figure 16-11 shows that sales after August 2009 report empty values.

Month	CY 2007	CY 2008	CY 2009	Total
January	794,248.24	656,766.69	580,901.05	**2,031,915.98**
February	891,135.91	600,080.00	622,581.14	**2,113,797.05**
March	961,289.24	559,538.52	496,137.87	**2,016,965.62**
April	1,128,104.82	999,667.17	678,893.22	**2,806,665.20**
May	936,192.74	893,231.96	1,067,165.23	**2,896,589.93**
June	982,304.46	845,141.60	872,586.20	**2,700,032.26**
July	922,542.98	890,547.41	1,068,396.58	**2,881,486.97**
August	952,834.59	721,560.95	338,971.06	**2,013,366.60**
September	1,009,868.98	963,437.23		**1,973,306.21**
October	914,273.54	719,792.99		**1,634,066.53**
November	825,601.87	1,156,109.32		**1,981,711.19**
December	991,548.75	921,709.14		**1,913,257.89**
Total	**11,309,946.12**	**9,927,582.99**	**5,725,632.34**	**26,963,161.45**

FIGURE 16-11 There are no sales after August 2009.

When the month is present on the report as in the report shown, the numbers are clear. A user would quickly understand that the last year is incomplete; therefore, they would not make a comparison between the total of 2009 against the total of previous years. Nevertheless, a developer could author some code that—despite being useful—makes the wrong decisions. Consider the following two measures:

```
PY Sales :=
CALCULATE (
    [Sales Amount],
    SAMEPERIODLASTYEAR ( 'Date'[Date] )
)

Growth :=
DIVIDE (
    [Sales Amount] - [PY Sales],
    [PY Sales]
)
```

A user might easily build a report like the one in Figure 16-12 and erroneously deduce that sales are decreasing dramatically for all the brands.

Calendar Year ∨	Brand	Sales Amount	PY Sales	Growth
CY 2009 ∨	A. Datum	282,029.42	463,721.61	-39.18%
	Adventure Works	423,639.36	892,674.52	-52.54%
	Contoso	1,478,194.20	2,369,167.68	-37.61%
	Fabrikam	1,111,065.95	1,993,123.48	-44.26%
	Litware	765,737.20	1,487,846.74	-48.53%
	Northwind Traders	87,281.65	469,827.70	-81.42%
	Proseware	546,032.88	763,586.23	-28.49%
	Southridge Video	241,796.89	294,635.04	-17.93%
	Tailspin Toys	90,391.24	97,193.87	-7.00%
	The Phone Company	298,658.25	355,629.36	-16.02%
	Wide World Importers	400,805.30	740,176.76	-45.85%
	Total	**5,725,632.34**	**9,927,582.99**	**-42.33%**

FIGURE 16-12 The report seems to indicate a dramatic drop in sales for all the brands.

The report does not perform a fair comparison between 2008 and 2009. For the selected year (2009), it reports the sales up to August 15, 2009, whereas for the previous year it considers the sales of the entire year, including September and later dates.

An appropriate comparison should exclusively consider sales that occurred before August 15 in all previous years, so to produce meaningful growth percentages. In other words, the data from previous years should be restricted to the dates up to the last day and month of sales in 2009. The cutoff date is the last date for which there are sales reported in the database.

As usual, there are several ways to solve the problem, and this section presents some of them. The first approach is to modify the PY Sales measure, so that it only considers the dates that happen to be before the last date of sales projected in the previous year. One option to author the code is the following:

```
PY Sales :=
VAR LastDateInSales =
    CALCULATETABLE (
        LASTDATE ( Sales[Order Date] ),
        ALL ( Sales )
    )
VAR LastDateInDate =
    TREATAS (
        LastDateInSales,
        'Date'[Date]
    )
VAR PreviousYearLastDate =
    SAMEPERIODLASTYEAR ( LastDateInDate )
VAR PreviousYearSales =
    CALCULATE (
        [Sales Amount],
        SAMEPERIODLASTYEAR ( 'Date'[Date] ),
        'Date'[Date] <= PreviousYearLastDate
    )
RETURN
    PreviousYearSales
```

The first variable computes the last *Order Date* in all sales. In the sample data model, it retrieves August 15, 2009. The second variable (*LastDateInDate*) changes the data lineage of the previous result to *Date[Date]*. This step is needed because time intelligence functions are expected to work on the date table. Using them on different tables might lead to wrong behaviors, as we will demonstrate later. Once *LastDateInDate* contains August 15, 2009, with the right data lineage, *SAMEPERIODLASTYEAR* moves this date one year back. Finally, *CALCULATE* uses this value to compute the sales in the previous year combining two filters: the current selection moved one year back and every day before August 15, 2008.

The result of this new formula is visible in Figure 16-13.

Calendar Year ⌄	Brand	Sales Amount	PY Sales	Growth
CY 2009 ⌄	A. Datum	282,029.42	281,929.56	0.04%
	Adventure Works	423,639.36	548,902.82	-22.82%
	Contoso	1,478,194.20	1,486,074.44	-0.53%
	Fabrikam	1,111,065.95	1,073,377.56	3.51%
	Litware	765,737.20	754,046.93	1.55%
	Northwind Traders	87,281.65	298,321.72	-70.74%
	Proseware	546,032.88	421,903.10	29.42%
	Southridge Video	241,796.89	176,612.65	36.91%
	Tailspin Toys	90,391.24	63,602.42	42.12%
	The Phone Company	298,658.25	221,633.71	34.75%
	Wide World Importers	400,805.30	415,097.96	-3.44%
	Total	**5,725,632.34**	**5,741,502.86**	**-0.28%**

FIGURE 16-13 Considering the right fraction of the year, the results are now comparable.

It is important to understand the reason why the previous formula requires *TREATAS*. An inexperienced DAX developer might write the same measure with this simpler code:

```
PY Sales Wrong :=
VAR LastDateInSales =
    CALCULATETABLE (
        LASTDATE ( Sales[Order Date] ),
        ALL ( Sales )
    )
VAR PreviousYearLastDate =
    SAMEPERIODLASTYEAR ( LastDateInSales )
VAR PreviousYearSales =
    CALCULATE (
        [Sales Amount],
        SAMEPERIODLASTYEAR ( 'Date'[Date] ),
        'Date'[Date] <= PreviousYearLastDate
    )
RETURN
    PreviousYearSales
```

To make matters worse, on the demo model we provide as an example, this latter measure and the previous measure return the same figures. Therefore, there is a bug that is not evident at first sight. Here is the problem: The result from *SAMEPERIODLASTYEAR* is a table of one column with the same data lineage as its input column. If one passes a column with the lineage of *Sales[Order Date]* to *SAMEPERIODLASTYEAR*, then the function must return a value that exists among the possible values of *Sales[Order Date]*. Being a column in *Sales*, *Order Date* is not expected to contain all the possible values. For example, if there are no sales during a weekend, then that weekend date is not present among the possible values of *Sales[Order Date]*. In that scenario, *SAMEPERIODLASTYEAR* returns blank.

Figure 16-14 shows what happens to the report by removing any transaction from August 15, 2008, from the *Sales* table, for demo purposes.

Calendar Year	Brand	Sales Amount	PY Sales Wrong	Growth
CY 2009 ⌄				
	A. Datum	282,029.42		
	Adventure Works	423,639.36		
	Contoso	1,478,194.20		
	Fabrikam	1,111,065.95		
	Litware	765,737.20		
	Northwind Traders	87,281.65		
	Proseware	546,032.88		
	Southridge Video	241,796.89		
	Tailspin Toys	90,391.24		
	The Phone Company	298,658.25		
	Wide World Importers	400,805.30		
	Total	**5,725,632.34**		

FIGURE 16-14 The boxed area contains the value of *PY Sales Wrong*, which is always blank.

Because the last date is August 15, 2009, moving this date one year back leads to August 15, 2008, which, on purpose, does not exist in *Sales[Order Date]*. Therefore, *SAMEPERIODLASTYEAR* returned a blank. Since *SAMEPERIODLASTYEAR* returned a blank, the second condition inside *CALCULATE* imposes that the date be less than or equal to blank. There is no date satisfying the condition; therefore, the *PY Sales Wrong* measure always returns blank.

In the example, we removed one date from *Sales* to show the issue. In the real world, the problem might happen on any date, if on the corresponding day in the previous year there were no sales. Remember: Time intelligence functions are expected to work on a well-designed date table. Using them on columns from different tables might lead to unexpected results.

Of course, once the overall logic becomes clearer, there can be many ways of expressing the same code. We proposed one version, but you should feel free to experiment.

Finally, scenarios like this one have a much better solution if one can update the data model. Indeed, computing the last date with sales every time a calculation is required and moving it back one year (or by whatever offset is needed) proves to be a tedious, error-prone task. A much better solution is to pre-calculate whether each date should be included in the comparison or not, and consolidate this value directly in the *Date* table.

One could create a new calculated column in the *Date* table, which indicates whether a given date should be included in the comparison with the last year or not. In other words, all dates before August 15 have a value of *TRUE*, whereas all the rows after August 15 have a value of *FALSE*.

The new calculated column can be authored this way:

```
'Date'[IsComparable] =
VAR LastDateInSales =
    MAX ( Sales[Order Date] )
VAR LastMonthInSales =
    MONTH ( LastDateInSales )
VAR LastDayInSales =
    DAY ( LastDateInSales )
VAR LastDateCurrentYear =
    DATE ( YEAR ( 'Date'[Date] ), LastMonthInSales, LastDayInSales )
VAR DateIncludedInCompare =
    'Date'[Date] <= LastDateCurrentYear
RETURN
    DateIncludedInCompare
```

Once the column is in place, the *PY Sales* measure can be authored much more simply:

```
PY Sales :=
CALCULATE (
    [Sales Amount],
    SAMEPERIODLASTYEAR ( 'Date'[Date] ),
    'Date'[IsComparable] = TRUE
)
```

Not only is this code easier to read and debug, it is also way faster than the previous implementation. The reason is that it is no longer necessary to use the complex code required to compute the last date in *Sales*, move it as a filter on *Date*, and then apply it to the model. The code is now executed with a simple filter argument of *CALCULATE* that checks for a *Boolean* value. The takeaway of this example is that it is possible to move a complex logic for a filter in a calculated column, which is computed during data refresh and not when a user is waiting for the report to come up.

Conclusions

As you have seen, this chapter does not include any new function of the language. Instead, we wanted to show that the same problem can be approached in several different ways. We have not covered the internals of the engine, which is an important topic to introduce optimizations. However, by performing a simple analysis of the code and simulating its behavior, it is oftentimes possible to consider a better formula for the same scenario.

Please remember that this chapter is not about patterns. You can freely use this code in your models, but do not assume that it is the best implementation of the pattern. Our goal was to lead you in thinking about the same scenario in different ways.

As you learn in the next chapters, providing unique patterns in DAX is nearly impossible. The code that runs faster in one data model might not be the top performer in a different data model, or even in the same model with a different data distribution.

If you are serious about optimizing DAX code, then be prepared for a deep dive in the internals of the engine, discovering all the most intricate details of the DAX query engines. This fascinating and complex trip is about to begin, as soon as you turn to the next page.

The DAX engines

The goal of the book up to this point has been to provide a solid understanding of the DAX language. On top of gaining further experience through practice, the next goal for you is to write efficient DAX and not just DAX that works. Writing efficient DAX requires understanding the internals of the engine. The next chapters aim to provide the essential knowledge to measure and improve DAX code performance.

More specifically, this chapter is dedicated to the internal architecture of the engines running DAX queries. Indeed, a DAX query can run on a model that is stored entirely in memory, or entirely on the original data source, or on a mix of these two options.

Starting from this chapter, we somewhat deviate from DAX and begin to discuss low-level technical details about the implementation of products that use DAX. This is an important topic, but you need to be aware that implementation details change often. We did our best to show information at a level that is not likely to change soon, carefully balancing detail level and usefulness with consistency over time. Nevertheless, given the pace at which technology runs these days, the information might be outdated within a few years. The most up-to-date information is always available online, in blog posts and articles.

New versions of the engines come out every month, and the query optimizer can change and improve the query execution. Therefore, we aim to teach how the engines work, rather than just provide a few rules about writing DAX code that would quickly become obsolete. We sometimes provide best practices, but remember to always double-check how our suggestions apply to your specific scenario.

Understanding the architecture of the DAX engines

The DAX language is used in several Microsoft products based on the Tabular technology. Yet, specific features might only be available in a few editions or license conditions. A Tabular model uses both DAX and MDX as query languages. This section describes the broader architecture of a Tabular model, regardless of the query language and of the limitations of specific products.

Every report sends queries to Tabular using either DAX or MDX. Despite the query language used, the Tabular model uses two engines to process a query:

- The **formula engine** (FE), which processes the request, generating and executing a query plan.

- The **storage engine** (SE), which retrieves data out of the Tabular model to answer the requests made by the Formula Engine. The Storage Engine has two implementations:

  - **VertiPaq** hosts a copy of the data in-memory that is refreshed periodically from the data source.

  - **DirectQuery** forwards queries directly to the original data source for every request. DirectQuery does not create an additional copy of data.

Figure 17-1 represents the architecture that executes a DAX or MDX query.

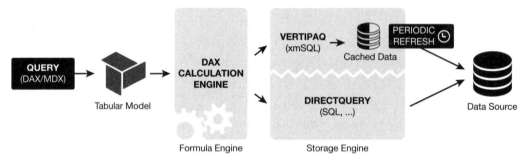

FIGURE 17-1 A query is processed by an architecture using a formula engine and a storage engine.

The formula engine is the higher-level execution unit of the query engine in a Tabular model. It can handle all the operations requested by DAX and MDX functions and can solve complex DAX and MDX expressions. However, when the formula engine must retrieve data from the underlying tables, it forwards part of the requests to the storage engine.

The queries sent to the storage engine might vary from a simple retrieval of the raw table data to more complex queries aggregating data and joining tables. The storage engine only communicates with the formula engine. The storage engine returns data in an uncompressed format, regardless of the original format of the data.

A Tabular model usually stores data using either the VertiPaq or the DirectQuery storage engine. However, composite models can use both technologies within the same data model and for the same tables. The choice of which engine to use is made by the engine on a by-query basis.

This book is exclusively focused on DAX. Be mindful that MDX uses the same architecture when it queries a Tabular model. This chapter describes the different types of storage engines available in a Tabular model, focusing more on the details of the VertiPaq engine because it is the native and faster engine for DAX.

Introducing the formula engine

The formula engine is the absolute core of the DAX execution. Indeed, the formula engine alone is able to understand the DAX language, though it understands MDX as well. The formula engine converts a DAX or MDX query into a query plan describing a list of physical steps to execute. The storage engine part of Tabular is not aware that its queries originated from a model supporting DAX.

Each step in the query plan corresponds to a specific operation executed by the formula engine. Typical operators of the formula engine include joins between tables, filtering with complex conditions, aggregations, and lookups. These operators typically require data from columns in the data model. In these cases, the formula engine sends a request to the storage engine, which answers by returning a datacache. A datacache is a temporary storage area created by the storage engine and read by the formula engine.

 Note Datacaches are not compressed; datacaches are plain in-memory tables stored in an uncompressed format, regardless of the storage engine they come from.

The formula engine always works with datacaches returned by the storage engine or with data structures computed by other formula engine operators. The result of a formula engine operation is not persisted in memory across different executions, even within the same session. On the other hand, datacaches are kept in memory and can be reused in following queries. The formula engine does not have a cache system to reuse results between different queries. DAX relies entirely on the cache features of the storage engine.

Finally, the formula engine is single-threaded. This means that any operation executed in the formula engine uses just one thread and one core, no matter how many cores are available. The formula engine sends requests to the storage engine sequentially, one query at a time. A certain degree of parallelism is available only within each request to the storage engine, which has a different architecture and can take advantage of multiple cores available. This is described in the next sections.

Introducing the storage engine

The goal of the storage engine is to scan the Tabular database and produce the datacaches needed by the formula engine. The storage engine is independent from DAX. For example, DirectQuery on top of SQL Server uses SQL as the storage engine. SQL was born much earlier than DAX. Although it might seem strange, the internal storage engine of Tabular (known as VertiPaq) is independent from DAX too. The overall architecture is very clean and sound. The storage engine executes exclusively queries allowed by its own set of operators. Depending on the kind of storage engine used, the set of operators might range from very limited (VertiPaq) to very rich (SQL). This affects the performance and the kind of optimizations that a developer should consider when analyzing query plans.

A developer can define the storage engine used for each table, using one of these three options:

- **Import:** Also called in-memory, or VertiPaq. The content of the table is stored by the VertiPaq engine, copying and restructuring the data from the data source during data refresh.

- **DirectQuery:** The content of the table is read from the data source at query time, and it is not stored in memory during data refresh.

- **Dual:** The table can be queried in both VertiPaq and DirectQuery. During data refresh the table is loaded in memory, but at query time the table may also be read in DirectQuery mode, with the most up-to-date information.

Moreover, a table in a Tabular model could be used as an aggregation for another table. Aggregations are useful to optimize storage engine requests, but not to optimize a bottleneck in the formula engine. Aggregations can be defined in both VertiPaq and DirectQuery, though they are commonly defined in VertiPaq to achieve the best query performance.

The storage engine features a parallel implementation. However, it receives requests from the formula engine, which sends them synchronously. Thus, the formula engine waits for one storage engine query to finish before sending the next one. Therefore, parallelism in the storage engine might be reduced by the lack of parallelism of the formula engine.

Introducing the VertiPaq (in-memory) storage engine

The VertiPaq storage engine is the native lower-level execution unit of the DAX query engine. In certain products it was officially named xVelocity In-Memory Analytical Engine. Nevertheless, it is widely known as VertiPaq, which is the original code name used during development. VertiPaq stores a copy of the data read from the data source in a compressed in-memory format based on a columnar database structure.

VertiPaq queries are expressed using an internal pseudo-SQL language called xmSQL. xmSQL is not a real query language, but rather a textual representation of a storage engine query. The intent of xmSQL is to give visibility to humans as to how the formula engine is querying VertiPaq. VertiPaq offers a very limited set of operators: In case the calculation requires a more complex evaluation within an internal data scan, VertiPaq can perform a callback to the formula engine.

The VertiPaq storage engine is multithreaded. The operations performed by the VertiPaq storage engine are very efficient and can scale up on multiple cores. A single storage engine query can increase its parallelism up to one thread for each segment of a table. We will describe segments later in this chapter. Considering that the storage engine can use up to one thread per column segment, one can benefit from the parallelism of the storage engine only when there are many segments involved in the query. In other words, if there are eight storage engine queries, running on a small table (one segment), they will run sequentially one after the other, instead of all in parallel, because of the synchronous nature of communication between the formula engine and the storage engine.

A cache system stores the results produced by the VertiPaq storage engine, holding a limited number of results—typically the last 512 internal queries per database, but different versions of the engine might use a different number. When the storage engine receives an xmSQL query identical to one already in cache, it returns the corresponding datacache without doing any scan of data in memory. The cache is not involved in security considerations because the row-level security system only influences the formula engine behavior, producing different xmSQL queries in case the user is restricted to seeing specific rows in a table.

A scan operation made by the storage engine is usually faster than the equivalent scan performed by the formula engine, even with a single thread available. This is because the storage engine is better optimized for these operations and because it iterates over compressed data; the formula engine, on the other hand, can only iterate over datacaches, which are uncompressed.

Introducing the DirectQuery storage engine

The DirectQuery storage engine is a generic definition, describing the scenario where the data is kept in the original data source instead of being copied in the VertiPaq storage. When the formula engine sends a request to the storage engine in DirectQuery mode, it sends a query to the data source in its specific query language. This is SQL most of the time, but it could be different.

The formula engine is aware of the presence of DirectQuery. Therefore, the formula engine generates a different query plan compared to VertiPaq because it can take advantage of more advanced functions available in the query language used by the data source. For example, SQL can manage string transformations such as *UPPER* and *LOWER*, whereas the VertiPaq engine does not have any string manipulation functions available.

Any optimization of the storage engine using DirectQuery requires an optimization of the data source—for example, using indexes in a relational database. More details about DirectQuery and the possible optimizations are available in the following white paper: https://www.sqlbi.com/whitepapers/directquery-in-analysis-services-2016/. The considerations are valid for both Power BI and Analysis Services because they share the same underlying engine.

Understanding data refresh

DAX runs on SQL Server Analysis Services (SSAS) Tabular, Azure Analysis Services (same as SSAS in this book), Power BI service (both on server and on the local Power BI Desktop), and in the Power Pivot for Microsoft Excel add-in. Technically, both Power Pivot for Excel and Power BI use a customized version of SSAS Tabular. Speaking about different engines is thus somewhat artificial: Power Pivot and Power BI are like SSAS although SSAS runs in a hidden mode. In this book, we do not discriminate between these engines; when we mention SSAS, the reader should always mentally replace SSAS with Power Pivot or Power BI. If there are differences worth highlighting, then we will note them in that specific section.

When SSAS loads the content of a source table in memory, we say that it processes the table. This takes place during the process operation of SSAS or during the data refresh in Power Pivot for Excel and Power BI. The table process for DirectQuery simply clears the internal cache without executing any access to the data source. On the other hand, when processing occurs in VertiPaq mode, the engine reads the content of the data sources and transforms it into the internal VertiPaq data structure.

VertiPaq processes a table following these few steps:

1. Reading of the source dataset, transformation into the columnar data structure of VertiPaq, encoding and compressing of each column.

2. Creating of dictionaries and indexes for each column.

3. Creating of the data structures for relationships.

4. Computing and compressing all the calculated columns and calculated tables.

The last two steps are not necessarily sequential. Indeed, a relationship can be based on a calculated column, or calculated columns can depend on a relationship because they use *RELATED* or *CALCULATE*. Therefore, SSAS creates a complex graph of dependencies to execute the steps in the correct order.

In the next sections, we describe these steps in more detail. We also cover the format of the internal structures created by SSAS during the transformation of the data source into the VertiPaq model.

Understanding the VertiPaq storage engine

The VertiPaq engine is the most common storage engine used in Tabular models. VertiPaq is used whenever a table is in Import storage mode. This is the common choice in many data models, and it is the only choice in Power Pivot for Excel. In composite models, the presence of tables or aggregations in dual storage mode also implies the use of the VertiPaq storage engine combined with DirectQuery.

For these reasons, a solid knowledge of the VertiPaq storage engine is a basic skill required to understand how to optimize both the memory consumption of the model and the execution time of the queries. In this section, we describe how the VertiPaq storage works.

Introducing columnar databases

VertiPaq is an in-memory columnar database. Being in-memory means that all the data handled by a model reside in RAM. But VertiPaq is not only in-memory; it is also a columnar database. Therefore, it is relevant to have a good understanding of what a columnar database is in order to correctly understand VertiPaq.

We think of a table as a list of rows, where each row is divided into columns. For example, consider the *Product* table in Figure 17-2.

Product

ID	Name	Color	Unit Price
1	Camcorder	Red	112.25
2	Camera	Red	97.50
3	Smartphone	White	100.00
4	Console	Black	112.25
5	TV	Blue	1,240.85
6	CD	Red	39.99
7	Touch screen	Blue	45.12
8	PDA	Black	120.25
9	Keyboard	Black	120.50

FIGURE 17-2 The figure shows the *Product* table, with four columns and nine rows.

Thinking of a table as a set of rows, we are using the most natural visualization of a table structure. Technically, this is known as a *row store*. In a row store, data is organized in rows. When the table is stored in memory, we might think that the value of the *Name* column in the first row is adjacent to the values of the *ID* and *Color* columns in the same row. On the other hand, the value in the second row of the *Name* column is slightly farther from the *Name* value in the first row because in between we find *Color* and *Unit Price* in the first row, and the value of the *ID* column in the second row. As an example, the following code is a schematic representation of the physical memory layout of a row store:

```
ID,Name,Color,Unit Price|1,Camcorder,Red,112.25|2,Camera,Red,97.50|3,Smartphone,
White,100.00|4,Console,Black,112.25|5,TV,Blue,1,240.85|6,CD,Red,39.99|7,
Touch screen,Blue,45.12|8,PDA,Black,120.25,9,Keyboard,Black,120.50
```

Imagine a developer needs to compute the sum of *Unit Price*: The engine must scan the entire memory area, reading many irrelevant values in the process. Imagine scanning the memory of the database sequentially: To read the first value of *Unit Price*, the engine needs to read (and skip) the first row of *ID*, *Name,* and *Color*. Only then does it find an interesting value. The same process is repeated for all the rows. Following this technique, the engine needs to read and ignore many columns to find the relevant values to sum.

Reading and ignoring values take time. In fact, if we asked someone to compute the sum of *Unit Price*, they would not follow that algorithm. Instead, as human beings, they would probably scan the first row in Figure 17-2 searching for the position of *Unit Price*, and then move their eyes down, reading the values one at a time and mentally accumulating them to produce the sum. The reason for this very natural behavior is that we save time by reading vertically instead of row-by-row.

A columnar database organizes data to optimize vertical scanning. To obtain this result, it needs a way to make the different values of a column adjacent to one another. In Figure 17-3 you can see the same *Product* table as organized by a columnar database.

Product Columns

ID	Name	Color	Unit Price
1	Camcorder	Red	112.25
2	Camera	Red	97.50
3	Smartphone	White	100.00
4	Console	Black	112.25
5	TV	Blue	1,240.85
6	CD	Red	39.99
7	Touch screen	Blue	45.12
8	PDA	Black	120.25
9	Keyboard	Black	120.50

FIGURE 17-3 The *Product* table organized column-by-column.

When stored in a columnar database, each column has its own data structure; it is physically separated from the others. Thus, the different values of *Unit Price* are adjacent to one another and distant from *Color*, *Name*, and *ID*. The following code is a schematic representation of the physical memory layout of a column store:

```
ID,1,2,3,4,5,6,7,8,9
Name,Camcorder,Camera,Smartphone,Console,TV,CD,Touch screen,PDA,Keyboard
Color,Red,Red,White,Black,Blue,Red,Blue,Black,Black
Unit Price,112.25,97.50,100.00,112.25,1240.85,39.99,45.12,120.25,120.50
```

With this data structure, computing the sum of *Unit Price* is much easier because the engine immediately goes to the structure containing *Unit Price*. There, it finds all the values needed to perform the computation next to each other. In other words, it does not have to read and ignore other column values: In a single scan, it obtains exclusively the useful numbers, and it can quickly aggregate them.

In our next scenario, instead of summing *Unit Price*, we compute the sum of *Unit Price* just for the Red products. You are encouraged to give this a try before reading on, in order to better understand the algorithm.

This is not so easy anymore; indeed, it is no longer possible to obtain the desired number by simply scanning the *Unit Price* column. What developers would typically do is scan the *Color* column, and whenever it is Red, retrieve the corresponding value in *Unit Price*. At the end, all the values would be summed up to compute the result.

Though very intuitive, this algorithm requires a constant move of the eyes from one column to the other in Figure 17-3, possibly using a finger as a guide to save the last scanned position of *Color*. It is not an optimized way of computing the value. The reason is that the engine needs to constantly jump from one memory area to another, resulting in poor performance. A better way—which only computers use—is to first scan the *Color* column, find the positions where the color is Red, and then scan the *Unit Price* column, summing only the values in the positions identified in the previous step.

This last algorithm is much better because it performs one scan of the first column and one scan of the second column, always accessing memory locations that are adjacent to one another—other than the jump between the scan of the first and second column. Sequential reading of memory is much faster than random access.

For a more complex expression, such as the sum of all products that are either Blue or Black with a price higher than US$50, things are even worse. This time, there is no possibility of scanning the column one at a time because the condition depends on way too many columns. As usual, trying on paper helps better understand the problem.

The simplest algorithm producing the desired result is to scan the table not on a column basis, but on a row basis instead. We naturally tend to scan the table row-by-row, though the storage organization is column-by-column. Although it is a very simple operation when executed on paper by a human, the same operation is extremely expensive if executed by a computer in RAM; indeed, it requires a lot of random reads of memory, leading to poorer performance than if computed doing a sequential scan.

As discussed, a columnar storage presents both pros and cons. Columnar databases provide very quick access to a single column; but as soon as one needs a calculation involving many columns, they need to spend some time—after having read the column content—to reorganize the information so that the final expression can be computed. Even though this example was very simple, it helps highlight the most important characteristics of column stores:

- Single-column access is very fast: It sequentially reads a single block of memory and then computes whatever aggregation is needed on that memory block.

- If an expression uses many columns, the algorithm is more complex because it requires the engine to access different memory areas at different times, keeping track of the progress in a temporary area.

- The more columns are needed to compute an expression, the harder it becomes to produce a result. At a certain point it becomes easier to rebuild the row storage out of the column store to compute the expression.

Column stores aim to reduce the read time. However, they spend more CPU cycles to rearrange the data when many columns from the same table are used. Row stores, on the other hand, have a more linear algorithm to scan data, but they result in many useless reads. As a rule, reducing reads at the cost of increasing CPU usage is a good deal, because with modern computers, it is always easier (and cheaper) to increase the CPU speed versus reducing I/O (or memory access) time.

Moreover, as we will see in the next sections, columnar databases have more options to reduce the amount of time spent scanning data. The most relevant technique used by VertiPaq is compression.

Understanding VertiPaq compression

In the previous section, you learned that VertiPaq stores each column in a separate data structure. This simple fact allows the engine to implement some extremely important compressions and encoding described in this section.

Note The actual details of the compression algorithm of VertiPaq are proprietary. Thus, we cannot publish them in a book. Yet what we explain in this chapter is already a good approximation of what takes place in the engine, and we can use it, for all intents and purposes, to describe how the VertiPaq engine stores data.

VertiPaq compression algorithms aim to reduce the memory footprint of a data model. Reducing the memory usage is a very important task for two very good reasons:

- A smaller model makes better use of the hardware. Why spend money on 1 TB of RAM when the same model, once compressed, can be hosted in 256 GB? Saving RAM is always a good option, if feasible.

- A smaller model is faster to scan. As simple as this rule is, it is very important when speaking about performance. If a column is compressed, the engine will scan less RAM to read its content, resulting in better performance.

Understanding value encoding

Value encoding is the first kind of encoding that VertiPaq might use to reduce the memory cost of a column. Consider a column containing the price of products, stored as integer values. The column contains many different values and a defined number of bits is required to represent all of them.

In the Figure 17-4 example, the maximum value of *Unit Price* is 216. At least 8 bits are required to store each integer value up to that number. Nevertheless, by using a simple mathematical operation, we can reduce the storage to 5 bits.

Reducing the number of bits needed

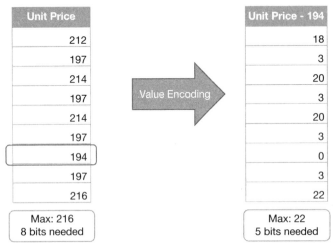

FIGURE 17-4 By using simple mathematical operations, VertiPaq reduces the number of bits needed for a column.

In the example, VertiPaq found out that by subtracting the minimum value (194) from all the values of the column, it could modify the range of the values in the column, reducing it to a range from 0 to 22. Storing numbers up to 22 requires fewer bits than storing numbers up to 216. While 3 bits might seem like an insignificant savings, when we multiply this by a few billion rows, it is easy to see that the difference can be important.

The VertiPaq engine is much more sophisticated than this. It can discover mathematical relationships between the values of a column, and when it finds them, it can use them to modify the storage. This reduces its memory footprint. Obviously, when using the column, it must reapply the transformation in the opposite direction to obtain the original value. Depending on the transformation, this can happen before or after aggregating the values. Again, this increases the CPU usage and reduces the number of reads, which is a very good option.

Value encoding only takes place for integer columns because it cannot be applied on strings or floating-point values. Be mindful that VertiPaq stores the *Currency* data type of DAX (also called Fixed Decimal Number) as an integer value. Therefore, currencies can be value-encoded too, whereas floating point numbers cannot.

Understanding hash encoding

Hash encoding (also known as dictionary encoding) is another technique used by VertiPaq to reduce the number of bits required to store a column. Hash encoding builds a dictionary of the distinct values of a column and then replaces the column values with indexes to the dictionary. In Figure 17-5 you can see the storage of the *Color* column, which uses strings and cannot be value-encoded.

Replacing data types with dictionary and indexes

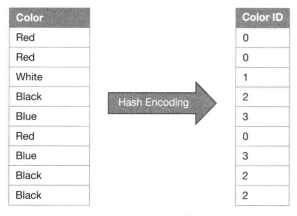

FIGURE 17-5 Hash encoding consists of building a dictionary and replacing values with indexes.

When VertiPaq encodes a column with hash encoding, it

- Builds a dictionary, containing the distinct values of the column.

- Replaces the values with integer numbers, where each number is the dictionary index of the original value.

There are some advantages in using hash encoding:

- All columns only contain integer values; this makes it simpler to optimize the internal code of the engine. Moreover, it also means that VertiPaq is data type independent.

- The number of bits used to store a single value is the minimum number of bits necessary to store an index entry. In the example provided, 2 bits are enough because there are only four different values.

These two aspects are of paramount importance for VertiPaq. It does not matter whether a column uses a string, a 64-bit integer, or a floating point to represent a value. All these data types can be hash encoded, providing the same performance in terms of speed of scanning and of storage space. The only difference might be in the size of the dictionary, which is typically very small when compared with the size of the original column itself.

The primary factor to determine the column size is not the data type. Instead, it is the number of distinct values of the column. We refer to the number of distinct values of a column as its *cardinality*. Repeating a concept this important is always a good thing: Of all the various aspects of an individual column, the most important one when designing a data model is its cardinality.

The lower the cardinality, the smaller the number of bits required to store a single value. Consequently, the smaller the memory footprint of the column. If a column is smaller, not only will it be possible to store more data in the same amount of RAM, but it will also be much faster to scan it whenever the engine needs to aggregate its values in a DAX expression.

Understanding Run Length Encoding (RLE)

Hash encoding and value encoding are two very good compression techniques. However, there is another complementary compression technique used by VertiPaq: Run Length Encoding (RLE). This technique aims to reduce the size of a dataset by avoiding repeated values. For example, consider a column storing in which quarter the sales took place, stored in the *Sales* table. This column might contain the string "Q1" repeated many times in contiguous rows, for all the sales in the same quarter. In such a case, VertiPaq avoids storing values that are repeated. It replaces them with a slightly more complex structure that contains the value only once, with the number of contiguous rows having the same value. This is shown in Figure 17-6.

RLE's efficiency strongly depends on the repetition pattern of the column. Some columns have the same value repeated for many rows, resulting in a great compression ratio. Other columns with quickly changing values produce a lower compression ratio. Data sorting is extremely important to improve the compression ratio of RLE. Therefore, finding an optimal sort order is an important step of the data refresh performed by VertiPaq.

Reducing rows using Run Length Encoding (RLE)

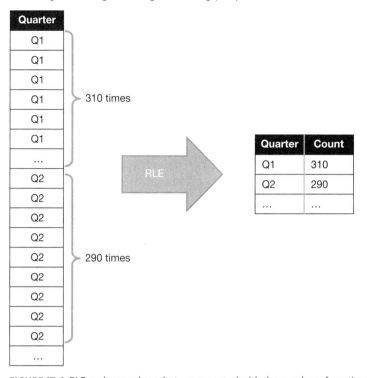

FIGURE 17-6 RLE replaces values that are repeated with the number of contiguous rows with the same value.

Finally, there could be columns in which the content changes so often that if VertiPaq tried to compress them using RLE, the compressed columns would end up using more space than the original columns. A great example of this is the primary key of a table. It has a different value for each row, resulting in an RLE version larger than the column itself. In cases like this, VertiPaq skips the RLE compression and stores the column as-is. Thus, the VertiPaq storage of a column never exceeds the original column size. Worst-case scenario, both would be the same size.

In the example, we have shown RLE working on a *Quarter* column containing strings. RLE can also process the already hash-encoded version of a column. Each column can have both RLE and either hash or value encoding. Therefore, the VertiPaq storage for a column compressed with hash encoding consists of two distinct entities: the dictionary and the data rows. The latter is the RLE-encoded result of the hash-encoded version of the original column, as shown in Figure 17-7.

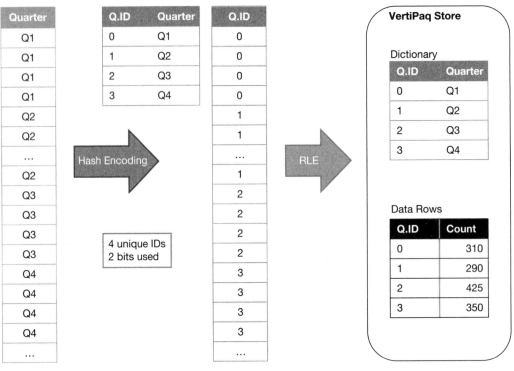

FIGURE 17-7 RLE is applied to the dictionary-encoded version of a column.

VertiPaq also applies RLE to value-encoded columns. In this case the dictionary is missing because the column already contains value-encoded integers.

The factors influencing the compression ratio of a Tabular model are, in order of importance:

1. The cardinality of the column, which defines the number of bits used to store a value.

2. The number of repetitions, that is, the distribution of data in a column. A column with many repeated values is compressed more than a column with very frequently changing values.

3. The number of rows in the table.

4. The data type of the column, which only affects the dictionary size.

Given all these considerations, it is nearly impossible to predict the compression ratio of a table. Moreover, while a developer has full control over certain aspects of a table—they can limit the number of rows and change the data types—these are the least important aspects. Yet as you learn in the next chapter, one can work on cardinality and repetitions too. This improves the compression and performance of a model.

Finally, it is worth noting that reducing the cardinality of a column also increases the chances of repetitions. For example, if a time column is stored at the second granularity, then the column contains up to 86,400 distinct values. If, on the other hand, the developer stores the same time column at the hour granularity, then not only have they reduced the cardinality, but they also introduced repeating values. Indeed, 3,600 seconds convert to one same hour. All this results in a much better compression ratio. On the other hand, changing the data type from *DateTime* to *Integer* or even *String* offers a negligible impact on column size.

Understanding re-encoding

SSAS must decide which algorithm to use to encode each column. More specifically, it needs to decide whether to use value or dictionary encoding. In order to make an educated decision, it reads a row sample during the first scan of the source, and it chooses a compression algorithm depending on the values found.

If the data type of the column is not *Integer*, then the choice is straightforward: SSAS goes for dictionary encoding. For integer values, it uses some heuristics, for example:

- If the numbers in the column increase linearly, it is probably a primary key and value encoding is the best option.

- If all numbers fall within a defined range of values, then value encoding is the way to go.

- If the numbers fall within a very wide range of values, with values very different from another, then dictionary encoding is the best choice.

Once the decision is made, SSAS starts to compress the column using the chosen algorithm. Unfortunately, it sometimes makes the wrong decision and finds this out only very late during processing. For example, SSAS might read a few million rows where the values are in the 100–201 range, so value encoding is the best choice. After those millions of rows, suddenly an outlier appears, such as a large number like 60,000,000. Obviously, the initial choice was wrong because the number of bits needed to store such a large number is huge. What should SSAS do then? Instead of continuing with the wrong choice, SSAS can decide to re-encode the column. This means that the entire column is re-encoded using dictionary encoding. This process might take a long time because SSAS needs to reprocess the whole column.

For very large datasets where processing time is important, a best practice is the following: the data distribution in the first set of rows read by SSAS should be of such quality that all types of values are represented. This in turn reduces re-encoding to a minimum. Developers do so by providing a quality sample in the first partition processed or by providing an encoding hint parameter to the column.

> **Note** The *Encoding Hint* property was introduced in Analysis Services 2017, and it is not available in all products.

Finding the best sort order

As we said earlier, RLE's efficiency strongly depends on the sort order of the table. All the columns of the same table are sorted the same way to keep integrity of the data at the table level. In large tables it is important to determine the best sorting of data to improve the efficiency of RLE and to reduce the memory footprint of the model.

When SSAS reads a table, it tries different sort orders to improve the compression. In a table with many columns, this is a very expensive operation. SSAS then sets an upper limit to the time it can spend finding the best sort order. The default can change with different versions of the engine. At printing time, the default is currently 10 seconds per million rows. One can modify its value in the *Processing-TimeboxSecPerMRow* entry in the configuration file of the SSAS service. Power BI and Power Pivot do not provide access to this value.

 Note   SSAS searches for the best sort order in the data, using a heuristic algorithm that certainly also considers the physical order of the rows it receives. For this reason, although one cannot force the sort order used by VertiPaq for RLE, it is possible to provide the engine with data sorted arbitrarily. The VertiPaq engine includes this sort order in the options to consider.

To attain maximum compression, one can set the value of *ProcessingTimeboxSecPerMRow* to 0, which means SSAS stops searching only when it finds the best compression factor. The benefit in terms of space usage and query speed can vary. On the other hand, processing will take much longer because the engine is being instructed to try all the possible sort orders before making a choice.

Generally, developers should put the columns with the least number of unique values first in the sort order because these columns are likely to generate many repeating values. Still, keep in mind that finding the best sort order is a very complex task. It only makes sense to spend time on this when the data model is really large (in the order of a few billion rows). Otherwise, the benefit obtained from these extreme optimizations is limited.

Once all the columns are compressed, SSAS completes the processing by building calculated columns, tables, hierarchies, and relationships. Hierarchies and relationships are additional data structures needed by VertiPaq to execute queries, whereas calculated columns and tables are added to the model by using DAX expressions.

Calculated columns, like all other columns, are compressed after they are computed. However, calculated columns are not the same as standard columns. Calculated columns are compressed during the final stage of processing, when all the other columns have already finished their compression. Consequently, VertiPaq does not consider calculated columns when choosing the best sort order for a table.

Consider creating a calculated column that results in a *Boolean* value. There being only two values, the calculated column can be compressed very well (1 bit is enough to store a *Boolean* value), and it is a very good candidate to be first in the sort order list. Indeed, doing this, the table shows all the *True* values first and only later the *False* values. Being a calculated column, the sort order is already defined by other columns; it might be the case that with the defined sort order, the calculated column frequently changes its value. In that case, the column ends up with less-than-optimal compression.

Whenever there is a chance to compute a column in DAX or in the data source (including Power Query), keep in mind that computing it in the data source results in slightly better compression. Many other factors may drive the choice of DAX instead of Power Query or SQL to calculate the column. For example, the engine automatically computes a calculated column in a large table depending on a column in a small table, whenever said small table has a partial or full refresh. This happens without having to reprocess the entire large table, which would be necessary if the computation were in Power Query or SQL. This is something to consider when looking for the optimal compression.

Note A calculated table has the same compression as a regular table, without the side effects described for calculated columns. However, creating a calculated table can be quite expensive. Indeed, a calculated table requires enough memory to keep a copy of the entire uncompressed table in memory before it is compressed. Carefully think before creating a large calculated table because of the memory pressure generated at refresh time.

Understanding hierarchies and relationships

As we said in the previous sections, at the end of table processing, SSAS builds two additional data structures: hierarchies and relationships.

There are two types of hierarchies: attribute hierarchies and user hierarchies. Hierarchies are data structures used primarily to improve performance of MDX queries and also to improve certain search operations in DAX. Because the concept of hierarchy is not present in the DAX language, hierarchies are not relevant to the topics of this book.

Relationships, on the other hand, play an important role in the VertiPaq engine; it is important to understand how they work for extreme optimizations. We will describe the role of relationships in a query in following chapters. Here, we are only interested in defining what relationships are, in terms of VertiPaq storage and behavior.

A relationship is a data structure that maps IDs from one table to row numbers in another table. For example, consider the columns *ProductKey* in *Sales* and *ProductKey* in *Product*. These two columns are used to build the relationship between the two tables. *Product[ProductKey]* is a primary key. Because it is a primary key, the engine used value encoding and no compression at all. Indeed, RLE could not reduce the size of a column in the absence of duplicated values. On the other hand, *Sales[ProductKey]* is likely to have been dictionary-encoded and compressed. This is because it probably contains many repetitions. Therefore, despite the columns having the same name and data type, their internal data structures are completely different.

Moreover, because they are part of a relationship, VertiPaq knows that queries are likely to use the columns very often placing a filter on *Product* and also expecting to filter *Sales*. VertiPaq would be very slow if—every time it needs to move a filter from *Product* to *Sales*—it had to perform the following: retrieve values from *Product[ProductKey]*, search them in the dictionary of *Sales[ProductKey]*, and finally retrieve the IDs of *Sales[ProductKey]* to place the filter.

Therefore, to improve query performance, VertiPaq stores relationships as pairs of IDs and row numbers. Given the ID of a *Sales[ProductKey]*, it can immediately find the corresponding rows of *Product* that match the relationship. Relationships are stored in memory, as any other data structure of VertiPaq. Figure 17-8 shows how the relationship between *Sales* and *Product* is stored in VertiPaq.

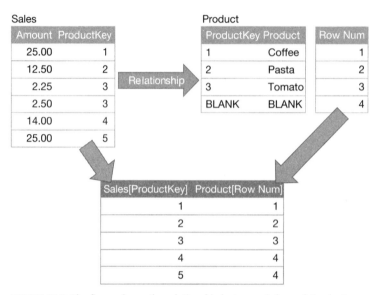

FIGURE 17-8 The figure shows the relationship between *Sales* and *Product*.

Even though the structure does not seem to be very intuitive, later in this chapter we describe how VertiPaq uses relationships and why relationships have this very specific structure. It would come naturally that it is a complex structure optimized for performance.

Understanding segmentation and partitioning

Compressing a table of several billion rows in one single step would be extremely memory-intensive and time-consuming. Therefore, the table is not processed as a single unit. Instead, during processing, SSAS splits the table into segments that contain 8 million rows each by default. When a segment is completely read, the engine starts to compress the segment while reading the next segment in the meantime.

It is possible to configure the segment size in SSAS using the *DefaultSegmentRowCount* entry in the configuration file of the service (or in the server properties in Management Studio). In Power BI Desktop and Power Pivot, the segment size has a set value of 1 million rows, and it cannot be changed.

Segmentation is important for several reasons, including query parallelisms and compression efficiency. When querying a table, VertiPaq uses the segments as the basis for parallelism: It uses one core per segment when scanning a column. By default, SSAS always uses one single thread to scan a table with 8 million rows or less. We start observing parallelism in action only on much larger tables.

The larger the segment, the better the compression. Having the option of analyzing more rows in a single compression step, VertiPaq can achieve better compression levels. On very large tables, it is important to test different segment sizes and measure the memory usage to achieve optimal compression. Keep in mind that increasing the segment size can negatively affect processing time: The larger the segment, the slower the processing.

Although the dictionary is global to the table, bit-sizing takes place at the segment level. Thus, if a column has 1,000 distinct values but only two distinct values are used in a specific segment, then that column will be compressed to a single bit for that segment.

If segments are small, then the parallelism at query time is increased. This is not always a good thing. While it is true that scanning the column is faster because more cores can do that in parallel, VertiPaq needs more time at the end of the scan to aggregate partial results computed by the different threads. If a partition is too small, then the time required for managing task switching and final aggregation is more than the time needed to scan the data, with a negative impact on the overall query performance.

During processing, the treatment of the first segment is particular if the table has only one partition. Indeed, the first segment can be larger than *DefaultSegmentRowCount*. VertiPaq reads twice the size of *DefaultSegmentRowCount* and starts to segment a table only if the table contains more rows. This does not apply to a partitioned table. If a table is partitioned, then all the segments are smaller than the default segment row count. Consequently, in SSAS a nonpartitioned table with 10 million rows is stored as a single segment. On the other hand, a table with 20 million rows uses three segments: two containing 8 million rows and one containing 4 million rows. In Power BI Desktop and Power Pivot, VertiPaq uses multiple segments for tables with more than 2 million rows.

Segments cannot exceed the partition size. If the partitioning schema of a model creates partitions of only 1 million rows, then all the segments will be smaller than 8 million rows; namely, they will be same as the partition size. Overpartitioning a table is a common mistake made by novices to optimize performance. What they obtain is the opposite effect: Creating too many small partitions typically lowers performance.

Using Dynamic Management Views

SSAS enables the discovery of all the information about the data model using Dynamic Management Views (DMV). DMVs are extremely useful to explore how a model is compressed, the space used by different columns and tables, the number of segments in a table, or the number of bits used by columns in different segments.

DMVs can run from inside SQL Server Management Studio. Regardless, we suggest you use DAX Studio; it offers a list of all DMVs in a simpler way without the need to remember them or to reopen this book looking for the DMV name. However, a more efficient way to use DMVs is with the free VertiPaq Analyzer tool (http://www.sqlbi.com/tools/vertipaq-analyzer/), which displays data from DMVs and organizes them in useful reports, as shown in Figure 17-9.

Row Labels	Cardinality	Table Size	Columns Total Size	Data Size	Dictionary Size	Columns Hierar	Encoding
⊞ ExchangeRate	773	63,144	63,064	6,224	45,520	11,320	Many
⊞ Geography	674	155,624	141,736	2,640	127,736	11,360	Many
⊟ Inventory	8,013,099	108,978,244	108,973,588	76,679,640	188,556	32,105,392	Many
Aging	7		15,780	14,312	1,372	96	HASH
CurrencyKey	1		1,476	64	1,348	64	HASH
Datekey	156		4,240,320	4,229,328	9,696	1,296	HASH
DaysInStock	115		7,126,300	7,122,512	2,828	960	HASH
ETLLoadID	1		1,476	64	1,348	64	HASH
InventoryKey	8,013,099		53,420,840	21,368,304	120	32,052,416	VALUE
LoadDate	1		1,416	64	1,288	64	HASH
MaxDayInStock	60		6,412,616	6,410,504	1,584	528	HASH
MinDayInStock	55		6,412,484	6,410,440	1,564	480	HASH

FIGURE 17-9 VertiPaq Analyzer shows statistics about a data model in an efficient manner.

Although DMVs use an SQL-like syntax, the full SQL syntax is not available. DMVs do not run inside SQL Server. They are only a convenient way to discover the status of SSAS and to gather information about data models.

There are different DMVs, divided into two main categories:

- **SCHEMA views:** These return information about SSAS metadata, such as database names, tables, and individual columns. They are used to gather information about data types, names, and similar data, including statistical information about numbers of rows and unique values stored in columns.

- **DISCOVER views:** They are intended to gather information about the SSAS engine and/or discover statistics information about objects in a database. For example, one can use views in the discover area to enumerate the DAX keywords, the number of connections and sessions that are currently open, or the traces running.

In this book, we do not describe the details of all the views because doing so would be going off topic. More information is available in Microsoft documentation on the web. Instead, we want to provide a few hints and point out the most useful DMVs related to databases used by DAX. Moreover, while many DMVs report useful information in many columns, in this book we describe the most interesting ones related to the internal structure.

A first useful DMV to discover the memory usage of all the objects in the SSAS instance is *DISCOVER_OBJECT_MEMORY_USAGE*. This DMV returns information about all the objects in all the databases in the SSAS instance. *DISCOVER_OBJECT_MEMORY_USAGE* is not limited to the current database. For example, the following query can be run in DAX Studio or SQL Server Management Studio:

```
SELECT * FROM $SYSTEM.DISCOVER_OBJECT_MEMORY_USAGE
```

Figure 17-10 shows a small excerpt of the result of the previous query. There are many more columns and rows, so analyzing this detailed information can be very time-consuming.

OBJECT_PARENT_PATH	OBJECT_ID	OBJECT_MEMORY_SHRINKABLE	OBJECT_MEMORY_NONSHRINKABLE	OBJECT_VER
GAP\AnalysisServicesWor...	HSDaxBook Sales...	0	0	
MessageManager	French (France)	0	37084	137967
Global	TMPersistenceSQ...	0	368	104775
	Global	0	6357634	
GAP\AnalysisServicesWor...	ID_TO_POS	0	0	

FIGURE 17-10 Partial result of the *DISCOVER_OBJECT_MEMORY_USAGE* DMV.

The output of the DMV is a table containing many rows that are very hard to read. The output structure is a parent/child hierarchy that starts with the instance name and ends with individual column information. Although the raw dataset is nearly impossible to read, one can build a Power Pivot data model on top of this query, implementing the parent/child hierarchy structure and browsing the full memory map of the instance. Kasper De Jonge published a workbook on his blog that does exactly this. It is available at http://www.powerpivotblog.nl/what-is-using-all-that-memory-on-my-analysis-server-instance/.

Other useful DMVs to check the current state of the Tabular engine are *DISCOVER_SESSIONS*, *DISCOVER_CONNECTIONS*, and *DISCOVER_COMMANDS*. These DMVs provide information about active sessions, connections, and executed commands. These views are used by an open source tool called SSAS Activity Monitor, available at https://github.com/RichieBzzzt/SSASActivityMonitor/tree/master/Download, that provides the same information (plus much more) in a more convenient way.

There are also DMVs that analyze the distribution of data in columns and tables, and the memory required for compressed data. These are *TMSCHEMA_COLUMN_STORAGES* and *DISCOVER_STORAGE_TABLE_COLUMNS*. The former is the more recent one; the latter is there for compatibility with older versions of the engine (compatibility level 1103 or lower).

Finally, a very useful DMV to analyze calculation dependency is *DISCOVER_CALC_DEPENDENCY*. This DMV can be used to create a graph of dependencies between calculations in the data model, including calculated columns, calculated tables, and measures. Figure 17-11 shows an excerpt of the result of this DMV.

OBJECT_TYPE	TABLE	OBJECT	EXPRESSION	REFERENCED_OBJECT_TYPE	REFERENCED_TABLE	REFERENCED_OBJECT
MEASURE	Sales	Sales Amo...	SUMX (Sales, Sales[Quantity] * Sales[Net Price])	COLUMN	Sales	Quantity
MEASURE	Sales	Sales Amo...	SUMX (Sales, Sales[Quantity] * Sales[Net Price])	COLUMN	Sales	Net Price
MEASURE	Sales	Total Cost	SUMX (Sales, Sales[Quantity] * Sales[Unit Cost])	TABLE	Sales	Sales
MEASURE	Sales	Total Cost	SUMX (Sales, Sales[Quantity] * Sales[Unit Cost])	COLUMN	Sales	Quantity
MEASURE	Sales	Total Cost	SUMX (Sales, Sales[Quantity] * Sales[Unit Cost])	COLUMN	Sales	Unit Cost

FIGURE 17-11 Partial result of the *DISCOVER_CALC_DEPENDENCY* DMV.

Understanding the use of relationships in VertiPaq

When a DAX query generates requests to the VertiPaq storage engine, the presence of relationships in the data model allows a quicker transfer of the filter context from one table to another. The internal implementation of a relationship in VertiPaq is worth knowing because relationships might affect the performance of a query even though most of the calculation happens in the storage engine.

To understand how relationships work, we start from the analysis of a query that only involves one table, *Sales*:

```
EVALUATE
ROW (
    "Result", CALCULATE (
        COUNTROWS ( Sales ),
        Sales[Quantity] > 1
    )
)

-- Result
-- 20016
```

A developer used to working with tables in relational databases might suppose that the engine iterates the *Sales* table, tests the value of the *Quantity* column for each row of *Sales*, and increments the returned value if the *Quantity* value is greater than 1. In fact, VertiPaq does it better: VertiPaq only scans the *Quantity* column because it already provides the number of rows for the entire table. Therefore, a single column scan is enough to solve the entire query.

If we write a similar query using the column of another table as a filter, then scanning a single column is no longer enough to produce the result. For example, consider the following query that counts the number of rows in *Sales* related to products of the Contoso brand:

```
EVALUATE
ROW (
    "Result", CALCULATE (
        COUNTROWS ( Sales ),
        'Product'[Brand] = "Contoso"
    )
)

-- Result
-- 37984
```

This time, we are using two different tables: *Sales* and *Product*. Solving this query requires a bit more effort. Indeed, because the filter is on *Product* and the table to aggregate is *Sales*, it is not possible to scan a single column.

If you are not used to columnar databases, you probably think that, to solve the query, the engine should iterate the *Sales* table, follow the relationship with *Product*, and sum 1 if the product brand is Contoso, 0 otherwise. This would be an algorithm like the following DAX code:

```
EVALUATE
ROW (
    "Result", SUMX (
        Sales,
        IF ( RELATED ( 'Product'[Brand] ) = "Contoso", 1, 0 )
    )
```

```
)

-- Result
-- 37984
```

Although this is a simple algorithm, it contains much more complexity than expected. Indeed, if we carefully think about the columnar nature of VertiPaq, we realize that this query involves three different columns:

- *Product[Brand]* used to filter the *Product* table.

- *Product[ProductKey]* used by the relationship between *Product* and *Sales*.

- *Sales[ProductKey]* used on the *Sales* side of the relationship.

Iterating over *Sales[ProductKey]*, searching the row number in *Product* scanning *Product[ProductKey]*, and finally gathering the brand in *Product[Brand]* would be extremely expensive. The process requires a lot of random reads to memory, with negative consequences on performance. Therefore, VertiPaq uses a completely different algorithm, optimized for columnar databases.

First, VertiPaq scans the *Product[Brand]* column and retrieves the row numbers of the *Product* table where *Product[Brand]* is Contoso. As shown in Figure 17-12, VertiPaq scans the *Brand* dictionary (1), retrieves the encoding of Contoso, and finally scans the segments (2) searching for the row numbers in the product table where the dictionary ID equals 0 (corresponding to Contoso), returning the indexes to the rows found (3).

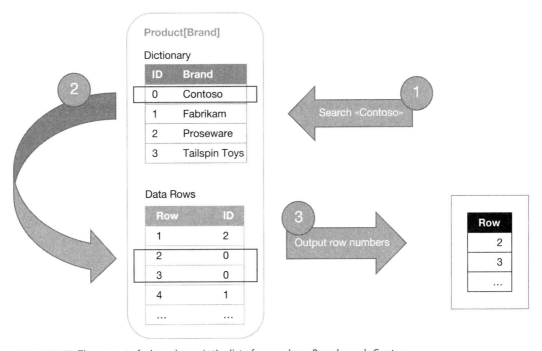

FIGURE 17-12 The output of a brand scan is the list of rows where *Brand* equals Contoso.

At this point, VertiPaq knows which rows in the *Product* table contain the given brand. The relationship between *Product* and *Sales* enables VertiPaq to translate the row numbers of *Product* in internal data IDs for *Sales[ProductKey]*. VertiPaq performs a lookup of the selected row numbers to determine the values of *Sales[ProductKey]* valid for those rows, as shown in Figure 17-13.

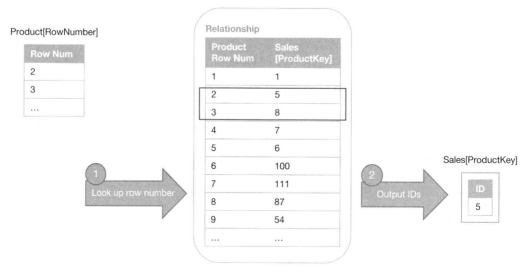

FIGURE 17-13 VertiPaq scans the product keys in the relationship to retrieve the IDs where brand equals Contoso.

The last step is to apply the filter on the *Sales* table. Since VertiPaq already has the list of values of *Sales[ProductKey]*, it is enough to scan the *Sales[ProductKey]* column to transform this list of values into row numbers and finally count them. If, instead of computing a *COUNTROWS*, VertiPaq had to perform the *SUM* of a column, then it would perform an additional step transforming row numbers into column values to perform the last step.

The important takeaway is that the cost of a relationship depends on the cardinality of the column that defines the relationship. Even though the previous query filtered only one brand, the cost of the relationship was the number of products for that brand. The lower the cardinality of a relationship, the better. When the cardinality of a relationship is above one million unique values, the end user can experience slower performance. A performance degradation is already measurable when the relationship has 100,000 unique values. VertiPaq aggregations can mitigate the impact of high-cardinality relationships by pre-aggregating data at a different granularity, removing the cost of traversing expensive relationships at query time. We briefly discuss aggregations later in this chapter.

Introducing materialization

Now that we have provided a basic explanation of how VertiPaq stores data in memory, we can describe what *materialization* is. Materialization is a step of the query execution that occurs when using columnar databases. Understanding when and how it happens is of paramount importance.

The basic principle about materialization is that every time the formula engine sends a request to the storage engine, the formula engine receives an uncompressed table that is generated dynamically by the storage engine. This special temporary table is called a *datacache*. A datacache is always the materialization of data that will be consumed by the formula engine, regardless of the storage engine used. Both VertiPaq and DirectQuery generate datacaches.

A large materialization happens when a single storage engine query produces a large datacache. The conditions for a DAX query to produce a large materialization depend on many factors; basically, whenever the storage engine is not able to execute all the operations required by the DAX query, the formula engine will do the work using a copy of the data owned by the storage engine. Be mindful that the formula engine cannot access the raw data directly, whether VertiPaq or DirectQuery. To access the raw data, the formula engine needs to ask the storage engine to retrieve the data and save it in a datacache. The amount and kind of materialization can be very different depending on the storage engine used. In this book, we only describe how to reduce the materialization in VertiPaq. For DirectQuery there could be differences between different data source drivers. Even so, the tools used to measure the materialization produced by the storage engine are the same used for VertiPaq.

The next chapters describe how to measure the materialization produced by a DAX query using specific tools and metrics. In this section, we just introduce the concept of materialization and how it relates to the result of a query. The cardinality of the result of every DAX query defines the optimal materialization. For example, the following query returns a single row, counting the number of rows in a table:

```
EVALUATE
ROW (
    "Result", COUNTROWS ( Sales )
)

-- Result
-- 100231
```

The optimal materialization for the previous query is a datacache with only one row. This means that the entire calculation is performed within the storage engine. The next query returns one row for each year; therefore, the optimal materialization is three rows, one for each year with sales:

```
EVALUATE
SUMMARIZECOLUMNS (
    'Date'[Calendar Year],
    "Sales Amount", [Sales Amount]
)

-- Calendar Year | Sales Amount
-- ----------------|---------------
-- CY 2007        | 11,309,946.12
-- CY 2008        |  9,927,582.99
-- CY 2009        |  9,353,814.87
```

Whenever the storage engine produces a single datacache with the same cardinality as the result of the DAX query, that is called a *late materialization*. If the storage engine produces more datacaches and/or the datacache produced has more rows than those displayed in the result, we have an *early materialization*. With a late materialization the formula engine does not have to aggregate data, whereas with an early materialization the formula engine must perform operations like joining and grouping, which result in slower queries for the end users.

Predicting materialization is not easy without a deep knowledge of the VertiPaq engine. For example, the materialization of the following query is optimal because the entire calculation is executed within the storage engine:

```
EVALUATE
VAR LargeOrders =
    CALCULATETABLE (
        DISTINCT ( Sales[Order Number] ),
        Sales[Quantity] > 1
    )
VAR Result =
    ROW (
        "Orders", COUNTROWS ( LargeOrders )
    )
RETURN
    Result

-- Orders
-- 8388
```

On the other hand, the next query creates a temporary table that corresponds to the number of unique combinations between customers and dates related to sales with a quantity greater than one (for a total of 6,290 combinations):

```
EVALUATE
VAR LargeSalesCustomerDates =
    CALCULATETABLE (
        SUMMARIZE ( Sales, Sales[CustomerKey], Sales[Order Date] ),
        Sales[Quantity] > 1
    )
VAR Result =
    ROW (
        "CustomerDates", COUNTROWS ( LargeSalesCustomerDates )
    )
RETURN
    Result

-- CustomerDates
-- 6290
```

The latter query has a materialization of 6,290 rows, even though there is only one row in the result. The two queries are similar: a table is evaluated and then its rows are counted. The reason why the former has an earlier materialization is because it involves a single column, whereas the calculation requiring the combinations of two columns cannot be solved by the storage engine by just scanning the two columns. In general, any operation involving a single column has higher chances of being solved in the storage engine, but it would be a mistake to believe that involving multiple columns is always an issue. For example, the following query has an optimal late materialization even though it multiplies two columns from two tables, *Sales* and *Product*:

```
DEFINE
    MEASURE Sales[Sales Amount] =
        SUMX (
            Sales,
            Sales[Quantity] * RELATED ( 'Product'[Unit Price] )
        )
EVALUATE
ROW ( "Sales Amount", [Sales Amount] )

-- Sales Amount
-- 33,690,148.51
```

In complex queries it is nearly impossible to obtain an optimal late materialization. Therefore, the effort for optimizing a query is reducing the materialization, pushing most of the workload to the storage engine, if possible.

Introducing aggregations

A data model can have multiple tables related to the same original raw data. The purpose of this redundancy is to offer alternative ways to the storage engine to retrieve the data faster. The tables used to this purpose are called *aggregations*.

An aggregation is nothing but a pregrouped version of the original table. By pre-aggregating data, one reduces the number of columns (hence, the number of rows) and replaces values with their aggregate.

As an example, consider the *Sales* table in Figure 17-14, which has one row for each date, product, and customer.

Sales

Date	Product	Customer	Quantity	Amount
2018-09-01	AV010	C092	3	29.97
2018-09-01	AV022	C092	1	16.40
2018-09-01	AV010	C054	2	19.98
2018-09-01	FL892	C248	1	190.00
2018-09-01	GT400	C127	1	999.00
2018-09-02	AV010	C115	3	29.97
2018-09-02	FL580	C127	1	790.00
2018-09-02	AV022	C772	2	32.80
2018-09-02	KB723	C614	2	59.98
2018-09-02	FL580	C614	1	790.00
...	...	...	...	...

FIGURE 17-14 The original *Sales* table has a high number of rows.

If a query requires the sum of *Quantity* or *Amount* by *Date*, the storage engine must evaluate and aggregate all the rows with the same *Date*. In VertiPaq this operation is relatively quick, thanks to the compression and the optimized algorithms that scan the memory. DirectQuery is usually much slower than VertiPaq to perform the same operation. Anyway, VertiPaq also requires time to scan billions of rows rather than millions of rows. Therefore, there could be an advantage in creating an alternate—smaller—table to use in place of the original one.

Figure 17-15 shows the content of a *Sales* table aggregated by *Date*. In this case, there is only one row for every date, and the *Quantity* and *Amount* columns store the sum of the values included in the original rows, pre-aggregated by *Date*.

Sales Agg Date

Date	Quantity	Amount
2018-09-01	8	1,255.35
2018-09-02	9	1,702.75
...	...	...

FIGURE 17-15 The *Sales Agg Date* table has one row for every date.

In an aggregated table, every column is either a "group by" or an aggregation of the original table. If a request to the storage engine only needs columns that are present in an aggregation table, then the engine uses the aggregation rather than the original source. The *Sales Agg Date* table shown in Figure 17-15 can be mapped as an aggregation of *Sales* by specifying the role of each column:

- *Date*: GroupBy *Sales[Date]*

- *Quantity*: Sum *Sales[Quantity]*

- *Amount*: Sum *Sales[Amount]*

The aggregation type must be specified for every column that is not a "group by." The aggregation types available are Count, Min, Max, Sum, and count rows of the table. A column in an aggregation table can only map native columns in the original table; it is not possible to specify an aggregation over a calculated column.

> **Important** Aggregations cannot be used to optimize the execution of complex calculations in DAX. The only purpose of aggregations is to reduce the execution time of storage engine queries. Aggregations can be useful for relatively small tables in DirectQuery, whereas aggregations for VertiPaq should be considered only for tables with billions of rows.

A table in a Tabular model can have multiple aggregations with different priorities in case there are multiple aggregations compatible with a specific storage engine request. Moreover, aggregations and original tables can be stored with different storage engines. A common scenario is storing aggregations in VertiPaq to improve the performance of large tables accessed through DirectQuery. Nevertheless, it is also possible to create aggregations in the same storage engine used for the original table.

Note There could be limitations in storage engines available for aggregations and original tables, depending on the version and the license of the product used. This section provides general guidance on the concept of aggregations, which are one of the tools to optimize performance of a DAX query as described in the following chapters.

Aggregations are powerful, but they require a lot of attention to detail. An incorrect definition of aggregations produces incorrect or inconsistent results. It is a responsibility of the data modeler to guarantee that a query executed in an aggregation produces the same result as an equivalent query executed on the original table. Aggregations are an optimization tool and should be used only whenever strictly necessary. The presence of aggregations requires additional work to define and maintain the aggregation tables in the data model. One should therefore use them only after having checked that a performance benefit exists.

Choosing hardware for VertiPaq

Choosing the right hardware is critical for a solution based on a Tabular model using the VertiPaq storage engine. Spending more does not always mean having a better machine. This section describes how to choose the right hardware for a Tabular model.

Since the introduction of Analysis Services 2012, we helped several companies adopt the new Tabular model in their solutions. A very common issue was that when going into production, performance was slower than expected. Worse, sometimes it was slower than in the development environments. Most of the times, the reason for that was incorrect hardware sizing, especially when the server was in a virtualized environment. As we will explain, the problem is not the use of a virtual machine in itself. Instead, the problem is more likely the technical specs of the underlying hardware. A very complete and detailed hardware-sizing guide for Analysis Services Tabular is available in the whitepaper titled "Hardware Sizing a Tabular Solution (SQL Server Analysis Services)" (http://msdn.microsoft.com/en-us/library/jj874401.aspx). The goal of this section is to provide a quick guide to understand the issues affecting many data centers when they host a Tabular solution. Users of Power Pivot or Power BI Desktop on a personal computer can skip the details about Non-Uniform Memory Access (NUMA) support, but all the other considerations are equally true for choosing the right hardware.

Hardware choice as an option

The first question is whether one can choose their hardware or not. The problem of using a virtual machine for a Tabular solution is that often the hardware has already been selected and installed. One can only influence the number of cores and the amount of RAM that are assigned to the server. Unfortunately, these parameters are not so relevant for performance. If there are limited choices available, one should collect information about the CPU model and clock of the host server as soon as possible. If this information is not accessible, ask for a small virtual machine running on the same host server and run the Task Manager: The Performance tab shows the CPU model and the clock rate. With this information, one can predict whether the performance will be worse than an average modern laptop. Unfortunately, chances are that many developers will be in that position. If so, then they must sharpen their political skills to convince the right people that running Tabular on that server is a bad idea. If the host server is a good machine, then one still needs to avoid the pitfall of running a virtual machine on different NUMA nodes (more on this later).

Set hardware priorities

If it is possible to influence the hardware selection, this is the order of priorities:

1. **CPU Clock and Model**: the faster, the better.

2. **Memory Speed:** the faster, the better.

3. **Number of Cores:** the higher, the better. Still, a few fast cores are way better than many slow cores.

4. **Memory Size.**

Disk I/O performance is not on the list. Indeed, it is not important at query time although it could have a role in improving the speed of a disaster recovery. There is only one condition (paging) where disk I/O affects performance, and we discuss it later in this section. However, the RAM of the system should be sized so that there will be no paging at all. Our reader should allocate the budget on CPU and memory speed, memory size, and not waste money on disk I/O bandwidth. The following sections include information to consider for such allocation.

CPU model

The most important factors that affect the speed of code running in VertiPaq are CPU clock and model. Different CPU models might have a different performance at the same clock rate, so considering the clock alone is not enough. The best practice is to run a benchmark measuring the different performance in queries that stress the formula engine. An example of such a query is the following:

```
DEFINE
VAR t1 =
    SELECTCOLUMNS ( CALENDAR ( 1, 10000 ), "x", [Date] )
VAR t2 =
    SELECTCOLUMNS ( CALENDAR ( 1, 10000 ), "y", [Date] )
VAR c =
    CROSSJOIN ( t1, t2 )
VAR result =
    COUNTROWS ( c )
EVALUATE
    ROW ( "x", result )
```

This query can run in DAX Studio or SQL Server Management Studio connected to any Tabular model; the execution is intentionally slow and does not produce any meaningful result. Using a query of a typical workload for a specific data model is certainly better because performance might vary on different hardware depending on the memory allocated to materialize intermediate results; the query in the preceding code block has a minimal use of memory.

For example, this query runs in 9.5 seconds on an Intel i7-4770K 3.5 GHz, and in 14.4 seconds on an Intel i7-6500U 2.5 GHz. These CPUs run a desktop workstation and a notebook, respectively. Do not assume that a server will be faster. You should always evaluate hardware performance by running the same test with the same version of the engine and looking at the results because they are often surprising.

In general, Intel Xeon processors used on a server are E5 and E7 series, and it is common to find clock speed around 2–2.4 GHz even with a very high number of cores available. You should look for a clock speed of 3 GHz or more. Another important factor is the L2 and L3 cache size: The larger, the better. This is especially important for large tables and relationships between tables based on columns that have more than 1 million unique values.

The reason why CPU and cache are so important for VertiPaq is clarified in Table 17-1, which compares the typical access time of data stored at different distances from the CPU. The column with human metrics represents the same difference using metrics that are easier for humans to understand.

TABLE 17-1 Expanded versions of the tables

Access	Access Time	Human Metrics
1 CPU cycle	0.3 ns	1 s
L1 cache	0.9 ns	3 s
L2 cache	2.8 ns	9 s
L3 cache	12.9 ns	43 s
RAM access	120 ns	6 min
Solid-state disk I/O	50–150 µs s	2–6 days
Rotational disk I/O	1–10 ms	1–12 months

As shown here, the fastest storage in a PC is not the RAM; it is the core cache. It should be clear that a large L2 cache is important, and the CPU speed plays a primary role in determining performance. The same table also clarifies why keeping data in RAM is so much better than accessing data in other, slower storage devices.

Memory speed

The memory speed is an important factor for VertiPaq. Every operation made by the engine accesses memory at a very high speed. When the RAM bandwidth is the bottleneck, performance counters report CPU usage instead of I/O waits. Unfortunately, there are no performance counters that monitor the time spent waiting for the RAM access. In Tabular, this amount of time can be relevant, and it is hard to measure.

In general, you should use RAM that has at least 1,833 MHz; however, if the hardware platform permits, you should select faster RAM—2,133 MHz or more.

Number of cores

VertiPaq splits execution on multiple threads only when the table involved has multiple segments. Each segment contains 8 million rows by default (1 million on Power BI and Power Pivot). A CPU with eight cores will not use all of them in a single query unless a table has at least 64 million rows, or 8 million rows in Power BI and Power Pivot.

For these reasons, scalability over multiple cores is effective only for very large tables. Raising the number of cores improves performance for a single query only when it hits a large table, 200 million rows or more. In terms of scalability (number of concurrent users), a higher number of cores might not improve performance if users access the same tables as they would contend access to shared RAM. A better way to increase the number of concurrent users is to use more servers in a load-balancing configuration.

The best practice is to get the maximum number of cores available on a single socket, getting the highest clock rate possible. Having two or more sockets on the same server is not good, even though Analysis Services Tabular recognizes the NUMA architecture. NUMA requires a more expensive inter-socket communication whenever a thread running on a socket accesses memory allocated by another socket. You can find more details about NUMA architecture in Hardware Sizing a Tabular Solution (SQL Server Analysis Services) at http://msdn.microsoft.com/en-us/library/jj874401.aspx.

Memory size

The entire volume of data managed by VertiPaq must be stored in memory. Additional RAM is required to execute process operations—unless there is a separate process server—and to execute queries. Optimized queries usually do not have a high request for RAM, but a single query can materialize temporary tables that could be very large. Database tables have a high compression rate, whereas materialization of intermediate tables during a single query generates uncompressed data.

Having enough memory only guarantees that a query will end by returning a result, but increasing available RAM does not produce any performance improvement. Cache used by Tabular does not increase just because there is more RAM available. However, a condition of low available memory might negatively affect query performance if the server starts paging data. Developers should have enough memory to store all the data of their database and to avoid materialization during query execution. More memory than this is a waste of resources.

Disk I/O and paging

You should not allocate budget on storage I/O for Analysis Services Tabular. This is very different from Multidimensional, where random I/O operation on disk occurs very frequently, especially in certain measures. In Tabular, there are no direct storage I/O operations during a query. The only event when this might happen is under low memory conditions. However, it is less expensive and more effective to provide more RAM to a server than trying to improve performance by increasing storage I/O throughput when there is systematic paging caused by low memory availability.

Best practices in hardware selection

You should measure performance before choosing the hardware for SSAS Tabular. It is common to observe a server running twice as slow as a development workstation, even if the server is very new. This is because a server designed to be scalable—especially for virtual machines—does not usually perform very well for activities made by a single thread. However, this type of workload is very common in VertiPaq. One will need time and numbers, doing a proper benchmark, to convince a company that a "standard server" could be the weak point of their entire BI solution.

Conclusions

In this first chapter about optimization we described the internal architecture of a Tabular engine, and we provided the basic information about how data is stored in VertiPaq. As you will see in the following chapters, this knowledge is of paramount importance to optimize your code.

These are the main topics you learned in the chapter:

- There are two engines inside a Tabular server: the formula engine and storage engine.

- The formula engine is the top-level query engine. It is very powerful but rather limited in terms of speed because it is single-threaded.

- There are two storage engines: VertiPaq and DirectQuery.

- VertiPaq is an in-memory columnar database. It stores information on a column-by-column basis, providing very quick access to single columns. Using multiple columns in a single DAX formula might require materialization.

- VertiPaq compresses columns to reduce the memory scan time. Optimizing a model means optimizing the compression by reducing the cardinality of a column as much as possible.

- Both VertiPaq and DirectQuery storage engines can coexist in the same model; this is called a composite model. A single query can use only VertiPaq, only DirectQuery, or both, depending on the storage model of the tables involved in the query.

Now that we have provided the basic knowledge about the internals of the engine, in the next chapter we start learning a few techniques to optimize VertiPaq storage to reduce both the size of a data model and its execution time.

Optimizing VertiPaq

The previous chapter introduced some of the internals of VertiPaq. That knowledge is useful to design and optimize a data model for a faster execution of DAX queries. While the previous chapter was more theoretical, in this chapter we move on to the more practical side. Indeed, this chapter describes the most important guidelines for saving memory and thereby improving the performance of a data model. The main objective in creating an efficient data model is to reduce the cardinality of columns in order to decrease the dictionary size, improve the compression, and speed up any iteration and filter.

The final goal of the chapter is optimizing a model. However, before going there, the first and most important skill to learn is the ability to evaluate the pros and cons of each design choice. *You should not follow any rules blindly without evaluating their impact.* For this reason, the first part of the chapter illustrates how to measure the size of each object in a model in memory. This is important when evaluating whether a decision made on a model was worth the effort or not, based on the memory impact of the decision.

Before moving on, we want to stress once more this important concept: *You should always test the techniques described in every data model.* Data distribution is important in VertiPaq. The very same *Sales* table structure may be compressed in different ways because of the data distribution, leading to different results for the same optimization techniques. Do not learn best practices. Instead, learn different optimization techniques, knowing in advance that not all of them will be applicable in every data model.

Gathering information about the data model

The first step for optimizing a data model is gathering information about the cost of the objects in the database. This section describes the tools and the techniques to collect all the data that help in prioritizing the possible optimizations of the physical structure.

Table 18-1 shows the pieces of information to collect from each object in a database.

In general, object size strongly depends on the number of unique values in the columns being used or referenced. For this reason, the number of unique values in a column, also known as column cardinality, is the single most important piece of information to gather from a database.

TABLE 18-1 Information to collect for each object in a database

Object	Information to Collect
Table	Number of rows
Column	Number of unique values Size of dictionary Size of data (total size of all segments)
Hierarchy	Size of hierarchy structure
Relationship	Size of relationship structure

In Chapter 17, "The DAX engines," we introduced the Dynamic Management Views (DMVs) to retrieve information about the objects in the VertiPaq storage engine. The following sections describe how to interpret the relevant information through VertiPaq Analyzer, which simplifies the collection of data from DMVs.

The first piece of information to consider in a data model is the size of each table, in terms of cardinality (number of rows) and size in memory. Figure 18-1 shows the Table section of VertiPaq Analyzer executed on a Contoso data model in Power BI. The model used in this example contains more tables and data than the simplified data model previously used throughout the book.

Row Labels	Cardinality	Table Size	Columns Total Size	Data Size	Dictionary Size	Columns Hierarchies Size
⊞ Channel	4	52,368	52,368	56	51,936	376
⊞ Currency	28	58,516	58,516	136	57,204	1,176
⊞ Customer	18,869	3,202,854	3,202,214	361,688	2,236,374	604,152
⊞ Date	2,556	510,280	510,280	38,400	404,584	67,296
⊞ DateTableTemplate_	1	35,268	35,172	56	34,828	288
⊞ ExchangeRate	773	63,144	63,064	6,224	45,520	11,320
⊞ Geography	674	155,624	141,736	2,640	127,736	11,360
⊞ Inventory	8,013,099	108,978,244	108,973,588	76,679,640	188,556	32,105,392
⊞ ITMachine	23,283	258,048	242,392	93,240	24,152	125,000
⊞ ITSLA	4,925	832,404	814,660	78,200	611,252	125,208
⊞ Machine	7,816	569,847	569,495	48,352	421,951	99,192
⊞ OnlineSales	12,627,608	254,159,572	254,115,436	133,076,608	56,877,668	64,161,360
⊞ Product	2,517	858,585	857,881	58,688	706,433	92,760
⊞ ProductCategory	8	52,980	52,980	56	52,436	488
⊞ ProductSubcategory	44	78,834	78,826	232	76,834	1,760
⊞ Promotion	28	95,816	95,816	256	94,192	1,368
⊞ Sales	3,406,089	75,214,220	75,208,028	50,401,856	9,408,932	15,397,240
⊞ SalesQuota	7,465,911	196,733,872	196,729,392	72,794,816	81,569,824	42,364,752
⊞ SalesTerritory	265	163,020	156,196	1,968	145,180	9,048
⊞ Scenario	3	53,522	53,522	56	53,114	352
⊞ Store	306	326,420	325,708	5,608	295,500	24,600
⊞ StrategyPlan	2,750,628	130,468,816	130,468,728	16,393,680	86,726,368	27,348,680
Grand Total	**34,325,435**	**772,922,254**	**772,805,998**	**350,042,256**	**240,210,574**	**182,553,168**

FIGURE 18-1 Details of tables shown in VertiPaq Analyzer.

The *Table Size* column represents the amount of memory used to store the compressed data in VertiPaq, whereas the *Cardinality* column shows the number of rows of each table. By drilling down a table name, it is possible to see the details of each column. At the column level, *Cardinality* shows the number of unique values in the entire table; however, the *Table Size* value is not available because each column only has the cost shown in *Columns Total* Size. For example, Figure 18-2 shows the columns available in the largest table of the data model, *SalesQuota*; note that the total size of each column is extremely variable within the same table.

Row Labels	Cardinality	Table Size	Columns Total Size	Data Size	Dictionary Size	Columns Hierarchies Size	Encoding
− SalesQuota	7,465,911	196,733,872	196,729,392	72,794,816	81,569,824	42,364,752	Many
ChannelKey	4		1,624	184	1,360	80	HASH
CurrencyKey	1		1,476	64	1,348	64	HASH
Datekey	36		431,632	429,712	1,584	336	HASH
ETLLoadID	1		1,476	64	1,348	64	HASH
GrossMarginQuota	944,795		67,753,032	17,578,832	42,615,800	7,558,400	HASH
LoadDate	1		1,416	64	1,288	64	HASH
ProductKey	2,516		11,996,128	11,900,032	75,920	20,176	HASH
RowNumber-2662979B-			120	0	120		VALUE
SalesAmountQuota	613,799		60,602,464	16,854,808	38,837,224	4,910,432	HASH
SalesQuantityQuota	1,101		182,004	151,952	21,204	8,848	HASH
SalesQuotaKey	7,465,911		49,772,920	19,909,136	120	29,863,664	VALUE
ScenarioKey	3		2,212	792	1,356	64	HASH
StoreKey	306		5,981,472	5,969,112	9,864	2,496	HASH
UpdateDate	1		1,416	64	1,288	64	HASH
+ SalesTerritory	265	163,020	156,196	1,968	145,180	9,048	Many
+ Scenario	3	53,522	53,522	56	53,114	352	Many
+ Store	306	326,420	325,708	5,608	295,500	24,600	Many
+ StrategyPlan	2,750,628	130,468,816	130,468,728	16,393,680	86,726,368	27,348,680	Many
Grand Total	34,325,435	772,922,254	772,805,998	350,042,256	240,210,574	182,553,168	Many

FIGURE 18-2 Details of tables and columns shown in VertiPaq Analyzer.

Each column reported by VertiPaq Analyzer carries a specific meaning described in the following list:

- **Cardinality:** Object cardinality; the number of rows in a table or the number of unique values in a column, depending on the level of detail in the report.

- **Rows:** Number of rows in the table. This metric is shown in the columns report (visible later in Figure 18-3) and not in the table report (in Figure 18-2), where the same information is available in the *Cardinality* metric, at the table detail level of the report.

- **Table Size:** Size of the table in bytes. This metric contains the sum of *Columns Total Size*, *User Hierarchies Size*, and *Relationships Size*.

- **Columns Total Size:** Size in bytes of a column. This metric contains the sum of *Data Size*, *Dictionary Size*, and *Columns Hierarchies Size*.

- **Data Size:** Size in bytes of all the compressed data in segments and partitions. It does not include dictionary and column hierarchies. This number depends on the compression of the column, which, in turn, depends on the number of unique values and the distribution of the data across the table.

- **Dictionary Size:** Size in bytes of dictionary structures. This number is only relevant for columns with hash encoding; it is a small fixed number for columns with value encoding. The dictionary size depends on the number of unique values in the column and on the average length of the strings in case of a text column.

- **Columns Hierarchies Size:** Size in bytes of the automatically generated attribute hierarchies for columns. These hierarchies are necessary to access a column in MDX, and they are also used by DAX to optimize filter and sort operations.

- **Encoding:** Type of encoding (hash or value) used for the column. The encoding of a column is selected automatically by the VertiPaq compression algorithm.

- **User Hierarchies Size:** Bytes of user-defined hierarchies. This structure is computed at the table level, and its values are only visible at the table level detail in a VertiPaq Analyzer report. The user hierarchy size depends on the number of unique values and on the average length of the strings of the columns used in the hierarchy itself.

- **Relationship Size:** Bytes of relationships between tables. The relationship size is related to the table on the many-side of a relationship. The size of a relationship depends on the cardinality of the columns involved in the relationship, although this is usually a tiny fraction of the cost of the table.

- **Table Size %:** Ratio of *Columns Total Size* versus *Table Size*.

- **Database Size %:** Ratio of *Table Size* versus *Database Size*, which is the sum of *Table Size* for all the tables.

- **Segments #:** Number of segments. All the columns of a table have the same number of segments of the table.

- **Partitions #:** Number of partitions. All the columns of a table have the same number of partitions of the table.

- **Columns #:** Number of columns.

Attribute hierarchies and column encoding

Two columns in VertiPaq Analyzer provide information that could be used to optimize large data models. We report the link to relevant documentation because we do not cover these optimizations in this book.

The attribute hierarchy size reported in *Columns Hierarchies Size* depends on the number of unique values in the column and on the average length of the strings, similarly to the dictionary size. However, the attribute hierarchy is created for both value and hash encoding, whereas the dictionary only exists for hash encoding. The attribute hierarchy creation can be disabled when the column is only used in aggregations and not as a filter or grouping condition. This optimization might require advanced settings. More details about the setting to disable attribute hierarchies are available at https://docs.microsoft.com/en-us/dotnet/api/microsoft.analysisservices.tabular.column.isavailableinmdx and https://blogs.msdn.microsoft.com/analysisservices/2018/06/08/new-memory-options-for-analysis-services/.

The *Encoding* selected for a column in the model might be changed by the developer. The data model can offer hints to suggest an encoding type to use. Usually, VertiPaq chooses the encoding that saves more memory; however, the developer might choose a specific encoding that may turn out to be more expensive in order to meet specific needs, like improving the speed of dynamic aggregations. A difference in query performance might be visible in tables with billions of rows, whereas it is usually not significant for tables with a few million rows. More details about encoding hints are available at https://docs.microsoft.com/en-us/sql/analysis-services/what-s-new-in-sql-server-analysis-services-2017?view=sql-server-2017#encoding-hints.

The first possible optimization using VertiPaq Analyzer reports is removing any columns that are not useful for the reports and that are expensive in memory. For example, the data shown in Figure 18-2 highlights that one of the most expensive columns of the *SalesQuota* table is *SalesQuotaKey*. *SalesQuotaKey* is not used in any report, and it is not required by the data model structure—as it happens for columns used in relationships. Indeed, the *SalesQuotaKey* column could be removed from the model without affecting any report and calculation, saving both refresh time and precious memory.

The process of identifying the most expensive columns is made simpler by using another report available in VertiPaq Analyzer shown in Figure 18-3. This Columns report shows all the columns in a flattened list where the reported name is the concatenation of the table and column names, sorting the list by descending *Columns Total Size*.

TableColumn	Rows	Cardinality	Columns Total Size	Database Size %
StrategyPlan-Amount	2,750,628	2,042,832	108,871,288	14.09 %
OnlineSales-OnlineSalesKey	12,627,608	12,627,608	84,154,472	10.89 %
OnlineSales-SalesOrderNumber	12,627,608	1,674,320	79,176,940	10.25 %
SalesQuota-GrossMarginQuota	7,465,911	944,795	67,753,032	8.77 %
SalesQuota-SalesAmountQuota	7,465,911	613,799	60,602,464	7.84 %
Inventory-InventoryKey	8,013,099	8,013,099	53,420,840	6.91 %
SalesQuota-SalesQuotaKey	7,465,911	7,465,911	49,772,920	6.44 %
Sales-SalesKey	3,406,089	3,406,089	22,707,424	2.94 %
StrategyPlan-StrategyPlanKey	2,750,628	2,750,628	18,337,680	2.37 %
OnlineSales-SalesOrderLineNumber	12,627,608	4,972	16,544,600	2.15 %
Sales-GrossMargin	3,406,089	118,821	13,750,552	1.78 %

FIGURE 18-3 Details of columns shown in VertiPaq Analyzer.

Two of the three most expensive columns of the entire Contoso data model, *OnlineSalesKey* and *SalesOrderNumber* in the *OnlineSales* table, are seldom used in a report at the aggregated level. Each of these two columns imported in VertiPaq requires 10% of the data size of the entire data model. By removing these two columns, it is possible to save 20% of the database size. Being aware of the cost of every column helps one choose what to keep in the data model and what is too expensive relative to its analytical value.

The reason why the report in Figure 18-3 shows *Rows* and *Cardinality* side-by-side is to help recognize columns that are unique in a table. When the two numbers are close or identical, it is not useful to create summarized results over a column unless it is the target of an aggregation, such as the *Amount* column in the *StrategyPlan* table.

Another important piece of information available in VertiPaq Analyzer is included in the Relationships report shown in Figure 18-4. This report makes it easy to identify expensive relationships present in a data model, even though there are no critical situations in this specific example.

Row Labels	Relationships Size	Max From Cardinality	Max To Cardinality
⊞ Machine	352	303	306
'Machine'[StoreKey] -> 'Store'[StoreKey]	352	303	306
⊞ OnlineSales	44,136	18,869	18,869
'OnlineSales'[CurrencyKey] -> 'Currency'[CurrencyKey]	8	1	28
'OnlineSales'[CustomerKey] -> 'Customer'[CustomerKey]	38,304	18,869	18,869
'OnlineSales'[Datekey] -> 'Date'[Datekey]	1,760	1,096	2,556
'OnlineSales'[ProductKey] -> 'Product'[ProductKey]	4,032	2,516	2,517
'OnlineSales'[PromotionKey] -> 'Promotion'[PromotionKey]	24	28	28
'OnlineSales'[StoreKey] -> 'Store'[StoreKey]	8	3	306
Grand Total	95,488	18,869	18,869

FIGURE 18-4 Size and cardinality of relationships shown in VertiPaq Analyzer.

In VertiPaq, relationships with a cardinality larger than 1 million unique values are particularly expensive, impacting the storage engine cost of any request involving that relationship. A common rule of thumb is to start paying attention to a relationship whenever its cardinality exceeds 100,000. Such relationships usually do not produce visible performance issues, but their presence starts to be measurable in hundreds of milliseconds and could create problems with any future growth of the database. While a single large relationship does not necessarily slow down a report visibly, its presence can undermine the performance of more complex calculations and reports.

An awareness of the cardinality of tables and columns is important in any further analyses of a DAX query's performance. While this information could be retrieved by running simple DAX queries, it is faster and more efficient to use a tool like VertiPaq Analyzer to collect this data automatically—spending more time evaluating the metrics obtained rather than manually running trivial queries on the data model.

Denormalization

The first optimization that can be applied to a data model is to denormalize data. Every relationship has a memory cost and an additional overhead when the engine transfers the filter from one table to another. Purely from a performance point of view, an optimal model would be one made of a single table. However, such an approach would be less than usable and would force a single granularity for all the measures. Thus, an optimal data model is organized as a star schema around each table defined for measures sharing the same granularity. For this reason, one should denormalize unnecessary related tables, thus reducing the number of columns and relationships in the data model.

The denormalization required in a data model for DAX is usually counterintuitive for anyone with some experience in data modeling for a relational database. For instance, consider a simple data model where a *Payment* table has two columns, *Payment Code* and *Payment Description*. In a relational database, a table with *Code* and *Description* is commonly used to avoid duplicating the description content in each row of a *Transactions* table. It is common practice to only store the *Payment Code* in *Transactions* to save space in a relational model.

Table 18-2 shows a denormalized version of the *Transactions* table. There are many rows with duplicated values of Credit Card and Cash in the *Payment Type Description* column.

TABLE 18-2 *Transactions* table with *Payment Type* denormalized in the *Code* and *Description* columns

Date	Amount	Payment Type Code	Payment Type Description
2015-06-21	100	00	Cash
2015-06-21	100	02	Credit Card
2015-06-22	200	02	Credit Card
2015-06-23	200	00	Cash
2015-06-23	100	03	Wire Transfer
2015-06-24	200	02	Credit Card
2015-06-25	100	00	Cash

By using a separate table containing all the payment types, it is possible to only store the *Payment Type Code* in the *Transactions* table, as shown in Table 18-3.

TABLE 18-3 *Transactions* table normalized, with *Payment Type Code* only

Date	Amount	Payment Type Code
2015-06-21	100	00
2015-06-21	100	02
2015-06-22	200	02
2015-06-23	200	00
2015-06-23	100	03
2015-06-24	200	02
2015-06-25	100	00

By storing the description of payment types in a separate table (see Table 18-4), there is only one row for each payment type code and description. That table in a relational database reduces the total amount of space required, by avoiding the duplication of a long string in the *Transactions* table.

TABLE 18-4 *Payment Type* table that normalizes *Code* and *Description*

Payment Type Code	Payment Type Description
00	Cash
01	Debit Card
02	Credit Card
03	Wire Transfer

However, this optimization, which works perfectly fine for a relational database, might be a bad choice in a data model for DAX. The VertiPaq engine automatically creates a dictionary for each column, which means that the *Transactions* table will not pay a cost for duplicated descriptions as would be the case in a relational model.

> **Note** Compression techniques based on dictionaries are also available in certain relational databases. For example, Microsoft SQL Server offers this feature through the clustered columnstore indexes. However, the default behavior of a relational database is to store data without using a dictionary-based compression.

In terms of space saving, the denormalization is always better by denormalizing a single column in a separate table; on the other hand, the denormalization of many columns in a single table—as is the case for the attributes of a *Product*—might be more expensive than using a normalized model. For example, we can compare the memory cost between a normalized and a denormalized model:

- Memory cost for normalized model:
    - Column *Transactions[Type Code]*
    - Column *Payments[Type Code]*
    - Column *Payments[Type Description]*
    - Relationship *Transactions[Type Code] – Payments[Type Code]*

- Memory cost for denormalized model:
    - Column *Transactions[Type Code]*
    - Column *Transactions[Type Description]*

The denormalized model removes the cost of the *Payments[Type Code]* column and the cost of the relationship on *Transactions[Type Code]*. However, the cost of the *Type Description* column is different between *Transactions* and *Payments* tables, and in a very large table, the difference might be in favor of the normalized model. However, usually the aggregation of a column performs better when a filter is applied to another column of the same table, rather than a filter on a column in another table connected through a relationship. Does this justify a complete denormalization of the data model into a single table? Absolutely not! In terms of usability, the star schema should be always the preferred choice because it is a good trade-off in terms of resource usage and performance.

A star schema contains a table for each business entity such as *Customer* and *Product*, and all the attributes related to an entity are completely denormalized in such tables. For example, the *Product* table should have attributes such as *Category*, *Subcategory*, *Model*, and *Color*. This model works well whenever the cardinality of the relationship is not too large. As mentioned before, 1 million unique values is the threshold to define a large cardinality for a relationship, although 100,000 unique values already classifies a relationship as a potential risk for the performance of the queries.

In order to understand why the cardinality of a relationship is important for performance, it is useful to know what happens by applying a filter on a column. Consider the schema in Figure 18-5, where there are relationships between the *Sales* table and *Product*, *Customer*, and *Date*. By querying the data model filtering customers by gender, the engine transfers the filter from *Customer* to *Sales* by specifying the list of customer keys that belong to each gender type included in the query. If there are

10,000 customers, any list generated by a filter cannot be larger than this number. However, if there are 6 million customers, a filter by a single gender type might generate a list of unique keys, resulting in around 3 million unique values for each gender. A large number of keys involved in a relationship always has an impact in performance, even though in absolute terms said impact also depends on the version of the engine and on the hardware being used (CPU clock, cache size, RAM speed).

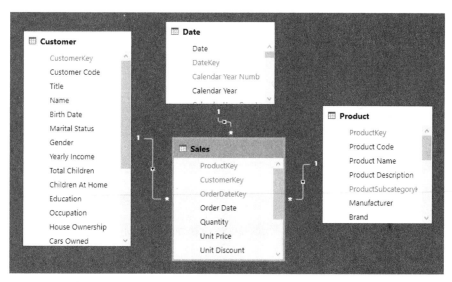

FIGURE 18-5 The *Sales* table has relationships with the *Product*, *Customer*, and *Date* tables.

What can be done to optimize the data model when a relationship involves millions of unique values? If the measured performance degradation is not compatible with the query latency requirements, one might consider other forms of denormalization that reduce the cardinality of the relationship or that remove entirely the need for a relationship in certain queries. In the previous example, one might consider denormalizing the *Gender* column in the *Sales* table, in the event it is the only case where they need to optimize performance. If there are more columns to optimize, consider creating another table with the columns of *Customer* table that users query often and that have a low cardinality (and a low selectivity).

For instance, consider a table called *Customer Info* with *Gender*, *Occupation*, and *Education* columns. If the cardinality of these columns is 2, 5, and 5 values, respectively, a table with all the possible combinations has 50 rows (2 × 5 × 5). A query on any of these columns will be much faster because the filter applied to *Sales* will have a very short list of values. In terms of usability, the user will see two groups of attributes for the same entity, corresponding to the two tables, *Customer* and *Customer Info*. This is not an ideal situation. For this reason, this optimization should only be considered when strictly necessary, unless the same result can be obtained by using the Aggregations feature in the Tabular model.

> **Important** The Aggregations feature is discussed later in this chapter. It is a feature that automates the creation of the underlying tables and relationships whose only purpose is to optimize the performance of the storage engine requests. As of April 2019, the Aggregations feature only works for tables stored in DirectQuery and cannot replace the techniques described in this section. This will be possible when the Aggregations also work for tables stored in VertiPaq.

It is important that both tables have a direct relationship with the *Sales* table, as shown in Figure 18-6.

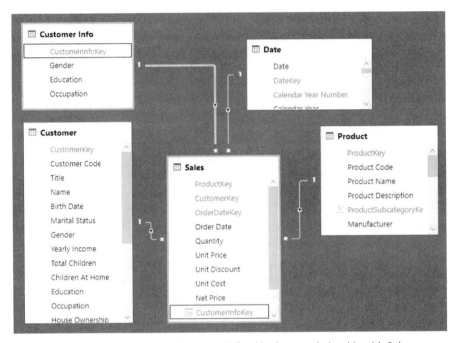

FIGURE 18-6 Both the *Customer* and *Customer Info* tables have a relationship with *Sales*.

The *CustomerInfoKey* column should be added to the *Sales* table before any data is imported into it so that it is a native column. As discussed in Chapter 17, native columns are better compressed than calculated columns. However, a calculated column could also be created with the following DAX expression:

```
Sales[CustomerInfoKey] =
LOOKUPVALUE (
    'Customer Info'[CustomerInfoKey],
    'Customer Info'[Gender], RELATED ( Customer[Gender] ),
    'Customer Info'[Occupation], RELATED ( Customer[Occupation] ),
    'Customer Info'[Education], RELATED ( Customer[Education] )
)
```

From a user experience perspective, the columns that are denormalized in the *Customer Info* table should be hidden from the *Customer* table. Showing the same attributes (*Gender, Occupation,* and *Education*) in two tables would generate confusion. However, by hiding these attributes from the *Customer* table, it is not possible to create a report with the list of customers with a certain *Occupation* without looking at the transactions in the *Sales* table. In order to avoid losing such features, the model should be enhanced including an inactive relationship, which can be activated if needed. We need specific measures to activate that relationship, as we will see later in the optimized *Sales Amount* measure. Figure 18-7 shows that there is an active relationship between the *Customer Info* table and the *Sales* table, and an inactive relationship between the *Customer Info* table and the *Customer* table.

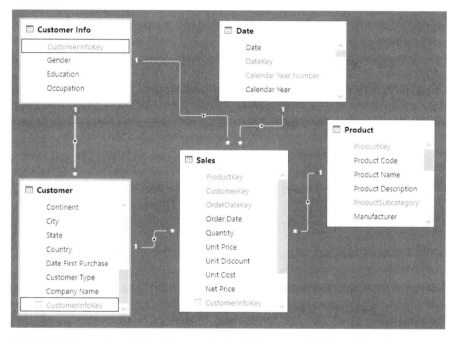

FIGURE 18-7 An inactive relationship connects the *Customer* and *Customer Info* tables.

The relationship between *Customer Info* and *Customer* can be activated whenever there is any other filter active in the *Customer* table. For example, consider the following definition of the *Sales Amount* measure:

```
Sales Amount :=
IF (
    ISCROSSFILTERED ( Customer[CustomerKey] ),
    CALCULATE (
        [Sales Internal],
        USERELATIONSHIP ( Customer[CustomerInfoKey], 'Customer Info'[CustomerInfoKey] ),
        CROSSFILTER ( Sales[CustomerInfoKey], 'Customer Info'[CustomerInfoKey], NONE )
    ),
    [Sales Internal]
)
```

The cross filter is only active in the *Customer* table when there is a filter on any column of the *Customer* table, unless the relationship between *Sales* and *Customer* is bidirectional. Indeed, when the cross filter is active, the relationship between *Customer* and *Customer Info* is enabled by using *USERELATIONSHIP*, automatically disabling the other relationship between *Customer Info* and *Sales*. Furthermore, the *CROSSFILTER* in the function is not necessary, but it is a good idea to keep it there; it highlights the intention to disable the filter propagation in the relationship between *Customer Info* and *Sales*. The idea is that, since the engine must process a list of *CustomerKey* values in any case, it is better to reduce such a filter by also including the attributes moved into *Customer Info*. However, when the user filters columns in *Customer Info* and not in *Customer*, the default active relationship uses a better relationship made with a lower number of unique values. Unfortunately, in order to optimize the use of the *Customer-Sales* relationship in a data model, this DAX pattern must be applied to all the measures that might involve *Customer Info* attributes. This is not necessary using Aggregations in the data model because the pattern is implemented automatically by the engine without requiring any effort in the DAX code.

Another very common scenario where a high cardinality in a relationship should be denormalized is that of a relationship between two large tables. For example, consider the *Sales Header* and *Sales Detail* tables in the data model in Figure 18-8.

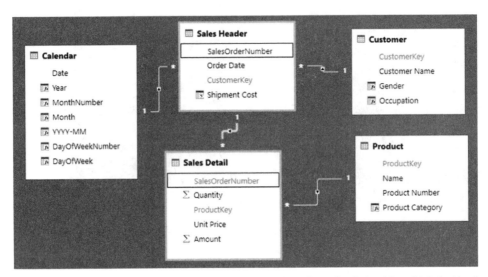

FIGURE 18-8 The *Customer* table filters *Sales Detail* transactions through relationships with *Sales Header*.

This situation is common because many normalized relational databases are composed of this same design. However, the relationship between *Sales Header* and *Sales Detail* is particularly dangerous for a DAX query because of the high number of unique values. Any query grouping the *Quantity* column (from *Sales Detail*) by *Customer[Gender]* transfers a filter from *Sales Header* to *Sales Detail* through the *SalesOrderNumber* column. A better design is possible by denormalizing in *Sales Detail* all the relationships stored in *Sales Header*. In practice, there should be two star schemas sharing the same dimensions. The only purpose of the denormalization is to avoid passing a filter through the relationship between *Sales Header* and *Sales Detail*, which no longer exists in the new design shown in Figure 18-9.

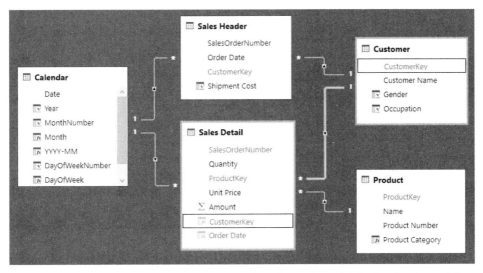

FIGURE 18-9 There are direct relationships between the *Sales Header* and *Sales Detail* tables, and *Customer* and *Calendar*.

Use the right degree of denormalization in a data model for DAX, especially for performance reasons. The best practices described in this section provide a good balance between usability and performance.

Columns cardinality

The cardinality of a column is the number of unique values that the column contains. This number is important to reduce the size of the column, which has a direct impact on VertiPaq scan performance. Another reason to reduce the cardinality of a column to a necessary minimum is that many DAX operations, such as iterations and filters, have an execution time that directly depends on this number. Often, the cardinality of a column is more important than the number of rows of the table containing the column.

The data model designer should identify the cardinality of a column and consider possible optimizations if the column is to be used in relationships, filters, or calculations. There are several common scenarios to consider:

- **Key of a relationship:** The cardinality of the column cannot be changed unless the cardinality of the related table is changed, too. See the "Denormalization" section, earlier in this chapter.

- **Numeric value aggregated in a measure:** Do not change the precision of a number if that number represents a quantity or the amount of a monetary transaction. However, if a number represents a measure with a floating-point value, one might consider removing the decimals that are not relevant. For example, when collecting temperatures, the value could be rounded down to the closest decimal digit; the removed part is probably lower than the precision of the measuring tool.

- **Low cardinality text description:** The only impact is on dictionary size in case the column has many unique values. There are no advantages in moving the column into a separate table because the dictionary would be the same. Keep this column if users need it.

- **High cardinality text notes:** Potentially different for every row of the table, but it is not a big issue if most of the rows have a blank value.

- **Pictures:** This column is required to display graphics in a client tool—for example, a picture of a product. This data type is not available in Power BI; storing the URL of an image that is loaded dynamically is a better alternative that saves memory.

- **Transaction ID:** This column has a high cardinality in a large table. Consider removing it if it is not necessary in DAX queries. If used in drill-through operations—for example, to see the transactions that form a particular aggregation—consider splitting the number/string into two or more parts, each with a smaller number of unique values.

- **Date and time:** Consider splitting the column into two parts. More on this in the following section in this chapter, "Handling date and time."

- **Audit columns:** A table in a relational database often has standard columns used for auditing purposes—for instance, timestamp and user of last update. These columns should not be imported in a model stored by VertiPaq, unless required for drill-through. In that case, consider splitting the timestamp following the same rules applied to date and time.

As a rule of thumb, consider that reducing the cardinality of a column saves memory and improves performance. Because reducing cardinality might imply losing information and/or accuracy, be careful in considering the implications of these optimizations.

Handling date and time

Almost any data model has one or more date columns. Every so often, the time is also an interesting dimension of analysis. Usually, these columns come from original *Datetime* columns in the data source. There are several best practices to optimize these types of columns.

First and foremost, date and time should be always split into two separate columns, without using calculated columns to do so. The split should take place by reading the original column in two different columns of the data model: one for the date, the other for the time. For example, reading a *TransactionExecution* column from a table in SQL Server, one should use the following syntax in a T-SQL query to create two columns, *TransactionDate* and *TransactionTime*:

```
...
CAST ( TransactionExecution AS DATE ) AS TransactionDate,
CAST ( TransactionExecution AS TIME ) AS TransactionTime,
...
```

It is very important to do this split operation; otherwise, the model would have a column in which dictionary and cardinality would increase every day. Moreover, analyzing a timestamp in Tabular is very hard. A *Date* table needs an exact match with the date, and the *Datetime* column would not work correctly in a relationship with the *Date* column of a *Date* table.

A *Date* column usually has a good granularity: 10 years correspond to less than 3,700 unique values, and even 100 years still fall within a manageable order of magnitude. Moreover, time intelligence functions require a complete calendar for each year considered, so removing days (for example, keeping only one day per month) is not an optimization to consider.

The *Time* column, on the other hand, should be subject to more considerations. With a *Time* column, one should consider creating a *Time* table, which contains one row for each point in the chosen granularity. The time should be rounded to the same granularity as the one chosen for the *Time* table. The *Time* table will make it easy to consider different time periods: for example, morning and evening, or 15-minute intervals. Depending on the data and the analysis required, the time could be rounded down to the closest hour or millisecond—even though the latter is very unlikely. Table 18-5 shows the different cardinality corresponding to different precision levels.

TABLE 18-5 Cardinality corresponding to different precision levels for a *Time* column

Precision	Cardinality
Hour	24
15 Minutes	96
5 Minutes	288
Minute	1,440
Second	86,400
Millisecond	86,400,000

Choosing the millisecond precision is usually the worst choice, and a precision down to the second still has a relatively high number of unique values. Most of the times the precision choice will be in a range between hours and minutes. At this point, one might think that the minute precision is a safe choice because it has a relatively low cardinality. However, remember that the compression of a column depends on the presence of duplicated values in contiguous rows. Thus, moving from a minute to 15-minute precision can have a big impact on the compression of large tables.

The choice between rounding to the closest second/minute or truncating the detail not needed for the analysis depends on analytical requirements. Here is an example of the T-SQL code that truncates a time to different precision levels:

```
-- Truncate to the second
DATEADD (
    MILLISECOND,
    - DATEPART ( MILLISECOND, CAST ( TransactionExecution AS TIME(3) ) ),
    CAST ( TransactionExecution AS TIME(3) )
)
```

```
-- Truncate to the minute
DATEADD (
    SECOND,
    - DATEPART (SECOND, CAST ( TransactionExecution AS TIME(0) ) ),
    CAST ( TransactionExecution AS TIME(0) )
)

-- Truncate to 5 minutes
--    change 5 to 15 to truncate to 15 minutes
--    change 5 to 60 to truncate to the hour
CAST (
    DATEADD (
        MINUTE,
        ( DATEDIFF (
            MINUTE,
            0,
            DATEADD (
                SECOND,
                - DATEPART ( SECOND, CAST ( TransactionExecution AS TIME(0) ) ),
                CAST ( TransactionExecution AS TIME(0) )
            )
        ) / 5 ) * 5,
        0
    ) AS TIME(0)
)
```

The following T-SQL code shows examples for rounding time instead of truncating it:

```
-- Round to the second
CAST ( TransactionExecution AS TIME(0) )

-- Round to the minute
CAST ( DATEADD (
    MINUTE,
    DATEDIFF (
        MINUTE,
        0,
        DATEADD ( SECOND, 30, CAST ( TransactionExecution AS TIME(0) ) )
    ),
    0
) AS TIME ( 0 ) )

-- Round to 5 minutes
--    change 5 to 15 to truncate to 15 minutes
--    change 5 to 60 to truncate to the hour
CAST ( DATEADD (
    MINUTE,
    ( DATEDIFF (
        MINUTE,
        0,
        DATEADD ( SECOND, 5 * 30, CAST ( TransactionExecution AS TIME(0) ) )
    ) / 5 ) * 5,
    0
) AS TIME ( 0 ) )
```

Similar transformations can be applied in Power Query when importing data, though for tables with millions of rows a transformation made in the original data source may provide better performance.

When storing millions of new rows every day in a single table, these details can make a big difference in memory usage and performance. At the same time, do not spend too much time optimizing a data model that does not require very high a level of compression; after all, reducing the precision means removing some information that will no longer be available for deeper insights if needed.

Calculated columns

A calculated column stores the result of a DAX expression evaluated row-by-row during a table refresh. For this reason, calculated columns might be considered as a possible way to optimize query execution time. However, a calculated column has hidden costs, and it is only a good optimization technique under specific conditions.

Calculated columns should be considered as viable options only in these two situations:

- **Group or filter data:** If a calculated column returns a value used to group or filter data, there is no alternative other than creating the same value before importing data into the data model. For example, the price of a product might be classified into Low, Medium, and High categories. This value is usually a string, especially when the user makes it available as a selection.

- **Precalculate complex formulas:** A calculated column can store the result of a complex calculation that is not sensitive to filters made at query time. However, it is very hard to establish when this produces a real computational advantage, and it is necessary to measure the presence of a real advantage at query time in order to justify its use.

Do not make the wrong assumption that any calculated column is faster than doing the same computation at query time. This is often inaccurate. Other times, the advantage is barely measurable and does not balance out the cost of the calculated column. There should be a relevant performance improvement at query time to justify a calculated column for optimization reasons. There are also many factors to consider when evaluating the cost/benefit ratio of a calculated column against an equivalent calculation made at runtime in a measure.

A calculated column is not as optimized as a native column. It might have a lower compression rate compared to native columns of the table because it does not take part in the heuristic that VertiPaq executes to find the optimal sort order of the data in each segment. Only a column storing a very low number of unique values might benefit from a good compression, but this is usually the result of logical conditions and not of numeric expressions.

For example, consider the case of a simple calculated column:

```
Sales[Amount] = Sales[Quantity] * Sales[Price]
```

If there are 100 unique values in *Quantity* and 1,000 unique values in *Price*, the resulting *Amount* column might have a cardinality between 1 and 100,000 unique values, depending on the actual values in the columns and on their distribution across table rows. Usually, the larger the number of rows in the table, the higher the number of unique values found in the *Amount* column—because of statistical distribution. With a dictionary that is one or two orders of magnitude larger than the original columns, the compression is usually worse. What about query performance? It depends, and it should be measured case-by-case in order to get a correct answer, considering the two possible calculations: one based on a calculated column and the other completely dynamic and based on measures.

A simple measure can sum the *Amount* calculated column:

```
TotalAmountCC := SUM ( Sales[Amount] )
```

The alternative dynamic implementation transfers the expressions of the calculated column in an iterator over the table:

```
TotalAmountM := SUMX ( Sales, Sales[Quantity] * Sales[Price] )
```

Is the cost of scanning the single *Sales[Amount]* column smaller than scanning the two original *Sales[Quantity]* and *Sales[Price]* columns? It is impossible to estimate this in advance, so it must be measured. Usually, the difference between these two options is only visible in very large tables. In small tables the performance might be very close, so the calculated column is not worth its memory footprint.

Most of the time, calculated columns used to compute aggregated values can be replaced by using the same expressions in iterators such as *SUMX* and *AVERAGEX*. In the previous example, *TotalAmountM* is a measure that dynamically executes the same expression defined in the calculated *Amount* column, used by the simple aggregation in *TotalAmountCC*.

A different evaluation is necessary when a context transition is present in an iterator. For example, consider the following DAX measure in a model where the *Sales Header* and *Sales Detail* tables are connected through a relationship:

```
AverageOrder :=
AVERAGEX (
    'Sales Header',
    CALCULATE (
        SUMX (
            'Sales Detail',
            'Sales Detail'[Quantity] * 'Sales Detail'[Unit Price]
        ),
        ALLEXCEPT ( 'Sales Detail', 'Sales Header' )
    )
)
```

In this case, the context transition within the loop can be very expensive, especially if the *Sales Header* table contains millions of rows or more. Storing the value in a calculated column will probably save a lot of execution time.

```
'Sales Header'[Amount] =
CALCULATE (
    SUMX (
        'Sales Detail',
        'Sales Detail'[Quantity] * 'Sales Detail'[Unit Price]
    )
)

AverageOrder :=
AVERAGEX (
    'Sales Header',
    'Sales Header'[Amount]
)
```

We will never grow tired of repeating that these examples are guidelines. One should measure the performance improvements of a calculated column and its related memory cost in order to decide whether to use it or not.

Consider that a calculated column can be avoided by creating the same value for a native column in the data source when populating the table—for example, using an SQL statement or a Power Query transformation. A useful calculated column should leverage the VertiPaq engine, providing a faster and more flexible way to compute a column than reading the entire table again from the data source. Usually, this happens when the calculated column expression aggregates rows from tables other than the one it belongs to; the previous *Amount* calculated column in the *Sales Header* table is an example of such condition.

Finally, a calculated column increases the time to refresh a data model especially because it is an operation that cannot scale on multiple threads, as explained in more detail in a following section, "Processing of calculated columns."

At this point, it should be clear that calculated columns are expensive for two reasons:

- **Memory:** The values are persisted using a nonoptimal compression.

- **Duration of Refresh:** The process of calculated columns is a sequential operation using a single thread, which results in a nonscalable operation also in large servers.

With that said, calculated columns prove useful in many scenarios. We do not want to pass on the message that calculated columns are always to be avoided. Instead, be aware of their cost and make an educated decision on whether to use them or not. In the next section we describe a good example where calculated columns really shine in improving performance.

Optimizing complex filters with *Boolean* calculated columns

It is worth mentioning a specific case where optimization is achieved using calculated columns. A logical expression used to filter a high-cardinality column can be consolidated using a calculated column that stores the result of the logical expression itself.

For example, consider the following measure:

```
ExpensiveTransactions :=
COUNTROWS (
    FILTER (
        Sales,
        VAR UnitPrice =
            IF (
                Sales[Unit Discount] > 0,
                RELATED ( 'Product'[Unit Price] ),
                Sales[Net Price]
            )
        VAR IsLargeTransaction = UnitPrice * Sales[Quantity] > 100
        VAR IsLargePrice = UnitPrice > 70
        VAR IsExpensive = IsLargeTransaction || IsLargePrice
        RETURN
            IsExpensive
    )
)
```

In case there are millions of rows in the *Sales* table, the filter iteration could be expensive. If the expression used in the filter does not depend on the existing filter context, as in this case, the result of the expression can be consolidated in a calculated column, applying a filter on that column in a *CALCULATE* statement instead. For example, the previous operation can be rewritten this way:

```
Sales[IsExpensive] =
VAR UnitPrice =
    IF (
        Sales[Unit Discount] > 0,
        RELATED ( 'Product'[Unit Price] ),
        Sales[Net Price]
    )
VAR IsLargeTransaction = UnitPrice * Sales[Quantity] > 100
VAR IsLargePrice = UnitPrice > 70
VAR IsExpensive = IsLargeTransaction || IsLargePrice
RETURN
    IsExpensive

ExpensiveTransactions :=
CALCULATE (
    COUNTROWS ( Sales ),
    Sales[IsExpensive] = TRUE
)
```

The calculated column containing a logical value (*TRUE* or *FALSE*) usually benefits from good compression and a low memory cost. It is also very effective at execution time because it applies a direct filter to the scan of the *Sales* table required to count the rows. In this case, the benefit at query time is usually evident. Just consider if it is worth the longer processing time for the column; that processing time must be measured before making a final decision.

Processing of calculated columns

The presence of one or more calculated columns slows down the refresh of any part of a table that is somewhat related to the calculated column. This section describes the reasons for that; it also provides background information on why an incremental refresh operation can be very expensive because of the presence of calculated columns.

Any refresh operation of a table requires recomputing all the calculated columns in the entire data model referencing any column of that table. For example, refreshing a partition of a table—as during any incremental refresh—requires a complete update of all the calculated columns stored in the table. Such a calculation is performed for all the rows of the table, even though the refresh only affects a single partition of the table. It does not matter whether the expression of the calculated column only depends on other columns of the same table; the calculated column is always computed for the entire table and not for a single partition.

Moreover, the expression of a calculated column might depend on the content of other tables. In this case, the calculated columns referencing a partially refreshed table must also be recalculated to guarantee the consistency of the data model. The cost for computing a calculated column usually depends on the number of rows of the table where the column is stored.

The process of a calculated column is a single-thread job, which iterates all the rows of the table to compute the column expression. In case there are several calculated columns, they are evaluated one at a time, making the entire operation a process bottleneck for large tables. For these reasons, creating a calculated column in a large table with hundreds of millions of rows is not a good idea. Creating tens of calculated columns in a large table can result in a very long processing time, adding minutes to the time required to process the native data.

Choosing the right columns to store

The previous section about calculated columns explained that storing a column that can be computed row-by-row using other columns of the same table is not always an advantage. The same consideration is also valid for native columns of the table. When choosing the columns to store in a table, consider the memory size and the query performance. Good optimizations of resource allocation (and memory in particular) are possible by doing the right evaluation in this area.

We consider the following types of columns in a table:

- **Primary or alternate keys:** The column contains a unique value for each row of the table.

- **Qualitative attributes:** The column can be text or number, used to group and/or filter rows in a table; for instance, name, color, city, country.

- **Quantitative attributes:** The number is a value used both as a filter (for example, less than a certain value) and as an argument in a calculation, such as price, amount, quantity.

- **Descriptive attributes:** The column contains text providing additional information about a row, but its content is never used to filter or to aggregate rows—for example, notes, comments.

- **Technical attributes:** Information recorded in the database for technical reasons, without a business value, such as username of last update, timestamp, GUID for replication.

The general principle is to try to minimize the cardinality of the columns imported into a table, not importing columns that have a high cardinality and that are not relevant for the analysis. However, every type of column deserves additional considerations.

The columns for **primary** or **alternate keys** are necessary if there are one or more one-to-many relationships with other tables. For instance, the product code and the product key columns of a table of products are certainly required columns. However, a table should not include a primary or alternate key column not used in a relationship with other tables. For example, the *Sales* table might have a unique identifier for each row in the original table. Such a column has a cardinality that corresponds to the number of rows of the *Sales* table. Moreover, a unique identifier is not necessary for relationships because no tables target *Sales* for a relationship. For these reasons, it is a very expensive column in terms of memory, and it should not be imported in memory. In a composite data model, a similar high-granularity column could be accessed only through DirectQuery without being stored in memory, as described later in the "Optimizing column storage" section of this chapter.

A table should always include **qualitative attributes** that have a low cardinality because they have a good compression and might be useful for the analysis. For example, the product category is a column that has a low cardinality, related to the *Product* table. In case there is a high cardinality, we should consider carefully whether to import the column or not because its storage memory cost can be high. The high selectivity might justify the cost, but we should check that filters in queries usually select a low number of values in that column. For instance, the production lot number might be a piece of information included in the *Sales* table that users want to filter at query time. Its high cost might be justified by a business need to apply this filter in certain queries.

All the **quantitative attributes** are generally imported to guarantee any calculation, although we might consider skipping columns providing redundant information. Consider the *Quantity*, *Price*, and *Amount* columns of a *Sales* table, where the *Amount* column contains the result of the product between *Quantity* and *Price*. We probably want to create measures that aggregate each of these columns; yet we will probably calculate the price as a weighted average considering the sum of amount and quantity, instead of a simple average of the price considering each transaction at the same level. This is an example of the measure we want to define:

```
Sum of Quantity := SUM ( Sales[Quantity] )

Sum of Amount    := SUM ( Sales[Amount] )

Average Price    := DIVIDE ( [Sum of Amount], [Sum of Quantity] )
```

By looking at these measures, we might say that we only need to import *Quantity* and *Amount* in the data model, without importing the *Price* column, which is not used by these measures. However, if we consider the cardinality of the columns, we start to have doubts. If there are 100 unique values in the *Quantity* column, and there are 10,000 unique values in the *Price* column, we might have up to 1,000,000 unique values in the *Amount* column. At this point, we might consider importing only the *Quantity* and *Price* columns, using the following definition of the measures in the data model; only *Sum of Amount* changes, the other two measures did not change:

```
Sum of Quantity := SUM ( Sales[Quantity] )

Sum of Amount   := SUMX ( Sales, Sales[Quantity] * Sales[Price] )

Average Price   := DIVIDE ( [Sum of Amount], [Sum of Quantity] )
```

The new definition of the *Sum of Amount* measure might be slower because it has to scan two columns instead of one. However, these columns might be smaller than the original *Amount*. Trying to predict the faster option is very hard because we should also consider the distribution of the values in the table, and not only the cardinality of the column. We suggest measuring the memory used and the performance in both scenarios before making a final decision. Based on our experience, removing the *Amount* column in a small data model can be more important for Power BI and Power Pivot. Indeed, the available memory in personal computers is usually more limited than that of a server, and a smaller memory footprint also produces a faster loading time opening the smaller file. At any rate, in a large table with billions of rows stored in an Analysis Services Tabular model, the performance penalty of the multiplication between two columns (*Quantity* and *Price*) could be larger than the increased memory scan time for the *Amount* column. In this case, the better response time for the queries justifies the higher memory cost to store the *Amount* column. Regardless, we should measure size and performance in each specific case because the distribution of data plays a key role in compression and affects any decision pertaining to it.

Note   Storing *Quantity* and *Price* instead of *Amount* is an advantage if the table is stored in VertiPaq, whereas it is not the suggested best practice for DirectQuery models. Moreover, if the table in VertiPaq contains billions of rows in memory, the *Amount* column can provide better query performance and it is compatible with future Aggregations over VertiPaq. More details in the section "Managing VertiPaq Aggregations" later in this chapter.

We should consider whether to import **descriptive attributes** or not. In general, they have a high storage cost for the dictionary of the column when imported in memory. A few examples of descriptive attributes are the *Notes* field in an invoice and the *Description* column in the *Product* table. Usually, these attributes are mainly used to provide additional information about a specific entity. Users hardly use this type of column to group or filter data; the typical use case is to get detailed drill-through information. The only issue with including these columns in the data model is their memory storage cost, mainly related to the column dictionary. If the column has many blank values and a low number of unique nonblank values in the table, then its dictionary will be small and the column cost will be more acceptable. Nevertheless, a column containing the transcription of conversations made in a call center is probably too expensive for a *Service Calls* table containing date, time, duration, and operator who managed the call. When the cost of storing descriptive attributes in memory is too expensive, we can consider only accessing them through DirectQuery in a composite data model.

A particular type of descriptive attribute is the information provided as detail for transactions in a drill-through operation. For example, the invoice number or the order number of a transaction is an attribute that has a high cardinality, but that could be important for some reports. In this case, we should consider the particular optimizations for drill-through attributes described in the next section, "Optimizing column storage."

Most of the time, there is no reason to import columns for **technical attributes**, such as timestamp, date, time, and operator of the last update. This information is mainly for auditing and forensic requirements. Unless we have a data model specifically built for auditing requirements, the need for this information is usually low in an analytical solution. However, technical attributes are good candidates for columns accessed only through DirectQuery in a composite data model.

Optimizing column storage

The best optimization for a column is to remove the column from a table entirely. In the previous section, we described when this decision makes sense based on the type of columns in a table. Once we define the set of columns that are part of the data model, we can still use optimization techniques in order to reduce the amount of memory used, even though each optimization comes with side effects. In case the composite data model feature is available, an additional option is that of keeping a column in the data source, only making it accessible through DirectQuery.

Using column split optimization

The memory footprint of a column can be lowered by reducing the column cardinality. In certain conditions, we can achieve this result by splitting the column into two or more parts. The column split cannot be obtained with calculated columns because that would require storing the original column in memory. We show examples of the split operation in SQL, but any other transformation tool (such as Power Query) can obtain the same result.

For instance, if there is a 10-character string (such as the values in *TransactionID*), we can split the column in two parts, five characters each (as in *TransactionID_High* and *TransactionID_Low*):

```
SELECT
    LEFT ( TransactionID, 5 ) AS TransactionID_High,
    SUBSTRING ( TransactionID, 6, LEN ( TransactionID ) - 5 ) AS TransactionID_Low,
    ...
```

In case of an integer value, we can use division and modulo for a number that creates an even distribution between the two columns. If there is an integer *TransactionID* column with numbers between 0 and 100 million, we can divide them by 10,000 as in the following example:

```
SELECT
    TransactionID / 10000 AS TransactionID_High,
    TransactionID % 10000 AS TransactionID_Low,
    ...
```

We can use a similar technique for decimal numbers. An easy split is separating the integer from the decimal part, although this might not produce an even distribution. For example, we can transform a *UnitPrice* decimal number column into *UnitPrice_Integer* and *UnitPrice_Decimal* columns:

```
SELECT
    FLOOR ( UnitPrice ) AS UnitPrice_Integer,
    UnitPrice - FLOOR ( UnitPrice ) AS UnitPrice_Decimal,
    ...
```

We can use the result of a column split as is in simple details reports or measures that restore the original value during the calculation. If available in the client tool, the Detail Rows feature allows us to control the drill-through operation, showing to the client the original column and hiding the presence of the two split columns.

> **Important**   The column split can optimize numbers aggregated in measures, using the separation between integer and decimal parts as in the previous example or similar techniques. However, consider that the aggregation operation will have to scan more than one column, and the total time of the operation is usually larger than with a single column. When optimizing for performance, saving memory might be not effective in this case, unless the dictionary is removed by enforcing value encoding instead of hash encoding for a currency or integer data type. A specific measurement is always required for a data model to validate if such optimization also works from a performance point of view.

Optimizing high-cardinality columns

A column with a high cardinality has a high cost because of a large dictionary, a large hierarchy structure, and a lower compression in encoding. The attribute hierarchy structure can be expensive and may be disabled under certain conditions. We describe how to disable attribute hierarchies in the next section.

If it is not possible to disable the hierarchy, or if this reduction is not enough for memory optimization, then consider the column split optimization for a high-cardinality column used in a measure. We can hide this optimization from the user by hiding the split columns and by adapting the calculation in measures. For example, if we optimize *UnitPrice* using the column split, we can create the *Sum of Amount* measure this way:

```
Sum of Amount :=
SUMX (
    Sales,
    Sales[Quantity] * ( Sales[UnitPrice_Integer] + Sales[UnitPrice_Decimal] )
)
```

Remember that the calculation will be more expensive, and only an accurate measurement of the performance of the two models (with and without column split optimization) can establish which one is better for a specific data model.

Disabling attribute hierarchies

The attribute hierarchy structure is required by MDX queries that reference the column as an MDX attribute hierarchy. This structure contains a sorted list of all the values of the column, and its creation might require a large amount of time during a refresh operation, including incremental ones. The size of this structure is measured in the *Columns Hierarchies Size* column of VertiPaq Analyzer. If a column is only used by measures and in drill-through results, and it is not shown to the user as an attribute to filter or group data, then the attribute hierarchy structure is not necessary because it is never used.

The *Available In MDX* property of a column disables the creation of the attribute hierarchy structure when set to *False*. By default, this property is *True*. The name of this property in TMSL and TOM is *isAvailableInMdx*. Depending on the development tool and on the compatibility level of the data model, this property might be not available. A tool that shows this property is Tabular Editor: https://github.com/otykier/TabularEditor/releases/latest.

The attribute hierarchy structure is also used in DAX to optimize sorting and filter operations. It is safe to disable the *isAvailableInMdx* property when a column is only used in a measure expression, it is not visible, and it is never used to filter or sort data. This property is also documented at https://docs.microsoft.com/en-us/dotnet/api/microsoft.analysisservices.tabular.column.isavailableinmdx.

Optimizing drill-through attributes

If a column contains data used only for drill-through operations, there are two possible optimizations. The first is the column split optimization; the second is keeping the columns accessible only through DirectQuery in a composite data model.

When the column is not being used in measures, there are no concerns about possible costs of the materialization of the original values. By leveraging the Detail Rows feature, it is possible to show the original column in the result of a drill-through operation, hiding the presence of the two split columns. However, it is not possible to use the original value as a filter or group-by column.

In a composite data model, the entire table can be made accessible through a DirectQuery request, whereas the columns used by relationships and measures can be included in an in-memory aggregation managed by the VertiPaq engine. This way, it is possible to get the best performance when aggregating data, whereas the query execution time will be longer when the drill-through attributes are requested to the data source via DirectQuery. The next section, "Managing VertiPaq Aggregations," provides more details about that feature.

Managing VertiPaq Aggregations

The VertiPaq storage engine can be used for managing aggregations over DirectQuery data sources—and in the future, also over large VertiPaq tables. Aggregations were initially introduced in late 2018 as a Power BI feature. That same feature could later be adopted by other products. The purpose of Aggregations is to reduce the cost of a storage engine request, removing the need for an expensive DirectQuery request in case the data is available in a smaller table containing aggregated data.

The Aggregations feature is not necessarily related to VertiPaq: it is possible to define aggregations in a DirectQuery model so that different tables are queried on the data source, depending on the granularity of a client request. However, the typical use case for Aggregations is defining them in a composite data model, where each table has three possible storage modes:

- **Import:** The table is stored in memory and managed by the VertiPaq storage engine.

- **DirectQuery:** The data is kept in the data source; at runtime, every DAX query might generate one or more requests to the data source, typically sending SQL queries.

- **Dual:** The table is stored in memory by VertiPaq and can also be used in DirectQuery, typically joining other tables stored in DirectQuery or Dual mode.

The principle of aggregations is to provide different options to solve a storage engine request. For example, a *Sales* table can store the details of each transaction, such as product, customer, and date. When one creates an aggregation by product and month, the aggregated table has a much smaller number of rows. The *Sales* table could also have more than one aggregation, each one with a precedence used in case of multiple aggregations compatible with the same request. Consider a case where the following aggregations are available in a model with *Sales*, *Product*, *Date*, and *Store*:

- *Product* and *Date*—precedence 50

- *Store* and *Date*—precedence 20

If a query required the total of sales by product brand and year, it would use the first aggregation. The same aggregation would be used when drilling down at the month or day level. Indeed, the aggregation that has the *Sales* data at the *Product* and *Date* granularity can solve any query that groups rows by using attributes included in these tables. With the same logic, a query aggregating data by store country and year will use the second aggregation created at the granularity of *Store* and *Date*. However, a query aggregating data by store country and product brand cannot use any existing aggregation. Such queries must use the *Sales* table that has all the details because none of the aggregations available have a granularity compatible with the request. If two or more aggregations are compatible with the request, the choice is made based on the precedence setting defined for each aggregation: The engine chooses the aggregation with the highest precedence. Table 18-6 recaps the aggregations used based on the query request in the examples described.

TABLE 18-6 Examples of aggregation used, based on query request

Query Request	Aggregation Used
Group by product brand and year	*Product* and *Date*
Group by product brand and month	*Product* and *Date*
Group by store country and year	*Store* and *Date*
Group by store country and month	*Store* and *Date*
Group by year	*Product* and *Date* (highest precedence)
Group by month	*Product* and *Date* (highest precedence)
Group by store country and product brand	No aggregation—query *Sales* table at detail level

The engine chooses the aggregation to use only considering the precedence order, regardless of the aggregation storage mode. Indeed, every aggregation has an underlying table that can be stored either in VertiPaq or in DirectQuery. Common sense would suggest that a VertiPaq aggregation should be preferred over a DirectQuery aggregation. Nevertheless, the DAX engine only follows precedence rules. If a DirectQuery aggregation has a higher precedence over a VertiPaq aggregation, and both are candidates to speed up a request, the engine chooses the DirectQuery aggregation. It is up to the developer to define a good set of precedence rules.

An aggregation can match a storage engine request depending on several conditions:

- Granularity of the relationships involved in the storage engine request.

- Matching of columns defined as GroupBy in the summarization type of the aggregation.

- Summarization corresponding to a simple aggregation of a single column.

- Presence of a Count summarization of the detail table.

These conditions might have an impact on the data model design. A model that imports all the tables in VertiPaq usually is designed to minimize the memory requirements. As described in the previous section, "Choosing the right columns to store," storing the *Quantity* and *Price* columns allows the developer to compute the *Amount* at query time using a measure such as:

```
Sales Amount := SUMX ( Sales, Sales[Quantity] * Sales[Price] )
```

This version of the *Sales Amount* measure might not use an aggregation with a Sum summarization type because the Sum summarization only references a single column. However, an aggregation could match the request if *Sales[Quantity]* and *Sales[Price]* have the GroupBy summarization and if there is a Count summarization of the *Sales* table. For complex expressions it could be hard to define an efficient aggregation, and this could impact the model and aggregation design.

Consider the following code as an educational example. If there are two Sum aggregations for the *Sales[Amount]* and *Sales[Cost]* columns, then a *Margin* measure should be implemented using the difference between two aggregations (*Margin1* and *Margin2*), instead of aggregating the difference computed row-by-row (*Margin3*).

```
Sales Amount := SUM ( Sales[Amount] )                        -- Can use Sum aggregations
Total Cost   := SUM ( Sales[Cost] )                          -- Can use Sum aggregations
Margin1      := [Sales Amount] - [Total Cost]                -- Can use Sum aggregations
Margin2      := SUM ( Sales[Amount] ) - SUM ( Sales[Cost] )  -- Can use Sum aggregations

Margin3 := SUMX ( Sales, Sales[Amount] - Sales[Cost] )    -- CANNOT use Sum aggregations
```

However, the *Margin3* measure could match an aggregation that defines the GroupBy summarization for the *Sales[Amount]* and *Sales[Cost]* columns and that also includes a Count summarization of the *Sales* table. Such aggregation would potentially also be useful for the previous definitions of the *Sales Amount* and *Total Cost* measures, even though it would be less efficient than a Sum aggregation on the specific column.

As of April 2019, the Aggregations feature is available for DirectQuery tables. While it is not possible to define aggregations for a table imported in memory, that feature might be implemented in the near future. At that point, all these combinations will become possible:

- DirectQuery aggregation over a DirectQuery table

- VertiPaq aggregation over a DirectQuery table

- VertiPaq aggregation over a VertiPaq table (not available as of April 2019)

The ability to create a VertiPaq aggregation over VertiPaq tables will provide a tool to optimize two scenarios for models imported in memory: very large tables (billions of rows) and relationships with a high cardinality (millions of unique values). These two scenarios can be managed by manually modifying the data model and the DAX code as described in the "Denormalization" section earlier in this chapter. The aggregations over VertiPaq tables will automate this process, resulting in better performance, reduced maintenance, and decreased development costs.

Conclusions

In this chapter we focused on how to optimize a data model imported in memory using the VertiPaq storage engine. The goal is to reduce the memory required for a data model, obtaining as a side effect an improvement in query performance. VertiPaq can also be used to store aggregations in composite models, combining the use of the DirectQuery and VertiPaq storage engines in a single model.

The main takeaways of this chapter are:

- Only import in memory the columns required for the analysis.

- Control columns cardinality, as a low cardinality column has better compression.

- Manage date and time in separate tables and store them at the proper granularity level for the analysis. Storing a precision higher than required (e.g., milliseconds) consumes memory and lowers query performance.

- Consider using VertiPaq to store in-memory aggregations for DirectQuery data sources in composite models.

Analyzing DAX query plans

DAX is a functional language with an advanced query engine that can use different storage engines. As is the case with many query languages, it is usually possible to get the same result using different DAX expressions, each one performing differently. Optimizing a measure or a query requires finding the most efficient way to obtain the desired result. In order to find a more efficient implementation for an expression, the first step is to identify the bottlenecks of the existing code.

This chapter describes the components of the DAX query engine in more detail, explaining how to obtain information about query plans and performance counters related to a particular DAX expression using DAX Studio. This knowledge is fundamental to optimize any DAX formula.

Capturing DAX queries

In order to analyze a query plan, it is necessary to execute a DAX query. A report in Power BI or Excel automatically generates queries that invoke measures included in the data model. Thus, optimizing a DAX measure requires analyzing and optimizing the DAX query that invokes that measure. Collecting the queries generated for a report is the first step in the DAX optimization journey. Indeed, a single slow report is likely to generate dozens of queries. The careful developer should find the slowest query out of them all, thus focusing on the biggest bottleneck first.

DAX Studio (http://daxstudio.org/) is a free open-source tool that offers several useful features to capture and analyze DAX queries. In the following example, see how DAX Studio connects to a Power BI data model to capture the queries generated by a report page.

The Power BI report shown in Figure 19-1 contains one visual that is slower to display. The table in the bottom-left corner with two columns (*Product Name* and *Customers*) requires a few seconds to be updated when the page is first opened and when the user changes the *Continent* slicer selection. We know this because we created the report on purpose. But how would one uncover the slowest visual in a report? DAX studio proves to be very helpful in this.

	A. Datum	Adventure Works	Contoso	Fabrikam	Litware	Northwind Traders	
	(Blank)	20.45K	44.50K	8.46K	14.23K	876.65	Red
	Proseware	Southridge Video	Tailspin Toys	The Phone Company	World Wide Importers		
	6.04K	3.79K	325.71	(Blank)	2.78K		
	A. Datum	Adventure Works	Contoso	Fabrikam	Litware	Northwind Traders	
	22.75K	80.95K	95.83K	82.16K	24.36K	94.99	Black
	Proseware	Southridge Video	Tailspin Toys	The Phone Company	World Wide Importers		
	73.49K	81.42K	5.24K	37.71K	94.08K		
	A. Datum	Adventure Works	Contoso	Fabrikam	Litware	Northwind Traders	
	1.93K	9.12K	17.64K	63.97K	14.78K	64.66K	Blue
	Proseware	Southridge Video	Tailspin Toys	The Phone Company	World Wide Importers		
	4.63K	1.42K	7.77K	(Blank)	27.42K		

Product Name	Customers
Adventure Works 26" 720p LCD HDTV M140 Silver	270
SV 16xDVD M360 Black	270
A. Datum SLR Camera X137 Grey	109
Total	**2160**

Continent

☐ Asia
☐ Europe
☐ North America

Sales   Empty page   +

FIGURE 19-1 A Power BI report with many visuals, one of which is slower to display.

DAX Studio can connect to a Power BI model by selecting the name of a Power BI Desktop file already opened on the same computer. This is shown in Figure 19-2.

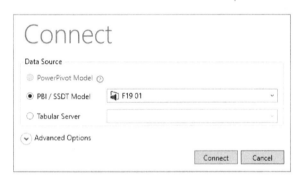

FIGURE 19-2 DAX Studio can connect to multiple types of Tabular models, including Power BI.

Once connected, DAX Studio can start capturing all the queries sent to the Tabular engine after the user activates the All Queries button in the Traces tab of the Home ribbon. This is visible in Figure 19-3.

FIGURE 19-3 The All Queries feature captures all the queries sent to the Tabular engine.

At this point, every action in the client might produce one or more queries. For example, Power BI generates at least one DAX query for every visual in the page. Figure 19-4 shows the queries captured in the sample from Figure 19-1 when selecting the Asia continent in the Continent slicer.

StartTime	Type	Duration	User	Database	Query
05:51:56	DAX	2,879	marco	F19 01	DEFINE VAR __DS0FilterTable = TREATAS({{'Asia"}
05:51:56	DAX	63	marco	F19 01	DEFINE VAR __DS0FilterTable = TREATAS({{'South
05:51:56	DAX	51	marco	F19 01	DEFINE VAR __DS0FilterTable = TREATAS({{'Prose
05:51:56	DAX	65	marco	F19 01	DEFINE VAR __DS0FilterTable = TREATAS({{'Adver
05:51:56	DAX	76	marco	F19 01	DEFINE VAR __DS0FilterTable = TREATAS({{'Adver
05:51:56	DAX	55	marco	F19 01	DEFINE VAR __DS0FilterTable = TREATAS({{'Cont
05:51:56	DAX	44	marco	F19 01	DEFINE VAR __DS0FilterTable = TREATAS({{'Wide
05:51:56	DAX	47	marco	F19 01	DEFINE VAR __DS0FilterTable = TREATAS({{'Wide
05:51:56	DAX	26	marco	F19 01	DEFINE VAR __DS0FilterTable = TREATAS({{'A. Da
05:51:56	DAX	43	marco	F19 01	DEFINE VAR __DS0FilterTable = TREATAS({{'Litwa

Output | Results | Query History | ▸ All Queries

FIGURE 19-4 The All Queries pane shows all the queries captured by DAX Studio.

Note DAX Studio listens to all the queries sent to the Tabular server. By connecting DAX Studio to Power BI Desktop, the queries are always executed by the same user on the same database. Different Power BI files require different connections and a different window in DAX Studio. However, a connection to Analysis Services (which requires administrative rights) will show queries executed by different users and on different databases. The query type will be MDX for any queries generated by a client like Excel. The *Duration* column shows the execution time in milliseconds, and the *Query* column contains the complete text of the query executed on the server.

You can easily check that the first query has a duration of around three seconds. All the remaining queries are very fast, thus not worth any further attention. In a real-world report you likely will notice more than one slow query. DAX Studio lets you quickly discover the slowest queries, focusing the attention on those and avoiding any waste of time on measures and queries that are quick enough.

When you double-click on a line in the All Queries list, the query is copied into the editor window. For example, Figure 19-5 shows the complete text of the first query in the previous list. When you press the highlighted Format Query button on the Home tab, the query is also formatted using the DAX Formatter web service.

Once a slow query is identified following these steps, it can be executed in DAX Studio multiple times. One would analyze its query plan and other metrics to evaluate the bottlenecks and to try changes that could improve performance. The following sections analyze very simple queries created from scratch for educational reasons, although the end goal is to also analyze queries captured from a real workload.

FIGURE 19-5 The Format Query button invokes DAX Formatter to format the DAX code in the editor.

Introducing DAX query plans

The DAX engine provides several details about how it executes a query in the query plan. However, "query plan" is a generic definition for a set of information including two different types of query plans (logical and physical) and a list of storage engine queries used by the physical query plan. Unless otherwise specified, the generic term "query plan" references the whole set of details available. These are introduced in this section and explained in more detail in the following part of the chapter.

In Chapter 17, "The DAX engines," we explained that there are two layers in the DAX query engine: the formula engine (FE) and the storage engine (SE). Every query result is produced by executing the following steps:

1. **Building an Expression Tree.** The engine transforms the query from a string to an expression tree, a data structure that is easier to manipulate for further optimization.

2. **Building a Logical Query Plan.** The engine produces a list of the logical operations required to execute the query. This tree of logical operators resembles the original query syntax. It is easy to find a correspondence between a DAX function and a similar operation in the logical query plan.

3. **Building a Physical Query Plan.** The engine transforms the logical query plan into a set of physical operations. A physical query plan is still a tree of operators, but the resulting tree can be different from the logical query plan.

4. **Executing the Physical Query Plan.** The engine finally executes the physical query plan, retrieving data from the SE and computing the query calculations.

The first step is not interesting to analyze performance. Steps 2 and 3 involve the formula engine, whereas step 4 also involves the storage engine (SE). Technically, step 3 is the most important for determining how the query works, even though the physical query plan is available only after the actual execution of a query (step 4). Therefore, it is necessary to wait for the execution of a query before being able to see its physical query plan. However, during the execution of step 4, there are other interesting pieces of information (SE requests) that are easier to read compared to the physical query plan. For this reason, we will see how the analysis of a query often starts from the analysis of the SE requests generated at step 4.

> **Note** Tabular can be queried in both MDX and DAX, even though its natural language is DAX. Nevertheless, the engine does not translate MDX into DAX. MDX queries generate both a logical and a physical query plan just as DAX queries do. Keep in mind that the same query written in DAX or in MDX typically produces different query plans despite returning similar results. Here the focus is on the DAX language; however, the information provided in this chapter is useful to analyze how Tabular handles MDX queries as well.

Collecting query plans

As explained in the previous section, a DAX query generates both a logical and a physical query plan. These plans describe the operations performed by the query engine in detail. Unfortunately, the query plan is only available in textual representation, not graphical visualization. Because of the complexity and length of a typical query plan, other tools and techniques should be used to optimize a DAX expression before starting to analyze the query plan in detail. However, it is important to understand the basics of a DAX query plan in order to both understand the behavior of the engine and quickly spot potential bottlenecks in longer and more complex query plans. We will now describe in greater detail the different parts of a query plan using a simple query. As you will see, even the simplest query produces rather complex plans.

As an example, consider this query executed in DAX Studio:

```
EVALUATE
{ SUM ( Sales[Quantity] ) }
```

The result of the table constructor is a table with one row and one column (*Value*), filled with the sum of the *Quantity* column for all the rows of the *Sales* table, as shown in Figure 19-6.

Value
140180

FIGURE 19-6 The result of a query with a simple table constructor with one row and one column.

The next sections describe the query plans generated and executed by this DAX query. Later on we will see how to obtain this information for any query. At this stage, just focus your attention on the role of the query plans, how they are structured, and the information they provide.

Introducing logical query plans

The logical query plan is a close representation of the DAX query expression tree. Figure 19-7 shows the logical query plan of the previous query.

Line	Logical Query Plan
1	AddColumns: RelLogOp DependOnCols()() 0-0 RequiredCols(0)(''[Value])
2	Sum_Vertipaq: ScaLogOp DependOnCols()() Integer DominantValue=BLANK
3	Scan_Vertipaq: RelLogOp DependOnCols()() 0-110 RequiredCols(86)('Sales'[Quantity])
4	'Sales'[Quantity]: ScaLogOp DependOnCols(86)('Sales'[Quantity]) Integer DominantValue=NONE

FIGURE 19-7 The logical query plan of a simple query.

Each line is an operator, and the following lines, indented, are the parameters of the operator. By ignoring the parameters for each operator for a moment, it is possible to envision a simpler structure:

```
AddColumns:
        Sum_Vertipaq:
                Scan_Vertipaq:
                'Sales'[Quantity]:
```

The outermost operator is *AddColumns*. It creates the one-row table with the *Value* column containing the value returned by the DAX query. The *Sum_VertiPaq* operator scans the *Sales* table and sums the *Sales[Quantity]* column. The two operators included within *Sum_Vertipaq* are *Scan_Vertipaq* and a reference to the scanned column.

This query plan in plain English would be: "Create a table with a column named *Value*, filled with the content of a *SUM* operation, performed by the storage engine by scanning the *Quantity* column in the *Sales* table."

The logical query plan shows what the DAX query engine plans to do in order to compute the results. Not surprisingly, it scans *Sales* summarizing *Quantity* using *SUM*. Clearly, more complex query plans will be harder to decode.

Introducing physical query plans

The physical query plan has a similar format to the logical query plan. Each line is an operator and its parameters are in subsequent lines, indented with one tab. Apart from this aesthetic similarity, the two query plans use completely different operators. Figure 19-8 shows the physical query plan generated by the previous DAX query.

Line	Records	Physical Query Plan
1		AddColumns: IterPhyOp LogOp=AddColumns IterCols(0)([Value])
2		SingletonTable: IterPhyOp LogOp=AddColumns
3	1	SpoolLookup: LookupPhyOp LogOp=Sum_Vertipaq Integer #Records=1 #KeyCo
4	1	ProjectionSpool<ProjectFusion<Copy>>: SpoolPhyOp #Records=1
5		Cache: IterPhyOp #FieldCols=0 #ValueCols=1

FIGURE 19-8 The physical query plan of a simple query.

Again, a simplified version of the query plan is possible by removing the parameters of each operator:

```
AddColumns:
        SingletonTable:
        SpoolLookup: LookupPhyOp
                ProjectionSpool<ProjectFusion<Copy>>: SpoolPhyOp
                        Cache: IterPhyOp
```

The first operator, *AddColumns*, builds the result table. Its first parameter is a *SingletonTable*, which is an operator returning a single-row table generated by the table constructor. The second parameter, *SpoolLookup*, searches for a value in the datacache obtained by a query sent to the storage engine. This is the most intricate part of DAX query plans. The physical query plan shows that it uses some data that was previously spooled by other SE queries, but it does not show exactly from which one. In other words, the code of an SE query cannot be obtained by reading the DAX query plan. It is possible to retrieve the queries sent to the storage engine, but matching them with the exact point in the query plan is only possible in simple DAX queries. In more complex—yet realistic—DAX operations, this association might require a longer analysis.

Before moving forward, it is important to highlight some important information included in the query plan:

```
ProjectionSpool<ProjectionFusion<Copy>>: SpoolPhyOp #Records=1
        Cache: IterPhyOp #FieldCols=0 #ValueCols=1
```

> **Note** In former versions of the Tabular engine that did not support composite models, the *ProjectionSpool* and *Cache* operators were called *AggregationSpool* and *VertiPaqResult*, respectively. Besides some differences in operator names, the structure of the physical query plan did not change much, and the same logic described in this chapter can be applied to older Tabular engines.

The *ProjectionSpool* operator represents a query sent to the storage engine; the next section will describe storage engine requests. The *ProjectionSpool* operator iterates the result of the query, showing the total number of rows iterated in the #Records=1 parameter. The number of records also represents the number of rows returned by the nested *Cache* operator.

The number of records is important for two reasons:

- It provides the size (in rows) of the datacache created by VertiPaq or DirectQuery. A large data-cache consumes more memory at query time and takes more time to scan.

- The iteration performed by *ProjectionSpool* in the formula engine runs in a single thread. When a query is slow and this number is large, it could indicate a bottleneck in the query execution.

Because of the importance of the number of records, DAX Studio reports it in the *Records* column of the query plan. We sometimes refer to the number of records as the *cardinality* of the operator.

Introducing storage engine queries

The previous physical query plan includes a *ProjectionSpool* operator that represents an internal query sent to the storage engine (SE). Because the model is in Import mode, DAX uses the VertiPaq SE, which receives queries in xmSQL. The following is the xmSQL query generated during the execution of the DAX query analyzed in the previous sections:

```
SET DC_KIND="AUTO";
SELECT
SUM ( 'DaxBook Sales'[Quantity] )
FROM 'DaxBook Sales';

'Estimated size ( volume, marshalling bytes ) : 1, 16'
```

The preceding code is a simplified version shown in DAX Studio, which removes a few internal details that are not relevant in performance analysis. The original xmSQL visible in SQL Server Profiler is the following:

```
SET DC_KIND="AUTO";
SELECT
SUM([DaxBook Sales (905)].[Quantity (923)]) AS [$Measure0]
FROM [DaxBook Sales (905)];

[Estimated size (volume, marshalling bytes): 1, 16]
```

This query aggregates all the rows of the *Sales* table, returning a single column with the sum of *Quantity*. The SE executes the entire aggregation operation, returning a small datacache (one row, one column) regardless of the size of the *Sales* table. The materialization required for this datacache is minimal. Moreover, the only data structures read by this query are those storing the *Quantity* column in the *Sales* table. A *Sales* table with hundreds of other columns would not affect the performance of this xmSQL query. The VertiPaq SE only scans columns included in the xmSQL query. If the model had been using DirectQuery, the query generated would have been a SQL query like the following one:

```
SELECT
SUM ( [Quantity] )
FROM Sales
```

Note From here on out, we will not cover the details of query plans using DirectQuery. As discussed in Chapter 17, optimizing DirectQuery requires an optimization of the data source. However, changes to the DAX query can improve the SQL code sent to the DirectQuery data source, so the same techniques for analyzing a query plan described for VertiPaq can also be applied to DirectQuery, even though the assumptions on the speed of the storage engine are no longer valid for DirectQuery.

Later in the chapter we will explain why measuring the execution time of each SE query is an important part of the optimization process. Keep in mind that VertiPaq performance is related to the size of the columns involved in a query, and not only to the number of rows of the table. Different columns can have different compression rates and different sizes in memory, resulting in different scan times.

Capturing profiling information

The previous section introduced the DAX query plans. This section describes the tools to capture these events and how to measure their duration, which are the first steps in DAX optimization.

The DAX engine has grown as part of Microsoft SQL Server Analysis Services. Analysis Services provides trace events that can be captured with the SQL Server Profiler tool or by intercepting extended events (xEvents). Other products such as Power Pivot and Power BI use the same engine, although these products do not have the same tools available as for Analysis Services to capture trace or extended events. For example, Power Pivot for Excel and Power BI Desktop have diagnostic options that save trace events on a file, which can be opened later with the same SQL Server Profiler tool.

However, the events generated by the engine require some massage to be useful for performance analysis; the SQL Server Profiler is a general-purpose tool that is not designed specifically for this task. On the other hand, DAX Studio reads and interprets Analysis Services events, summarizing relevant information in an easier way. This is why we strongly suggest using DAX Studio as a primary tool to edit, test, and optimize DAX queries and expressions. A later section includes a description of SQL Server Profiler, providing more details to the readers interested in understanding the internal details. DAX Studio collects the same events as SQL Server Profiler, processing them and displaying summarized information in a very efficient way.

Using DAX Studio

As explained at the beginning of this chapter, DAX Studio can also capture DAX queries sent to the Tabular engine. Indeed, DAX Studio can execute any valid DAX query, including those captured by DAX Studio itself. The DAX query syntax is explained in Chapter 13, "Authoring queries." DAX Studio collects trace events generated by one or more queries executed from within DAX Studio and displays the relevant information about the query plans and storage engine. DAX Studio can connect to Power BI, Analysis Services, and Power Pivot for Excel.

Before analyzing a query in DAX Studio, we must enable the Query Plan and Server Timings options in the Traces tab of the Home tab, as shown in Figure 19-9.

FIGURE 19-9 The Query Plan and Server Timings options enable the tracing features in DAX Studio.

When the user enables these options, DAX Studio shows the Query Plan and Server Timings panes next to the Output and Results pane, which is visible by default. DAX Studio connects to the DAX engine as if it were a profiler, and it captures the trace events described in the next section. It automatically only filters the events related to the executed query, so we do not have to worry if there are other concurrent users active on the same server.

The Query Plan pane displays the two query plans generated by the query, as shown in Figure 19-10. The physical query plan is in the upper half of the pane, and the logical query plan is in the lower half. The physical query plan is usually the most important to analyze when looking for a performance bottleneck in the formula engine. For this reason, this list also provides a column containing the number of records iterated by a spool operation (which is an iteration performed by the formula engine, usually over a datacache). This way, we can easily recognize which operations iterate over a large number of records in a complex query plan. We will describe how to use this information later in Chapter 20, "Optimizing DAX."

Line	Records	Physical Query Plan
1		AddColumns: IterPhyOp LogOp=AddColumns IterCols(0)(''[Value])
2		SingletonTable: IterPhyOp LogOp=AddColumns
3	1	SpoolLookup: LookupPhyOp LogOp=Sum_Vertipaq Integer #Records=1 #KeyCols=111 #ValueCols=1 DominantValue=BLANK
4	1	ProjectionSpool<ProjectFusion<Copy>>: SpoolPhyOp #Records=1
5		Cache: IterPhyOp #FieldCols=0 #ValueCols=1

Line		Logical Query Plan
1		AddColumns: RelLogOp DependOnCols()() 0-0 RequiredCols(0)(''[Value])
2		Sum_Vertipaq: ScaLogOp DependOnCols()() Integer DominantValue=BLANK
3		Scan_Vertipaq: RelLogOp DependOnCols()() 0-110 RequiredCols(86)('Sales'[Quantity])
4		'Sales'[Quantity]: ScaLogOp DependOnCols(86)('Sales'[Quantity]) Integer DominantValue=NONE

FIGURE 19-10 The Query Plan pane displays the Physical Query Plan and the Logical Query Plan.

The Server Timings pane in Figure 19-11 shows information related to SE queries and how the execution time splits between FE and SE.

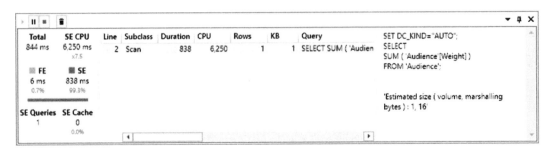

FIGURE 19-11 The Server Timings pane displays a summary of timings information and the details of the storage engine queries.

Note The SE query displayed in Figure 19-11 is applied to a model with 4 billion rows to show high CPU consumption. The model used for this example is not included in the companion files for the book.

The following metrics are found on the left side of the Server Timings pane:

- **Total:** Elapsed time for the complete DAX query. It corresponds to the Duration of the *Query End* event.

- **SE CPU:** Sum of the CPU Time value for all the VertiPaq scan events. It also reports the degree of parallelism of VertiPaq operations (number of cores used in parallel).

- **FE:** Time elapsed in the formula engine, in milliseconds and as a percentage of the Total time.

- **SE:** Time elapsed in the storage engine, in milliseconds and as a percentage of the Total time.

- **SE Queries:** Number of queries sent to the storage engine.

- **SE Cache:** Number of storage engine queries resolved by the storage engine cache, displayed as an absolute number and as a percentage of the SE Queries value.

The list in the center shows the SE queries executed, and the panel on the right side displays the complete code of the SE query selected in the center list. By default, the list includes only one row for each query, hiding the *VertiPaq Scan Internal* and other cache events that are always visible in SQL Server Profiler. We can show/hide these more detailed events by enabling the Cache, Internal, and Batch buttons of the Server Timings group on the Home tab from Figure 19-9. However, these events are usually not necessary in the performance analysis and are thus hidden by default.

A DAX performance analysis usually starts from the results displayed in the Server Timings pane. If the query spent more than 50% of the execution time in FE, then we might analyze the query plans first, looking for the most expensive operations in the FE. Otherwise, when most of the execution time is spent in SE, then we will look for the most expensive SE queries in the center list of the Server Timings pane.

Information provided in the *Duration* and *CPU* columns is helpful to identify performance bottlenecks in a query. Both values are in milliseconds. The *Duration* is the time elapsed between the start and the end of the request made to the SE. The *CPU* column shows the total amount of time consumed by one core. If the *CPU* number is larger than *Duration*, it means that more cores have been used in parallel to complete the operation.

The parallelism of an operation is obtained by dividing *CPU* by *Duration*. When this number is close to the total number of cores in the server, we cannot improve performance by increasing the parallelism. In this example, we used a system with eight cores. Thus, with a parallelism of 7.5, the query has reached the limits of the hardware. A concurrent user would not be able to get optimal performance executing a long-running query and would also slow down other users. In this condition, more cores would improve the speed of the query. In case the parallelism of a query is much smaller than the number of cores available, there would not be any benefit from providing more cores to the Tabular engine.

The parallelism is computed only for SE operations because the FE runs in a single thread. Formula engine operations cannot benefit from parallel execution.

The *Rows* and *KB* columns show the estimated number of rows and size of the result (datacache) provided by each SE query. Because every datacache must be consumed by the FE in a single thread, a datacache with a large cardinality might be responsible for a slow FE operation. Moreover, the size of a datacache represents the memory cost required by the materialization of a set of data in an uncompressed format; indeed, the FE only consumes uncompressed data. The SE cost to create a large datacache is usually caused by the need to allocate and write uncompressed data in memory. Therefore, reducing the need for the materialization of a datacache is important to lower the volume of data exchanged between SE and FE, reducing memory pressure and improving both query performance and scalability.

 Note   The *Rows* and *KB* columns show an estimated value that can sometimes be wrong. The exact number of rows returned by an SE query is available in the physical query plan. It is reported in the *Records* column of the *ProjectionSpool* event consuming a *Cache* element. The exact size of a datacache is not available, but it can be approximated proportionally to the ratio between *Records* in the query plan and the estimated *Rows* of the SE query.

DAX Studio allows sorting of the queries by any column, making it easy to find the most expensive queries when they are sorted by *CPU*, *Duration*, *Rows*, or *KB*, depending on the ongoing investigation. DAX Studio makes finding the bottlenecks in a DAX query more productive. It does not optimize DAX by itself, but it simplifies the optimization task. In the remaining part of the book we will use DAX Studio as a reference. However, the same information could also be obtained by using SQL Server Profiler, which would be more expensive.

Using the SQL Server Profiler

The SQL Server Profiler tool is installed as part of the SQL Server Management environment, which can be freely downloaded from https://docs.microsoft.com/en-us/sql/ssms/download-sql-server-management-studio-ssms. SQL Server Profiler can be connected to an Analysis Services instance and collects all the events related to a DAX query execution. SQL Server Profiler can also load a file containing a trace session produced by the same SQL Server Profiler, or by other services such as Power Pivot for Excel and Power BI Desktop. This section explains how to use SQL Server Profiler in case DAX Studio cannot be used for any reason. However, you can skip this section if DAX Studio is available. We provide it as a reference because it can be interesting to understand the underlying behavior of the events involved in performance analysis.

In order to catch DAX query plans and storage engine queries, it is necessary to configure a new trace session selecting the interesting events for a DAX query. This is shown in Figure 19-12.

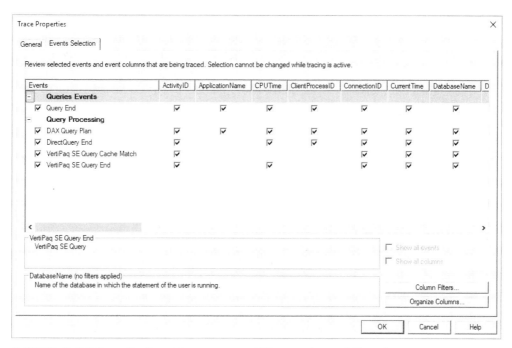

FIGURE 19-12 SQL Server Profiler settings to capture DAX query plans and SE queries.

There are five classes of events required to collect the same information used by DAX Studio:

- **Query End:** Event fired at the end of a query. One might include the *Query Begin* event too, but we suggest only catching *Query End* because it contains the execution time.

- **DAX Query Plan:** Event fired after the query engine has computed the query plan. It contains a textual representation of the query plan. This event class includes two different subclasses, *Logical Plan* and *Physical Plan*. For each query, the engine generates both classes: one logical query plan and one physical query plan.

- **DirectQuery End:** Event fired when the DirectQuery engine answers a query. As with the *Query End* event, to gather timing information we suggest including the end event of the queries executed by the DirectQuery engine.

- **VertiPaq SE Query Cache Match:** Event fired when a VertiPaq query is resolved by looking at the cache data. It is useful in order to see how much of your query performs real computations and how much of it just does cache lookups.

- **VertiPaq SE Query End:** Event fired when the VertiPaq engine answers a query. As with the *Query End* event, to gather timing information, we suggest including the end event of the queries executed by the VertiPaq storage engine.

Tip Once you select the events needed, it is a good idea to organize columns (clicking the Organize Columns button you see in Figure 19-12), and to save a template of the selections made, so you do not have to repeat the same selection every time you start a new session. You can save a trace template by using the File / Templates / New Template menu in SQL Server Profiler.

Note In a production environment, one should filter the events of a single user session. Otherwise, all the events of different queries executed at the same time would be visible, which makes it harder to analyze events related to a single query. By running the Profiler in a development or test environment where there are no other active users, only the events related to the query executed for the performance tests would be visible without any background noise. DAX Studio automatically filters the events related to a single query analyzed, removing any background noise without requiring any further actions.

In order to see the sequence of events fired, we analyze what has happened by running the query used to generate the SE query displayed in Figure 19-11 using DAX Studio over a large table (over 4 billion rows):

```
EVALUATE
ROW ( "Result", SUM ( Audience[Weight] ) )
```

The log window of the SQL Server Profiler shows the result, visible in Figure 19-13.

EventClass	EventSubclass	Duration	CPUTime
DAX Query Plan	1 - DAX VertiPaq Logical Plan		
VertiPaq SE Query End	10 - Internal VertiPaq Scan	837	6250
VertiPaq SE Query End	0 - VertiPaq Scan	838	6250
DAX Query Plan	2 - DAX VertiPaq Physical Plan		
Query End	3 - DAXQuery	844	0

FIGURE 19-13 Trace events captured in a SQL Server Profiler session for a simple DAX query.

Even for such a simple query, the DAX engine fires five different events:

1. A *DAX VertiPaq Logical Plan* event, which is the logical query plan.

2. An *Internal VertiPaq Scan* event, which corresponds to an SE query. There could be more than one internal event (subclass 10) for each *VertiPaq Scan* event (subclass 0).

3. A *VertiPaq Scan* event, which describes a single SE query received by the FE.

4. A DAX *VertiPaq Physical Plan* event, which is the physical query plan.

5. A final *Query End* event, which returns the query duration of the complete DAX query. The CPU time reported by this event should be ignored. It should be close to the time spent in the FE but is not as accurate as the calculation explained later.

All the events show both CPU time and duration, expressed in milliseconds. *CPU Time* is the amount of CPU time consumed to answer the query, whereas *Duration* is the time the user has had to wait for their result. When *Duration* is lower than *CPU Time*, the operation has been executed in parallel on many cores. When *Duration* is greater than *CPU Time*, the operation had to wait for other operations (usually logged in different events) to be completed.

> **Note** The accuracy of the *CPU Time* and *Duration* columns is not very reliable for values lower than 16 milliseconds, and *CPU Time* can be less accurate than that in conditions of high parallelism. Moreover, these timings might depend on other operations in progress on the same server. It is a common practice to run the same test multiple times in order to create an average of the execution time of single operations, especially when one needs accurate numbers. However, if only looking for an order of magnitude, one might just ignore differences under 100 milliseconds.

Considering the sequence of events, the logical query plan precedes all the SE queries (VertiPaq scans), and only after their execution is the physical query plan raised. In other words, the physical query plan is an actual query plan and not an estimated one. Indeed, it contains the number of rows processed by any iteration in the FE, though it does not provide information about the CPU time and duration of each step in the query plan.

Logical and physical query plans do not provide any timing information, which are only available in the other events gathered by the Profiler. Information provided in the *CPU Time* and *Duration* columns is the same shown in *CPU* and *Duration* by DAX Studio for SE queries. However, the calculation of the time spent in the FE displayed in DAX Studio requires some more work using SQL Server Profiler.

The *Query End* event only provides the total elapsed time for a DAX query in the *Duration* column, summing both the FE and SE durations. The *VertiPaq* scan events provide the time spent in the SE. The elapsed time in FE is obtained by subtracting the duration of all the SE queries from the duration of the entire DAX query provided in the *Query End* event.

As shown in Figure 19-13, the *Query End* event had a *Duration* of 844 milliseconds. The time spent in the SE was 838 milliseconds. There was only one SE query, which lasted 838 milliseconds; only consider the VertiPaq *Scan* event, ignoring internal ones. The difference is 6 milliseconds, which is the amount of time spent in the FE. In case of multiple SE queries, their execution time must be aggregated to calculate the total amount of time spent in the SE, which must be subtracted from the total duration to get the amount of time spent in the FE.

Finally, the SQL Server Profiler can save and load a trace session. SQL Server Profiler cannot connect to Power Pivot for Excel, but it can open a trace file saved by Power Pivot for Excel or Power BI Desktop. However, Power Pivot for Excel has an Enable Power Pivot Tracing check box in the Settings dialog box that generates a TRC file; TRC is the extension for trace file. The events captured in the profiler session saved this way cannot be customized; they also usually include more event types than those required to analyze DAX query plans. DAX Studio cannot load a trace session but can connect directly to all the tools including Power Pivot for Excel without any limitation.

Reading VertiPaq storage engine queries

In the previous sections, we described some details of the physical and logical query plans. Although these plans are useful in some scenarios, the most interesting part of a query plan is the set of VertiPaq SE queries.

In this section we describe how to read the VertiPaq SE queries and understand what happens in VertiPaq to execute an xmSQL query. This information is useful to solve a bottleneck in the VertiPaq storage engine. However, reading these queries is useful to also understand what happens in the FE: If a calculation is not performed by the SE, it must be computed in the FE. Because the number of SE queries is usually smaller than the rows in the query plan, it is more productive to always start analyzing the SE queries regardless of the detected bottleneck type.

Introducing xmSQL syntax

In the previous section, we introduced a simple SE query described in a simplified xmSQL syntax, which is the same as displayed by DAX Studio:

```
SELECT
SUM ( Sales[Quantity] )
FROM Sales;
```

This syntax would be quite similar in standard ANSI SQL:

```
SELECT
SUM ( Quantity )
FROM Sales;
```

Every xmSQL query involves a *GROUP BY* condition, even if this is not explicitly stated as part of its syntax. For example, the following DAX query returns the list of unique values of the *Color* column in the *Product* table:

```
EVALUATE VALUES ( 'Product'[Color] )
```

It results in this xmSQL query; note that no *GROUP BY* appears in the query:

```
SELECT Product[Color]
FROM Product;
```

The corresponding query in ANSI SQL would have a *GROUP BY* condition:

```
SELECT Color
FROM Product
GROUP BY Color
```

The reason we compare the xmSQL to an ANSI SQL query with *GROUP BY* instead of *DISTINCT*—which would be possible for the previous example—is that most of the time xmSQL queries also include aggregated calculations. For example, consider the following DAX query:

```
EVALUATE
SUMMARIZECOLUMNS (
    Sales[Order Date],
    "Revenues", CALCULATE ( SUM ( Sales[Quantity] ) )
)
```

This is the corresponding xmSQL query sent to the SE:

```
SELECT Sales[Order Date], SUM ( Sales[Quantity] )
FROM Sales;
```

In ANSI SQL there would be a *GROUP BY* condition for the *Order Date* column:

```
SELECT [Order Date], SUM ( Quantity )
FROM Sales
GROUP BY [Order Date]
```

An xmSQL query never returns duplicated rows. When a DAX query runs over a table that does not have a unique key, the corresponding xmSQL query includes a special *RowNumber* column that keeps the rows unique. However, the *RowNumber* column is not accessible in DAX. For example, consider this DAX query:

```
EVALUATE Sales
```

It generates the following xmSQL code:

```
SELECT Sales[RowNumber], Sales[column1], Sales[column2], ... ,Sales[columnN]
FROM Sales
```

Aggregation functions

xmSQL includes the following aggregation operations:

- *SUM* sums the values of a column.

- *MIN* returns the minimum value of a column.

- *MAX* returns the maximum value of a column.

- *COUNT* counts the number of rows in the current *GROUP BY*.

- *DCOUNT* counts the number of distinct values of a column.

The behavior of *SUM*, *MIN*, *MAX*, and *DCOUNT* is similar. For example, the following DAX query returns the number of unique customers for each order date:

```
EVALUATE
SUMMARIZECOLUMNS (
    Sales[Order Date],
    "Customers",  DISTINCTCOUNT ( Sales[CustomerKey] )
)
```

It generates the following xmSQL code:

```
SELECT Sales[Order Date], DCOUNT ( Sales[CustomerKey] )
FROM Sales;
```

Which corresponds to this ANSI SQL query:

```
SELECT [Order Date], COUNT ( DISTINCT CustomerKey )
FROM Sales
GROUP BY [Order Date]
```

The *COUNT* function does not have an argument. Indeed, it computes the number of rows for the current group. For example, consider the following DAX query that counts the number of products for each color:

```
EVALUATE
SUMMARIZECOLUMNS (
    'Product'[Color],
    "Products", COUNTROWS ( 'Product' )
)
```

This is the xmSQL code sent to the SE:

```
SELECT Product[Color], COUNT ( )
FROM Product;
```

A corresponding ANSI SQL query could be the following:

```
SELECT Color, COUNT ( * )
FROM Product
GROUP BY Color
```

Other aggregation functions in DAX do not have a corresponding xmSQL aggregation function. For example, consider the following DAX query using *AVERAGE*:

```
EVALUATE
SUMMARIZECOLUMNS (
    'Product'[Color],
    "Average Unit Price", AVERAGE ( 'Product'[Unit Price] )
)
```

The corresponding xmSQL code includes two aggregations: one for the numerator and one for the denominator of the division that will compute a simple average in the FE:

```
SELECT Product[Color], SUM ( Product[Unit Price] ), COUNT ( )
FROM Product
WHERE Product[Unit Price] IS NOT NULL;
```

Converting the xmSQL query in ANSI SQL, we would write:

```
SELECT Color, SUM ( [Unit Price] ), COUNT ( * )
FROM Product
WHERE Product[Unit Price] IS NOT NULL
GROUP BY Color
```

Arithmetical operations

xmSQL includes simple arithmetical operations: +, −, *, / (sum, subtraction, multiplication, division). These operations work on single rows, whereas the FE usually performs arithmetical operations between the results of aggregations. It is common to see arithmetical operations in the expression used by an aggregation function. For example, the following DAX query returns the sum of the product of *Quantity* by *Unit Price* calculated row-by-row for the *Sales* table:

```
EVALUATE
{ SUMX ( Sales, Sales[Quantity] * Sales[Unit Price] ) }
```

It generates the following xmSQL code:

```
WITH
    $Expr0 := ( Sales[Quantity] * Sales[Unit Price] )
SELECT
SUM ( @$Expr0 )
FROM Sales;
```

The *WITH* statement introduces expressions associated with symbolic names (starting with the *$Expr* prefix) that are referenced later in the remaining part of the query. For example, in the previous code the *$Expr0* expression corresponds to the multiplication between *Quantity* and *Unit Price* that is later evaluated for each row of the *Sales* table, summing the result in the aggregated value.

The previous xmSQL code corresponds to this ANSI SQL query: .

```
SELECT SUM ( [Quantity] * [Unit Price] )
FROM Sales
```

xmSQL can also execute casts between data types to perform arithmetical operations. It is important to remember that these operations only happen within a row context, from the point of view of a DAX expression.

Filter operations

An xmSQL query can include filters in a *WHERE* condition. The performance of a filter depends on the cardinality of the conditions applied (this will be discussed in more detail later in the section "Understanding scan time").

For example, consider the following query that returns the sum of the *Quantity* column for all sales with a unit price equal to 42:

```
EVALUATE
CALCULATETABLE (
    ROW ( "Result", SUM ( Sales[Quantity] ) ),
    Sales[Unit Price] = 42
)
```

The resulting xmSQL query is the following:

```
SELECT SUM ( Sales[Quantity] )
FROM Sales
WHERE Sales[Unit Price] = 420000;
```

Note   The reason why the value in the *WHERE* condition is multiplied by 10,000 is because the *Unit Price* column is stored as a *Currency* data type (also known as *Fixed Decimal Number* in Power BI). That number is stored as an *Integer* in VertiPaq, so the FE performs the conversion to a decimal number by dividing the result by 10,000. Such division is not visible, neither in the query plan nor in the xmSQL code.

The *WHERE* condition might include a test with more than one value. For example, consider a small variation of the previous query that sums either the quantity or the sales with a unit price equal to 16 or 42. You see this in the following DAX query:

```
EVALUATE
CALCULATETABLE (
    ROW ( "Result", SUM ( Sales[Quantity] ) ),
    OR ( Sales[Unit Price] = 16, Sales[Unit Price] = 42 )
)
```

The xmSQL uses the *IN* operator to include a list of values:

```
SELECT SUM ( Sales[Quantity] )
FROM Sales
WHERE Sales[Unit Price] IN ( 16000, 42000 );
```

Any filter condition in xmSQL only includes existing values of the column. For example, if a DAX condition references a value that does not exist in the column, the resulting xmSQL code will include a condition that will filter out all the rows. For example, if neither 16 nor 42 existed in the *Sales* table, the previous xmSQL query could be not invoked at all from the FE or would become something like:

```
SELECT SUM ( Sales[Quantity] )
FROM Sales
WHERE Sales[Unit Price] IN ( );
```

The result of such an xmSQL query will always be empty.

It is important to remember that xmSQL is a textual representation of an SE query. The actual structure is more optimized. For example, when the list of values allowed for a column is very long, the xmSQL reports a few values, highlighting the total number of values passed internally to the query. This happens quite often for time intelligence functions. For example, consider the following DAX query that returns the sum of the quantity for one year of sales:

```
EVALUATE
CALCULATETABLE (
    ROW ( "Result", SUM ( Sales[Quantity] ) ),
    Sales[Order Date] >= DATE ( 2006, 1, 1 ) && Sales[Order Date] <= DATE ( 2006, 12, 31 )
)
```

Using a recent version of the DAX engine, it generates the following xmSQL query:

```
SELECT SUM ( Sales[Quantity] )
FROM Sales
WHERE Sales[Order Date] >= 38718.000000
  VAND Sales[Order Date] <= 39082.000000
```

DAX represents date and time values as floating-point numbers. For this reason, the comparison of the *Order Date* column happens with two numbers corresponding to the two dates used in the filter argument of the DAX expression.

However, older versions of the DAX engine might produce the following xmSQL query instead:

```
SELECT SUM ( Sales[Quantity] )
FROM Sales
WHERE Sales[Order Date] IN ( 38732.000000, 38883.000000, 38846.000000, 38997.000000,
38809.000000, 38960.000000, 38789.000000, 38923.000000, 39074.000000, 38752.000000..[365
total values, not all displayed] ) ;
```

In this case, instead of a range condition, the xmSQL query has a bitmap index that identifies all the values included in the filter. The *WHERE / IN* condition represents such a bitmap index, only reporting in the xmSQL code a sample of the values followed by the total number of values in the column. In order to obtain the list of values for a range, another xmSQL query might be executed before:

```
SELECT Sales[Order Date]
FROM Sales
WHERE Sales[Order Date] >= 38718.000000
    VAND Sales[Order Date] <= 39082.000000
```

The actual xmSQL query generated in this last example might be more complex, including a callback to the FE to transform the result of the *DATE* function into the corresponding floating-point value. More information about these callbacks is included in the section "Understanding *CallbackDataID*" later in this chapter.

Join operators

The xmSQL code can execute *JOIN* conditions when a DAX query involves multiple tables connected by relationships in the data model. For example, consider the following DAX query returning the sum of the *Quantity* column in the *Sales* table for each *Color* name in the *Product* table:

```
EVALUATE
SUMMARIZECOLUMNS (
    'Product'[Color],
    "Sales",  SUM ( Sales[Quantity] )
)
```

If there is a one-to-many relationship between the *Product* and *Sales* tables in the data model, the corresponding xmSQL code includes a *LEFT OUTER JOIN* between the two tables, as shown in the following SE query:

```
SELECT Product[Color], SUM ( Sales[Quantity] )
FROM Sales
    LEFT OUTER JOIN Product ON Sales[ProductKey] = Product[ProductKey];
```

The *ON* condition of the *JOIN* automatically includes the columns that define the relationship in the data model. For each relationship involved in the query, there is one join in xmSQL.

Temporary tables and shallow relationships in batch events

VertiPaq can execute xmSQL queries whose result is kept in memory for another xmSQL query without being consumed by the FE. This improves the query performance because this temporary result is not materialized for the SE. If the temporary table is used in a different xmSQL operation, there should be a *Batch* operation in the VertiPaq storage engine grouping the different SE queries executed. For example, consider the following DAX query computing the average yearly income of customers that made at least one purchase in the corresponding year:

```
EVALUATE
CALCULATETABLE (
    SUMMARIZECOLUMNS (
        'Date'[Calendar Year],
        "Yearly Income", AVERAGE ( Customer[Yearly Income] )
    ),
    CROSSFILTER ( Sales[CustomerKey], Customer[CustomerKey], BOTH )
)
```

The presence of the bidirectional filter between the *Sales* and *Customer* tables activates a special behavior of the SE, which generates a query executed in different steps of a *Batch* statement. In DAX Studio, the *Batch* event is hidden by default, but it can be activated to see the *Batch* event after one or more *Scan* events. This is shown in Figure 19-14.

Line	Subclass	Duration	CPU	Rows	KB	Query
2	Scan	3	0	14,228	56	DEFINE TABLE '$TTable3' := SELEC
4	Scan	0	0	18,880	3	DEFINE TABLE '$TTable4' := SELEC
6	Scan	5	0	3	1	DEFINE TABLE '$TTable1' := SELEC
7	Batch	9	0			DEFINE TABLE '$TTable3' := SELEC

FIGURE 19-14 SE events captured in DAX Studio enabling the Batch filter in Server Timings.

The *Batch* reported at line 7 includes all the *Scan* events reported in lines 2, 4, and 6. The SE query of each *Scan* event is separated by a comma, but the *Batch* event could have additional statements like the one highlighted in the complete code of the *Batch* event that follows. The *CREATE SHALLOW RELATION* statement implements the behavior of the bidirectional filter at the SE level, optimizing the execution of a DAX query involving one or more bidirectional filters:

```
--
-- This query is also the first Scan event processed
--
DEFINE TABLE '$TTable3' :=
SELECT
    Customer[CustomerKey], Date[Calendar Year]
FROM Sales
    LEFT OUTER JOIN Customer
        ON Sales[CustomerKey]=Customer[CustomerKey]
    LEFT OUTER JOIN Date
        ON Sales[OrderDateKey]=Date[DateKey],


--
-- This directive does not generate any Scan event
--
CREATE SHALLOW RELATION '$TRelation1' MANYTOMANY
    FROM Customer[CustomerKey] TO '$TTable3'[Customer$CustomerKey],


--
-- This query is the second Scan event processed
--
DEFINE TABLE '$TTable4' :=
SELECT
    SIMPLEINDEXN ( '$TTable3'[Customer$CustomerKey] )
FROM '$TTable3',


--
-- This query is the third and last Scan event processed for this batch
--
DEFINE TABLE '$TTable1' :=
```

```
SELECT
    '$TTable3'[Date$Calendar Year],
    SUM ( '$TTable2'[$Measure0] ), SUM ( '$TTable2'[$Measure1] )
FROM '$TTable2'
    INNER JOIN '$TTable3'
        ON '$TTable2'[Customer$CustomerKey]='$TTable3'[Customer$CustomerKey]

REDUCED BY

'$TTable2' :=
SELECT
    Customer[CustomerKey],
    SUM ( Customer[Yearly Income] ),
    SUM ( ( PFDATAID ( Customer[Yearly Income] ) <> 2 ) )
FROM Customer
WHERE
Customer[CustomerKey] ININDEX '$TTable4'[$Index1];
```

Only the last *DEFINE TABLE* statement in a batch generates a result returned to the FE, correspond-ing to the *$TTable2* query. All the previous *DEFINE TABLE* statements generate temporary tables used later within the same batch. It is worth noting that the last query starts from *DEFINE TABLE $TTable1* and ends at the end of the batch, including the *REDUCED BY* clause. *REDUCED BY* is a syntax defining a subquery within the same SE request rather than requiring a separate SE query executed within the same batch, like *$TTable3* and *$TTable4* in this batch. The result of a temporary table defined within *DEFINE TABLE* before the last one in the batch could contain binary information that is never returned as a DAX result. For example, the *SIMPLEINDEXN* function generates an index structure, so that a following query can use that index to apply a filter to a column through the *ININDEX* operator. These temporary tables are not returned to the FE; they are only kept in the SE with an efficient structure used only to improve the internal evaluation of other SE queries.

Understanding scan time

After having described the syntax of xmSQL queries, it is time to consider the work performed by the storage engine to execute such statements.

VertiPaq performs a complete scan of each column involved in an SE query. There could be more iterations for a column, depending on the request. Because there are no indexes, the time required to complete a scan depends on the memory footprint of the column, which depends on the number of unique values in the column, on their distribution across the rows, and on the number of rows in the table. The importance of these factors depends on the aggregation function used in the xmSQL query. For example, consider a large table with four columns: *Date*, *Time*, *Age*, and *Score*. The table has 4 billion rows, so that we can observe relevant differences in execution time. We executed the following DAX queries for each column:

```
EVALUATE
ROW ( "Sum", SUM ( Example[<column name>] ) )

EVALUATE
ROW (
    "Distinct Count",
    CALCULATE (
        DISTINCTCOUNT ( Example[<column name>] ),
        NOT ISBLANK ( Example[<column name>] )
    )
)
```

> **Note** The second query includes a *NOT ISBLANK* condition that is required to obtain an SE query to execute the query. If the query did not have a filter, the number of distinct values in a column would have been retrieved from the metadata of the model, without actually executing any SE request.

We are not interested in the values returned by these queries. We are only interested in the time spent in the SE, which for these simple queries is always close to the entire execution time of the DAX queries. Table 19-1 shows the results where we reported, for each column:

- **Memory (MB):** The memory footprint of the column for the entire table (4 billion rows).

- **Distinct Values:** The number of unique values in the column, obtained by executing the *DISTINCTCOUNT* aggregation function in DAX.

- **SUM (ms):** The execution time of the query that applies the *SUM* aggregation to the column.

- **DISTINCTCOUNT (ms):** The execution time of the query that applies the *DISTINCTCOUNT* aggregation to the column.

TABLE 19-1 Column size, cardinality, and execution time of aggregation functions

Column	Memory (MB)	Distinct Values	SUM (ms)	DISTINCTCOUNT (ms)
Date	0.03	1,588	9	20
Age	165.26	96	146	333
Score	2,648.40	9,766,664	837	**4,288**
Time	6,493.57	1,439	**1,330**	4,102

At first sight, a few results might appear counterintuitive. Usually, the larger the number of unique values in a column, the slower the query. In this case, *Date* is faster than *Age*, which has a smaller number of unique values. Moreover, the *Time* column, which has a cardinality similar to *Date*, has a difference in performance of at least one order of magnitude compared to *Date*. The reasons for these differences are the different compression rates, derived by different sort orders of the columns.

The *Date* column always has the faster execution time. This is because the 4 billion rows have been processed as reading rows sorted by date. Even without partitioning, this created segments with one or two unique values each. Thus, all the rows in each segment had a very high compression rate, as is made clear by the memory used by the *Date* column.

The *Age* column has the second-best performance for both *SUM* and *DISTINCTCOUNT*. This column has a larger memory footprint than *Date* because there are different *Age* values for each *Date*, and rows are sorted by *Date* first.

The *Score* and *Time* columns have a slower performance. The performance of *SUM* depends mainly on the memory footprint, whereas *DISTINCTCOUNT* is also sensitive to the number of distinct values in the column. The reason for that is the different calculation algorithm used for these two aggregations.

The important concept here is that we can obtain a different performance for an SE query depending on the memory footprint of a column. We can optimize a VertiPaq SE query by reducing the memory footprint of the columns used. We can obtain that by using columns with a smaller number of unique values, or with a different sort order of the data source, or by reducing the number of rows in the table, or by applying other techniques that we will describe in the remaining part of this book.

Understanding *DISTINCTCOUNT* internals

The use of the *DISTINCTCOUNT* function in a DAX expression generates multiple *VertiPaq Scan Internal* events for a single *VertiPaq Scan* event. We can see internal events by enabling the Internal button in the Server Timings group of DAX Studio.

Consider the following DAX query:

```
EVALUATE
ROW (
    "Distinct Count",
    CALCULATE (
        DISTINCTCOUNT ( Example[Score] ),
        Example[Score] <> 0
    )
)
```

Table 19-2 shows the complete list of *VertiPaq Scan* events generated by the preceding query.

TABLE 19-2 *VertiPaq Scan* events for a DAX query with a *DISTINCTCOUNT* measure

Line	Subclass	Duration	CPU	Query
1	Internal	4,269	31,641	SELECT Example[Score] FROM Example;
2	Internal	4,269	31,641	SELECT Example[Score] FROM Example;
3	Internal	19	31,766	SELECT COUNT( ) FROM $DCOUNT_DATACACHE;
4	Scan	4,288	31,766	SELECT DCOUNT (Example[Score]) FROM Example;

The last line includes the SE query requested by the FE. However, internally the query is split into two subqueries. The first result is duplicated in two identical rows (see the content of the *Duration* and *CPU* columns). The following is the xmSQL code of the first internal subquery, which retrieves the list of unique values in the *Score* column of the *Example* table:

```
SELECT Example[Score]
FROM Example
WHERE Example[Score] <> 0;
```

The result of this SE query is a list of the unique values in the *Score* column of the *Example* table. The next step is to count how many rows are in this list. In other words, counting the rows returned by the internal query provides the correct result to the original query. This particular xmSQL query just references a special table named *$DCOUNT_DATACACHE*, which references the previous result from an SE query:

```
SELECT COUNT ( )
FROM $DCOUNT_DATACACHE;
```

Table 19-2 also shows that the duration of the *Scan* event corresponds to the sum of the duration of the two internal events, although the duplicated event only counts once. Regarding the *CPU Time*, it is always the same in all the events of the same query. The parallelism ratio you can evaluate by dividing *CPU Time* by *Duration* is around seven, which means that up to eight threads in parallel were executed. The next section presents a deeper discussion about parallelism within an SE query.

Understanding parallelism and datacache

Every SE query described by an xmSQL statement returns a result called a datacache, which is a single uncompressed table in memory. The result of an SE query can be completely materialized in memory, or its rows can be consumed during the iteration without them persisting. Usually, we refer to a datacache when this result is materialized, which is the case most of the time in complex queries.

The execution of the SE query can be parallelized among many cores, using different execution threads. The number of threads used depends on the hardware and on the physical structure of the columns involved in the query. The VertiPaq engine assigns one thread to each segment involved in a single scan operation as described in the section, "Understanding segmentation and partitioning" in Chapter 17. When the operation runs on multiple threads, every thread creates a partial result. Only when all the threads complete their execution will VertiPaq consolidate these results into a single final datacache. The FE will then consume the datacache in a single thread. It is also for this reason that the result of an SE query requires such a consolidation. You can see the parallel processing and consolidation behavior described in a schema in Figure 19-15.

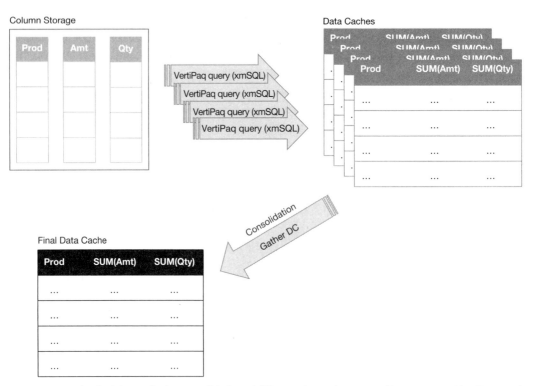

FIGURE 19-15 The final datacache is a consolidation of different datacaches created by concurrent VertiPaq queries when the engine parallelizes execution.

A segment should not be too small because the consolidation process requires time. The efficiency of running scan operations in multiple threads should balance the overhead of the consolidation, but this is not possible if the segments are too small. As a side effect, VertiPaq operations on small tables cannot get the benefits of multiple cores: The consolidation process would be more expensive than the gain provided by the parallelization of small tables.

It is useful to remember that the SE query only provides data to the FE. In a simple scenario, we have the following steps:

1. The SE receives an xmSQL query.

2. The SE executes the scan operations potentially on many threads, creating one datacache per thread.

3. The SE consolidates the different datacaches into a single, final datacache.

4. The FE consumes the datacache in a single thread.

5. The FE can use the same datacache in different steps of the query plan.

In the Profiler, you will always see the SE events before the query plan. The physical query plan always appears at the end of the events related to a query. The logical query plan can be preceded by a few SE queries. When this is the case, it is because the DAX engine itself sends queries to retrieve information about the size and density of columns. The DAX engine uses this information to create a better query plan. Using DAX Studio, you cannot see such a behavior because this tool shows query plans and SE queries in different parts of the user interface.

Understanding the VertiPaq cache

The DAX formula engine does not have a cache, whereas the VertiPaq storage engine has one: the VertiPaq cache. Its primary goal is to improve the performance of multiple requests of the same datacache within the same query. Its secondary goal is to improve the performance of different DAX queries requesting the same datacache. It is important to understand the goals of the VertiPaq cache in order to analyze its behavior and evaluate its efficiency.

For example, consider the following DAX query:

```
EVALUATE
ADDCOLUMNS (
    VALUES ( Example[Date] ),
    "A", CALCULATE ( SUM ( Example[Amt] ) ),
    "Q", CALCULATE ( SUM ( Example[Qty] ) )
)
```

The result of the query includes two columns, *A* and *Q*, summing the *Amt* and *Qty* columns of the *Example* table for each *Date*. We are going to run the query twice, analyzing the different execution time of the two runs. Table 19-3 shows the sequence of *Scan* events for the first execution, enabling both *Cache* and *Internal* events in DAX Studio.

TABLE 19-3 *VertiPaq* events for the first execution of a DAX query with two aggregations

Line	Subclass	Duration	CPU	Query
1	Internal	1,796	13,516	SELECT Example[Date], SUM (Example[Amt]), SUM (Example[Qty]), COUNT () FROM Example;
2	Scan	1,796	13,516	SELECT Example[Date], SUM (Example[Amt]), SUM (Example[Qty]), COUNT () FROM Example;
3	Internal	6	31	SELECT Example[Date], COUNT () FROM Example;
4	Scan	6	31	SELECT Example[Date] FROM Example;

The second execution of the same query produces a different result because the second execution can benefit from the VertiPaq cache of the first run. This result is visible in Table 19-4.

TABLE 19-4 *VertiPaq* events for the second execution of a DAX query with two aggregations

Line	Subclass	Duration	CPU	Query
1	Cache	0	0	SELECT Example[Date], SUM (Example[Amt]), SUM (Example[Qty]), COUNT ( ) FROM Example;
2	Scan	0	0	SELECT Example[Date], SUM (Example[Amt]), SUM (Example[Qty]), COUNT ( ) FROM Example;
3	Cache	0	0	SELECT Example[Date], COUNT ( ) FROM Example;
4	Scan	0	0	SELECT Example[Date] FROM Example;

The duration of the second execution is zero milliseconds. The reason is that the second time the query was run, a datacache containing the required data was already available in the VertiPaq cache. Therefore, the engine did not execute any VertiPaq query; instead it simply retrieved the result from the cache.

The *Cache* and *Internal* events are disabled by default in DAX Studio, so the typical result visible when hitting the cache for SE queries is shown in Table 19-5. The only visible events are the *Scan* events, with a duration of 0 milliseconds.

TABLE 19-5 *VertiPaq Scan* events visible for a DAX query with two aggregations

Line	Subclass	Duration	CPU	Query
2	Scan	0	0	SELECT Example[Date], SUM (Example[Amt]), SUM (Example[Qty]), COUNT ( ) FROM Example;
4	Scan	0	0	SELECT Example[Date] FROM Example;

The VertiPaq engine only reuses data in cache when the cardinality is the same and the columns are a subset of a previous query. This algorithm is very simple because the lookup in the VertiPaq cache must not be an overhead of the memory scan operation that it is trying to avoid. For this reason, the VertiPaq cache only keeps in memory a limited number of datacaches. Therefore, there is no guarantee that a request will hit the cache, even when the query plan repeats the same storage query multiple times within the same DAX query. Nevertheless, in most conditions the VertiPaq cache satisfies several of the requests that occur within a short period.

> **Note** VertiPaq ignores row-level security settings. The DAX formula engine manages the role-based security and generates different VertiPaq storage engine queries depending on security settings and user credentials. For this reason, the VertiPaq cache is a global resource and shares the results between different users and sessions. The FE guarantees the correctness of the result, generating different SE queries depending on the requirements.

When analyzing performance, it is important to clear the cache before running a query. In order to find bottlenecks and areas of improvement for a query plan, it is better to observe the time required to complete a scan in memory, simulating the worst-case scenario (empty cache). Because of the reduced size of the VertiPaq cache, missing the cache is a frequent event on a busy server with many concurrent users running queries.

DAX Studio provides two techniques to clear the cache before executing a query:

- Clicking the Clear Cache button on the Home tab to clear the cache on the DAX engine before executing a query with the Run Query button.

- Selecting the Clear Cache then Run button on the Home tab so that the cache gets cleared before each Run execution.

The Run and Clear Cache then Run buttons are shown in Figure 19-16.

FIGURE 19-16 The Home tab in DAX Studio has several options to clear the cache of the DAX engine.

DAX Studio internally sends a clear cache command to the DAX engine using the following XMLA command, which removes the cache of results related to the specified database. This example clears the cache of the Contoso database:

```
<ClearCache xmlns="http://schemas.microsoft.com/analysisservices/2003/engine">
```

```
    <Object>
        <DatabaseID>Contoso</DatabaseID>
    </Object>
</ClearCache>
```

Understanding *CallbackDataID*

The VertiPaq SE only supports a limited set of operators and functions in xmSQL. Thus, it is up to the FE to execute any operation not directly supported by the SE. However, when a complex calculation is required within a VertiPaq iterator, the SE may call the FE using a special xmSQL function called *CallbackDataID*.

The operators supported in xmSQL include the basic mathematical operations (sum, subtraction, multiplication, and division) but do not include mathematical functions such as square root (*SQRT* in DAX), or conditional logic such as the *IF* function. If you include an expression that is not supported by xmSQL in an iterator, then the query plan generates an xmSQL query containing a special function: *CallbackDataID*. During the iteration, the SE calls the FE for every row, passing the DAX expression and the values of its members as arguments.

For example, consider the sum of rounded values in this DAX query:

```
EVALUATE
ROW (
    "Result", SUMX ( Sales, ROUND ( Sales[Line Amount], 0 ) )
)
```

In this expression, the SE cannot evaluate the *ROUND* function. Therefore, the query plan generates the following xmSQL statement:

```
WITH
    $Expr0 := [CallbackDataID ( ROUND ( Sales[Line Amount]] ), 0 ) ]
                ( PFDATAID ( Sales[Line Amount] ) )
SELECT
    SUM ( @$Expr0 )
FROM Sales;
```

The *CallbackDataID* function contains the DAX expression that rounds a value to the closest integer. This expression is evaluated for the *Line Amount* column in the *Sales* table for the current row. The *PFDATAID* syntax is not relevant for analyzing the logic we are describing now. The SE calls the *CallbackDataID* function for each row of the *Sales* table. The result of the xmSQL query is a datacache with only one row, corresponding to the aggregated result. Even though the FE is single threaded, when the SE calls the FE through a *CallbackDataID*, the parallelism of the SE is not affected. Indeed, there could be multiple instances of the FE executed in parallel, one for each thread of the SE.

Parallelism of *CallbackDataID* and possible alternatives

In order to understand how the parallelism interacts with *CallbackDataID* and the associated cost, consider what could happen if the *CallbackDataID* were not available. We might have a query plan requesting a datacache with the value of the *Line Amount* column for all the rows of the *Sales* table, using an xmSQL query such as the following:

```
SELECT
    Sales[Line Amount], COUNT( )
FROM Sales;
```

The datacache obtained by the FE would contain one row for each unique value of the *Line Amount* column and the number of rows having this value in the *Sales* table (returned by *COUNT*). Using this information, the FE would apply the *ROUND* function to the value of *Line Amount* for each row of the datacache, multiplying that result by the number of occurrences of the *Line Amount* value in the *Sales* table. The result provided by the FE would be identical, but the SE should create a much larger datacache than the one-row datacache obtained by the xmSQL query with the *CallbackDataID*. Remember that the SE often materializes the entire datacache in memory, and that this would be in an uncompressed format. Then the FE would iterate this datacache sequentially in a single thread. This would result in poor performance and a larger memory consumption.

The execution using *CallbackDataID* is less expensive in terms of memory (the datacache materialized only has one row) and is more scalable. If the *VertiPaq Scan* operation spans on multiple threads, calls made to the FE through *CallbackDataID* use a thread instance of the FE. In other words, we can imagine that every running thread has its own instance of the FE—even within the same query. The only sequential operation is the consolidation made by the SE on the datacaches created by the running threads. However, this operation will be very fast because it consolidates different datacaches only containing one column each.

From a performance point of view, *CallbackDataID* has three other implications:

- Expressions solved through *CallbackDataID* calls are more expensive than expressions solved by internal operators of the SE. There is an **overhead associated with each call to** *CallbackDataID*.

- In a trace session, **a *VertiPaq SE* event includes the time spent in the FE by a *CallbackDataID* call**. Consider that optimizing an SE query that has a long execution time might require you to reduce or to remove the calls to *CallbackDataID* made by xmSQL queries.

- The **SE cache does not save datacaches** produced by an xmSQL query **containing *CallbackDataID* calls**. Therefore, the presence of *CallbackDataID* in an xmSQL function should be carefully evaluated when the storage executes it in an iteration.

> **Important** The FE is single-threaded, but when the SE calls the FE through *CallbackDataID*, the execution of the code in the FE is parallelized through the several threads created by the SE. The parallelism provided by this technique reduces overall *Duration*, but *CPU Time* might increase because of the *CallbackDataID* calls overhead.

In order to understand the performance impact of *CallbackDataID*, consider the following DAX query that sums the result of a division made row by row:

```
EVALUATE
{
    SUMX (
        Example,
        IF (
            Example[Denominator] <> 0,
            Example[Numerator] / Example[Denominator]
        )
    )
}
```

The *IF* function avoids a calculation error in case one row contains a zero value in the denominator column. The xmSQL query sent to the SE is similar to the following one:

```
WITH
    $Expr0 := [CallbackDataID (
        IF (
            Example[Denominator] <> 0,
            Example[Numerator] / Example[Denominator]
        ) ]
        ( PFDATAID ( Example[Numerator] ), PFDATAID ( Example[Denominator] ) ) )
SELECT
    SUM ( @$Expr0 )
FROM Example;
```

We executed a corresponding DAX query on our *Example* table with 4 billion rows, obtaining the SE events shown in Table 19-6.

TABLE 19-6 *VertiPaq Scan* events with a *CallbackDataID* including an *IF* function in DAX

Line	Subclass	Duration	CPU	Rows	Query
1	Internal	8,379	64,234	1	WITH $Expr0 := [**CallbackDataID** (IF (Example[Denominator] <> 0, ...
2	Scan	8,379	64,234	1	WITH $Expr0 := [**CallbackDataID** (IF (Example[Denominator] <> 0, ...

The parallelism ratio (*CPU Time* divided by *Duration*) is close to eight because we used a server with eight cores. The important point is that different threads executed parallel calls to the FE. In previous chapters, we have seen that in DAX the *DIVIDE* function can replace the specific *IF* condition used to check whether the denominator of a division is equal to zero. We can see what happens if we use *DIVIDE* instead of *IF* in this example. The DAX query is the following:

```
EVALUATE
{
    SUMX (
        Example,
        DIVIDE ( Example[Numerator], Example[Denominator] )
    )
}
```

The *DIVIDE* function does not have a corresponding syntax in xmSQL, so we have a *CallbackDataID* in the corresponding xmSQL query sent to the engines in this case too:

```
WITH
    $Expr0 := [CallbackDataID (
        DIVIDE ( Example[Numerator], Example[Denominator] ) ]
        ( PFDATAID ( Example[Numerator] ), PFDATAID ( Example[Denominator] ) )
SELECT
    SUM ( @$Expr0 )
FROM Example;
```

Table 19-7 shows the SE events obtained from running the query over the same 4-billion-row table used in the previous example.

TABLE 19-7 *VertiPaq Scan* events with a *CallbackDataID* including a *DIVIDE* function in DAX

Line	Subclass	Duration	CPU	Rows	Query
1	Internal	6,790	51,984	1	WITH $Expr0 := [**CallbackDataID** (IF (Example[Denominator] <> 0, ...
2	Scan	6,790	51,984	1	WITH $Expr0 := [**CallbackDataID** (IF (Example[Denominator] <> 0, ...

Using *DIVIDE* instead of *IF*, we obtained a 19% performance improvement in both *Duration* and *CPU Time*. However, despite the parallelism achieved with this technique, the overhead of *CallbackDataID* is still high because the SE calls a function in the FE. If we remove the *CallbackDataID* completely, this overhead disappears. In this case, this is possible by simply applying a filter so that the iteration ignores rows containing zero in the *Denominator* column. This is possible with the following DAX query:

```
EVALUATE
{
    CALCULATE (
        SUMX (
            Example,
            Example[Numerator] / Example[Denominator]
        ),
        Example[Denominator] <> 0
    )
}
```

The corresponding syntax in xmSQL for this entire DAX expression does not use *CallbackDataID*:

```
WITH
    $Expr0 := Example[Numerator] / Example[Denominator]
SELECT
    SUM ( @$Expr0 )
FROM Example
WHERE Example[Denominator] <> 0;
```

The resulting SE events shown in Table 19-8 demonstrate an improvement of more than 50% compared to the performance of the *DIVIDE* version.

TABLE 19-8 *VertiPaq Scan* events without *CallbackDataID* to execute a safe division in DAX

Line	Subclass	Duration	CPU	Rows	Query
1	Internal	3,108	23,859	1	WITH $Expr0 := Example[Numerator] / Example[Denominator], ...
2	Scan	3,108	23,859	1	WITH $Expr0 := Example[Numerator] / Example[Denominator], ...

This last version also offers another advantage by avoiding the use of *CallbackDataID*. The VertiPaq cache now keeps the datacache for future executions, which is not possible when the xmSQL query includes a *CallbackDataID*. If we execute the last DAX query twice, the second execution produces the events shown in Table 19-9.

TABLE 19-9 *VertiPaq Scan* events without *CallbackDataID* hitting the SE cache

Line	Subclass	Duration	CPU	Rows	Query
1	Cache	0	0	1	WITH $Expr0 := Example[Numerator] / Example[Denominator], ...
2	Scan	0	0	1	WITH $Expr0 := Example[Numerator] / Example[Denominator], ...

In general, a careful developer should avoid or at least reduce to a minimum the number of calls to *CallbackDataID* made by the SE. We will show some examples of this optimization in Chapter 20.

Profiler limitations for *CallbackDataID* in Analysis Services 2012/2014

There are important limitations in profiler events generated by Analysis Services 2012 and 2014 when the xmSQL query includes *CallbackDataID*. The internal DAX expression passed to *CallbackDataID* might include subquery statements in DAX generating further requests to the SE. Unfortunately, versions of Analysis Services released before 2015 only provide information about these subqueries in the logical query plan. The physical query plan does not include the subexpression included within *CallbackDataID*. The SE queries executed to evaluate these subexpressions do not fire any event visible in the profiler. Analysis Services, Excel, and Power BI Desktop versions released since 2016 do not have this problem.

Reading DirectQuery storage engine queries

This section describes how to read the DirectQuery SE queries. These queries are expressed in the SQL language accepted by the data source. It is advisable to read the previous section about VertiPaq storage engine queries before reading this section to understand the similarities and differences between the two.

For example, consider the following DAX query:

```
EVALUATE
SUMMARIZECOLUMNS (
    Sales[Order Date],
    "Total Quantity", SUM ( Sales[Quantity] )
)
```

When executed in a DirectQuery model, the DAX engine generates a single SE query sent to the data source in SQL language, like the following one:

```
SELECT
    TOP (1000001) [t4].[Order Date],
    SUM ( CAST ( [t4].[Quantity] as BIGINT ) ) AS [a0]
FROM (
    select [StoreKey],
           [ProductKey],
           ... // other columns of the tables omitted here
    from [dbo].[Sales] as [$Table]
) AS [t4]
GROUP BY [t4].[Order Date]
```

The presence of a *TOP* condition limits the number of rows transferred from the data source to the DAX engine. If the number of rows returned is identical to the parameter of the *TOP* condition, then the DAX query fails because it is not able to retrieve the full set of data from the data source. For this reason the argument of *TOPN* is 1,000,001 when the limit of rows accepted by DirectQuery is 1,000,000. This limit avoids the consumption of too much memory because the entire result of the SE query should be loaded in memory in an uncompressed way after being transferred from the data source to the DAX engine.

 Note   The limit or rows accepted in a storage engine request using DirectQuery is 1,000,000 by default. This number can be modified in the *MaxIntermediateRowsetSize* configuration setting available in Analysis Services but not in Power BI. More details about this behavior are available in the article at https://www.sqlbi.com/articles/tuning-query-limits-for-directquery/.

Figure 19-17 shows an example of the information retrieved for SQL SE queries sent to a DirectQuery data source. The *Duration* column shows the time in milliseconds spent waiting for the data source to provide the result of the SQL query. The *CPU* is usually a low number, if not 0, because it should report the cost to the DirectQuery engine to retrieve the result, but it ignores the effective cost on the data source. In order to evaluate the actual *CPU* consumption on the data source, it is necessary to analyze the query running on the data source engine—for example, by using SQL Server Profiler for Microsoft SQL Server databases.

Total	SE CPU	Line	Subclass	Duration	CPU	Rows	KB	Query
3,140 ms	0 ms	1	SQL	3,132	0			SELECT TOP (1000001) [t
	x0.0							

FE	SE
8 ms	3,132 ms
0.3%	99.7%

SE Queries	SE Cache
1	0
	0.0%

FIGURE 19-17 DirectQuery SE queries are displayed as SQL queries.

The SQL event in Figure 19-17 does not have any information for the columns *Rows* and *KB*; indeed, the *SQL* events do not have an estimate of the result in terms of rows and memory as it happens for xmSQL queries sent to VertiPaq.

Finally, the result of a DirectQuery SE query is never persisted in the storage engine cache, therefore, the *SE Cache* counter is always zero for a DirectQuery data model.

Analyzing composite models

In a composite model the same DAX query can generate a mix of VertiPaq and DirectQuery SE queries. For example, consider the following DAX query executed in a model where the *Sales* table has a Direct-Query storage mode and all the other tables have a Dual storage mode:

```
EVALUATE
ADDCOLUMNS (
    VALUES ( 'Date'[Calendar Year] ),
    "Quantity", CALCULATE ( SUM ( Sales[Quantity] ) )
)
```

The *ADDCOLUMNS* function usually generates at least two SE queries: one for the *VALUES* function and the other to compute the sum of sales quantity by calendar year. The screenshot in Figure 19-18 shows two storage queries of different types, indeed.

Total	SE CPU	Line	Subclass	Duration	CPU	Rows	KB	Query
3,271 ms	0 ms	1	SQL	3,264	0			SELECT TOP (1000001) [t1]
	x0.0	3	Scan	0	0	10	1	SELECT 'Date'[Calendar Yea

FE	SE
7 ms	3,264 ms
0.2%	99.8%

SE Queries	SE Cache
2	0
	0.0%

FIGURE 19-18 DirectQuery SE are displayed as SQL queries.

The sum of quantity by calendar year requires that a SQL query (displayed at line 1) be sent to the DirectQuery data source. The list of *Calendar Year* names requested by *VALUES* is provided by the xmSQL VertiPaq SE query at line 3.

When analyzing a composite model, pay attention to the *Subclass* column that identifies the type of SE used. SQL always corresponds to a DirectQuery data source, which is usually slower than VertiPaq and can be optimized by using aggregations. This is described in the next section.

Using aggregations in the data model

As described in Chapter 18, "Optimizing VertiPaq," the presence of aggregations in a data model can improve the performance of the SE query. Aggregations can be defined in both VertiPaq and Direct-Query, providing alternative ways to execute an SE query. When there are aggregations available, the engine tries to rewrite an original SE query into a different one using an aggregation. This rewriting attempt is successful when there is a compatible aggregation. Whenever the rewriting attempt fails because of the lack of a compatible aggregation, the engine executes the original SE query.

DAX Studio can show the rewriting attempts to match an aggregation. These details might be useful to understand why an existing aggregation is not used when this was expected. For example, consider the following query executed in a composite model:

```
EVALUATE
SUMMARIZECOLUMNS (
    'Date'[Calendar Year],
    "Qty", SUM ( Sales[Quantity] ),
    "Qty Red", CALCULATE (
        SUM ( Sales[Quantity] ),
        'Product'[Color] = "Red"
    )
)
```

The model has an aggregation for the *Sales* table with the granularity of *Date* and *Customer*. The query computes two expressions for each calendar year: *Qty* is the sum of the quantity for all the orders made in the reported year, and *Qty Red* is the quantity for the orders of red products made in the same year. The screenshot in Figure 19-19 shows the SE queries reported by DAX Studio executing the preceding DAX query.

Total	SE CPU	Line	Subclass	Duration	CPU	Rows	KB	Query
2.366 ms	16 ms	1	RewriteAttempted	0				\<matchFound>
	x0.0	3	Scan	1	0	10	1	SELECT 'Date'[Calendar Year], SU
▓ FE	▓ SE	4	RewriteAttempted	0				\<attemptedFailed>
12 ms	2.354 ms	5	SQL	2.353	16			SELECT TOP (1000001) [t1].[Cal
0.5%	99.5%							
SE Queries	SE Cache							
2	0							
	0.0%							

FIGURE 19-19 Use of aggregations reported by *RewriteAttempted* events in DAX Studio.

There are two *RewriteAttempted* subclass events describing the evaluation made by the DAX engine before generating the SE query. The *Qty* calculation requires a filter by year; this request is compatible with the existing aggregation (which groups by *Date* and *Customer*). This is reported in Line 1 and the details about the match found are reported in the details of the event shown in Figure 19-20.

FIGURE 19-20 A matching aggregation reports the use of aggregations reported by *RewriteAttempted* events in DAX Studio.

Because the aggregation is a table imported in memory, the engine generates the following VertiPaq SE query reported at Line 3 in Figure 19-19:

```
SELECT
    'Date'[Calendar Year],
    SUM ( 'Sales_Agg'[Quantity] )
FROM 'Sales_Agg'
    LEFT OUTER JOIN 'Date' ON 'Sales_Agg'[Order Date]='Date'[Date];
```

The *RewriteAttempted* event at line 4 in Figure 19-19 does not find a matching aggregation for the *Qty Red* calculation, which requires a filter by *Date* and *Product*. In this case the *Sales* original table (whose storage is DirectQuery) must be queried directly without using any aggregation, as shown in the details in Figure 19-21.

FIGURE 19-21 Failed matching of aggregations reported by *RewriteAttempted* events in DAX Studio.

Because the *Sales* table has a DirectQuery storage, the engine generates an SQL query reported on line 5. The longer duration (more than two seconds) is normal and expected. Aggregations can be considered to improve the performance of DAX queries whose bottleneck is the SE. Aggregations are usually not useful for bottlenecks in the FE.

Reading query plans

At the beginning of this chapter, we described the two types of query plans available in DAX: logical and physical. In reality, we do not use these query plans often because we focus our attention on the SE queries first. We can analyze the performance of the SE queries to find issues caused by the SE and/or by the materialization of large datacaches in memory. SE queries are much easier to read than DAX query plans.

In this section, we describe some of the important behaviors to check in a query plan in order to identify performance bottlenecks. A complete and detailed coverage of all the operators used in logical and physical query plans is beyond the scope of this book. The goal here is to understand the relationships between a query plan and the SE queries, thus improving one's ability to find bottlenecks and to improve query performance.

A query plan usually generates more than one SE query. The FE combines the results of different datacaches, doing operations like joins between temporary tables. Consider the following DAX query; it returns a table with the quantity sold for each product color, only for transactions with a *Net Price* greater than 1,000:

```
EVALUATE
CALCULATETABLE (
    ADDCOLUMNS (
        ALL ( Product[Color] ),
        "Units", CALCULATE (
            SUM ( Sales[Quantity] )
        )
    ),
    Sales[Net Price] > 1000
)
ORDER BY Product[Color]
```

The result visible in Figure 19-22 includes all the unique values of *Color*, including those without any unit sold. In order to do that, the approach of the DAX engine is different from the one we would expect in plain SQL language; this is because of the different technique used to join tables in the SE. We will highlight this difference later; pay attention to the process for now.

Color	Units
Azure	
Black	551
Blue	575
Brown	64
Gold	
Green	403
Grey	421
Orange	58

FIGURE 19-22 The result of *ADDCOLUMNS* includes rows with a blank value in the *Units* column.

The logical query plan shown in Figure 19-23 includes three *Scan_Vertipaq* operations, two of which correspond to two datacaches provided by SE queries.

Line	Logical Query Plan
1	Order: RelLogOp DependOnCols()() 1-2 RequiredCols(1, 2)('Product'[Color], "[Units])
2	CalculateTable: RelLogOp DependOnCols()() 1-2 RequiredCols(1, 2)('Product'[Color], "[Units])
3	AddColumns: RelLogOp DependOnCols()() 1-2 RequiredCols(1, 2)('Product'[Color], "[Units])
4	Scan_Vertipaq: RelLogOp DependOnCols()() 1-1 RequiredCols(1)('Product'[Color])
5	Sum_Vertipaq: ScaLogOp DependOnCols(1)('Product'[Color]) Integer DominantValue=BLANK
6	Scan_Vertipaq: RelLogOp DependOnCols(1)('Product'[Color]) 2-113 RequiredCols(1, 88)('Product'[Color], 'Sales'[Quantity])
7	'Sales'[Quantity]: ScaLogOp DependOnCols(88)('Sales'[Quantity]) Integer DominantValue=NONE
8	Filter_Vertipaq: RelLogOp DependOnCols()() 0-0 RequiredCols(0)('Sales'[Net Price])
9	Scan_Vertipaq: RelLogOp DependOnCols()() 0-0 RequiredCols(0)('Sales'[Net Price])
10	GreaterThan: ScaLogOp DependOnCols(0)('Sales'[Net Price]) Boolean DominantValue=NONE
11	'Sales'[Net Price]: ScaLogOp DependOnCols(0)('Sales'[Net Price]) Currency DominantValue=NONE
12	Constant: ScaLogOp DependOnCols()() Currency DominantValue=1000
13	ColPosition<'Product'[Color]>: ScaLogOp DependOnCols(1)('Product'[Color]) String DominantValue=NONE

FIGURE 19-23 Logical query plan of a simple DAX query.

The two *Scan_Vertipaq* operations at lines 4 and 6 require different sets of columns. The third *Scan_Vertipaq* operation at line 9 is used for a filter, and it does not generate a separate datacache. Its logic is included in one of the other two SE queries generated.

The *Scan_Vertipaq* at line 4 only uses the product color, whereas the *Scan_Vertipaq* at line 6 includes product color and sales quantity, which are two columns in two different tables. When this happens, a join between two or more tables is required.

After the logical query plan, the profiler receives the events from the SE. The corresponding xmSQL queries are the following:

```
SELECT
    Product[Color],
    SUM ( Sales[Quantity] )
FROM Sales
    LEFT OUTER JOIN Product ON Sales[ProductKey] = Product[ProductKey]
WHERE Sales[Net Price] > 1000;

SELECT Product[Color] FROM Product;
```

The first SE query retrieves a table containing one row for each color that has at least one unit sold at a price greater than 1,000 in the *Sales* table. In order to do that, the query joins *Sales* and *Product* using the *ProductKey* column. The second xmSQL statement returns the list of all the product colors, independent of the *Sales* table. These two queries generate two different datacaches, one with two columns (product color and sum of quantity) and another with only one column (the product color).

At this point, we might wonder why a second query is required. Why is the first xmSQL not enough? The reason is that the *LEFT JOIN* in xmSQL has *Sales* on the left side and *Product* on the right side. In plain SQL code, we would have written another query:

```
SELECT
    Product.Color,
    SUM ( Sales.Quantity )
FROM Product
LEFT OUTER JOIN Sales
    ON Sales.ProductKey = Product.ProductKey
WHERE Sales.NetPrice > 1000
GROUP BY Product.Color
ORDER BY Product.Color;
```

Having the *Product* table on the left side of a *LEFT JOIN* would produce a result that includes all the product colors. However, the SE can only generate queries between tables with a relationship in the data model, and the resulting join in xmSQL always puts the table that is on the many-side of the relationship on the left side of the join condition. This guarantees that even though there are missing product keys in the *Product* table, the result will also include sales for those missing products; these sales will be included in a row with a blank value for all the product attributes, in this case the product color.

Now that we have seen why the DAX engine produces two SE queries for the initial DAX query, we can analyze the physical query plan shown in Figure 19-24, where we can find more information about the query execution.

Line	Records	Physical Query Plan
1		PartitionIntoGroups: IterPhyOp LogOp=Order IterCols(1, 2)('Product'[Color], '[Units]) #Groups=1 #Rows=16
2	1	AggregationSpool<Order>: SpoolPhyOp #Records=1
3		AddColumns: IterPhyOp LogOp=AddColumns IterCols(1, 2)('Product'[Color], '[Units])
4	16	Spool_Iterator<SpoolIterator>: IterPhyOp LogOp=Scan_Vertipaq IterCols(1)('Product'[Color]) #Records=16 #<
5	16	ProjectionSpool<ProjectFusion< >>: SpoolPhyOp #Records=16
6		Cache: IterPhyOp #FieldCols=1 #ValueCols=0
7	10	SpoolLookup: LookupPhyOp LogOp=Sum_Vertipaq LookupCols(1)('Product'[Color]) Integer #Records=10 #Ke
8	10	ProjectionSpool<ProjectFusion<Copy>>: SpoolPhyOp #Records=10
9		Cache: IterPhyOp #FieldCols=1 #ValueCols=1
10		ColPosition<'Product'[Color]>: LookupPhyOp LogOp=ColPosition<'Product'[Color]>ColPosition<'Product'[Colo

FIGURE 19-24 Physical query plan of a simple DAX query.

The physical query plan uses the *Cache* operator (line 6 and 9) to indicate where it is consuming a datacache provided by the SE. Unfortunately, it is not possible to see the corresponding SE query for each operation. Nevertheless, at least in simple cases like the one considered, we can figure out this association by looking at other pieces of information. For example, one *Cache* only has one column obtained with a group operation, whereas the other *Cache* has two columns: one that is the result of a group operation and the other that is the result of an aggregation (the sum of the quantity). In the physical query plan, *#ValueCols* reports the number of columns that are the result of an aggregation, whereas *#FieldCols* reports the number of other columns used to group the result. By looking at the columns consumed by each *Cache* node, it is often possible to identify the corresponding xmSQL query even though it is a time-consuming process in complex query plans. In this example, the *Cache* node at line 6 returns a column with 16 product color names; on the other hand, the *Cache* node at line 9 only returns 10 rows and two columns, only with the product color names that have at least one transaction in *Sales* within the condition specified for *Net Price* (which must be greater than 1,000).

The *ProjectionSpool<>* operation consumes the datacaches corresponding to *Cache* nodes in the physical query plan. Here we can find an important piece of information: the number of records iterated, which corresponds to the number of rows in the datacache used. This number follows the *#Records* attribute, which is also reported in the *Records* column in DAX Studio. We can find the same *#Records* attribute in parent nodes of the query plan—a place where the type of aggregation performed by the engine is also available if there is one. In this example, the *Cache* at line 9 has two columns: one is *Product[Color]* and the other is the result of a sum aggregation. This information is available in the *LogOp* argument of the *Spool_Iterator* and *SpoolLookup* nodes at lines 4 and 7, respectively.

At this point, we can recap what we are reading in the query plans and the SE queries:

1. The FE consumes two datacaches, corresponding to *Cache* nodes in the physical query plan.

2. The FE iterates over the list of product colors, which is a table containing 16 rows and one column. This is the datacache obtained by the second SE query. Do not make assumptions about the order of the SE queries in the profiler.

3. For each row of this datacache (a product color), the FE executes a lookup in the other datacache containing the product colors and the quantity sold for each color; this is a table with two columns and 10 rows.

The entire process executed by the FE is sequential and single-threaded. The FE sends one request at a time to the SE. The SE might parallelize the query, but the FE does not send multiple requests in parallel to the SE.

 Note The FE and the SE are subject to optimizations and improvements made in new releases. The behavior described might be different in newer versions of the DAX engine.

The FE can combine different results by using the lookup operation described in the previous query plan or other set operators. In any case, the FE executes this operation sequentially. For this reason, we might expect longer execution times by combining large datacaches or by performing a lookup for millions of rows in a large lookup datacache. A simple and effective way to identify these potential bottlenecks in the physical query plan is to look for the highest number of records in the operators of a logical query plan. For this reason, DAX Studio extracts that number from the query plan, making it easier to sort query plan operators by using the number of records iterated. It is possible to sort the rows by this number by clicking the *Records* column shown in Figure 19-24. We will show a more detailed example of this approach in Chapter 20.

The presence of relationships in the data model is important in order to obtain better performance. We can examine the behavior of a join between two tables when a relationship is not available. For example, consider a query returning the same result as the previous example, but operating in a data model that does not have a relationship between the *Product* and *Sales* tables. We need a DAX query such as the following; it uses the virtual relationship pattern shown in Chapter 15, "Advanced relationships," in the section "Transferring a filter using *INTERSECT*":

```
DEFINE
    MEASURE Sales[Units] =
        CALCULATE (
            SUM ( Sales[Quantity] ),
            INTERSECT (
                ALL ( Sales[ProductKey] ),
                VALUES ( 'Product'[ProductKey] )
            ),
            -- Disable the existing relationship between Sales and Product
            CROSSFILTER ( Sales[ProductKey], 'Product'[ProductKey], NONE )
        )
EVALUATE
ADDCOLUMNS (
    ALL ( 'Product'[Color] ),
    "Units", [Units]
)
ORDER BY 'Product'[Color]
```

The function in the *Units* measure definition is equivalent to a relationship between *Sales* and *Product*. The resulting query plan is more complex than the previous one because there are many more operations in both the logical and the physical query plans. Without doing a dump of the complete query plan, which would be too long for a book, we can summarize the behavior of the query plan in these logical steps:

1. Retrieves the list of *ProductKey* values for each product color.

2. Sums the *Quantity* value for each *ProductKey*.

3. For each color, aggregates the *Quantity* of the related *ProductKey* values.

The FE executes four SE queries, as shown in Figure 19-25.

Line	Subclass	Duration	CPU	Rows	KB	Query
2	Scan	1	0	2.238	18	SELECT
4	Scan	0	0	19	1	SELECT
6	Scan	1	0	2.517	10	SELECT
8	Scan	2	0	2.238	35	SELECT

FIGURE 19-25 SE queries executed for a DAX calculation using a virtual relationship with *INTERSECT*.

The following are the complete xmSQL statements of the four SE queries:

```
SELECT
Sales[ProductKey]
FROM Sales;

SELECT
Product[Color]
FROM Product;
```

```
SELECT
Product[ProductKey], Product[Color]
FROM Product;

SELECT
Sales[ProductKey], SUM ( Sales[Quantity] )
FROM Sales
WHERE      Sales[ProductKey] IN ( 490, 479, 528, 379, 359, 332, 374, 597, 387,
                            484..[158 total values, not all displayed] );
```

The *WHERE* condition highlighted in the last SE query might seem useless because the DAX query does not apply a filter over products. However, usually in the real world there are other filters active on products or other tables. The query plan tries to only extract the quantities sold of products that are relevant to the query, lowering the size of the datacache returned to the FE. When there are similar *WHERE* conditions in the SE, the only concern is the size of the corresponding bitmap index moved back and forth between the FE and the SE.

The FE has to group all the products belonging to each color. The performance of this join performed at the FE level mainly depends on the number of products and secondarily on the number of colors. Once again, the size of a datacache is the first and most important element to consider when we look for a performance bottleneck in the FE.

We considered the virtual relationship using *INTERSECT* for educational purposes. We wanted to display the SE queries required for a join condition resolved mainly by the FE. However, whenever possible, if a physical relationship is not available, *TREATAS* should be considered as a more optimized alternative. Consider this alternative implementation of the previous DAX query:

```
DEFINE
    MEASURE Sales[Units] =
        CALCULATE (
            SUM ( Sales[Quantity] ),
            TREATAS (
                VALUES ( 'Product'[ProductKey] ),
                Sales[ProductKey]
            ),
            -- Disable the existing relationship between Sales and Product
            CROSSFILTER ( Sales[ProductKey], 'Product'[ProductKey], NONE )
        )
EVALUATE
ADDCOLUMNS (
    ALL ( 'Product'[Color] ),
    "Units", [Units]
)
ORDER BY 'Product'[Color]
```

As shown in Figure 19-26, there are only three SE queries generated instead of four. Remember that *Batch* is just a recap of the previous *Scan* events. Moreover, the size of the datacaches is smaller because one result alone has 2,517 rows corresponding to the number of products in the *Product* table. In the previous implementation using *INTERSECT*, there were a larger number of queries returning thousands of rows. All of these datacaches must be consumed by the FE.

Line	Subclass	Duration	CPU	Rows	KB	Query
2	Scan	1	0	2,517	10	DEFINE TABLE '$TTa
4	Scan	2	0	16	1	DEFINE TABLE '$TTa
5	Batch	4	16			DEFINE TABLE '$TTa
7	Scan	0	0	19	1	SELECT 'Product'[Co

FIGURE 19-26 SE queries executed for a DAX calculation using a virtual relationship with *TREATAS*.

The following is the content of the *Batch* event at line 5, which includes the first two *Scan* events (lines 2 and 4):

```
DEFINE TABLE '$TTable3' := SELECT
'Product'[ProductKey], 'Product'[Color]
FROM 'Product',

CREATE SHALLOW RELATION '$TRelation1' MANYTOMANY
FROM 'Sales'[ProductKey] TO '$TTable3'[Product$ProductKey],

DEFINE TABLE '$TTable1' := SELECT
    '$TTable3'[Product$Color],
    SUM ( '$TTable2'[$Measure0] )
FROM '$TTable2'
    INNER JOIN '$TTable3' ON '$TTable2'[Sales$ProductKey]='$TTable3'[Product$ProductKey]
REDUCED BY
'$TTable2' := SELECT
    'Sales'[ProductKey],
    SUM ( 'Sales'[Quantity] ) AS [$Measure0]
FROM 'Sales';
```

The performance advantage of *TREATAS* is that it moves the execution of the operation to the SE, thanks to the *CREATE SHALLOW RELATION* statement highlighted in the previous code. This way, there is no need to materialize more data for the SE. Indeed, the join is executed within the FE, which reduces the number of lines of the physical query plan—from the 37 required by *INTERSECT* (not displayed in the book for brevity) to the 10 required by *TREATAS*. This results in a query plan very similar to the one shown in Figure 19-24.

Analyzing complex and longer query plans would require another book, considering the length of the query plans involved. More details about the internals of the query plans are available in the white papers "Understanding DAX Query Plans" (http://www.sqlbi.com/articles/understanding-dax-query-plans/) and "Understanding Distinct Count in DAX Query Plans" (http://www.sqlbi.com/articles/understanding-distinct-count-in-dax-query-plans/).

Conclusions

As you have seen, diving into the complexity of query plans opens up a whole new world. In this chapter we barely scratched the surface of query plans, and a deeper analysis would require twice the size of this book. The good news is that in most—if not all—scenarios, going into more detail turns out to be useless.

An experienced DAX developer who aims to write optimal code should be able to focus their attention on the low-hanging fruit that can be discovered very quickly by looking at the most relevant parts of the query plan:

- In the physical query plan, the presence of a large number of rows scanned indicates the materialization of large datasets. This suggests that the query is memory-hungry and potentially slow.

- Most of the time, the VertiPaq queries include enough information to figure out the overall algorithm of the calculation. Whatever is not computed in a VertiPaq query, it must be computed by the formula engine. Knowing this enables you to get a clear idea of the whole query process.

- *CallbackDataID* presence indicates iterations at the row level where your code requires calculations that are too complex for VertiPaq storage engine. *CallbackDataIDs* by themselves are not totally bad. Nevertheless, removing them almost always results in better performance.

- VertiPaq and DirectQuery models are different. When using DirectQuery, the performance of DAX is strongly connected to the performance of the data source. It makes sense to use Direct-Query if and only if the underlying data source is specifically optimized for the kind of queries generated by the DirectQuery storage engine.

In the next chapter, we are going to use the knowledge gained in this and previous chapters to provide a few guided optimization processes.

Optimizing DAX

This is the last chapter of the book, and it is time to use all the knowledge you have gained so far to explore the most fascinating DAX topic: optimizing formulas. You have learned how the DAX engines work, how to read a query plan, and the internals of the formula engine and of the storage engine. Now all the pieces are in place and you are ready to learn how to use that information to write faster code.

There is one very important warning before approaching this chapter. Do not expect to learn best practices or a simple way to write fast code. Simply stated: There is no way in DAX to write code that is always the fastest. The speed of a DAX formula depends on many factors, the most important of which unfortunately is not in the DAX code itself: It is data distribution. You have already learned that VertiPaq compression strongly depends on data distribution. The size of a column (hence, the speed to scan it) depends on its cardinality: the larger, the slower. Thus, the very same formula might behave differently when executed on one column or another.

You will learn how to measure the speed of a formula, and we will provide you with several examples where rewriting the expression differently leads to a faster execution time. Learn all these examples for what they are—examples that might help you in finding new ideas for your code. Do not take them as golden rules, because they are not.

We are not teaching you rules; we are trying to teach you how to find the best rules in the very specific scenario that is your data model. Be prepared to change them when the data model changes or when you approach a new scenario. Flexibility is key when optimizing DAX code: flexibility, a deep technical knowledge of the engine, and a good amount of creativity, to be prepared to test formulas and expressions that might be not so intuitive.

Finally, all the information we provide in this book is valid at the time of printing. New versions of the engine come on the market every month, and the development team is always working on improving the DAX engine. So be prepared to measure different numbers for the examples of the book in the version of the engine you will be running and be prepared to use different optimization methods if necessary. If one day you measure your code and reach the educated conclusion that "Marco and Alberto are wrong; this code runs much faster than their suggested code," that will be our brightest day, because we will have been able to teach you all that we know, and you are moving forward in writing better DAX code than ours.

Defining optimization strategies

The optimization process for a DAX query, expression, or measure requires a strategy to reproduce a performance issue, identify the bottleneck, and remove it. Initially, you always observe a slowness in a complex query, but optimizing a complicated expression including several DAX measures is more involved than optimizing one measure at a time. For this reason, the approach we suggest is to isolate the slowest measure or expression first, and optimize it in a simpler query that reproduces the issue with a shorter query plan.

This is a simple to-do list you should follow every time you want to optimize DAX:

1. Identify a single DAX expression to optimize.

2. Create a query that reproduces the issue.

3. Analyze server timings and query plan information.

4. Identify bottlenecks in the storage engine or formula engine.

5. Implement changes and rerun the test query.

You can see a more complete description of each of these steps in the following sections.

Identifying a single DAX expression to optimize

If you have already found the slowest measure in your model, you probably can skip this section and move to the following one. However, it is common to get a performance issue in a report that might generate several queries. Each of these queries might include several measures. The first step is to identify a single DAX expression to optimize. Doing this, you reduce the reproduction steps to a single query and possibly to a single measure returned in the result.

A complete refresh of a report in Power BI or Reporting Services or of a Microsoft Excel workbook typically generates several queries in either DAX or MDX (PivotTables and charts in Excel always generate the latter). When a report generates several queries, you have to identify the slowest query first. In Chapter 19, "Analyzing DAX query plans," you saw how DAX Studio can intercept all the queries sent to the DAX engine and identify the slowest query looking at the largest *Duration* amount.

If you are using Excel, you can also use a different technique to isolate a query. You can extract the MDX query it generates by using OLAP PivotTable Extensions, a free Excel add-in available at https://olappivottableextensions.github.io/.

Once you extract the slowest DAX or MDX query, you have to further restrict your focus and isolate the DAX expression that is causing the slowness. This way, you will concentrate your efforts on the right area. You can reduce the measures included in a query by modifying and executing the query interactively in DAX Studio.

For example, consider the following table result in Power BI with four expressions (two distinct counts and two measures) grouped by product brand, as shown in Figure 20-1.

Brand	Count of ProductKey	Sales Amount	Margin %	Count of Order Number
A. Datum	132	251,211,515.57	58.42%	131413
Adventure Works	192	518,462,059.16	51.31%	310083
Contoso	710	871,501,804.63	53.19%	462805
Fabrikam	267	627,751,182.08	54.38%	53309
Litware	264	416,239,414.35	51.73%	118500
Northwind Traders	47	151,481,923.36	52.33%	131667
Proseware	244	312,763,353.13	54.06%	51063
Southridge Video	192	183,482,982.39	49.53%	570613
Tailspin Toys	144	42,801,223.58	48.83%	688390
The Phone Company	152	174,742,660.20	52.23%	29852
Wide World Importers	173	254,953,905.77	52.39%	49745
Total	**2517**	**3,805,392,024.21**	**53.03%**	**1663351**

FIGURE 20-1 Simple visualization in Power BI generated by a DAX query with four expressions.

The report generates the following DAX query, captured by using DAX Studio:

```
EVALUATE
TOPN (
    502,
    SUMMARIZECOLUMNS (
        ROLLUPADDISSUBTOTAL ( 'Product'[Brand], "IsGrandTotalRowTotal" ),
        "DistinctCountProductKey", CALCULATE (
            DISTINCTCOUNT ( 'Product'[ProductKey] )
        ),
        "Sales_Amount", 'Sales'[Sales Amount],
        "Margin__", 'Sales'[Margin %],
        "DistinctCountOrder_Number", CALCULATE (
            DISTINCTCOUNT ( 'Sales'[Order Number] )
        )
    ),
    [IsGrandTotalRowTotal], 0,
    'Product'[Brand], 1
)
ORDER BY
    [IsGrandTotalRowTotal] DESC,
    'Product'[Brand]
```

You should reduce the query by trying one calculation at a time, to locate the slowest one. If you can manipulate the report, you might just include one calculation at a time. By accessing the DAX code, it is enough to comment or remove three of the four columns calculated in the *SUMMARIZECOLUMNS* function (*DistinctCountProductKey*, *Sales_Amount*, *Margin__*, and *DistinctCountOrder_Number*), finding the slowest one before proceeding. In this case, the most expensive calculation is the last one. The following query takes up 80% of the time required to compute the original query, meaning that the distinct count over *Sales[Order Number]* is the most expensive operation in the entire report:

```
EVALUATE
TOPN (
    502,
    SUMMARIZECOLUMNS (
        ROLLUPADDISSUBTOTAL ( 'Product'[Brand], "IsGrandTotalRowTotal" ),
```

```
//          "DistinctCountProductKey", CALCULATE (
//              DISTINCTCOUNT ( 'Product'[ProductKey] )
//          ),
//          "Sales_Amount", 'Sales'[Sales Amount],
//          "Margin__", 'Sales'[Margin %],
          "DistinctCountOrder_Number", CALCULATE (
              DISTINCTCOUNT ( 'Sales'[Order Number] )
          )
      ),
      [IsGrandTotalRowTotal], 0,
      'Product'[Brand], 1
)
ORDER BY
      [IsGrandTotalRowTotal] DESC,
      'Product'[Brand]
```

Another example is the following MDX query generated by the pivot table in Excel as seen in Figure 20-2:

```
SELECT {
    [Measures].[Sales Amount],
    [Measures].[Total Cost],
    [Measures].[Margin],
    [Measures].[Margin %]
  } DIMENSION PROPERTIES PARENT_UNIQUE_NAME, HIERARCHY_UNIQUE_NAME ON COLUMNS,
NON EMPTY HIERARCHIZE(
    DRILLDOWNMEMBER(
        { { DRILLDOWNMEMBER(
                { { DRILLDOWNLEVEL(
                        { [Date].[Calendar].[All] },,, include_calc_members )
                } },
            { [Date].[Calendar].[Year].&[CY 2008] },,, include_calc_members )
        } },
        { [Date].[Calendar].[Quarter].&[Q4-2008] },,, include_calc_members )
    )
)
DIMENSION PROPERTIES PARENT_UNIQUE_NAME,HIERARCHY_UNIQUE_NAME ON ROWS
FROM [Model]
CELL PROPERTIES VALUE, FORMAT_STRING, LANGUAGE, BACK_COLOR, FORE_COLOR, FONT_FLAGS
```

Row Labels	Sales Amount	Total Cost	Margin	Margin %
⊞ CY 2007	1,415,298,561.42	656,812,625.98	758,485,935.44	53.59%
⊟ CY 2008				
⊞ Q1-2008	249,328,405.72	121,389,562.10	127,938,843.62	51.31%
⊞ Q2-2008	321,749,612.47	147,214,171.80	174,535,440.67	54.25%
⊞ Q3-2008	323,449,998.92	147,948,797.33	175,501,201.59	54.26%
⊟ Q4-2008				
October 2008	97,130,506.81	44,062,202.41	53,068,304.40	54.64%
November 2008	96,777,975.30	50,656,942.35	46,121,032.95	47.66%
December 2008	100,890,113.59	52,797,506.05	48,092,607.54	47.67%
⊞ CY 2009	1,200,766,849.99	566,553,987.10	634,212,862.89	52.82%
Grand Total	3,805,392,024.21	1,787,435,795.12	2,017,956,229.09	53.03%

FIGURE 20-2 Simple pivot table in Excel that generates an MDX query with four measures.

You can reduce the measures either in the pivot table or directly in the MDX code. You can manipulate the MDX code by reducing the list of measures in braces. For example, you reduce the code to only the *Sales Amount* measure by modifying the list, as in the following initial part of the query:

```
SELECT
{ [Measures].[Sales Amount] }
DIMENSION PROPERTIES PARENT_UNIQUE_NAME, HIERARCHY_UNIQUE_NAME ON COLUMNS,
...
```

Regardless of the technique you use, once you identify the DAX expression (or measure) that is responsible for a performance issue, you need a reproduction query to use in DAX Studio.

Creating a reproduction query

The optimization process requires a query that you can execute several times, possibly changing the definition of the measure in order to evaluate different levels of performance.

If you captured a query in DAX or MDX, you already have a good starting point for the reproduction (repro) query. You should try to simplify the query as much as you can, so that it becomes easier to find the bottleneck. You should only keep a complex query structure when it is fundamental in order to observe the performance issue.

Creating a reproduction query in DAX

When a measure is constantly slow, you should be able to create a repro query producing a single value as a result. Using *CALCULATE* or *CALCULATETABLE*, you can apply all the filters you need. For example, you can execute the *Sales Amount* measure for November 2008 using the following code, obtaining the same result ($96,777,975.30) you see in Figure 20-2 for that month:

```
EVALUATE
{
    CALCULATE (
        [Sales Amount],
        'Date'[Calendar Year] = "CY 2008",
        'Date'[Calendar Year Quarter] = "Q4-2008",
        'Date'[Calendar Year Month] = "November 2008"
    )
}
```

You can also write the previous query using *CALCULATETABLE* instead of *CALCULATE*:

```
EVALUATE
CALCULATETABLE (
    { [Sales Amount] },
    'Date'[Calendar Year] = "CY 2008",
    'Date'[Calendar Year Quarter] = "Q4-2008",
    'Date'[Calendar Year Month] = "November 2008"
)
```

The two approaches produce the same result. You should consider *CALCULATETABLE* when the query you use to test the measure is more complex than a simple table constructor.

Once you have a repro query for a specific measure defined in the data model, you should consider writing the DAX expression of the measure as local in the query, using the *MEASURE* syntax. For example, you can transform the previous repro query into the following one:

```
DEFINE
    MEASURE Sales[Sales Amount] =
        SUMX ( Sales, Sales[Quantity] * Sales[Net Price] )
EVALUATE
CALCULATETABLE (
    { [Sales Amount] },
    'Date'[Calendar Year] = "CY 2008",
    'Date'[Calendar Year Quarter] = "Q4-2008",
    'Date'[Calendar Year Month] = "November 2008"
)
```

At this point, you can apply changes to the DAX expression assigned to the measure directly into the query statement. This way, you do not have to deploy a change to the data model before executing the query again. You can change the query, clear the cache, and run the query in DAX Studio, immediately measuring the performance results of the modified expression.

Creating query measures with DAX Studio

DAX Studio can generate the *MEASURE* syntax for a measure defined in the model by using the Define Measure context menu item. The latter is available by selecting a measure in the Metadata pane, as shown in Figure 20-3.

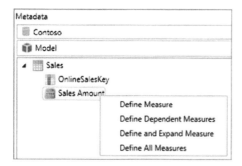

FIGURE 20-3 Screenshot of how a user would access the "Define Measure" menu item.

If a measure references other measures, all of them should be included as query measures in order to consider any possible change to the repro query. The Define Dependent Measures feature includes the definition of all the measures that are referenced by the selected measure, whereas Define and Expand Measure replaces any measure reference with the corresponding measure expression. For example, consider the following query that just evaluates the *Margin %* measure:

```
EVALUATE
{ [Margin %] }
```

By clicking Define Measure on *Margin %*, you get the following code, where there are two other references to *Sales Amount* and *Margin* measures:

```
DEFINE
    MEASURE Sales[Margin %] =
        DIVIDE ( [Margin], [Sales Amount] )
EVALUATE
{ [Margin %] }
```

Instead of repeating the Define Measure action on all the other measures, you can click on Define Dependent Measures on *Margin %*, obtaining the definition of all the other measures required; this includes *Total Cost*, which is used in the *Margin* definition:

```
DEFINE
    MEASURE Sales[Margin] = [Sales Amount] - [Total Cost]
    MEASURE Sales[Sales Amount] =
        SUMX ( Sales, Sales[Quantity] * Sales[Net Price] )
    MEASURE Sales[Total Cost] =
        SUMX ( Sales, Sales[Quantity] * Sales[Unit Cost] )
    MEASURE Sales[Margin %] =
        DIVIDE ( [Margin], [Sales Amount] )
EVALUATE
{ [Margin %] }
```

You can also obtain a single DAX expression without measure references by clicking Define and Expand Measure on *Margin %*:

```
DEFINE
    MEASURE Sales[Margin %] =
        DIVIDE (
            CALCULATE (
                CALCULATE ( SUMX ( Sales, Sales[Quantity] * Sales[Net Price] ) )
                    - CALCULATE ( SUMX ( Sales, Sales[Quantity] * Sales[Unit Cost] ) )
            ),
            CALCULATE ( SUMX ( Sales, Sales[Quantity] * Sales[Net Price] ) )
        )
EVALUATE
{ [Margin %] }
```

This latter technique can be useful to quickly evaluate whether a measure includes nested iterators or not, though it could generate very verbose results.

Creating a reproduction query in MDX

In certain conditions, you have to use an MDX query to reproduce a problem that only happens in MDX and not in DAX. The same DAX measure, executed in a DAX or in an MDX query, generates different query plans; it might display a different behavior depending on the language of the query. However in this case too, you can define the DAX measure local to the query. That way, it is more efficient to edit and run again. For instance, you can define the *Sales Amount* measure local to the MDX query using the *WITH MEASURE* syntax:

```
WITH
    MEASURE Sales[Sales Amount] = SUMX ( Sales, Sales[Quantity] * Sales[Unit Price] )
SELECT {
    [Measures].[Sales Amount],
    [Measures].[Total Cost],
    [Measures].[Margin],
    [Measures].[Margin %]
} DIMENSION PROPERTIES PARENT_UNIQUE_NAME, HIERARCHY_UNIQUE_NAME ON COLUMNS,
NON EMPTY HIERARCHIZE(
    DRILLDOWNMEMBER(
        { { DRILLDOWNMEMBER(
                { { DRILLDOWNLEVEL(
                        { [Date].[Calendar].[All] },,, include_calc_members )
                } },
            { [Date].[Calendar].[Year].&[CY 2008] },,, include_calc_members )
        } },
        { [Date].[Calendar].[Quarter].&[Q4-2008] },,, include_calc_members
    )
)
DIMENSION PROPERTIES PARENT_UNIQUE_NAME,HIERARCHY_UNIQUE_NAME ON ROWS
FROM [Model]
CELL PROPERTIES VALUE, FORMAT_STRING, LANGUAGE, BACK_COLOR, FORE_COLOR, FONT_FLAGS
```

As you see, in MDX you must use *WITH* instead of *DEFINE*, which is how you can rename the syntax generated by DAX Studio if you optimize an MDX query. The syntax after *MEASURE* is always DAX code, so you will follow the same optimization process for an MDX query. Regardless of the repro query language (either DAX or MDX), you always have a DAX expression to optimize, which you can define within a local *MEASURE* definition.

Analyzing server timings and query plan information

Once you have a repro query, you run it and collect information about execution time and query plan. You saw in Chapter 19 how to read the information provided by DAX Studio or SQL Server Profiler. In this section, we recap the steps required to analyze a simple query in DAX Studio.

For example, consider the following DAX query:

```
DEFINE
    MEASURE Sales[Sales Amount] =
        SUMX ( Sales, Sales[Quantity] * Sales[Unit Price] )
EVALUATE
ADDCOLUMNS (
    VALUES ( 'Date'[Calendar Year] ),
    "Result", [Sales Amount]
)
```

If you execute this query in DAX Studio after clearing the cache and enabling Query Plan and Server Timings, you obtain a result with one row for each year in the *Date* table, and the total of *Sales Amount* for sales made in that year. The starting point for an analysis is always the Server Timings pane, which displays information about the entire query, as shown in Figure 20-4.

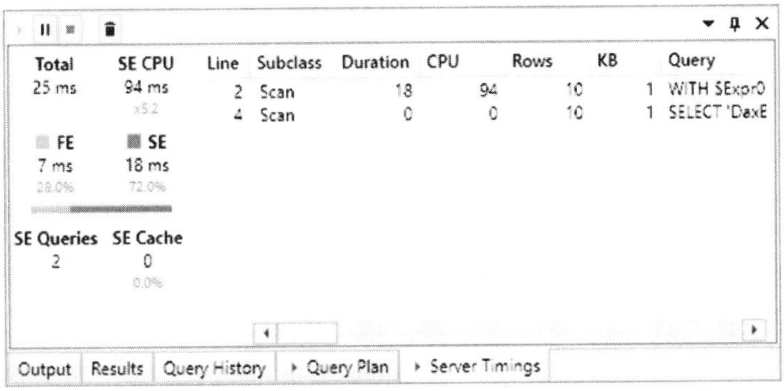

FIGURE 20-4 Server Timings pane after a simple query execution.

Our query returned the result in 25 ms (*Total*), and it spent 72 percent of this time in the storage engine (*SE*), whereas the formula engine (*FE*) only used up 7 ms of the total time. This pane does not provide much information about the formula engine internals, but it is rich in details on storage engine activity. For example, there were two storage engine queries (*SE Queries*) that consumed a total of 94 ms of processing time (*SE CPU*). The *CPU* time can be larger than *Duration* thanks to the parallelism of the storage engine. Indeed, the engine used 94 ms of logical processors working in parallel, so that the duration time is a fraction of that number. The hardware used in this test had 8 logical processors, and the parallelism degree of this query (ratio between *SE CPU* and *SE*) is 5.2. The parallelism cannot be higher than the number of logical processors you have.

The storage engine queries are available in the list, and you can see that a single storage engine operation (the first one) consumes the entire duration and *CPU* time. By enabling the display of *Internal* and *Cache* subclass events, you can see in Figure 20-5 that the two storage engine queries were actually executed by the storage engine.

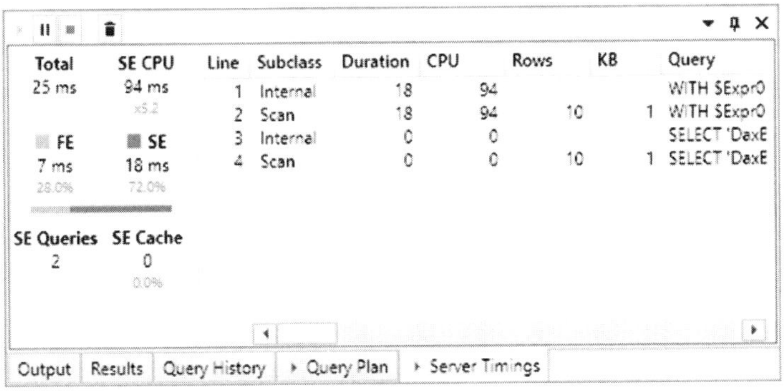

FIGURE 20-5 Server Timings pane with internal subclass events visible.

If you execute the same query again without clearing the cache, you see the results in Figure 20-6. Both storage engine queries retrieved the values from the cache (*SE cache*), and the storage engine queries resolved in the cache are visible in the *Subclass* column.

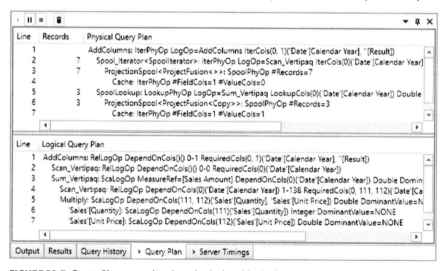

Total	SE CPU	Line	Subclass	Duration	CPU	Rows	KB	Query
6 ms	0 ms	1	Cache					WITH $Expr0
	x0.0	2	Scan	0	0	10	1	WITH $Expr0
FE	SE	3	Cache					SELECT 'DaxE
6 ms	0 ms	4	Scan	0	0	10	1	SELECT 'DaxE
100.0%	0.0%							

SE Queries	SE Cache
2	2
	100.0%

Output Results Query History ▸ Query Plan ▸ Server Timings

FIGURE 20-6 Server Timings pane with cache subclass events visible, after second execution of the same DAX query.

Usually, we will use the repro query with a cold cache (clearing the cache before the execution), but in some cases it is important to evaluate whether a given DAX expression can leverage the cache in an upcoming request or not. For this reason, the *Cache* visualization in DAX Studio is disabled by default, and you enable it on demand.

At this point, you can start looking at the query plans. In Figure 20-7 you see the physical and logical query plans of the query used in the previous example.

The physical query plan is the one you will use more often. In the query of the previous example, there are two datacaches—one for each storage engine query. Every *Cache* row in the physical query plan consumes one of the datacaches available. However, there is no simple way to match the correspondence between a query plan operation and a datacache. You can infer the datacache by looking at the columns used in the operations requiring a *Cache* result (the *Spool_Iterator* and *SpoolLookup* rows, in Figure 20-7).

Line	Records	Physical Query Plan
1		AddColumns: IterPhyOp LogOp=AddColumns IterCols(0, 1)('Date'[Calendar Year], "[Result])
2	7	Spool_Iterator<SpoolIterator>: IterPhyOp LogOp=Scan_Vertipaq IterCols(0)('Date'[Calendar Year]
3	7	ProjectionSpool<ProjectFusion<>>: SpoolPhyOp #Records=7
4		Cache: IterPhyOp #FieldCols=1 #ValueCols=0
5	3	SpoolLookup: LookupPhyOp LogOp=Sum_Vertipaq LookupCols(0)('Date'[Calendar Year]) Double
6	3	ProjectionSpool<ProjectFusion<Copy>>: SpoolPhyOp #Records=3
7		Cache: IterPhyOp #FieldCols=1 #ValueCols=1

Line	Logical Query Plan
1	AddColumns: RelLogOp DependOnCols()() 0-1 RequiredCols(0, 1)('Date'[Calendar Year], "[Result])
2	Scan_Vertipaq: RelLogOp DependOnCols()() 0-0 RequiredCols(0)('Date'[Calendar Year])
3	Sum_Vertipaq: ScaLogOp MeasureRef=[Sales Amount] DependOnCols(0)('Date'[Calendar Year]) Double Domin
4	Scan_Vertipaq: RelLogOp DependOnCols(0)('Date'[Calendar Year]) 1-138 RequiredCols(0, 111, 112)('Date'[Ca
5	Multiply: ScaLogOp DependOnCols(111, 112)('Sales'[Quantity], 'Sales'[Unit Price]) Double DominantValue=N
6	'Sales'[Quantity]: ScaLogOp DependOnCols(111)('Sales'[Quantity]) Integer DominantValue=NONE
7	'Sales'[Unit Price]: ScaLogOp DependOnCols(112)('Sales'[Unit Price]) Double DominantValue=NONE

Output Results Query History ▸ Query Plan ▸ Server Timings

FIGURE 20-7 Query Plan pane showing physical and logical query plans.

An important piece of information available in the physical query plan is the column showing the number of records processed. As you will see, when optimizing bottlenecks in the formula engine, it might be useful to identify the slowest operation in the formula engine by searching for the line with the largest number of records. You can sort the rows by clicking the *Records* column header, as you see in Figure 20-8. You restore the original sort order by clicking the *Line* column header.

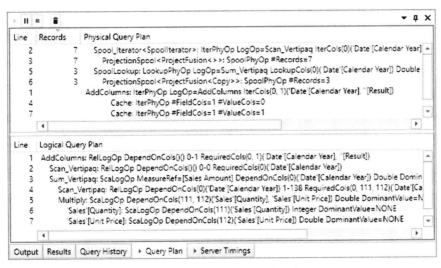

FIGURE 20-8 Steps in physical query plan sorted by *Records* column.

Identifying bottlenecks in the storage engine or formula engine

There are many possible optimizations usually available for any query. The first and most important step is to identify whether a query spends most of the time in the formula engine or in the storage engine. A first indication is available in the percentages provided by DAX Studio for FE and SE. Usually, this is a good starting point, but you also have to identify the distribution of the workload in both the formula engine and the storage engine. In complex queries, a large amount of time spent in the storage engine might correspond to a large number of small storage engine queries or to a small number of storage engine queries that concentrate the most of the workload. As you will see, these differences require different approaches in your optimization strategy.

When you identify the execution bottleneck of a query, you should also prioritize the optimization areas. For example, there might be different inefficiencies in the query plan resulting in a large formula engine execution time. You should identify the most important inefficiency and concentrate on that first. If you do not follow this approach, you might end up spending time optimizing an expression that only marginally affects the execution time. Sometimes the more efficient optimizations are simple but hidden in counterintuitive context transitions or in other details of the DAX syntax. You should always measure the execution time before and after each optimization attempt, making sure that you obtain a real advantage and that you are not just applying some optimization pattern you found on the web or in this book without any real benefit.

Finally, remember that even if you have an issue in the formula engine, you should always start your analysis by looking at the storage engine queries. They provide valuable information about the content and size of the datacaches used by the formula engine. Reading the query plan that describes the operations made by the formula engine is a very complex process. It is easier to consider that the formula engine will use the content of datacaches and will have to do all the operations required to produce the result of a DAX query that has not already been produced by the storage engine. This approach is especially efficient for large and complex DAX queries. Indeed, these might generate thousands of lines in a query plan, but a relatively small number of datacaches produced by storage engine queries.

Implementing changes and rerunning the test query

Once the bottlenecks have been identified, the next step is to change the DAX expressions and/or the data model, so that the query plan is more efficient. Running the test query again, it is possible to verify that the improvement is effective, starting the search for the next bottleneck and continuing the loop restarting at the step "Analyzing server timings and query plan information." This process will continue until the performance is optimal or there are no further possible improvements that are worth the effort.

Optimizing bottlenecks in DAX expressions

A longer execution time in the storage engine is usually the consequence of one or more of the following causes (explained in more detail in Chapter 19):

- **Longer scan time.** Even for a simple aggregation, a DAX query must scan one or more columns. The cost for this scan depends on the size of the column, which depends on the number of unique values and on the data distribution. Different columns in the same table can have very different execution times.

- **Large cardinality.** A large number of unique values in a column affects the *DISTINCTCOUNT* calculation and the filter arguments of the *CALCULATE* and *CALCULATETABLE* functions. A large cardinality can also affect the scan time of a column, but it could be an issue by itself regardless of the column data size.

- **High frequency of *CallbackDataID*.** A large number of calls made by the storage engine to the formula engine can affect the overall performance of a query.

- **Large materialization.** If a storage engine query produces a large datacache, its generation requires time (allocating and writing RAM). Moreover, its consumption (by the formula engine) is also another potential bottleneck.

In the following sections, you will see several examples of optimization. Starting with the concepts you learned in previous chapters, you will see a typical problem reproduced in a simpler query and optimized.

Optimizing filter conditions

Whenever possible, a filter argument of a *CALCULATE/CALCULATETABLE* function should always filter columns rather than tables. The DAX engine has improved over the years, and several simple table filters are relatively well optimized in 2019 or newer engine versions. However, expressing a filter condition by columns rather than by tables is always a best practice.

For example, consider the report in Figure 20-9 that compares the total of *Sales Amount* with the sum of the sales transactions larger than $1,000 (*Big Sales Amount*) for each product brand.

Brand	Sales Amount	Big Sales Amount (slow)
A. Datum	251,211,515.57	63,063,695.61
Adventure Works	518,462,059.16	204,706,066.50
Contoso	871,501,804.63	390,591,570.37
Fabrikam	627,751,182.08	296,193,218.97
Litware	416,239,414.35	228,117,264.38
Northwind Traders	151,481,923.36	133,573,773.58
Proseware	312,763,353.13	116,288,985.19
Southridge Video	183,482,982.39	20,706,704.07
Tailspin Toys	42,801,223.58	290,849.14
The Phone Company	174,742,660.20	24,106,049.40
Wide World Importers	254,953,905.77	89,883,001.77
Total	**3,805,392,024.21**	**1,567,521,178.98**

FIGURE 20-9 *Sales Amount* and *Big Sales Amount* reported by product brand.

Because the filter condition in the *Big Sales Amount* measure requires two columns, a trivial way to define the filter is by using a filter over the *Sales* table. The following query computes just the *Big Sales Amount* measure in the previous report, generating the server timings results visible in Figure 20-10:

```
DEFINE
    MEASURE Sales[Big Sales Amount (slow)] =
        CALCULATE (
            [Sales Amount],
            FILTER (
                Sales,
                Sales[Quantity] * Sales[Net Price] > 1000
            )
        )
EVALUATE
SUMMARIZECOLUMNS (
    ROLLUPADDISSUBTOTAL ( 'Product'[Brand], "IsGrandTotalRowTotal" ),
    "Big_Sales_Amount", 'Sales'[Big Sales Amount (slow)]
)
```

Total	SE CPU	Line	Subclass	Duration	CPU	Rows	KB	Query
144 ms	563 ms	2	Scan	58	203	3.937	47	WITH $Expr0 := (
	x4.4	4	Scan	37	188	3.937	16	SELECT 'DaxBook
▮ FE	▮ SE	6	Scan	34	172	1	1	WITH $Expr0 := (
15 ms	129 ms							
10.4%	89.6%							

SE Queries	SE Cache
3	0
	0.0%

FIGURE 20-10 Server Timings running the query for the *Big Sales Amount (slow)* measure.

Because *FILTER* is iterating a table, this query is generating a larger datacache than necessary. The result in Figure 20-9 only displays 11 brands and one additional row for the grand total. Nevertheless, the query plan estimates that the first two datacaches return 3,937 rows, which is the same number as reported also in the Query Plan pane visible in Figure 20-11.

Line	Records	Physical Query Plan
7		Union: IterPhyOp LogOp=Union IterCols(0, 1, 2, 3)('Product'[Bran
8		GroupSemijoin: IterPhyOp LogOp=GroupSemiJoin IterCols(0, 1
9	11	Spool_Iterator<SpoolIterator>: IterPhyOp LogOp=Sum_Vert
10	11	AggregationSpool<AggFusion<Sum>>: SpoolPhyOp #Re
11		CrossApply: IterPhyOp LogOp=Sum_Vertipaq IterCols(0
12	3,937	Spool_MultiValuedHashLookup: IterPhyOp LogOp=F
13	3,937	ProjectionSpool<ProjectFusion<>>: SpoolPhyOp
14		Cache: IterPhyOp #FieldCols=3 #ValueCols=0
15		Cache: IterPhyOp #FieldCols=3 #ValueCols=1
16		GroupSemijoin: IterPhyOp LogOp=GroupSemiJoin IterCols(0, 1
17	1	Spool_Iterator<SpoolIterator>: IterPhyOp LogOp=Sum_Vert
18	1	ProjectionSpool<ProjectFusion<Copy>>: SpoolPhyOp #F
19		Cache: IterPhyOp #FieldCols=0 #ValueCols=1

FIGURE 20-11 Query Plan pane running the query for *Big Sales Amount (slow)* measure.

The formula engine receives a much larger datacache than the one required for the query result because there are two additional columns. Indeed, the xmSQL query at line 2 is the following:

```
WITH
    $Expr0 := ( CAST ( PFCAST ( 'DaxBook Sales'[Quantity] AS  INT ) AS  REAL )
                 * PFCAST ( 'DaxBook Sales'[Net Price] AS  REAL )  )
SELECT
    'DaxBook Product'[Brand],
    'DaxBook Sales'[Quantity],
    'DaxBook Sales'[Net Price],
    SUM ( @$Expr0 )
FROM 'DaxBook Sales'
    LEFT OUTER JOIN 'DaxBook Product'
        ON 'DaxBook Sales'[ProductKey]='DaxBook Product'[ProductKey]
WHERE
  ( COALESCE ( ( CAST ( PFCAST ( 'DaxBook Sales'[Quantity] AS  INT ) AS  REAL )
    * PFCAST ( 'DaxBook Sales'[Net Price] AS  REAL ) )  ) > COALESCE ( 1000.000000 ) );
```

The structure of the xmSQL query at line 4 in Figure 20-10 is similar to the previous one, just without the *SUM* aggregation. The presence of a table filter in *CALCULATE* results in this side effect in the query plan because the semantic of the filter includes all the columns of the *Sales* expanded table (expanded tables are described in Chapter 14, "Advanced DAX concepts").

The optimization of the measure only requires a column filter. Because the filter expression uses two columns, a row context requires a table with just those two columns to produce a corresponding and more efficient filter argument to *CALCULATE*. The following query implements the columns filter adding *KEEPFILTERS* to keep the same semantic as the previous version, generating the server timings results visible in Figure 20-12:

```
DEFINE
    MEASURE Sales[Big Sales Amount (fast)] =
        CALCULATE (
            [Sales Amount],
            KEEPFILTERS (
                FILTER (
                    ALL (
                        Sales[Quantity],
                        Sales[Net Price]
                    ),
                    Sales[Quantity] * Sales[Net Price] > 1000
                )
            )
        )
EVALUATE
SUMMARIZECOLUMNS (
    ROLLUPADDISSUBTOTAL ( 'Product'[Brand], "IsGrandTotalRowTotal" ),
    "Big_Sales_Amount", 'Sales'[Big Sales Amount (fast)]
)
```

Total	SE CPU	Line	Subclass	Duration	CPU	Rows	KB	Query
72 ms	391 ms	2	Scan	42	188	14	1	WITH $Expr0 := (C
	x5.9	4	Scan	24	203	1	1	WITH $Expr0 := (C
FE	**SE**							
6 ms	66 ms							
8.3%	91.7%							
SE Queries	**SE Cache**							
2	0							
	0.0%							

FIGURE 20-12 Server Timings when running the query for the *Big Sales Amount (fast)* measure.

The DAX query runs faster, but what is more important is that there is only one datacache for the rows of the result, excluding the grand total, which still has a separate xmSQL query. The materialization of the datacache at line 2 in Figure 20-12 only returns 14 estimated rows, when there are only 11 in the actual count visible in the Query Plan pane in Figure 20-13.

Line	Records	Physical Query Plan
7		Union: IterPhyOp LogOp=Union IterCols{0, 1, 2, 3}('Product'[Bran
8		GroupSemijoin: IterPhyOp LogOp=GroupSemiJoin IterCols{0, 1
9	11	Spool_Iterator<SpoolIterator>: IterPhyOp LogOp=Sum_Vert
10	11	ProjectionSpool<ProjectFusion<Copy>>: SpoolPhyOp #R
11		Cache: IterPhyOp #FieldCols=1 #ValueCols=1
12		GroupSemijoin: IterPhyOp LogOp=GroupSemiJoin IterCols{0, 1
13	1	Spool_Iterator<SpoolIterator>: IterPhyOp LogOp=Sum_Vert
14	1	ProjectionSpool<ProjectFusion<Copy>>: SpoolPhyOp #R
15		Cache: IterPhyOp #FieldCols=0 #ValueCols=1

FIGURE 20-13 Query Plan pane running the query for *Big Sales Amount (fast)* measure.

The reason for this optimization is that the query plan can create a much more efficient calculation in the storage engine without returning additional data to the formula engine because of the semantic required by a table filter. The following is the xmSQL query at line 2 in Figure 20-12:

```
WITH
    $Expr0 := ( CAST ( PFCAST ( 'DaxBook Sales'[Quantity] AS  INT ) AS  REAL )
                  * PFCAST ( 'DaxBook Sales'[Net Price] AS  REAL )  )
SELECT
    'DaxBook Product'[Brand],
    SUM ( @$Expr0 )
FROM 'DaxBook Sales'
    LEFT OUTER JOIN 'DaxBook Product'
        ON 'DaxBook Sales'[ProductKey]='DaxBook Product'[ProductKey]
WHERE
  ( COALESCE (  ( CAST ( PFCAST ( 'DaxBook Sales'[Quantity] AS  INT ) AS  REAL )
    * PFCAST ( 'DaxBook Sales'[Net Price] AS  REAL )  )  ) > COALESCE ( 1000.000000 ) );
```

The datacache no longer includes the *Quantity* and *Net Price* columns, and its cardinality corresponds to the cardinality of the DAX result. This is an ideal condition for minimal materialization. Keeping the filter conditions using columns rather than tables is an important effort to achieve this goal.

The important takeaway of this section is that you should always pay attention to the rows returned by storage engine queries. When their number is much bigger than the rows included in the result of a DAX query, there might be some overhead caused by the additional work performed by the storage engine to materialize datacaches and by the formula engine to consume such datacaches. Table filters are one of the most common reasons for excessive materialization, though they are not always responsible for bad performance.

Note   When you write a DAX filter, consider the cardinality of the resulting filter. If the cardinality using a table filter is identical to a column filter and the table filter does not expand to other tables, then the table filter can be used safely. For example, there is not usually much difference between filtering a *Date* table versus the *Date[Date]* column.

Optimizing context transitions

The storage engine can only compute simple aggregations and simple grouping over columns of the model. Anything else must be computed by the formula engine. Every time there is an iteration and a corresponding context transition, the storage engine materializes a datacache at the granularity level of the iterated table. If the expression computed during the iteration is simple enough to be solved by the storage engine, the performance is typically good. Otherwise, if the expression is too complex, a large materialization and/or a *CallbackDataID* might occur as we demonstrate in the following example. In these scenarios, simplifying the code by reducing the number of context transitions and by reducing the granularity of the iterated table greatly helps in improving performance. For example, consider a *Cashback* measure that multiplies the *Sales Amount* by the *Cashback %* attribute assigned to each *Customer* based on an algorithm defined by the marketing department. The report in Figure 20-14 displays the *Cashback* amount for each country.

Country	Cashback (slow)	Cashback (fast)
Australia	1,169,963.12	1,169,963.12
Canada	372,901.28	372,901.28
France	442,965.22	442,965.22
Germany	749,048.18	749,048.18
United Kingdom	1,003,561.31	1,003,561.31
United States	1,785,417.75	1,785,417.75
Total	**5,523,856.86**	**5,523,856.86**

FIGURE 20-14 *Cashback* reported by customer country.

The easiest and most intuitive way to create the *Cashback* measure is also the slowest, which multiplies the *Cashback %* by the *Sales Amount* for each customer, summing the result. The following query computes the slowest *Cashback* measure in the previous report, generating the server timings results visible in Figure 20-15:

```
DEFINE
    MEASURE Sales[Cashback (slow)] =
        SUMX (
            Customer,
            [Sales Amount] * Customer[Cashback %]
        )
EVALUATE
SUMMARIZECOLUMNS (
    ROLLUPADDISSUBTOTAL ( 'Customer'[Country], "IsGrandTotalRowTotal" ),
    "Cashback", 'Sales'[Cashback (slow)]
)
```

Total	SE CPU	Line	Subclass	Duration	CPU	Rows	KB	Query
46 ms	110 ms	2	Scan	24	94	18,872	295	WITH $Expr0 := (C
	x3.8	4	Scan	3	16	32	1	WITH $Expr0 := (
▓ FE	▓ SE	6	Scan	0	0	18,872	295	WITH $Expr0 := (C
17 ms	29 ms	8	Scan	2	0	1	1	WITH $Expr0 := (
37.0%	63.0%							

SE Queries	SE Cache
4	1
	25.0%

FIGURE 20-15 Server Timings running the query for the *Cashback (slow)* measure reported by country.

The queries at lines 2 and 4 of Figure 20-15 compute the result at the *Country* level, whereas the queries at lines 6 and 8 run the same task for the grand total. We will focus exclusively on the first two storage engine queries. In order to check whether the estimation for the rows materialized is correct, you can look at the query plan in Figure 20-16. This could be surprising, because it seems that a few storage engine queries are not used at all.

Line	Records	Physical Query Plan
1		AddColumns: IterPhyOp LogOp=AddColumns IterCols(0)(``[BLANK])
2		SingletonTable: IterPhyOp LogOp=AddColumns
3		Constant: LookupPhyOp LogOp=Constant Integer 0
4		AddColumns: IterPhyOp LogOp=AddColumns IterCols(0)(``[BLANK])
5		SingletonTable: IterPhyOp LogOp=AddColumns
6		Constant: LookupPhyOp LogOp=Constant Integer 0
7		Union: IterPhyOp LogOp=Union IterCols(0, 1, 2, 3)('Customer'[Country], ``[IsGr
8		GroupSemijoin: IterPhyOp LogOp=GroupSemiJoin IterCols(0, 1, 2)('Custome
9	29	Spool_Iterator<SpoolIterator>: IterPhyOp LogOp=Sum_Vertipaq IterCols(
10	29	ProjectionSpool<ProjectFusion<Copy>>: SpoolPhyOp #Records=29
11		Cache: IterPhyOp #FieldCols=1 #ValueCols=1
12		GroupSemijoin: IterPhyOp LogOp=GroupSemiJoin IterCols(0, 1, 2)('Custome
13	1	Spool_Iterator<SpoolIterator>: IterPhyOp LogOp=Sum_Vertipaq #Record
14	1	ProjectionSpool<ProjectFusion<Copy>>: SpoolPhyOp #Records=1
15		Cache: IterPhyOp #FieldCols=0 #ValueCols=1

FIGURE 20-16 Query Plan pane running the query for the *Cashback (slow)* measure reported by country.

The query plan in Figure 20-16 only reports two *Cache* nodes, which correspond to lines 4 and 8 of the Server Timings pane in Figure 20-15. This is another example of why looking at the query plan could be confusing. The formula engine is actually doing some other work, but the execution within a *CallbackDataID* is not always reported in the query plan, and this is one of those cases. This is the xmSQL query at line 4 of Figure 20-15, which returns 29 effective rows instead of the estimated 32:

```
WITH
    $Expr0 := ( [CallbackDataID ( SUMX ( Sales, Sales[Quantity]] * Sales[Net Price]] ) )
                ] ( PFDATAID ( 'DaxBook Customer'[CustomerKey] ) )
            * PFCAST ( 'DaxBook Customer'[Cashback %] AS  REAL )  )
SELECT
    'DaxBook Customer'[Country],
    SUM ( @$Expr0 )
FROM 'DaxBook Customer';
```

The DAX code passed to *CallbackDataID* must be computed for each customer by the formula engine, which receives the *CustomerKey* as argument. You can see the additional storage engine queries, but the corresponding query plan is not visible in this case. Therefore, we can only imagine what the query plan does by looking at the other storage engine query at line 2 of Figure 20-15:

```
WITH
    $Expr0 := ( CAST ( PFCAST ( 'DaxBook Sales'[Quantity] AS  INT ) AS  REAL )
            * PFCAST ( 'DaxBook Sales'[Net Price] AS  REAL )  )
SELECT
    'DaxBook Customer'[CustomerKey],
    SUM ( @$Expr0 )
FROM 'DaxBook Sales'
    LEFT OUTER JOIN 'DaxBook Customer'
        ON 'DaxBook Sales'[CustomerKey]='DaxBook Customer'[CustomerKey];
```

The result of this xmSQL query only contains two columns: the *CustomerKey* and the result of the *Sales Amount* measure for that customer. Thus, the formula engine uses the result of this query to provide a result to the *CallbackDataID* request of the former query.

Once again, instead of trying to describe the exact sequence of operations performed by the engine, it is easier to analyze the result of the storage engine queries, checking whether the materialization is larger than what is required for the query result. In this case the answer is yes: the DAX query returns only 6 visible countries, whereas a total of 29 countries were computed by the formula engine. In any case, there is a huge difference with the materialization of 18,872 customers produced by the latter xmSQL query analyzed. Is it possible to push more workload to the storage engine, aggregating the data by country instead of by customer? The answer is yes, by reducing the number of context transitions. Consider the original *Cashback* measure: the expression executed in the row context depends on a single column of the *Customer* table (*Cashback %*):

```
Sales[Cashback (slow)] :=
SUMX (
    Customer,
    [Sales Amount] * Customer[Cashback %]
)
```

Because the *Sales Amount* measure can be computed for a group of customers that have the same *Cashback %*, the optimal cardinality for the *SUMX* iterator is defined by the unique values of the *Cashback %* column. The following optimized version just replaces the first argument of *SUMX* using the unique values of *Cashback %* visible in the filter context:

```
DEFINE
    MEASURE Sales[Cashback (fast)] =
        SUMX (
            VALUES ( Customer[Cashback %] ),
            [Sales Amount] * Customer[Cashback %]
        )
EVALUATE
SUMMARIZECOLUMNS (
    ROLLUPADDISSUBTOTAL ( 'Customer'[Country], "IsGrandTotalRowTotal" ),
    "Cashback", 'Sales'[Cashback (fast)]
)
```

This way, the materialization is much smaller, as visible in Figure 20-17. However, even though the number of rows materialized is significantly smaller, the overall execution time is similar if not larger; remember that a difference of a few milliseconds should not be considered relevant.

Total	SE CPU	Line	Subclass	Duration	CPU	Rows	KB	Query
49 ms	204 ms	2	Scan	24	63	288		5 WITH $Expr0 := (C
	x4.9	4	Scan	18	141	9		1 WITH $Expr0 := (C

FE	SE
7 ms	42 ms
14.3%	85.7%

SE Queries	SE Cache
2	0
	0.0%

FIGURE 20-17 Server Timings running the query for *Cashback (fast)* reported by country.

This time there is a single xmSQL query to compute the amount by country. This is the xmSQL query at line 2 of Figure 20-17:

```
WITH
    $Expr0 := ( CAST ( PFCAST ( 'DaxBook Sales'[Quantity] AS  INT ) AS  REAL )
             * PFCAST ( 'DaxBook Sales'[Net Price] AS  REAL )  )
SELECT
    'DaxBook Customer'[Country],
    'DaxBook Customer'[Cashback %],
    SUM ( @$Expr0 )
FROM 'DaxBook Sales'
    LEFT OUTER JOIN 'DaxBook Customer'
        ON 'DaxBook Sales'[CustomerKey]='DaxBook Customer'[CustomerKey];
```

The result of this query contains three columns: *Country*, *Cashback %*, and the corresponding *Sales Amount* value. Thus, the formula engine multiplies *Cashback %* by *Sales Amount* for each row, aggregating the rows belonging to the same country. The result presents an estimated count of 288 rows, whereas there are only 65 rows consumed by the formula engine. This is visible in the query plan in Figure 20-18.

Line	Records	Physical Query Plan
7		Union: IterPhyOp LogOp=Union IterCols(0, 1, 2, 3)('Customer'[Country], '[IsGran
8		GroupSemijoin: IterPhyOp LogOp=GroupSemiJoin IterCols(0, 1, 2)('Customer'[
9	6	Spool_Iterator<SpoolIterator>: IterPhyOp LogOp=SumX IterCols(0)('Custon
10	6	AggregationSpool<Sum>: SpoolPhyOp #Records=6
11		Extend_Lookup: IterPhyOp LogOp=Multiply IterCols(0, 1)('Customer'[C
12	65	Spool_Iterator<SpoolIterator>: IterPhyOp LogOp=Sum_Vertipaq Ite
13	65	ProjectionSpool<ProjectFusion<Copy>>: SpoolPhyOp #Records=
14		Cache: IterPhyOp #FieldCols=2 #ValueCols=1
15		ColValue<'Customer'[Cashback %]>: LookupPhyOp LogOp=ColValu

FIGURE 20-18 Query Plan pane running the query for *Cashback (fast)* reported by country.

Even though it is not evident, this measure is faster than the original measure. Having a smaller footprint in memory, it performs better in more complex reports. This is immediately visible by using a slightly different report like the one in Figure 20-19, grouping the *Cashback* measure by product brand instead of by customer country.

Brand	Cashback (slow)	Cashback (fast)
A. Datum	477,910.16	477,910.16
Adventure Works	1,025,695.46	1,025,695.46
Contoso	1,464,170.77	1,464,170.77
Fabrikam	196,534.01	196,534.01
Litware	531,080.24	531,080.24
Northwind Traders	1,046,681.00	1,046,681.00
Proseware	111,461.75	111,461.75
Southridge Video	357,256.48	357,256.48
Tailspin Toys	203,818.73	203,818.73
The Phone Company	50,731.91	50,731.91
Wide World Importers	58,516.35	58,516.35
Total	**5,523,856.86**	**5,523,856.86**

FIGURE 20-19 *Cashback* reported by product brand.

The following query computes the slowest *Cashback* measure in the report shown in Figure 20-19, generating the server timings results visible in Figure 20-20:

```
DEFINE
    MEASURE Sales[Cashback (slow)] =
        SUMX (
            Customer,
            [Sales Amount] * Customer[Cashback %]
        )
EVALUATE
SUMMARIZECOLUMNS (
    ROLLUPADDISSUBTOTAL ( Product[Brand], "IsGrandTotalRowTotal" ),
    "Cashback", 'Sales'[Cashback (slow)]
)
```

Total	SE CPU	Line	Subclass	Duration	CPU	Rows	KB	Query
415 ms	922 ms	2	Scan	227	797	192,514	2,257	WITH $Expr0 := (CAST (PF
	x3.6	4	Scan	4	0	18,869	148	SELECT 'DaxBook Customer
■ FE	■ SE	6	Scan	22	109	18,872	295	WITH $Expr0 := (CAST (PF
158 ms	257 ms	8	Scan	4	16	1	1	WITH $Expr0 := ([Callbac
38.1%	61.9%							

SE Queries	SE Cache
4	0
	0.0%

FIGURE 20-20 Server Timings running the query for *Cashback (slow)* reported by brand.

There are a few differences in this query plan, but we focus on the materialization of 192,514 rows produced by the following xmSQL query at line 2 of Figure 20-20:

```
WITH
    $Expr0 := ( CAST ( PFCAST ( 'DaxBook Sales'[Quantity] AS  INT ) AS  REAL )
              * PFCAST ( 'DaxBook Sales'[Net Price] AS  REAL )  )
SELECT
    'DaxBook Customer'[CustomerKey],
    'DaxBook Product'[Brand],
    SUM ( @$Expr0 )
FROM 'DaxBook Sales'
    LEFT OUTER JOIN 'DaxBook Customer'
        ON 'DaxBook Sales'[CustomerKey]='DaxBook Customer'[CustomerKey]
    LEFT OUTER JOIN 'DaxBook Product'
        ON 'DaxBook Sales'[ProductKey]='DaxBook Product'[ProductKey];
```

The reason for the larger materialization is that now, the inner calculation computes *Sales Amount* for each combination of *CustomerKey* and *Brand*. The estimated count of 192,514 rows is confirmed by the actual count visible in the query plan in Figure 20-21.

Line	Records	Physical Query Plan
16		CrossApply: IterPhyOp LogOp=Sum_Vertipaq IterCols(0, 2)(Product [Brand], 'Cu
17	18,869	Spool_MultiValuedHashLookup: IterPhyOp LogOp=Scan_Vertipaq LookupCols
18	18,869	AggregationSpool<GroupBy>: SpoolPhyOp #Records=18869
19	18,869	Spool_Iterator<SpoolIterator>: IterPhyOp LogOp=Scan_Vertipaq IterCols
20	18,869	ProjectionSpool<ProjectFusion<>>: SpoolPhyOp #Records=18869
21		Cache: IterPhyOp #FieldCols=3 #ValueCols=0
22	192,514	Spool_Iterator<SpoolIterator>: IterPhyOp LogOp=Sum_Vertipaq IterCols(0, 2)
23	192,514	ProjectionSpool<ProjectFusion<Copy>>: SpoolPhyOp #Records=192514
24		Cache: IterPhyOp #FieldCols=2 #ValueCols=1

FIGURE 20-21 Query Plan pane running the query for the *Cashback (slow)* measure reported by country.

When the test query is using the faster measure, the materialization is much smaller and the query response time is also much faster. The execution of the following DAX query produces the server timings results visible in Figure 20-22:

```
DEFINE
    MEASURE Sales[Cashback (fast)] =
        SUMX (
            VALUES ( Customer[Cashback %] ),
            [Sales Amount] * Customer[Cashback %]
        )
EVALUATE
SUMMARIZECOLUMNS (
    ROLLUPADDISSUBTOTAL ( Product[Brand], "IsGrandTotalRowTotal" ),
    "Cashback", 'Sales'[Cashback (fast)]
)
```

Total	SE CPU	Line	Subclass	Duration	CPU	Rows	KB	Query
48 ms	172 ms	2	Scan	26	125	126		2 WITH $Expr0 := (CAST (PF(
	x4.3	4	Scan	14	47	9		1 WITH $Expr0 := (CAST (PF(

FE	SE
8 ms	40 ms
16.7%	83.3%

SE Queries	SE Cache
2	0
	0.0%

FIGURE 20-22 Server Timings running the query for *Cashback (fast)* reported by brand.

The materialization is three orders of magnitude smaller (126 rows instead of 192,000), and the total execution time is 9 times faster than the slow version (it was 415 milliseconds and it is 48 milliseconds with the fast version). Because these differences depend on the cardinality of the report, you should focus on the formula that minimizes the work in the formula engine by computing most of the aggregations in the storage engine. Reducing the number of context transitions is an important step to achieve this goal.

> **Note** Excessive materialization generated by unnecessary context transitions is the most common performance issue in DAX measures. Using table filters instead of column filters is the second most common performance issue. Therefore, making sure that your DAX measures do not have these two problems should be your priority in an optimization effort. By inspecting the server timings, you should be able to quickly see the symptoms by looking at the materialization size.

Optimizing *IF* conditions

An *IF* function is always executed by the formula engine. When there is an *IF* function within an iteration, there could be a *CallbackDataID* involved in the execution. Moreover, the engine might evaluate the arguments of the *IF* regardless of the result of the condition in the first argument. Even though the result is correct, you might pay the full cost of processing all the possible solutions. As usual, there could be different behaviors depending on the version of the DAX engine used.

Optimizing *IF* in measures

Conditional statements in a measure could trigger a dangerous side effect in the query plan, generating the calculation of every conditional branch regardless of whether it is needed or not. In general, it is a good idea to avoid or at least reduce the number of conditional statements in expressions evaluated for measures, applying filters through the filter context whenever possible.

For example, the report in Figure 20-23 displays a *Fam. Sales* measure that only considers customers with at least one child at home. Because the goal is to display the value for individual customers, the first implementation (slow) does not work for aggregations of two or more customers (Total row is blank), whereas the alternative, faster implementation also works at aggregated levels.

Date		Manufacturer	CustomerKey	Name	Sales Amount	Fam. Sales (slow)	Fam. Sales (fast)
5/10/2007 5/10/2007		☐ Adventure Works					
		☐ Contoso, Ltd	12189	Jai, Austin	1,599.90	1,599.90	1,599.90
		☐ Fabrikam, Inc.	12190	Moore, Megan	1,599.90		
		☐ Litware, Inc.	12192	Raji, Gilbert	1,599.90		
Category		■ Northwind Traders	12193	Garcia, Emily	1,599.90		
☐ Audio		☐ Proseware, Inc.	12194	Flores, Alexis	1,599.90	1,599.90	1,599.90
☐ Cameras and camcorders		☐ Wide World Importers	12195	Cook, Shelby	1,599.90	1,599.90	1,599.90
☐ Cell phones			12196	Mohamed, X...	3,199.80	3,199.80	3,199.80
☐ Computers		Class	12197	Roberts, Carlos	1,599.90	1,599.90	1,599.90
☐ Games and Toys		☐ Deluxe	12198	Cook, Cole	1,599.90	1,599.90	1,599.90
■ Home Appliances		☐ Economy	12199	Sanders, Jac...	1,599.90	1,599.90	1,599.90
☐ Music, Movies and Audio Bo...		■ Regular	**Total**		**17,598.90**		**12,799.20**
☐ TV and Video							

FIGURE 20-23 *Fam. Sales* reported by product brand.

The following query computes the *Fam. Sales (slow)* measure in a report similar to the one in Figure 20-1. For each customer, an *IF* statement checks the number of children at home to filter customers classified as a family. The execution of the following DAX query produces the server timings results visible in Figure 20-22:

```
DEFINE
    MEASURE Sales[Fam. Sales (slow)] =
        VAR ChildrenAtHome = SELECTEDVALUE ( Customer[Children At Home] )
        VAR Result =
            IF (
                ChildrenAtHome > 0,
                [Sales Amount]
            )
        RETURN Result
EVALUATE
CALCULATETABLE (
    SUMMARIZECOLUMNS (
        ROLLUPADDISSUBTOTAL (
            ROLLUPGROUP (
                'Customer'[CustomerKey],
                'Customer'[Name]
            ), "IsGrandTotalRowTotal"
```

```
    ),
        "Fam__Sales__slow_", 'Sales'[Fam. Sales (slow)]
    ),
    'Product Category'[Category] = "Home Appliances",
    'Product'[Manufacturer] = "Northwind Traders",
    'Product'[Class] = "Regular",
    DATESBETWEEN (
        'Date'[Date],
        DATE ( 2007, 5, 10 ),
        DATE ( 2007, 5, 10 )
    )
)
ORDER BY
    [IsGrandTotalRowTotal] DESC,
    'Customer'[CustomerKey],
    'Customer'[Name]
```

Total	SE CPU	Line	Subclass	Duration	CPU	Rows	KB	Query
55 ms	32 ms	2	Scan	0	0	2,559	20	SELECT 'DaxB
	x1.4	4	Scan	4	0	18,869	664	SELECT 'DaxB
■ FE	■ SE	6	Scan	5	16	18,869	74	SELECT 'DaxB
32 ms	23 ms	9	Scan	14	16	18,872	295	WITH $Expr0
58.2%	41.8%							

SE Queries	SE Cache
4	0
	0.0%

FIGURE 20-24 Server Timings running the query for *Fam. Sales (slow)* reported by customer.

The query is not that slow, but we wanted a query result with a small number or rows because the focus is mainly on the materialization required. We can avoid looking at the query plan, which is already 62 lines long, because the information provided in the Server Timings pane already highlights several facts:

- Even though the DAX result only has 7 rows, the rows materialized in three xmSQL queries have more than 18,000 rows, a number close to the number of customers.

- The materialization produced by the storage engine query at line 4 in Figure 20-24 includes information about the number of children at home computed for each customer.

- The materialization produced by the storage engine query at line 9 in Figure 20-24 includes the *Sales Amount* measure computed for each customer.

- The grand total is not computed by any storage engine query, so it is the formula engine that aggregates the customers to obtain that number.

This is the storage engine query at line 4 in Figure 20-24. It provides the information required by the formula engine to filter customers based on the number of children at home:

```
SELECT
    'DaxBook Customer'[CustomerKey],
    SUM ( ( PFDATAID ( 'DaxBook Customer'[Children At Home] ) <> 2 ) ),
    MIN ( 'DaxBook Customer'[Children At Home] ),
```

```
        MAX ( 'DaxBook Customer'[Children At Home] ),
    COUNT ( )
FROM 'DaxBook Customer';
```

This result is used as an argument to the following storage engine query at line 9 in Figure 20-24 in order to filter an estimate of 7,368 customers that have at least one child at home:

```
WITH
    $Expr0 := ( CAST ( PFCAST ( 'DaxBook Sales'[Quantity] AS  INT ) AS  REAL )
                  * PFCAST ( 'DaxBook Sales'[Net Price] AS  REAL ) )
SELECT
    'DaxBook Customer'[CustomerKey],
    SUM ( @$Expr0 )
FROM 'DaxBook Sales'
    LEFT OUTER JOIN 'DaxBook Customer'
        ON 'DaxBook Sales'[CustomerKey]='DaxBook Customer'[CustomerKey]
    LEFT OUTER JOIN 'DaxBook Date'
        ON 'DaxBook Sales'[OrderDateKey]='DaxBook Date'[DateKey]
    LEFT OUTER JOIN 'DaxBook Product'
        ON 'DaxBook Sales'[ProductKey]='DaxBook Product'[ProductKey]
    LEFT OUTER JOIN 'DaxBook Product Subcategory'
        ON 'DaxBook Product'[ProductSubcategoryKey]
            ='DaxBook Product Subcategory'[ProductSubcategoryKey]
    LEFT OUTER JOIN 'DaxBook Product Category'
        ON 'DaxBook Product Subcategory'[ProductCategoryKey]
            ='DaxBook Product Category'[ProductCategoryKey]
WHERE
    'DaxBook Customer'[CustomerKey]
        IN ( 2241, 13407, 5544, 7787, 11090, 7368, 17055, 16636, 1329, 12914..
            [7368 total values, not all displayed] )
VAND 'DaxBook Date'[Date] = 39212.000000
VAND 'DaxBook Product'[Manufacturer] = 'Northwind Traders'
VAND 'DaxBook Product'[Class] = 'Regular'
VAND 'DaxBook Product Category'[Category] = 'Home Appliances';
```

The estimated number of rows in this result is wrong, because there are only 7 rows received in the previous storage engine query. This is visible in the query plan; however, it might not be trivial to find the corresponding xmSQL query for each *Cache* node in the query plan shown in Figure 20-25.

Line	Records	Physical Query Plan
31		EmptyTable: IterPhyOp LogOp=Constant
32	7	Spool_Iterator<SpoolIterator>: IterPhyOp LogOp=Sum_Vertipaq IterCols(4)('Customer'[CustomerKey])
33	7	ProjectionSpool<ProjectFusion<Copy>>: SpoolPhyOp #Records=7
34		Cache: IterPhyOp #FieldCols=1 #ValueCols=1

FIGURE 20-25 Server Timings running the query for the *Fam. Sales (slow)* measure reported by customer.

The previous storage engine query receives a filter over the *CustomerKey* column. The formula engine requires a materialization of such a list of values in *CustomerKey* in order to provide the corresponding filter in a storage engine query. However, the materialization of a large number of customers in the formula engine is likely to be the bigger cost for this query. The size of this materialization depends on the number of customers. Therefore, a model with hundreds of thousands or millions of customers would make the performance issue evident. In this case you should look at the size of the materialization rather than just the execution time. The latter is still relatively quick. Understanding whether the materialization is efficient is important to create a formula that scales up well with a growing number of rows in the model.

The *IF* statement in the measure can only be evaluated by the formula engine. This requires either materialization like in this example, or *CallbackDataID* calls, which we describe later. A better approach is to apply a filter to the filter context using *CALCULATE*. This removes the need to evaluate an *IF* condition for every cell of the query result.

When the test query is using the faster measure, the materialization is much smaller and the query response time is also much shorter. The execution of the following DAX query produces the server timings results visible in Figure 20-26:

```
DEFINE
    MEASURE Sales[Fam. Sales (fast)] =
        CALCULATE (
            [Sales Amount],
            KEEPFILTERS ( Customer[Children At Home] > 0 )
        )
EVALUATE
CALCULATETABLE (
    SUMMARIZECOLUMNS (
        ROLLUPADDISSUBTOTAL (
            ROLLUPGROUP (
                'Customer'[CustomerKey],
                'Customer'[Name]
            ), "IsGrandTotalRowTotal"
        ),
        "Fam__Sales__fast_", 'Sales'[Fam. Sales (fast)]
    ),
    'Product Category'[Category] = "Home Appliances",
    'Product'[Manufacturer] = "Northwind Traders",
    'Product'[Class] = "Regular",
    DATESBETWEEN (
        'Date'[Date],
        DATE ( 2007, 5, 10 ),
        DATE ( 2007, 5, 10 )
    )
)
ORDER BY
    [IsGrandTotalRowTotal] DESC,
    'Customer'[CustomerKey],
    'Customer'[Name]
```

Total	SE CPU	Line	Subclass	Duration	CPU	Rows	KB	Query
47 ms	94 ms	2	Scan	0	0	2,559	20	SELECT 'DaxBo
	x3.8	4	Scan	13	94	18,872	295	WITH $Expr0 :=
▊ FE	▊ SE	6	Scan	3	0	18,869	74	SELECT 'DaxBo
22 ms	25 ms	8	Scan	9	0	1	1	WITH $Expr0 :=
46.8%	53.2%							

SE Queries	SE Cache
4	0
	0.0%

FIGURE 20-26 Server Timings running the query for *Fam. Sales (fast)* reported by customer.

Even though there are still four storage engine queries, the query at line 4 in Figure 20-24 is no longer used. The query at line 4 in Figure 20-26 corresponds to the query at line 9 in Figure 20-24. It includes the filter over the number of children, highlighted in the last two lines of the following xmSQL query:

```
WITH
    $Expr0 := ( CAST ( PFCAST ( 'DaxBook Sales'[Quantity] AS  INT ) AS  REAL )
                * PFCAST ( 'DaxBook Sales'[Net Price] AS  REAL )  )
SELECT
    'DaxBook Customer'[CustomerKey],
    SUM ( @$Expr0 )
FROM 'DaxBook Sales'
    LEFT OUTER JOIN 'DaxBook Customer'
        ON 'DaxBook Sales'[CustomerKey]='DaxBook Customer'[CustomerKey]
    LEFT OUTER JOIN 'DaxBook Date'
        ON 'DaxBook Sales'[OrderDateKey]='DaxBook Date'[DateKey]
    LEFT OUTER JOIN 'DaxBook Product'
        ON 'DaxBook Sales'[ProductKey]='DaxBook Product'[ProductKey]
    LEFT OUTER JOIN 'DaxBook Product Subcategory'
        ON 'DaxBook Product'[ProductSubcategoryKey]
                ='DaxBook Product Subcategory'[ProductSubcategoryKey]
    LEFT OUTER JOIN 'DaxBook Product Category'
        ON 'DaxBook Product Subcategory'[ProductCategoryKey]
                ='DaxBook Product Category'[ProductCategoryKey]
WHERE
    'DaxBook Date'[Date] = 39212.000000
VAND 'DaxBook Product'[Manufacturer] = 'Northwind Traders'
VAND 'DaxBook Product'[Class] = 'Regular'
VAND 'DaxBook Product Category'[Category] = 'Home Appliances'
VAND ( PFCASTCOALESCE ( 'DaxBook Customer'[Children At Home] AS  INT )
        > COALESCE ( 0 )  );
```

This different query plan has pros and cons. The advantage is that the formula engine bears a lower workload, not having to transfer the filter of customers back and forth between storage engine queries. The price to pay for this is that the execution of the filters is applied at the storage engine level, which results in an increased cost moving from a former 32 ms of *SE CPU* time to the current 94 ms of *SE CPU* time.

Another side effect of the new query plan is the additional storage engine query at line 8 in Figure 20-26; this query computes the aggregation at the grand total without having to perform such aggregation in the formula engine, as was the case in the slower measure. The code is similar to the previous xmSQL query, without the aggregation by *CustomerKey*.

As a rule of thumb, replacing a conditional statement with a filter argument in *CALCULATE* is usually a good idea, prioritizing a smaller materialization rather than looking at the execution time for small queries. This way, the expression is usually more scalable with larger data models. However, you should always evaluate the performance in specific conditions, analyzing the metrics provided by DAX Studio using different implementations; you might otherwise choose an implementation that, in a particular scenario, turns out to be slower and not faster.

Choosing between *IF* and *DIVIDE*

A very common use of the *IF* statement is to make sure that an expression is only evaluated with valid arguments. For example, an *IF* function can validate the denominator of a division to avoid a division by zero. For this specific condition, the *DIVIDE* function provides a faster alternative. It is interesting to consider why the code is faster by analyzing the different executions with DAX Studio.

The report in Figure 20-27 displays an *Average Price* measure by customer and brand.

Brand	CustomerKey	Average Price (slow)	Average Price (fast)
Southridge Video	8	35.22	35.22
Tailspin Toys	8	34.22	34.22
A. Datum	9	551.76	551.76
Adventure Works	9	425.11	425.11
Contoso	9	492.78	492.78
Litware	9	1,343.16	1,343.16
Northwind Traders	9	1,047.21	1,047.21
Total		**216.98**	**216.98**

FIGURE 20-27 *Average Price* reported by product brand and customer.

The following query computes the *Average Price (slow)* measure in the report shown in Figure 20-27. For each combination of product brand and customer, it divides the sales amount by the sum of quantity—only if the latter is not equal to zero. The execution of this DAX query produces the server timings results visible in Figure 20-28:

```
DEFINE
    MEASURE Sales[Average Price (slow)] =
        VAR Quantity = SUM ( Sales[Quantity] )
        VAR SalesAmount = [Sales Amount]
        VAR Result =
            IF (
                Quantity <> 0,
                SalesAmount / Quantity
            )
        RETURN Result
EVALUATE
TOPN (
    502,
    SUMMARIZECOLUMNS (
        ROLLUPADDISSUBTOTAL (
            ROLLUPGROUP (
                'Customer'[CustomerKey],
                'Product'[Brand]
            ), "IsGrandTotalRowTotal"
        ),
        "Average_Price__slow_", 'Sales'[Average Price (slow)]
    ),
    [IsGrandTotalRowTotal], 0,
```

```
    'Customer'[CustomerKey], 1,
    'Product'[Brand], 1
)
ORDER BY
    [IsGrandTotalRowTotal] DESC,
    'Customer'[CustomerKey],
    'Product'[Brand]
```

Total	SE CPU	Line	Subclass	Duration	CPU	Rows	KB	Query
2.338 ms	859 ms	2	Scan	204	750	192.514	3.761	WITH $Expr0 := (CAST
	x3.9	4	Scan	1	0	14	1	SELECT 'DaxBook Produ
▓ FE	▓ SE	6	Scan	1	0	18.872	148	SELECT 'DaxBook Custo
2.119 ms	219 ms	8	Scan	13	109	1	1	WITH $Expr0 := (CAST
90.6%	9.4%							

SE Queries	SE Cache
4	0
	0.0%

FIGURE 20-28 Server Timings running the query for *Average Price (slow)* reported by product brand and customer.

Though the result of the query is limited to 500 rows, the materialization of the datacaches returned by the storage engine queries is much larger. The following xmSQL query is executed at line 2 in Figure 20-28, and returns one row for each combination of customer and brand:

```
WITH
    $Expr0 := ( CAST ( PFCAST ( 'DaxBook Sales'[Quantity] AS  INT ) AS  REAL )
                * PFCAST ( 'DaxBook Sales'[Net Price] AS  REAL )  )
SELECT
    'DaxBook Customer'[CustomerKey],
    'DaxBook Product'[Brand],
    SUM ( @$Expr0 ),
    SUM ( 'DaxBook Sales'[Quantity] )
FROM 'DaxBook Sales'
    LEFT OUTER JOIN 'DaxBook Customer'
        ON 'DaxBook Sales'[CustomerKey]='DaxBook Customer'[CustomerKey]
    LEFT OUTER JOIN 'DaxBook Product'
        ON 'DaxBook Sales'[ProductKey]='DaxBook Product'[ProductKey];
```

The query does not have any filter; therefore, the formula engine evaluates every row returned by this datacache, sorting the result and choosing the first 500 rows to return. This is certainly the most expensive part of the storage engine execution, which consumes 90% of the query duration time. The other three storage engine queries return the list of product brands (line 4), the list of customers (line 6), and the value of sales amount and quantity at the grand total level (line 8). However, these queries are less important in the optimization process. What matters is the formula engine cost required to execute the *IF* condition on more than 190,000 rows. The query plan resulting from the slow version of the measure has more than 80 lines (not reported here), and it consumes every datacache multiple times. This is a side effect of having different execution branches in an *IF* statement.

The optimization of the *Average Price* measure is based on replacing the *IF* function with *DIVIDE*. The execution of the following DAX query produces the server timings results visible in Figure 20-29:

```
DEFINE
    MEASURE Sales[Average Price (fast)] =
        VAR Quantity = SUM ( Sales[Quantity] )
        VAR SalesAmount = [Sales Amount]
        VAR Result =
            DIVIDE (
                SalesAmount,
                Quantity
            )
        RETURN Result
EVALUATE
TOPN (
    502,
    SUMMARIZECOLUMNS (
        ROLLUPADDISSUBTOTAL (
            ROLLUPGROUP (
                'Customer'[CustomerKey],
                'Product'[Brand]
            ), "IsGrandTotalRowTotal"
        ),
        "Average_Price__fast_", 'Sales'[Average Price (fast)]
    ),
    [IsGrandTotalRowTotal], 0,
    'Customer'[CustomerKey], 1,
    'Product'[Brand], 1
)
ORDER BY
    [IsGrandTotalRowTotal] DESC,
    'Customer'[CustomerKey],
    'Product'[Brand]
```

Total	SE CPU	Line	Subclass	Duration	CPU	Rows	KB	Query
413 ms	751 ms	2	Scan	218	688	192,514	3,761	WITH $Expr0 := (CAS
	x3.2	4	Scan	14	63	1	1	WITH $Expr0 := (CAS

FE	SE
181 ms	232 ms
43.8%	56.2%

SE Queries	SE Cache
2	0
	0.0%

FIGURE 20-29 Server Timings running the query for *Average Price (fast)* reported by product brand and customer.

The query now runs in 413 milliseconds, saving more than 80% of the execution time. At first sight, there being only two storage engine queries instead of four might seem like a good reason for the improved performance. However, this is not really the case. Overall, the *SE CPU* time did not change significantly, and the larger materialization is still there. The optimization is obtained by a shorter and more efficient query plan, which has only 36 lines instead of more than 80 generated by the slower query. In other words, *DIVIDE* reduces the size and complexity of the query plan, saving time in the formula engine execution by almost one order of magnitude.

Optimizing *IF* in iterators

Using the *IF* statement within a large iterator might create expensive callbacks to the formula engine. For example, consider a *Discounted Sales* measure that applies a 10% discount to every transaction that has a quantity greater than or equal to 3. The report in Figure 20-30 displays the *Discounted Sales* amount for each product brand.

Brand	Sales Amount	Discounted Sales (slow)	Discounted Sales (scalable)
A. Datum	251,211,515.57	242,822,223.32	242,822,223.32
Adventure Works	518,462,059.16	501,169,853.87	501,169,853.87
Contoso	871,501,804.63	842,438,948.01	842,438,948.01
Fabrikam	627,751,182.08	606,861,928.96	606,861,928.96
Litware	416,239,414.35	402,383,288.37	402,383,288.37
Northwind Traders	151,481,923.36	146,432,377.72	146,432,377.72
Proseware	312,763,353.13	302,307,008.81	302,307,008.81
Southridge Video	183,482,982.39	177,362,856.28	177,362,856.28
Tailspin Toys	42,801,223.58	41,376,146.41	41,376,146.41
The Phone Company	174,742,660.20	168,915,267.19	168,915,267.19
Wide World Importers	254,953,905.77	246,451,374.64	246,451,374.64
Total	**3,805,392,024.21**	**3,678,521,273.59**	**3,678,521,273.59**

FIGURE 20-30 *Discounted Sales* reported by product brand.

The following query computes the slower *Discounted Sales* measure in the previous report, generating the server timings results visible in Figure 20-31:

```
DEFINE
    MEASURE Sales[Discounted Sales (slow)] =
        SUMX (
            Sales,
            Sales[Quantity] * Sales[Net Price] * IF (
                Sales[Quantity] >= 3,
                .9,
                1
            )
        )
EVALUATE
SUMMARIZECOLUMNS (
    ROLLUPADDISSUBTOTAL ( 'Product'[Brand], "IsGrandTotalRowTotal" ),
    "Sales_Amount", 'Sales'[Sales Amount],
    "Discounted_Sales__slow_", 'Sales'[Discounted Sales (slow)]
)
ORDER BY
    [IsGrandTotalRowTotal] DESC,
    'Product'[Brand]
```

Total	SE CPU	Line	Subclass	Duration	CPU	Rows	KB	Query
142 ms	438 ms	2	Scan	77	172	14	1	WITH SExpr0 := ((CAS
	x3.3	4	Scan	56	266	1	1	WITH SExpr0 := ((CAS

FE	SE
9 ms	133 ms
6.3%	93.7%

SE Queries	SE Cache
2	0
	0.0%

FIGURE 20-31 Server Timings running the query for *Discounted Sales (slow)* reported by product brand.

The *IF* statement executed in the *SUMX* iterator produces two storage engine queries with a *CallbackDataID* call. The following is the xmSQL query at line 2 of Figure 20-31:

```
WITH
    $Expr0 := ( ( CAST ( PFCAST ( 'DaxBook Sales'[Quantity] AS INT ) AS REAL )
                    * PFCAST ( 'DaxBook Sales'[Net Price] AS REAL ) )
                    * [CallbackDataID ( IF ( Sales[Quantity]] >= 3, .9, 1 ) ) ]
                        ( PFDATAID ( 'DaxBook Sales'[Quantity] ) ) ) ,
    $Expr1 := ( CAST ( PFCAST ( 'DaxBook Sales'[Quantity] AS INT ) AS REAL )
                    * PFCAST ( 'DaxBook Sales'[Net Price] AS REAL ) )
SELECT
    'DaxBook Product'[Brand],
    SUM ( @$Expr0 ),
    SUM ( @$Expr1 )
FROM 'DaxBook Sales'
    LEFT OUTER JOIN 'DaxBook Product'
        ON 'DaxBook Sales'[ProductKey]='DaxBook Product'[ProductKey];
```

The presence of a *CallbackDataID* comes with two consequences: a slower execution time compared to the storage engine performance and the unavailability of the storage engine cache. The datacache must be computed every time and cannot be retrieved from the cache in subsequent requests. The second issue could be more important than the first one, as is the case for this example.

The *CallbackDataID* can be removed by rewriting the measure in a different way, summing the value of two *CALCULATE* statements with different filters. For example, the *Discounted Sales* measure can be rewritten using two *CALCULATE* functions, one for each percentage, filtering the transactions that share the same multiplicator. The following DAX query implements a version of *Discounted Sales* that does not rely on any *CallbackDataID*. The code is longer and requires *KEEPFILTERS* to provide the same semantic as in the original measure, producing the server timings results visible in Figure 20-32:

```
DEFINE
    MEASURE Sales[Discounted Sales (scalable)] =
        CALCULATE (
            SUMX (
                Sales,
                Sales[Quantity] * Sales[Net Price]
            ) * .9,
            KEEPFILTERS ( Sales[Quantity] >= 3 )
        ) + CALCULATE (
```

```
        SUMX (
            Sales,
            Sales[Quantity] * Sales[Net Price]
        ),
        KEEPFILTERS ( NOT ( Sales[Quantity] >= 3 ) )
    )
EVALUATE
SUMMARIZECOLUMNS (
    ROLLUPADDISSUBTOTAL ( 'Product'[Brand], "IsGrandTotalRowTotal" ),
    "Sales_Amount", 'Sales'[Sales Amount],
    "Discounted_Sales__slow_", 'Sales'[Discounted Sales (scalable)]
)
```

Total	SE CPU	Line	Subclass	Duration	CPU	Rows	KB	Query
159 ms	751 ms	2	Scan	34	94	14		1 WITH $Expr0 := (CAST
	x5.1	4	Scan	26	141	14		1 WITH $Expr0 := (CAST
FE	SE	6	Scan	37	172	14		1 WITH $Expr0 := (CAST
13 ms	146 ms	8	Scan	14	94	1		1 WITH $Expr0 := (CAST
8.2%	91.8%	10	Scan	15	109	1		1 WITH $Expr0 := (CAST
		12	Scan	20	141	1		1 WITH $Expr0 := (CAST

SE Queries	SE Cache
6	0
	0.0%

FIGURE 20-32 Server Timings running the query for *Discounted Sales (scalable)* by product brand for the first time.

Actually, in this simple query the result is not faster at all. The query required 159 milliseconds instead of the 142 milliseconds of the "slow" version. However, we called this measure "scalable." Indeed, the important advantage is that a second execution of the last query with a warm cache produces the results visible in Figure 20-33, whereas multiple executions of the query for the "slow" version always produce a result similar to the one shown in Figure 20-31.

Total	SE CPU	Line	Subclass	Duration	CPU	Rows	KB	Query
8 ms	0 ms	2	Scan	0	0	14		1 WITH $Expr0 := (CAS
	x0.0	4	Scan	0	0	14		1 WITH $Expr0 := (CAS
FE	SE	6	Scan	0	0	14		1 WITH $Expr0 := (CAS
8 ms	0 ms	8	Scan	0	0	1		1 WITH $Expr0 := (CAS
100.0%	0.0%	10	Scan	0	0	1		1 WITH $Expr0 := (CAS
		12	Scan	0	0	1		1 WITH $Expr0 := (CAS

SE Queries	SE Cache
6	6
	100.0%

FIGURE 20-33 Server Timings running the query for *Discounted Sales (scalable)* by product brand a second time.

The Server Timings in Figure 20-33 show that there is no *SE CPU* cost after the first execution of the query. This is important when a model is published on a server and many users open the same reports: Users experience a faster response time, and the memory and CPU workload on the server side is reduced. This optimization is particularly relevant in environments with a fixed reserved capacity, such as Power BI Premium and Power BI Report Server.

The rule of thumb is to carefully consider the *IF* function in the expression of an iterator with a large cardinality because of the possible presence of *CallbackDataID* in the storage engine queries. The next section includes a deeper discussion on the impact of *CallbackDataID*, which might be required by many other DAX functions used in iterators.

Note The *SWITCH* function in DAX is similar to a series of nested *IF* functions and can be optimized in a similar way.

Reducing the impact of *CallbackDataID*

In Chapter 19, you saw that the *CallbackDataID* function in a storage engine query can have a huge performance impact. This is because it slows down the storage engine execution, and it disables the use of the storage engine cache for the datacache produced. Identifying the *CallbackDataID* is important because this is often the reason behind a bottleneck in the storage engine, especially for models that only have a few million rows in their largest table (scan time should typically be in the order of magnitude of 10–100 milliseconds).

For example, consider the following query where the *Rounded Sales* measure computes its result rounding *Unit Price* to the nearest integer. The report in Figure 20-34 displays the *Rounded Sales* amount for each product brand.

Brand	Rounded Sales (slow)	Rounded Sales (fast)
A. Datum	251,231,956.00	251,231,956.00
Adventure Works	518,414,395.00	518,414,395.00
Contoso	871,357,864.00	871,357,864.00
Fabrikam	627,737,296.00	627,737,296.00
Litware	416,210,111.00	416,210,111.00
Northwind Traders	151,497,660.00	151,497,660.00
Proseware	312,741,659.00	312,741,659.00
Southridge Video	183,564,219.00	183,564,219.00
Tailspin Toys	42,843,104.00	42,843,104.00
The Phone Company	174,730,262.00	174,730,262.00
Wide World Importers	254,943,149.00	254,943,149.00
Total	**3,805,271,675.00**	**3,805,271,675.00**

FIGURE 20-34 *Rounded Sales* reported by product brand.

The simpler implementation of *Rounded Sales* applies the *ROUND* function to every row of the *Sales* table. This results in a *CallbackDataID* call, which slows down the execution, thus lowering performance. The following query computes the slowest *Rounded Sales* measure in the previous report, generating the server timings results visible in Figure 20-35:

```
DEFINE
    MEASURE Sales[Rounded Sales (slow)] =
        SUMX (
            Sales,
            Sales[Quantity] * ROUND ( Sales[Net Price], 0 )
        )
EVALUATE
TOPN (
    502,
```

```
    SUMMARIZECOLUMNS (
        ROLLUPADDISSUBTOTAL ( 'Product'[Brand], "IsGrandTotalRowTotal" ),
        "Rounded_Sales", 'Sales'[Rounded Sales (slow)]
    ),
    [IsGrandTotalRowTotal], 0,
    'Product'[Brand], 1
)
ORDER BY
    [IsGrandTotalRowTotal] DESC,
    'Product'[Brand]
```

Total	SE CPU	Line	Subclass	Duration	CPU	Rows	KB	Query
632 ms	3,500 ms	2	Scan	326	1,703	14	1	WITH SExpr0 := (C
	x5.6	4	Scan	300	1,797	1	1	WITH SExpr0 := (C

FE	SE
6 ms	626 ms
0.9%	99.1%

SE Queries	SE Cache
2	0
	0.0%

FIGURE 20-35 Server Timings running the query for *Rounded Sales (slow)*.

The two storage engine queries at lines 2 and 4 compute the value for each brand and for the grand total, respectively. This is the xmSQL query at line 2 of Figure 20-35:

```
WITH
    $Expr0 := ( CAST ( PFCAST ( 'DaxBook Sales'[Quantity] AS  INT ) AS  REAL )
            * [CallbackDataID ( ROUND ( Sales[Net Price]], 0 ) ) ]
                        ( PFDATAID ( 'DaxBook Sales'[Net Price] ) ) )
SELECT
    'DaxBook Product'[Brand],
    SUM ( @$Expr0 )
FROM 'DaxBook Sales'
    LEFT OUTER JOIN 'DaxBook Product'
        ON 'DaxBook Sales'[ProductKey]='DaxBook Product'[ProductKey];
```

The *Sales* table contains more than 12 million rows, and each storage engine query computes an equivalent amount of *CallbackDataID* calls to execute the *ROUND* function. Indeed, the formula engine executes the *ROUND* operation to remove the decimal part of the *Unit Price* value. Based on the Server Timings report, we can estimate that the formula engine executes around 7,000 *ROUND* functions per millisecond. It is important to keep these numbers in mind, so that you can evaluate whether or not the cardinality of an iterator generating *CallbackDataID* calls would benefit from some amount of optimization. If the table contained 12,000 rows instead of 12 million rows, the priority would be to optimize something else. However, optimizing the measure in the current model requires reducing the number of *CallbackDataID* calls.

We aim to reduce the number of *CallbackDataID* calls by refactoring the measure. By looking at the information provided by VertiPaq Analyzer, we know that the *Sales* table has more than 12 million rows, whereas the *Net Price* column in the *Sales* table has less than 2,500 unique values. Accordingly, the formula can compute the same result by multiplying the rounded value of each unique *Unit Price* value by the sum of *Quantity* for all the *Sales* transaction with the same *Unit Price*.

> **Note** You should always use the statistics of your data model during DAX optimization. A quick way to obtain these numbers for a data model is by using VertiPaq Analyzer (http://www.sqlbi.com/tools/vertipaq-analyzer/).

The following optimized version of *Rounded Sales* materializes up to 2,500 rows computing the sum of *Quantity* iterating the unique values of *Unit Price*:

```
DEFINE
    MEASURE Sales[Rounded Sales (fast)] =
        SUMX (
            VALUES ( Sales[Net Price] ),
            CALCULATE ( SUM ( Sales[Quantity] ) ) * ROUND ( Sales[Net Price], 0 )
        )
EVALUATE
TOPN (
    502,
    SUMMARIZECOLUMNS (
        ROLLUPADDISSUBTOTAL ( 'Product'[Brand], "IsGrandTotalRowTotal" ),
        "Rounded_Sales", 'Sales'[Rounded Sales (fast)]
    ),
    [IsGrandTotalRowTotal], 0,
    'Product'[Brand], 1
)
ORDER BY
    [IsGrandTotalRowTotal] DESC,
    'Product'[Brand]
```

This way, the formula engine executes the *ROUND* function using the result of the datacache returning the sum of *Quantity* for each *Net Price*. Despite a larger materialization compared to the slow version, the time required to obtain the solution is reduced by almost one order of magnitude. Moreover, the results provided by the storage engine queries can be reused in following executions because the storage engine cache will store the result of xmSQL queries that do not have any *CallbackDataID* calls.

Total	SE CPU	Line	Subclass	Duration	CPU	Rows	KB	Query
51 ms	297 ms	2	Scan	30	219	3,863	46	SELECT '
	x7.1	4	Scan	12	78	2,472	39	SELECT '

FE	SE
9 ms	42 ms
17.6%	82.4%

SE Queries	SE Cache
2	0
	0.0%

FIGURE 20-36 Server Timings running the query for *Rounded Sales (fast)*.

The following is the xmSQL query at line 2 of Figure 20-36. This query returns the *Net Price* and the sum of the *Quantity* for each brand and does not have any *CallbackDataID* calls:

```
SELECT
    'DaxBook Product'[Brand],
    'DaxBook Sales'[Net Price],
    SUM ( 'DaxBook Sales'[Quantity] )
FROM 'DaxBook Sales'
    LEFT OUTER JOIN 'DaxBook Product'
        ON 'DaxBook Sales'[ProductKey]='DaxBook Product'[ProductKey];
```

In this latter version, the rounding is executed by the formula engine and not by the storage engine through the *CallbackDataID*. Be mindful that a very large number of unique values in *Net Price* would require a bigger materialization, up to the point where the previous version could be faster with a different data distribution. If *Net Price* had millions of unique values, a benchmark comparison between the two solutions would be required in order to determine the optimal solution. Moreover, the result could be different depending on the hardware. Rather than assuming that one technique is better than another, you should always evaluate the performance using a real database and not just a sample before making a decision.

Finally, remember that most of the scalar DAX functions that do not aggregate data require a *CallbackDataID* if executed in an iterator. For example, *DATE, VALUE*, most of the type conversions, *IFERROR, DIVIDE*, and all the rounding, mathematical, and date/time functions are only implemented in the formula engine. Most of the time, their presence in an iterator generates a *CallbackDataID* call. However, you always have to check the xmSQL query to verify whether a *CallbackDataID* is present or not.

Optimizing nested iterators

Nested iterators in DAX cannot be merged into a single storage engine query. Only the innermost iterator can be executed using a storage engine query, whereas the outer iterators typically require either a larger materialization or additional storage engine queries.

For example, consider another *Cashback* measure named *"Cashback Sim."* that simulates a cashback for each customer using the current price of each product multiplied by the historical quantity and the cashback percentage of each customer. The report in Figure 20-37 displays the *Cashback Sim.* amount for each country.

Country	Cashback Sim. (slow)	Cashback Sim. (medium)	Cashback Sim. (fast)
Australia	1,308,420.16	1,308,420.16	1,308,420.16
Canada	398,393.28	398,393.28	398,393.28
France	489,314.08	489,314.08	489,314.08
Germany	828,920.45	828,920.45	828,920.45
United Kingdom	1,110,960.36	1,110,960.36	1,110,960.36
United States	1,912,379.56	1,912,379.56	1,912,379.56
Total	**6,048,387.89**	**6,048,387.89**	**6,048,387.89**

FIGURE 20-37 *Cashback Sim.* reported by customer country.

The first and slowest implementation iterates the *Customer* and *Product* tables in order to retrieve the cashback percentage of the customer and the current price of the product, respectively. The innermost iterators retrieve the quantity sold for each combination of customer and product, multiplying it by *Unit Price* and *Cashback %*. The following query computes the slowest *Cashback Sim.* measure in the previous report, generating the server timings results visible in Figure 20-38:

```
DEFINE
    MEASURE Sales[Cashback Sim. (slow)] =
        SUMX (
            Customer,
            SUMX (
                'Product',
                SUMX (
                    RELATEDTABLE ( Sales ),
                    Sales[Quantity] * 'Product'[Unit Price] * Customer[Cashback %]
                )
            )
        )
EVALUATE
TOPN (
    502,
    SUMMARIZECOLUMNS (
        ROLLUPADDISSUBTOTAL ( 'Customer'[Country], "IsGrandTotalRowTotal" ),
        "Cashback Sim. (slow)", 'Sales'[Cashback Sim. (slow)]
    ),
    [IsGrandTotalRowTotal], 0,
    'Customer'[Country], 1
)
ORDER BY
    [IsGrandTotalRowTotal] DESC,
    'Customer'[Country]
```

Total	SE CPU	Line	Subclass	Duration	CPU	Rows	KB	Query
12,891 ms	11,516 ms	2	Scan	5,575	11,484	12,527,442	97,871	SELECT
	x2.1	4	Scan	0	0	2,517	20	SELECT
▩ FE	▩ SE	6	Scan	3	16	18,869	74	SELECT
7,305 ms	5,586 ms	8	Scan	3	0	32	1	WITH S
56.7%	43.3%	10	Scan	0	0	12,527,442	97,871	SELECT
		12	Scan	3	16	18,869	74	SELECT
SE Queries	SE Cache	14	Scan	2	0	1	1	WITH S
7	1							
	14.3%							

FIGURE 20-38 Server Timings running the query for the *Cashback Sim. (slow)* measure reported by country.

The execution cost is split between the storage engine and the formula engine. The former pays a big price to produce a large materialization, whereas the latter spends time consuming that large set of materialized data. The storage engine queries at lines 2 and 10 of Figure 20-38 are identical and materialize the following columns for the entire *Sales* table: *CustomerKey, ProductKey, Quantity,* and *RowNumber*:

```
SELECT
    'DaxBook Customer'[CustomerKey],
    'DaxBook Product'[ProductKey],
    'DaxBook Sales'[RowNumber],
    'DaxBook Sales'[Quantity]
```

```
FROM 'DaxBook Sales'
    LEFT OUTER JOIN 'DaxBook Customer'
        ON 'DaxBook Sales'[CustomerKey]='DaxBook Customer'[CustomerKey]
    LEFT OUTER JOIN 'DaxBook Product'
        ON 'DaxBook Sales'[ProductKey]='DaxBook Product'[ProductKey];
```

The *RowNumber* is a special column inaccessible to DAX that is used to uniquely identify a row in a table. These four columns are used in the formula engine to compute the formula in the innermost iterator, which considers the sales for each combination of *Customer* and *Product*. The query at line 2 creates the datacache that is also returned at line 10, hitting the cache. The presence of this second storage engine query is caused by the need to compute the grand total in *SUMMARIZECOLUMNS*. Without the two levels of granularity in the result, half the query plan and half the storage engine queries would not be necessary.

The DAX measure iterates two tables (*Customer* and *Product*) producing all the possible combinations. For each combination of customer and product, the innermost *SUMX* function iterates only the corresponding rows in *Sales*. The formula also considers the combinations of *Customer* and *Product* that do not have any rows in the *Sales* table, potentially wasting precious CPU time. The query plan shows that there are 2,517 products and 18,869 customers; these are the same numbers estimated for the storage engine queries at lines 4 and 6 in Figure 20-38, respectively. Therefore, the formula engine performs 1,326,280 aggregations of the rows materialized by the *Sales* table, as shown in the excerpt of the query plan in Figure 20-39. The *Records* column shows the number of rows iterated by consumed datacaches returned by storage engine queries (see the *Cache* nodes at lines 28, 33, and 36) or computed by other formula engine operations (see the *CrossApply* node at line 23).

Line	Records	Physical Query Plan
20	1,326,280	Spool_Iterator<SpoolIterator>: IterPhyOp LogOp=SumX IterCols(2, 27, 29, 45)('Customer'[CustomerKey].
21	1,326,280	AggregationSpool<Sum>: SpoolPhyOp #Records=1326280
22		Extend_Lookup: IterPhyOp LogOp=Multiply IterCols(27, 45, 168)('Customer'[Cashback %], 'Product'[
23		CrossApply: IterPhyOp LogOp=Multiply IterCols(27, 45, 168)('Customer'[Cashback %], 'Product'[U
24	18,869	Spool_MultiValuedHashLookup: IterPhyOp LogOp=Scan_Vertipaq LookupCols(2)('Customer'[C
25	18,869	AggregationSpool<GroupBy>: SpoolPhyOp #Records=18869
26	18,869	Spool_Iterator<SpoolIterator>: IterPhyOp LogOp=Scan_Vertipaq IterCols(0, 2, 27)('Custom
27	18,869	ProjectionSpool<ProjectFusion<>>: SpoolPhyOp #Records=18869
28		Cache: IterPhyOp #FieldCols=3 #ValueCols=0
29	2,517	Spool_MultiValuedHashLookup: IterPhyOp LogOp=Scan_Vertipaq LookupCols(29)('Product'[Pro
30	2,517	AggregationSpool<GroupBy>: SpoolPhyOp #Records=2517
31	2,517	Spool_Iterator<SpoolIterator>: IterPhyOp LogOp=Scan_Vertipaq IterCols(28, 29, 45)('Prod
32	2,517	ProjectionSpool<ProjectFusion<>>: SpoolPhyOp #Records=2517
33		Cache: IterPhyOp #FieldCols=3 #ValueCols=0
34	12,527,442	Spool_Iterator<SpoolIterator>: IterPhyOp LogOp=Scan_Vertipaq IterCols(2, 29, 153, 168)('Cust
35	12,527,442	ProjectionSpool<ProjectFusion<>>: SpoolPhyOp #Records=12527442
36		Cache: IterPhyOp #FieldCols=4 #ValueCols=0

FIGURE 20-39 Query Plan pane running the query for the *Cashback Sim. (slow)* measure reported by country.

Although the DAX code iterates the tables, the xmSQL code only retrieves the columns of the tables uniquely representing one row of each table. This reduces the number of columns materialized, even though the cardinality of the tables iterated is larger than necessary. At this point, there are two important considerations:

- The cardinality of the iterators is larger than required. Thanks to the context transition, it is possible to reduce the cardinality of the outer iterators; that way, the query context considers all the rows in *Sales* for a given combination of *Unit Price* and *Cashback %*, instead of each combination of product and customer.

- Removing nested iterators would produce a better query plan, also removing expensive materialization.

The first consideration should suggest applying the technique previously described to optimize the context transitions. Indeed, the *RELATEDTABLE* function is like a *CALCULATETABLE* without filter arguments that only performs a context transition. The first variation to the DAX measure is a "medium" version that iterates the *Cashback %* and *Unit Price* columns, instead of iterating by *Customer* and *Product*. The semantic of the query is still the same because the innermost expression only depends on these columns:

```
DEFINE
    MEASURE Sales[Cashback Sim. (medium)] =
        SUMX (
            VALUES ( Customer[Cashback %] ),
            SUMX (
                VALUES ( 'Product'[Unit Price] ),
                SUMX (
                    RELATEDTABLE ( Sales ),
                    Sales[Quantity] * 'Product'[Unit Price] * Customer[Cashback %]
                )
            )
        )
EVALUATE
TOPN (
    502,
    SUMMARIZECOLUMNS (
        ROLLUPADDISSUBTOTAL ( 'Customer'[Country], "IsGrandTotalRowTotal" ),
        "Cashback Sim. (medium)", 'Sales'[Cashback Sim. (medium)]
    ),
    [IsGrandTotalRowTotal], 0,
    'Customer'[Country], 1
)
ORDER BY
    [IsGrandTotalRowTotal] DESC,
    'Customer'[Country]
```

Figure 20-40 shows that the execution of the "medium" version is orders of magnitude faster than the "slow" version, thanks to a smaller granularity and a simpler dependency between tables iterated and columns referenced.

Total	SE CPU	Line	Subclass	Duration	CPU	Rows	KB	Query
105 ms	375 ms	2	Scan	52	234	18,774	221	WITH SE
	x4.1	4	Scan	39	141	2,444	29	WITH SE

FE	SE
14 ms	91 ms
13.3%	86.7%

SE Queries	SE Cache
2	0
	0.0%

FIGURE 20-40 Server Timings running the query for the *Cashback Sim. (medium)* measure reported by country.

The two storage engine queries provide a result for each of the cardinalities of the result. The following is the storage query at line 2, whereas the similar query at line 4 does not include the *Country* column and is used for the grand total:

```
WITH
    $Expr0 := (  ( CAST ( PFCAST ( 'DaxBook Sales'[Quantity] AS  INT ) AS  REAL )
                    * PFCAST ( 'DaxBook Product'[Unit Price] AS  REAL )  )
                    * PFCAST ( 'DaxBook Customer'[Cashback] AS  REAL )  )
SELECT
    'DaxBook Customer'[Country],
    'DaxBook Customer'[Cashback],
    'DaxBook Product'[Unit Price],
    SUM ( @$Expr0 )
FROM 'DaxBook Sales'
    LEFT OUTER JOIN 'DaxBook Customer'
        ON 'DaxBook Sales'[CustomerKey]='DaxBook Customer'[CustomerKey]
    LEFT OUTER JOIN 'DaxBook Product'
        ON 'DaxBook Sales'[ProductKey]='DaxBook Product'[ProductKey];
```

The "medium" version of the *Cashback Sim.* measure still contains the same number of nested iterators, potentially considering all the possible combinations between the values of the *Unit Price* and *Cashback %* columns. In this simple measure, the query plan is able to establish the dependencies on the *Sales* table, reducing the calculation to the existing combinations. However, there is an alternative DAX syntax to explicitly instruct the engine to only consider the existing combinations. Instead of using nested iterators, a single iterator over the result of a *SUMMARIZE* enforces a query plan that does not compute calculations over non-existing combinations. The following version named "improved" could produce a more efficient query plan in complex scenarios, even though in this example it generates the same result and query plan:

```
MEASURE Sales[Cashback Sim. (improved)] =
    SUMX (
        SUMMARIZE (
            Sales,
            'Product'[Unit Price],
            Customer[Cashback %]
        ),
        CALCULATE ( SUM ( Sales[Quantity] ) )
            * 'Product'[Unit Price] * Customer[Cashback %]
    )
```

The "medium" and "improved" versions of the *Cashback Sim.* measure can easily be adapted to use existing measures in the innermost calculations. Indeed, the "improved" version uses a *CALCULATE* function to compute the sum of *Sales[Quantity]* for a given combination of *Unit Price* and *Cashback %*, just like a measure reference would. You should consider this approach to write efficient code that is easier to maintain. However, a more efficient version is possible by removing any nested iterators.

Note A measure definition often includes aggregation functions such as *SUM*. With the exception of *DISTINCTCOUNT*, simple aggregation functions are just a shorter syntax for an iterator. For example, *SUM* internally invokes *SUMX*. Hence, a measure reference in an iterator often implies the execution of another nested iterator with a context transition in the middle. When this is required by the nature of the calculation, this is a necessary computational cost. When the nested iterators are additive like the two nested *SUMX/SUM* of the *Cashback Sim. (improved)* measure, then a consolidation of the calculation may be considered to optimize the performance; however, this could affect the readability and reusability of the measure.

The following "fast" version of the *Cashback Sim.* measure optimizes the performance, at the cost of reducing the ability to reuse the business logic of existing measures:

```
DEFINE
    MEASURE Sales[Cashback Sim. (fast)] =
        SUMX (
            Sales,
            Sales[Quantity]
                * RELATED ( 'Product'[Unit Price] )
                * RELATED ( Customer[Cashback %] )
        )
EVALUATE
TOPN (
    502,
    SUMMARIZECOLUMNS (
        ROLLUPADDISSUBTOTAL ( 'Customer'[Country], "IsGrandTotalRowTotal" ),
        "Cashback Sim. (fast)", 'Sales'[Cashback Sim. (fast)]
    ),
    [IsGrandTotalRowTotal], 0,
    'Customer'[Country], 1
)
ORDER BY
    [IsGrandTotalRowTotal] DESC,
    'Customer'[Country]
```

Figure 20-41 shows the server timings information of the "fast" version, which saves more than 50% of the execution time compared to the "medium" and "improved" versions.

Total	SE CPU	Line	Subclass	Duration	CPU	Rows	KB	Query
47 ms	140 ms	2	Scan	24	31	32	1	WITH SE
	x3.6	4	Scan	15	109	1	1	WITH SE

FE	SE
8 ms	39 ms
17.0%	83.0%

SE Queries	SE Cache
2	0
	0.0%

FIGURE 20-41 Server Timings running the query for the *Cashback Sim. (fast)* measure reported by country.

The measure with a single iterator without context transitions generates the following simple storage engine query, reported at line 2 of Figure 20-41:

```
WITH
    $Expr0 := ( ( CAST ( PFCAST ( 'DaxBook Sales'[Quantity] AS  INT ) AS  REAL )
                            * PFCAST ( 'DaxBook Product'[Unit Price] AS  REAL ) )
                            * PFCAST ( 'DaxBook Customer'[Cashback] AS  REAL ) )
SELECT
    'DaxBook Customer'[Country],
    SUM ( @$Expr0 )
FROM 'DaxBook Sales'
    LEFT OUTER JOIN 'DaxBook Customer'
        ON 'DaxBook Sales'[CustomerKey]='DaxBook Customer'[CustomerKey]
    LEFT OUTER JOIN 'DaxBook Product'
        ON 'DaxBook Sales'[ProductKey]='DaxBook Product'[ProductKey];
```

Using the *RELATED* function does not require any *CallbackDataID*. Indeed, the only consequence of *RELATED* is that it enforces a join in the storage engine to enable the access to the related column, which typically has a smaller performance impact compared to a *CallbackDataID*. However, the "fast" version of the measure is not suggested unless it is critical to obtain the last additional performance improvement and to keep the materialization at a minimal level.

Avoiding table filters for *DISTINCTCOUNT*

We already mentioned that filter arguments in *CALCULATE/CALCULATETABLE* functions should be applied to columns instead of tables. The goal of this example on the same topic is to show you an additional query plan pattern that you might find in server timings. A side effect of a table filter is that it requires a large materialization to the storage engine, to enable the formula engine to compute the result. However, for non-additive expressions, the query plan might generate one storage engine query for each element included in the granularity of the result. The *DISTINCTCOUNT* aggregation is a simple and common example of a non-additive expression.

For example, consider the report in Figure 20-42 that shows the number of customers that made purchases over $1,000 (*Customers 1k*) for each product name.

Product Name	Customers 1k (slow)	Customers 1k (fast)
A. Datum SLR Camera 35" X358 Pink	59	59
A. Datum SLR Camera 35" X358 Silver	112	112
A. Datum SLR Camera 35" X358 Silver Grey	182	182
A. Datum SLR Camera M135 Black	115	115
A. Datum SLR Camera M136 Silver	116	116
A. Datum SLR Camera M137 Grey	117	117
A. Datum SLR Camera M138 Silver Grey	91	91
Total	**18,852**	**18,852**

FIGURE 20-42 Customers with purchase amounts over $1,000 for each product.

The filter condition in the *Customers 1k* measure requires two columns. The less efficient way to implement such a condition is by using a filter over the *Sales* table. The following query computes the *Customers 1k* measure in the previous report, generating the server timings results visible in Figure 20-43:

```
DEFINE
    MEASURE Sales[Customers 1k (slow)] =
        CALCULATE (
            DISTINCTCOUNT ( Sales[CustomerKey] ),
            FILTER (
                Sales,
                Sales[Quantity] * Sales[Net Price] > 1000
            )
        )
EVALUATE
TOPN (
    502,
    SUMMARIZECOLUMNS (
        ROLLUPADDISSUBTOTAL ( 'Product'[Product Name], "IsGrandTotalRowTotal" ),
        "Customers_1k__slow_", 'Sales'[Customers 1k (slow)]
    ),
    [IsGrandTotalRowTotal], 0,
    'Product'[Product Name], 1
)
ORDER BY
    [IsGrandTotalRowTotal] DESC,
    'Product'[Product Name]
```

Total	SE CPU	Line	Subclass	Duration	CPU	Rows	KB	Query
45,944 ms	192,450 ms	2	Scan	37	172	13,432	53	SELECT 'DaxBook P
	x4.7	6	Scan	35	156	1	1	SELECT DCOUNT (
FE	SE	10	Scan	39	156	1	1	SELECT DCOUNT (
4,832 ms	41,112 ms	14	Scan	33	141	1	1	SELECT DCOUNT (
10.5%	89.5%	18	Scan	31	109	1	1	SELECT DCOUNT (
		22	Scan	32	188	1	1	SELECT DCOUNT (
SE Queries	SE Cache	26	Scan	32	219	1	1	SELECT DCOUNT (
1,093	0	30	Scan	33	141	1	1	SELECT DCOUNT (
	0.0%	34	Scan	33	172	1	1	SELECT DCOUNT (

FIGURE 20-43 Server Timings running the query for the *Customers 1k (slow)* measure.

This query generates a large number of storage engine queries—one query for each product included in the result. Because each storage engine query requires 100 to 200 milliseconds, there are a total of several minutes of CPU cost, and the latency is below one minute just because of the parallelism of the storage engine.

The first xmSQL query at line 2 of Figure 20-43 returns the list of product names, including *Quantity* and *Net Price* for the sales transactions of that product. Indeed, even though there are only 1,091 products used at least once in the *Sales* table in transactions with an amount greater than $1,000, the granularity of the datacache is larger because it also includes additional details other than the product name, returning more rows for the same product:

```
SELECT
    'DaxBook Product'[Product Name],
    'DaxBook Sales'[Quantity],
    'DaxBook Sales'[Net Price]
FROM 'DaxBook Sales'
    LEFT OUTER JOIN 'DaxBook Product'
        ON 'DaxBook Sales'[ProductKey]='DaxBook Product'[ProductKey]
WHERE
    ( COALESCE (  ( CAST ( PFCAST ( 'DaxBook Sales'[Quantity] AS  INT ) AS  REAL )
                        * PFCAST ( 'DaxBook Sales'[Net Price] AS  REAL ) ) )
      > COALESCE ( 1000.000000 )
    );
```

There are 1,091 xmSQL queries that are very similar to the one at line 6 of Figure 20-43 and return a single value obtained with a distinct count aggregation. In this case, the filter condition has all the combinations of *Quantity* and *Net Price* that return a value greater than 1,000 for the Adventure Works 52" LCD HDTV X790W Silver product:

```
SELECT
    DCOUNT ( 'DaxBook Sales'[CustomerKey] )
FROM 'DaxBook Sales'
    LEFT OUTER JOIN 'DaxBook Product'
        ON 'DaxBook Sales'[ProductKey]='DaxBook Product'[ProductKey]
WHERE
    ( COALESCE (  ( CAST ( PFCAST ( 'DaxBook Sales'[Quantity] AS  INT ) AS  REAL )
                        * PFCAST ( 'DaxBook Sales'[Net Price] AS  REAL ) ) )
      > COALESCE ( 1000.000000 )
    )
VAND (
        'DaxBook Product'[Product Name],
        'DaxBook Sales'[Quantity],
        'DaxBook Sales'[Net Price] )
    IN {
        ( 'Adventure Works 52" LCD HDTV X790W Silver', 2, 1592.200000 ) ,
        ( 'Adventure Works 52" LCD HDTV X790W Silver', 4, 1432.980000 ) ,
        ( 'Adventure Works 52" LCD HDTV X790W Silver', 1, 1273.760000 ) ,
        ( 'Adventure Works 52" LCD HDTV X790W Silver', 3, 1480.746000 ) ,
        ( 'Adventure Works 52" LCD HDTV X790W Silver', 4, 1512.590000 ) ,
        ( 'Adventure Works 52" LCD HDTV X790W Silver', 3, 1592.200000 ) ,
        ( 'Adventure Works 52" LCD HDTV X790W Silver', 3, 1353.370000 ) ,
        ( 'Adventure Works 52" LCD HDTV X790W Silver', 4, 1273.760000 ) ,
        ( 'Adventure Works 52" LCD HDTV X790W Silver', 1, 1480.746000 ) ,
        ( 'Adventure Works 52" LCD HDTV X790W Silver', 1, 1592.200000 )
    ..[24 total tuples, not all displayed]};
```

Indeed, the following xmSQL query at line 10 of Figure 20-43 only differs from the latter in the final filter condition, which includes valid combinations of *Quantity* and *Net Price* for the Contoso Washer & Dryer 21in E210 Blue product:

```
SELECT
    DCOUNT ( 'DaxBook Sales'[CustomerKey] )
FROM 'DaxBook Sales'
    LEFT OUTER JOIN 'DaxBook Product'
        ON 'DaxBook Sales'[ProductKey]='DaxBook Product'[ProductKey]
WHERE
    ( COALESCE ( ( CAST ( PFCAST ( 'DaxBook Sales'[Quantity] AS  INT ) AS  REAL )
                        * PFCAST ( 'DaxBook Sales'[Net Price] AS  REAL ) ) )
        > COALESCE ( 1000.000000 )
    )
VAND (
        'DaxBook Product'[Product Name],
        'DaxBook Sales'[Quantity],
        'DaxBook Sales'[Net Price] )
    IN {
        ( 'Contoso Washer & Dryer 21in E210 Blue', 2, 1519.050000 ) ,
        ( 'Contoso Washer & Dryer 21in E210 Blue', 2, 1279.200000 ) ,
        ( 'Contoso Washer & Dryer 21in E210 Blue', 2, 1359.150000 ) ,
        ( 'Contoso Washer & Dryer 21in E210 Blue', 4, 1487.070000 ) ,
        ( 'Contoso Washer & Dryer 21in E210 Blue', 3, 1439.100000 ) ,
        ( 'Contoso Washer & Dryer 21in E210 Blue', 3, 1519.050000 ) ,
        ( 'Contoso Washer & Dryer 21in E210 Blue', 3, 1359.150000 ) ,
        ( 'Contoso Washer & Dryer 21in E210 Blue', 2, 1599.000000 ) ,
        ( 'Contoso Washer & Dryer 21in E210 Blue', 1, 1439.100000 ) ,
        ( 'Contoso Washer & Dryer 21in E210 Blue', 3, 1279.200000 )
        ..[24 total tuples, not all displayed]};
```

The presence of multiple similar storage engine queries is also visible in the Query Plan pane shown in Figure 20-44. Each row starting at line 15 corresponds to a single datacache with just one column produced by one of the storage engine queries described before.

Line	Records	Physical Query Plan
7		PartitionIntoGroups: IterPhyOp LogOp=Order IterCols(0, 1, 2, 3)('Product'[Product Name],
8	1	AggregationSpool<Order>: SpoolPhyOp #Records=1
9		PartitionIntoGroups: IterPhyOp LogOp=TopN IterCols(0, 1, 2, 3)('Product'[Product Na
10	1	AggregationSpool<Top>: SpoolPhyOp #Records=1
11		Union: IterPhyOp LogOp=Union IterCols(0, 1, 2, 3)('Product'[Product Name], "[Is
12		GroupSemijoin: IterPhyOp LogOp=GroupSemiJoin IterCols(0, 1, 2)('Product'[P
13	1,091	Spool_Iterator<SpoolIterator>: IterPhyOp LogOp=DistinctCount_Vertipaq I
14	1,091	ProjectionSpool<ProjectFusion<Copy>>: SpoolPhyOp #Records=1091
15		Cache: IterPhyOp #FieldCols=0 #ValueCols=1
16		Cache: IterPhyOp #FieldCols=0 #ValueCols=1
17		Cache: IterPhyOp #FieldCols=0 #ValueCols=1
18		Cache: IterPhyOp #FieldCols=0 #ValueCols=1
19		Cache: IterPhyOp #FieldCols=0 #ValueCols=1
20		Cache: IterPhyOp #FieldCols=0 #ValueCols=1

FIGURE 20-44 Query Plan pane running the query for *Customers 1k (slow)*.

The presence of the table filter applied to the filter context forces a query plan that is not efficient. In this case, a table filter produces multiple storage engine queries instead of a single large materialization. However, the optimization required is always the same: Column filters are better than table filters in *CALCULATE* and *CALCULATETABLE*. The optimized version of the *Customer 1k* measure applies a filter over the two columns *Quantity* and *Net Price*, using *KEEPFILTERS* in order to use the filter semantic of the original measure. The following query produces the Server Timings results visible in Figure 20-45:

```
DEFINE
    MEASURE Sales[Customers 1k (fast)] =
        CALCULATE (
            DISTINCTCOUNT ( Sales[CustomerKey] ),
            KEEPFILTERS (
                FILTER (
                    ALL (
                        Sales[Quantity],
                        Sales[Net Price]
                    ),
                    Sales[Quantity] * Sales[Net Price] > 1000
                )
            )
        )
EVALUATE
TOPN (
    502,
    SUMMARIZECOLUMNS (
        ROLLUPADDISSUBTOTAL ( 'Product'[Product Name], "IsGrandTotalRowTotal" ),
        "Customers_1k__fast_", 'Sales'[Customers 1k (fast)]
    ),
    [IsGrandTotalRowTotal], 0,
    'Product'[Product Name], 1
)
ORDER BY
    [IsGrandTotalRowTotal] DESC,
    'Product'[Product Name]
```

Total	SE CPU	Line	Subclass	Duration	CPU	Rows	KB	Query
97 ms	453 ms	4	Scan	59	281	1,091	13	SELECT '
	x5.7	8	Scan	21	172	1	1	SELECT

FE	SE
17 ms	80 ms
17.5%	82.5%

SE Queries	SE Cache
2	0
	0.0%

FIGURE 20-45 Server Timings running the query for *Customers 1k (fast)*.

The column filter in *CALCULATE* simplifies the query plan, which now only requires two storage engine queries—one for each granularity level of the result (one product versus total of all products). The following is the xmSQL query at line 4 in Figure 20-45:

```
SELECT
    'DaxBook Product'[Product Name],
    DCOUNT ( 'DaxBook Sales'[CustomerKey] )
FROM 'DaxBook Sales'
```

```
        LEFT OUTER JOIN 'DaxBook Product'
            ON 'DaxBook Sales'[ProductKey]='DaxBook Product'[ProductKey]
WHERE
        ( COALESCE (  ( CAST ( PFCAST ( 'DaxBook Sales'[Quantity] AS  INT ) AS  REAL )
                            * PFCAST ( 'DaxBook Sales'[Net Price] AS  REAL ) )  )
          > COALESCE ( 1000.000000 )
        );
```

The datacache obtained corresponds to the result of the DAX query. The formula engine does not have to do any further processing. This is an optimal condition for the performance of this query. The lesson here is that the number of storage engine queries can also matter. A large number of storage engine queries might be the result of a bad query plan. Non-additive measures combined with table filters or bidirectional filters could be one of the reasons for this behavior, impacting performance in a negative way.

Avoiding multiple evaluations by using variables

When a DAX expression evaluates the same subexpression multiple times, it is usually a good idea to store the result of the subexpression in a variable, referencing the variable name in following parts of the original DAX expression. The use of variables is a best practice which improves code readability and can provide a better and more efficient query plan—with just some exceptions described later in this section.

For example, the report in Figure 20-46 shows a *Sales YOY %* measure computing the percentage difference between the value of *Sales Amount* displayed in the row of the report and the corresponding value in the previous year.

Year	Sales Amount	Sales YOY % (slow)	Sales YOY % (fast)
~~October 2007~~	~~105,525,001.15~~		
November 2007	108,008,618.91		
December 2007	110,436,896.10		
CY 2008	**1,189,326,612.81**	**-15.97%**	**-15.97%**
January 2008	79,431,234.29	-28.85%	-28.85%
February 2008	85,088,461.45	-27.11%	-27.11%
March 2008	84,808,709.97	-27.07%	-27.07%
April 2008	105,627,816.67	-16.83%	-16.83%
May 2008	109,011,089.35	-19.01%	-19.01%
June 2008	107,110,706.45	-12.13%	-12.13%
Total	**3,805,392,024.21**	**0.00%**	**0.00%**

FIGURE 20-46 Difference in sales year over year reported by year and month.

The *Sales YOY %* measure uses other measures internally. In order to be able to modify each part of the calculation, it is useful to include all the underlying measures using the Define Dependent Measure feature in DAX Studio. The following query computes the original *Sales YOY % (slow)* measure in the previous report, generating the server timings results visible in Figure 20-47:

```
DEFINE
    MEASURE Sales[Sales PY] =
        CALCULATE (
```

```
                    [Sales Amount],
                    SAMEPERIODLASTYEAR ( 'Date'[Date] )
                )
        MEASURE Sales[Sales YOY (slow)] =
            IF (
                NOT ISBLANK ( [Sales Amount] ) && NOT ISBLANK ( [Sales PY] ),
                [Sales Amount] - [Sales PY]
            )
        MEASURE Sales[Sales Amount] =
            SUMX (
                Sales,
                Sales[Quantity] * Sales[Net Price]
            )
        MEASURE Sales[Sales YOY % (slow)] =
            DIVIDE (
                [Sales YOY (slow)],
                [Sales PY]
            )
EVALUATE
TOPN (
    502,
    SUMMARIZECOLUMNS (
        ROLLUPADDISSUBTOTAL (
            ROLLUPGROUP (
                'Date'[Calendar Year Month],
                'Date'[Calendar Year Month Number]
            ), "IsGrandTotalRowTotal"
        ),
        "Sales_YOY____slow_", 'Sales'[Sales YOY % (slow)]
    ),
    [IsGrandTotalRowTotal], 0,
    'Date'[Calendar Year Month Number], 1,
    'Date'[Calendar Year Month], 1
)
ORDER BY
    [IsGrandTotalRowTotal] DESC,
    'Date'[Calendar Year Month Number],
    'Date'[Calendar Year Month]
```

Total	SE CPU	Line	Subclass	Duration	CPU	Rows	KB	Query
172 ms	625 ms	2	Scan	24	156	7,569	119	WITH SE:
	x4.6	4	Scan	0	0	2,559	20	SELECT '(
▨ FE	▨ SE	6	Scan	1	0	2,556	10	SELECT '(
35 ms	137 ms	8	Scan	26	109	2,559	40	WITH SE:
20.3%	79.7%	10	Scan	29	125	7,569	119	WITH SE:
		12	Scan	0	0	731	3	SELECT '(
SE Queries	SE Cache	14	Scan	0	0	7,569	60	SELECT '(
14	4	16	Scan	21	141	2,559	40	WITH SE:
	28.6%	18	Scan	13	0	1	1	WITH SE:

FIGURE 20-47 Server Timings running the query for the *Sales YOY % (slow)* measure.

The description of the query plan includes 1,819 rows, not reported here. Moreover, there are four storage engine queries retrieved by the storage engine cache (*SE Cache*), even though we executed a clear cache command before running the query. This indicates that different parts of the query plan generate different requests for the same storage engine query. Although the cache improves the performance of the storage engine request, the presence of such redundancy in the query plan is an indicator that there is room for further improvements.

When a query plan is so complex and there are many storage engine queries, it is a good idea to review the DAX code and reduce redundant evaluations by using variables. Indeed, redundant evaluations could be responsible for these duplicated requests. In general, the DAX engine should be able to locate similar subexpressions executed within the same filter context, and reuse their results without multiple evaluations. However, the presence of logical conditions such as *IF* and *SWITCH* creating different branches of execution can easily stop this internal optimization.

For example, consider the *Sales YOY (slow)* measure implementation: the *Sales Amount* and *Sales PY* measures are executed in different branches of the evaluation. The first argument of the *IF* function must always be evaluated, whereas the second argument should only be evaluated whenever the first argument evaluates to *TRUE*. A DAX expression that is present in both the first and the second argument might be evaluated twice in the query plan, which might not consider the result obtained for the first argument as something that can be reused when evaluating the second argument. The technical reasons why this happens and when it turns out to be preferable are outside the scope of this book.

The following excerpt of the previous query highlights the measure references that might be evaluated twice because they are in both the first and the second argument:

```
MEASURE Sales[Sales YOY (slow)] =
    IF (
        NOT ISBLANK ( [Sales Amount] ) && NOT ISBLANK ( [Sales PY] ),
        [Sales Amount] - [Sales PY]
    )
```

By storing the values returned by the two measures *Sales Amount* and *Sales PY* in two variables, it is possible to instruct the DAX engine to enforce a single evaluation of the two measures before the *IF* condition, reusing the result in both the first and the second argument. The following excerpt of the *Sales YOY (fast)* measure shows how to implement this technique in the DAX code:

```
MEASURE Sales[Sales YOY (fast)] =
    VAR SalesPY = [Sales PY]
    VAR SalesAmount = [Sales Amount]
    RETURN
        IF (
            NOT ISBLANK ( SalesAmount ) && NOT ISBLANK ( SalesPY ),
            SalesAmount - SalesPY
        )
```

The following query includes a full implementation of the *Sales YOY (fast) %* measure, which internally relies on *Sales YOY (fast)* instead of *Sales YOY (slow)*. The execution of the query produces the server timings results visible in Figure 20-48:

```
DEFINE
    MEASURE Sales[Sales PY] =
        CALCULATE (
```

```
            [Sales Amount],
            SAMEPERIODLASTYEAR ( 'Date'[Date] )
        )
    MEASURE Sales[Sales YOY (fast)] =
        VAR SalesPY = [Sales PY]
        VAR SalesAmount = [Sales Amount]
        RETURN
            IF (
                NOT ISBLANK ( SalesAmount ) && NOT ISBLANK ( SalesPY ),
                SalesAmount - SalesPY
            )
    MEASURE Sales[Sales Amount] =
        SUMX (
            Sales,
            Sales[Quantity] * Sales[Net Price]
        )
    MEASURE Sales[Sales YOY % (fast)] =
        DIVIDE (
            [Sales YOY (fast)],
            [Sales PY]
        )
EVALUATE
TOPN (
    502,
    SUMMARIZECOLUMNS (
        ROLLUPADDISSUBTOTAL (
            ROLLUPGROUP (
                'Date'[Calendar Year Month],
                'Date'[Calendar Year Month Number]
            ), "IsGrandTotalRowTotal"
        ),
        "Sales_YOY____fast_", 'Sales'[Sales YOY % (fast)]
    ),
    [IsGrandTotalRowTotal], 0,
    'Date'[Calendar Year Month Number], 1,
    'Date'[Calendar Year Month], 1
)
ORDER BY
    [IsGrandTotalRowTotal] DESC,
    'Date'[Calendar Year Month Number],
    'Date'[Calendar Year Month]
```

Total	SE CPU	Line	Subclass	Duration	CPU	Rows	KB	Query
95 ms	359 ms	2	Scan	23	109	7,569	119	WITH S
	x4.6	4	Scan	0	0	2,559	20	SELECT
FE	SE	6	Scan	1	16	2,556	10	SELECT
17 ms	78 ms	8	Scan	25	109	2,559	40	WITH S
17.9%	82.1%	10	Scan	0	0	7,569	60	SELECT
		12	Scan	12	47	1	1	WITH S
SE Queries	SE Cache	14	Scan	0	0	2,559	20	SELECT
8	1	16	Scan	17	78	1	1	WITH S
	12.5%							

FIGURE 20-48 Server Timings running the query for *Sales YOY % (fast)*.

The description of the query plan includes 488 rows (not reported here), reducing the complexity of the query plan by 73%; the previous query plan was 1,819 rows long. The new query plan reduces the cost for the storage engine in terms of both execution time and number of queries, and it also reduces the execution time in the formula engine. Overall, the optimized measure reduces the execution time by about 50%, but the optimization could be even bigger in more complex models and expressions. If the same optimization were applied to nested measures, the improvement might be exponential.

However, pay attention to possible side effects of assigning variables before conditional statements. Only the subexpressions used in the first argument can be assigned to variables defined before an *IF* or *SWITCH* statement; otherwise, the effect could be the opposite, enforcing the evaluation of expressions that would otherwise be ignored. You should follow these guidelines:

- When the same DAX expression is evaluated multiple times within the same filter context, assign it to a variable and reference the variable instead of the DAX expression.

- When a DAX expression is evaluated within the branches of an *IF* or *SWITCH*, whenever necessary assign the expression to a variable within the conditional branch.

- Do not assign a variable outside an *IF* or *SWITCH* statement if the variable is only used within the conditional branch.

- The first argument of *IF* and *SWITCH* can use variables defined before *IF* and *SWITCH* without it affecting performance.

More examples about these guidelines are included in this article: https://www.sqlbi.com/articles/optimizing-if-and-switch-expressions-using-variables/

Implementing alternative conditional statements

In the last example we used a simple *IF* statement to show a possible optimization using variables. While using variables is a best practice, it is worth mentioning that there are alternative ways to express the same conditional logic in DAX. For example, whenever an *IF* function returns a numeric value and the expression of the second argument does not raise an execution error when the condition of the first argument is *TRUE*, it is possible to convert this code:

```
IF ( <condition>, <expression> )
```

Into:

```
<expression> * <condition>
```

For example, the *Sales YOY (fast)* measure can be implemented using this expression:

```
MEASURE Sales[Sales YOY (fast)] =
    ( [Sales Amount] - [Sales PY] )
        * ( NOT ISBLANK ( [Sales Amount] ) && NOT ISBLANK ( [Sales PY] ) )
```

The result produces only 208 rows in the query plan, despite a very similar query duration. Nevertheless, in more complex models the reduction of the query plan might have more visible benefits. However, different versions of the engine will tend to produce different results. Consider this alternative coding style one of the options available in case you need to further optimize your code. Do not apply such techniques without checking the effects on performance and query plans, verifying whether they improve performance and whether they are worth reducing the readability of your code.

Conclusions

The lesson in this last chapter (to be honest, in the entire book) is that you must consider all the factors that affect a query plan in order to find the real bottleneck. Looking at the percentages of FE and SE shown in server timings is a good starting point, but you should always investigate the reason behind the numbers. Tools like DAX Studio and VertiPaq Analyzer provide you with the ability to measure the effects of a bad query plan, but these are only clues and pieces of evidence pointing to the reasons for a slow query.

Welcome to the DAX world!

Index

Numbers

DAX (Data Analysis eXpressions)

R

S

Marco Russo and **Alberto Ferrari** are the founders of sqlbi.com, where they regularly publish articles about Microsoft Power BI, Power Pivot, DAX, and SQL Server Analysis Services. They have worked with DAX since the first beta version of Power Pivot in 2009 and, during these years, sqlbi.com became one of the major sources for DAX articles and tutorials. Their courses, both in-person and online, are the major source of learning for many DAX enthusiasts.

They both provide consultancy and mentoring on business intelligence (BI) using Microsoft technologies. They have written several books and papers about Power BI, DAX, and Analysis Services. They constantly help the community of DAX users providing content for the websites daxpatterns.com, daxformatter.com, and dax.guide.

Marco and Alberto are also regular speakers at major international conferences, including Microsoft Ignite, PASS Summit, and SQLBits. Contact Marco at marco.russo@sqlbi.com, and contact Alberto at alberto.ferrari@sqlbi.com